Lecture Notes in Computer Science 16788

Founding Editors

Gerhard Goos
Juris Hartmanis

Editorial Board Members

Elisa Bertino, *Purdue University, West Lafayette, IN, USA*
Wen Gao, *Peking University, Beijing, China*
Bernhard Steffen, *TU Dortmund University, Dortmund, Germany*
Moti Yung, *Columbia University, New York, NY, USA*

The series Lecture Notes in Computer Science (LNCS), including its subseries Lecture Notes in Artificial Intelligence (LNAI) and Lecture Notes in Bioinformatics (LNBI), has established itself as a medium for the publication of new developments in computer science and information technology research, teaching, and education.

LNCS enjoys close cooperation with the computer science R & D community, the series counts many renowned academics among its volume editors and paper authors, and collaborates with prestigious societies. Its mission is to serve this international community by providing an invaluable service, mainly focused on the publication of conference and workshop proceedings and postproceedings. LNCS commenced publication in 1973.

Maciej Paszynski · Amanda S. Barnard ·
Yongjie Jessica Zhang

Editors

Computational Science – ICCS 2026 Workshops

26th International Conference, ICCS 2026
Hamburg, Germany, June 29 – July 1, 2026
Proceedings, Part III

Springer

Editors
Maciej Paszynski
AGH University of Kraków
Kraków, Poland

Amanda S. Barnard
Australian National University
Canberra, ACT, Australia

Yongjie Jessica Zhang
Carnegie Mellon University
Pittsburgh, PA, USA

ISSN 0302-9743   ISSN 1611-3349 (electronic)
Lecture Notes in Computer Science
ISBN 978-3-032-29914-7   ISBN 978-3-032-29915-4 (eBook)
https://doi.org/10.1007/978-3-032-29915-4

This Springer imprint is published by the registered company Springer Nature Switzerland AG
The registered company address is: Gewerbestrasse 11, 6330 Cham, Switzerland

If disposing of this product, please recycle the paper.

Preface

Welcome to the Workshops on Computational Science, which were co-organized with the 26th International Conference on Computational Science (ICCS 2026 - https://www.iccs-meeting.org/iccs2026/), held from 30 June to 1 July 2026 at DESY (Deutsches Elektronen-Synchrotron), in Hamburg, Germany.

This 26th edition, jointly organized by the University of Amsterdam (UvA) and the University of Tennessee at Knoxville (UTK), was a fully in-person event—as was the previous edition in Singapore. Despite the many challenges of our present times, we have strived to keep the ICCS community as dynamic, creative, and productive as possible. We are proud to present these proceedings as a testament to that effort.

Founded in 1959, DESY is a publicly funded research center of the Helmholtz Association and one of the world's leading accelerator centers. With 3000 staff members, of whom 1300 are scientists, DESY conducts ground-breaking matter research, leveraging DESY research infrastructures, such as the X-ray radiation source PETRA III, but also its international involvement, for example, in CERN experiments. This very data-intensive strand of research builds upon efficient data-centric computing and data streaming infrastructures, in particular DESY's Interdisciplinary Data & Analysis Facility (IDAF), and upon matter-oriented computing and data management research and development. This interplay of infrastructures, research, and development enables unprecedented scientific insights into more than 200 PBs of data that are being managed by DESY—from the interaction of elementary particles to nanomaterials and biomolecular processes. With these capabilities and capacities, DESY has become a magnet for thousands of guest researchers and was particularly happy to welcome ICCS participants in 2026!

The Workshops on Computational Science are a set of thematic workshops organized by experts in a particular area of Computational Science. These workshops are specifically intended to provide a forum for the discussion of novel and more focused topics in the field of Computational Science among an international group of researchers, and to strengthen the application of Computational Science in particular disciplines.

We are proud to note that this 26th edition, with 23 workshops (the Workshops on Computational Science), and over 300 participants, kept to the tradition and high standards of previous editions.

The theme for 2026, **"At the Forefront of Science through Computation and Data"**, highlighted the role of Computational Science in assisting multidisciplinary research.

ICCS is well known for its lineup of keynote speakers. The keynotes for 2026 were:

- **George Karniadakis**, Brown University, USA
- **Amanda Randles**, Duke University, USA
- **Luis M. Rocha**, Binghamton University – State University of New York, USA
- **Christian Schroer**, DESY|University of Hamburg, Germany
- **Hareesha Narayana Shirankallu**, Bosch Global Software Technologies GmbH, Germany

- **Estela Suarez**, Jülich Supercomputing Centre|University of Bonn, Germany

This year, the Workshops on Computational Science registered 353 submissions, of which 133 were accepted as full papers, and 46 as short papers. There were on average 2.5 single-blind reviews per submission.

We would like to thank all committee members from the main track and workshops for their contribution to ensuring a high standard for the accepted papers. We would also like to thank *Springer, Elsevier,* and *Intellegibilis* for their support. Finally, we appreciate all the local organizing committee members for their hard work in preparing this conference.

We hope you enjoyed the conference and the beautiful city of Hamburg.

July 2026

Maciej Paszynski
Amanda S. Barnard
Yongjie Jessica Zhang

Organization

Program Committee – Workshops on Computational Science - Chair

Maciej Paszynski   AGH University of Krakow, Poland

Program Committee – Workshops on Computational Science

Amanda S. Barnard   Australian National University, Australia
Yongjie Jessica Zhang   Carnegie Mellon University, USA

Program Committee – General Chair

Derek Groen   Brunel University of London, UK

Program Committee – Local Chair at DESY

Philipp Neumann   DESY|University of Hamburg, Germany

Program Committee – Main Track

Michael H. Lees   University of Amsterdam, The Netherlands
Michael J. Puma   Columbia University, USA

Program Committee – Chairs Emeritus

Peter M. A. Sloot   University of Amsterdam, The Netherlands
Jack J. Dongarra   University of Tennessee, USA

Sponsorship Chair

Alan Serrano   Brunel University of London, UK

Early Career Engagement Chair

Valeria Krzhizhanovskaya   University of Amsterdam, The Netherlands

Workshop Chairs

Advances in High-Performance Computational Earth Sciences: Numerical Methods, Frameworks & Applications - IHPCES

Takashi Shimokawabe   University of Tokyo, Japan
Kohei Fujita   University of Tokyo, Japan
Dominik Bartuschat   FAU Erlangen-Nürnberg, Germany

Artificial Intelligence and High-Performance Computing for Advanced Simulations - AIHPC4AS

Maciej Paszynski   AGH University of Krakow, Poland
Maciej Woźniak   AGH University of Krakow, Poland
David Pardo   Basque Center for Applied Mathematics &
                                           University of the Basque Country, Spain
Victor Calo   Curtin University, Australia
Quanling Deng   Tsinghua University, China
Sergio Rojas   Monash University, Australia

Artificial Intelligence for Network Analysis in Biology and Beyond - AI4NetBio

Marianna Milano   University Magna Graecia of Catanzaro, Italy
Pietro Hiram Guzzi   University Magna Graecia of Catanzaro, Italy

Biomedical and Bioinformatics Challenges for Computer Science - BBC

Mario Cannataro   University Magna Graecia of Catanzaro, Italy
Giuseppe Agapito   University Magna Graecia of Catanzaro, Italy
Riccardo Dondi   Università degli Studi di Bergamo, Italy
Rodrigo Weber dos Santos   Universidade Federal de Juiz de Fora, Brazil
Italo Zoppis   University of Milano-Bicocca, Italy
Chiara Zucco   University Magna Graecia of Catanzaro, Italy
Pietro Cinaglia   University Magna Graecia of Catanzaro, Italy

Computational Health - CompHealth

Sergey Kovalchuk	ITMO University, Russia
Georgiy Bobashev	RTI International, USA
Anastasia Angelopoulou	University of Westminster, UK

Computational Methods for Petascale Research - CompPet

Graeme Andrew Stewart	DESY, Germany

Computational Modeling and Artificial Intelligence for Social Systems - CMAISS

Tanzhe Tang	University of Amsterdam, Netherlands
Jaeyoung Kwak	Nanyang Technological University, Singapore

Computational Optimization, Modelling and Simulation - COMS

Xin-She Yang	Middlesex University London, UK
Slawomir Koziel	Reykjavik University, Iceland
Leifur Leifsson	Purdue University, USA

Computational Psychology and Mental Health - ComPsy

Valeria Epelbaum	University of Amsterdam, Netherlands
Sophie Engels	Northeastern University, USA

Computer Vision in the Era of Large Neural Models - CV-LNM

Bogusław Cyganek	AGH University of Krakow, Poland
Bogdan Kwolek	AGH University of Krakow, Poland
Radek Silhavy	Tomas Bata University in Zlín, Czechia

Computing and Data Science for Materials Discovery and Design - CDMDD

Ulf Schiller	University of Delaware, USA
Roderick Melnik	Wilfrid Laurier University, Canada
Luca Ghiringhelli	Karlsruhe Institute of Technology, Germany
Xiao Xue	University College London, UK

Credible Multiscale Modelling and Simulation - MMS

Diana Suleimenova	Brunel University of London, UK
Bartosz Bosak	Poznań Supercomputing and Networking Center, Poland
Derek Groen	Brunel University of London, UK
Gábor Závodszky	University of Amsterdam, Netherlands
Wouter Edeling	CWI Amsterdam, Netherlands
Ulf Schiller	University of Delaware, USA

Large Language Models related Intelligent Decision-Making in the Digital Economy Era - LLM-IDM

Yong Shi	Chinese Academy of Sciences, China
Yunlong Mi	Central South University, China
Wei Li	American Express, Singapore
Luyao Zhu	AI Singapore, National University of Singapore, Singapore
Yi Qu	Chinese Academy of Sciences, China
Jinyuan Feng	Chinese Academy of Sciences, China

Machine Learning and Data Assimilation for Dynamical Systems - MLDADS

Rossella Arcucci	Imperial College London, UK
Sibo Cheng	École nationale des Ponts et Chaussées, France
Martin Weissmann	University of Vienna, Austria
Tijana Janjic	KU Eichstaett-Ingolstadt, Germany
Rochelle Schneider	European Space Agency, Italy/UK

Multi-Criteria Decision-Making: Methods, Applications, and Innovations - MCDM

Wojciech Sałabun	West Pomeranian University of Technology, Szczecin, Poland
Jarosław Wątróbski	University of Szczecin, Poland

Navigating Trustworthy and Autonomous Modelling of Complex Systems: AI Meets Computational Science - TAMCS

Yani Xue	Brunel University of London, UK

Numerical Algorithms and Computer Arithmetic for Computational Science - NACA

Paweł Gepner	Warsaw University of Technology, Poland
Ewa Deelman	USC Information Sciences Institute, USA
Hatem Ltaief	King Abdullah University of Science and Technology, Saudi Arabia

Quantum Computing - QCW

Karol Capała	AGH University of Krakow, Poland
Katarzyna Rycerz	AGH University of Krakow, Poland
Marian Bubak	AGH University of Krakow|University of Amsterdam, Poland|Netherlands

Retrieval-Augmented Generation - RAGW

Aleksander Smywiński-Pohl	AGH University of Krakow, Poland
Magdalena Król	AGH University of Krakow, Poland

Simulations of Flow and Transport: Modeling, Algorithms and Computation - SOFTMAC

Shuyu Sun	Tongji University, China
Jingfa Li	Yangtze University, China
James Liu	Colorado State University, USA

Smart Systems: Bringing Together Computer Vision, Sensor Networks and Artificial Intelligence - SmartSys

Pedro J. S. Cardoso	University of Algarve, Portugal
Roberto Lam	University of Algarve, Portugal
João M. F. Rodrigues	University of Algarve, Portugal
Jaime A. Martins	University of Algarve, Portugal
Jânio Monteiro	University of Algarve, Portugal

Solving Problems with Uncertainties - SPU

Vassil Alexandrov	STFC Hartree Centre, UK
Aneta Karaivanova	IPP-BAS, Bulgaria

Teaching Computational Science - WTCS

Evguenia Alexandrova	STFC Hartree Centre, UK
Vassil Alexandrov	STFC Hartree Centre, UK

Reviewers

Tesfamariam Mulugeta Abuhay	University of Illinois Chicago, USA
Giuseppe Agapito	Università Magna Graecia di Catanzaro, Italy
Adriano Agnello	STFC Hartree Centre, UK
Elisabete Alberdi	University of the Basque Country UPV/EHU, Spain
Luis Alexandre	Universidade da Beira Interior and NOVA LINCS, Portugal
Vassil Alexandrov	STFC Hartree Centre, UK
Evguenia Alexandrova	STFC Hartree Centre, UK
Shaukat Ali	Simula Research Laboratory|Oslo Metropolitan University, Norway
Julen Alvarez-Aramberri	University of the Basque Country (UPV/EHU), Spain
Domingos Alves	University of São Paulo, Brazil
Sergey Alyaev	NORCE, Norway
Anastasia Anagnostou	Brunel University of London, UK
Anastasia Angelopoulou	University of Westminster, UK
Hideo Aochi	BRGM, France

Rossella Arcucci	Imperial College London, UK
Olivia Atkins	Imperial College London, UK
Paula Bajdor	Warsaw University of Technology, Poland
Krzysztof Banaś	AGH University of Krakow, Poland
Luca Barillaro	Magna Graecia University of Catanzaro, Italy
João Barroso	INESC TEC, Portugal
Dominik Bartuschat	FAU Erlangen-Nürnberg, Germany
Anton Barty	DESY, Germany
Pouria Behnoudfar	Curtin University, Australia
Jörn Behrens	University of Hamburg, Germany
Gebrail Bekdas	Istanbul University, Turkey
Sana Ben Abdallah Ben Lamine	University of Manouba, Tunisia
Stefano Beretta	San Raffaele Telethon Institute for Gene Therapy (SR-TIGET), Italy
Gabriele Bertoli	University of Florence, Italy
John Betts	Monash University, Australia
Piotr Biskupski	IBM, Poland
Rafał Bistroń	Jagiellonian University, Poland
Georgiy Bobashev	RTI International, USA
Klavdiya Bochenina	ITMO University, Russia
Johan Bollen	University of Amsterdam, Netherlands
Carlos Bordons	University of Seville, Spain
Denny Borsboom	University of Amsterdam, Netherlands
Bartosz Bosak	Poznań Supercomputing and Networking Center, Poland
Lorella Bottino	University Magna Graecia Catanzaro, Italy
Wojciech Bożejko	Wrocław University of Technology, Poland
Isabel Sofia Brito	Instituto Politécnico de Beja, Portugal
Marian Bubak	AGH University of Krakow|University of Amsterdam, Poland|Netherlands
Keith Butler	University College London, UK
Aleksander Byrski	AGH University of Krakow, Poland
Cristiano Cabrita	Universidade do Algarve, Portugal
Xing Cai	Simula Research Laboratory, Norway
Carlos T. Calafate	Universitat Politècnica de València, Spain
Mario Cannataro	University Magna Graecia of Catanzaro, Italy
Haobin Cao	Brunel University of London, UK
Karol Capała	AGH University of Krakow, Poland
Pedro J. S. Cardoso	Universidade do Algarve, Portugal
Stefano Casarin	Houston Methodist Hospital, USA
Ida Caspary	Imperial College London, UK
Federico Castagna	Brunel University of London, UK

Gregoire Cattan	IBM, Poland
Nicholas Chancellor	Durham University, UK
Sibo Cheng	École nationale des Ponts et Chaussées, France
Su Fong Chien	MIMOS Berhad, Malaysia
Marta Chinnici	ENEA, Italy
Leszek J Chmielewski	Warsaw University of Life Sciences, Poland
Bastien Chopard	University of Geneva, Switzerland
Michał Choraś	Bydgoszcz University of Science and Technology, Poland
Pietro Cinaglia	University Magna Graecia of Catanzaro, Italy
Andrew Clelland	Imperial College London, UK
Ian Collier	UKRI-STFC, UK
Noélia Correia	Universidade do Algarve, Portugal
Adriano Cortes	Federal University of Rio de Janeiro, Brazil
Ana Cortes	Universitat Autònoma de Barcelona, Spain
Enrique Costa-Montenegro	Universidad de Vigo, Spain
David Coster	Max Planck Institute for Plasma Physics, Germany
Carlos Cotta	Universidad de Málaga, Spain
Peter Coveney	University College London, UK
Matteo Croci	Basque Center for Applied Mathematics & Ikerbasque, Spain
Daan Crommelin	CWI Amsterdam, Netherlands
Attila Csikász-Nagy	King's College London|Pázmány Péter Catholic University, UK
Zhiji Cui	University of Birmingham, UK
António Cunha	University of Trás-os-Montes and Alto Douro, Portugal
Joshua Curtiss	Northeastern University, USA
Bogusław Cyganek	AGH University of Krakow, Poland
Jakub Czartowski	Trinity College Dublin, Ireland
Pasqua D'Ambra	IAC-CNR, Italy
Dong Dai	University of Delaware, USA
Lisandro Dalcin	CONICET, Argentina
Haluk Damgacioglu	Medical University of South Carolina, USA
Bhaskar Dasgupta	University of Illinois Chicago, USA
Derek de Beurs	University of Amsterdam, Netherlands
Ewa Deelman	USC Information Sciences Institute, USA
Quanling Deng	Australian National University, Australia
Abhijnan Dikshit	Purdue University, USA
Riccardo Dondi	Università degli Studi di Bergamo, Italy
Rafal Drezewski	AGH University of Krakow, Poland

Wojciech Drożdż	University of Szczecin, Poland
Hans du Buf	University of Algarve, Portugal
Jacek Długopolski	AGH University of Krakow, Poland
Rob E. Loke	Amsterdam University of Applied Sciences, Netherlands
Wouter Edeling	Vrije Universiteit Amsterdam, Netherlands
Nahid Emad	Paris-Saclay University, France
Christian Engelmann	Oak Ridge National Laboratory, USA
Sophie Engels	Northeastern University, USA
Valeria Epelbaum	University of Amsterdam, Netherlands
Aniello Esposito	Hewlett Packard Enterprise, Switzerland
Fedra Rosita Falvo	University Magna Graecia of Catanzaro, Italy
Jingzhong Fang	Brunel University of London, UK
Giuseppe Fedele	University of Calabria, Italy
Jinyuan Feng	Chinese Academy of Sciences, China
Yinchu Feng	University of Birmingham, UK
Paweł Forczmański	West Pomeranian University of Technology, Szczecin, Poland
Piotrek Frackiewicz	Pomeranian University, Poland
Bogdan Franczyk	Leipzig University, Germany
Kohei Fujita	University of Tokyo, Japan
Takeshi Fukaya	Hokkaido University, Japan
Wlodzimierz Funika	AGH University of Krakow, Poland
Frank Gaede	DESY, Germany
Teresa Galvão	University of Porto, Portugal
Luis Garcia-Castillo	Universidad Carlos III de Madrid, Spain
Bartłomiej Gardas	Jagiellonian University, Poland
Piotr Gawron	Nicolaus Copernicus Astronomical Centre - Polish Academy of Sciences, Poland
Bernhard Geiger	Know-Center GmbH, Austria
Paweł Gepner	Warsaw University of Technology, Poland
Luca Ghiringhelli	Karlsruhe Institute of Technology, Germany
Maziar Ghorbani	Brunel University of London, UK
Raffaele Giancotti	University of Calabria, Italy
Alexandrino Gonçalves	Polytechnic University of Leiria, Portugal
Simon Goodchild	STFC, UK
Yuriy Gorbachev	Soft-Impact LLC, Russia
Pawel Gorecki	University of Warsaw, Poland
Derek Groen	Brunel University of London, UK
Joel Guerreiro	Universidade do Algarve, Portugal
Tobias Guggemos	University of Vienna, Austria
Serge Guillas	University College London, UK

Manish Kumar Gupta	Harish-Chandra Research Institute, India
Piotr Gurgul	AGH University of Krakow, Poland
Oscar Gustafsson	Linköping University, Sweden
Juntao Han	Brunel University of London, UK
Laura Harbach	Brunel University of London, UK
Alexander Heinecke	Intel Parallel Computing Lab, USA
Teiko Heinosaari	University of Jyväskylä, Finland
Marcin Hernes	Wrocław University of Economics, Poland
Jiale Hong	Donghua University, China
Maximilian Höb	Leibniz-Rechenzentrum der Bayerischen Akademie der Wissenschaften, Germany
Huda Ibeid	Intel Corporation, USA
Marcin Iwanowski	Warsaw University of Technology, Poland
Alireza Jahani	Brunel University of London, UK
Tijana Janjic	Katholische Universität Eichstätt-Ingolstadt, Germany
Jaroslaw Jankowski	West Pomeranian University of Technology, Poland
Peter Janku	Tomas Bata University in Zlín, Czechia
Jiří Jaroš	Brno University of Technology, Czechia
Dorota Jelonek	Czestochowa University of Technology, Poland
Chao Jiang	University of Birmingham, UK
Zihan Jiang	Tongji University, China
Geethu Joy	Middlesex University Dubai, United Arab Emirates
John Kang	San Diego State University, USA
Aneta Karaivanova	IPP-BAS, Bulgaria
Gregor Kasieczka	Universität Hamburg, Germany
Robin Kennedy-Reid	STFC Hartree Centre, UK
Bartłomiej Kizielewicz	The National Institute of Telecommunications, Poland
Haruo Kobayashi	Gunma University, Japan
Łukasz Kobyliński	IPI PAN, Poland
Marcel Koch	Karlsruhe Institute of Technology, Germany
Ivan Kondov	Karlsruhe Institute of Technology, Germany
Georgy Kopanitsa	Tomsk Polytechnic University, Russia
Pavankumar Koratikere	Purdue University, USA
Varun Kotte	Adobe, USA
Sergey Kovalchuk	ITMO University, Russia
Slawomir Koziel	Reykjavik University, Iceland
Rafał Kozik	Bydgoszcz University of Science and Technology, Poland

Joanna Kołodziejczyk	National Institute of Telecommunications, Poland
Ronald Kriemann	Max Planck Institute for Mathematics in the Sciences, Germany
Valeria Krzhizhanovskaya	University of Amsterdam, Netherlands
Marek Kubalcik	Tomas Bata University in Zlín, Czechia
Sebastian Kuckuk	Friedrich-Alexander-Universität Erlangen-Nürnberg, Germany
Ryszard Kukulski	IT4Innovations National Supercomputing Center, Poland
Krzysztof Kurowski	Poznań Supercomputing and Networking Center, Poland
Marcin Kuta	AGH University of Krakow, Poland
Jaeyoung Kwak	Nanyang Technological University, Singapore
Bogdan Kwolek	AGH University of Krakow, Poland
Roberto Lam	Universidade do Algarve, Portugal
Ilaria Lazzaro	University Magna Graecia of Catanzaro, Italy
Paola Lecca	University of Bozen-Bolzano, Italy
Mike Lees	University of Amsterdam, Netherlands
Lili Lei	Nanjing University, China
Leifur Leifsson	Purdue University, USA
Kenneth Leiter	Army Research Laboratory, USA
Marek Lempart	VŠB-Technical University of Ostrava, Czechia
Yu Leng	Los Alamos National Lab, USA
Paulina Lewandowska	IT4Innovations National Supercomputing Center, Czechia
Jingfa Li	Yangtze University, China
Tao Li	Henan Normal University, China
James Liu	Colorado State University, USA
Zhao Liu	National Super Computer Center in Wuxi, China
Marcelo Lobosco	Federal University of Juiz de Fora, Brazil
Jay Lofstead	Sandia National Laboratories, USA
Petra Loncar	Imperial College London, UK
Chu Kiong Loo	University of Malaya, Malaysia
Stefan Luding	University of Twente, Netherlands
Piotr Luszczek	University of Tennessee Knoxville, USA
Pedro M. M. Guerreiro	Universidade do Algarve, Portugal
Wenyue Ma	Nanyang Technological University, Singapore
Luca Magri	Imperial College London, UK
Anirban Mandal	Renaissance Computing Institute, USA
Livia Marcellino	University of Naples Parthenope, Italy
Tomas Margalef	Universitat Autònoma de Barcelona, Spain
Osni Marques	Lawrence Berkeley National Laboratory, USA

Ignacio Martinez-Moyano	Argonne National Laboratory, USA
Andreia Martinho	Tufts University, USA
Maria Chiara Martinis	Università Magna Graecia di Catanzaro, Italy
Jaime A. Martins	University of Algarve, Portugal
Michele Martone	Max-Planck-Institut für Plasmaphysik, Germany
Pawel Matuszyk	Baker Hughes Inc., USA
Krzysztof Małecki	West Pomeranian University of Technology, Poland
Jon McCullough	Queen's University Belfast, UK
Sina Mehrdad	Imperial College London, UK
Wagner Meira Jr.	Universidade Federal de Minas Gerais, Brazil
Roderick Melnik	Wilfrid Laurier University, Canada
Ivan Merelli	Institute for Biomedical Technologies - National Research Council, Italy
Jakub Mielczarek	Jagiellonian University, Poland
Marianna Milano	Università Magna Graecia di Catanzaro, Italy
Jaroslaw Miszczak	Institute of Theoretical and Applied Informatics, Polish Academy of Sciences, Poland
Fernando Monteiro	Polytechnic Institute of Bragança, Portugal
Jânio Monteiro	University of Algarve, Portugal
Andrew Moore	University of California Santa Cruz, USA
Anabela Moreira Bernardino	Polytechnic Institute of Leiria, Portugal
Eugénia Moreira Bernardino	Polytechnic Institute of Leiria, Portugal
Leonid Moroz	Warsaw Technology University, Poland
Dariusz Mrozek	Silesian University of Technology, Poland
Peter Mueller	IBM Zurich Research Laboratory, Switzerland
Judit Munoz-Matute	University of the Basque Country, Spain
Hiromichi Nagao	University of Tokyo, Japan
Kengo Nakajima	University of Tokyo, Japan
Kesra Nermend	University of Szczecin, Poland
Philipp Neumann	DESY and University of Hamburg, Germany
Sinan Melih Nigdeli	Istanbul University, Turkey
Joseph O'Connor	University of Edinburgh, UK
Lidia Ogiela	AGH University of Krakow, Poland
Ángel Javier Omella	University of the Basque Country (UPV/EHU), Spain
Kenji Ono	RIIT, Kyushu University, Japan
Eneko Osaba	TECNALIA Research & Innovation, Spain
Aziz Ouaarab	Cadi Ayyad University, Morocco
Joanna Paliszkiewicz	Warsaw University of Life Sciences, Poland
Jose Palma	University of Murcia, Spain
Shaowu Pan	Rensselaer Polytechnic Institute, USA

Wei Pan	European Centre for Medium-Range Weather Forecasts, UK
George Papadimitriou	University of Southern Californa, USA
Nikela Papadopoulou	University of Glasgow, UK
Dário Passos	CENTRA-IST, Portugal
Zbigniew Pastuszak	University of Maria Curie-Skłodowska, Poland
Anna Paszynska	Jagiellonian University, Poland
Maciej Paszynski	AGH University of Krakow, Poland
Łukasz Pawela	Institute of Theoretical and Applied Informatics – Polish Academy of Sciences, Poland
Frank Phillipson	TNO, Netherlands
Anna Pietrenko-Dabrowska	Gdańsk University of Technology, Poland
Armando Pinho	University of Aveiro, Portugal
Yuri Pirola	Università degli Studi di Milano-Bicocca, Italy
Paweł Poczekajło	Koszalin University of Technology, Poland
Valeria Popello	University Magna Graecia of Catanzaro, Italy
Cristina Portales	Universidad de Valencia, Spain
Simon Portegies Zwart	Leiden University, Netherlands
Anna Procopio	Università Magna Graecia di Catanzaro, Italy
Małgorzata Przybyła-Kasperek	University of Silesia in Katowice, Poland
Michal Ptaszynski	Kyoto Institute of Technology, Japan
Ubaid Ali Qadri	Science and Technology Facilities Council, UK
Yi Qu	Chinese Academy of Sciences, China
Antonio Rago	University of Southern Denmark, Denmark
Jordan Ramassamy-Moutoussamy	University of Toulouse, France
Raul Ramirez	Tecnológico de Monterrey, Mexico
Célia Ramos	University of Algarve, Portugal
Vishwas Rao	Argonne National Laboratory, USA
Francesco Renzini	University of Milan, Italy
Jorge Ribeiro	Instituto Politécnico Viana do Castelo, Portugal
Robin Richardson	Netherlands eScience Center, Netherlands
Heike Riel	IBM Research - Zurich, Switzerland
João M.F. Rodrigues	Universidade do Algarve, Portugal
Daniel Rodriguez	University of Alcalá, Spain
Marcin Rogowski	Saudi Aramco, Saudi Arabia
Sergio Rojas	Monash University, Australia
Albert Romkes	South Dakota School of Mines and Technology, USA
Cosmina Rosca	Petroleum-Gas University of Ploiesti, Romania
Tommaso Ruga	University of Calabria, Italy
Tomasz Rybotycki	IBS PAN, CAMK PAN, AGH, Poland

Katarzyna Rycerz	AGH University of Krakow, Poland
Emre Sahin	STFC Hartree Centre, UK
Takeshi Saitoh	Kyushu Institute of Technology, Japan
Shinji Sako	Nagoya Institute of Technology, Japan
Federica Saldano	University "Magna Graecia" of Catanzaro, Italy
Özlem Salehi	Özyeğin University, Turkey
Ayşin Sancı	Altinay, Turkey
Jaromir Savelka	Carnegie Mellon University, USA
Wojciech Sałabun	West Pomeranian University of Technology, Szczecin, Poland
Robert Schaefer	AGH University of Krakow, Poland
Rafał Scherer	Częstochowa University of Technology, Poland
Ulf Schiller	University of Delaware, USA
Thomas Schincariol	University of Konstanz, Germany
Kilian Schwarz	DESY, Germany
Paulina Sepulveda	Pontificia Universidad Católica de Valparaíso, Chile
Marzia Settino	Università Magna Graecia di Catanzaro, Italy
Mostafa Shahriari	Basque Center for Applied Mathematics, Spain
Andrii Shekhovtsov	National Institute of Telecommunications, Poland
Takashi Shimokawabe	University of Tokyo, Japan
Alexander Shukhman	Orenburg State University, Russia
Bhargav Sriram Siddani	Lawrence Berkeley National Laboratory, USA
Marcin Sieniek	AGH University of Krakow, Poland
Radek Silhavy	Tomas Bata University in Zlín, Czechia
Haozhen Situ	South China Agricultural University, China
Leszek Siwik	AGH University of Krakow, Poland
Oskar Slowik	Center for Theoretical Physics PAS, Poland
Tomasz Sluzalec	AGH University of Krakow, Poland
Bogdan Smolka	Silesian University of Technology, Poland
Maciej Smołka	AGH University of Krakow, Poland
Michalis Smyrnakis	Hartree Centree, UK
Aleksander Smywiński-Pohl	AGH University of Krakow, Poland
Baoye Song	Shandong University of Science and Technology, China
Robert Staszewski	University College Dublin, Ireland
Graeme Andrew Stewart	DESY, Germany
Magdalena Stobinska	University of Gdańsk|Institute of Physics, Polish Academy of Sciences, Poland
Barbara Strug	Jagiellonian University, Poland
Diana Suleimenova	Brunel University of London, UK
Jing Sun	Delft University of Technology, Netherlands

Shuyu Sun	Tongji University, China
Martin Swain	Aberystwyth University, UK
Katarzyna Szopik-Depczyńska	University of Szczecin, Poland
Lidia Sánchez-González	Universidad de León, Spain
Tseden Taddese	STFC Hartree Centre, UK
Claude Tadonki	Mines ParisTech/CRI - Centre de Recherche en Informatique, France
Tanzhe Tang	University of Amsterdam, Netherlands
Osamu Tatebe	University of Tsukuba, Japan
Michela Taufer	University of Tennessee Knoxville, USA
Jamie Taylor	CUNEF Universidad, Spain
Kasim Terzic	University of St Andrews, UK
Jannis Teunissen	Centrum Wiskunde & Informatica, KU Leuven, Netherlands
Sue Thorne	UKRI Science and Technology Facility Council, UK
Francis Ting	XJTLU, China
Paweł Topa	AGH University of Krakow, Poland
Paolo Trunfio	University of Calabria, Italy
Popello Valeria	University Magna Graecia of Catanzaro, Italy
Eirik Valseth	South Dakota School of Mines and Technology, USA
Vítor V. Vasconcelos	University of Amsterdam, Netherlands
Mayank Verma	Delhi Technological University, India
Muñoz Martinez Victor	University of Málaga, Spain
Milana Vuckovic	European Centre for Medium-Range Weather Forecasts, UK
Cheng Wang	Heriot-Watt University, UK
Jian-Xun Wang	Cornell University, USA
Jinhong Wang	Imperial College London, UK
Kun Wang	Imperial College London, UK
Peng Wang	NVIDIA, China
Shaoni Wang	University of Groningen, Netherlands
Logan Ward	Argonne National Laboratory, USA
Rodrigo Weber dos Santos	Universidade Federal de Juiz de Fora, Brazil
Mei Wen	National University of Defense Technology, China
Wendy Winnard	UKRI STFC, UK
Christoph Wissing	DESY, Germany
Konrad Wojtasik	Politechnika Wrocławska, Poland
Maciej Wołoszyn	AGH University of Krakow, Poland
Maciej Woźniak	AGH University of Krakow, Poland

Michał Wroński	NASK - National Research Institute, Poland
Han Wu	Brunel University of London, UK
Jarosław Wąs	AGH University of Krakow, Poland
Jarosław Wątróbski	University of Szczecin, Poland
Linglin Xia	Nanchang University, China
Dunhui Xiao	Tongji University, China
Yuanchao Xu	Kyoto University, Japan
Xiao Xue	University College London, UK
Yani Xue	Brunel University of London, UK
Abuzer Yakaryilmaz	University of Latvia, Latvia
Xin-She Yang	Middlesex University, UK
Yehor Yudin	Bangor University, UK
Sebastian Zając	SGH Warsaw School of Economics, Poland
Małgorzata Zajęcka	AGH University of Krakow, Poland
Justyna Zawalska	ACC Cyfronet AGH, Poland
Wei Zhang	Huazhong University of Science and Technology, China
Yifan Zhang	City University of Hong Kong (Dongguan), China
Yicun Zhen	Hohai University, China
Hao Zhou	Queensland University of Technology, Australia
Qiyao Zhou	Paris-Saclay University, France
Yihang Zhou	Imperial College London, UK
Kewei Zhu	University College London, UK
Beata Zielosko	University of Silesia in Katowice, Poland
Ewa Ziemba	University of Economics in Katowice, Poland
Paweł Ziemba	University of Szczecin, Poland
Bartosz Ziółko	AGH University of Krakow, Poland
Italo Zoppis	University of Milano-Bicocca, Italy
Chiara Zucco	University Magna Graecia of Catanzaro, Italy
Ester Zumpano	University of Calabria, Italy
Pavel Zun	ITMO University, Russia
Gabor Závodszky	University of Amsterdam, Netherlands
José Álvarez Macías	Universidad de Huelva, Spain
Marcin Łoś	AGH University of Krakow, Poland
Grażyna Ślusarczyk	Jagielonian University, Poland
Karol Życzkowski	Jagiellonian University, Poland
Tibor Žingora	Masaryk University, Czechia

Contents

Machine Learning and Data Assimilation for Dynamical Systems

Multi-Criteria Decision-Making: Methods, Applications, and Innovations

**Navigating Trustworthy and Autonomous Modelling of Complex
Systems: AI Meets Computational Science**

Numerical Algorithms and Computer Arithmetic for Computational Science

Credible Multiscale Modelling and Simulation

A Scalable Numerical Framework for Predicting Particle Transport in Bifurcating Vascular Networks

Md Zaheen Tamzeed Kabir and Jon McCullough[✉] [iD]

Queen's University Belfast, University Road, Belfast BT7 1NN, Northern Ireland, UK
{mkabir01,jon.mccullough}@qub.ac.uk

Abstract. Cardiovascular diseases remain the predominant cause of death worldwide. Although computational fluid dynamics is an effective tool for predicting hemodynamics and drug particle transport in arteries, its clinical adoption remains limited due to the complexity of the workflow and computational limitations. This paper presents a scalable approach for predicting hemodynamic parameters and particle exit fractions in large networks from results obtained for ideal bifurcations. A total of 828 3D CFD simulations, combined with particle tracking, were performed on a high-performance computing environment with variations of inlet velocity, particle density, inlet and outlet diameters, and bifurcation angles on Y and T-shaped bifurcations. The simulation dataset was used to train three ML algorithms: Linear Regression, k-Nearest Neighbour, and Random Forest Regression for the prediction of velocity and particle exit fraction at the bifurcation outlets. Larger vascular networks were built by successively combining predictions from single bifurcation variants, thereby reducing computational costs. Our model successfully predicted the distributions of particle exit fraction and velocity in larger networks with better accuracy and reduced runtime than a 1D model of a realistic hepatic artery geometry and a reconstructed model.

Keywords: Machine Learning (ML) · Computational Fluid Dynamics (CFD) · Bifurcating Vessels · Multiscale Modelling · Lagrangian Particle Tracking (LPT)

1 Introduction

Approximately 523 million people worldwide suffer from cardiovascular disease (CVD), resulting in a significant public health burden and a primary cause of illness and death in all age divisions [1]. Personalised therapies remain one of the significant challenges in drug delivery applications, notably in treating CVDs, primarily due to the complexity of an individual's vascular structure [2]. Computational Fluid Dynamics (CFD) has been widely used by clinical researchers to predict the behaviour of blood flow and drug particle deposition in arteries, which would be highly difficult to obtain experimentally [3, 4]. However, the application of CFD in clinical settings remains limited largely due to high computational costs, limitations in MRI/CT image segmentation, and data protection policies [5, 6].

© The Author(s), under exclusive license to Springer Nature Switzerland AG 2026
M. Paszynski et al. (Eds.): ICCS 2026 Workshops, LNCS 16788, pp. 3–18, 2026.
https://doi.org/10.1007/978-3-032-29915-4_1

In recent times, CFD coupled with data-driven machine learning (ML) or deep learning (DL) has proven to be an alternative to overcome computational costs. A CFD-ML approach developed by Malek et al. [7] investigated left coronary artery (LCA) bifurcations with varying stenosis severity and location using computational fluid dynamics (CFD) to calculate hemodynamic parameters. A dataset of 6,858 synthetic coronary artery geometries was generated, and fourteen machine learning regression models were trained using the CFD-derived results. Among these models, the Decision Tree Regressor and K-Nearest Neighbour showed the best performance for predicting total average wall shear stress (TAWSS) and oscillatory shear Index (OSI), closely matching the CFD outputs. Another similar approach was found in blood flow modelling of a simplified 2D vessel containing magnetic nanocarriers for cancer therapy. The CFD-derived data were used to train machine learning models predict fluid velocity [8]. One study that combines CFD with the discrete element method (DEM) for resolving suspended particles and ML techniques was reported by Islam et al. [9]. Here, the authors performed coupled CFD–DEM simulations of pharmaceutical aerosol flow in both idealised and realistic airway models to capture the interaction between the continuum phase (airflow) and the discrete phase (particles). Similar to the work of [9], Francis et al. [10] performed CFD simulations of particle transport in an acinar region of the lung to determine the striking velocity and impact time for three particle diameters under both healthy and diseased (high surface tension) conditions in lung airways. The resulting CFD data for these two hemodynamic parameters were used to train machine learning classifiers that accurately identified the optimal particle diameter required to achieve desirable striking velocities and impact times. Lin et al. [11] performed 3D CFD simulations on 1,000 subject-specific aortic geometries. The authors investigated the distributions of velocity, pressure, and wall shear stress (WSS). The authors then trained deep neural networks on the CFD outputs to predict velocity magnitude and direction, pressure, and WSS for unseen geometries. The prediction models in their study were further compared against an additional 100 geometries and showed good agreement (deviation of 3–5%). In an attempt to reduce computation time, 1D segmentation of coronary vessels combined with an ML approach was applied by Coenen et al. [12] for predicting fractional flow reserve for diagnosing CVDs, reducing computational time by 5–10 min per patient. Another attempt to reduce computation was made by Ko et al. [13]. One-dimensional flow and pressure distributions were predicted using a reduced-order fluid model in coronary trees.

Although CFD coupled with an ML/DL approach is a promising way to reduce computational time, it also requires substantial time to run simulations on larger vascular networks and to generate the training dataset. Furthermore, it is extremely difficult to obtain such a dataset without substantial simplification of the underlying physics, which might omit critical information of interest [14, 15]. For example, 1D models homogenise the flow profile across a domain, leading to a failure to capture local particle deposition [14].

In this paper, we introduce a scalable approach for predicting flow behavior and particle transport in large vascular networks based on CFD with particle tracking and ML. Conceptually, CFD results for flow and particle transport in a single bifurcation are used to train an ML model, reducing the complexity of generating this dataset. Larger networks are then efficiently constructed by chaining together multiple bifurcation variants. Figures 1 and 2 outline the steps taken by this approach.

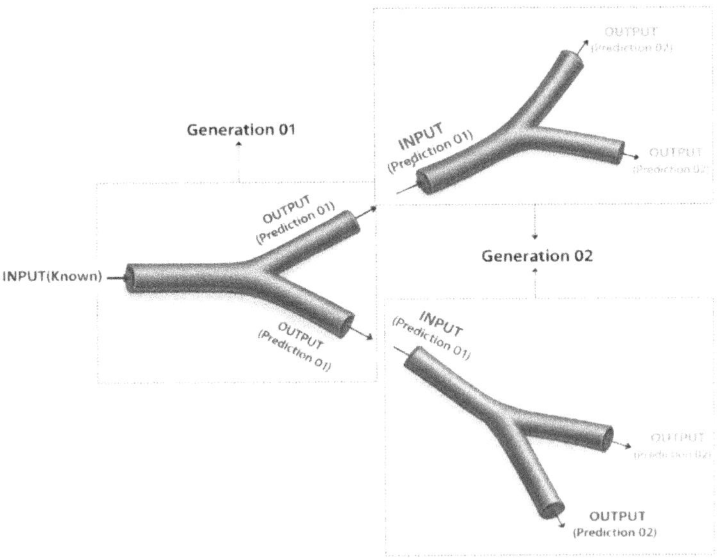

Fig. 1. Graphical overview of our multiscale model for predicting flow in large networks

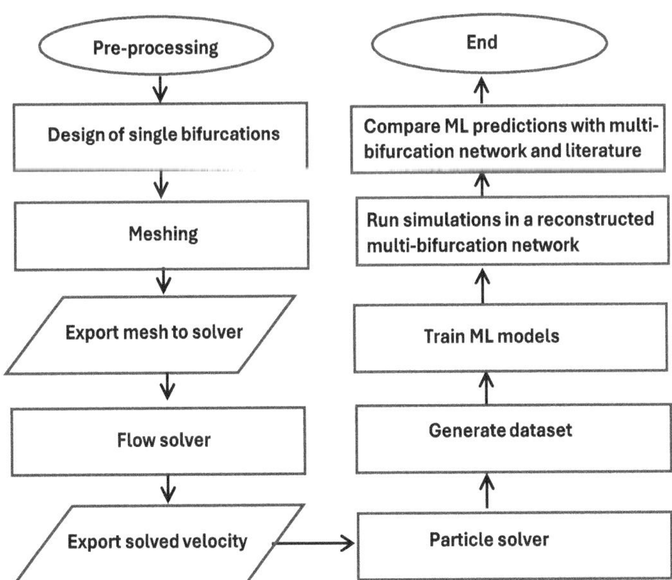

Fig. 2. The systematic workflow of the complete methodology for predicting particle trajectories in large networks

2 Methodology

The workflow for the current study is presented in Fig. 2. A total of 93 geometries with varying parameters of Y and T bifurcations were constructed using SOLIDWORKS 2024 [16]. The numerical simulations were performed on the compute nodes of the NI-HPC high-performance computing (HPC) cluster Kelvin2 [17]. The CFD simulations were performed using an open-source CFD software, OpenFOAM version 8.0 [18]. The ML models were trained using an open-source Python library, scikit learn [19].

2.1 Governing Equations

2.1.1 Modelling Blood Flow

The incompressible, steady, laminar momentum and continuity equations were numerically solved using the finite volume method (FVM) for modelling blood flow.

$$\rho_f \left(\frac{\partial \vec{v}_f}{\partial t} + \vec{v}_f . \nabla \vec{v}_f \right) = -\vec{\nabla P} + \rho_f \vec{g} + \mu \nabla^2 \vec{v}_f \tag{1}$$

$$\nabla . \vec{v}_f = 0 \tag{2}$$

where ρ_f is the density of blood, $\vec{v}$ Velocity of the fluid phase, P is the pressure of blood, and μ is the dynamic viscosity. The rheology of blood was assumed to be a Newtonian fluid and rigid-wall conditions were applied. The problem was assumed to be a steady state and was solved using the semi-implicit method for the pressure-linked equation (SIMPLE) algorithm to resolve pressure-velocity coupling using the simpleFoam solver in OpenFOAM.

2.1.2 Modelling Particle Transport (Lagrangian Particle Tracking)

The particle transport was modelled using the Lagrangian Particle Tracking (LPT) solver particleFoam in OpenFOAM. The particle trajectories were predicted by the equations of Newton's second law in the known fluid domain obtained from the simpleFoam solver.

$$\frac{d v_p}{dt} = \frac{\sum F}{m_p} = \frac{F_{drag} + F_{gravity}}{m_p} \tag{3}$$

where, m_p is the mass of the particle and v_p is the particle velocity. The forces acting on individual particles were determined by Newton's second law of motion. $\sum F$ is the summation of the considered dominant forces in this case - hydrodynamic drag (F_{drag}) and gravity force ($F_{gravity}$). Other forces were neglected due to problem specification and computational demand. The drag force is defined in Eq. 4 [20].

$$F_{drag} = m_p \frac{\rho_p d_p^2}{18\mu} \frac{24}{C_D Re_p} \left(v_f - v_p\right) \tag{4}$$

where, C_D is the drag coefficient, ρ_p is the density of the particle, Re_p is the particle Reynolds number, $(v_f - v_p)$ is the relative velocity between the fluid and the particle. In this study, the laminar flow regime with micron-sized spherical particles was considered. Hence, the particle Reynolds number was assumed to be less than 1000, and the Schiller-Naumann correlation was applied to model the viscous and inertial effects accurately. The drag coefficient C_D [20] is now expressed in Eq. 5.

$$C_D = \frac{24}{Re_p} \left(1 + 0.15 Re_p^{0.687}\right), for\ Re_p < 1000 \tag{5}$$

The gravity force is defined as

$$F_{gravity} = \frac{4}{3} \pi r_p^3 \rho_p g \tag{6}$$

The Stokes number (St) [21] is a dimensionless number that is significant in defining the behavior of particles dispersed in the flow. The Stokes number is represented in Eq. (7)

$$St = \frac{\rho_p d_p^2 v_f}{18\mu l_0} \tag{7}$$

here the characteristic dimension l_0 is defined by the inlet diameter of the domain.

2.2 Computational Domain

The geometric parameters and boundary conditions for both Y and T bifurcation are described in Table 1 and Fig. 3. The inlet velocity was examined at three levels (0.212 m/s, 0.30 m/s, and 0.36 m/s) to vary the Reynolds number from approximately 150 to 1000 while maintaining the flow in the laminar regime. The particle density varied across three levels (1050 kg/m³, 1100 kg/m³, 1150 kg/m³) to investigate the effects of neutrally buoyant, positively buoyant, and negatively buoyant particles. For the Y bifurcation, Θ_1 was varied between angles 50°, 70°, 90°, 110°, 150° and for the T bifurcation, Θ_2 was varied between 50°, 70°, 90°, 110°, 130°, 150° respectively. The diameters were varied with different combinations. For the Y bifurcation, D was varied over 10 levels, and for the T bifurcation, 7 levels were used, ranging from 1.5 to 8 mm. Constant length (L1 (60 mm), L2 (25 mm), L3 (25 mm)) was retained.

Table 1. Geometric parameters

Y Bifurcation		T Bifurcation	
Parameter	Notation	Parameter	Notation
Inlet Diameter	I	Inlet Diameter	I
Outlet 01 Diameter	D_1	Outlet 01 Diameter	D_1
Outlet 02 Diameter	D_2	Outlet 02 Diameter	D_2
Parent Vessel Length	L_1	Parent Vessel Length	L_1
Daughter Vessel 01 Length	L_2	Daughter Vessel 01 Length	L_2
Daughter Vessel 02 Length	L_3	-	-
Bifurcation Angle	Θ_1	Bifurcation Angle	Θ_2

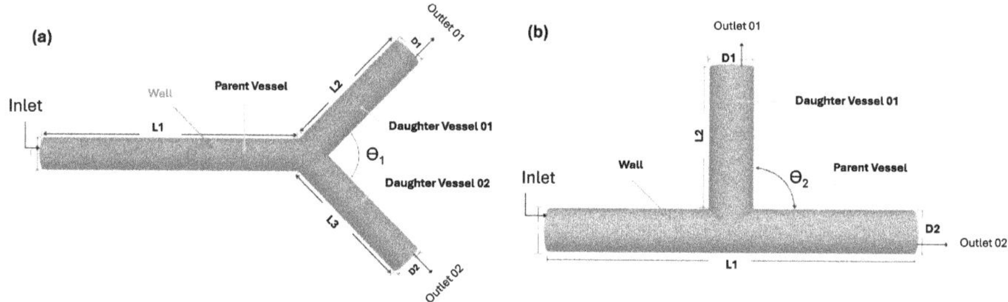

Fig. 3. Representative computational domains used for CFD simulations: (a) Y Bifurcation, (b) T Bifurcation. Gravity was oriented downwards in the vertical plane.

The mesh was generated using tetrahedral elements with inflation layers to accurately capture the quantities of interest at the outlets, resulting in 776,384 elements and an average cell size of 0.34 mm. A grid convergence study was performed to confirm that the results were independent of the mesh construction at this scale. The rheology of blood was assumed to be a Newtonian fluid [22] with a density of 1100 kg/m^3 and a dynamic viscosity of 0.003 Pa.s [23]. A total of ten thousand spherical particles with 1.6 μm diameter were injected at the inlets of both the Y- and T-bifurcation geometries, and a one-way coupling assumption was adopted for fluid particle interaction with ideal wall collision.

2.3 Machine Learning Implementation

To reduce the complexity and computational cost of simulations across a large vascular network, our approach builds the training dataset by varying the geometry and boundary conditions of Y- and T-shaped bifurcation fragments. The variations in geometry and boundary conditions are shown in Table 1. The results obtained from these single bifurcations are used to build the training dataset and generate predictions for generation 01 bifurcations. The predictions from generation 01 bifurcations were used as inputs for generation 02 bifurcation fragments to create a larger network, as illustrated in Fig. 1. The dataset obtained from the simulation results was used to train three ML models: Linear Regression (LR), k-Nearest Neighbour (kNN), and Random Forest Regression (RFR).

The metrics used to compare the performance of the ML algorithms were the Mean Squared Error (MSE), Root Mean Squared Error (RMSE), Mean Absolute Error (MAE) and the Coefficient of Determination (R^2).

$$MSE = \frac{1}{n} \sum_{i=1}^{n} (y_i - y_i')^2 \tag{8}$$

$$RMSE = \sqrt{MSE} \tag{9}$$

$$MAE = \frac{1}{n} \sum_{i=1}^{n} |y_i - y_i'| \tag{10}$$

$$R^2 = 1 - \frac{\sum_{i=1}^{n} (y_i - y_i')^2}{\sum_{i=1}^{n} (y_i - y'')^2} \tag{11}$$

where n is the number of observations, y_i is the actual value and $y_i\prime$ is the predicted value, and y'' is the mean of actual values.

The performance of our scalable prediction model was compared with flow simulation results from the multi-bifurcation domain P1, illustrated in Fig. 4, and the realistic hepatic artery domain of [24]. The velocity and exit fractions from outlets 01, 02, 03, and 04 were the parameters used to compare ML predictions with CFD-LPT simulations on P1. Table 2 summarises the output parameters in the study.

Table 2. Output parameters of interest

Parameter	Notation	Parameter	Notation
Velocity (outlet 1)	V1	Exit fraction (outlet 1)	EF1
Velocity (outlet 2)	V2	Exit fraction (outlet 2)	EF2
Velocity (outlet 3)	V3	Exit fraction (outlet 3)	EF3
Velocity (outlet 4)	V4	Exit fraction (outlet 4)	EF4

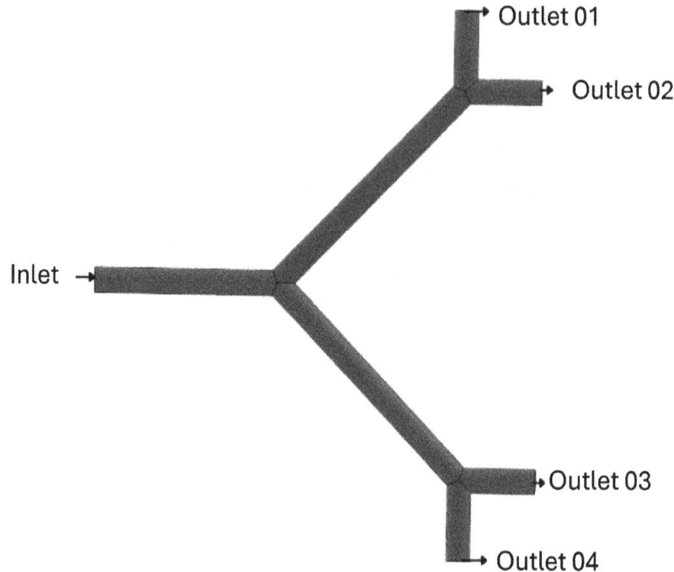

Fig. 4. (Multi-bifurcation) Model P1, which is used to evaluate the performance of the ML framework.

3   Results

3.1   Validation

To validate the accuracy of the simpleFoam and particleFoam solvers, the results were compared with those of the in-vitro experiments by Bushi et al. [23] and the computational studies of Param et al. [25] in a replicated domain of a Y bifurcation (specific details can be found in the supplementary dataset). Steady-state condition was used for the simulation of the fluid phase, and a Reynolds number (Re) of 500 was imposed at the inlet. The flow ratio ($Q1/Q2$) was varied at the outlets by varying the pressure at outlet 02 and retaining constant pressure at outlet 01, where $Q1$ and $Q2$ are the flow rates in outlets 01 and 02. Ten thousand neutrally buoyant spherical particles were injected at the inlet with particle diameters of 0.6 mm, assuming one-way coupling between particle and fluid. The exit fraction at the outlets was calculated by Eq. (12)

$$Exit\ Fraction\ (\%) = \frac{Number\ of\ particles\ exiting\ from\ an\ outlet}{Number\ of\ injected\ particles} \tag{12}$$

A comparison of the results obtained from the current study and the literature is shown in Fig. 5. The results obtained from present study showed a similar trend to the literature validating the accuracy of the solver.

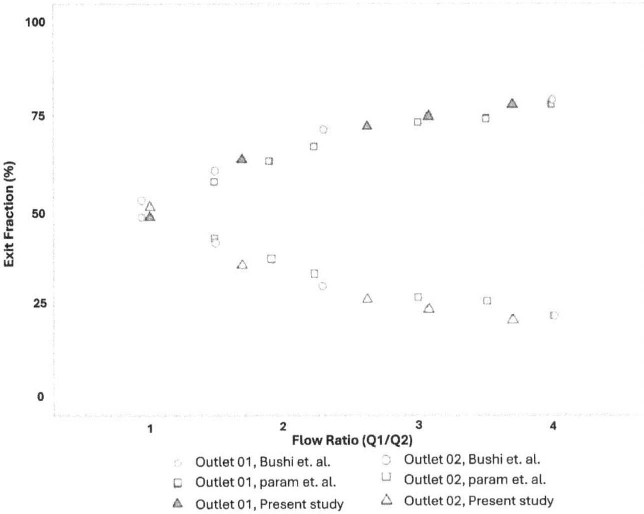

Fig. 5. Comparison of particle exit fraction between the present study and the experiments of Param et al. [25] and Bushi et al. [23].

3.2 Performance of ML Algorithms for Single Bifurcations

The CFD-LPT results were used to train ML models for predicting the output parameters (velocity, particle exit fraction) for a single bifurcation. Detailed results on CFD-LPT simulations are available in the data availability section. Table 3 demonstrates the performance of ML algorithms for generation 01 bifurcations. The best overall performance in predicting four output parameters (velocity at outlets 01 and 02 and exit fraction at outlets 01 and 02) for a generation 01 bifurcation was achieved with the RFR algorithm. Slightly weaker performance was observed for both kNN and LR, though both had most R^2 values above 0.98. The performance of the ML algorithms was further analysed by comparing CFD-LPT simulation results with ML predictions. Figure 6 compares the predicted velocity at outlet 01 from the ML approach and CFD-LPT simulations using different ML algorithms. As shown in Fig. 6, the predicted values from the RFR algorithm closely follow the actual values (CFD-LPT), as expected, given that the ML algorithms were trained on data from generation 01 bifurcations. kNN began showing slight deviations, and LR had the lowest accuracy of the three algorithms.

Table 3. Performance metrics of ML algorithms

Algorithm	Parameter	MSE	RMSE	MAE	R^2
LR	V1	0.0002	0.0143	0.0116	0.9697
	V2	8.8e-05	0.0093	0.0069	0.9840
	EF1	9.0008	3.0001	2.4049	0.9913
	EF2	9.7504	3.1225	2.5295	0.9914
RFR	V1	1.1E-06	0.0010	0.0007	0.9998
	V2	1.8E-06	0.0013	0.0008	0.9996
	EF1	0.1748	0.4181	0.2358	0.9998
	EF2	0.2531	0.5031	0.2822	0.9997
kNN Regression	V1	8.8E-05	0.0094	0.0044	0.9869
	V2	0.0001	0.0104	0.0048	0.9803
	EF1	12.4237	3.5247	1.5920	0.9880
	EF2	12.6909	3.5624	1.6585	0.9888

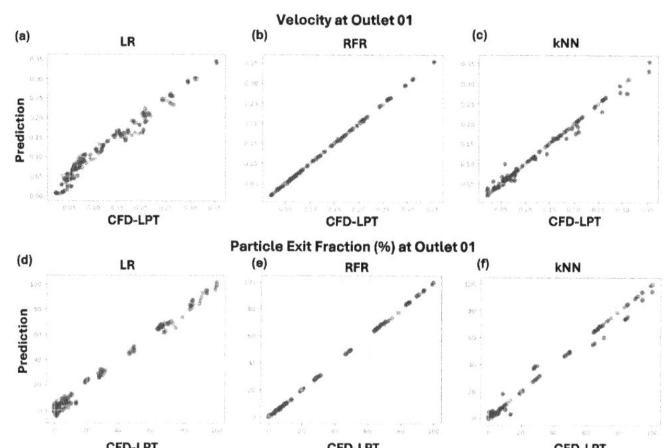

Fig. 6. Comparison of predicted and computed velocities from algorithms (a) LR (b) RFR, (c) kNN and exit fractions from algorithms (d) LR, (e) RFR, (f) kNN at outlet 01 for generation 01 bifurcations

3.3   Performance of Scalable ML Model

3.3.1   Comparison with P1

The predicted results from generation 02 bifurcations were compared with the results of CFD-LPT simulations carried out on the performance evaluation model P1 (Fig. 4). Contrary to generation 01 predictions, the overall best performance in velocity prediction was observed by the LR (RMSE 0.031) and RFR (0.034) regression for generation 02 bifurcations. The worst outcome was observed by the kNN (RMSE 0.29) algorithm. LR (RMSE 6.61) and RFR (RMSE 10.49) show better performance in predicting exit fractions. The weakest performance in predicting both parameters for generation 02 bifurcations was observed by the kNN (RMSE 38.73) algorithm.

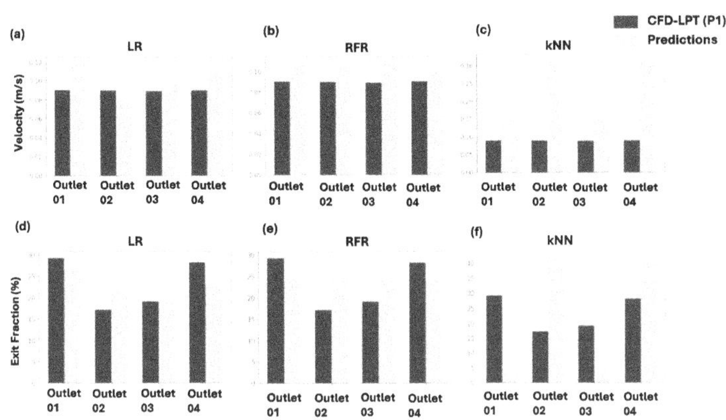

Fig. 7. Comparison of predicted and computed velocities from algorithms (a) LR, (b) RFR, (c) kNN and exit fractions from algorithms (d) LR, (e) RFR, (f) kNN at four outlets for generation 02 bifurcations

3.3.2 Comparison with Literature

To evaluate the performance of our model with flow in a more realistic vasculature, we generated a representation of the hepatic arterial domain presented in Fig. 8 of Umbarkar and Kleinstreuer [24]. We represented the Proper hepatic artery (PHA), right hepatic artery (RHA) and left hepatic artery (LHA) in our model as two generations of Y-bifurcations using the RFR algorithm, as it performed best in generation 01 (RMSE 0.4181 for EF1). A comparison of the results of normalised particle exit fraction at the four hepatic artery outlets found in [24] (ignoring particles exiting via the gastroduo-denal artery-GDA) and the developed prediction model is shown in Table 4. Similar geometric and flow profiles to [24] were given as inputs in our prediction model. Whilst the absolute values of exit fraction are different to the 3D results obtained by Umbarkar and Kleinstreuer [24], our model correctly predicts the order of outlet exit fractions and that the D3 saw significantly greater particles exiting compared to the other outlets. This latter result was not observed in the 1D results presented by [24] in conjunction with their 3D data. Although the geometric domain is different, considering curves and angles, the prediction of the distribution of particles was successfully achieved using the developed prediction model.

Table 4. Comparison of our predictive model with literature results for a hepatic arterial domain. The literature data has been normalised to ignore the particles leaving via the GDA to ensure a fair comparison with our results

Outlet	Exit Fraction (%) [24] 1D model (Normalised)	Exit Fraction (%) [24] 3D model (Normalised)	Exit Fraction (%) Prediction Model (RFR)
D1	27.19	17.56	10.42
D2	20.62	21.77	18.84
D3	27.71	39.99	46.27
D4	24.49	20.68	14.34

Table 5. Comparison of Computing Requirements

Computation	Umbarkar and Kleinstreuer [24]	Our Model
1D Model	2.67 GHz CPU, 6GB RAM (Runtime 60 min), for four cardiac cycles)	-
3D Model	10 processors, 40 GB RAM, 3.33 GHz (Runtime 4 days), for four cardiac cycles)	60 processors, 60 GB RAM, 2.45 GHz (Runtime 9 days, for the entire campaign of CFD-LPT simulations)
ML Model		8 Processors, 32 GB RAM, 2.3 GHz (Runtime 40 s for single generation training and evaluation)

4 Discussion

The primary objective of our approach was to develop a prediction model using a dataset comprising CFD-LPT results from geometric and flow variations from Y- and T-bifurcation fragments, thereby reducing the need for time and resource-intensive simulations over a large domain.

All ML algorithms showed good performance on generation 01 bifurcations, as expected. However, the key challenge was predicting the output parameters for second-generation bifurcations, as the model had to make predictions in an entirely new environment that it had not encountered before and may not have been fully represented in the training data. Nonetheless, our prediction model successfully predicted the distribution of particle exit fraction in a replicated condition of a realistic geometric domain of [24], which the 1D model was unable to adequately represent. The 1D analysis reported by Umbarkar and Kleinstreuer [24] required approximately 1% of the computational time compared to 3D simulations. Although the simulations for generating the training dataset took significantly longer, the ML predictions required a fraction of the runtime of both the 1D and 3D models of [24] and achieved better accuracy than the 1D models.

The ML based model generated the predictions in Table 4 in under 3 min of compute time.

The LR and RFR demonstrated the best predictive accuracy, whereas kNN showed the poorest performance in predicting particle exit fraction when compared to P1. This is primarily due to the complexity of setting up the number of neighbours (k value). A large k value risks averaging over very different target values (bad smoothing), while a small k risks fitting to local noise instead of the true trend [26].

From Fig. 7, an even distribution of particles was observed from the RFR algorithm for the P1 model. This was primarily due to RFR having an R2 score of almost 0.9999 for each of the output parameters of interest, and an even distribution of particles was observed in the simulation across geometries with a D1/D2 ratio of 1. Because the P1 model has a D1/D2 ratio of 1, an even distribution was predicted. In contrast, the domain of [24] had a D1/D2 ratio of 1.20 and, therefore, a uneven distribution between exit fractions were predicted when this was used as an input to our ML model. Nonetheless, the ML model only represents the underlying patterns present within the training data. The relative order of 3D particle exit fractions seen in [24] was replicated by the predictions made by our framework.

Although full-scale 3D CFD-LPT simulations were conducted, several simplifications were considered due to computational limitations. The assumption of blood as a Newtonian fluid and rigid walls is one limitation in this study. Another limitation is the assumption of steady-state flow and the one-way coupling assumption for particle tracking. The flow behaviour was primarily governed by the geometric domain [27]. However, steady-state simulations did not capture the pulsatile characteristics of the flow, and variations in particle density had a negligible influence due to $St < 1$ under the one-way coupling assumption.

Although generation 01 prediction models showed accurate results, the results of generation 02 predictions were limited. A significant challenge in improving prediction accuracy in later generations of bifurcations is incorporating temporally and spatially varying flow profiles from the larger domain into the simulations of fragmented subdomains. A skewed velocity distribution was observed at the junction points of second-generation bifurcations when simulations were conducted on P1. Figure 8 shows the velocity distribution of model P1. As particle trajectories largely depend on the flow, this certainly affects the distribution of particle deposition. Incorporating further variation in geometric and flow parameters may include unforeseen profiles into the training dataset.

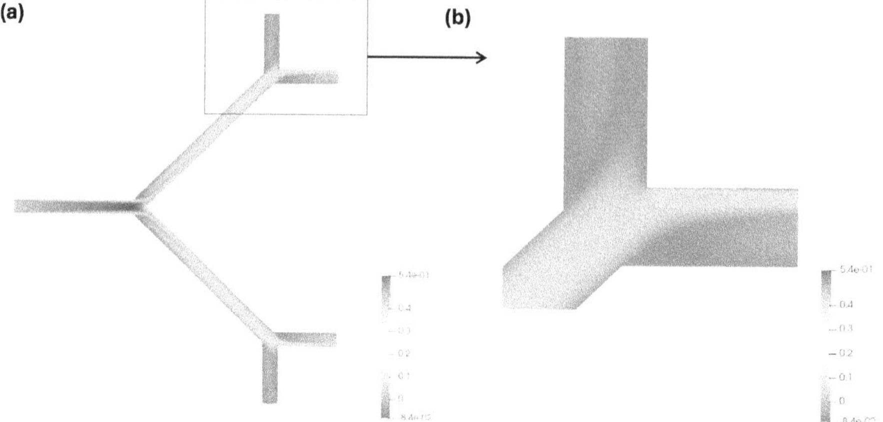

Fig. 8. Velocity distribution (x direction) of (a) model P1 and observed (b) skewed profile

As a preliminary step, the present work represents an initial approach using an ML framework. Improved data handling in the ML model would increase the efficiency of generating particle distribution predictions in large vascular networks with multiple bifurcation components. Other predictive modelling approaches, such as Artificial Neural Networks (ANNs), Convolutional Neural Networks (CNNs), and Physics-Informed Neural Networks (PINNs), remain unexplored and could offer further benefits to the presented framework. With various combinations of Y and T bifurcations, including fragments from patient-specific geometries, an entire tree of vascular network may be reconstructed. Thus, further investigation of a larger vascular network is still required.

5 Conclusion

In this paper, a scalable framework for predicting flow characteristics and particle transport in bifurcating vascular networks was constructed by training an ML model on output from 3D CFD-LPT simulations. By successively combining simulation results from smaller bifurcation variants, a larger network was represented in a modular fashion. This approach enables rapid evaluation of flow dynamics and particle transport while substantially reducing computational requirements and demonstrating improved predictive capability compared to conventional one-dimensional modelling approaches. Furthermore, our framework substantially decreases the computational burden of dataset generation by avoiding full-network simulations. Although certain limitations had to be considered, there remain several areas in which the current framework could be further refined. In our future work, we wish to incorporate the pulsatile nature of flow with more realistic vessel shapes and explore PINNs in larger networks.

Acknowledgments. We are grateful for the use of the computing resources from the Northern Ireland High Performance Computing (NI-HPC) service funded by EPSRC (EP/T022175).

Data Availability. All mesh files and scripts and supplementary dataset are available at: https://github.com/Zaheenman/CFD_DPM__ML_Vascular_Repository.

Disclosure of Interests.   The authors have no competing interests to declare that are relevant to the content of this article.

References

1. Nedkoff, L., Briffa, T., Zemedikun, D., Herrington, S., Wright, F.L.: Global trends in atherosclerotic cardiovascular disease. Clin. Ther. **45**(11), 1087–1091 (2023). https://doi.org/10.1016/j.clinthera.2023.09.020
2. Cicha, I.: The Grand Challenges in Cardiovascular Drug Delivery. [Specialty Grand Challenge]. Frontiers in Drug Delivery, Volume 1 – 2021. https://doi.org/10.3389/fddev.2021.784731. (2021)
3. Lee, B.-K. Computational Fluid Dynamics in Cardiovascular Disease. KCJ **41**(8), 423–430, https://doi.org/10.4070/kcj.2011.41.8.423 (2011)
4. Meschi, S.S., Farghadan, A., Arzani, A.: Flow topology and targeted drug delivery in cardiovascular disease. J. Biomech. **119**, 110307 (2021). https://doi.org/10.1016/j.jbiomech.2021.110307
5. Zhong, L., Zhang, J.-M., Su, B., Tan, R.S., Allen, J.C., Kassab, G.S.: Application of Patient-Specific Computational Fluid Dynamics in Coronary and Intra-Cardiac Flow Simulations: Challenges and Opportunities. [Review]. Frontiers in Physiology, Volume 9 - 2018, https://doi.org/10.3389/fphys.2018.00742 (2018)
6. Kurtcuoglu, V., Poulikalos, D.: Principles and challenges of computational fluid dynamics in medicine. In: 9th MICCAI Workshop on Computational Biomechanics for Medicine, pp. 14–22, October 2006
7. Malek, S., Eskandari, A., Sharbatdar, M.: Machine learning-based prediction of hemodynamic parameters in left coronary artery bifurcation: A CFD approach. Heliyon **11**(2) (2025)
8. Alqarni, A.A., Alqarni, M., Felemban, M.F., Algahtani, F.S., Alzubaidi, M.A., Shukr, B.S.: Advanced hybrid numerical-machine learning computational study on fluid flow modeling in magnetic nanocarriers for targeted drug delivery. Case Stud. Thermal Eng. **59**, 104497 (2024)
9. Islam, M.S., Larpruenrudee, P., Rahman, M.M., Li, G., Husain, S., Munir, A., et al.: Pharmaceutical aerosol transport in airways: a combined machine learning (ML) and discrete element model (DEM) approach. Powder Technol. **448**, 120271 (2024)
10. Francis, I., Saha, S.C.: Computational fluid dynamics and machine learning algorithms analysis of striking particle velocity magnitude, particle diameter, and impact time inside an acinar region of the human lung. Physics of Fluids, **34**(10) (2022)
11. Lin, D., Kenjereš, S.: Towards fast and reliable estimations of 3D pressure, velocity and wall shear stress in aortic blood flow: CFD-based machine learning approach. Comput. Biol. Med. **191**, 110137 (2025)
12. Coenen, A., Lubbers, M.M., Kurata, A., Kono, A., Dedic, A., Chelu, R.G., et al.: Fractional flow reserve computed from noninvasive CT angiography data: diagnostic performance of an on-site clinician-operated computational fluid dynamics algorithm. Radiology **274**(3), 674–683 (2015)
13. Ko, B.S., Cameron, J.D., Munnur, R.K., Wong, D.T., Fujisawa, Y., Sakaguchi, T., et al.: Noninvasive CT-derived FFR based on structural and fluid analysis: a comparison with invasive FFR for detection of functionally significant stenosis. JACC: Cardiovascular Imaging, **10**(6), 663–673 (2017)
14. Kuprat, A.P., Jalali, M., Jan, T., Corley, R.A., Asgharian, B., Price, O., et al.: Efficient bidirectional coupling of 3D Computational Fluid-Particle Dynamics and 1D Multiple Path Particle Dosimetry lung models for multiscale modeling of aerosol dosimetry. J. Aerosol. Sci. **151**, https://doi.org/10.1016/j.jaerosci.2020.105647 (2021)

15. Longest, P.W., Bass, K., Dutta, R., Rani, V., Thomas, M.L., El-Achwah, A., et al.: Use of computational fluid dynamics deposition modeling in respiratory drug delivery. Expert Opin. Drug Deliv. **16**(1), 7–26 (2019). https://doi.org/10.1080/17425247.2019.1551875

16. Dassault Systèmes: SOLIDWORKS. Dassault Systèmes, Vélizy-Villacoublay. https://www.solidworks.com. Accessed 02 Apr 2026

17. Northern Ireland High Performance Computing (NI-HPC). Kelvin2 HPC Service. https://ni-hpc.ac.uk/Kelvin2/. Accessed 02 Apr 2026

18. Jasak, H.: OpenFOAM: Open source CFD in research and industry. Int. J. Naval Archit. Ocean Eng. **1**(2), 89–94 (2009). https://doi.org/10.2478/IJNAOE-2013-0011

19. Kramer, O.: Scikit-learn. In Machine learning for evolution strategies, pp. 45–53. Springer (2016)

20. Arefin, N.M., Good, B.C.: Emboli Transport in a Full-Length Patient-Specific Aorta: Assessment of Abdominal Organ Injury Risk During Cardiopulmonary Bypass. medRxiv, 2025.2006. 2007.25329120 (2025)

21. Ferrante, A., Elghobashi, S.: 3 - Physics of two-way coupling in particle-laden homogeneous isotropic turbulence. In: S. Subramaniam, & S. Balachandar (eds.), Modeling Approaches and Computational Methods for Particle-Laden Turbulent Flows, pp. 81–109. Academic Press (2023)

22. De Nisco, G., Lodi Rizzini, M., Verardi, R., Chiastra, C., Candreva, A., De Ferrari, G., et al.: Modelling blood flow in coronary arteries: Newtonian or shear-thinning non-Newtonian rheology? Comput. Methods Programs Biomed. **242**, 107823 (2023). https://doi.org/10.1016/j.cmpb.2023.107823

23. Bushi, D., Grad, Y., Einav, S., Yodfat, O., Nishri, B., Tanne, D.: Hemodynamic evaluation of embolic trajectory in an arterial bifurcation. Stroke **36**(12), 2696–2700 (2005). https://doi.org/10.1161/01.STR.0000190097.08862.9a

24. Umbarkar, T.S., Kleinstreuer, C.: Computationally efficient fluid-particle dynamics simulations of arterial systems. Commun. Comput. Phys. **17**(2), 401–423 (2015)

25. Khalili Param, H., Tofighian, H., Mokhlesabadi, M., Nabaei, M., Farnoud, A.: Targeted drug delivery during radioembolization in a comprehensive hepatic artery system: a computational study. Comput. Math. Appl. **135**, 193–205 (2023). https://doi.org/10.1016/j.camwa.2023.02.007

26. Zhang, S. Challenges in KNN Classification. IEEE Trans. Knowl. Data Eng. 1. https://doi.org/10.1109/TKDE.2021.3049250 (2021)

27. Geers, A., Larrabide, I., Morales, H., Frangi, A.: Comparison of steady-state and transient blood flow simulations of intracranial aneurysms. In 2010 Annual International Conference of the IEEE Engineering in Medicine and Biology, pp. 2622–2625. IEEE (2010)

Adaptive Resolution Scheme for Non-additive Molecular Three-Body Potentials

Jose Alfonso Pinzon Escobar[1]([✉]) [iD] and Philipp Neumann[2,3] [iD]

[1] Chair for High Performance Computing, Helmut Schmidt University, Hamburg, Germany
jose.pinzon@hsu-hh.de
[2] High Performance Computing & Data Science, University of Hamburg, Hamburg, Germany
philipp.neumann@desy.de
[3] IT-Department, Deutsches Elektronen-Synchrotron, Hamburg, Germany

Abstract. This work proposes the use of Adaptive Resolution Schemes (AdResS) in molecular dynamics simulations that include three-body interactions described by the Axilrod-Teller-Muto (ATM) potential. It is known that the computation of three-body forces greatly increases the number of calculations, which is the motivation to investigate appropriate speedup techniques. In this work, AdResS is used to allow for the computation of three-body interactions only within a portion of the simulation domain. This is implemented using force resolution regions, such that across the domain three-body forces are introduced smoothly from a pure two-body force region. The proposed scheme is tested using a relevant number of single-site, Lennard-Jones molecules in homogeneous case studies. In order to measure performance, the achieved speedup is expressed in terms of the geometric configuration of the force resolution regions where the three-body forces are calculated. These tests were carried out at node-level to measure the parallel and AdResS speedups using several force resolution region configurations with increasing portions of three-body presence. It is shown that AdResS, for three-body interactions, introduces inconsistencies in simple ensemble averages, like the temperature and density, which require the use of correction schemes. In this work we make use of the thermodynamic force for the correction of artificial density gradients in our simulations, which originate from a pressure difference induced by the coarse interactions.

Keywords: Molecular simulations · Adaptive resolution · Three-body interactions

1 Introduction

Molecular dynamics simulations are of increasing importance in the modeling of phenomena at the atomic level. The computation of interatomic forces requires a great portion of the computational effort within a simulation. Commonly, only short-range interactions are explicitly computed. Additionally, the calculated forces are limited to those within pairs of molecules. It is known that these limitations result in discrepancies between experimental and simulation results, e.g. for simple fluids. These differences can be corrected by introducing short-range, three-body interactions, such that the potential energy is given by

$$U = U\left(r_{ij}\right) + U\left(r_{ij}, r_{jk}, r_{ik}\right), \tag{1}$$

where r_{ij}, r_{jk}, r_{ik} are distances between particle pairs. Here, $U\left(r_{ij}\right)$ is described by the Lennard-Jones (LJ) potential [7], and $U\left(r_{ij}, r_{jk}, r_{ik}\right)$ is described by the ATM potential [3,12]. The interactions are truncated at a distance r_c, the cutoff radius. The computation of $U\left(r_{ij}, r_{jk}, r_{ik}\right)$ dramatically increases the runtime and computational effort required by the simulation. Therefore, it is of interest to investigate techniques which allow for a faster calculation of these forces. In this work, the use of AdResS [15,16] is proposed to speed up simulations that include the calculation of three-body interactions. Our technique builds on the fundamental AdResS literature for pairwise interactions, therefore combining two separate fields in a novel fashion. This could be used in the case of inhomogeneous scenarios, where the liquid phase is of main interest, or where the formation of vapor-liquid interfaces has to be studied instead of the behavior of the entire system.

This work is organized as follows. A theoretical overview of three-body interactions, AdResS, and molecular dynamics concepts used in our experiments is given in Sect. 2, together with implementation details. In the following sections performance measurements are used to determine an appropriate force resolution region configuration for AdResS-enabled simulations. Subsequently, we present thermodynamic results generated using simulations of LJ fluids, as well as a discussion of the effects AdResS has on these thermodynamic properties. Using similar AdResS configurations, we show how the thermodynamic force could be used to correct unwanted effects on the ensemble averages. Finally, we give a conclusion and a perspective on future work.

2 Theoretical Background

2.1 Three-Body Forces in MD

The triple dipole described by the ATM potential contributes 5–10% of the total energy of a fluid in the liquid phase [5]. Additionally, it has been reported that introducing three-body computations can reduce the error of surface tension calculations with respect to experimental results from about 19% to 2.2%, see [4]. For this reason, the ATM potential has been introduced to inhomogeneous simulations of the vapor-liquid phases of LJ fluids [17] and argon [18]. These facts highlight the importance of using three-body forces in molecular dynamics simulations.

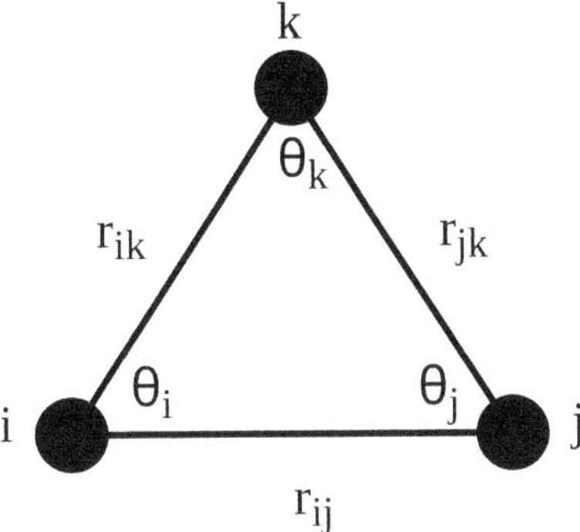

Fig. 1. Triangular configuration formed by three atoms i, k, j. The interactions are truncated if any of the distances r_{ij}, r_{jk}, r_{ik} are larger than r_c.

The ATM potential is given by

$$U_{ijk} = \nu \left(\frac{1 + \cos\theta_i \cos\theta_j \cos\theta_k}{\left(r_{ij}r_{jk}r_{ik}\right)^3} \right), \tag{2}$$

where ν is a molecular model-dependent constant. The angles $\theta_i, \theta_j, \theta_k$ and lengths r_{ij}, r_{jk}, r_{ik} are associated with the triangular configuration formed by an atomic triplet, as shown in Fig. 1.

The dependence on the angles can be removed using the law of cosines, which also allows for the implementation of Newton's third law [10] to significantly reduce the required force calculations. For instance, a reduction factor of 9 can be achieved in some cases [14]. In this work, the interactions are truncated if any of the three sides of the triangular configuration are larger than a cutoff radius r_c, as for instance in [2,13].

2.2 Adaptive Resolution

AdResS is used with the purpose of reducing the computational effort required by the calculation of the forces in molecular dynamics. This is achieved by reducing the level of resolution of the molecules. Originally, it has been applied to reducing the degrees of freedom (DoFs) by coarsening a multi-site molecule to a single site located at the center of mass [15]. The coarse interactions are computed using a corresponding coarse potential, for instance following the procedure given in [11].

Here, certain aspects of AdResS are used to introduce three-body interactions to a region of the domain, without requiring DoF reduction nor the use of coarse-grain potentials as the one proposed in [9]. The used approach is illustrated in Fig. 2. Three force resolution regions are used to transition from pure, two-body interactions, $\boldsymbol{F} = \boldsymbol{F}_{ij}$, to a two- and three-body scheme, $\boldsymbol{F} = \boldsymbol{F}_{ij} + \boldsymbol{F}_{ijk}$. The former corresponds to the coarse force (CF) region, and the latter to the full force (FF). These are connected by a hybrid force (HF) region, where $\boldsymbol{F} = \boldsymbol{F}_{ij} + w\left(x\right)\boldsymbol{F}_{ijk}$ via a weight function $w\left(x\right)$, as in regular AdResS.

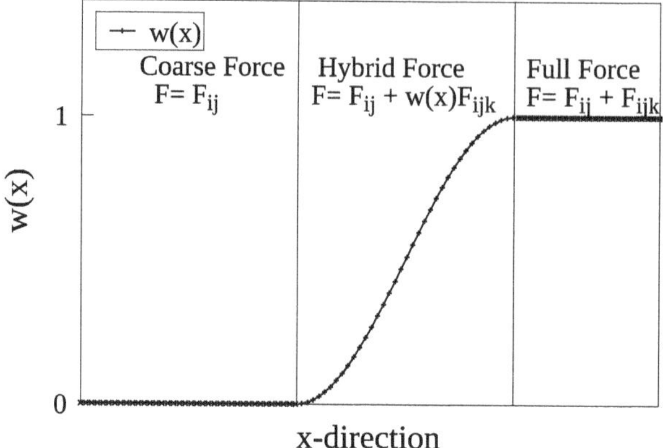

Fig. 2. The CF and FF regions are connected via an HF region. A weight function, $w\left(x\right)$, smoothly introduces $\boldsymbol{F}_{ijk}$ to the domain. The x-direction can be any of the principal physical directions of a 3D domain.

In the HF region, the transition from CF to FF is enabled via $w\left(x\right)$, the weight function given by

$$w(x) = \begin{cases} 0 & x \in \text{CF} \\ \cos^2\left[\left(\frac{\pi}{2\,d_{HF}}\right)(x - d_{FF})\right] & x \in \text{HF} \\ 1 & x \in \text{FF,} \end{cases} \tag{3}$$

as in [20], and where d_{HF} and d_{FF} are the widths of the HF and FF regions respectively, and x is the position of a given molecule. It allows for a smooth introduction of the three-body forces into the simulation.

Using this proposed scheme, it is attempted to reproduce fluid properties in a slab of the domain with two- and three-body interactions. These properties should match those of a reference simulation, where three-body interactions were used across the complete domain. In the AdResS simulation, the FF slab has to be sufficiently wide to allow for meaningful physical results, as well as for a significant reduction of the computational effort.

2.3   Algorithmic Implementation

The three-body computations, as described in Sect. 2.1, are combined with the AdResS aspects of Sect. 2.2 to speed up the computation of three-body interactions. It is assumed that the atomic triplets can be found efficiently, for instance through the use of the linked cells algorithm and appropriate cell traversing routines, as in [14].

The implementation is described in Algorithm 1. In the context of this work, the molecules are sorted into cells. At least one of the involved cells must be fully or partially inside the HF or FF regions. A molecular triplet can be sorted into a single, a pair, or a triplet of cells. Based on the spatial distribution sketched in Fig. 2, determining to which resolution region a molecular triplet belongs to, is a fundamental task. For this reason, before traversing the molecules, the cells are used to determine if the computation of three-body forces is required. If this is the case, then Algorithm 1 is used to compute the required interactions.

Our approach is limited to flat interfaces, splitting the domain over a unique dimension x. In traditional AdResS, as given e.g. in [15], the center of mass for a multi-site molecule is used for the computation of $w(x)$. In our case, this approach is discouraged, because the center of mass would need to be computed for every triplet. This would greatly increase the overhead, which would drastically reduce the achieved performance. Therefore, we make use of the average position over x, i.e. $\bar{x}$, of a given atomic triplet. This is given by

$$\bar{x} = \frac{1}{3}\left(x_1 + x_2 + x_3\right) \tag{4}$$

where x_1, x_2, x_3 are the x-direction components of the positions of each of the three molecules. In this way, the value of the weight function can be determined as $w(\bar{x})$. However, the choice of (4) above COM was made for performance reasons only. In our tested scenarios using equal mass, single-site molecules, the two methods are equivalent and yield the same results.

Algorithm 1 Computation of ATM Forces using AdResS

Require: At least on cell partially/fully in HF or FF
 1: **for all** molecular triplets in cells **do**
 2:      Find $\bar{x}$ with (4)
 3:      Determine which resolution region
 4:      Calculate $w(\bar{x})$ with (3)
 5:      Compute $\boldsymbol{F} = \boldsymbol{F}_{ij} + w(\bar{x})\,\boldsymbol{F}_{ijk}$
 6: **end for**

2.4   Measured Property

Here, we describe the measured thermodynamic properties for the validation of the proposed AdResS and three-body methodology. Our main focus is to measure the particle distribution, as well as thermal and mechanical equilibrium. The density and temperature can be directly measured over the x-dimension of the domain via binning on every time step. Their average over the time steps can then be presented. In this way, a profile for both functions, $\langle \rho(x) \rangle$ and $\langle T(x) \rangle$, can be generated. Further details can be found in [1].

Mechanical equilibrium can be described by the pressure. As mentioned in Sect. 2.1, this property is greatly affected by the presence of three-body interactions, as compared to the results obtained only with two-body forces, e.g. in [2], where pure LJ results are compared to those including the ATM potential. Thus, measuring the pressure can allow for a better understanding of the effects of AdResS on the simulation domain. In order to generate a pressure profile, the pressure tensor, $\bar{\mathbf{P}}$, has to be measured over x. Here, the Irving-Kirkwood representation is used

$$\bar{\mathbf{P}}\left(x\right) = \rho\left(x\right)\kappa_B T\mathbf{1} + \frac{1}{2A}\left\langle\sum_{i=1}^{N-1}\sum_{j>i}^{N} \boldsymbol{r}_{ij}\otimes\boldsymbol{F}_{ij}\frac{1}{|x_{ij}|}\theta\left(\frac{x-x_i}{x_{ij}}\right)\theta\left(\frac{x_j-x}{x_{ij}}\right)\right\rangle,$$
$$(5)$$

where θ is a Heaviside function, x indicates the discrete bin centers positions, x_i and x_j the positions of particles i and j over the x-dimension, A is the bin surface area perpendicular to x, and $\otimes$ stands for the outer product between two vectors. The first term on the r.h.s. of (5) stands for the ideal gas part of P, in analogy to the global pressure value commonly used in molecular dynamics. The second r.h.s. term is referred to as the virial or excess contribution. In equilibrium, the off-diagonal terms of $\bar{\mathbf{P}}$ are zero. Then the remaining diagonal terms can be split into two different components called the normal and tangential parts [1, 19],

$$p_N\left(x\right) = P_{zz} \tag{6}$$

$$p_T\left(x\right) = \frac{1}{2}\left(P_{xx} + P_{yy}\right) \tag{7}$$

where P_{xx}, P_{yy}, P_{zz} are the three diagonal terms of $\bar{\mathbf{P}}$. In equilibrated, homogeneous regions the equality $p_N = p_T$ is fulfilled and $p_N = \text{constant}$ over x.

In this context, we make use of $\bar{\mathbf{P}}$ to measure the local effects of AdResS on the pressure in the FF and HF regions. The main focus is on measuring and reproducing $p_N\left(x\right)$ with different values widths of the FF and HF slabs, and comparing the obtained results to those of a reference simulation with ATM forces everywhere. Together with $\rho\left(x\right)$ and $T\left(x\right)$, these ensemble averages illustrate the effects of AdResS over fundamental ensemble averages.

3 Results

Here we present results for simulations involving single-site LJ fluids. As mentioned before, the pairwise forces are given by the LJ potential, while the ATM potential describes the three-body interactions. This section starts by using homogeneous scenarios for the measurement of the speedup in the context of the configuration of the force resolution regions, i.e. the width of the regions where $\boldsymbol{F}_{ijk}$ is computed. These studies are useful for finding a proper width to the FF and HF regions, while allowing for meaningful performance gains. This is followed by the presentation of thermodynamic averages and correlation functions as given in Sect. 2.4, comparing simulations with three-body computations across the whole domain to those with the optimal configurations found with the speedup studies.

Throughout this section, we make use of LJ-reduced units for all given quantities. This reduction scheme can be found in [1]. The used molecular model is set to LJ parameters of $\epsilon = 1$ and $\sigma = 1$, and a mass $m = 1$. For all cases, the ATM parameter is set to $\nu = 0.072$ as in [2]. The simulations were carried out using our in-house molecular dynamics simulation software, LauraMD [14]. It is programmed in C++ and parallelized using OpenMP.

3.1   Speedup

AdResS is used to reduce the computational effort of computing the forces in a simulation. In [8], this was measured in terms of the speedup gained in terms of the region configuration.

Similarly, here we use the fraction v, given by

$$v = \frac{V_{HF} + V_{FF}}{V_{Total}},\tag{8}$$

to indicate the portion of the total domain's volume V_{Total}, where the three-body forces have to be computed, i.e., the sum of the FF and HF volumes, V_{FF} and V_{HY} respectively. The limit cases are $v = 1$, where $\boldsymbol{F}_{ijk}$ is computed over all the domain and $v = 0$, where no three-body forces are present at all. Given that only slab geometries are used in this work, v can be also expressed in terms of the widths of the HF and FF, respectively d_{HF} and d_{FF}.

With this in mind, the achieved AdResS-speedup for a given configuration can be measured via

$$S_{AdResS} = \frac{t_{3B}}{t_{3B AdResS}},\tag{9}$$

where the runtimes correspond to the computation of the three-body forces, and t_{3B} is the limit case for $v = 1.0$, while $t_{3B AdResS}$ is the corresponding runtime for a scenario with a known v-value.

In this context, v determines the total computational effort. Opposed to the methodology given in [8], for this case there is no reduction of the degrees of freedom (the number of sites), therefore we cannot directly use the speedup relation given therein. However, we can use a similar procedure by measuring several v-values to determine the value that allows for a large total FF + HF volume while retaining a large speedup. In theory, it would be expected for S_{AdResS} and t to be linear functions of v. However, the AdResS functionalities add overhead, which hampers down the performance.

The AdResS and parallel speedups were measured for a box domain with $a = 40$. A total of $N = 20,000$ molecules were used, and the linked cells algorithm was used with $r_c = 2.5$ and a total of $4,096$ cells with periodic boundary conditions on all domain borders. The phase space was first equilibrated for $50,000$ time steps and $\Delta t = 0.01$, to guarantee an even distribution of the molecules across the domain. This was followed by a production phase of 20 time steps to measure the runtime, t, of the routine which computes the three-body forces.

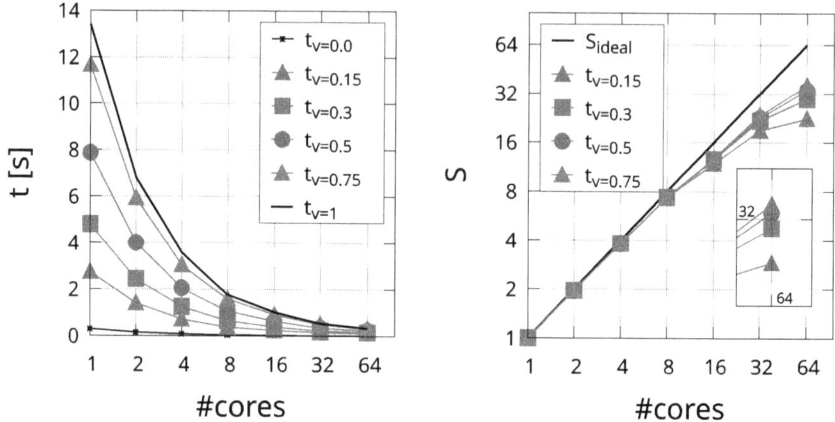

Fig. 3. Strong scaling and parallel speedup for a domain with side length $a = 40$ and $N = 20,000$ molecules, measured over 20 steps. Several v-values are tested. A lower value of v means that the ATM potential is computed in a smaller portion of the domain. For $v = 0.0$, the given runtime shows the overhead introduced by the AdResS functionalities. On the right-hand side, a magnification of the highest core count is given within the figure.

The parallel performance results are given in Fig. 3 for increasing proportions of v. For all cases V_{FF} was maintained at 10% of V_{Total}, with the remaining v-portion being assigned to V_{HF}. All configurations were run 5 times, and the average of these runs is presented. Their respective standard deviations are negligible. The runtimes for the limiting cases, $v = 0.0$ and $v = 1.0$, are given for comparison.

As expected, decreasing values of v allow for a faster production run. However, the overhead seems to accumulate as v increases. This is more noticeable at low core counts, where it is seen that for $v = 0.75$ the runtime does not decrease linearly with v. A similar case is found for $v = 0.5$, which is above the 50% expected time reduction. From Fig. 3, we learn that $v = 0.3$ allows for a scenario with good speedup, while being close to the theoretical runtime reduction.

As the core count increases, these differences become less apparent, since also the reference time is decreased. Therefore, it is important to measure the performance in terms of the AdResS speedup for varying number of cores. This is given in Fig. 4. The runtime of a simulation with $v = 1.0$ was used as t_{3B} at different core counts, and used in (9) as the full three-body reference simulation. The tested values are then $v = \{0.15, 0.3, 0.5, 0.75, 1.0\}$. A higher v together with the overhead results in a reduced performance, for instance at $v = 0.5$. However, for all core counts the scenario $v = 0.3$ allows for a production run twice as fast as t_{3B}. These results can help decide what proportion of three-body computation domain should be used to guarantee a significant performance increase. In this context, we see a small v, could allow for noticeable performance gains while retaining sufficient FF domain to generate meaningful results.

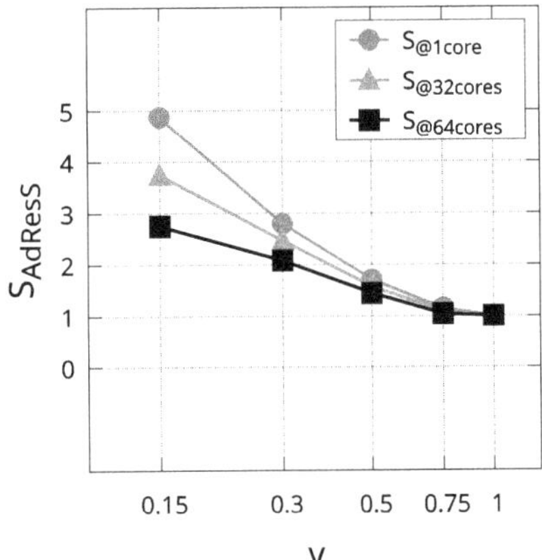

Fig. 4. AdResS-Speedup for several core counts and v-values. Higher values of v reduce the achieved performance gain, as seen e.g. for $v = 0.5$. For each core count, the corresponding t_{3B} was used with $v = 1.0$, as given in (9).

3.2   Thermodynamical Results

This section presents results which measure the properties described in Sect. 2.4, e.g. the pressure tensor components. The AdResS-enabled simulations were configured following the insight obtained from Sect. 3.1, such that the force resolution regions can be optimally configured. In this sense, the FF and HF regions were set using $v \in \{0.3, 0.5, 1.0\}$ and $v = 1.0$ is used as a reference. As before, for the other configurations of v, FF is set to 10% of V_{Total} while only the proportion of HF varies.

These simulation runs were configured as before. The time step was set to $\Delta t = 0.003$ with $T = 1.2$. After every step, a velocity scaling thermostat was used to adjust the temperature. The given properties were sampled over $50,000$ time steps, using a total of 500 bins. As mentioned in Sect. 2, it is known that the ATM potential can have large effects on the pressure of the system [4]. Therefore, the given results are based on measuring $p_N(x)$ over the simulation domain, since for a homogeneous region it is expected that $p_N = $ constant.

These results are given in Fig. 5, for the aforementioned v-values. The FF region is constant for all cases and indicated by the two solid lines, while HF varies with v. The borders for each v-value are indicated by the differently dashed lines. Profiles for $T(x)$, $\rho(x)$, and $p_N(x)$ are provided as time averages. The results for $v = 1.0$ are used as a pure three-body reference.

It is seen that AdResS introduces artificial density gradients towards the FF region. While the density values in CF appear closer to the original bulk density ρ_0, the gradients generate visible deviations as the three-body forces are introduced. A similar case is observed in $T(x)$, where a slight deviation with respect to the reference is observed. Nevertheless, this appears to be below 5% of the bulk temperature $T = 1.2$ and is assumed to have negligible effects on the other measured properties. However, major AdResS effects can be observed

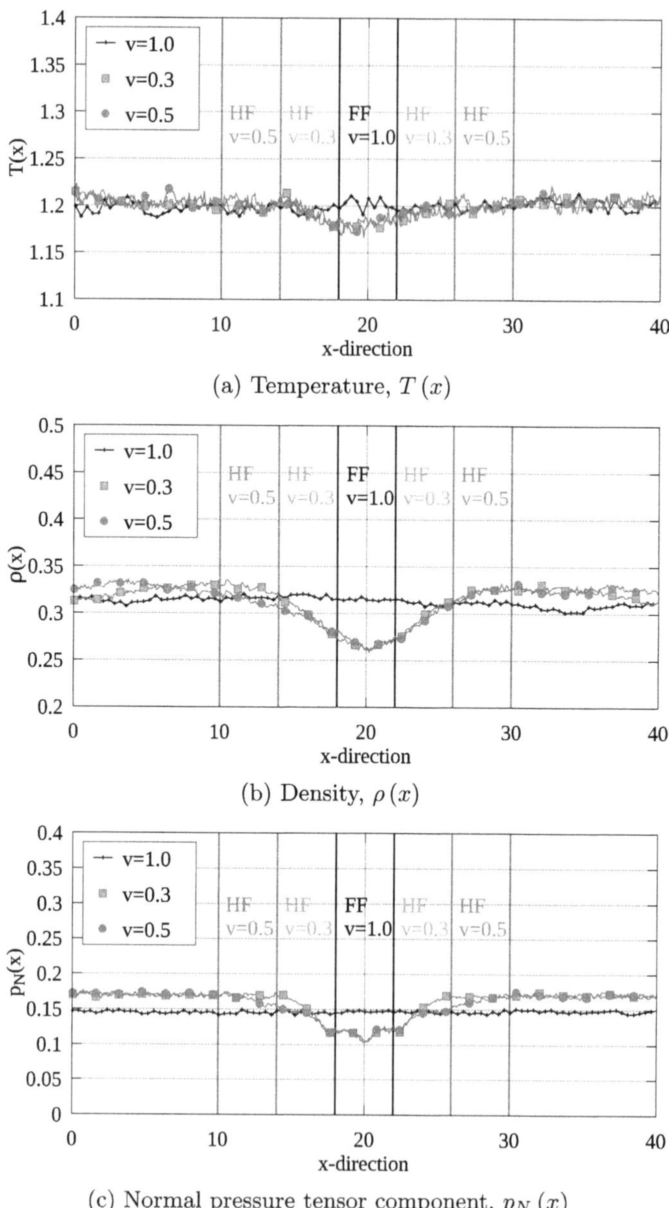

(a) Temperature, $T(x)$

(b) Density, $\rho(x)$

(c) Normal pressure tensor component, $p_N(x)$

Fig. 5. (a) Temperature profile, (b) density profile, and (c) normal pressure component, $p_N(x)$, of $\bar{\mathbf{P}}$, for $v \in \{1.0, 0.5, 0.3\}$. The force resolution region borders are correspondingly labeled by v value, as well as using solid lines for FF and dashed lines for HF. The values of $v = 1.0$ correspond to the pure three-body reference. These profiles were sampled using 500 bins for $50,000$ time steps. The use of AdResS generates computational artifacts in the sampled profiles with respect to the reference $v = 1.0$.

in the $p_N(x)$ profile. Both tested scenarios deviate greatly from the reference p_N value, particularly at the FF region. Noticeably, the bulk value at the CF region also deviates from that of $v = 1.0$. Since the density, $\rho(x)$, contributes to the ideal part of $\bar{\mathbf{P}}$ as given in (5), a density correcting scheme was used as a possible correction to the p_N deviations observed in Fig. 5.

3.3 Thermodynamic Force

Algorithm 2 Thermodynamic Force Computation

Require: *sampling, stride, step,* α, ρ_0
  for all *step* in simulation **do**
      ⋮
    Sample $\rho(x)$
    if $(step > sampling)$ & $(step \bmod stride = 0)$ **then**
      Compute $\boldsymbol{F}^i_{Th.}$ using (10)
    end if
    Apply $\boldsymbol{F}^i_{Th.}$ to all molecules
      ⋮
  end for

The encountered issues in Fig. 5 are very similar to those found in the implementation of traditional, DoF-reducing AdResS. For instance, artificial density gradients have been reported in AdResS implementations [15]. As mentioned before, the direct relation between $\bar{\mathbf{P}}$ and $\rho(x)$ could be used to investigate correction schemes of benefit to both properties.

A standard approach, e.g. [6], to fixing these issues makes use of an iterative method to compute a correction of the density via its gradient, such that

$$\mathbf{F}^{i+1}_{Th.}(x) = \mathbf{F}^i_{Th.}(x) - \frac{\alpha}{\rho_0^2}\left(\nabla \rho^i(x)\right), \tag{10}$$

where α is a given constant, and ρ_0 is the bulk density, which is known a priori.

The thermodynamic force is computed using the methodology described in [6,20]. Our implementation is given in Algorithm 2. The $F_{th.}$ update is done on every *stride* steps. At the beginning of the simulation, a *sampling* number of steps is allowed before the first update, $\boldsymbol{F}^0_{Th.}$, so that a smooth density profile is obtained. Once the *sampling* threshold is surpassed, $\boldsymbol{F}^i_{Th.}$ is updated every *stride* number of steps using (10). Since $\rho(x)$ is sampled using bins, the same approach is used for $\boldsymbol{F}_{Th.}(x)$. For this, central differences are used to compute $\nabla \rho(x)$. Once the updated iterate $\boldsymbol{F}^i_{Th.}(x)$ is stored in every bin, its value is linearly interpolated and applied to every molecule. The computation of $\boldsymbol{F}_{Th.}$ can be finalized either with a convergence criterion or after a total number of steps.

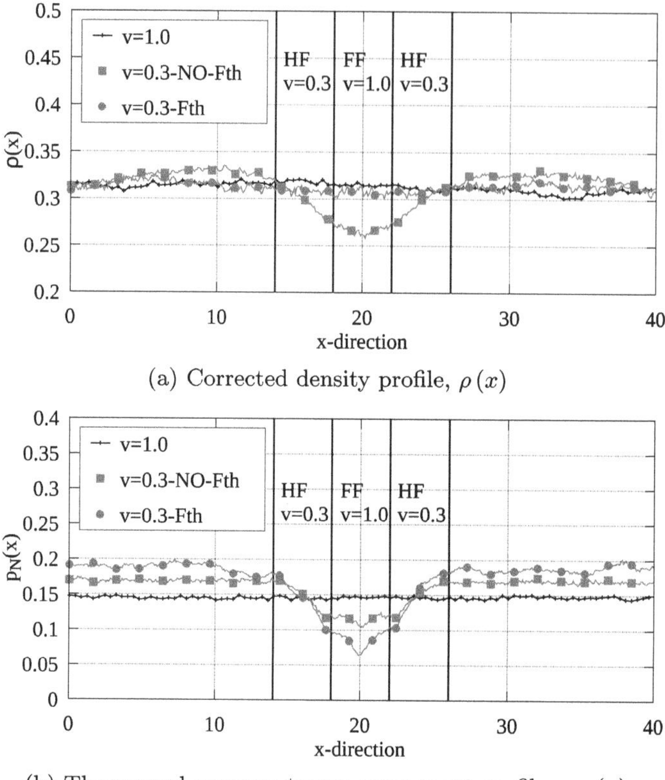

(a) Corrected density profile, $\rho\left(x\right)$

(b) The normal pressure tensor component profile, $p_N\left(x\right)$

Fig. 6. (a) Correction to the density profile and (b) effects on the normal component. Although $\boldsymbol{F}_{Th.}$ corrected the density over x, the sampled values of p_N show that the thermodynamic force had negative effects on this property. The FF region is indicated by solid black lines, and the HF region by dashed lines.

Tests were performed using the $v = 0.3$ configuration. A first *sampling* run of $20,000$ steps was used to generate a smooth density profile, and *stride* was set to 100 steps. This was followed by an $F_{th.}$ calculation and property sampling production run of $50,000$ steps, during which the thermodynamic force was updated following Algorithm 2. The value of $\alpha = 0.01$ was heuristically determined with test runs.

The results are given in Fig. 6 for the density and normal pressure tensor component profiles, $\rho\left(x\right)$ and $p_N\left(x\right)$ respectively. As expected, $\boldsymbol{F}_{Th.}$ successfully corrected the deviations of $\rho\left(x\right)$ observed in Fig. 5. The resulting profile closely follows the reference value of $v = 1.0$. However, the obtained values of $p_N\left(x\right)$ seem to be negatively affected by $\boldsymbol{F}_{Th.}$. It can be seen that the value in the CF region also seems to be affected by the use of the thermodynamic force. The reasons for this are a matter of ongoing investigation.

4 Conclusion and Outlook

In this work an AdResS approach for the computation of three-body interactions was presented, since these computations greatly increase the workload and impact the runtime. It was shown that it is possible to reduce the workload by restricting the calculation of three-body forces to only a portion of the domain via the use of AdResS.

Simple LJ fluids were used to test the described AdResS and three-body implementation. Moreover, the presented results show that in some cases it is possible to speed up the simulation fivefold when compared to a reference case with three-body forces present everywhere. The performance gains were presented in terms of a fraction v, which quantifies the portion of the domain where three-body interactions are computed. Although in theory the AdResS speedup is a linear function of v, this is different in the multicore case, where the overall computational load saturates earlier for smaller values of v. We have investigated and quantified these speedups for the provided scenarios. Therefore, parallel studies were carried out to determine appropriate values of v for which there are sufficient performance gains while still allowing for the generation of meaningful physical results.

We proposed several correlation functions and ensemble averages for the validation of the proposed methodology. These showed that AdResS introduced non-physical artifacts to the two- and three-body regions. Specifically, the density profile was visibly affected by the use of AdResS, which introduced unwanted density gradients around the interface borders. These are commonly reported in the AdResS literature and are corrected using a thermodynamic force scheme. The latter was introduced in this work via an iterative approach. With it the density profile was corrected, but the measured pressure tensor components were not successfully reproduced.

Nevertheless, it was shown that there is great speedup to be achieved by the use of AdResS in the context of three-body forces. Additionally, further work will be done on determining how to introduce the thermodynamic force to the computation of the pressure tensor, this could help correct the negative effects on the normal pressure tensor component. And on how the thermodynamic force affects the temperature of the AdResS with three-body simulations. Our studies were limited to single phase molecular systems, however three-body forces are of great interest in multi-phase simulations. Thus, ongoing work will target the possible use of AdResS in the vapor-liquid phase interaction for which appropriate correcting schemes might need to be developed.

Acknowledgments. Support, including resources by hpc.bw, funded by dtec.bw – Digitalization and Technology Research Center of the Bundeswehr, is acknowledged. dtec.bw is funded by the European Union – NextGenerationEU. The project has been supported by the BMBF project 3xa, 16ME0653, which has been financed by the European Union.

Disclosure of Interests. The authors have no competing interests to declare.

References

1. Allen, M.P., Tildesley, D.J.: Computer Simulation of Liquids. Oxford University Press, June 2017. ISBN: 9780198803195. https://doi.org/10.1093/oso/9780198803195.001.0001

2. Attard, P.: Simulation results for a fluid with the Axilrod-Teller triple dipole potential. Phys. Rev. A **45**, 5649–5653 (1992). https://doi.org/10.1103/PhysRevA.45.5649

3. Axilrod, B.M., Teller, E.: Interaction of the van der waals type between three atoms. J. Chem. Phys. **11**(6), 299–300 (1943). ISSN: 0021-9606. https://doi.org/10.1063/1.1723844

4. Barker, J.A.: Surface tension and atomic interactions in simple liquids. Molecular Phys. **80**(4), 815–820 (1993). https://doi.org/10.1080/00268979300102671

5. Barker, J.A., Fisher, R.A., Watts, R.O.: Liquid argon: Monte Carlo and molecular dynamics calculations. Molecular Phys. **21**(4), 657–673 (1971). https://doi.org/10.1080/00268977100101821

6. Fritsch, S., et al.: Adaptive resolution molecular dynamics simulation through coupling to an internal particle reservoir. Phys. Rev. Lett. **108**, 170602 (2012). https://doi.org/10.1103/PhysRevLett.108.170602

7. Zollweg, J.A., Johnson, J.K., Gubbins, K.E.: The Lennard-Jones equation of state revisited. Mol. Phys. **78**(3), 591–618 (1993). https://doi.org/10.1080/00268979300100411

8. Junghans, C., Agarwal, A., Site, L.D.: Computational efficiency and Amdahl's law for the adaptive resolution simulation technique. Comput. Phys. Commun. **215**, 20–25 (2017). ISSN: 0010-4655. https://doi.org/10.1016/j.cpc.2017.01.030

9. Larini, L., Lu, L., Voth, G.A.: The multiscale coarse-graining method. VI. Implementation of three-body coarse-grained potentials. J. Chem. Phys. **132**(16), 164107 (2010). ISSN: 0021-9606. https://doi.org/10.1063/1.3394863

10. Marcelli, G.: The role of three-body interactions on the equilibrium and non-equilibrium properties of fluids from molecular simulation, January 2001. https://doi.org/10.25916/sut.26273536.v1

11. Moore, T.C., Iacovella, C.R., McCabe, C.: Derivation of coarse-grained potentials via multistate iterative Boltzmann inversion. J. Chem. Phys. **140**(22), 224104 (2014). https://doi.org/10.1063/1.4880555

12. Muto, Y.: Force between nonpolar molecules. Proc. Phys.-Math. Soc. Jpn. **17**(6), 629–631 (1943). ISSN: 0370-1239

13. Nitzke, I., Lishchuk, S.V., Vrabec, J.: Long-range corrections for molecular simulations with three-body interactions. J. Chem. Theory Comput. **21**(1), 1–4 (2025), PMID: 39686577. https://doi.org/10.1021/acs.jctc.4c01250

14. Pinzón Escobar, J.A., et al.: Linked cell traversal algorithms for three-Body interactions in molecular dynamics. Comput. Phys. Commun. **321**, 110028 (2026). ISSN: 0010-4655. https://doi.org/10.1016/j.cpc.2026.110028

15. Praprotnik, M., Site, L.D., Kremer, K.: Adaptive resolution molecular-dynamics simulation: Changing the degrees of freedom on the fly. J. Chem. Phys. **123**(22), 224106 (2005). ISSN: 0021-9606. https://doi.org/10.1063/1.2132286

16. Praprotnik, M., et al.: Adaptive resolution simulation of liquid water. J. Phys. Condensed Matter **19**(29), 292201 (2007). https://doi.org/10.1088/0953-8984/19/29/292201

17. Sadus, R.J.: Exact calculation of the effect of three-body Axilrod–Teller interactions on vapour–liquid phase coexistence. Fluid Phase Equilibria **144**(1), 351–359 (1998). ISSN: 0378-3812. https://doi.org/10.1016/S0378-3812(97)00279-3

18. Sadus, R.J., Prausnitz, J.M.: Three-body interactions in fluids from molecular simulation: Vapor–liquid phase coexistence of argon. J. Chem. Phys. **104**(12), 4784–4787 (1996). ISSN: 0021-9606. https://doi.org/10.1063/1.471172
19. Walton, J.P.R.B., et al.: The pressure tensor at the planar surface of a liquid. Molecular Phys. **48**(6), 1357–1368 (1983). https://doi.org/10.1080/00268978300100971
20. Wang, H., Schütte, C., Site, L.D.: Adaptive Resolution Simulation (AdResS): A Smooth Thermodynamic and Structural Transition from Atomistic to Coarse Grained Resolution and Vice Versa in a Grand Canonical Fashion. J. Chem. Theory Comput. **8**(8) (2012), PMID: 26592127, pp. 2878–2887. https://doi.org/10.1021/ct3003354

From Formal Specifications to Executable Simulations: A Computation-Driven Metasystem for Agent-Based Modeling

Francisco Mesas[1]([✉]) [iD], Manel Taboada[1] [iD], Francisco Epelde[2] [iD],
Eduardo Cabrera[3] [iD], Alvaro Wong[3] [iD], and Dolores Rexachs[3] [iD]

[1] Escuelas Universitarias Gimbernat (EUG), Computer Science School, Universitat Autonoma de Barcelona, Sant Cugat del Vallès, Barcelona, Spain
{francisco.mesas,manel.taboada}@eug.es

[2] Internal Medicine Department, Parc Taulí Hospital Universitari, Institut d'Investigació i Innovació Parc Taulí (I3PT-CERCA), Universitat Autònoma de Barcelona, Sabadell, Spain
fepelde@tauli.cat

[3] Computer Architecture and Operating System Department, Universitat Autonoma de Barcelona, Barcelona, Spain
{eduardocesar.cabrera,alvaro.wong,dolores.rexachs}@uab.cat
https://webs.uab.cat/hpc4eas/

Abstract. Agent-Based Modeling and Simulation (ABMS) has become a widely used approach for analyzing complex systems in multidisciplinary fields such as healthcare and hospital Emergency Departments (EDs). However, the adoption of this methodology is often hampered by monolithic implementations in which domain knowledge is tightly intertwined with computational logic, limiting the long-term reusability and adaptability of simulation models. Inspired by Lego®'s modularity, this paper presents a metasystem based on a modular architecture centered on an agent metagenerator. The proposed approach conceptually encapsulates the definitions of the agents in brick-style agents, decomposing each agent into six canonical blocks. These blocks are independent of the target programming language, ensuring a clear separation between conceptual specifications defined by domain experts and their computational implementation by engineers and technicians. This separation of concerns facilitates multidisciplinary collaboration by enabling experts to explicitly define agent behavior through standardized specifications. Unlike large-scale data-driven approaches, all agent decisions are explicitly defined and calibrated using a small, controlled dataset, preserving transparency and traceability between the conceptual model and the resulting computational behavior. The proposed metasystem is validated through a proof-of-concept implementation using a simplified ED case study. The results suggest that the architecture prevents re-monolithization while enhancing modularity, providing a solid foundation for reusable, traceable, and scientifically grounded ABMS.

M. Paszynski et al. (Eds.): ICCS 2026 Workshops, LNCS 16788, pp. 34–42, 2026.
https://doi.org/10.1007/978-3-032-29915-4_3

Keywords: Agent Based Modeling · Software Architecture for Simulation · Complex Systems Simulation · Healthcare Computing · Digital Twins

1   Introduction

Simulation allows the study of complex systems, including heterogeneous and uncertain systems, and communication between multiple entities answering "what-if" questions that would be difficult to explore. Agent-Based Modeling and Simulation (ABMS) represents actors individually, each with its own internal state and interaction capability, enabling the simulated system to capture emergent properties arising from individual interactions [3,11].

It is important to clarify that ABMS is a computation-driven simulation technique: agent behavior is derived from formally specified computational rules rather than inferred from large data-driven models. ABMS prioritizes explicit representation of mechanisms and causal interactions [7], and can work with limited data to validate system behavior.

ABMS has been successfully applied in numerous studies in various domains, including social, biophysical, industrial and in the field of health to support decision making [5,9]. In hospital Emergency Departments (EDs), the presence of diverse patients with varying needs, medical staff with different roles, shared resources, and limited decision-making time creates a complex system that can be represented using ABMS [12]. In this paper, EDs are used as a representative case study to illustrate the proposed approach.

This modeling approach allows the creation of customized environments based on the requirements of the system under study and supports the replication of real-world behavior, separating the conceptual description of the system provided by domain experts from its computational implementation while preserving their correspondence.

However, most ABMS implementations are monolithic, with agent behavior, interaction logic, and environment configuration tightly coupled within a single codebase, making it difficult to reuse and reconfigure components, as noted by several authors who also explore different modular approaches [1,2,6,8]. For example, in EDs, phlebotomy certification is required in the United States but not in Spain, where nurses perform the same task. In monolithic systems, supporting such differences requires changes across multiple interconnected agents, complicating adaptation to different regulations, workflows, and organizational structures [6,15].

The concept of a metasystem architecture and the notion of agent bricks as encapsulated, reusable components, analogous to Lego®pieces, were introduced. A methodology based on standardized specification tables was formalized to capture expert knowledge, agent behavior, and interaction logic. A new component has been incorporated into the architecture: the Metagenerator, the automated mechanism that transforms specification tables into operational agent bricks. The term "meta" denotes that this component operates at a higher level of abstraction, generating executable agents from formal specifications rather than directly encoding agent behavior.

This paper introduces the Metagenerator and describes how it completes the metasystem pipeline. First, it defines a formal six-block model for agent specification: State, Inputs, Decision Logic, Actions, Interactions, and Lifecycle, providing a complete description of any agent within the metasystem. Second, it formalizes the Metagenerator as the component that automates the transformation of specification tables into agent bricks. Finally, although the proof-of-concept is illustrated using a NetLogo-based [14] ED model, the architectural issues are not specific to this platform or domain but are common ABMS challenges.

The remainder of this article is structured as follows: Sect. 2 analyzes the limitations of monolithic ABMS using an ED case study and introduces a metasystem aimed at generating independent agents to achieve modularity. Section 3 presents the Metagenerator and describes its architecture, as well as the mechanisms used to prevent re-monolithization. Section 4 details the internal architecture and operation of an agent brick. Section 5 presents a simplified case implemented using the proposed metasystem architecture. Finally, Sect. 6 summarizes the main contributions and outlines future work.

2   From Monolithic Simulators to Modular Metasystems

This section analyzes a monolithic simulation system to motivate the need for an architectural change and the introduction of a Metagenerator. The analysis starts from a different case study of an existing ABMS. The objective is to highlight the difficulties that arise when such models must be adapted, extended, or reused in contexts different from those for which they were originally developed.

2.1   The Monolithic Simulator

Despite the satisfactory results obtained in multiple studies, it remains extremely difficult to adapt many ABMS to new contexts with different behaviors, regulations, and organizational structures [2,6]. This limitation is widely observed across ABMS models reported in the literature, many of which operate in a predominantly monolithic manner [1,8,13]. Such designs introduce significant constraints in terms of adaptability, extensibility, and reuse.

To illustrate this general limitation, we consider a case study based on a previously developed ABMS [4]. However, as in many existing ABMS implementations, adapting the model to different contexts remains costly and complex. These limitations motivate the modular approach introduced next (the metasystem of agent bricks) and the Metagenerator described in Sect. 3.

2.2   The Metasystem Concept

To address these limitations, a modular architectural approach is introduced, inspired by the composability of Lego® blocks. This approach defines agent-based models in terms of standardized (i.e., internally consistent and formally defined within the metasystem), self-contained components called agent bricks, whose relationships are explicitly specified through formal specification tables. Each agent brick encapsulates all the elements that define an agent: State, Inputs, Decision Logic, Actions, Interactions, and Lifecycle as detailed in Sect. 4.

3   The Metagenerator: Automated Agent Brick Generation

The modular architecture proposed in the previous section requires mechanisms to automate the transformation of high-level definitions into executable specifications. This is the role of the Agent Metagenerator. This work contributes an architectural and methodological advance for ABMS, rather than an algorithmic one, by defining a formally constrained pipeline that prevents implicit dependencies regardless of implementation details. This section describes how information is introduced through specification tables, transformed into independent agent bricks, and kept from re-monolithizing.

3.1   Architectural Overview

The Metagenerator bridges the conceptual and computational models by transforming domain-expert specification tables into a canonical agent description (state variables, admissible inputs, decision rules, actions, interaction channels, and lifecycle policies) before any simulator-specific code is produced. It then validates the tables, identifies dependencies, and generates independent modules materialized as agent bricks. With a communication layer for message exchange between agents (the *message hub*), these modules are assembled into a functional simulator; the *message hub* is an architectural communication abstraction introduced by the metasystem, independent of NetLogo's native communication mechanisms.

3.2   Metagenerator Pipeline

At the core of the metasystem is the Metagenerator, which defines agents in a platform-agnostic language. For example, a rule describing how a patient reacts to a triage notification is translated into an explicit decision procedure and a corresponding message-handling interface in the generated agent brick. The resulting bricks implement each agent type's formal specification while remaining platform-independent.

The construction of canonical agent bricks follows two main processing stages:

Stage 1: Table Parsing and Validation. The Metagenerator processes all the information from the specification tables and compiles it into canonical JSON for each agent type. The JSON contains the agent state (internal variables and attributes), inputs, decision logic, actions, interactions, and lifecycle. At this stage, consistency is ensured to avoid errors during the specification process.

Stage 2: Dependency Resolution. Interactions between agents create dependencies between agent bricks. The Metagenerator builds a dependency graph to capture these relationships and determine which interfaces each agent brick must expose. Dependencies are resolved at the interface level, ensuring that agent bricks remain independent and interact through well-defined communication channels, enabling modular composition and preventing hidden coupling. Conceptually, the Metagenerator can be seen as analogous to an oracle, in the sense that it has a global view of all specifications and resolves dependencies prior to execution, while remaining external to the runtime simulation.

Once dependencies have been resolved at the conceptual level, the canonical representation is transformed into executable code through backend-specific generation stages:

Stage 3: Code Generation. For each agent type, the Metagenerator produces a module consisting of four files, following the naming conventions defined in previous work [10]. Although this step may differ for other target languages, the current implementation uses NetLogo.

Stage 4: Assembly. A Python-based assembler script collects all generated modules, resolves `__includes` directives, merges global variable declarations, and produces a single executable `main.nlogo` file. This step is necessary because NetLogo does not natively support multi-file project structures [10].

4   Agent Bricks: The Block Architecture

In ABMS, agents are represented by their states, their ability to perceive the environment, make decisions, and interact. Figure 1 shows the architecture defined for the agent brick generated by the Agent Metagenerator. This architecture provides a formal description of the agent, allowing clean, traceable, and reproducible behavior analysis, and avoiding the black-box approach commonly found in other systems.

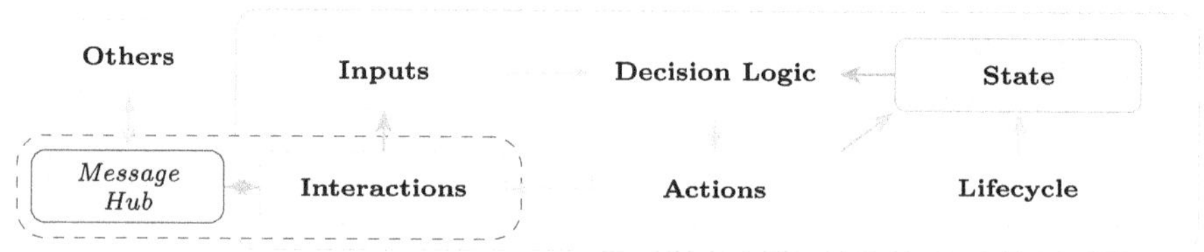

Fig. 1. Internal architecture of an Agent Brick

At the core of the agent is the **Lifecycle**, which controls when agents exist, whether they are created dynamically or remain fixed, and the conditions under which they are activated or change roles (for example, an experienced doctor reasoning differently from an inexperienced one).

Once agents are created, their **State** captures all conditions at a given time, including state variables, their attributes, and internal memory. The state reflects the sequence of events that has led to the current situation and can, in turn, trigger reactions through the decision logic.

Decision Logic contains the complete agent logic, including rules, finite-state machines, and constraints defined in the specification tables. At each simulation step, the agent determines whether to act reactively or proactively.

Once a decision is selected, its effects are realized through the actions block. **Actions** constitute the only mechanism through which an agent can affect the system and include movement, resource requests, and mediated updates to other agents. The Metagenerator generates a dedicated procedure for each declared action, ensuring that all effects on the simulation remain explicit and auditable.

Communication between agents is handled through the **Interactions block**, which specifies communication partners and channels, referred to in this article as the *message hub*. For example, in a waiting room scenario, a message broadcast through loudspeakers may be perceived by multiple agents, even if it is only relevant to one, allowing others to ignore it or react differently.

Finally, agents only have access to the information defined in the **Input** block, which determines what they can perceive and interpret. A *message hub*-based communication mechanism is used to deliver events to the agent, ensuring that it only receives input that it is allowed to observe.

Together, these six blocks define everything an agent requires to function independently. This structure also enables the creation of controlled test environments in which inputs and outputs can be simulated using an oracle that injects predefined messages. Individual agents can then be executed and validated in isolation, ensuring that they correctly process messages and make decisions, while accounting for the stochastic nature of the system.

5 Methodology and Proof-of-Concept Validation

The metasystem is validated through a proof of concept that targets the agent blocks. Accordingly, the case study should be interpreted as a structural validation of the architecture. Three aspects are analyzed: whether the model effectively supports agent specification, whether the separation between the conceptual and computational layers is maintained in practice, and whether execution can occur without hidden monolithic dependencies.

The scenario used is an ED. A simplified state machine is implemented for a patient, and all interactions are handled through message centers, enabling full traceability. Each simulation cycle represents one minute. Patient arrivals are generated from a real dataset fitted to a Poisson distribution. The simulation runs for 6400 cycles, with adjustable initial conditions. The patient transitions through four states: waiting, queuing, being seen, and discharged. State transitions occur either due to internal changes or incoming messages. The inputs include the environmental context, the current simulation time, and received messages. Interactions are intentionally kept to a minimum.

The same six-block logic is also applied to resources. The simplest resources are represented as part of the environmental state, while more complex ones, those requiring their own decision logic, are modeled as service agents. This provides a practical solution that avoids making the abstraction overly rigid.

Although code generation is intended to be automatic, the proof-of-concept implements the final step manually to validate the abstraction; artifacts and datasets will be released in future work.

6 Conclusions

The difficulty of reusing ABMS-based simulators with monolithic structures has increased over time. Based on both the literature and the accumulated experience with the ED model, a metasystem is proposed that formally separates the conceptual model from the computational model, preventing implementations that diverge from the underlying conceptual specification.

Six blocks have been introduced to describe the behavior of the agent. This structure helps to formalize expert knowledge and facilitates traceability between conceptual and computational models. All agent-independent decisions are made explicit, distinguishing this approach from others based on large volumes of data and untraceable models. The approach relies on calibration using a small, controlled dataset, positioning itself at the intersection of computation and data as a driver of scientific progress, while avoiding methods in which the decision logic cannot be traced back to the conceptual level of the model.

The Metagenerator enforces this architecture throughout the analysis process, from formal data collection in specification tables to the final simulator. It validates definitions, resolves dependencies, and generates reusable, encapsulated modules. This reduces the risk of reintroducing monolithic behavior by maintaining a clear separation between agents. This is particularly important in distributed decision domains such as EDs, where regulations can change and significantly affect agents and, consequently, the model.

The results suggest that the proposed six-block agent abstraction is sufficient to support executable simulations in the investigated scenario. At this stage, the translation of specifications into code is performed manually to avoid dependence on tooling, reinforcing the idea that each agent is an independent entity with a communication mechanism (*message hub*) and maintains a contract between the conceptual model and the simulation. Further validation across domains and platforms remains future work.

Future work involves implementing automatic generation from the specification tables of the already developed digital twin model and extending the metasystem to other platforms and simulation languages. This opens the door to create digital twins and performing new analyzes in other domains such as urban planning and public transportation systems.

Acknowledgements. This research has been supported by the Agencia Estatal de Investigación (AEI), Spain and the Fondo Europeo de Desarrollo Regional (FEDER) UE, under contract PID2023-146978OB-I00.

Disclosure of Interests. The authors have no competing interests to declare that are relevant to the content of this article.

References

1. Abo-Hamad, W., Arisha, A.: Simulation-based framework to improve patient experience in an emergency department. Eur. J. Oper. Res. **224**(1), 154–166 (2013). https://doi.org/10.1016/j.ejor.2012.07.028
2. Berger, U., et al.: Towards reusable building blocks for agent-based modelling and theory development. Environ. Modelling Softw. **175**, 106003 (2024). https://doi.org/10.1016/j.envsoft.2024.106003
3. Bonabeau, E.: Agent-based modeling: methods and techniques for simulating human systems. Proc. Natl. Acad. Sci. U.S.A. **99**(Suppl 3), 7280–7287 (2002). https://doi.org/10.1073/pnas.082080899
4. Cabrera, E., Taboada, M., Iglesias, M.L., Epelde, F., Luque, E.: Optimization of healthcare emergency departments by agent-based simulation. Procedia CS **4**, 1880–1889 (2011). https://doi.org/10.1016/j.procs.2011.04.204
5. Comis, M., Cleophas, C., Büsing, C.: Patients, primary care, and policy: agent-based simulation modeling for health care decision support. Health Care Manag. Sci. **24**(4), 799–826 (2021). https://doi.org/10.1007/s10729-021-09556-2
6. Filatova, T., et al.: Agentblocks: A community platform for sharing, comparing, and improving reusable building blocks for (agent-based) models. J. Artif. Soc. Soc. Simul. **28**(4), 11 (2025). https://doi.org/10.18564/jasss.5831
7. Gao, C., et al.: Large language models empowered agent-based modeling and simulation: a survey and perspectives. Humanities Soc. Sci. Commun. **11**(1), 1259 (2024). https://doi.org/10.1057/s41599-024-03611-3
8. Godfrey, T., et al.: Supporting emergency department risk mitigation with a modular and reusable agent-based simulation infrastructure. In: 2023 Winter Simulation Conference (WSC), pp. 162–173. IEEE (2023). https://doi.org/10.1109/WSC60868.2023.10407894
9. He, J., Hou, X.Y., Toloo, S., Patrick, J.R., Fitz Gerald, G.: Demand for hospital emergency departments: a conceptual understanding. World J. Emerg. Med. **2**(4), 253–261 (2011). https://doi.org/10.5847/wjem.j.1920-8642.2011.04.002
10. Mesas, F., Taboada, M., Rexachs, D., Epelde, F., Wong, A., Luque, E.: A customizable agent-based simulation framework for emergency departments. In: Computational Science – ICCS 2025, pp. 46–53 (2025). https://doi.org/10.1007/978-3-031-97635-3_6
11. Monks, T., Currie, C.S.M., Onggo, B.S., Robinson, S., Kunc, M., Taylor, S.J.E.: Strengthening the reporting of empirical simulation studies: introducing the stress guidelines. J. Simul. **13**(1), 55–67 (2019). https://doi.org/10.1080/17477778.2018.1442155
12. Samadbeik, M., et al.: Patient flow in emergency departments: a comprehensive umbrella review of solutions and challenges across the health system. BMC Health Serv. Res. **24**(1), 274 (2024). https://doi.org/10.1186/s12913-024-10725-6

13. Taboada, M., Cabrera, E., Luque, E., Epelde, F., Iglesias, M.L.: A decision support system for hospital emergency departments designed using agent-based modeling and simulation. In: 2012 IEEE 13th International Conference on Information Reuse & Integration (IRI) (2012). https://doi.org/10.1109/IRI.2012.6303032
14. Wilensky, U.: Netlogo. http://ccl.northwestern.edu/netlogo/ (1999), center for Connected Learning and Computer-Based Modeling, Northwestern University. Evanston, IL
15. Zschaler, S., et al.: On simulation reuse in healthcare applications. Simulation **102**(2), 149–165 (2026). https://doi.org/10.1177/00375497251383912

Transport Network Topology as a Determinant of Forced Displacement Dynamics: Case Study of Rail-Based Evacuation from Ukraine

Ivana Malčić[1]([✉]), Derek Groen[1,2], Valeria Krzhizhanovskaya[1], and Diana Suleimenova[2]

[1] University of Amsterdam, Amsterdam, The Netherlands
`ivana.malcic@student.uva.nl`
[2] Brunel University of London, Uxbridge, UK
`diana.suleimenova@brunel.ac.uk`

Abstract. Conflict-induced displacement is strongly shaped by transportation networks, yet most displacement models represent mobility as continuous or distance-based, neglecting network constraints such as corridor structure, connectivity, and capacity. This limits the ability of existing approaches to capture evacuation dynamics in situations where movement is mediated by infrastructure-specific determinants.

This paper presents an agent-based model of infrastructure-constrained forced displacement that explicitly represents a real-world railway network. Implemented in Flee 3, the model simulates displacement during the early phase of the 2022 Russian invasion of Ukraine by dynamically generating agents in response to conflict-onset data from ACLED and routing movement exclusively along operational rail corridors toward railway-accessible border checkpoints. Simulations cover the period from February to June 2022, producing daily arrival counts at eight major border crossings for validation against a curated empirical dataset.

The model achieves strong overall fit, with a median across-camp average relative difference (ARD) of 0.31 and sustained post-surge errors below 20% for most corridors. Beyond aggregate fit, the results reveal a clear two-phase structural transition. During the initial surge, flows are distributed across multiple corridors, with no single route consistently dominant. In the stabilized phase, flows consolidate sharply, indicating persistent single-corridor dominance. Ultimately, the findings suggest displacement trajectories are not governed by distance or conflict intensity alone, but by network topology, asymmetric capacity constraints, and endogenous corridor competition.

Keywords: forced displacement · agent-based modeling · Ukraine · network-constrained mobility · evacuation dynamics · railway networks · Flee 3

M. Paszynski et al. (Eds.): ICCS 2026 Workshops, LNCS 16788, pp. 43–57, 2026.
https://doi.org/10.1007/978-3-032-29915-4_4

1 Introduction

Conflict-induced displacement is an increasingly prominent feature of global population mobility, referring to the involuntary movement of people escaping armed conflict, political instability, or systematic human rights violations [1]. The 2022 invasion of Ukraine triggered one of the most rapid and large-scale displacement events in modern history, with millions fleeing their homes and crossing into neighboring countries.

Unlike voluntary migration, conflict-induced displacement is characterized by sudden onset, limited individual choice, and strong dependence on infrastructure, humanitarian responses, and institutional actions. These conditions pose challenges for quantitative modeling, particularly during early phases when movements are rapid, unpredictable, and uncoordinated. In large-scale evacuations, infrastructure is not merely a passive medium; it actively structures mobility by enabling, constraining, and redirecting flows. Likewise, transport modes play distinct roles in this process: rail systems operate along fixed corridors and enable coordinated high-capacity movement, while road-based transport tends to be more decentralized and allows adaptive routing. Despite these differences, relatively little modeling work explicitly accounts for transport modality in displacement dynamics.

To fill this gap, the present paper investigates the role of railway networks in shaping large-scale forced displacement, using the 2022 Russian invasion of Ukraine as a case study. To this end, an agent-based model is developed using Flee 3 [2], embedding an operational railway network and coupling it with conflict-onset dynamics and population distributions. Displaced individuals are represented as agents moving from conflict-affected areas to border checkpoints along realistic rail corridors. The simulation covers the early phase of the invasion (February 22 to June 22, 2022) and generates daily arrival counts at major border crossings, which are validated against observed data.

Overall, this work investigates how explicitly modeling railway infrastructure alters our understanding of forced displacement during conflict. In particular, it assesses whether network-constrained evacuation dynamics can reproduce observed refugee flows and reveal structural consolidation effects. By analyzing corridor hierarchy, flow concentration, and the emergence of dominant routes, we show how network topology actively governs displacement trajectories.

2 Related Work

Agent-based models (ABMs) are widely used to simulate forced displacement in contexts such as natural disasters and armed conflict. Early models largely relied on distance-driven mobility assumptions, with individuals moving toward safety along the shortest paths. More recent approaches incorporate greater behavioral heterogeneity and social interactions, enabled by increased computational capacity [3,4].

Insights from transport geography show that physical constraints such as topography, node-link structures, and grade limitations shape land transport networks, imposing a natural convergence of routes that create a certain degree of centrality [5]. These properties are particularly pronounced in railway systems, which operate along fixed corridors and impose limited routing flexibility alongside station-level bottlenecks. Such structural characteristics are not fully represented in mode-agnostic displacement models. The use of rail transport for medical evacuations, cross-border displacement, and logistic support has been directly observed during the ongoing conflict in Ukraine, where the railway network has proven to be indispensable for large-scale evacuation efforts [6]. Empirical studies further document their use in large-scale medical evacuation and humanitarian operations [7].

Recent work by Mehrab et al. [3,8] examines forced displacement dynamics in Ukraine using agent-based approaches that capture adaptive decision-making under crisis conditions and explore the impact of environmental and social factors on displacement trajectories. Beyond displacement modeling, large-scale agent-based transportation frameworks have been developed to analyze evacuation dynamics in road-based contexts. Wolshon et al. [9] applied the TRANSIMS microscopic framework to study megaregional hurricane evacuations. Similarly, MATSim (Multi-Agent Transport Simulation) [10] provides a large-scale agent-based platform widely used for urban and regional transport analysis.

Despite these advances, a key limitation across displacement and transport modeling approaches is the lack of integration between conflict-driven migration dynamics and infrastructure-explicit mobility constraints. Some displacement models [3,8] incorporate behavioral and spatial processes but typically do not constrain movement using transport infrastructure, while transport frameworks such as TRANSIMS and MATSim explicitly represent transport network topology but are not equipped to capture conflict-induced displacement. This abstraction may ultimately lead to miss-estimation of corridor-level flows and higher uncertainty in route allocation. In contrast, the present study addresses this gap by integrating infrastructure-constrained mobility with conflict-driven displacement dynamics in a unified modeling framework to examine how these processes jointly shape displacement patterns.

3 Methodology

Agent-based modeling (ABM) provides a suitable framework for this study as it allows the simultaneous representation of network-level physical constraints together with individual-level behavioral drivers. By explicitly modeling heterogeneous agents, ABMs can reproduce evacuation dynamics including queue formation at stations, congestion spillovers to secondary checkpoints, and route rerouting under capacity pressure [11].

3.1 Modeling Framework

Flee is an agent-based modeling framework designed to simulate conflict-driven displacement under crisis conditions, with explicit representation of movement processes and destination constraints [2,12].

Agent Decision-Making and Movement Rules. In Flee, displacement is modeled as a two-stage process consisting of conflict-driven agent generation and network-constrained movement. Generation of agents at conflict zones is triggered dynamically following conflict onset: once a conflict-zone node becomes active, a fraction of the local population representing civilians initiating displacement is released into the network.

At each discrete time step, agents first decide whether to move according to probabilistic decision rules depending on their current location type; agents in conflict zones move with probability `conflict_movechance`, whereas agents in transit locations move with `default_movechance`. Those in camps stay there, representing people who crossed the border.

If an agent decides to move, it evaluates a set of reachable destinations determined by `awareness_level`. In Flee, route choice is based on weighted routing, combining distance decay, destination attractiveness, and capacity constraints. For our model, this can be summarized as

$$A_j \propto \frac{w_j}{d_{ij}^{\alpha}} \cdot C_j,$$

where d_{ij} denotes the network distance from the current location i to destination j, α is given by `distance_power`, w_j represents destination attractiveness, primarily determined by `camp_weight`, and C_j captures capacity effects which reduce attractiveness as occupancy approaches capacity, controlled by `capacity_scaling`.

Agents then probabilistically select a destination based on the normalized attractiveness score and proceed following a planned route toward it. Movement is executed incrementally along the network, with daily travel distances bounded by `max_move_speed`. Movement is strictly constrained to the underlying railway network: agents can only traverse predefined links between nodes, and no off-network routing is permitted.

Node Creation: Camps, Conflict Zones and Towns. The railway network was represented as a set of discrete locations connected by passenger rail links, with nodes grouped into three Flee-native categories: conflict zones, towns, and camps, as described in Table 1. To reduce complexity while preserving national connectivity, one representative train station was selected per oblast. Camps were defined at major railway-accessible border crossings shown in Table 2. Conflict onset dates for each conflict-zone node were assigned using data from the Armed Conflict Location and Event Data Project (ACLED) [13]. The simulation covers the period from February 22, 2022 to June 22, 2022 (120 days), while the initial populations at each node were estimated using aggregated demographic data reported at the oblast level. The full list of modeled locations with their associated attributes is available in the supplementary repository [14].

Table 1. Classification and attributes of model locations.

Category	Description	Key attributes
Conflict zones	Major railway stations located in or near active conflict areas during the simulation period, serving as primary departure points for displaced agents.	Geographic coordinates; administrative region; location type; population; conflict start date.
Camps	Railway-accessible border checkpoints functioning as final safe destinations. Agent movement terminates upon arrival. Each camp is assigned a `camp_weight` reflecting relative reception capacity.	Geographic coordinates; administrative region; location type; capacity; camp weighting factor.
Towns	Intermediate stations located in areas unaffected by conflict. These nodes facilitate network connectivity but do not directly generate displacement.	Geographic coordinates; administrative region; location type; population.

Table 2. Border camps grouped by destination country.

Destination country	Camps/border checkpoints
Poland	Mostyska–Przemyśl; Yahodyn–Dorohusk; Volodymyr-Volynskyi–Hrubieszów
Hungary	Chop (Druzhba)–Záhony
Slovakia	Mukachevo–Košice
Moldova	Reni–Giurgiuleşti; Mohyliv-Podilskyi–Volchinets
Romania	Vadul–Siret–Vicşani

Railway Network Construction. Figure 1 shows the full set of modeled nodes and links used in the simulation, including conflict zones, towns, and border camps, corresponding to the three principal evacuation corridors described below.

The network was constructed by identifying major rail corridors across the country and compiling inter-regional links from open railway data and verified schedules. Realistic distances (km) were assigned using geodesic estimates along railway alignments to preserve plausible travel times and network scale. The final topology reflects three principal corridors:

East-West long-haul routes connecting major eastern centers to western regions (e.g., Kharkiv-Kyiv; Dnipro-Kropyvnytskyi-Vinnytsia-Lviv).

South-West transit corridors linking coastal cities to border checkpoints via Odesa (e.g., Kherson-Mykolaiv-Odesa-Reni).

Western border approaches enabling cross-border movement into Poland, Slovakia, and Hungary (e.g., Lviv-Mostyska; Mukachevo-Košice; Uzhhorod-Chop).

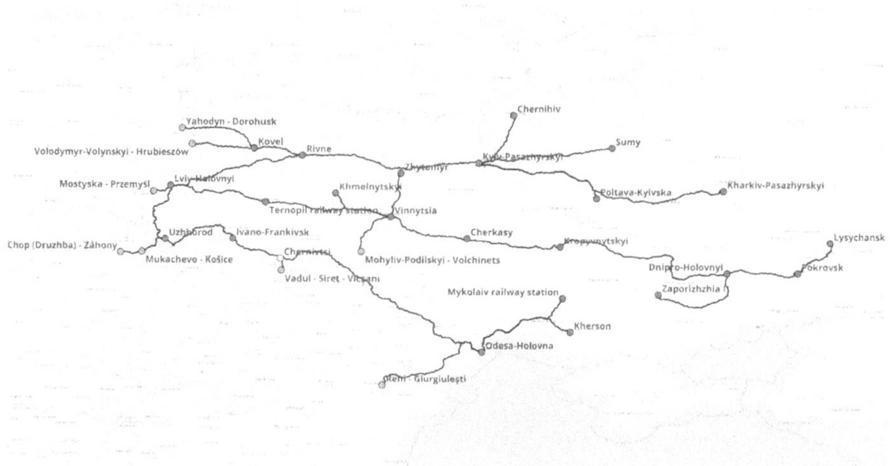

Fig. 1. Map of Ukraine with red nodes representing train stations (conflict zones), yellow nodes representing towns, and green nodes representing border checkpoints (camps). The base map is derived from OpenStreetMap and used under the Open Database License (ODbL).

3.2   Assumptions, Parameters and Model Validation

The simulation relied on selected parameters in `simsetting.yml`, chosen to reflect evacuation conditions listed in Table 3.

Location Capacities. In Flee, each location is associated with a population or capacity parameter that constrains how many agents can be generated from, or absorbed by, that node over time. For conflict-zone nodes, the population parameter represents the pre-war civilian population, determining the upper bound on the total number of agents that can be generated, or displaced, from each location. For camp nodes, the capacity parameter represents an aggregate approximation of the maximum number of arrivals that can be accommodated over the simulation period. Capacity assignments reflect the relative scale of border infrastructure, staffing, and onward transport options, informed by host-country context and qualitative reports from the early phase of the conflict. Major railway crossings were therefore assigned substantially higher capacities than smaller or less-connected checkpoints.

Camp Weights. In addition to absolute capacity limits, Flee allows destination attractiveness to be modulated through the `camp_weight` parameter, biasing movement probabilities towards more desired camps. This separation enables the model to distinguish between where agents preferentially travel from how many arrivals a location can ultimately absorb. In this model, camp weights were assigned on a relative scale to reflect differences in attractiveness within

Table 3. Key simulation parameters and rationale.

Parameter	Bounds	Value	Description and rationale
max_move_speed	$[0, \infty)$	700.0	Maximum daily travel distance (km), reflecting intercity rail transport capacity.
max_walk_speed	$[0, \infty)$	35.0	Maximum daily walking distance (km), representing short access segments to stations or camps.
awareness_level	$[1, 3]$	3	Agents evaluate destinations up to three network links away, approximating route planning based on available connections and information.
distance_power	$[0, 1]$	0.7	Controls the influence of distance on destination choice, biasing agents toward shorter routes while allowing other factors to influence decisions.
conflict_movechance	$[0, 1]$	1.0	Daily probability of leaving conflict zones. A value of 1.0 ensures immediate displacement upon conflict exposure.
default_movechance	$[0, 1]$	0.4	Baseline daily movement probability outside conflict zones, capturing gradual and anticipatory displacement dynamics.
capacity_scaling	$[0, 1]$	0.8	Controls how rapidly destination attractiveness decreases as capacity is approached, representing congestion and administrative constraints.

the same border region. Weighting factors account for arbitrary differences in connectivity to onward transport networks, perceived economic opportunity, and host-country's institutional capacity; for example, the Mostyska–Przemyśl crossing is assigned a higher value than Volodymyr-Volynskyi–Hrubieszów crossing, reflecting its stronger rail connectivity and higher observed throughput.

Validation Data Construction. In absence of an external curated rail crossing dataset, a custom validation dataset was constructed by combining multiple country-specific border statistics with additional rail-use evidence and cross-checking the result against an aggregate benchmark.

1. **Border crossing data analysis.** Daily counts of border crossings were collected for each neighboring country over the period February–June 2022 using official national statistics and reports [15–19].
2. **Estimation of train use.** Because border statistics do not report transport mode, the proportion of refugees traveling by train was estimated using two credible independent survey-based assessments conducted in Poland and Slovakia during mid-March 2022. Both surveys report that approximately 18% of respondents entering Poland and Slovakia used rail transport [20,21]. For modeling purposes, this value was rounded to 20% to account for uncertainty in survey-based estimates.

3. **Camp-level cross-validation.** Estimated rail-based arrivals per country were further disaggregated to individual border checkpoints (camps) and cross-checked against additional qualitative and quantitative sources, including reports on railway operations, humanitarian logistics, and observed congestion at specific crossings.
4. **Aggregate plausibility check.** To assess overall consistency, daily rail-based arrival estimates were aggregated over the full simulation period, yielding a total of 1,380,232 individuals. This figure was compared against an independent benchmark of roughly 1.3 million derived from total registered refugees by June 2022 multiplied by the assumed 20% rail share. The agreement between these values (within 5%) provides a robust plausibility check for the constructed dataset.

To operationalize the data, the estimated rail share was applied to daily country-level border crossing totals and then distributed across multiple railway-accessible checkpoints according to observed usage patterns informed by reported train frequencies, infrastructure capacity, and qualitative accounts of evacuation flows from media reports.

3.3   Evaluation Metrics

To assess how rail-based evacuation patterns consolidate into dominant routes over time, two complementary dimensions were evaluated: (i) structural concentration of flows across corridors and (ii) model–validation data agreement at the camp level. Interpretive guidance for the concentration measures and the ARD metric is provided in the Supplementary Information (Appendix B).

Corridor Concentration Metrics. Rail-based displacement does not distribute uniformly across all border crossings, as flows may be directed to a limited number of high-capacity corridors. To quantify this hierarchical organization, daily camp-bound arrivals were aggregated by destination country. Let $F_i(t)$ denote total arrivals to corridor i on day t, and define corridor shares as

$$s_i(t) = \frac{F_i(t)}{\sum_j F_j(t)}. \tag{1}$$

Because $\sum_i s_i(t) = 1$, concentration measures reflect structural distribution independently of total evacuation volume. Three complementary metrics were computed.

Concentration Ratio (CR1). The concentration ratio, here interpreted as the dominance index,

$$H(t) = \max_i s_i(t) \tag{2}$$

captures the share of displaced people absorbed by the single largest corridor. This measure directly quantifies whether evacuation is governed by one structurally dominant route.

Herfindahl–Hirschman Index (HHI). The HHI,

$$HHI(t) = \sum_i s_i(t)^2,\tag{3}$$

measures overall concentration across all corridors. Unlike CR1, which isolates only the largest share, HHI captures the cumulative contribution of secondary corridors.

Gini Coefficient. The Gini coefficient measures inequality across $\{s_i(t)\}$, capturing disparity between dominant and marginal corridors and therefore emphasizing relative imbalance in the full distribution.

These three metrics distinguish between (i) single-corridor dominance, (ii) system-wide concentration, and (iii) inequality across competing routes, and are together used to analyze emergent corridor hierarchy.

Error Metric (ARD). Model–validation data agreement was evaluated using the Average Relative Difference (ARD), following prior Flee validation practice [22].

Let $S_k(t)$ denote simulated arrivals and $D_k(t)$ observed arrivals at camp k on day t, then the daily ARD is defined as

$$E(t) = \frac{\sum_k |S_k(t) - D_k(t)|}{\sum_k D_k(t)}.\tag{4}$$

This formulation aggregates absolute deviations across camps and normalizes by total observed arrivals, yielding a dimensionless measure of proportional system-level mismatch. ARD values are context-dependent, and as such need to be interpreted with regards to the specific application; a useful reference range can be obtained via prior studies using Flee which reported acceptable ARD values on the order of 0.2–0.4 [22].

4 Results

4.1 Camp-Level Model Fit

The model error exhibits a clear temporal structure. During the initial phase (approximately days 1–20), daily relative errors are elevated across most corridors. After this transient adjustment period, errors decline substantially and remain low for the remainder of the simulation. From early May onward, median daily ARD across camps remains below 0.2, as seen in Fig. 2, indicating stable alignment once displacement flows settle.

Error dynamics also vary systematically across corridors. From Fig. 3, it is visible that high-throughput evacuation corridors such as Mostyska–Przemyśl and Vadul-Siret–Vicșani exhibit comparatively balanced and stable error patterns after the early surge. In contrast, peripheral camps, including Mohyliv–Volchinets and Reni–Giurgiulești, display greater temporal volatility.

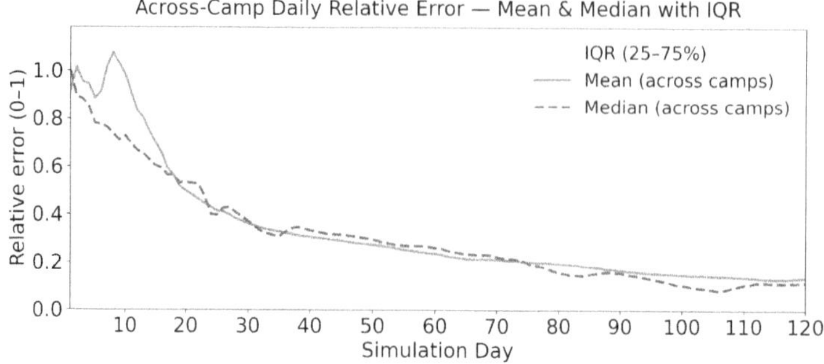

Fig. 2. Across-camp ARD showing mean, median, and inter-quartile range of daily errors between simulated and observed arrivals.

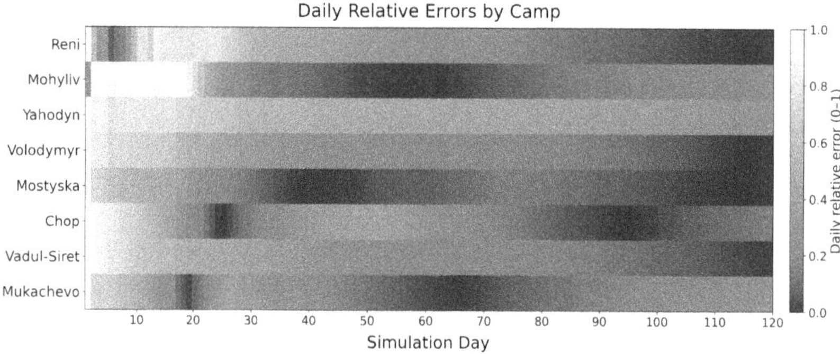

Fig. 3. Heatmap of daily relative errors for each simulated border checkpoint (camp) over the 120-day simulation period (ARD camp-specific components). Camp names are abbreviated for compactness; full names can be found in Table 2

Cumulative arrivals in Fig. 4 confirm these patterns. High-throughput corridors such as Mostyska–Przemyśl and Vadul–Siret–Vicşani track observed data closely over most of the simulation, whereas peripheral lower-volume corridors show larger early deviations and slower convergence.

High-Throughput Corridors. The strongest and most consistent agreement is observed along major evacuation routes. Mostyska–Przemyśl exhibits the lowest mean and median ARD (0.169 and 0.095), indicating sustained alignment across the full simulation horizon. Vadul–Siret–Vicşani shows similarly stable behavior, with moderate median (0.259) and limited variability relative to peripheral routes. For these corridors, discrepancies are largely confined to the early surge period.

Intermediate Corridors. Mukachevo–Košice (median ARD 0.203), Chop (Druzhba)–Záhony (median 0.204), and Volodymyr-Volynskyi–Hrubieszów

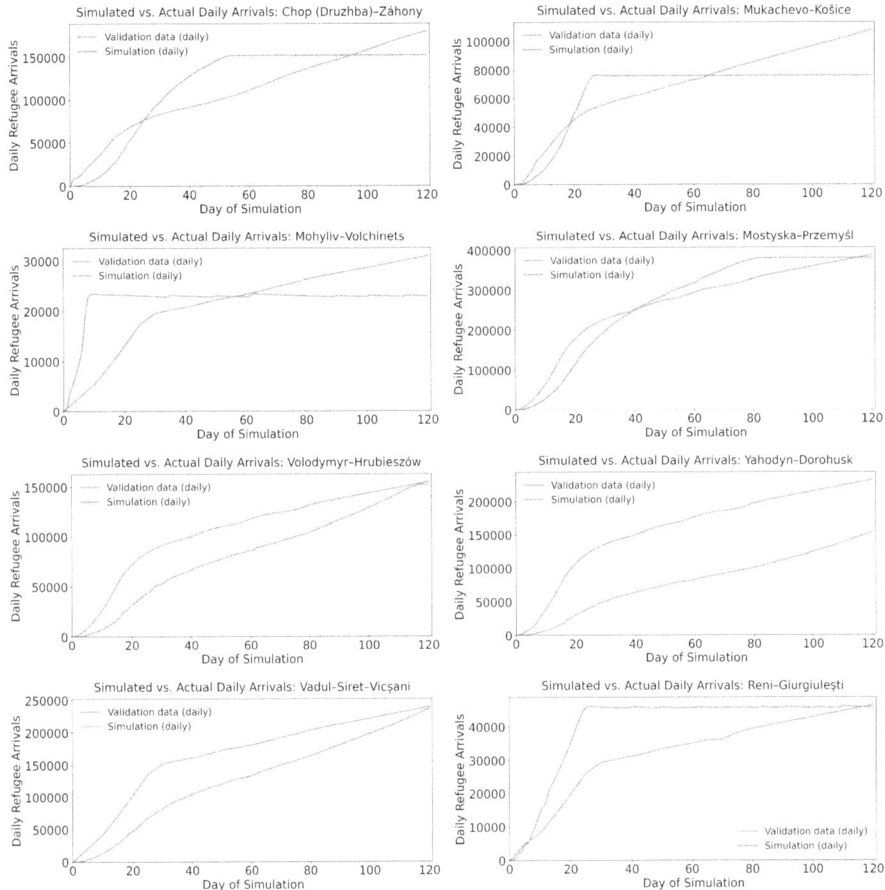

Fig. 4. Simulated versus observed cumulative daily refugee arrivals for each border camp over the 120-day simulation period.

(median 0.269) display low error and low variability, with means and medians following closely together. These corridors show stable but less precise alignment compared to the highest-volume routes.

Peripheral/Low-Volume Corridors. Greater variability is observed in lower-volume routes. Yahodyn–Dorohusk shows persistently elevated deviation, with the highest mean and median ARD (0.555 and 0.530), reflecting sustained under-prediction. Mohyliv-Podilskyi–Volchinets is characterized by pronounced variability rather than systematic bias, with the largest maximum error (4.313) but a substantially lower median (0.165), indicating occasional but extreme deviations. Reni–Giurgiulești (median ARD 0.283) exhibits a similar early overshoot followed by slower growth. Across these peripheral corridors discrepancies extend beyond the initial shock phase and are more temporally volatile.

Full descriptive statistics of the daily ARD time series for each camp are provided in Supplementary Table S1 (see Supplementary Appendix C).

4.2 Corridor Hierarchy

During the early phase (days 1–14), evacuation flows are distributed. The mean dominance index is $H = 0.485$, indicating that the largest corridor captures less than half of daily camp-bound flow on a typical day. Early-phase corridor shares are relatively balanced: Poland (mean share 0.363) and Moldova (0.325) both function as major channels, while Romania, Hungary, and Slovakia retain consistent secondary participation. By contrast, in the stabilized phase (days 30–120), flows consolidate sharply. Mean dominance increases to 0.634, and concentration metrics rise substantially (Gini: $0.373 \to 0.619$; HHI: $0.352 \to 0.507$), reflecting a transition toward persistent single-corridor dominance. Poland-bound routes capture an average share of 0.634 and are dominant on 98.9% of stabilized-phase days, while Romania emerges as a stable secondary corridor (mean share 0.275). Other corridors become marginal. The full distribution of daily dominance values $H(t)$ is reported in Supplementary Appendix C, Table S2 (Table 4).

Table 4. Corridor concentration metrics by phase.

Phase	Mean H	Mean Gini	Mean HHI
Early (1–14)	0.485	0.373	0.352
Stabilized (30–120)	0.634	0.619	0.507

Per-corridor metrics further reinforce this structural shift. In the early phase, Poland is dominant on 64.3% of days, but Moldova also exhibits substantial activity (active on 100% of days). In the stabilized phase, however, dominance becomes nearly exclusive: Poland accounts for almost all dominant days, while Hungary, Moldova, and Slovakia display reduced activation frequency and low share variability. Share standard deviations decline for dominant corridors, indicating increased temporal stability. Activation timing further highlights the rapid onset of corridor competition: all major corridors exceed their activation thresholds within the first two days of the simulation, confirming that hierarchy does not emerge from delayed availability. Comprehensive dominance distributions, activation thresholds, and per-corridor structural statistics for both phases are reported in Supplementary Tables S2–S5 (Supplementary Appendix C).

4.3 Model Performance and Comparison

To contextualize model performance, the results are also compared with prior work on forced displacement and existing Flee-based studies. At the aggregate level, we compare our results to the Ukraine-specific Network Agency model [3].

Mehrab et al. report a root mean squared percentage error (RMSPE) of 0.24 and a Pearson correlation coefficient (PCC) of 0.98 for aggregate daily outflows, whereas the present model yields an RMSPE of 0.27 and a PCC of 0.993. This indicates similar accuracy even without explicit social influence mechanisms, and using a purely rail-constrained network, thus supporting the finding that infrastructure topology is a first-order determinant of displacement patterns. Metric-level comparison below the aggregate level, however, is not possible because Mehrab et al. do not report corridor-level or camp-level error distributions, and their model does not disaggregate by transport mode.

The results can also be interpreted in the context of prior Flee validation studies. Existing work shows that model performance improves as additional information on routing, destination attractiveness, and capacity constraints is incorporated. In particular, Suleimenova and Groen [22] report consistently higher ARD values for simpler configurations, suggesting that reduced formulations (e.g., distance-only or fixed-attractiveness assumptions) would yield weaker agreement with observed data. The median across-camp ARD value of 0.31 obtained in our model lies within the range reported across historical Flee applications [2] and compares favorably with crisis-specific studies such as the Tigray case [23]. This is notable given the structural complexity of the present case, which combines a large transport network, a high-speed mobility regime, and a custom validation dataset.

5   Discussion

The results indicate that rail-based displacement dynamics exhibits a two-phase structure: an early surge regime followed by structural consolidation. The early phase reflects not only empirical volatility but also an initialization effect of the modeling framework.

In the first weeks, flows are distributed across multiple corridors, routing patterns fluctuate, and model–data error peaks. This arises from two interacting mechanisms. First, real-world displacement is inherently unstable immediately after escalation, with uncertainty, congestion spillovers, and rapid rerouting. Second, the model undergoes a transient "warm-up": at $t = 0$ camps are empty and therefore highly attractive, while capacity constraints have not yet taken effect. As agents accumulate at border nodes, capacity scaling progressively reshapes destination probabilities, amplifying early routing differences and increasing ARD. Incorporating time-dependent movement behavior or improved initialization in future work may therefore reduce early-phase discrepancies.

From approximately the first month onward, the system enters a more stable regime. Flows consolidate onto high-capacity corridors, peripheral crossings become episodic, and ARD remains low. This structural consolidation is further reflected in the emergence of a clear corridor hierarchy. High-capacity routes consistently dominate system-level flows, while secondary corridors remain active but contribute marginally, indicating that displacement becomes increasingly governed by network topology and capacity asymmetries over time.

The validation results place the model in the context of prior work: aggregate-level accuracy is similar to that reported in recent Ukraine-specific modeling, while camp-level ARD values fall within the range observed across historical Flee applications. The present model, however, additionally resolves corridor-level structure, allowing explicit examination of route hierarchy.

Several limitations remain. Movement parameters were calibrated heuristically rather than estimated from independent data, and assumptions such as fixed rail use and static capacities significantly simplify time-varying operational conditions. Moreover, the simplification of the rail network to one station per oblast may omit important local feeder dynamics that could influence route choice and the timing of arrivals.

Nonetheless, the framework is structurally transferable. It relies on three core elements—transport network topology, conflict-driven agent generation, and capacity-driven destination attractiveness—which can be adapted to other contexts given appropriate data. In particular, the network representation can be extended to multimodal systems, while conflict and population inputs can be derived from region-specific datasets, although the relative importance of infrastructure constraints may vary across settings, particularly where transport networks are less centralized.

The distinction between surge and stabilization phases also has practical implications. During the early phase, flexibility is critical: temporarily expanding throughput across multiple crossings and rapidly reallocating transport capacity can help mitigate congestion and spillovers. In the later phase, system performance depends on the reliability of dominant corridors, as disruptions at major hubs are likely to propagate across the network. Maintaining capacity at high-throughput crossings, while preserving secondary routes as contingency options, is therefore key.

Supplementary Information and Code Availability: Supplementary Information, as well as the input information, output results and figures as well as code can be found at [14].

References

1. Sironi, A., Bauloz, C. and Emmanuel, M. (eds.): Glossary on Migration, International Migration Law, No. 34, International Organization for Migration, Geneva (2019)
2. Ghorbani, M., et al.: Flee 3: Flexible agent-based simulation for forced migration. J. Comput. Sci. **81**, 102371 (2024)
3. Mehrab, Z., et al.: Network Agency: An Agent-based Model of Forced Migration from Ukraine. In: Proceedings of the 23rd International Conference on Autonomous Agents and Multiagent Systems (AAMAS), pp. 1372–1380 (2024)
4. Pan, X., Han, C.S., Dauber, K., Law, K.H.: A multi-agent based framework for the simulation of human and social behaviors during emergency evacuations. AI Soc. **22**(2), 113–132 (2007)

5. Rodrigue, J.-P., Comtois, C., Slack, B.: The Geography of Transport Systems, 4th edn. Routledge, New York (2016)

6. The European Correspondent. Freedom travels by train (2024). https://europeancorrespondent.com/en/r/freedom-travels-by-train. Accessed 9 Aug 2025

7. Walravens, S., et al.: Characteristics of medical evacuation by train in Ukraine, 2022. JAMA Netw. Open **6**(6), e2319726 (2023)

8. Mehrab, Z., et al.: An agent-based framework to study forced migration: A case study of Ukraine. PNAS Nexus **3**(3), pgae080 (2024)

9. Wolshon, B., et al.: Agent-based modeling for evacuation traffic analysis in megaregion road networks. Proc. Comput. Sci. **52**, 908–913 (2015)

10. Horni, A., Nagel, K., Axhausen, K.W. (eds.): The Multi-Agent Transport Simulation MATSim, Ubiquity Press (2016)

11. Xu, Z., Bai, Q., Shao, Y., Hu, A., Dong, Z.: A review on passenger emergency evacuation from multimodal transportation hubs. J. Traffic Transp. Eng. (Engl. Ed.) **9**(4), 571–590 (2022)

12. Groen, D., Suleimenova, D., Bell, D.: Flee Documentation (2023). https://flee.readthedocs.io/en/master/, Accessed 9 Aug 2025

13. Armed Conflict Location and Event Data Project (ACLED). Ukraine Conflict Event Data (2025). https://acleddata.com/, Accessed 9 Aug 2025

14. Malcic, I.: Supplementary Information: Transport Network Topology as a Determinant of Forced Displacement Dynamics: Case Study of Rail-Based Evacuation from Ukraine (2026). https://doi.org/10.5281/zenodo.18762088

15. Urbán, F.: Characteristics of migration from Ukraine to Hungary in the last decade. Hung. Law Enforcement **1**, 205–217 (2023)

16. Duszczyk, M., Kaczmarczyk, P.: The war in Ukraine and migration to Poland: outlook and challenges. Intereconomics **57**(3), 164–170 (2022)

17. UNICEF. UNICEF in Romania: Support for Refugee Children, Women and Families from Ukraine (2022). https://www.unicef.org/romania/stories/unicef-support-romania-refugee-children-women-and-families-coming-ukraine

18. ACTED. Ukraine Conflict: How We Support Refugees in Moldova (2022). https://www.acted.org/en/ukraine-conflict-how-we-support-refugees-in-moldova/

19. UNHCR. Ukraine Refugee Situation: Slovakia Refugee Data Portal (2025). https://data.unhcr.org/en/situations/ukraine/location/10785

20. Statistics Poland and World Health Organization. Health of refugees from Ukraine in Poland 2022: Household survey and behavioural insights research, Warsaw, Poland (2023)

21. International Organization for Migration. Ukraine Response 2022 – Slovakia: Displacement patterns, needs and intentions survey (2022)

22. Suleimenova, D., Groen, D.: How policy decisions affect refugee journeys in South Sudan: a study using automated ensemble simulations. J. Artif. Soc. Soc. Simul. **23**(1), 1 (2020)

23. Suleimenova, D., Low, W., Groen, D.: An agent-based forced displacement simulation: A case study of the Tigray crisis, Lecture Notes in Computer Science, pp. 83–89 (2022). https://doi.org/10.1007/978-3-031-08760-8_7

Satellite-Based Conflict Damage Detection: Siamese CNNs for Forced Displacement Planning in Ukraine

Taulant Matarova[✉] and Diana Suleimenova[iD]

Department of Computer Science, Brunel University of London, London, UK
`taulantsyle@outlook.com`, `diana.suleimenova@brunel.ac.uk`

Abstract. Forced displacement due to armed conflict is an escalating global challenge, with over 117 million people displaced worldwide in 2025. Traditional damage assessment methods are slow, resource-intensive, and often impractical in active conflict zones. We present a Siamese Convolutional Neural Network for binary building damage detection using freely available Sentinel-2 medium-resolution satellite imagery. Using pre- and post-conflict image pairs from the Copernicus Data Space Ecosystem and UNOSAT building damage annotations, we evaluate eight model variants across four ResNet backbone depths with a Multilayer Perceptron classification head, tested across twenty-two conflict-affected Ukrainian regions. Our best-performing model, a Siamese ResNet-101 with an MLP head, achieves an Area Under the ROC Curve of 0.911 and an Average Precision of 0.888, demonstrating strong detection capability without high-resolution commercial imagery. We analyse the model's utility for both outward and inward humanitarian displacement planning and discuss its potential integration with agent-based models for simulating forced displacement scenarios. Our results demonstrate that resource-efficient, publicly available satellite data can support data-driven humanitarian planning at scale.

Keywords: Siamese CNN · Damage Detection · Satellite Imagery · Population Displacement

1 Introduction

Forced displacement is one of the defining humanitarian challenges of the twenty-first century. By June 2025, more than 117 million people were forcibly displaced worldwide due to armed conflict, violence, climate-related disasters, and socio-political instability [1]. The escalation of the war in Ukraine following the full-scale invasion of February 2022 illustrates the speed and scale at which contemporary conflicts generate displacement, uprooting millions of internally displaced persons and refugees, and placing severe pressure on humanitarian systems [2]. In such contexts, rapid, data-driven decision-making is essential for

M. Paszynski et al. (Eds.): ICCS 2026 Workshops, LNCS 16788, pp. 58–72, 2026.
https://doi.org/10.1007/978-3-032-29915-4_5

allocating resources, planning evacuation and relocation pathways, and preparing host regions.

Effective response requires two complementary forms of operational planning: *outward displacement planning*, which addresses immediate population flight, and *inward displacement planning*, which supports safe return and resettlement [3,4]. Both depend critically on timely and accurate spatial information about building damage, as the distribution and severity of infrastructure destruction shape habitability, infrastructure functionality, and displacement patterns [5].

Traditional damage assessments rely on ground surveys and expert interpretation of imagery. Although reliable, these methods are slow, resource-intensive, and often infeasible in active conflict zones. Large-scale crises, such as the 2010 Haiti earthquake, required weeks of coordinated mapping efforts, highlighting the persistent challenge of timely assessment [6,7]. Remote sensing offers a scalable alternative by enabling observation without direct human access.

Very high-resolution (VHR) commercial imagery enables detailed building-level damage classification [8], but high costs and access constraints limit its operational utility for many humanitarian actors. Medium-resolution imagery from the European Space Agency's Sentinel-2 constellation provides a compelling alternative. It delivers multispectral imagery at 10 m ground sampling distance with a five-day revisit cycle and free, open access through the Copernicus Data Space Ecosystem [9,10]. Despite its coarser resolution, its temporal frequency, spectral richness, and zero-cost availability make it attractive for large-scale humanitarian monitoring.

Siamese Convolutional Neural Networks (CNNs) have emerged as a powerful approach for change detection in remote sensing, learning discriminative representations from paired pre- and post-event imagery through shared-weight architectures [11–13]. While prior studies have focused predominantly on VHR data [14,15], the application of Siamese CNNs to medium-resolution imagery remains underexplored. Moreover, systematic comparisons of backbone architectures and classification heads are limited, and integration with operational humanitarian workflows has not been comprehensively addressed.

To bridge these gaps, this paper presents a systematic evaluation of Siamese CNN architectures for binary building damage detection using freely available Sentinel-2 imagery, with explicit relevance to displacement planning. We (1) construct curated datasets from conflict-affected regions using Copernicus Emergency Management Service activations and United Nations Operational Satellite Applications Programme (UNOSAT) annotations [16], (2) benchmark eight model variants based on four ResNet backbones (ResNet-34, ResNet-50, ResNet-101, ResNet-152) with a Multilayer Perceptron classification head, (3) demonstrate competitive performance without reliance on costly VHR imagery, and (4) outline pathways for integrating automated damage mapping into displacement simulation and humanitarian decision-support systems, including the agent-based Flee simulation toolkit [17].

The remainder of the paper is structured as follows. Section 2 reviews the literature on displacement planning, remote sensing-based damage assessment, and Siamese CNN-based change detection. Section 3 describes the study area, data sources, preprocessing pipeline, and the Siamese CNN approach with its model configurations. Section 4 presents the experimental results and discusses the humanitarian implications, limitations, and directions for future work (Section 5). Finally, Section 6 concludes the paper.

2   Related Work

Forced displacement driven by armed conflict reflects a complex interaction of security conditions, economic pressures, and social networks [18,19]. As humanitarian actors seek scalable, data-driven decision-support tools, computational approaches to displacement modelling have gained prominence [20]. Agent-based models (ABMs) are particularly influential, with approaches such as Flee simulating refugee movement along transportation networks under conflict pressure across multiple crises [17,21], though these require spatially granular inputs often incomplete or delayed in operational contexts. Statistical and machine learning methods have similarly been applied using conflict event data, socioeconomic indicators, and satellite-derived variables [6,20,22], including CNN-based route accessibility assessment from satellite imagery [23] and broader ML enhancements to ABMs [24,25]. Nevertheless, research has focused primarily on outward displacement, with limited attention to return planning. Survey evidence from Ukraine highlights persistent uncertainty over housing damage and local safety [26], underscoring the importance of timely building damage information for both flight and return decisions.

Satellite remote sensing provides a scalable mechanism for such spatial evidence. Conflict damage assessment has relied on expert interpretation of optical and synthetic aperture radar imagery since the early 2000s [16], with deep learning substantially accelerating this process. Benchmarks such as xBD standardised large-scale datasets for building damage classification from VHR imagery, enabling convolutional and transformer-based architectures [8], though dependence on commercial VHR data constrains cost-efficiency and scalability. Medium-resolution imagery remains comparatively underexplored. Existing studies demonstrate the feasibility of combining Sentinel-1 and Sentinel-2 data or applying recurrent networks to multitemporal Sentinel-2 imagery for urban change detection [27–29], yet translating medium-resolution signals into actionable building-level damage estimates remains difficult [30].

Siamese neural networks, originally developed for signature verification and metric learning [11,12], offer a weight-sharing approach to change detection in paired imagery, enforcing consistent feature representations across co-registered pre- and post-event inputs. In remote sensing, these models demonstrate strong change-detection capability with further gains from recurrent components and attention mechanisms, primarily in VHR settings [14,15,31], and perform competitively against early-fusion approaches when labelled data are limited [13].

Backbone selection also shapes performance: ResNets enable deeper architectures through skip connections [32], with variants such as ResNet-50, -101, and -152 balancing accuracy and cost [33]. VGG-16 remains competitive in transfer learning despite higher parameter counts [34], and comparative surveys emphasise backbone choice for downstream performance [35]. However, systematic benchmarking of Siamese CNNs with varied backbones for binary building damage detection using medium-resolution Sentinel-2 imagery in conflict settings remains absent.

Overall, although displacement modelling, satellite-based damage assessment, and deep learning are increasingly converging, an operational gap persists. The lack of systematically evaluated, resource-efficient damage detection approaches tailored to medium-resolution imagery and explicitly aligned with displacement planning workflows. This study addresses that gap by evaluating Siamese CNN-based building damage detection using Sentinel-2 imagery and examining its integration into humanitarian simulation and decision-support systems.

3 Methods

The ongoing conflict in Ukraine, which escalated to full-scale war in February 2022, has caused extensive damage to both urban and rural infrastructure [27]. To monitor and analyse this impact, Sentinel-2A Level-2A imagery was obtained from the Copernicus Data Space Ecosystem [10]. Each tile is approximately 1 GB and provides surface reflectance at 10 m ground sampling distance. Four spectral bands were retained for analysis: B02 (Blue, 490 nm), B03 (Green, 560 nm), B04 (Red, 665 nm), and B08 (Near-Infrared (NIR), 842 nm). The visible RGB bands enable full-colour composites, while the NIR band provides additional phenological information for the deep learning model, as healthy vegetation strongly reflects in NIR whereas damaged or disturbed surfaces do not [36]. Sentinel-1 imagery was deliberately excluded to limit the dataset size, making it more feasible for humanitarian organisations with restricted storage capacity.

Building damage labels were obtained from UNOSAT assessment shapefiles covering the 2022 Ukraine conflict [16], as individual buildings cannot be reliably distinguished at Sentinel-2 resolution through visual inspection alone. Only first-instance assessments with available shapefiles (`.shp`) were included; updated reports were excluded to avoid label inconsistencies. Pre-damage images were selected from any date prior to 24 February 2022, while post-damage images corresponded to the exact date of the report, preventing mislabelling of undamaged buildings as damaged. Images were visually inspected to minimise cloud coverage, though small residual clouds were retained to improve the model's robustness to atmospheric artefacts.

After data quality checks, 22 out of 25 conflict-affected regions were retained for modelling. These regions were selected to capture diverse conflict intensities and geographic contexts, maximising the representativeness of the trained models. Labels describe building-level damage assessments recorded during the 2022 Ukraine conflict. Table 1 summarises the complete dataset specification.

3.1 Preprocessing and Exploratory Data Analysis

All preprocessing used the GDAL library [37] within a Conda environment [38]. Coordinate reference systems of each image pair and its shapefile were verified and reprojected where necessary. Bands were merged into a four-channel TIF file (RGB + NIR) and visually inspected in QGIS [39]. Three regions were removed: Borodyanka (insufficient before/after overlap), Sievierodonetsk (single damage label), and Moshchun (a single large contiguous mask block). Points in Mykolaiv that fell outside the image boundary were removed manually.

Table 1. Dataset and Sentinel-2 configuration details.

Field	Description
Dataset	Sentinel-2 Level-2A images
Resolution	10 m per pixel
Bands used	B02 (Blue, 490 nm), B03 (Green, 560 nm),
	B04 (Red, 665 nm), B08 (NIR, 842 nm)
Images	25 pre-conflict, 25 post-conflict
Labels	UNOSAT building damage assessment shapefiles
Portals	https://browser.dataspace.copernicus.eu/;
	https://unosat.org/products
Regions	Borodyanka*, Bucha, Volnovakha, Trostianets, Sumy, Shchastia,
	Rubizhne, Okhtyrka, Mykolaiv, Moshchun*, Melitopol,
	Makariv, Lysychansk, Kremenchuk, Kramatorsk,
	Kherson, Kharkiv, Avdiivka, Antonivka, Chernihiv,
	Hostomel, Irpin, Vorzel, Azovstal industrial,
	Sievierodonetsk*

* Removed during preprocessing (see Sect. 3.1).

Rasterising labels. Shapefile damage points were buffered by 50 m before rasterisation to reduce misalignment at 10 m pixel resolution. Binary masks assigned each pixel a value of 1 (damage) or 0 (no damage). Bounding boxes were computed from the image geotransform as:

$$x_{\max} = x_{\min} + W \times p_x \tag{1}$$

$$y_{\min} = y_{\max} + H \times p_y \tag{2}$$

where $(x_{\min}, y_{\max})$ is the top-left origin, W and H are image dimensions in pixels, and p_x, p_y are pixel sizes.

Patching and dataset construction. Each of the 22 valid region triplets (before image, after image and mask as shown in Fig. 1) was converted into aligned 64 × 64 pixel patches covering 640 × 640 m on the ground, capturing local road and building context while limiting dilution of damage signals. A patch was labelled *damaged* if any mask pixel equalled 1. Up to 1,000 damaged and 1,000 non-damaged patches per region were stored in compressed .npz format (see Data Availability Statement for further details).

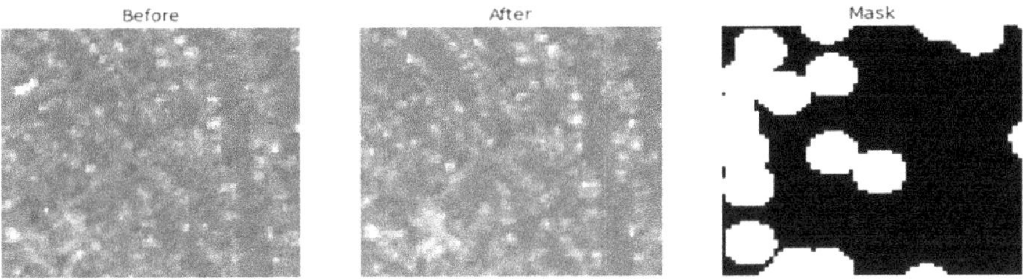

Fig. 1. Representation of the patch triplet from Avdiivka: (left) pre-conflict Sentinel-2A image acquired before 24 February 2022, (centre) post-conflict image acquired on the UNOSAT report date, and (right) corresponding binary damage mask (white indicates damage, black indicates no damage).

Exploratory analysis then identified 2,578 and 2,253 entirely black (invalid) patches in either the before or after channels, respectively, which were removed. The remaining 19,422 non-damaged patches were downsampled to 4,000. The 3,252 damaged patches were increased to 4,000 by augmentation of randomly selected patches via vertical flip, horizontal flip, and 90° rotation, adding 748 patches. 17 duplicate pairs were identified and removed across both classes, and the non-damaged patches were trimmed to match the damaged patches, yielding a balanced final dataset of 3,984 damaged and 3,984 non-damaged patches.

Figure 2 shows that 46.5 % of damaged patches had less than 5 % of their area covered by damage labels, motivating a deep learning approach over simple thresholding. To confirm this, principal component analysis (PCA) reduced the dimensionality of damaged images to 86 components explaining 80 % of variance. K-means clustering ($k = 2$) yielded a silhouette score of 0.1904, indicating minimal linear separability (Fig. 3). The dataset was split 60/20/20 into training, validation, and test subsets, which were used across the eight model variants for fair comparison.

3.2   Siamese CNN Architecture

The Siamese CNN passes before and after image patches independently through a shared ResNet backbone. The first convolutional layer, which expects 3 RGB channels, was extended to a fourth NIR channel by copying the layer and averaging the RGB weights, enabling the model to exploit NIR features from the RGB prior. The ResNet backbone captures multi-scale spatial representations inherently through its hierarchical convolutional stages: shallow layers encode fine-grained edge and texture features at sub-patch spatial scales, while deeper residual stages aggregate semantically richer representations at progressively coarser

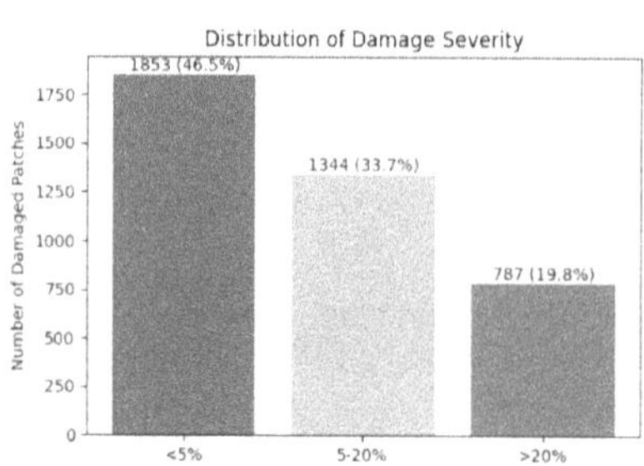

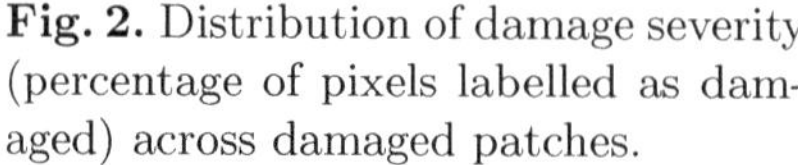

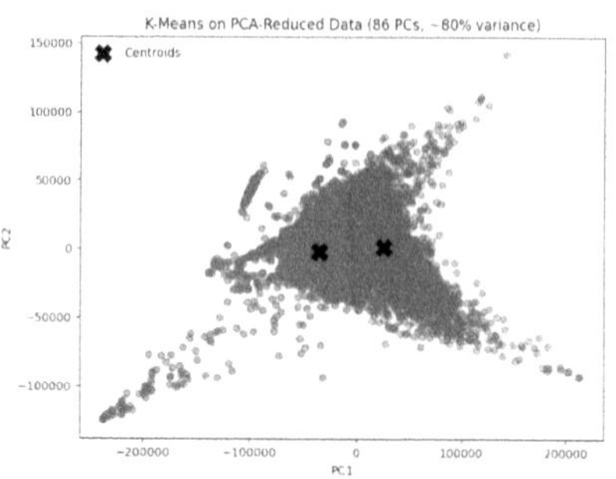

Fig. 2. Distribution of damage severity (percentage of pixels labelled as damaged) across damaged patches.

Fig. 3. K-means clustering on PCA-reduced features of damaged patches, showing minimal cluster separation (silhouette score = 0.1904).

scales. The 64×64 pixel patch (640×640 m on the ground) defines the operational inference scale, bridging the 10 m pixel resolution of Sentinel-2 imagery to the neighbourhood-block level at which damage assessments are produced. This patch-to-neighbourhood scale coupling is a deliberate design choice that positions the model's outputs for direct integration with city- and regional-scale displacement simulations. The preprocessing pipeline, implemented in Python using NumPy and Rasterio within a Conda environment, operates across these scales. GDAL reprojection and band merging are performed at the full-tile scale ($\sim 100 \times 100$ km), binary mask rasterisation at the 10 m pixel scale, and patch extraction and `.npz` serialisation at the 64×64 pixel scale. The final fully connected classification layer was removed.

After extracting features f_{before} and f_{after}, a 4D combined vector is constructed:

$$f_{\text{combined}} = \left[f_{\text{before}};\ f_{\text{after}};\ |f_{\text{before}} - f_{\text{after}}|;\ f_{\text{before}} \odot f_{\text{after}} \right] \tag{3}$$

where $\odot$ denotes element-wise product, capturing individual context, magnitude of change, and feature similarity. These combined features are passed to a Multilayer Perceptron (MLP) head with Gaussian Error Linear Unit (GELU) activation [40]:

$$\text{GELU}(x) = 0.5\, x \left(1 + \tanh\left[\sqrt{\tfrac{2}{\pi}}\, (x + 0.044715\, x^3) \right] \right) \tag{4}$$

and `BatchNorm1d` [41] after each linear layer, defined as:

$$y = \frac{x - \text{E}[x]}{\sqrt{\text{Var}[x] + \varepsilon}} \cdot \gamma + \beta \tag{5}$$

where $\text{E}[x]$ and $\text{Var}[x]$ are the batch mean and variance, ε is a small constant for numerical stability, and γ, β are learnable affine parameters. The output is a single logit with a damage threshold of 0.5 (sigmoid output). Eight architectures were evaluated across ResNet backbone depths (34, 50, 101, 152) and MLP head configurations, as listed in Table 2.

Table 2. Incremental improvement results. Model numbers correspond to training iterations, backbone and MLP head configurations are listed. Dropout rates are shown in parentheses.

Model	ResNet	MLP Head	Accuracy
0	34	$2048\,(0.5) \rightarrow 1024\,(0.2) \rightarrow 256$	0.8338
1	50	$8192\,(0.5) \rightarrow 1024\,(0.2) \rightarrow 256$	0.8369
2	50	$8192\,(0.5) \rightarrow 4096\,(0.2) \rightarrow 1024\,(0.2) \rightarrow 256$	0.8331
3	101	$8192\,(0.5) \rightarrow 4096\,(0.2) \rightarrow 1024\,(0.2) \rightarrow 256$	**0.8507**
4	101	$8192\,(0.6) \rightarrow 4096\,(0.2) \rightarrow 1024\,(0.2) \rightarrow 256$	0.8344
5	152	$8192\,(0.6) \rightarrow 4096\,(0.2) \rightarrow 1024\,(0.2) \rightarrow 256$	0.8375
6	152	$8192\,(0.5) \rightarrow 4096\,(0.2) \rightarrow 1024\,(0.2) \rightarrow 256$	0.8319
7	101	$8192\,(0.5) \rightarrow 4096\,(0.2) \rightarrow 1024\,(0.2) \rightarrow 256^{*}$	0.8394

*Model 7 uses backbone learning rate 10^{-3} (vs. 10^{-4} for all others).

3.3   Training Setup

Data loading, training, and evaluation used PyTorch [42] with a fixed random seed. Sentinel-2 surface reflectance values (stored scaled by 10,000) were divided by 10,000, then z-score normalised per channel using training-set statistics:

$$z = \frac{x - \mu}{\sigma + \epsilon}, \quad \epsilon = 10^{-8} \tag{6}$$

where μ and σ are per-channel mean and standard deviation computed on training data only. Normalisation was applied across all splits via the `PairsDataset` class, which supplies batched (before, after, label) triplets to PyTorch `DataLoader` objects.

Training ran for up to 40 epochs with early stopping (patience $= 5$, minimum improvement $= 10^{-6}$), meaning training halts if validation loss does not improve by at least 10^{-6} over 5 consecutive epochs [42]. The loss function was `BCEWithLogitsLoss` [41]:

$$\ell(x, y) = -\big[y \cdot \log \sigma(x) + (1 - y) \cdot \log(1 - \sigma(x))\big], \quad \sigma(x) = \frac{1}{1 + e^{-x}} \tag{7}$$

The Adam optimiser [43] used separate learning rates for the backbone (10^{-4}) and MLP head (10^{-3}), with L2 weight decay of 10^{-4} and gradient clipping at a maximum norm of 1.5. All models were trained on a GPU.

3.4   Evaluation Metrics

All models were trained and evaluated on the same pre-split dataset, with a fixed random seed to ensure a fair comparison. They were assessed using standard classification metrics, including Precision, Recall, F1 score, Area Under the Receiver Operating Characteristic (AUROC) curve, and Average Precision (AP) from the precision-recall curve. For a binary class i, these metrics are defined as:

$$Precision_i = \frac{TP_i}{TP_i + FP_i}, Recall_i = \frac{TP_i}{TP_i + FN_i} \tag{8}$$

$$F1_i = 2 \cdot \frac{Precision_i \cdot Recall_i}{Precision_i + Recall_i} \tag{9}$$

4   Results

All models triggered early stopping at epoch 6 (except Model 7 at epoch 13), indicating rapid overfitting given the dataset size and suggesting that backbone capacity is constrained by the availability of labelled training data. Table 3 summarises performance across all eight variants ranked by AP. Model 3, a Siamese ResNet-101 with a four-layer MLP head, achieved the highest AP (0.888), AUROC (0.911), and test accuracy (0.851), indicating the strongest discrimination between damaged and non-damaged patches across all evaluated configurations.

Table 3. Model performance ranked by average precision (AP), Area Under the Curve (AUC), and Accuracy (ACC). ND = no-damage class, D = damage class, P = precision, R = recall.

Model	AP	AUC	ACC	ND-P	ND-R	ND-F1	D-P	D-R	D-F1
3	**0.888**	**0.911**	**0.851**	0.895	0.794	0.842	0.815	0.907	0.859
2	0.878	0.900	0.833	0.865	0.789	0.825	0.806	0.877	0.840
6	0.876	0.906	0.832	0.866	0.785	0.824	0.804	0.878	0.839
7	0.874	0.899	0.839	0.872	0.795	0.832	0.812	0.883	0.846
0	0.872	0.896	0.834	0.850	0.811	0.830	0.819	0.857	0.838
1	0.870	0.902	0.837	0.882	0.778	0.827	0.801	0.896	0.846
5	0.869	0.904	0.838	0.883	0.778	0.827	0.802	0.897	0.847
4	0.865	0.897	0.834	0.869	0.788	0.826	0.806	0.881	0.842

Model 3's confusion matrices (Fig. 4) confirm high damaged-patch recall (D-Recall = 0.907) alongside accurate non-damaged classification (ND-Recall = 0.794), with a slight bias toward the damaged class attributable to training-time oversampling. The ROC curve (Fig. 5a) lies consistently above all other models, confirming the highest AUROC, while the precision-recall curve (Fig. 5b) shows a performance advantage that widens notably at recall values above 0.80, indicating an optimal balance of sensitivity and specificity for patch-level building damage detection.

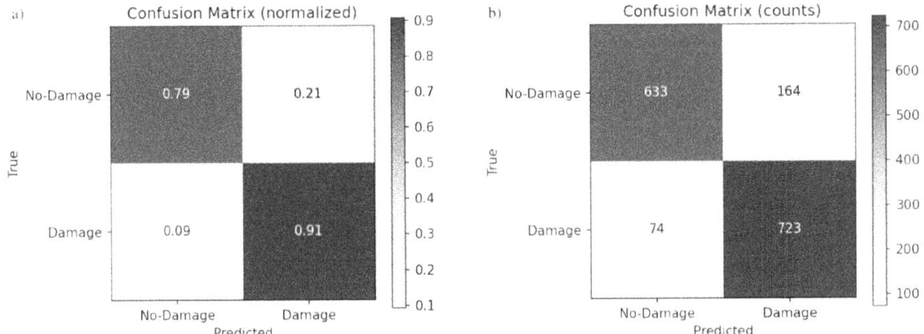

Fig. 4. Confusion matrices for Model 3: (a) row-normalised per-class recall rates (D-Recall = 0.907, ND-Recall = 0.794); (b) absolute prediction totals across No-Damage and Damage classes.

The model exhibited robustness to seasonal variation, successfully distinguishing genuine damage signals from spectral differences attributable to vegetation and phenological change between pre- and post-conflict acquisitions. The underperformance of deeper ResNet-152 variants relative to ResNet-101 is most plausibly attributed to dataset scale: larger parameter counts are harder to fine-tune without overfitting on limited labelled data, corroborated by the rapid early-stopping behaviour observed across all variants.

5   Discussions

5.1   Displacement Planning Applications

In the immediate aftermath of conflict escalation, outward displacement planning requires rapid identification of unsafe areas. The model's damage probability map, generated at 64×64-pixel resolution (approximately $0.41\,\mathrm{km}^2$ footprints), provides a spatially continuous raster suitable for prioritising evacuation corridors, identifying safe passage routes, and allocating emergency resources. Due to training-time oversampling, the model exhibits a slight bias toward the damaged class, producing fewer false negatives at the expense of some false positives, an operationally appropriate trade-off in emergency contexts where underestimating danger carries higher costs than issuing precautionary alerts. A single Sentinel-2 scene covering roughly $100\,\mathrm{km} \times 100\,\mathrm{km}$ can be processed within hours of acquisition, enabling near-real-time spatial intelligence infeasible through ground-based surveys in active conflict zones, while the five-day revisit frequency supports near-continuous monitoring of damage dynamics.

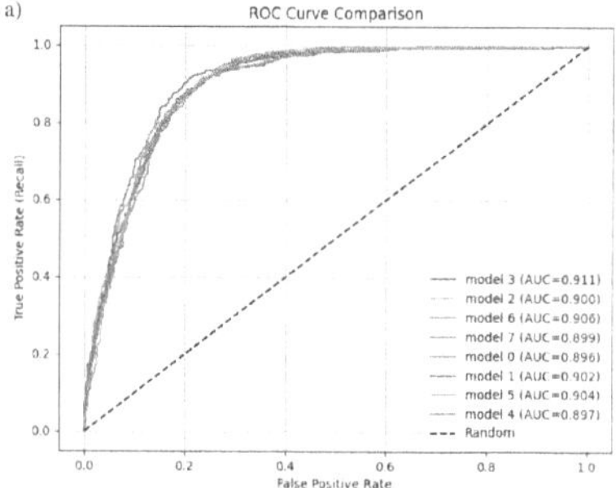
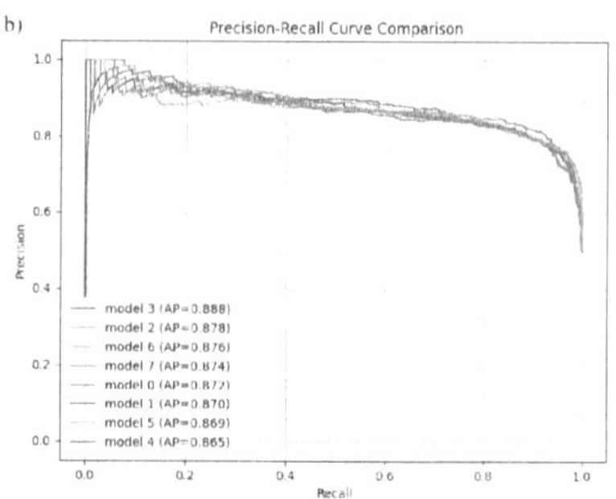

Fig. 5. Evaluation curves for all models: (a) ROC curves, with Model 3 achieving the highest AUROC = 0.911; (b) precision-recall curves, with Model 3 achieving the highest AP = 0.888.

For inward displacement and return planning, spatially comprehensive damage assessments are equally critical. UNHCR intention surveys in Ukraine (2022–2024) consistently identify housing damage and physical safety as primary barriers to return [26]. Housing condition is also a strong predictor of reintegration success [44], while delayed return imposes measurable economic burdens on host communities [45]. The Siamese CNN model provides a regularly updatable, large-scale building damage assessment that can complement ground-based housing surveys and inform return facilitation strategies. Given the model's false positive rate, outputs should be treated as an initial spatial screening tool rather than definitive household-level evidence, used to prioritise secondary field verification, the approach can substantially reduce the cost and time of systematic damage assessment, enabling coverage of conflict-affected territories that would otherwise exceed humanitarian resource capacity.

5.2   Integration with Agent-Based Displacement Models

A natural extension of this work is integration with an agent-based displacement simulation toolkit, namely Flee [21]. The damage probability maps generated by the Siamese CNN could serve as dynamic data layers within ABM simulations, providing near real-time information about building damage intensity that influences agent decision-making and route accessibility within the simulation environment. This integration would address one of the primary data limitations of current ABM-based displacement models: the difficulty of obtaining timely, spatially granular information about conflict-affected infrastructure. Conceptually, the approach extends the framework proposed by Suleimenova et al. [23], who identify CNNs applied to satellite imagery as a mechanism for updating route accessibility parameters in Flee simulations. In addition, the potential for continuous integration, drawing inspiration from real-time detection frameworks [46], could enable ABMs to ingest dynamically evolving damage layers as new Sentinel-2 imagery becomes available, rather than relying on periodic static snapshots.

5.3   Limitations and Future Work

Several limitations constrain the generalisability and operational readiness of the presented approach. The model was trained and evaluated exclusively on Ukrainian conflict data, and transfer to regions with substantially different settlement patterns, building typologies (e.g., informal settlements, mud-brick construction), or environmental backgrounds may degrade performance and requires explicit cross-theatre validation. Pre- and post-conflict image pairs acquired under different seasonal and atmospheric conditions can introduce spectral artefacts that confound damage signals. Z-score normalisation mitigates some radiometric variation, but residual seasonal and phenological differences, particularly between summer pre-event and winter post-event acquisitions, may influence predictions. A further source of noise arises from the resolution mismatch between UNOSAT annotations derived from VHR commercial imagery and the Sentinel-2 patches used for training: the 50 m spatial buffering applied to convert building-level annotations to patch-level labels introduces boundary noise and may cause undamaged patches near damaged areas to be mislabelled. At the granularity of a 64×64-pixel Sentinel-2 patch (approximately $0.41 \, km^2$), assessments are necessarily at neighbourhood-block rather than individual building level, limiting utility for fine-grained return planning at the household scale. Finally, although the preprocessing pipeline applies cloud masking via the Sentinel-2 Scene Classification Layer, prolonged cloud cover can introduce temporal gaps in damage monitoring that may be operationally critical.

Several promising directions for future work emerge from these limitations. Expanding training data to additional conflict regions, including Syria, Yemen, Gaza, and the Iran-Iraq border region, where sustained conflict has produced large-scale infrastructure damage and Sentinel-2 imagery is freely available, would enable rigorous cross-theatre generalisation assessment and is a prerequisite for operational deployment beyond Ukraine. The consequences of regional conflict dynamics on Iran and Persian Gulf states represent a further candidate application context given the absence of systematic medium-resolution damage detection studies in these areas. Integrating Sentinel-1 SAR data as a complementary input modality [27] would mitigate the cloud-cover limitation and improve damage signal robustness. Architectural enhancements including attention mechanisms, recurrent classification heads for temporal feature integration, and multi-scale feature pyramids offer clear pathways for improving performance on medium-resolution imagery [15,31]. Finally, end-to-end integration of the damage detection pipeline with ABM displacement simulations represents an important applied research target with direct humanitarian impact.

6   Conclusion

This paper presented a Siamese CNN approach for binary building damage detection using freely available Sentinel-2 medium-resolution satellite imagery, motivated by the operational needs of humanitarian displacement planning in conflict-affected regions. Eight model variants combining four ResNet backbone architectures with a four-dimensional combined feature representation and MLP classification heads were systematically evaluated on 7,968 balanced patches spanning 22 Ukrainian cities and regions annotated with UNOSAT damage assessments. The best-performing Siamese ResNet-101 achieved an AUROC of 0.911 and AP of 0.888 on the held-out test split, demonstrating strong damage detection capability from publicly available medium-resolution data without reliance on costly commercial VHR imagery. Architectural analysis revealed that ResNet-101 with a four-layer MLP head provides the optimal capacity-regularisation balance at this dataset scale, with deeper ResNet-152 backbones yielding diminishing returns due to limited training data. We further analysed the operational utility of the resulting damage probability maps for both outward and inward humanitarian displacement planning and discussed integration pathways with agent-based displacement simulations, establishing a compelling foundation for resource-efficient, scalable conflict damage assessment using open satellite data.

Data Availability Statement. The code for all eight model variants and hardware specifications are available at https://github.com/TMatarova/S2_urban_damage_detector_siamese. The dataset and pretrained weights for the best-performing model are additionally archived on Zenodo at https://zenodo.org/records/19441105.

Disclosure of Interests. The authors have no competing interests to declare that are relevant to the content of this article.

References

1. UNHCR: Figures at a Glance. UNHCR, Geneva (2025). https://www.unhcr.org/about-unhcr/overview/figures-glance
2. IOM: Ukraine Internal Displacement Report. General Population Survey. International Organization for Migration (2024). https://dtm.iom.int/reports/ukraine-internal-displacement-report
3. Black, R., Gent, S.: Sustainable return in post-conflict contexts. Int. Migr. **44**(3), 15–38 (2006)
4. Özerdem, A., Payne, L.: Ethnic minorities and sustainable refugee return and reintegration in Kosovo. Confl. Secur. Dev. **19**(4), 403–425 (2019)
5. Ramazani, R., et al.: War, displacement, and the best location for temporary sheltering: A qualitative study. BMC Public Health **22**(1), 2099 (2022)
6. Lu, X., Bengtsson, L., Holme, P.: Predictability of population displacement after the 2010 Haiti earthquake. Proc. Natl. Acad. Sci. U.S.A. **109**(29), 11576–11581 (2012)
7. Winkler, N.E., et al.: Critical failings in humanitarian response: a cholera outbreak in Kumer Refugee Camp. Ethiopia. BMJ Glob. Health **9**(12), e015585 (2024)
8. Gupta, R.: Creating xBD: a dataset for assessing building damage from satellite imagery. In: Proc. IEEE/CVF CVPR Workshops (2019)
9. European Space Agency: Sentinel-2 User Handbook. ESA Standard Document, Issue 1 Rev. 2 (2015). https://sentinels.copernicus.eu/documents/247904/685211/Sentinel-2_User_Handbook

10. Copernicus Data Space Ecosystem: Copernicus Data Space Ecosystem (2025). https://dataspace.copernicus.eu
11. Bromley, J., et al.: Signature verification using a "Siamese" time-delay neural network. In: Series in Machine Perception and Artificial Intelligence, pp. 25–44. World Scientific (1994)
12. Chopra, S., Hadsell, R., LeCun, Y.: Learning a similarity metric discriminatively, with application to face verification. In: Proc. IEEE CVPR, vol. 1, pp. 539–546 (2005)
13. Daudt, R.C., Le Saux, B., Boulch, A.: Fully convolutional Siamese networks for change detection. In: Proc. IEEE ICIP, pp. 4063–4067 (2018)
14. Yang, L., Chen, Y., Song, S., Li, F., Huang, G.: Deep Siamese networks based change detection with remote sensing images. Remote Sens. **13**(17), 3394 (2021)
15. Wu, C., et al.: Building damage detection using U-Net with attention mechanism from pre- and post-disaster remote sensing datasets. Remote Sens. **13**(5), 905 (2021)
16. UNITAR-UNOSAT: Ukraine: Building Damage Assessment Maps (Collection). United Nations Satellite Centre, Geneva (2022). https://unosat.org/products
17. Suleimenova, D., Bell, D., Groen, D.: A generalized simulation development approach for predicting refugee destinations. Sci. Rep. **7**, 13377 (2017)
18. Schon, J.: Motivation and opportunity for conflict-induced migration: an analysis of Syrian migration timing. J. Peace Res. **56**(1), 12–27 (2018)
19. Urbański, M.: Comparing push and pull factors affecting migration. Economies **10**(1), 21 (2022)
20. Hoffmann Pham, K., Luengo-Oroz, M.: Predictive modelling of movements of refugees and internally displaced people: towards a computational framework. J. Ethn. Migr. Stud. **49**(2), 408–444 (2022)
21. Ghorbani, M., et al.: Flee 3: flexible agent-based simulation for forced migration. J. Comput. Sci. **81**, 102371 (2024)
22. Huynh, B.Q., Basu, S.: Forecasting internally displaced population migration patterns in Syria and Yemen. Disaster Med. Public Health Prep. **14**(3), 302–307 (2019)
23. Suleimenova, D., Xue, Y., Tas, A., Low, W.: AI-enhanced agent-based modelling approach for forced displacement predictions. In: ICCS 2025 Workshops. LNCS, vol. 15911, pp. 79–86. Springer, Cham (2025)
24. Dehkordi, M.A.E., Lechner, J., Ghorbani, A., Nikolić, I., Chappin, É.: Using machine learning for agent specifications in agent-based models and simulations: a critical review and guidelines. J. Artif. Soc. Soc. Simul. **26**(1), 9 (2023)
25. Monti, R.P., Dasgupta, T., Cattaneo, M., Pan, W.: On learning agent-based models from data. Sci. Rep. **13**(1), 9268 (2023)
26. UNHCR: Lives on Hold: Intentions and Perspectives of Refugees, Refugee Returnees and IDPs from Ukraine #5. UNHCR, Geneva (2024). https://data.unhcr.org/en/documents/details/106738
27. Aimaiti, Y., Sanon, C., Koch, M., Baise, L.G., Moaveni, B.: War-related building damage assessment in Kyiv, Ukraine, using Sentinel-1 radar and Sentinel-2 optical images. Remote Sens. **14**(24), 6239 (2022)
28. Papadomanolaki, M., Vakalopoulou, M., Karantzalos, K.: Detecting urban changes with recurrent neural networks from multitemporal Sentinel-2 data. In: Proc. IEEE IGARSS, pp. 4971–4974 (2019)
29. Papadomanolaki, M., Vakalopoulou, M., Karantzalos, K.: Urban change detection based on semantic segmentation and fully convolutional LSTM networks. ISPRS Ann. Photogramm. Remote Sens. Spatial Inf. Sci. V-2-2020, 541–547 (2020)

30. Sticher, V., Wegner, J.D., Pfeifle, B.: Toward the remote monitoring of armed conflicts. PNAS Nexus **2**(6) (2023)
31. Chen, H., Wu, C., Du, B., Zhang, L., Wang, L.: Change detection in multisource VHR images via deep Siamese convolutional multiple-layers recurrent neural network. IEEE Trans. Geosci. Remote Sens. **58**(4), 2848–2864 (2020)
32. He, K., Zhang, X., Ren, S., Sun, J.: Deep residual learning for image recognition. In: Proc. IEEE CVPR, pp. 770–778 (2016)
33. Nagpal, P., Bhinge, S.A., Shitole, A.: A comparative analysis of ResNet architectures. In: Proc. IEEE SMART GENCON (2022)
34. Simonyan, K., Zisserman, A.: Very deep convolutional networks for large-scale image recognition. In: Proc. ICLR (2015)
35. Elharrouss, O., Akbari, Y., Almaadeed, N., Al-Maadeed, S.: Backbones-review: Feature extractor networks for deep learning and deep reinforcement learning approaches. Comput. Sci. Rev. **53**, 100645 (2024)
36. National Aeronautics and Space Administration: Reflected Near-Infrared Waves. NASA Science (2010). https://science.nasa.gov/ems/08_nearinfraredwaves
37. GDAL/OGR Contributors: GDAL/OGR Geospatial Data Abstraction Software Library. Open Source Geospatial Foundation (2023). https://gdal.org
38. Conda Developers: Managing environments. Conda documentation (2025). https://docs.conda.io/projects/conda/en/stable/user-guide/tasks/manage-environments.html
39. QGIS Development Team: QGIS Geographic Information System. Open Source Geospatial Foundation (2023). https://qgis.org
40. Lee, M.: Mathematical analysis and performance evaluation of the GELU activation function in deep learning. J. Math. (2023)
41. PyTorch. PyTorch documentation (2025). https://docs.pytorch.org
42. Paszke, A.: PyTorch: An imperative style, high-performance deep learning library. In: Advances in Neural Information Processing Systems, vol. 32, pp. 8024–8035 (2019)
43. Kingma, D.P., Ba, J.: Adam: A method for stochastic optimization (2014). arXiv:1412.6980
44. Zavisca, J.R., Mitchneck, B., Gerber, T.P.: Housing and integration of internally displaced persons: The case of Ukraine in 2018. Front. Hum. Dyn. **5** (2023)
45. Verme, P., Schuettler, K.: The impact of forced displacement on host communities: a review of the empirical literature in economics. J. Dev. Econ. **150**, 102606 (2021)
46. Redmon, J., Divvala, S., Girshick, R., Farhadi, A.: You only look once: Unified, real-time object detection. In: Proc. IEEE CVPR, pp. 779–788 (2016)

A Reproducible Multiscale Workflow for Socioecological Indicator Calculation in European Agriculture

Alan Bernardo Palacio[1]([✉])[iD], Antonio Espinosa[1][iD], and Joan Marull[2][iD]

[1] Universitat Autònoma de Barcelona, Barcelona, Spain
`alan.palacio@autonoma.cat, antoniomiguel.espinosa@uab.cat`
[2] Minuartia, Barcelona, Spain
`joan.marull@minuartia.com`

Abstract. We present a reproducible computational workflow that transforms official European statistics (Eurostat), CORINE Land Cover, and Copernicus High Resolution Layers into spatially explicit sustainability indicators for any European NUTS2 region. The workflow performs three computational steps: (i) mass-balance-preserving dasymetric downscaling from NUTS2 regions to H3 hexagons ($\approx 0.74\,\mathrm{km}^2$), enabling re-aggregation to arbitrary administrative boundaries; (ii) computation of socio-metabolic indicators—Energy Return on Investment (EROI), Energy-Landscape Integration Assessment (ELIA), and greenhouse gas (GHG) emissions—with explicit, configurable coefficients; and (iii) Shapley-value decomposition attributing observed indicator changes to land-area, intensity, and composition factors. Applied to three NUTS2 regions (NL23 Flevoland, ES53 Illes Balears, ITF2 Molise) over 2010–2020, composition shifts consistently dominate observed sustainability transitions (57–90%), while land-area and intensity changes together account for less than half. The workflow is implemented in Python and all coefficients are versioned, enabling transparent cross-regional comparison and independent replication.

Keywords: Multiscale modelling · Shapley decomposition · Dasymetric downscaling · Sustainability indicators · European agriculture

1 Introduction

Agricultural sustainability assessment requires methods that compare environmental performance across diverse regions using consistent indicators. In practice, however, assessments rely on partial metrics (e.g., yield per hectare, emissions intensity) or region-specific narratives that make cross-regional comparison difficult [1]. Decision-makers need transparent, reproducible tools that quantify sustainability consequences using well-accepted indicators across different agricultural systems.

© The Author(s), under exclusive license to Springer Nature Switzerland AG 2026
M. Paszynski et al. (Eds.): ICCS 2026 Workshops, LNCS 16788, pp. 73–80, 2026.
https://doi.org/10.1007/978-3-032-29915-4_6

This paper presents a computational workflow that makes sustainability indicators *comparable, auditable, and reproducible* across European regions. The workflow addresses a specific research question: *How do socioecological sustainability indicators evolve across regions, and what factors drive the observed transitions?*

Our contributions are:

1. A *multiscale downscaling pipeline* that allocates NUTS2-level statistics to H3 hexagons ($\approx 0.74\,\text{km}^2$) using dasymetric weights, preserving mass balance by construction and enabling re-aggregation to arbitrary boundaries (municipalities, watersheds, custom zones).
2. An *integrated indicator computation module* producing socio-metabolic indicators (EROI, ELIA), GHG emissions, and nutrient balances, with all coefficients explicit and configurable.
3. A *Shapley-based attribution pipeline* that decomposes observed indicator changes into land-area, intensity, and composition contributions with axiomatic fairness guarantees.

2   Related Work

Existing frameworks each cover part of this space: agri-economic models (CAPRI [2], FSSIM [3]) capture policy responses at coarse resolution; land-use platforms (LUISA [4], CLUE-S [5]) model transitions without metabolic accounting; ecosystem-service tools (InVEST [6]) evaluate endpoints post-scenario without attribution; socio-metabolic frameworks (MuSIASEM [7], HANPP [8]) offer fund–flow theory but lack spatialisation and decomposition pipelines. No existing workflow combines mass-balance-preserving multiscale downscaling, socio-metabolic indicators, and Shapley attribution in a single auditable pipeline.

3   Data and Study Areas

We evaluate three NUTS2 regions—the Nomenclature of Territorial Units for Statistics level 2, a standardised European classification typically covering 3,000–15,000 km^2 [9]. NUTS2 is the finest level at which Eurostat systematically reports crop areas, livestock numbers, and production volumes. These three regions were specifically chosen to test the workflow's robustness across a vast gradient of European geographic and agricultural contexts: *NL23 Flevoland* (central Netherlands) represents flat, highly intensive arable and dairy farming on reclaimed coastal polders; *ES53 Illes Balears* (western Mediterranean, Spain) provides a closed island ecosystem under severe water stress and tourism-driven land-use pressure; and *ITF2 Molise* (southern Italy) serves as a case study for rugged, mountainous topography with lower-intensity traditional cereal cultivation and sheep grazing.

We analyse 2010–2020 (11 years). Land cover uses CORINE Land Cover (CLC) [10] epochs with linear interpolation between available years. Eurostat [9] provides annual agricultural statistics via datasets `agr_r_animal`, `apro_cpsh1`, and `aact_eaa01`. For 2017 onwards, we incorporate Copernicus High Resolution Layers (HRL) [11,12] at 10 m resolution as supplementary allocation weights for downscaling.

4   Methods

Figure 1 shows the workflow. Data from Eurostat, CLC, and HRL are harmonised, downscaled to hexagonal cells, used to compute indicators, and finally decomposed via Shapley values to attribute observed changes.

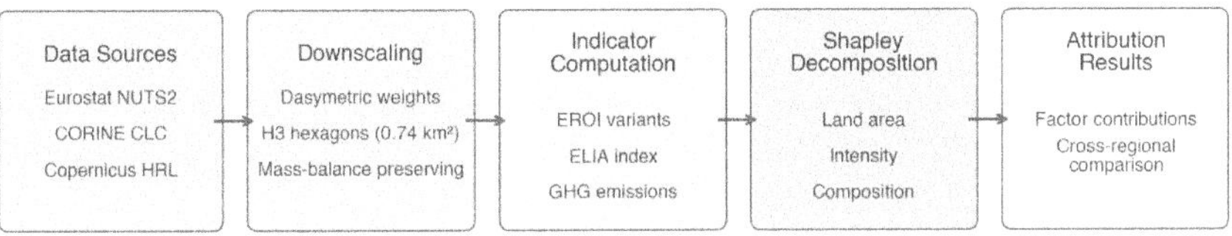

Fig. 1. Computational workflow. Official statistics (Eurostat), land cover (CORINE CLC), and high-resolution layers (Copernicus HRL) are harmonised, downscaled to H3 hexagons preserving mass balance, used to compute socio-metabolic and emissions indicators, and decomposed via Shapley values into land, intensity, and composition contributions.

4.1   Multiscale Dasymetric Downscaling

Official statistics are reported at NUTS2 scale, too coarse to identify sub-regional patterns. To enable finer analysis while preserving official totals, we use *dasymetric mapping* [14]—a spatial disaggregation technique that distributes aggregate quantities to finer zones using ancillary data as allocation weights. Each NUTS2 total X_r for quantity type c (e.g., wheat area, cattle count) is allocated to H3 hexagons [13] (resolution 8, $\approx 0.74\,\mathrm{km}^2$/cell):

$$w_{h,c} = \frac{\mathrm{suit}_{h,c}\,(1 - \mathrm{builtup}_h)}{\sum_{h' \in r} \mathrm{suit}_{h',c}\,(1 - \mathrm{builtup}_{h'})}, \qquad \hat{x}_h = w_{h,c} \cdot X_r \qquad (1)$$

where $\mathrm{suit}_{h,c} \in [0,1]$ is the suitability of hexagon h for quantity c, derived from CLC land-cover classes (e.g., arable land is suitable for crops, pasture for livestock), and $\mathrm{builtup}_h \in [0,1]$ is the built-up fraction from the Global Human Settlement Layer [15], which excludes urban areas from agricultural allocation. By construction $\sum_{h \in r} \hat{x}_h = X_r$, preserving official totals exactly.

This step enables re-aggregation to any spatial boundary (municipalities, watersheds, custom policy zones) while maintaining consistency with NUTS2 statistics. It also reveals intra-regional variation: within NL23, hexagon-level EROI ranges from 0.32 to 0.61, identifying hotspots invisible in the aggregate value of 0.45.

4.2 Indicator Computation

Following IPCC tiering principles [16], we distinguish Tier 1 indicators (accounting-based, directly derived from data) from Tier 2 indicators (coefficient-based proxies). All GHG values are CO_2-equivalents using AR5 Global Warming Potentials (CH_4=28, N_2O=265). LSU (Livestock Standard Units) follows Eurostat coefficients [9].

EROI. Energy Return on Investment measures energy yield relative to energy invested [17]. We compute: EROI $= E_{out}/(E_{ext} + E_{int})$, where E_{out} is metabolisable energy in products (MJ/yr), E_{ext} represents external fossil/industrial inputs, and E_{int} represents internally cycled biomass. Values below 1 are typical in fossil-subsidised agriculture (Tier 1).

ELIA. The Energy-Landscape Integrated Analysis index [1, 18] integrates energy storage E, metabolic organisation I (efficiency of energy flows), and landscape structure L (spatial heterogeneity of land cover):

$$\text{ELIA} = \left(\frac{E \cdot I \cdot L}{\kappa} \right)^{1/3} \tag{2}$$

where κ is a normalisation constant calibrated for cross-regional comparability (Tier 1).

GHG. Total emissions combine livestock sources (enteric fermentation, manure management) and land-based sources (fertiliser, soil N_2O, machinery):

$$\text{GHG}_{total} = \sum_i N_i \cdot g_i + \sum_j A_j \cdot g_j \tag{3}$$

where N_i is the head count of livestock species i, g_i is the emission factor per head (kg CO_2e/head/yr, IPCC Tier 1 defaults), A_j is the area (ha) of land-use class j, and g_j is the emission factor per hectare (kg CO_2e/ha/yr, Tier 2).

4.3 Shapley Decomposition of Indicator Changes

To attribute observed indicator changes to underlying drivers, we apply Shapley-value decomposition [19]. Any aggregate indicator I (GHG, energy) is expressed as a function of three factors, chosen as an *accounting factorisation* of the indicator identity: land area (A, total agricultural ha), intensity (f, yield or stocking density per ha in LSU), and composition (c, species mix). This is a deliberate modelling choice for attribution, not a claim that these are the only causal forces or that they are statistically independent; latent drivers act through changes in A, f, c, or remain outside the model scope.

For an observed change $\Delta I = I_{t_1} - I_{t_0}$, the Shapley value of factor k is:

$$C_k = \frac{1}{3!} \sum_{\pi \in \Pi} \left[I(S_\pi^k \cup \{k\}) - I(S_\pi^k) \right] \tag{4}$$

where Π is the set of all orderings, S_π^k the set of factors applied before k in ordering π, and $k \in \{\text{land}, \text{intensity}, \text{composition}\}$. Each of the $2^3 = 8$ counterfactual states (e.g., $A_{2020}, f_{2010}, c_{2010}$) is evaluated by recomputing the full indicator model. By construction: $C_{\text{land}} + C_{\text{intensity}} + C_{\text{composition}} = \Delta I$, providing symmetric, axiomatically fair attribution [19].

4.4 Uncertainty and Implementation

CORINE achieves $\geq 85\%$ thematic accuracy. Downscaled hexagon values are estimates; aggregate errors approach zero by construction at NUTS2 scale. Tier 2 emission coefficients carry $\pm 30\%$ uncertainty [16]; Tier 1 indicators (EROI, ELIA) support reliable cross-regional comparisons, while Tier 2 outputs (GHG) should be interpreted directionally. Under $\pm 30\%$ coefficient perturbation, composition remains the largest Shapley contributor in all regions. The workflow is implemented in Python 3.11 (GeoPandas, H3-py). All coefficients are stored in versioned YAML files.

5 Results

5.1 Spatial Discretisation

Figure 2 shows the downscaling result. NL23's intensive arable system produces high EROI values (green), while ITF2 and ES53 show greater heterogeneity reflecting their mixed agricultural systems.

5.2 Shapley Decomposition Across Three Regions

Table 1 presents the three-level Shapley decomposition for all regions. In every case, composition is the dominant contributor, explaining 57–90% of observed GHG changes and 57–84% of energy changes. Land-area contributions are small (1–11%), reflecting the stability of European agricultural land over this decade. Intensity contributes a moderate share (8–28% for GHG, 13–41% for energy), largest in ITF2 where yield changes accompanied the composition shift.

The pattern is consistent but not uniform. ES53 shows the strongest composition dominance ($\geq 84\%$), ITF2 the weakest for energy (57%) where yield changes also contributed. In NL23, dairy cattle (58% in 2010) shifted toward sheep/goats (17% by 2020); this compositional change—not land loss or intensity reduction—explains most GHG decline. ES53 crop data are partially missing in Eurostat; its results primarily reflect livestock dynamics.

6 Discussion and Conclusions

We presented a reproducible multiscale workflow—dasymetric downscaling, indicator computation, and Shapley decomposition—for computing and comparing socioecological sustainability indicators across European NUTS2 regions.

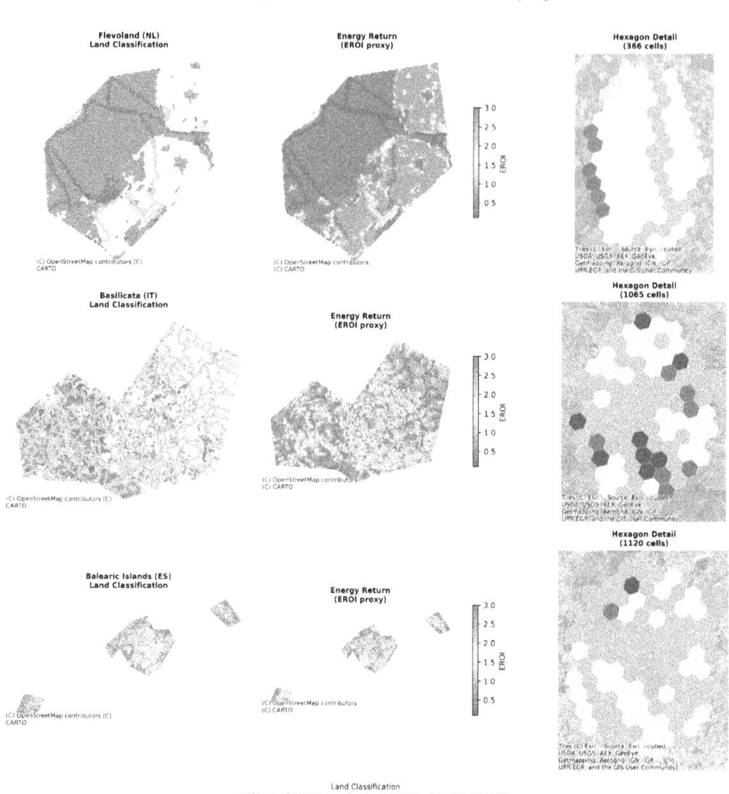

Fig. 2. Hexagonal tessellation for three NUTS2 regions. Left: dominant CLC land class. Centre: EROI proxy (green = higher). Right: hexagon close-ups over satellite imagery. (Color figure online)

Table 1. Three-level Shapley decomposition of observed 2010–2020 changes for all three NUTS2 regions. Values are percentage contributions to the total observed change in each indicator; rows sum to 100%.

Region	Indicator	C_{land} (%)	$C_{\text{int.}}$ (%)	$C_{\text{comp.}}$ (%)	Dominant
NL23 Flevoland	GHG	11.1	13.2	75.7	composition
	Energy	15.0	20.3	64.7	composition
ES53 Illes Balears	GHG	1.5	8.2	90.3	composition
	Energy	2.1	13.8	84.1	composition
ITF2 Molise	GHG	2.3	27.8	69.8	composition
	Energy	3.0	40.6	56.5	composition

Composition shifts explain 57–90% of observed GHG transitions across three contrasting regions. Current CAP eco-schemes primarily target land management and area payments, which account for a minority of observed variation. Effective decarbonisation may require support for *species transition*—helping farmers shift production mix. The framework does not model market demand, price responses, or trade adjustments.

The multiscale step enables sub-regional analysis (municipalities, watersheds) while preserving consistency with official statistics. Hexagon-level resolution reveals intra-regional patterns invisible in aggregate data.

GHG accounting is territorial; trade-displaced emissions are not captured. Tier 2 coefficients carry $\pm 30\%$ uncertainty [16]; composition dominance may not generalise to regions with rapid land conversion. Future work will focus on verification against independent data sources, Monte Carlo sensitivity analysis, and extending the framework to prospective scenarios.

Acknowledgement. This work has been granted by the Ministerio de Ciencia e Innovación MCIN AEI/10.13039/501100011033 under contract PID2023-146193OB-100.

Disclosure of Interests. The authors declare no competing interests.

References

1. Marull, J., Font, C., Padró, R., Tello, E., Panazzolo, A.: Assessing landscapes socio-ecological functionality. Land Use Policy **131**, 106558 (2023)
2. Britz, W., Witzke, P. (eds.): CAPRI Model Documentation. https://www.capri-model.org/
3. Louhichi, K., et al.: FSSIM, a bio-economic farm model for EU farming systems. Agric. Syst. **108**, 1–21 (2012)
4. Lavalle, C.: A high resolution land use/cover modelling framework for Europe. LNCS, vol. 6782, pp. 60–75 (2011). Springer
5. Verburg, P.H., et al.: Modeling the spatial dynamics of regional land use: the CLUE-S model. Environ. Manage. **30**, 391–405 (2002)
6. Sharp, R., et al.: InVEST User Guide/The Natural Capital Project. https://naturalcapitalproject.stanford.edu/software/invest
7. Giampietro, M., Mayumi, K., Sorman, A.H.: The Metabolic Pattern of Societies. Routledge (2012)
8. Haberl, H., et al.: Quantifying and mapping the human appropriation of net primary production. PNAS **104**(31), 12942–12947 (2007)
9. Eurostat: Eurostat database (agriculture and regional statistics). https://ec.europa.eu/eurostat
10. Copernicus Land Monitoring Service: CORINE Land Cover (CLC). https://land.copernicus.eu/pan-european/corine-land-cover
11. Copernicus Land Monitoring Service: High Resolution Layer – Grassland. https://land.copernicus.eu/en/products/high-resolution-layer-grassland
12. Copernicus Land Monitoring Service: High Resolution Layer – Imperviousness. https://land.copernicus.eu/en/products/high-resolution-layer-imperviousness
13. Uber Technologies: H3: Hexagonal Hierarchical Geospatial Indexing System. https://h3geo.org/

14. Eicher, C.L., Brewer, C.A.: Dasymetric mapping and areal interpolation. Cart. Geogr. Inf. Sci. **28**(2), 125–138 (2001)
15. European Commission, JRC: Global Human Settlement Layer (GHSL). https://ghsl.jrc.ec.europa.eu/
16. IPCC: 2019 Refinement to the 2006 IPCC Guidelines for National GHG Inventories (2019). https://www.ipcc-nggip.iges.or.jp/public/2019rf/
17. Hall, C.A.S., Balogh, S., Murphy, D.J.R.: What is the minimum EROI that a sustainable society must have? Energies **2**(1), 25–47 (2009)
18. Padró, R., Marull, J., Tello, E., et al.: Towards an energy-landscape integrated analysis? Landscape Urban Plan. **203**, 103905 (2020)
19. Shapley, L.S.: A value for n-person games. In: Kuhn, H.W., Tucker, A.W. (eds.) Contributions to the Theory of Games, vol. II, pp. 307–317. Princeton UP (1953)

Cross-validation-Based Hierarchical Decision Tree Framework for Dispersed Data Classification

Benjamin Agyare Addo[1] and Małgorzata Przybyła-Kasperek[1,2]

[1] University of Silesia in Katowice, Institute of Computer Science, Będzińska 39, 41-200 Sosnowiec, Poland
{benjamin.addo,malgorzata.przybyla-kasperek}@us.edu.pl
[2] Constantine the Philosopher University in Nitra, Trieda Andreja Hlinku 1, 949 01 Nitra, Slovakia

Abstract. The proliferation of fragmented, high-dimensional data across independent sources renders centralized classification impractical due to structural and privacy constraints. Existing hierarchical frameworks often worsen these challenges by taking part of the already limited test data for validation, reducing the reliability of final evaluation. This paper introduces a hierarchical decision tree architecture for dispersed sources that removes the need to extract a validation subset from the test data during global training. The method uses a two-level learning strategy. At the local level, decision trees are trained independently on each table using stratified cross-validation, and out-of-fold probability estimates are generated for all training objects to ensure reliable, leakage-free predictions. These vectors represent the predictive behaviour of each local view. At the global level, probability vectors from all sources are concatenated into a unified representation used to train a global decision tree that integrates information across views and produces the final classification. Experimental evaluation on multiclass benchmark datasets with varying levels of dispersion shows that the proposed method achieves performance comparable to other hierarchical and ensemble approaches designed for distributed data. The comparison included methods that train separate local classifiers and combine their outputs at the decision level. The results demonstrate that the hierarchical strategy based on cross-validation makes more effective use of limited and fragmented information while maintaining a strict separation between training and testing data. As a result, the global classifier is trained in a fully leakage-free manner and remains robust even when individual local tables contain only a small or highly uneven set of features.

Keywords: Dispersed Data Classification · Stacking · Local and Global Models · Ensemble Learning

1 Introduction

Machine learning has become indispensable for high-stakes predictive analytics, particularly in domains such as smart agriculture where complex, multi-modal feature sets are used to classify plant health. However, the increasing fragmentation of real-world data across disparate sensor nodes makes traditional centralized learning impractical due to privacy constraints and communication latency [15]. This has necessitated a shift toward decentralized paradigms, most notably Federated Learning (FL) [1,3,6] and Ensemble Learning (EL) [2,12,13], which allow for collaborative model training or fusion without requiring raw data aggregation [9,10].

Classification in these dispersed environments can be effectively achieved by constructing a global model that aggregates class probability vectors generated by independent local models. This architecture treats local diagnostic confidences as high-level features, significantly reducing communication overhead while maintaining data privacy and accommodating heterogeneous sensor formats. Prior research has explored this via decision trees with bagging [7,8] or K-nearest neighbor algorithms [4]. Such approaches are particularly valuable in "Small Data" scenarios where local sampling is essential to derive meaningful results from limited samples [14].

The core contribution of this paper is a structured hierarchical learning framework specifically tailored for fragmented data environments. Unlike existing stacking strategies that often require centralized data access or an explicit validation split of the test data for higher-level training, our approach utilizes a cross-validation-driven strategy to generate out-of-fold probability vectors. This ensures that the global decision tree is trained in a strictly leakage-free manner, preserving the integrity of the test set exclusively for final evaluation. By eliminating the need to partition limited datasets for validation, the proposed framework addresses critical constraints related to data locality and evaluation reliability in multi-source classification.

Building upon the dual-level architectures introduced in [8], this study investigates a methodology that employs cross-validation at the local level to produce robust probability features for a second-level global decision tree. This design aims to enhance classification performance in high-dimensional, multiclass settings while ensuring that every available data point is utilized effectively without compromising experimental validity. The remainder of the paper is organized as follows: Sect. 2 details the proposed hierarchical model; Sect. 3 describes the experimental setup and datasets; Sect. 4 discusses the results; and Sect. 5 provides concluding remarks and future research directions.

2 Model

This research addresses a classification problem where data is distributed across multiple autonomous sources rather than a centralized repository. Each source provides a partial and potentially heterogeneous perspective on a single underlying phenomenon. We define a collection of dispersed local decision tables

$\mathcal{D} = \{D_1, D_2, \ldots, D_n\}$, where each source i is represented as $D_i = (U_i, A_i, d)$. Here, U_i denotes the local object set, A_i represents the conditional attributes specific to that source, and d is a shared decision attribute. These tables are typically maintained by independent entities—such as distinct medical clinics or financial branches—meaning that while the attribute sets A_i may differ or partially overlap, the objective d remains consistent across the entire system.

Learning in such a fragmented environment presents significant challenges, primarily due to the potential for inter-source inconsistencies. Because each agent only observes a subset of the global attribute space, the same object might be associated with conflicting decision values across different tables. This necessitates a robust integration strategy that can resolve these contradictions and extract a coherent global signal without requiring the movement of raw, sensitive data to a central location.

To resolve these complexities, we propose a two-level hierarchical decision tree framework. The first level operates locally and independently on each decision table. For every source, we construct an ensemble of decision trees using a localized training strategy. These models do not merely output a hard classification; instead, they generate a probability vector for every object. The dimensionality of this vector corresponds to the number of decision classes, where each component reflects the estimated likelihood of an object belonging to a specific class based on the evidence available at that specific local site.

The second level of the framework acts as an integrator for the information synthesized by the local agents. For each object x, the probability vectors generated by all n sources are concatenated into a unified global feature representation. This resultant vector captures the collective, multi-perspective evidence provided by the distributed system. A global decision tree is then trained on these concatenated vectors using the true labels. By treating local probabilistic outputs as high-level features, the global model learns the relative reliability of each source and produces the final classification decision.

2.1 Local Level and Out-of-Fold Strategy

A critical requirement for the global model is the ability to generalize to unseen data without falling victim to information leakage. If the global model were trained on the same local predictions used to evaluate the local models, it would likely overfit to local training errors. To prevent this, we implement an out-of-fold (OOF) prediction strategy grounded in K-fold cross-validation. For each local table D_i, the object set U_i is partitioned into K disjoint, stratified folds.

During the training phase, for each fold $k \in \{1, \ldots, K\}$, a local tree $Tree_{i,k}$ is trained on the data contained in the remaining $K - 1$ folds. This model is then applied to the held-out fold to generate posterior probabilities $P_{i,l}^{(k)}(x) = \text{predict\_proba}(Tree_{i,k}, x)$. By iterating this process across all K folds, we obtain an out-of-fold probability vector $\hat{P}_i(x)$ for every training object in U_i. This ensures that every feature provided to the global level was generated by a model that did not have access to that specific object during its own training phase.

2.2   Global Level Integration

Once the local processing is complete, the framework transitions to the global stage. The individual out-of-fold probability vectors from each source are concatenated to form a single global representation $V(x) = [\hat{P}_1(x)|\hat{P}_2(x)|\ldots|\hat{P}_n(x)]$. This creates a global feature matrix $\mathbf{S} = \{V(x) \mid x \in \bigcup_{i=1}^{n} U_i\}$ which serves as the input for the global stage of the hierarchy.

The global decision tree, $Tree_{\text{global}}$, is trained using this matrix $\mathbf{S}$ and the corresponding decision labels. The role of the global model is to learn decision rules that effectively combine probabilistic evidence from multiple dispersed sources. During the inference phase, any new object to be classified follows the same pipeline: local models generate probability scores, which are then fused and processed by the global tree to yield the final predicted label $\hat{y}$.

3   Experimental Methodology

The proposed framework was evaluated using three multiclass benchmark datasets from the UC Irvine Machine Learning Repository: Vehicle Silhouettes, Soybean Large, and Lymphography. These datasets were selected for their high-dimensional feature spaces and varying levels of class complexity. While these datasets are originally centralized, we adapted them to simulate the dispersed data scenarios common in real-world distributed systems.

For the Vehicle Silhouettes and Lymphography datasets, we employed a stratified random split, allocating 70% of the instances for training and 30% for testing. The Soybean dataset was used with its original training and test partitions. Table 1 summarizes the structural characteristics of these data sets, including the number of conditional attributes and decision classes.

Table 1. Characteristics of the benchmark datasets

Dataset	Training set	Test set	Attributes	Classes
Vehicle Silhouettes	592	254	18	4
Soybean	307	376	35	19
Lymphography	104	44	18	4

To simulate dispersion, the training attributes were partitioned into five different configurations consisting of 3, 5, 7, 9, and 11 local tables. Each table contained a unique subset of conditional attributes but maintained the full set of training objects. We ensured that while some attributes were shared between tables to simulate overlapping views, the majority were distributed to create fragmented perspectives. Notably, object identifiers were not shared across tables to prevent direct row-matching, forcing the models to rely on the shared decision logic.

The complexity of each local table varied inversely with the degree of dispersion. In configurations with only 3 tables, each agent possessed a significant portion of the total attribute space (approximately 6 to 12 attributes). Conversely, in the 11-table configuration, the feature space was highly fragmented, with some agents possessing as few as three attributes. This variation allowed us to test the framework's ability to maintain predictive power even when individual sources provided extremely limited information.

3.1   Evaluation Methodology

To ensure the scientific validity of our findings, model training and evaluation followed a strictly separated procedure designed to prevent any form of information leakage. The local-level models were trained exclusively on the training data using an out-of-fold (OOF) prediction strategy, where each local table was partitioned into K folds to iteratively train decision trees on $K-1$ subsets while generating class probability predictions for the held-out fold. This exhaustive process resulted in a complete set of OOF probability vectors for all training objects, which served as the foundational features for the global training matrix. The global decision tree was subsequently trained using only these out-of-fold representations and their corresponding true class labels, ensuring that no portion of the test set was accessed during any stage of model construction. Final performance evaluation was conducted by applying the ensemble of local models and the trained global decision tree to the entirely independent test set, with each experimental configuration repeated five times to mitigate variability from random data partitioning and report stable average results.

Classification performance was rigorously assessed using a suite of standard evaluation metrics to capture different facets of model effectiveness. Overall classification accuracy (acc) was utilized to measure the total proportion of correctly identified test instances, while precision and recall were employed to evaluate prediction reliability and the model's ability to identify all relevant instances of specific classes, respectively. To provide a single metric that balances these two often-competing objectives, the F-measure was calculated as the harmonic mean: $\text{F-measure} = 2 \cdot \frac{\text{Precision} \cdot \text{Recall}}{\text{Precision} + \text{Recall}}$

Furthermore, given the potential for class imbalance in the benchmark datasets, we prioritized balanced accuracy ($bacc$), which computes the average recall across all decision classes. This ensures that the model's performance on minority classes is not overshadowed by the majority class, providing a more equitable assessment of the hierarchical framework's predictive power.

4   Results and Discussion

This section presents the experimental results and comparative analysis of the proposed hierarchical framework. We first evaluate the sensitivity of the model to local tree depth before conducting a global comparison against established baseline methods.

Table 2. Comparative results of precision, recall, F-measure, balanced accuracy ($bacc$), and accuracy (acc) across Vehicle, Soybean, and Lymphography datasets.

Agent No.	Metric	Vehicle Silhouettes				Soybean				Lymphography			
		4	6	8	10	4	6	8	10	4	6	8	10
3	Prec.	0.693	0.687	0.652	0.690	0.748	0.715	0.704	0.707	0.689	0.653	0.620	0.625
	Recall	0.665	0.676	0.644	0.672	0.718	0.693	0.701	0.672	0.707	0.665	0.651	0.637
	F-m.	0.670	0.674	0.641	0.672	0.683	0.662	0.671	0.642	0.679	0.629	0.625	0.601
	$bacc$	0.655	0.664	0.632	0.659	0.673	0.620	0.626	0.614	0.511	0.478	0.469	0.459
	acc	0.665	0.676	0.644	0.672	0.718	0.693	0.701	0.672	0.707	0.665	0.651	0.637
5	Prec.	0.665	0.696	0.681	0.668	0.822	0.806	0.765	0.769	0.694	0.704	0.711	0.680
	Recall	0.656	0.695	0.665	0.669	0.829	0.799	0.772	0.773	0.726	0.740	0.730	0.716
	F-m.	0.654	0.694	0.666	0.664	0.815	0.789	0.754	0.755	0.705	0.717	0.713	0.693
	$bacc$	0.639	0.669	0.649	0.649	0.776	0.760	0.730	0.710	0.520	0.530	0.523	0.514
	acc	0.656	0.695	0.665	0.669	0.829	0.799	0.772	0.773	0.726	0.740	0.730	0.716
7	Prec.	0.673	0.666	0.680	0.701	0.796	0.779	0.791	0.755	0.685	0.632	0.594	0.551
	Recall	0.677	0.659	0.669	0.691	0.797	0.796	0.809	0.776	0.702	0.651	0.628	0.581
	F-m.	0.671	0.659	0.672	0.694	0.781	0.779	0.792	0.756	0.684	0.630	0.609	0.561
	$bacc$	0.655	0.639	0.649	0.666	0.773	0.785	0.792	0.766	0.505	0.469	0.449	0.416
	acc	0.677	0.659	0.669	0.691	0.797	0.796	0.809	0.776	0.702	0.651	0.628	0.581
9	Prec.	0.681	0.690	0.676	0.682	0.766	0.803	0.753	0.743	0.691	0.670	0.688	0.655
	Recall	0.674	0.680	0.662	0.669	0.744	0.773	0.720	0.722	0.712	0.712	0.698	0.670
	F-m.	0.670	0.682	0.665	0.674	0.735	0.771	0.712	0.713	0.685	0.688	0.688	0.658
	$bacc$	0.659	0.662	0.646	0.651	0.678	0.714	0.674	0.664	0.512	0.508	0.500	0.481
	acc	0.674	0.680	0.662	0.669	0.744	0.773	0.720	0.722	0.712	0.712	0.698	0.670
11	Prec.	0.657	0.645	0.649	0.651	0.718	0.751	0.731	0.734	0.707	0.714	0.716	0.715
	Recall	0.654	0.635	0.641	0.639	0.694	0.710	0.720	0.710	0.726	0.730	0.740	0.749
	F-m.	0.649	0.633	0.643	0.640	0.685	0.705	0.704	0.701	0.699	0.706	0.717	0.725
	$bacc$	0.638	0.622	0.622	0.622	0.641	0.650	0.653	0.648	0.523	0.527	0.532	0.539
	acc	0.654	0.635	0.641	0.639	0.694	0.710	0.720	0.710	0.726	0.730	0.740	0.749

The performance of the proposed architecture was evaluated across various local tree depths ($d \in \{4, 6, 8, 10\}$) using balanced accuracy ($bacc$) as the primary metric. Table 2 provides a detailed breakdown of these results across the Vehicle Silhouettes, Soybean, and Lymphography datasets for different levels of data dispersion.

The Friedman test indicated no globally significant difference in results across the four investigated depths ($\chi^2(3, 15) = 2.84, p = 0.41$), suggesting that the ensemble method maintains structural resilience regardless of minor depth variations. However, comparative analysis of the performance distributions in shows that $d = 6$ and $d = 8$ exhibit greater stability and higher median values than the

Table 3. Comprehensive performance comparison across datasets. Best results in blue; second best in red.

No. of Tables	Metric	Vehicle Silhouettes					Soybean Dataset					Lymphography Dataset				
		AB	DT	NB	DLB	CVB	AB	DT	NB	DLB	CVB	AB	DT	NB	DLB	CVB
3	bacc	0.628	0.669	0.513	0.696	0.664	0.158	0.878	0.864	0.668	0.673	0.596	0.532	0.467	0.855	0.511
	acc	0.646	0.677	0.520	0.717	0.676	0.202	0.823	0.699	0.793	0.718	0.386	0.773	0.682	0.791	0.707
5	bacc	0.619	0.678	0.500	0.695	0.669	0.114	0.050	0.071	0.739	0.776	0.682	0.563	0.457	0.842	0.530
	acc	0.630	0.693	0.504	0.721	0.695	0.177	0.086	0.083	0.830	0.829	0.545	0.818	0.659	0.774	0.740
7	bacc	0.518	0.699	0.484	0.655	0.666	0.064	0.056	0.056	0.664	0.792	0.268	0.520	0.424	0.679	0.505
	acc	0.520	0.717	0.484	0.683	0.691	0.135	0.105	0.041	0.803	0.809	0.386	0.750	0.614	0.748	0.702
9	bacc	0.441	0.665	0.459	0.665	0.662	0.082	0.046	0.099	0.588	0.714	0.374	0.478	0.472	0.570	0.512
	acc	0.441	0.681	0.457	0.682	0.680	0.110	0.124	0.135	0.745	0.773	0.545	0.682	0.682	0.591	0.712
11	bacc	0.551	0.656	0.450	0.636	0.638	0.077	0.104	0.066	0.669	0.653	0.368	0.478	0.683	0.848	0.539
	acc	0.547	0.673	0.441	0.649	0.654	0.133	0.133	0.086	0.779	0.720	0.523	0.682	0.523	0.783	0.749

shallower $d = 4$ configuration. Post-hoc Wilcoxon each-pair signed-rank tests confirmed these differences as statistically significant ($p = 0.031$ and $p = 0.027$, respectively). Conversely, the transition to $d = 10$ yielded a p-value of 0.18, indicating diminishing returns. Thus, a maximum depth of 6 or 8 is optimal for balancing predictive power while avoiding overfitting.

To evaluate effectiveness, the Cross-Validation-Based (CVB) model was compared against centralized models (AdaBoost, Decision Tree, Naive Bayes) using majority voting, alongside a dual-level bagging (DLB) method [8]. Table 3 illustrates that the CVB model consistently achieves superior performance, frequently outperforming baselines by substantial margins.

This architectural advantage is most evident in the Soybean dataset, where standard models suffer performance collapse as fragmentation increases. In contrast, CVB effectively integrates sparse local features. Statistical validation using the Friedman test ($\chi^2(74, 4) = 138.22, p < 0.000001$) and post hoc Wilcoxon tests confirm that CVB provides a significantly more robust and stable classification framework than traditional voting mechanisms.

5   Summary

This paper investigated the problem of classification in dispersed data environments, where data are distributed across multiple local sources with heterogeneous feature spaces and a shared decision attribute. To address the limitations of existing hierarchical approaches that rely on explicit validation splits of the test set, a two level hierarchical decision tree framework was proposed. The method leverages stratified cross validation at the local level to generate out-of-fold probability predictions, which serve as reliable and leakage free inputs for training a global decision tree. By constructing the global model solely from training data derived probability vectors, the framework preserves the integrity of the test set for unbiased evaluation while maximizing the use of available data.

Experimental results on several benchmark multiclass datasets with varying degrees of dispersion demonstrate that the proposed approach is effective in integrating information from fragmented views and performs competitively across different performance measures. The findings suggest that hierarchical decision trees combined with cross validation based stacking provide a robust and interpretable solution for learning from dispersed data without requiring data centralization or additional validation partitions.

Future work will focus on exploring alternative global learners, analyzing the impact of different cross validation strategies, and extending the framework to more complex real world scenarios with stronger class imbalance and higher dimensional feature spaces.

References

1. Firouzi, R., Rahmani, R., Kanter, T.: Federated learning for distributed reasoning on edge computing. Procedia Comput. Sci. **184**, 419–427 (2021)
2. Ksieniewicz, P., Zyblewski, P., Burduk, R.: Fusion of linear base classifiers in geometric space. Knowl.-Based Syst. **227**, 107231 (2021)
3. Lewy, D., Mańdziuk, J., Ganzha, M., Paprzycki, M.: StatMix: Data augmentation method that relies on image statistics in federated learning. In: International Conference on Neural Information Processing, pp. 574–585. Springer, Singapore (2022)
4. Marfo, K.F., Przybyła-Kasperek, M.: Radial basis function network for aggregating predictions of k-nearest neighbors local models generated based on independent data sets. Procedia Comput. Sci. **207**, 3234–3243 (2022)
5. Michalski, R.S., Chilausky, R.L.: Knowledge acquisition by encoding expert rules versus computer induction from examples: a case study involving soybean pathology. Int. J. Hum Comput Stud. **51**(2), 239–263 (1999)
6. Pedrycz, W.: Advancing federated learning with granular computing. Fuzzy Inform. Eng. **15**(1), 1–13 (2023)
7. Przybyła-Kasperek, M., Addo, B.A.: Novel hierarchical decision tree frameworks introducing tree method bagging stump integration and height optimization. In: International Conference on Computational Science, pp. 3–11. Springer, Switzerland (2025)
8. Przybyła-Kasperek, M., Addo, B.A., Kusztal, K.: Dual-level decision tree-based model for dispersed data classification. In: Marcinkowski, B., et al. (eds.) Harnessing Opportunities: Reshaping ISD in the Post-COVID-19 and Generative AI Era (ISD2024 Proceedings). University of Gdańsk (2024). https://doi.org/10.62036/ISD.2024.44
9. Rahim, N., El-Sappagh, S., Rizk, H., El-Serafy, O.A., Abuhmed, T.: Information fusion-based Bayesian optimized heterogeneous deep ensemble model based on longitudinal neuroimaging data. Appl. Soft Comput. **162**, 111749 (2024)
10. Seydi, S.T., Saeidi, V., Kalantar, B., Ueda, N., van Genderen, J.L., Maskouni, F.H., Aria, F.A.: Fusion of the multisource datasets for flood extent mapping based on ensemble convolutional neural network model. Journal of Sensors **2022**(1), 2887502 (2022)
11. Siebert, J.P.: Vehicle recognition using rule based methods (1987)

12. Trajdos, P., Burduk, R.: Ensemble of classifiers based on score function defined by clusters and decision boundary of linear base learners. Knowl.-Based Syst. **303**, 112411 (2024)
13. Węgier, W., Koziarski, M., Woźniak, M.: Multicriteria classifier ensemble learning for imbalanced data. IEEE Access **10**, 16807–16818 (2022)
14. Yu, L., Li, M.: A case-based reasoning driven ensemble learning paradigm for financial distress prediction with missing data. Appl. Soft Comput. **137**, 110163 (2023)
15. Yurochkin, M., Agarwal, M., Ghosh, S., Redewald, K., Hoang, N., Khazaeni, Y.: Bayesian nonparametric federated learning of neural networks. In: International Conference on Machine Learning, pp. 7252–7261 (2019). PMLR
16. Zwitter, M., Soklic, M.: Lymphography domain. University Medical Center, Institute of Oncology, Ljubljana, Yugoslavia (1988)

Large Language Models Related Intelligent Decision-Making in the Digital Economy Era

Feature Extractor Comparison for Distribution Matching Framework in Dataset Distillation

Muyang Li[1,2] ![ORCID], Zeheng He[3], Yi Qu[2,4(✉)], and Yong Shi[2,4]

[1] School of Computer Science and Technology, University of Chinese Academy of Sciences, Beijing 100190, China
[2] Research Center on Fictitious Economy and Data Science, Chinese Academy of Sciences, Beijing 100190, China
`quyi@ucas.ac.cn`
[3] Faculty of Information Technology, Monash University, Melbourne, VIC 3168, Australia
[4] School of Economics and Management, University of Chinese Academy of Sciences, Beijing 100190, China

Abstract. Dataset distillation is a technique to generate compact synthetic datasets which enable efficient model training and knowledge transfer. It relies on two critical procedures in distribution matching frameworks: feature extraction and distribution alignment. Previous studies have less attention on systematical investigations about how different feature extractors influence the performance of distilled datasets. To enrich research in this filed, this paper conducts comprehensive comparison of four feature extractors including convolutional neural network (CNN), ResNet-18, multilayer perceptron (MLP) and lightweight Vision Transformer (ViT), and further analyzes the impact of dynamic or fixed feature extractors. Experimental results indicates the optimal performance of ConvNet and finding that slight pre-training of feature extractors using image classification tasks can promote the performance of distilled datasets. This work provides empirical guidance for appropriate feature extractors selection in distribution matching frameworks of dataset distillation.

Keywords: Dataset distillation · Distribution matching · Feature extractor selection · Representation Learning

1 Introduction

As a thriving research field in computer vision, dataset distillation has been attracting increasingly significant research interests. The main challenge of dataset distillation lies in how to transfer crucial information from the original dataset $\mathcal{T}$ to the distilled one $\mathcal{S}$. Several frameworks have been proposed for dataset distillation problem, including bi-level optimization framework [12],

M. Paszynski et al. (Eds.): ICCS 2026 Workshops, LNCS 16788, pp. 93–103, 2026.
https://doi.org/10.1007/978-3-032-29915-4_8

kernel-based optimization framework [9], parameter matching framework [1,15] and distribution matching framework [14,16].

By considering dataset $\mathcal{X}$ as a sample of the distribution $\mathcal{D}_\mathcal{X}(\mathcal{X} \in \{\mathcal{S}, \mathcal{T}\})$, the workflow of distribution matching framework (Fig. 1) can be described as follows [14]:

Step 1: Extracts representation vectors via feature extractors from datasets $\mathcal{T}$ and $\mathcal{S}$ respectively.

Step 2: Construct the dataset $\mathcal{S}$ by matching these two distributions $\mathcal{D}_\mathcal{T}$ and $\mathcal{D}_\mathcal{S}$.

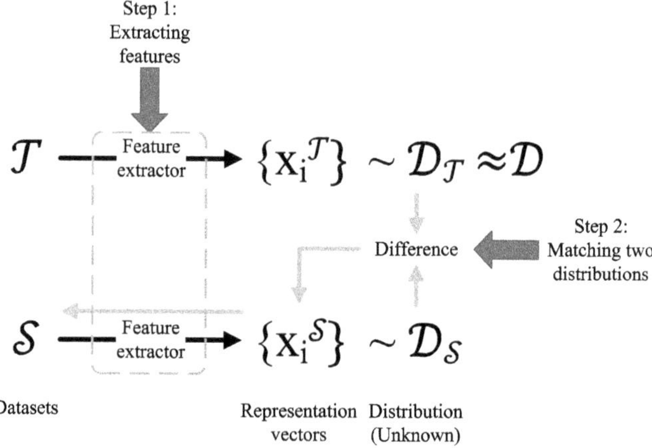

Fig. 1. Workflow of distribution matching framework. *Black arrows indicate the forward propagation process, orange arrows represent the backward propagation process.* (Color figure online)

The procedure of training a neural network can be regarded as the network learning the distribution of the dataset [3]. Thus the distribution matching framework can be considered as extracting the distribution of the dataset $\mathcal{T}$ and reconstructing the distribution in the dataset $\mathcal{S}$.

Existing works have mainly focused on the design of matching target while ignoring the importance of feature extraction [11,13,14]. In [16], the author provides a brief comparison regarding the performance of distilled dataset with respect to the training epoch iteration.

In this paper, we propose that different feature extractor impact the performance of distilled dataset. To verify the validity of this opinion, we carefully compare the performance of distilled dataset under different feature extractors. We select MLP, ConvNet, ResNet-18 and lightweight ViT as candidates.

The remainder of this paper is organized as follows: In Sect. 2, we will review some existing works on distribution matching approach. Section 3 will introduce the experimental setup and details. The experimental results and relevant discussions will be presented in Sect. 4. Finally, Sect. 5 will conclude the work of this paper.

2   Related Work

2.1   Dataset Distillation

As illustrated in Sect. 1, dataset distillation refers to the task of constructing another dataset $\mathcal{S}$ for a given dataset $\mathcal{T}$, such that $\mathcal{S}$ serves as an alternative to $\mathcal{T}$ [12]. Here alternative means that a neural network trained on $\mathcal{S}$ can achieve comparable performance to one trained on $\mathcal{T}$. This process involves distilling the essential knowledge from the original dataset $\mathcal{T}$ into a smaller synthetic dataset $\mathcal{S}$, which retains the critical statistical properties and representational power required to train models with equivalent efficacy.

Mathematically, the goal of dataset distillation can be expressed as:

$$\mathbb{E}_{(x,y)\sim\mathcal{D}}[\mathrm{loss}(f_{\mathcal{S}}(x), y)] \approx \mathbb{E}_{(x,y)\sim\mathcal{D}}[\mathrm{loss}(f_{\mathcal{T}}(x), y)] \tag{1}$$

Here $\mathcal{D}$ is the real distribution of dataset $\mathcal{T}$, $f_{\mathcal{X}}$ describes the neural network trained on dataset $\mathcal{X}$ ($\mathcal{X} = \mathcal{T}/\mathcal{S}$), thus $\mathbb{E}_{(x,y)\sim\mathcal{D}}[\mathrm{loss}(f(x), y)]$ represents the expectation risk of model f.

Distribution matching (DM) framework aims to achieve dataset distillation by aligning the distributions of the synthesized dataset $\mathcal{S}$ and the original dataset $\mathcal{T}$.

2.2   Distribution Matching

The vanilla DM method synthesizes the distilled dataset $\mathcal{S}$ based on the optimization of the Maximum Mean Discrepancy (MMD) [4], minimizing the MSE between the mean of the data representation distributions in $\mathcal{T}$ and $\mathcal{S}$. The MMD between two distributions is defined by:

$$\mathrm{MMD} = \sup_{\|\psi\|_{\mathcal{H}}\leq 1} (\mathbb{E}_{\mathcal{T}}[\psi(x)]) - (\mathbb{E}_{\mathcal{S}}[\psi(x)]) \tag{2}$$

Here $\psi(\cdot)$ is the feature extractor, $\mathbb{E}_{\mathcal{X}}(\mathcal{X} = \mathcal{T}/\mathcal{S})$ refers to the expectation calculated based on dataset $\mathcal{X}$. In practical applications, the empirical estimate of the MMD is used [14].

$$S^* = \arg\min_{\mathcal{S}} \mathbb{E}\left\| \frac{1}{|\mathcal{T}|} \sum_{i=1}^{|\mathcal{T}|} \psi(x_i) - \frac{1}{|\mathcal{S}|} \sum_{i=1}^{|\mathcal{S}|} \psi(x_i) \right\|^2 \tag{3}$$

Furthermore, Improvements to vanilla DM mainly focus on two categories. One is extracting more features: CAFE [11] aligns all feature maps in the same feature extractor between samples in $\mathcal{T}$ and $\mathcal{S}$; Improved distribution matching (IDM) [16] enhances image minibatches and increases feature extractors, adding crossentropy loss to alignment features. The other is using better alignment methods: Inspired by transfer learning, M^3D maps the distribution to a reproducing kernel Hilbert space to measure distribution distance [13]. In existing research, the Wasserstein distance is also used for better alignment result [8].

3   Experiments

3.1   Experiment Settings

All experiments are conducted on dataset CIFAR-10 [6], which consists of 10 classes, each class contains 5,000 32×32 images.

In [14], the author utilizes the first $n-1$ layers of the ConvNet as the feature extractor and treats the last fully connected layer as a classifier. In this paper, following a similar approach, we also regard the first $n-1$ layers of the neural network as the feature extractor, and take their output as the representation of the input data.

We select ConvNet [7], ResNet-18 [5], MLP [10] and lightweight ViT as feature extractors. The ConvNet consists of three identical convolution blocks, each has a 3×3 convolution layer, an instance normalization layer, a ReLU activation operation and an average pooling operation sequentially (see Fig. 2). The MLP in our experiment consists of 2 hidden layers, both have 128 hidden dimensions with activation function ReLU. The ResNet-18 is the standard original form. The lightweight ViT network takes input images of size 32×32, with each patch sized 4×4. The output dimension of the embedding layer in this network is 192. It consists of 12 transformer blocks, where the dimension of the feed-forward network within each transformer block is 768. For the multi-head attention mechanism, the network incorporates 12 attention heads (Table 1).

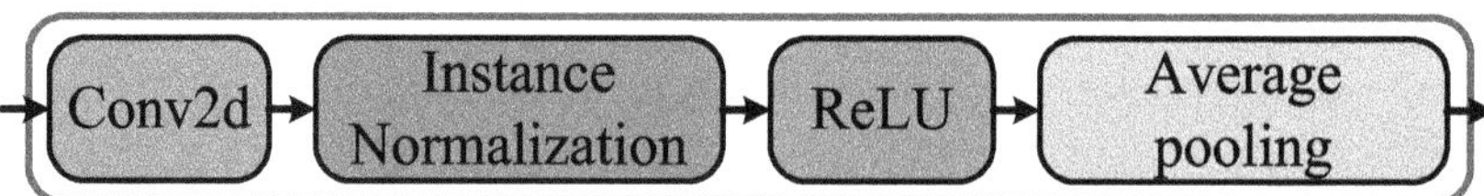

Fig. 2. One convolution block of ConvNet.

In the experiments of this paper, two kinds of feature extractors are used: the fixed feature extractors and the dynamic ones. The fixed feature extractors refer to those whose parameters remain frozen throughout the entire experiment. Specifically, they are the embedding layers of corresponding pre-training neural networks. In contrast, when a dynamic feature extractor is used for feature extraction, it always starts with a specified neural network that is randomly initialized. After training the network for the given number of epochs, its embedding layers are employed as the feature extractor.

Table 1. Hyperparameters of lightweight ViT

Hyperparameters	Values
input size	32×32
patch size	4×4
transformer blocks	12
feed-forward dimension	768
embedding dimension	192
number of heads	12

3.2 Experimental Content

In this section, we explain the specific experimental details. This study comprises three sets of experiments, as outlined below:

The first set of experiments compares the performance differences of distilled datasets under various combinations of feature extractors and networks. For networks, we select ConvNet and ResNet-18. The feature extractors are dynamic ConvNet and ResNet-18, both of which are trained on the CIFAR-10 dataset for 0, 1, 2, and 3 epochs respectively.

The second set of experiments focuses on the performance of the distilled dataset generated from using dynamic and fixed feature extractor. The performance evaluation is conducted by training ConvNet. The feature extractors in this part include ConvNet, ResNet-18, and MLP, all of which are trained on the CIFAR-10 dataset for 0, 1, 2, and 3 epochs respectively.

The third set of experiments compares the influence of different pre-training epochs of feature extractors on the performance of the distilled dataset, with the performance evaluation implemented by training ConvNet. The feature extractors include ConvNet, ResNet-18, MLP, and lightweight ViT. For fixed feature extractor, they are trained on the CIFAR-10 dataset for 0 5, 10, 50, and 100 epochs respectively. For dynamic feature extractors, they are trained on the CIFAR-10 dataset for 0, 1, 2, and 3 epochs respectively. Due to constraints on training time, lightweight ViT is not included in the dynamic feature extractors in this experiment set.

A summary of the above experimental contents is provided in Table 2.

4   Results and Discussion

4.1   Comparison Between Different Network-Feature Extractor Combinations

Figure 3 demonstrates the performance of distilled dataset in experiment set 1. The figure shows that using ConvNet as the feature extractor and training the ConvNet (the blue bar) exhibits the optimal performance across all scenarios where the number of pre-training epochs is 0, 1, 2, and 3. The performance of

Table 2. Summary of experiments

Experiment set	Network	Feature extractor	Fixed/Dynamic	Epochs
Architecture	ConvNet	ConvNet	Dynamic	0,1,2,3
		ResNet-18		
	ResNet-18	ConvNet		
		ResNet-18		
Dynamic/Fixed	ConvNet	ConvNet	Dynamic	
			Fixed	
		ResNet-18	Dynamic	
			Fixed	
		MLP	Dynamic	
			Fixed	
Epoch	ConvNet	ConvNet	Fixed	
		ResNet-18		0,1,2,3,4,5
		MLP		10,50,100
		lightweight ViT		

the ConvNet-ConvNet combination does not show a significant increase with the growth of the pre-training epochs of the feature extractor. However, the performance of the other three combinations is relatively poor when the pre-training epochs of the feature extractor are 0 ($\leq 20\%$), but there is a notable improvement ($\geq 20\%$) once the pre-training epochs exceed 0. We argue that this indicates that a slight pre-training of the feature extractor can effectively enhance the performance of the distilled dataset.

4.2   Comparison Between Dynamic and Fixed Feature Extractor

Figure 4 demonstrates the performance of distilled dataset in experiment set 2.

As shown in the figure, when the feature extractor is ConvNet, there is no significant difference in the performance of the distilled dataset between the dynamic ConvNet and the fixed ConvNet. However, both consistently outperform the distilled datasets generated by other feature extractors.

When the feature extractor is ResNet-18, increasing the pre-training epochs from 0 to 3 consistently improves the performance of the distilled dataset, and the performance improvement of the dynamic ResNet-18 is significantly greater than that of the fixed ResNet-18.

When the feature extractor is MLP, the dynamic MLP yields a well-performing distilled dataset only when the pre-training epoch is 0, with such performance even approaching that of the best-performing ConvNet feature extractor. In contrast, the fixed MLP results in relatively poor performance of the distilled dataset but still better than that with feature extractor ResNet-18. It is also worth noting that due to the strong fitting capacity of MLP, even

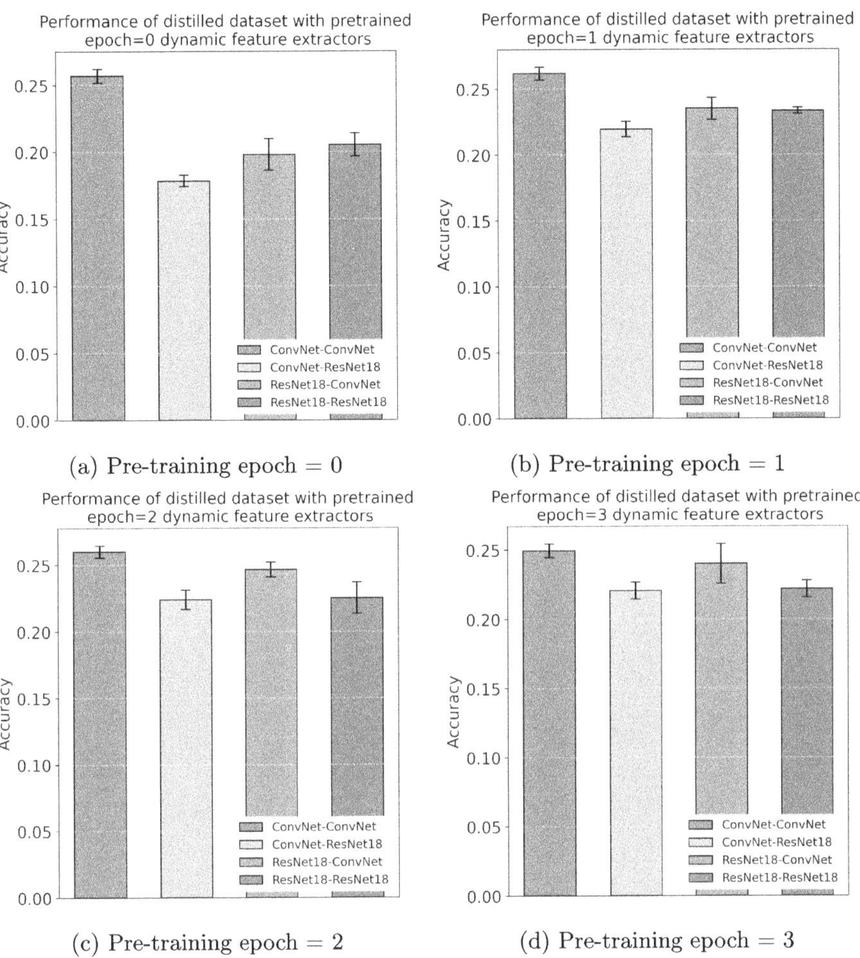

(a) Pre-training epoch = 0

(b) Pre-training epoch = 1

(c) Pre-training epoch = 2

(d) Pre-training epoch = 3

Fig. 3. Performance of dynamic feature extractor with different pre-training epochs. *The legends have form "network-feature extractor"*

though the small-scale MLP is used, the use of pre-trained MLP embedding layers as feature extractors ultimately led to gradient explosion in all experiments, as detailed in Fig. 4b-4d. Therefore, the possibility of using the embedding layers of pre-training MLPs as feature extractors is not discussed further in this paper.

4.3 Comparison Between Different Training Epoch of Fixed Feature Extractor

Figure 5, 6 and 7 illustrate the performance of dataset distillation tasks using the embedding layers of fixed neural networks trained for different epochs as

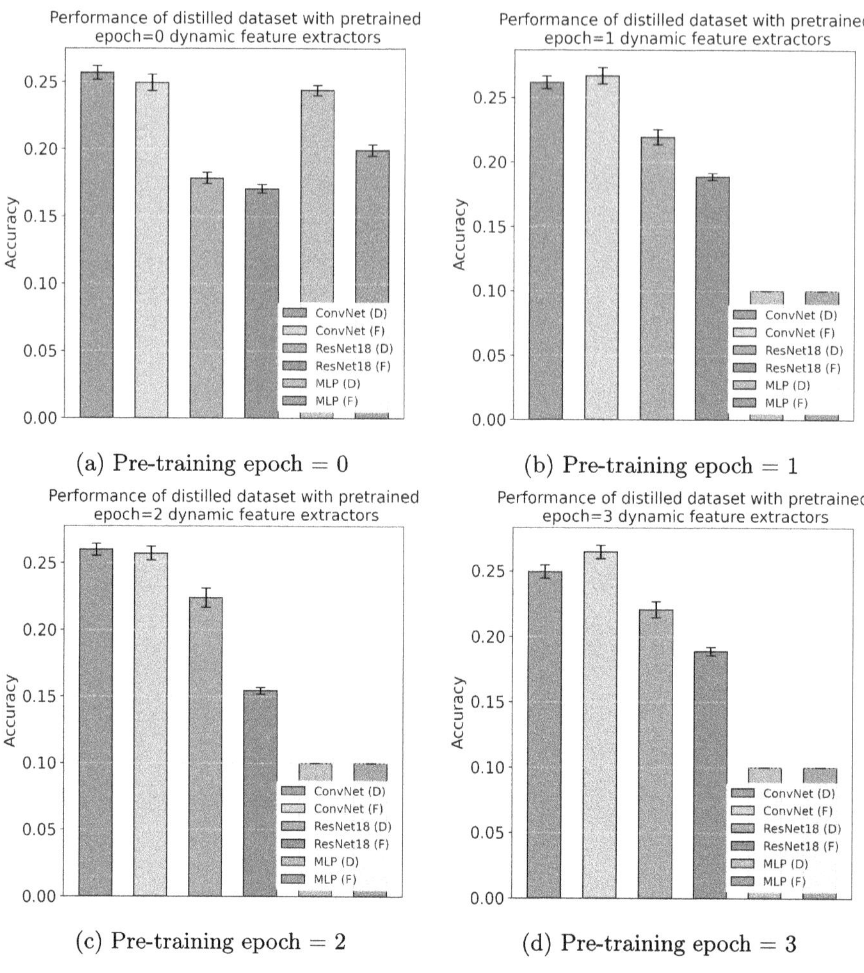

(a) Pre-training epoch = 0

(b) Pre-training epoch = 1

(c) Pre-training epoch = 2

(d) Pre-training epoch = 3

Fig. 4. Comparison between dynamic and fixed feature extractor with network ConvNet. *The legends has form "feature extractor(Dynamic/Fixed)"*

feature extractors. In this section, we will discuss performance of each feature extractors, respectively.

For ConvNet, Fig. 5a shows that when a fixed ConvNet is employed as the feature extractor, the best distillation performance is achieved at 5 training epochs, followed by that at 0 epochs. When the number of epochs exceeds 5, the performance of the dataset distillation task is even worse than that of the random ConvNet at 0 epochs; moreover, a larger number of training epochs leads to additional time cost. We attribute this phenomenon to overfitting caused by large training epochs and the downstream task of "classification", which drives data from different classes to be as divergent as possible in the representation space. To further investigate, we conducted a more detailed comparison of Con-

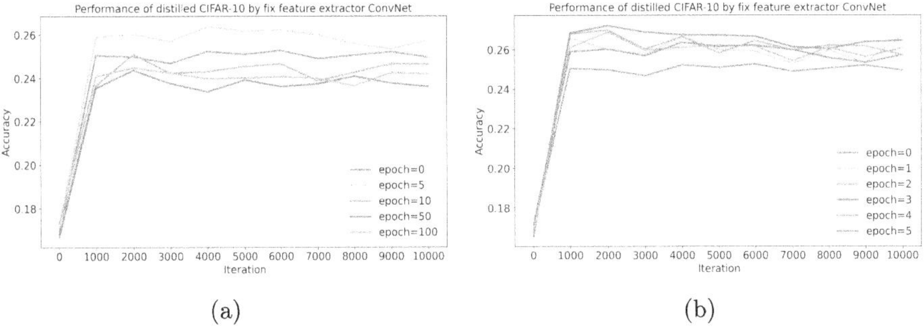

Fig. 5. Performance of fixed trained feature extractor ConvNet.

vNet feature extractors with pre-training epochs ranging from 0 to 5, and the results are presented in Fig. 5b. The results indicate that the feature extractor with 3 pre-training epochs outperforms those with 1, 2, 4, and 5 pre-training epochs in the dataset distillation task, while the latter perform better than the random feature extractor with 0 pre-training epochs. Therefore, we conclude that when using ConvNet as the feature extractor, all produce relatively optimal hyperparameters.

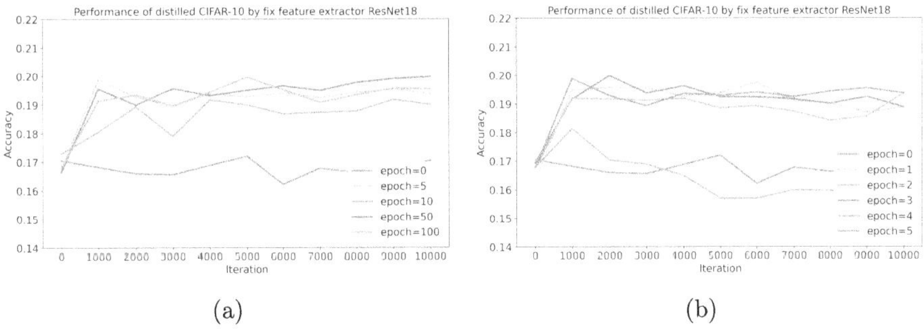

Fig. 6. Performance of fixed trained feature extractor ResNet-18.

For ResNet, Figure 6b demonstrates that the random feature extractor with 0 pre-training epochs exhibits significantly inferior performance in the dataset distillation task compared to pre-training feature extractors, and the performance of the dataset distillation task shows an upward trend as the number of pre-training epochs increases.

For lightweight ViT, Fig. 7b reveals that it seems that there is no significant correlation between the performance of the dataset distillation task and the number of pre-training epochs for lightweight ViT as a feature extractor. We hypothesize that this phenomenon is directly associated with the fact that the

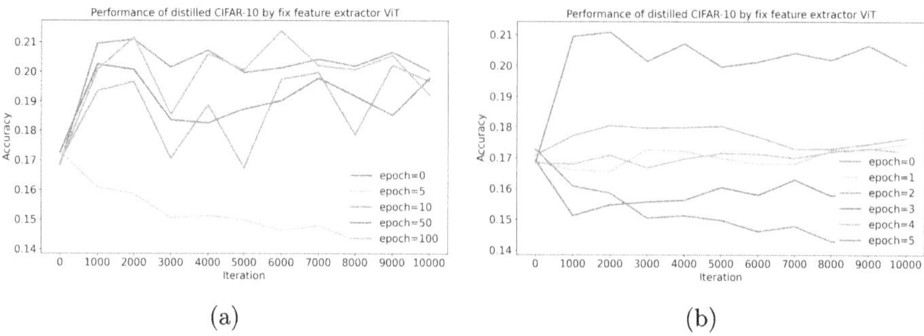

Fig. 7. Performance of fixed trained feature extractor ViT.

lightweight ViT model can only exhibit strong representational capabilities when pre-training on a large volume of data [2].

5   Conclusion and Future Work

This paper conducts a comparative study on the impact of different feature extractors on the performance of distilled datasets obtained through the distribution matching framework for dataset distillation tasks. The comparison reveals that ConvNet achieves the optimal performance among ConvNet, ResNet-18, MLP, and lightweight ViT. Meanwhile, slight pre-training (1-3 epochs) of feature extractors using image classification tasks can significantly enhance the performance of distilled datasets.

The comparison of feature extractors in this paper has certain limitations. This work lacks the exploration of precision structures in feature extractors, and the downstream tasks for pre-training feature extractors only contain image classification. In future research, we aim to conduct the precision structures of feature extractors to investigate how different micro-structures influence their performance. Additionally, we will leverage autoregressive encoder architectures to add image reconstruction and other generative tasks into downstream tasks, thereby examining the impact of diverse downstream tasks on the efficacy of pre-training feature extractors.

Acknowledgment. This study has been funded by Key Projects of National Natural Science Foundation of China (#72231010, #71932008).

References

1. Cazenavette, G., Wang, T., Torralba, A., Efros, A.A., Zhu, J.Y.: Dataset distillation by matching training trajectories. In: Proceedings of the IEEE/CVF Conference on Computer Vision and Pattern Recognition (CVPR) Workshops, pp. 4750–4759 (2022)
2. Dosovitskiy, A., et al.: An image is worth 16x16 words: Transformers for image recognition at scale (2021). https://arxiv.org/abs/2010.11929
3. Goodfellow, I., Bengio, Y., Courville, A.: Deep Learning. MIT Press (2016). http://www.deeplearningbook.org
4. Gretton, A., Borgwardt, K.M., Rasch, M.J., Schölkopf, B., Smola, A.: A kernel two-sample test. J. Mach. Learn. Res. **13**(null), 723–773 (2012)
5. He, K., Zhang, X., Ren, S., Sun, J.: Deep residual learning for image recognition. In: Proceedings of the IEEE Conference on Computer Vision and Pattern Recognition, pp. 770–778 (2016)
6. Krizhevsky, A., Hinton, G.: Learning multiple layers of features from tiny images (2009)
7. LeCun, Y., Bottou, L., Bengio, Y., Haffner, P.: Gradient-based learning applied to document recognition. Proc. IEEE **86**(11), 2278–2324 (2002)
8. Li, M., Xue, J., Shi, Y.: Dataset distillation via kantorovich-rubinstein dual of wasserstein distance. In: Paszynski, M., Barnard, A.S., Zhang, Y.J. (eds.) Computational Science - ICCS 2025 Workshops, pp. 293–306. Springer, Cham (2025)
9. Nguyen, T., Chen, Z., Lee, J.: Dataset meta-learning from kernel ridge-regression. In: International Conference on Learning Representations (2021)
10. Rosenblatt, F.: The perceptron: a probabilistic model for information storage and organization in the brain. Psychol. Rev. **65**(6), 386 (1958)
11. Wang, K., et al.: Cafe: learning to condense dataset by aligning features. In: Proceedings of the IEEE/CVF Conference on Computer Vision and Pattern Recognition (CVPR), pp. 12196–12205, June 2022
12. Wang, T., Zhu, J.Y., Torralba, A., Efros, A.A.: (2018). arXiv:1811.10959 Dataset distillation. arXiv preprint
13. Zhang, H., Li, S., Wang, P., Zeng, D., Ge, S.: M3d: Dataset condensation by minimizing maximum mean discrepancy. In: Proceedings of the AAAI Conference on Artificial Intelligence 38(8), pp. 9314–9322, March 2024. https://doi.org/10.1609/aaai.v38i8.28784. https://ojs.aaai.org/index.php/AAAI/article/view/28784
14. Zhao, B., Bilen, H.: Dataset condensation with distribution matching. In: Proceedings of the IEEE/CVF Winter Conference on Applications of Computer Vision (WACV), pp. 6514–6523 (2023)
15. Zhao, B., Mopuri, K.R., Bilen, H.: Dataset condensation with gradient matching, (2020). arXiv:2006.05929 arXiv preprint
16. Zhao, G., Li, G., Qin, Y., Yu, Y.: Improved distribution matching for dataset condensation. In: Proceedings of the IEEE/CVF Conference on Computer Vision and Pattern Recognition (CVPR), pp. 7856–7865 (2023)

Machine Learning and Data Assimilation for Dynamical Systems

Composite Reward Design in PPO-Driven Adaptive Filtering

A. Burkan Bereketoglu$^{(\boxtimes)}$ iD

Department of Informatics, University of Sussex, Brighton BN1 9QJ, UK
a.bereketoglu@sussex.ac.uk

Abstract. Model-free and reinforcement learning-based adaptive filtering methods are gaining traction for denoising in dynamic, nonstationary environments such as wireless signal channels, biomedical monitoring, and sensor networks. Traditional filters such as LMS, RLS, Wiener, and Kalman are often limited by assumptions of stationarity, the need for exact noise statistics, or fragile parameter tuning. This paper proposes an adaptive filtering framework using Proximal Policy Optimization (PPO), guided by a composite reward that balances SNR improvement, MSE reduction, and residual smoothness. We frame adaptive filtering as a Markov decision process and train a PPO agent to adjust filter coefficients directly in response to changing noise. Experiments on synthetic nonstationary signals with diverse noise types show that the PPO agent generalizes beyond its training distribution. Moreover, real-world analysis is made and evaluated on ECG recordings from the MIT-BIH Noise Stress Test Database corrupted by baseline wander, electrode motion, and muscle artifacts. The learned PPO policy achieves real-time inference and slightly outperforms strong classical baselines on ECG denoising. These results demonstrate the viability of policy-gradient reinforcement learning as a computationally efficient and flexible tool for adaptive filtering in nonlinear, time-varying dynamical systems.

Keywords: Reinforcement learning · Adaptive filtering · Noise reduction · PPO

1 Introduction

Wireless communication systems, biomedical devices, and sensor networks often operate in noisy, time-varying environments where effective denoising is critical. Adaptive filters such as LMS [1], RLS [2], Wiener [2], and Kalman filters [3] are widely used, but they can struggle in highly dynamic scenarios due to rigid assumptions. LMS requires careful step-size tuning and assumes relatively stationary noise; RLS is memory-intensive and may become unstable under impulsive interference; Wiener filtering is optimal only under stationary assumptions with known statistics; and Kalman filters demand accurate state-space models and noise covariances. In practice, classical filters often cannot fully cope with rapidly shifting or uncertain noise conditions without manual re-calibration.

M. Paszynski et al. (Eds.): ICCS 2026 Workshops, LNCS 16788, pp. 107–114, 2026.
https://doi.org/10.1007/978-3-032-29915-4_9

Reinforcement learning (RL) offers a data-driven alternative for adaptive signal filtering. Instead of relying on a fixed model, an RL agent learns to adjust filter parameters through interaction with the environment and feedback through a reward signal. Unlike supervised approaches, RL does not require ground-truth clean signals at run-time and can continually adapt online to new noise conditions. Policy-gradient methods such as Proximal Policy Optimization (PPO) [4] are particularly suitable because they support continuous actions and use conservative clipped updates that improve training stability. PPO uses a clipped surrogate objective to stabilize training, addressing the risk of divergence in high-variance environments, and naturally handles continuous action spaces (e.g., filter weight adjustments). Recent advances in RL techniques (e.g., intrinsic reward-based exploration via random network distillation [11]) can further improve an agent's ability to discover effective filtering policies in complex or hard-exploration scenarios. In this work, PPO is combined with a composite reward design to learn adaptive filtering policies that remain robust under changing and previously unseen noise conditions.

2   Background and Related Work

Classical adaptive filters such as LMS and RLS are gradient-based/recursive algorithms that update filter weights to minimize instantaneous error. Their performance degrades under nonstationary or impulsive noise due to reliance on fixed learning rates and assumptions of Gaussian noise statistics. Kalman filters offer recursive minimum-variance estimation in state-space models but rely on accurate process and measurement noise covariances; adaptive Kalman variants exist, but they often resort to heuristic tuning. Wiener filters, derived by solving the Wiener–Hopf equations for stationary signal and noise with known second-order statistics, provide the optimal linear filter in the mean-square sense [2]. However, Wiener filters are not suitable for time-varying noise and require prior knowledge of signal and noise correlation functions, which is impractical in many real-time systems.

Recently, RL-based approaches have emerged to tackle adaptive filtering and noise reduction without explicit modeling. Oh *et al.* [5] first showed that a model-free RL (Q-learning) agent can outperform classical channel estimators under uncertain conditions. Xie *et al.* [6] developed an RL-driven fractional order filter that is robust against impulsive (non-Gaussian) noise. RL has also been combined with model-based filtering: Lin *et al.* [7] and He *et al.* [8] introduced reinforcement learning to adapt Kalman filter parameters online in nonstationary environments, and Marino and Guglieri [9] integrated an RL strategy with a Kalman filter for improved drone navigation under noise. More recently, Luo *et al.* [10] applied deep RL to generative fixed-filter active noise control, demonstrating the potential of RL in active noise cancellation. These studies collectively indicate that RL-based adaptive filters can yield significant performance gains in dynamic noise scenarios by continually learning and adjusting filtering policies. Moreover, improvements in RL algorithms themselves (such as enhanced exploration strategies [11]) are directly relevant to adaptive filtering, as better exploration enables an agent to find more effective filtering strategies even in complicated or highly nonstationary environments.

3   Problem Formulation

Let $x(t)$ denote the clean signal and $n(t)$ a stochastic, possibly nonstationary noise process. The observed signal is

$$y(t) = x(t) + n(t), \tag{1}$$

and the goal is to produce an estimate $\hat{x}(t)$ that minimizes distortion over time. We frame adaptive filtering as a Markov decision process (MDP):

- **State**: a feature representation of the recent noisy signal together with the current baseline-filter output.
- **Action**: a continuous update applied to the adaptive filter parameters.
- **Reward**: a composite performance signal balancing reconstruction quality and temporal stability.

The agent learns a policy π that maximizes long-term filtering performance under changing noise statistics.

4   PPO Framework and Composite Reward

PPO is well suited to adaptive filtering because its clipped surrogate objective [4]

$$L_{\mathrm{CLIP}}(\theta) = \mathbb{E}_t\Big[\min\big(r_t(\theta)A_t,\ \mathrm{clip}(r_t(\theta), 1 - \epsilon, 1 + \epsilon)A_t\big)\Big] \tag{2}$$

constrains policy changes and improves robustness when the reward landscape changes with the noise process. PPO also supports continuous action spaces, making it natural for coefficient-update policies.

We use the composite reward that combines three complementary objectives

$$R(t) = \alpha\,\Delta\mathrm{SNR}(t) - \beta\,\mathrm{MSE}(t) - \gamma\,\mathcal{S}(t), \tag{3}$$

where $\Delta\mathrm{SNR}(t)$ is the improvement in signal-to-noise ratio, $\mathrm{MSE}(t)$ is the reconstruction error, and $\mathcal{S}(t)$ is a residual smoothness penalty. Where it penalizes temporal changes in the residual correction between consecutive steps, encouraging stable coefficient updates and suppressing oscillatory behavior, similar to a total variation, but not TV in signal processing sense.

During training, the MSE term is computed using clean reference signals available in simulation or labeled evaluation data. However, the PPO agent does *not* receive the clean signal as part of its observation. Its state is constructed from the noisy input window together with the output of a baseline adaptive filter. Thus, the current framework is best interpreted as an offline-trained, online-deployed adaptive filtering approach: reference signals are used to shape the reward during training, but the learned policy runs without them at inference time.

Policy Architecture. The PPO agent uses an actor-critic architecture with a recurrent policy network. The actor is implemented as a single-layer LSTM with hidden size 128 that processes the observation sequence and outputs the mean of a Gaussian action distribution through a linear projection layer. The policy variance is parameterized by a learnable log-standard deviation vector shared across actions. Actions correspond to continuous coefficient updates applied to the adaptive FIR filter. The critic is implemented as a feed-forward network consisting of a linear layer with 128 hidden units, a ReLU activation, and a final linear layer producing the state-value estimate.

Training Details and Stability. Training uses the Adam optimizer with learning rate 3×10^{-4}, discount factor $\gamma = 0.99$, clipping parameter $\epsilon = 0.2$, and 10 optimization epochs per policy update. Gradient norms are clipped to 0.5, and numerical safeguards are applied through observation and variance clamping. The recurrent architecture allows the policy to exploit temporal correlations in the signal, which is important for nonstationary noise processes.

5   Experimental Setup

5.1   Synthetic Signals

We first evaluate the proposed method on a synthetic denoising task. The clean signal $x(t)$ is a sum of time-varying sinusoids with drifting amplitudes and multiple harmonics over 2048 samples.

$$x(t) = \sum_{i=1}^{N} A_i(t) \cdot \sin(2\pi f_i t + \phi_i)$$

Additive noise is drawn from Gaussian, Laplacian, impulse, pink, brown, and uniform distributions. PPO is trained only on Gaussian noise and evaluated on all noise types to test generalization. The agent observes a sliding window of recent noisy samples together with the corresponding baseline-filter output. Actions are coefficient updates applied to a finite impulse response (FIR) filter. We compare PPO with LMS, RLS, Wiener, and Kalman filters, each tuned by grid search.

The advantage is computed using baseline-subtracted returns:

$$A_t = R_t - V(s_t), \quad \text{with} \quad R_t = \sum_{l=0}^{T-t-1} \gamma^l r_{t+l}$$

where $V(s_t)$ is the value network's estimate. Generalized advantage estimation (GAE) is omitted for simplicity and stability.

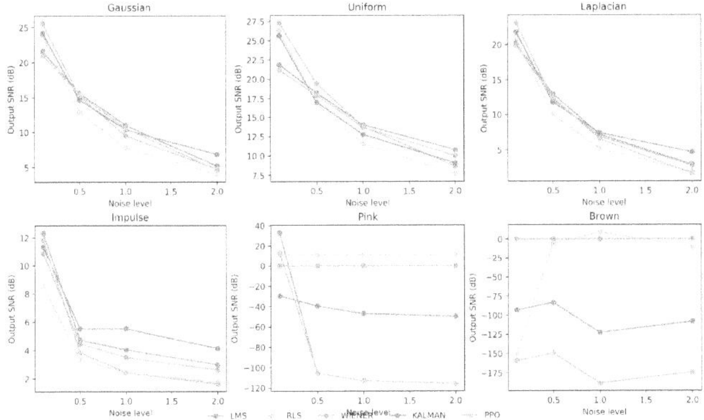

Fig. 1. Synthetic noise generalization across six noise families.

5.2   Real ECG Dataset

To evaluate performance on real-world signals, we use the MIT-BIH Noise Stress Test Database (NSTDB) available through PhysioNet [12,13]. The dataset provides clean ECG recordings together with standardized physiological noise sources including baseline wander (bw), electrode motion (em), and muscle arti-fact (ma). These disturbances represent common artifacts encountered in mobile ECG monitoring. Following standard ECG denoising practice, noisy signals are generated by combining clean ECG recordings with the corresponding NSTDB noise sources. This yields a controlled but realistic evaluation setting with real physiological morphology and realistic artifact structure. The PPO policy is trained on ECG recordings with corresponding noise and then evaluated on other recordings of ECG disturbances without additional fine-tuning.

6   Results

6.1   Synthetic Generalization

Figure 1 evaluates generalization to unseen noise families. PPO is trained only on Gaussian noise but remains competitive under uniform, Laplacian, and impulse noise. Pink and Brown noise are more challenging for all methods due to their strong low-frequency structure.

6.2   Real ECG Performance

Table 1 reports mean held-out SNR on real ECG data. PPO achieves the highest SNR across all three ECG noise conditions, slightly outperforming RLS while clearly exceeding LMS, Wiener, and Kalman.

Figure 2 provides qualitative ECG reconstructions. PPO consistently sup-presses noise while preserving QRS morphology and larger-scale waveform shape.

Table 1. Mean held-out SNR (dB) on real ECG signals.

Method	BW	EM	MA
LMS	12.2	10.6	9.4
RLS	14.1	12.6	10.4
Wiener	7.3	6.9	7.2
Kalman	5.6	5.5	5.9
PPO	**14.4**	**13.2**	**10.8**

Table 2. Impact of reward components on PPO filtering performance.

Reward	SNR	Gen.	Stab.
Full	**16.6**	✓	✓
No smoothness	< 0	✗	✗
No MSE	12.8	✓	borderline

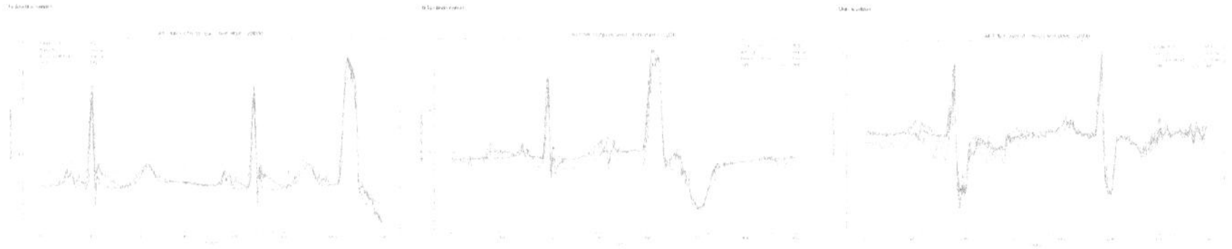

Fig. 2. Filtering performance on real ECG signals under baseline wander, electrode motion, and muscle artifact noise. PPO closely tracks the clean waveform and remains competitive with the strongest classical baseline, RLS, across all three settings.

The gains are modest relative to RLS, but they are consistent across all three artifact classes, which is a more credible and practically meaningful result than a large single-noise improvement.

6.3   Runtime on ECG Data

In addition to denoising quality, we evaluate computational efficiency on the ECG setting. Figure 3 shows average inference time per method for bw, em, and ma noise. PPO runs in approximately 1 ms per inference, substantially faster than RLS and Kalman in our implementation and close to the cost of the lighter baselines. This supports the claim that PPO-based filtering remains feasible for real-time deployment after offline training.

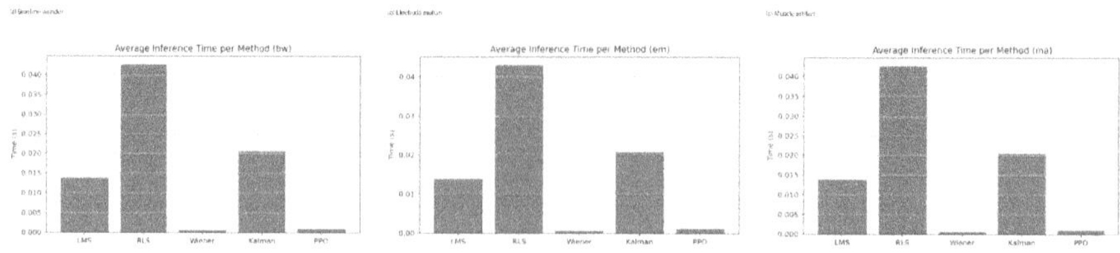

Fig. 3. Average inference time per method on ECG denoising tasks with baseline wander, electrode motion, and muscle artifact noise. PPO retains real-time performance while remaining markedly faster than RLS.

6.4   Training Behaviour and Stability

Training was stable over 1000 episodes, and the composite reward was essential to that stability. Figure 4 shows that the SNR gain term increases steadily during training while both the MSE term and the smoothness penalty decrease. The episode reward also improves consistently, and the actor/critic optimization dynamics stabilize after the initial exploration phase.

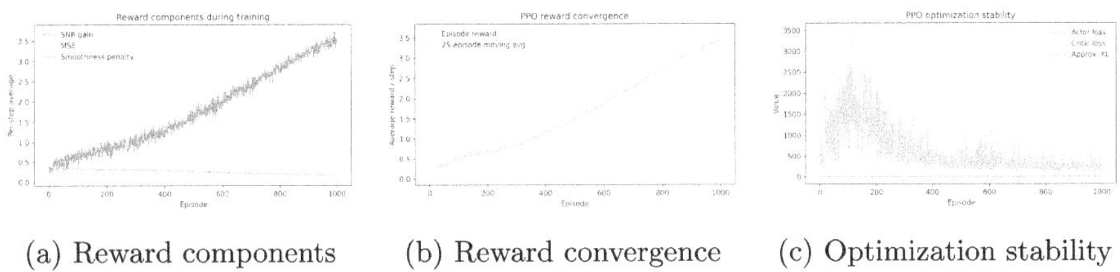

   (a) Reward components   (b) Reward convergence   (c) Optimization stability

Fig. 4. Training diagnostics for the PPO agent. The SNR gain increases over training, the MSE and smoothness penalties decrease, the episode reward improves steadily, and the actor/critic optimization remains stable after the initial exploration phase.

6.5   Ablation Study

We performed controlled ablation experiments to isolate the effect of reward components. Results are summarized in Table 2. Here, *Smoothness* denotes the temporal residual-change penalty.

These ablations confirm that removing either the MSE term or the smoothness component degrades stability and harms generalization, validating the need for the composite reward design.

7   Discussion

Experiments on real ECG signals provide insight on that, policies trained on synthetic mixtures or some split of real data still generalize and outperform on real biological signals, also clean reference signals are not directly shown to agent, and do not require them in inference time. Moreover, model's robustness on unseen noise indicates that the agent learns a transferable filtering policy rather than overfitting to a specific distribution. However, model requires a baseline model for path-finding, which might be mitigated with gamma parameter tuning. In that sense, the present framework is supervised in training but reference-free in deployment.

More broadly, the results show that PPO can learn coefficient-update policies that remain robust across multiple artifact types while preserving real-time inference speed. The remaining limitation is that training still depends on reference filters. Future work should therefore study unsupervised or self-supervised reward formulations and evaluate the same framework on additional biomedical and RF datasets.

8   Conclusion

This paper introduced a PPO-driven adaptive filtering framework based on a composite reward combining SNR improvement, MSE reduction, and residual smoothness. By formulating adaptive filtering as a Markov decision process, the agent learns coefficient-update policies that adapt to changing noise conditions rather than relying on fixed analytical update rules.

Experiments on synthetic signals and real ECG recordings show that PPO-based filtering generalizes beyond its training distribution, achieves the highest SNR among the tested methods on ECG denoising, and retains real-time inference cost. These findings support reinforcement learning as a practical tool for adaptive signal processing in dynamic and nonstationary environments.

References

1. Widrow, B., Stearns, S.D.: Adaptive Signal Processing. Prentice-Hall, Englewood Cliffs (1985)
2. Haykin, S.: Adaptive Filter Theory, 5th edn. Pearson Education, Upper Saddle River (2013)
3. Kalman, R.E.: A new approach to linear filtering and prediction problems. J. Basic Eng. **82**(1), 35–45 (1960)
4. Schulman, J.: Proximal policy optimization algorithms (2017). arXiv:1707.06347
5. Oh, M.: Channel estimation via successive denoising in MIMO-OFDM systems: a reinforcement learning approach. In: Proc. IEEE ICC (2021)
6. Xie, X., et al.: A fractional filter based on reinforcement learning for effective tracking under impulsive noise. Neurocomputing **516**, 155–168 (2023)
7. Lin, H.: Adaptive filtering algorithm based on reinforcement learning. In: Proc. CCDC, pp. 5268–5272 (2024)
8. He, P.: Reinforcement learning adaptive Kalman filter for AE signal's AR-mode denoise. In: Proc. IEEE ICICN (2023)
9. Marino, F., Guglieri, G.: Beyond static obstacles: integrating Kalman filter with reinforcement learning for drone navigation. Aerospace **11**(5) (2024)
10. Luo, Z., et al.: GFANC-RL: reinforcement learning-based generative fixed-filter active noise control. Neural Networks **180**, 106687 (2024)
11. Burda, Y.: Exploration by random network distillation. In: Proc. ICLR (2019)
12. Goldberger, A.L., Amaral, L.A.N., Glass, L., Hausdorff, J.M., Ivanov, P.C., Mark, R.G., Mietus, J.E., Moody, G.B., Peng, C.-K., Stanley, H.E.: PhysioBank, PhysioToolkit, and PhysioNet: components of a new research resource for complex physiologic signals. Circulation **101**(23), e215–e220 (2000)
13. Moody, G.B., Muldrow, W.E., Mark, R.G.: Noise stress test for arrhythmia detectors. Comput. Cardiol., 381–384 (1984)

Mechanistic Interpretability Tool for AI Weather Models

Kirsten I. Tempest[1(✉)] [iD], Matthias Beylich[1] [iD], and George C. Craig[1,2] [iD]

[1] Meteorological Institute Munich, Ludwig-Maximilians-Universität, 80333 Munich, Germany
`k.tempest@physik.uni-muenchen.de`
[2] Deutsches Zentrum für Luft- und Raumfahrt, Oberpfaffenhofen, Germany

Abstract. Artificial Intelligence (AI) weather models are improving rapidly, and their forecasts are already competitive with long-established traditional Numerical Weather Prediction (NWP). To build confidence in this new methodology, it is critical that we understand how these predictions are generated. This is a huge challenge as these AI weather models remain largely black boxes. In other areas of Machine Learning (ML), mechanistic interpretability has emerged as a framework for understanding ML predictions by analysing the building blocks responsible for them. Here we present an open-source, highly adaptable tool which incorporates concepts from mechanistic interpretability. The tool organises internal latent representations from the model processor and allows for initial analyses, including cosine similarity and Principal Component Analysis (PCA), enabling the user to identify directions in latent space potentially associated with meteorological features. Applying our tool to the graph neural network GraphCast, we present preliminary case studies for mid-latitude synoptic-scale waves and specific humidity. These demonstrate the tool's ability to identify linear combinations of latent channels that appear to correspond to interpretable features.

Keywords: Mechanistic Interpretability · AI Weather Models · Visualisation Tool

1 Introduction

Data-driven global weather forecast models developed in recent years are already competitive with traditional NWP, which has decades of research and development behind it. A major milestone was reached when AI models [2,7] surpassed the forecast skill of the world-leading European Centre for Medium-Range Weather Forecasts (ECMWF) High RESolution forecast (HRES) [10]. Recent developments include foundation models such as Aurora [3], and models designed for probabilistic forecasting such as AIFS-CRPS [8]. The improvements in skill over time are tracked in the WeatherBench database [13].

The architectures of AI models and their resulting predictive capabilities are diverse. For example, GraphCast employs a graph neural network to produce a

M. Paszynski et al. (Eds.): ICCS 2026 Workshops, LNCS 16788, pp. 115–127, 2026.
https://doi.org/10.1007/978-3-032-29915-4_10

deterministic forecast, whereas AIFS-CRPS, a transformer-based model, generates ensemble members that sample a probability distribution. Despite these differences, these models share a common architectural framework. This consists of an encoding stage, a processor stage comprising multiple steps, including blocks that facilitate information exchange between locations, and a multilayer perceptron (MLP) operating on the latent space at each location, and finally a decoder stage which maps the learned representation back into gridded meteorological variables for humans to understand. This is quite different from conventional numerical integration, which evolves the physical variables through a sequence of time-steps to produce forecasts.

Traditional NWP systems have large and complex codebases, which are built on our understanding of physical processes in the atmosphere, as well as in other Earth system components. AI weather models on the other hand are optimised to reproduce a training dataset, without regard to prior physical knowledge. By iteratively adjusting the weights (often millions, if not a billion as in Aurora [3]) of the model during the training process, algorithms are created which allow the model to interpret input data and generate a meaningful output. This learning process allows the model to exploit any relevant relationships present in the weather data to be used in the production of the forecast, not just those programmed in. The trained model might make use of connections and concepts which are not yet understood or discovered by humans. This raises the question: how can we understand the internal workings of AI weather models?

There have been various studies analysing AI weather models. In a recent survey [17], these approaches have been grouped into post-hoc interpretability techniques, and those where the design of the model is inherently interpretable. The former, relevant for understanding a broad range of models without altering the model itself, includes perturbation-based methods, where the input features are systematically modified and the predictions examined. Game theory based and gradient-based attribution methods have also been attempted. Although these methods provide insight, they remain specific to scenarios and models; a comprehensive understanding of how predictions are made, and what connections are learned, is missing. This is vital to build trust for integration of such models into operational weather prediction, and might lead to new scientific discoveries.

Mechanistic interpretability seeks to reverse engineer neural networks by understanding interpretable features and the circuits that connect them [11]. Features, which are meaningful patterns in the data, can be identified to correspond with directions in the latent space. By identifying features at different stages in the processor, it is possible to learn algorithms in the weights of the model which are used to get to the final output. For example, a vision model classifies an image of a dog's head correctly by identifying eyes, snout, fur and tongue [12]. Mechanistic interpretability has been used as a framework in fields such as Large Language Models [6,18], but has not yet been applied extensively to AI weather models. Initial work [9] has used sparse autoencoders to identify features in GraphCast, and has shown examples including surface heating in arid regions corresponding to directions in the latent space. This shows the potential of mechanistic interpretability techniques for understanding AI weather models.

Here we present an exploratory visualisation tool that leverages mechanistic interpretability concepts to investigate the latent space of AI weather models. By providing a structured interface, the tool enables millions of data points to be efficiently organised and interpreted, facilitating rapid idea and hypothesis generation. The tool is open-source and has been designed for ease of customisation, allowing users to extend supported model configurations and incorporate additional analyses.

Section 2 provides an overview of the tool design and methods, including the model and data used. Section 3 presents two case studies, one focusing on mid-latitude synoptic-scale waves and the other on specific humidity and how they correspond to directions in the latent space. The paper is then concluded in Sect. 4.

2   Design and Method Overview

2.1   Design

We propose a visualisation tool that can be used by both meteorologists and computer scientists to identify complex connection pathways within AI weather models. This requires the structured organisation and analysis of millions of data points.

In order to identify meaningful directions in the latent space, we begin by selecting a geographical region, one that contains a meteorologically relevant feature. Latent feature vectors within this region are then analysed.

The tool comprises the following components:

1. Specify initial parameters.
   - Select the model configuration and forecast time (t).
   - Choose whether to apply the latent space translator.
   - Select T, the number of maximally activated latent channels to display and use in analysis.
2. Select location.
   - Choose the meteorological variable to be displayed on the two maps. The first map shows the input data at the forecast initialisation time, $f(t_{\mathrm{init}})$, and the second shows the increment of the atmospheric state between initialisation and forecast time, $f(t) - f(t_{\mathrm{init}})$.
   - Define a circular geographic region of interest.
3. Extract latent feature vectors and perform initial analysis.
   - Latent feature vectors are loaded for all processor steps and mesh nodes, and the mesh nodes within the selected area are identified.
   - The T most strongly activated latent channels are selected, and global maps of their activations are plotted for the selected processor step, P.
4. Perform further analysis.
   - Cosine similarity analysis.

- Principal Component Analysis (PCA), with user-specified number of components, C.

We use Streamlit [16], an open-source app framework available as a Python package. It avoids a backend due to being able to add widgets in the same manner as declaring a variable. The aim is for scientists to use this open-source tool, provide feedback, or develop their own versions by forking the GitHub repository and customising it with their own data and analysis methods. We hope this allows for fast development in the field of AI weather model interpretability.

2.2 GraphCast

To demonstrate the visualisation tool, we will examine the GraphCast model [7]. This model is capable of producing high-quality forecasts while being relatively compact in size. The input reanalysis dataset it is trained on, ERA5 [5], is open-source, and can therefore aid in investigating connections between directions and features.

For our initial analysis, we use the pretrained small version of GraphCast, with $1°C$ resolution. However, the tool will function for other configurations of GraphCast, and can be extended for use with other AI weather models.

As we focus exclusively on latent representations, the model is run for a single time step (6 h in the case of GraphCast). Consequently, the time difference between initialisation and forecast is fixed at 6 h.

Processor Step The processor stage of GraphCast is made up of 16 processor steps, each consisting of a deep graph neural network operating on a multi-mesh, where nodes are connected by edges of varying lengths. The multi-mesh is constructed by combining icosahedral meshes of differing resolution, from the base mesh with 12 nodes to the finest resolution which has 40,962 nodes. In the small version used in this paper, the finest resolution contains 10,242 nodes.

Within each processor step, edge representations are first updated using information from adjacent mesh nodes. The mesh nodes are then updated by aggregating information from incoming edges. The resulting node representations are then normalised and updated via residual connections. This message-passing procedure is repeated iteratively.

Latent Feature Vectors We are interested in the latent feature vectors at each mesh node across the globe, extracted at the end of each processor step. These are of length 512, and whose individual entries we refer to as channels. For the small version of GraphCast, there are 10,242 mesh nodes at each processor step, with feature vectors of length 512. As such, there are a total of 83,902,464 latent data points to visualise and understand.

Meteorologically interpretable feature vectors may be arbitrary linear combinations of the channels in the latent space, and their orientation may be transformed between different processor steps. To compare the latent feature vectors consistently across these steps, the tool provides an option to apply an affine transformation, referred to as a translator, to the latent feature vectors [1]. Whenever intermediate processor steps are analysed in this paper, the translator is applied so that the basis is the same as that of the final processor step.

2.3 Analysis

Cosine Similarity Cosine Similarity is the normalised dot product of two vectors, $\bar{A}$ and $\bar{B}$ [15],

$$\frac{\bar{A} \cdot \bar{B}}{\|\bar{A}\| \|\bar{B}\|}. \tag{1}$$

It is bounded between -1 and 1, whereby a value of 1 means that the vectors are perfectly aligned, -1 indicates that they are oppositely aligned, and 0 denotes that they are orthogonal and therefore not similar at all.

In this analysis, the channels with the highest activations are selected to create a vector of length T at every mesh node. A node is then chosen at random from within the selected region, and the vector at that node is compared with all other mesh nodes globally. The analysis is then repeated, but comparing the full latent feature vector rather than shortening it to the most activated channels.

Principal Component Analysis (PCA) PCA is used to project data onto a lower-dimensional space defined by C principal components that capture the greatest variance [14]. This enables the most prominent features to be found.

In this analysis, the data in the selected geographical region is used to fit the principal components, and the global data is then transformed into this new basis. The amount of variance each principal component captures is calculated, as well as the channels that contribute most to each principal component vector.

3 Results: Case Studies

Two case studies are presented to illustrate the capabilities of the tool for interpreting AI weather models. In each case, a geographical region containing a relevant meteorological feature is identified, along with the latent channels maximally activated within that region. Global maps of these channel activations, as well as the resulting cosine similarity and PCA analyses, are then visualised to assess whether possible connections can be identified between the latent feature vectors and meteorological features.

As our primary aim is to identify directions associated with such features, we focus on the final (16th) processor step unless otherwise stated. Furthermore, we use the top 15 maximally activated latent channels T, and for PCA, the $C = 8$ leading components are extracted.

3.1 Mid-Latitude Synoptic-Scale Waves

We first identify directions associated with synoptic-scale waves in the mid-latitudes. A trough of low pressure is selected at $40°N$, $100°W$, indicated by the black circle with radius $20°$ in Fig. 1. The initial forecast time analysed is 2016-03-09 at 18:00 UTC, and the last ERA5 input (initial condition) is 6 h before, at 12:00 UTC (Fig. 1a). The residual (Fig. 1b) represents the 6 h forecast increment generated by the AI model.

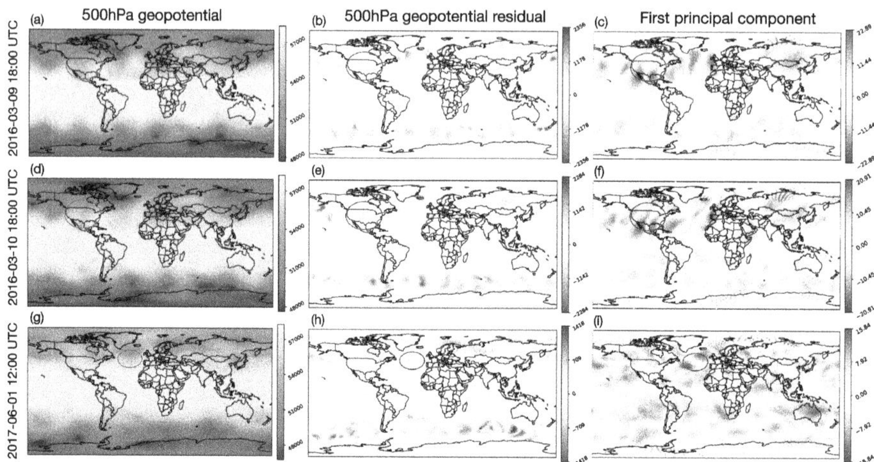

Fig. 1. Global fields for three forecast times, t: (a-c) 2016-03-09 18:00 UTC, (d-f) 2016-03-10 18:00 UTC, and (g-i) 2017-06-01 12:00 UTC. The left column (a,d,g) shows the 500hPa geopotential ($m^2\,s^{-2}$) at the forecast initialisation time, t_{init}. The middle column (b,e,h) shows the corresponding residual ($f(t) - f(t_{\mathrm{init}})$), and the right column (c,f,i) the first principal component. The circled region highlights the area used for analysis. For the first two rows, the circle is centred at $40°N$, $100°W$ and has a radius of $20°$. In the bottom row, the circle is centred at $46°N$, $30°W$ and has a radius of $12.59°$.

The first principal component in Fig. 1c shows a pronounced alternating dipole structure in the Northern mid-latitudes, particularly in the West. This suggests that a dipole (negative activation to the west, positive activation to the east) is associated with each trough. Focusing on the two troughs nearest the western edge of the domain, it is seen that the eastern trough extends further south. Similarly, the dipoles extend further south. Although the dipoles are weaker in the east, the connection is still evident. Dipole structures are also present in the Southern Hemisphere, but are considerably weaker than that observed in the Northern Hemisphere.

To investigate how the connection evolves over time, Fig. 1d-f shows the same fields 24 h later. This period is associated with a significant blocking event [4], which slows the eastward propagation of waves, with movement occurring primarily south of Greenland. It is observed that the low geopotential has shifted eastward there, accompanied by a corresponding shift in the dipole structure.

The last row of Fig. 1 shows a forecast from a different time of year (2017-06-01 12:00 UTC) to assess whether the dipole structure in the principal component persists when the synoptic-scale waves are not as clearly defined. At a trough (of radius 12.59°) at $46°N$, $30°W$, the same dipole structure is observed, but tilted in the opposite direction to the previous case. Furthermore, the strong alternating dipole structure across the Northern Hemisphere is less pronounced.

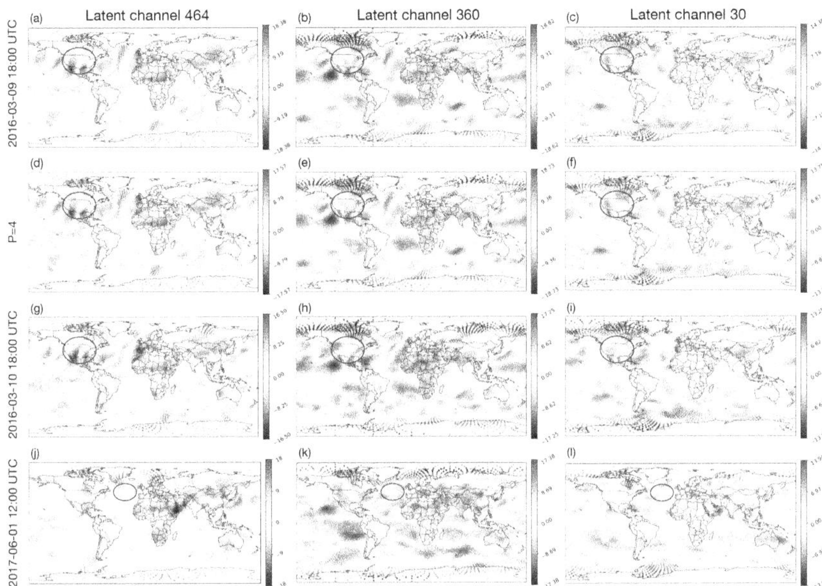

Fig. 2. Spatial structure of selected latent channels for three forecast times. Rows (a-c), (g-i) and (j-l) show the activation of channels 464, 360 and 30, respectively, at the last (16th) processor step for forecast times 2016-03-09 18:00 UTC, 2016-03-10 18:00 UTC and 2017-06-01 12:00 UTC. Second row from top (d-f) corresponds to the same forecast time as (a-c), but shows an earlier processor step ($P = 4$). Circles correspond to the same locations as in Fig. 1.

The top three channels contributing to the first principal component at the first forecast time of 2016-03-09 18:00 UTC are shown in Fig. 2, and Table 1 details the top contributing channels for all forecast times from Fig. 1. There is general consistency in the channels contributing to the first principal component across forecast times, although the ranking is not identical. When a distinct trough is present in the geopotential, the dipole structure is prominent in both channels 464 and 360, and, to a lesser extent, in channel 30, where the activation signs are reversed. Additional patterns are also seen in the raw channels. For example, channel 360 is often strongly activated over most of Africa. Finally, we look at the latent channels at an earlier processor step. Figure 2d-f shows the latent channels at processor step four for the forecast time of 2016-03-09 18:00 UTC. There are only minute differences; the earlier processor step already shows the broad structure observed in the final processor step.

Table 1. Top channels contributing to the first principal component at the final processor step, $P = 16$, for the synoptic wave case. Descending order, with 1 contributing most. Channels in bold occur at least twice.

Date and time of forecast	1	2	3	4	5	6
2016-03-09 18:00 UTC	**464**	**360**	**33**	239	**269**	**30**
2016-03-10 18:00 UTC	**464**	**360**	**33**	**126**	**30**	**269**
2017-06-01 12:00 UTC	**360**	19	**30**	**126**	183	426

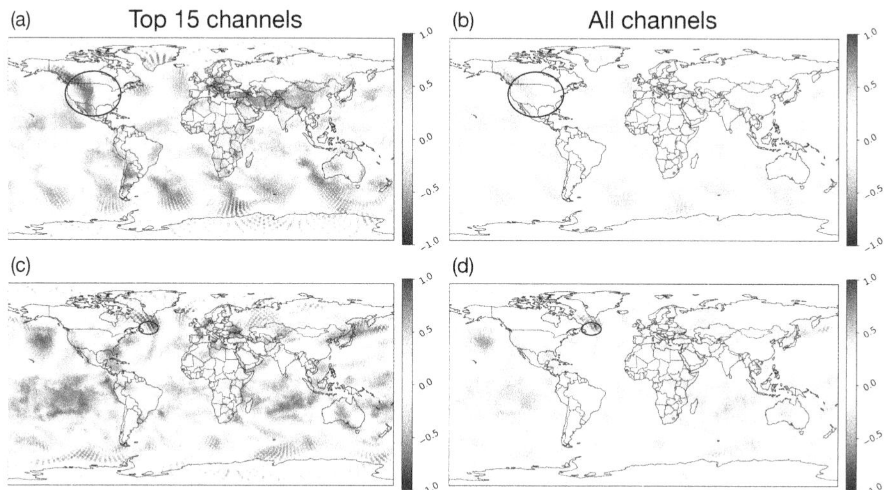

Fig. 3. Cosine similarity of the latent feature vectors for the forecast at 2016-03-09 18:00 UTC, evaluated using two regions indicated by black circles; (a-b) analysis region is as in top two rows of Fig. 1, and (c-d) analysis region is centred at $50°N$, $48°W$ and has a radius of $5.81°$. Left column (a,c) shows similarity computed using the 15 most activated channels, whereas the right column (b,d), uses the full set of channels.

The cosine similarity diagnostic is used to identify regions with similar latent space vectors. At first glance, the cosine similarity using the previously selected region over North America (Fig. 3a,b) does not yield obviously interpretable patterns. However, when a different region in the mid-latitudes is selected from the same forecast, a pattern of synoptic-scale waves emerges (Fig. 3c,d). Interestingly, this pattern does not include the North American trough, perhaps because geopotential values are not sufficiently low. When the entire vector is used for the cosine similarity as in Fig. 3d, the same pattern as in Fig. 3c emerges, but with reduced magnitude.

3.2 Specific Humidity

Next, we identify directions in the latent space associated with specific humidity. Figure 4 shows the ERA5 input data for specific humidity (a,c) and the first principal component (b,d) for two dates and times, one in winter and one in summer (rows). A region of radius $20°$ is selected, centred at $15°N$, $15°E$, which includes the strong moisture gradient of the Sahel region of Africa.

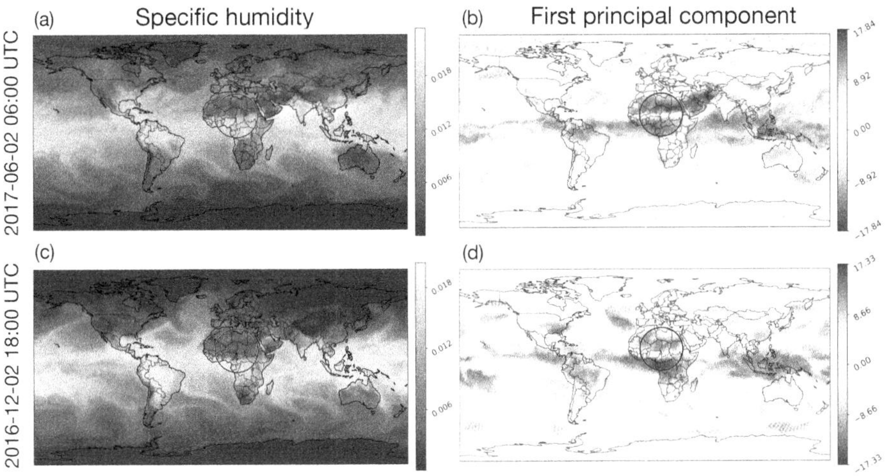

Fig. 4. Global fields for two forecast times, t: (a-b) 2017-06-02 06:00 UTC and (c-d) 2016-12-02 18:00 UTC. The left column (a,c) shows the 1000hPa specific humidity ($kgkg^{-1}$) at the forecast initialisation time, t_{init}, and the right column (b,d), the first principal component. The circled region highlights the area used for analysis. For both rows, the circle is centred at $15°N$, $15°E$ and has a radius of $20°$.

A clear correlation between the first principal component and the specific humidity is observed. This is evident north of the Gulf of Guinea. For example, on 2017-06-02 at 06:00 UTC, there is a relatively high specific humidity of approximately 0.015 kg/kg reaching up to the Northern borders of Nigeria. In contrast, on 2016-12-02 at 18:00 UTC, those levels of specific humidity extend only half way up the country. Similarly, a strong activation in the principal component is seen for the full extent of Nigeria on 2017-06-02 and only half way up on 2016-12-02. A clear correlation is also seen over Australia. The correspondence between the principal component and the meteorological data is also visible over the oceans. For example, the swirl on 2016-12-02 in the Atlantic is captured, as well as the prong-like structure in the Eastern Pacific. These correlations are strongest in the lower latitudes, weakening at higher latitudes, around 50°.

As before, the channels contributing to the first principal component are detailed in Table 2, and the top three from the first row are shown in Fig. 5 for the two forecast dates. Once again, there is a noticeable consistency over the two times, with all but one of the top six channels appearing in both forecasts, although not in the same order. Apart from a clear break at the equator and a strong activation either side of this in channels 33 and 172, distinct spatial patterns are less evident in the individual channels than for the synoptic wave feature. It is furthermore worth noting that a couple of channels appearing in Table 1 also occur in Table 2.

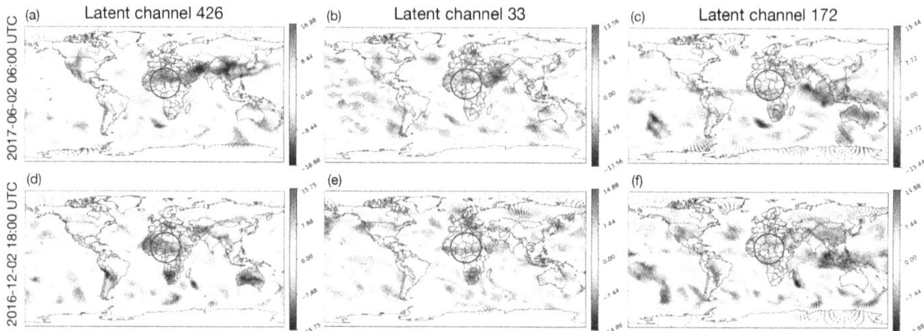

Fig. 5. Spatial structure of selected latent channels for two forecast times. Rows (a-c) and (d-f) show the activation of channels 426, 33 and 172, respectively, at the last (16th) processor step for forecast times 2017-06-02 06:00 UTC and 2016-12-02 18:00 UTC. Circles correspond to the same location as in Fig. 4.

Table 2. Top channels contributing to the first principal component at the final processor step, $P = 16$, for the specific humidity case. Descending order, with 1 contributing most. Channels in bold occur twice.

Date and time of forecast	1	2	3	4	5	6
2017-06-02 06:00 UTC	**426**	**172**	33	**464**	**19**	**183**
2016-12-02 18:00 UTC	**183**	**172**	**464**	**19**	**426**	360

3.3   Discussion

From the two case studies, we have identified possible connections between directions in the latent space and meteorological features. This illustrates the usefulness of the tool for exploring the latent space of the processor stage in AI weather models and generating hypotheses for further investigation.

Across the case studies, some components of the tool were more informative than others. In particular, PCA was effective at identifying prominent structures in the latent space and highlighting the channels that contributed most strongly to them. In both cases, each of the two features studied were associated with a set of frequently identified channels, although not always in the same order. Furthermore, although the two features we studied are not directly related, and are of importance in different geographical regions, some channels contributed strongly to both features e.g. channels 360 and 464. This might suggest a physical relationship between specific humidity and mid-latitude synoptic-scale waves, since they are represented in part by the same underlying features, although it could also indicate polysemantic neurons.

The ability to quickly generate visualisations of the latent space for different regions and then relate them to the atmospheric state resulted in the two case studies presented here, and suggests several avenues for further investigation using more quantitative techniques. For instance, our initial results suggest that AI weather models may represent the Northern and Southern Hemispheres differently, which may reflect differences in land-sea distribution. Although parts of some channels could be interpreted, other activated regions remained difficult to explain. For example, in channel 360, a recurring dipole activation was observed in the mid-latitudes, while strong activation over Africa remained unexplained.

Another application of the visualisation tool that has not been explored extensively here is how the latent space evolves across processor steps. In the one example shown in Fig. 2, it was observed that differences between steps four and sixteen were minimal, suggesting that certain large-scale features may already be established at earlier processor steps.

4   Conclusion

We have presented a tool to support mechanistic interpretability research in AI weather models, which currently supports the graph neural network GraphCast. The tool enables systematic organisation and visualisation of large-scale meteorological and latent data, while also supporting initial analyses. It is open source and available online at GitHub.

The aim of the tool is to enable rapid visual exploration of the model's latent space, to generate hypotheses that can motivate later, more detailed analysis using quantitative methods on large data sets. The use of the tool has been demonstrated in two case studies. In both cases, qualitative associations were observed between directions in the latent space and meteorological features, specifically mid-latitude synoptic-scale waves and specific humidity. These results highlight the potential to identify further feature-direction correspondences and to develop a deeper understanding of those already identified. In turn, this could enable the construction of a dictionary of interpretable latent features. Which could then support the analysis of how feature-associated directions evolve across processor steps and lead to the identification of circuits, ultimately contributing to a more comprehensive understanding of how AI weather models generate their predictions.

Development of the tool is ongoing, with current work focused on accommodating transformer-based models, and on supporting visualisations across selected forecast times.

Code and Data Availability. The visualisation tool developed in this work is open source and available at https://github.com/ktempestuous/latent_space_visualiser_weather_models. The repository includes instructions for installation, configuration, and extension to additional model architectures. In addition, sample data is accessible to use with the tool.

The ERA5 reanalysis dataset used in this study is publicly available from ECMWF at https://www.ecmwf.int/en/forecasts/datasets/.

Latent feature datasets were created by running the GraphCast model available at https://github.com/google-deepmind/graphcast with the small configuration, and extracting the latent features after each processor step.

Acknowledgement. The authors thank the computing resources and support of the Physics department at LMU, as well as fruitful discussions with colleagues for advancing this topic.

Disclosure of Interests. The authors have no competing interests to declare that are relevant to the content of this article.

References

1. Beylich, M., Tempest, K.I., Craig, G.C.: Interpretability of AI weather models via intermediate decoding (2026). To be submitted
2. Bi, K., Xie, L., Zhang, H., Chen, X., Gu, X., Tian, Q.: Accurate medium-range global weather forecasting with 3D neural networks. Nature **619**(7970), 533–538 (2023). https://doi.org/10.1038/s41586-023-06185-3. https://www.nature.com/articles/s41586-023-06185-3
3. Bodnar, C., et al.: A foundation model for the Earth system. Nature **641**(8065), 1180–1187 (2025). https://doi.org/10.1038/s41586-025-09005-y
4. Hauser, S., Teubler, F., Riemer, M., Knippertz, P., Grams, C.M.: Towards a holistic understanding of blocked regime dynamics through a combination of complementary diagnostic perspectives. Weather Climate Dynam. **4**(2), 399–425 (2023). https://doi.org/10.5194/wcd-4-399-2023. https://wcd.copernicus.org/articles/4/399/2023/
5. Hersbach, H., et al.: The Era5 global reanalysis. Q. J. R. Meteorol. Soc. **146**(730), 1999–2049 (2020). https://doi.org/10.1002/qj.3803. https://rmets.onlinelibrary.wiley.com/doi/abs/10.1002/qj.3803
6. Kissane, C., Krzyzanowski, R., Bloom, J.I., Conmy, A., Nanda, N.: Interpreting attention layer outputs with sparse autoencoders (2024). https://arxiv.org/abs/2406.17759
7. Lam, R., et al.: Learning skillful medium-range global weather forecasting. Science **382**(6677), 1416–1421 (2023). https://doi.org/10.1126/science.adi2336. https://www.science.org/doi/abs/10.1126/science.adi2336
8. Lang, S., et al.: AIFS-CRPS: Ensemble forecasting using a model trained with a loss function based on the continuous ranked probability score. https://doi.org/10.48550/arXiv.2412.15832, http://arxiv.org/abs/2412.15832

9. MacMillan, T., Ouellette, N.T.: Towards mechanistic understanding in a data-driven weather model: internal activations reveal interpretable physical features (2025). https://arxiv.org/abs/2512.24440
10. European Centre for Medium-Range Weather Forecasts, E.C.: Medium-range forecasts: Forecasts up to 15 days ahead (2026). https://www.ecmwf.int/en/forecasts/documentation-and-support/medium-range-forecasts. Accessed 13 Feb 2026
11. Olah, C.: Mechanistic interpretability, variables, and the importance of interpretable bases. https://www.transformer-circuits.pub/2022/mech-interp-essay (June 27 2022). Accessed 13 Feb 2026
12. Olah, C., Cammarata, N., Schubert, L., Goh, G., Petrov, M., Carter, S.: Zoom in: An introduction to circuits. https://distill.pub/2020/circuits/zoom-in/ (2020). Accessed 13 Feb 2026
13. Rasp, S., et al.: Weatherbench 2: a benchmark for the next generation of data-driven global weather models. Journal of Advances in Modeling Earth Syst. **16**(6), e2023MS004019 (2024). https://doi.org/10.1029/2023MS004019, https://agupubs.onlinelibrary.wiley.com/doi/abs/10.1029/2023MS004019, e2023MS004019 2023MS004019
14. scikit-learn developers: sklearn.decomposition.pca — scikit-learn 1.8.0 documentation (2025). https://scikit-learn.org/stable/modules/generated/sklearn.decomposition.PCA.html. Accessed 14 Feb 2026
15. scikit-learn developers: sklearn.metrics.pairwise.cosine similarity — scikit-learn 1.8.0 documentation (2025). https://scikit-learn.org/stable/modules/generated/sklearn.metrics.pairwise.cosine_similarity.html. Accessed 14 Feb 2026
16. Streamlit: Streamlit — a faster way to build and share data apps (2026). https://streamlit.io. Accessed 14 Feb 2026
17. Yang, R., et al.: Interpretable machine learning for weather and climate prediction: A review. Atmos. Environ. **338**, 120797 (2024). https://doi.org/10.1016/j.atmosenv.2024.120797. https://www.sciencedirect.com/science/article/pii/S1352231024004722
18. Zhao, H., Yang, F., Shen, B., Lakkaraju, H., Du, M.: Towards uncovering how large language model works: an explainability perspective (2024). https://arxiv.org/abs/2402.10688

Adjoint-Based Optimization with Quantized Local Reduced-Order Models for Spatiotemporally Chaotic Systems

Defne Ege Ozan[1(✉)] [iD], Antonio Colanera[2] [iD], and Luca Magri[1,3] [iD]

[1] Department of Aeronautics, Imperial College London, London SW7 2AZ, UK
`{d.ozan,l.magri}@imperial.ac.uk`
[2] International School for Advanced Studies (SISSA), Via Bonomea 265, 34136 Trieste, Italy
[3] Politecnico di Torino, DIMEAS, Corso Duca degli Abruzzi, 24, 10129 Torino, Italy

Abstract. We introduce a computationally efficient and accurate reduced-order modelling approach for the optimization of spatiotemporally chaotic systems. The proposed method combines quantized local reduced-order modelling with adjoint-based optimization. We employ the methodology in a variational data assimilation problem for the chaotic Kuramoto-Sivashinsky equation and show that it successfully reconstructs the full trajectory for up to 0.25 Lyapunov times given full state measurements at the final time. The proposed algorithm provides $\times 3.5$ speed-up when compared to the full-order model. The proposed method opens up new possibilities for the reduced-order modelling of spatiotemporally chaotic systems.

Keywords: Reduced-order modelling · Adjoint methods · Data assimilation · Spatiotemporal chaos

1 Introduction

Fluid systems that are of scientific and engineering interest are typically described by partial differential equations (PDEs), which often have spatiotemporally chaotic solutions [7]. Accurate solutions of these PDEs typically require fine discretizations that yield high-dimensional state representations in order to resolve the underlying multi-scale dynamics. The resulting high computational cost for the simulation of these systems motivates the development of reduced-order modelling (ROM) approaches, which aim to discover low-dimensional models that can be utilized to predict the system behaviour with some approximation error [13]. In dissipative systems, which are common in fluids, the ROM approach becomes viable, as the trajectories are attracted to a low-dimensional manifold.

ROMs are especially appealing in gradient-based optimization, where repeated forward simulations are required to reach convergence. Adjoint methods

M. Paszynski et al. (Eds.): ICCS 2026 Workshops, LNCS 16788, pp. 128–135, 2026.
https://doi.org/10.1007/978-3-032-29915-4_11

are central in this context. The adjoint formulation enables the computation of gradients of an objective functional with respect to many design parameters at a cost that is essentially independent of the number of parameters e.g., [5, 10, 12], unlike tangent-linear or finite-difference approaches whose cost scales with the parameter dimension. In data assimilation, an alternative class of approaches is based on sequential filtering, most notably the ensemble Kalman filter (EnKF); a general EnKF formalism is presented in [11].

In this paper, we leverage the recently developed quantized local reduced-order models (ql-ROMs) [2] for gradient-based optimization, which overcomes the challenge of designing a single global ROM for the entire state space. In this approach, the manifold is quantized via unsupervised clustering, and intrusive local ROMs are built for each cluster. The switching between the local models is enabled via a change of basis using assignment functions. We derive the adjoint of the ql-ROM, where a similar coordinate transformation exists between the local adjoint variables. We demonstrate the application of this method in a variational data assimilation problem of a prototypical spatiotemporally chaotic system, where the objective is to infer the initial condition of a trajectory given observations.

The remainder of the paper is organized as follows. In Sect. 2, we present the proposed methodology. Specifically, Sect. 2.1 summarizes the ql-ROM algorithm, Sect. 2.2 derives the adjoint of the ql-ROM and Sect. 2.3 embeds it within a gradient-based optimization framework for variational data assimilation problems. The methodology is demonstrated on the spatiotemporally chaotic solutions of the Kuramoto-Sivashinsky (KS) equation in Sect. 3. Section 4 concludes the paper.

2   Methodology

In this section, we outline the proposed workflow to enable adjoint-based optimization with quantized local reduced-order models (ql-ROMs). The approach consists of three building blocks: the construction of local intrusive ROMs on a quantized state space, the derivation of the corresponding adjoint with appropriate jump/coordinate transformations at cluster switches, and the integration of this adjoint within a variational data assimilation loop to update the initial condition. The overall workflow is shown in Fig. 1.

2.1   Quantized Reduced-Order Models (ql-ROMs)

We consider the spatial discretization of a PDE which results in the following system of ordinary differential equations

$$\dot{\boldsymbol{u}} = \boldsymbol{f}(\boldsymbol{u}), \quad \boldsymbol{u} \in \mathbb{R}^N, \quad \boldsymbol{u}(t = 0) = \boldsymbol{u}_0 \tag{1}$$

where $\boldsymbol{u}$ is the state vector, $\dot{\boldsymbol{u}} = d\boldsymbol{u}/dt$ is its time derivative, $\boldsymbol{f}$ is the nonlinear operator that describes the evolution of the state vector in time, and N the

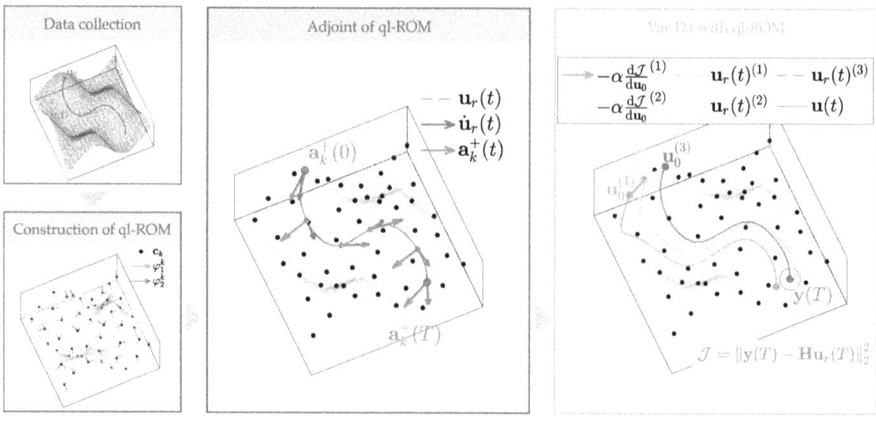

Fig. 1. Overview of adjoint-based optimization with quantized local reduced-order models (ql-ROMs): (1) data collection; (2) phase-space quantization and local basis/model construction; (3) ql-ROM adjoint integrated backward in time with jump/coordinate-transformation at cluster switches; (4) variational data assimilation using the ql-ROM direct–adjoint loop to update the initial condition.

dimension of the full-order state. Given a dataset of M snapshots $\{\boldsymbol{u}(t_m)\}_{m=0}^{M}$, where $t_m = m\Delta t$ with Δt being the time step, the method first partitions this data into K clusters with centroids $\boldsymbol{c}_k \in \mathbb{R}^N$, $k = 1, 2, \ldots, K$. Here, we employ K-means for this purpose, which is an unsupervised machine learning method for clustering data based on a distance metric, e.g., the Euclidean distance from the centroid. The cluster affiliation function then assigns a snapshot to the closest cluster using this metric, where the centroid acts as the mean of the cluster. In the next step, we project $\boldsymbol{u}$ on a basis defined by a centroid $\boldsymbol{c}_k$ and orthonormal basis vectors $\boldsymbol{V}_k \in \mathbb{R}^{N \times r_k}$ such that

$$\boldsymbol{u} = \boldsymbol{c}_k + \boldsymbol{V}_k \boldsymbol{a}_k, \tag{2}$$

where $\boldsymbol{a}_k \in \mathbb{R}^{r_k}$ are the coordinates in this new basis. The objective of reduced-order modelling is to build an accurate model with $r_k \ll N$. (When we set the number of clusters $K = 1$, this formulation becomes equivalent to the global modelling approach.) We determine

$$\boldsymbol{a}_k = \boldsymbol{V}_k^\top (\boldsymbol{u} - \boldsymbol{c}_k). \tag{3}$$

Here, we employ proper orthogonal decomposition (POD) [7] to obtain the local bases $\boldsymbol{V}_k$ in each cluster. Using Galerkin projection of the dynamics onto the chosen basis vector, we obtain a model for the time evolution of $\boldsymbol{a}_k$ for each cluster

$$\dot{\boldsymbol{a}}_k = \boldsymbol{g}_k(\boldsymbol{a}_k), \quad \boldsymbol{a}_k \in \mathbb{R}^{r_k}, \quad \boldsymbol{a}_k(0) = \boldsymbol{V}_k^\top (\boldsymbol{u}_0 - \boldsymbol{c}_k). \tag{4}$$

The advantage of the ql-ROM approach is that the dynamics are modelled locally, which means that as the trajectory moves along the state space, the cluster affiliations change. The coordinate transformation for switch from cluster i to cluster j is given by

$$a_j(t) = V_j^\top V_i a_i(t) + V_j^\top (c_i - c_j). \tag{5}$$

For further details about the algorithm, we refer the reader to [2,3].

2.2   Adjoint of Ql-ROM

Given a model of the system's dynamics, adjoint-based optimization relies on a direct–adjoint loop: the system is integrated forward in time, the dynamics are linearized along the resulting trajectory, and the corresponding adjoint equations are integrated backward to evaluate gradients e.g., [6,10].

Consider a scalar objective function

$$\mathcal{J} = \tilde{\mathcal{J}}(u(T)), \tag{6}$$

and the ql-ROM dynamics (4). Our goal is to compute the sensitivity of the objective function to the initial condition, i.e., to compute the gradient $d\mathcal{J}/du_0$. Since $a_0 = V_{k(0)}^\top (u_0 - c_{k(0)})$, it is sufficient to compute $d\mathcal{J}/da_0$ and then map it to $d\mathcal{J}/du_0$ by a constant transformation. We define the Lagrangian

$$\mathcal{L} = \mathcal{J} - \langle a^+, \dot{a} - g(a) \rangle = \tilde{\mathcal{J}}(a(T)) - \int_0^T a^{+\top} (\dot{a} - g(a))\, dt, \tag{7}$$

where a^+ are the adjoint variables. Stationarity of $\mathcal{L}$ with respect to a_0 yields, within each active cluster k,

$$\dot{a}_k^+ = -\left(\frac{dg_k(a_k)}{da_k}\right)^\top a_k^+, \tag{8}$$

with terminal condition $a^+(T) = d\tilde{\mathcal{J}}/da(T)$. The term $dg_k(a_k)/da_k \in \mathbb{R}^{r_k \times r_k}$ in Eq. (8) is the Jacobian of the local reduced-order model.

When the direct trajectory switches from cluster i to cluster j at time T_s, the adjoint satisfies the corresponding jump/coordinate transformation

$$a_i^+(T_s^-) = V_i^\top V_j\, a_j^+(T_s^+), \tag{9}$$

consistent with the direct coordinate change (5). This transformation follows from splitting the integral in Eq. (7) at the switching time, and collecting the boundary terms resulting from integration by parts of each subinterval. The reduced gradient follows as

$$\frac{d\mathcal{J}}{da_0} = a^+(0), \tag{10}$$

and $d\mathcal{J}/du_0$ is obtained via the fixed mapping da_0/du_0.

In this derivation we assume that the switching time is insensitive to the initial condition, i.e. $dT_s/da_0 \approx 0$. We verify this assumption in Fig. 2(a). Accounting for event-time sensitivity would require a differentiable switching mechanism and additional terms [1,8].

2.3   Variational Data Assimilation with Ql-ROMs

We consider an application in variational data assimilation e.g., [15], where we plug the adjoint of the ql-ROM developed in the previous section in a gradient-based optimization scheme. We consider the problem of inferring the unknown initial condition $\boldsymbol{u}_0$ of a trajectory given some observations at the final time T. We want to minimize the objective function

$$\mathcal{J} = ||\boldsymbol{y}(T) - \boldsymbol{H}\boldsymbol{u}(T)||_2^2, \tag{11}$$

where $\boldsymbol{y} \in \mathbb{R}^p$ are the observations and $\boldsymbol{H} \in \mathbb{R}^{p \times N}$ is the observation matrix that maps the full state to the observations space. (In this formulation, uncertainties can be captured by using a covariance matrix and bias in the objective function e.g., [11].) Starting with an initial guess for $\boldsymbol{u}_0$, we propagate the ql-ROM's Eq. (4) forward in time. We linearize the ql-ROM around this trajectory, i.e., compute the local Jacobian at each time step, and integrate the adjoint Eq. (8) backward in time, obtaining $d\mathcal{J}/d\boldsymbol{u}_0$. We update the initial condition using steepest gradient descent

$$\boldsymbol{u}_0^{(i+1)} = \boldsymbol{u}_0^{(i)} - \alpha \frac{d\mathcal{J}}{d\boldsymbol{u}_0}^{(i)}, \tag{12}$$

where i is the iteration step and α is the step size. The procedure is repeated until convergence. We perform the optimization in the full space by updating $\boldsymbol{u}_0$ (rather than the reduced coordinates $\boldsymbol{a}(0)$). This allows the cluster-affiliation map to be re-evaluated at each iteration, so that the sequence of active local models can adapt during the optimization and the algorithm can converge to the correct trajectory.

3   Application to Spatio-temporal Chaos

We demonstrate the developed methodology on a prototypical spatiotemporally chaotic system. The Kuramoto-Sivashinsky (KS) equation is a 1D PDE that arises in a variety of physical phenomena including flame front instabilities [14] and chemical reaction-diffusion equations [9]. The equation is described by

$$\frac{\partial u}{\partial t} + u\frac{\partial u}{\partial x} + \frac{\partial^2 u}{\partial x^2} + \nu\frac{\partial^4 u}{\partial x^4} = 0 \tag{13}$$

where $u(x,t) : [0, L] \times [0, \infty) \to \mathbb{R}$ is the velocity on a periodic domain of length L, i.e., $u(x,t) = u(x+L,t)$. Letting $\nu = 1$, the dynamical behaviour of the system is determined by the domain length L. Following a spectral discretization with 128 Fourier modes, the time integration is performed by a fourth-order exponential time differencing Runge-Kutta method (ETDRK4) [4] with a time step of $\Delta t = 0.05$. For the adjoint equations, we employ a discrete time formulation of the equations derived in Sect. 2.2.

For data generation, we choose $L = 20\pi$, which results in a chaotic regime with a Lyapunov (LT) of approximately 11.8 time units (235 time steps). The system is initialized by setting $u(x, 0) = \cos(x)$. We discard the first 5×10^3 time steps as transient, and we utilize the next 10^5 time steps in training and the next 10^4 time steps in testing. Following the analysis of [2], we set the number of clusters $K = 10$ and build local ROMs using $r_k = 30$ POD modes for each cluster.

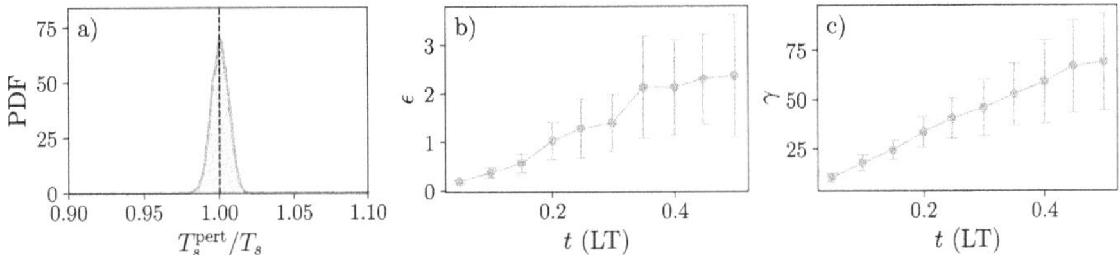

Fig. 2. Sensitivity of the switching time and accuracy of the adjoint sensitivity computed using the quantized local reduced model in comparison to the full-order model. (a) Estimated PDF of the normalized T_s in the ql-ROM, by perturbing the initial condition with random noise with standard deviation 10^{-3}. (b) the relative ℓ_2-norm of the error between these two gradient vectors, denoted by ϵ, and (c) the cosine similarity between these two gradient vectors, denoted by γ. The error bars indicate the mean and ± 1 standard deviation of 50 randomly initialized runs within the test set.

First, we verify the accuracy of the sensitivity computation using the ql-ROM. For this purpose, we use an objective function $\mathcal{J} = \|\boldsymbol{u}(T)\|_2^2$, which is the ℓ_2-norm of the final state. Figure 2 reports (a) the probability density function (PDF) of the normalized T_s obtained from randomly perturbed initial conditions, the accuracy of the ql-ROM adjoint sensitivity $d\mathcal{J}/d\boldsymbol{u}_0$ with respect to the full-order model one via two error metrics (b) the relative ℓ_2-norm of the error between these two gradient vectors, denoted by ϵ, and (c) their cosine similarity, denoted by γ. Since gradient-based optimization primarily depends on the search direction, the cosine similarity is particularly informative in practice.

As expected in chaotic systems, for short time horizons ~ 0.25 LT, the gradient remains accurate, while it gradually loses accuracy as the time horizon increases.

Second, we consider the variational data assimilation problem described in Sect. 2.3 for trajectories of length $T = 0.25$ LT. We assume full state measurements, i.e., the observation operator is the identity matrix $\boldsymbol{H} = I_{N \times N}$. The ql-ROM is initialized from a random snapshot on the chaotic attractor, and the initial condition is updated via gradient descent using the adjoint-based gradient. The results are shown in Fig. 3, where we plot the predicted trajectory at the beginning of the optimization, after 100 iterations, and at the end of the optimization after 1000 iterations. The method successfully recovers the true trajectory with decreasing error near the measurement time. Furthermore, the ql-ROM methodology is significantly more computationally efficient compared to the full-order model. Adjoint-based optimization with the full-order model

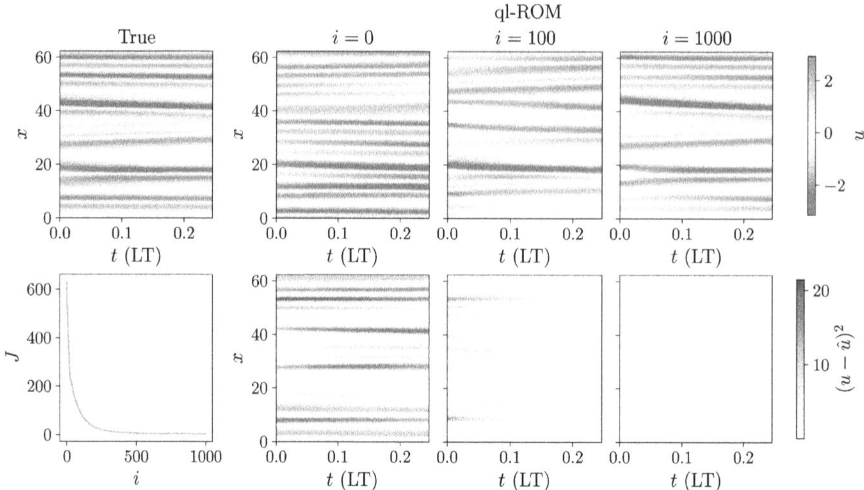

Fig. 3. Variational data assimilation on the Kuramoto-Sivashinsky equation using the adjoint of the quantized local reduced-order model. The method reconstructs the true trajectory from measurements at the final time $T = 0.25$ LT following the convergence of the optimization objective, $\mathcal{J}$.

takes approximately $26\,$s for 100 iterations, whereas with the model reduction enabled by the ql-ROM, this computation time is reduced to approximately $7.4\,$s for 100 iterations, overall resulting in $\times 3.5$ speed-up (results obtained on Intel Xeon(R) Gold 5218R CPU at $2.10\,$GHz $\times$ 80). We expect the cost of the adjoint method to scale with the cost of running two forward simulations. Reducing the state dimension from 128 to 30 would ideally yield a speed-up of about $\times 4.3$, which, in our numerical experiments, is reduced to $\times 3.5$ due to the overhead associated with the cluster switching operations.

4   Conclusion

We introduced a computationally efficient reduced-order framework for adjoint-based optimization of spatiotemporally chaotic systems. The proposed method combines quantized local reduced-order modelling with adjoint-based optimization at a fraction of the full-order cost. We demonstrated the methodology on a variational data assimilation problem for the chaotic Kuramoto-Sivashinsky equation, showing that it can successfully reconstruct the full trajectory over horizons up to 0.25 Lyapunov times from full state measurements at the final time. The proposed algorithm achieves an overall speed-up of $\times 3.5$ compared to the full-order model. In this paper, we used K-means for clustering and obtained the dynamics of the local reduced-order variables using Galerkin projection of the original PDE on local proper orthogonal decomposition modes. These choices are convenient but not essential: alternative clustering strategies and reduced modelling paradigms can be incorporated within the same quantized local and adjoint-based workflow. This method opens up new possibilities for efficient optimization, control, and data assimilation of spatiotemporally chaotic systems.

Acknowledgement. The authors acknowledge funding from the ERC Starting Grant No. PhyCo 949388.

Disclosure of Interests. The authors have no competing interests to declare that are relevant to the content of this article.

References

1. di Bernardo, M., Budd, C.J., Champneys, A.R., Kowalczyk, P.: Piecewise-smooth Dynamical Systems: theory and applications. Appl. Math. Sci. Springer London (2008). https://doi.org/10.1007/978-1-84628-708-4
2. Colanera, A., Magri, L.: Quantized local reduced-order modeling in time (ql-ROM). Comput. Methods Appl. Mech. Eng. **447**, 118393 (2025). https://doi.org/10.1016/j.cma.2025.118393
3. Colanera, A., Magri, L.: Towards extreme event prediction of turbulent flows with quantized local reduced-order models (2025). https://doi.org/10.48550/ARXIV.2511.04586
4. Cox, S.M., Matthews, P.C.: Exponential time differencing for stiff systems. J. Comput. Phys. **176**(2), 430–455 (2002). https://doi.org/10.1006/jcph.2002.6995
5. Giles, M.B., Pierce, N.A.: An introduction to the adjoint approach to design. Flow Turbul. Combust. **65**(3/4), 393–415 (2000). https://doi.org/10.1023/A:1011430410075
6. Gunzburger, M.D.: Perspectives in flow control and optimization. Soc. Ind. Appl. Math. (2002). https://doi.org/10.1137/1.9780898718720
7. Holmes, P., Lumley, J.L., Berkooz, G.: Turbulence, Coherent Structures, Dynamical Systems and Symmetry, 1 edn. Cambridge University Press (1996). https://doi.org/10.1017/CBO9780511622700
8. Kong, N.J., Payne, J.J., Zhu, J., Johnson, A.M.: Saltation matrices: the essential tool for linearizing hybrid dynamical systems. arXiv (2024). https://doi.org/10.1109/JPROC.2024.3440211
9. Kuramoto, Y.: Diffusion-induced chaos in reaction systems. Prog. Theor. Phys. Suppl. **64**, 346–367 (1978). https://doi.org/10.1143/PTPS.64.346
10. Magri, L.: Adjoint methods as design tools in thermoacoustics. Appl. Mech. Rev. **71**(2), 020801 (2019). https://doi.org/10.1115/1.4042821
11. Nóvoa, A., Racca, A., Magri, L.: Inferring unknown unknowns: regularized bias-aware ensemble Kalman filter. Comput. Methods Appl. Mech. Eng. **418**, 116502 (2024). https://doi.org/10.1016/j.cma.2023.116502
12. Ozan, D.E., Magri, L.: Data-driven computation of adjoint sensitivities without adjoint solvers: An application to thermoacoustics. Phys. Rev. Fluids **9**(10), 103902 (2024). https://doi.org/10.1103/physrevfluids.9.103902
13. Quarteroni, A., Rozza, G., Manzoni, A.: Certified reduced basis approximation for parametrized partial differential equations and applications. J. Math. Ind. **1**(1), 3 (2011). https://doi.org/10.1186/2190-5983-1-3
14. Sivashinsky, G.I.: On flame propagation under conditions of stoichiometry. SIAM J. Appl. Math. **39**(1), 67–82 (1980). https://doi.org/10.1137/0139007
15. Zaki, T.A.: Turbulence from an observer perspective. Annu. Rev. Fluid Mech. **57**(1), 311–334 (2025). https://doi.org/10.1146/annurev-fluid-030424-114735

Particle Filter Data Assimilation for Reconstructing Latent Hospital Care Pathways Under Partial Observability

Laith Ahmad[(✉)] [iD] and Sergey V. Kovalchuk [iD]

ITMO University, Saint Petersburg, Russia
`475790@niuitmo.ru, kovalchuk@itmo.ru`

Abstract. Hospital information systems record large volumes of clinical events, yet these records provide only a partial and asynchronous view of patient movement through care processes. Logged timestamps typically reflect administrative completion rather than true inter-department transitions, making direct reconstruction of care pathways unreliable.

We model daily ambulatory cardiology care pathways as partially observed stochastic dynamical systems. Department-level dynamics are represented using data-driven first- and second-order Markov transition models learned from multi-year hospital data (2015–2019), comprising 5,308 visit-level episodes across 51 departments. Latent department trajectories are reconstructed from sparse and noisy observations using a particle filter data assimilation framework that integrates structural transition priors with partial evidence. The transition model incorporates empirical termination behavior derived from observed episode statistics.

Reconstruction performance is evaluated via temporal holdout validation, training on 2015–2018 data and testing on 2019 episodes. Under representative sparse-observation conditions (stride 4, correctness 0.8), sequential assimilation improves reconstruction accuracy from 0.274 to 0.551 in-sample and from 0.289 to 0.518 out-of-sample. Gains persist across alternative sparsity and noise regimes, with larger improvements observed under increased observational degradation.

Complementary Bluetooth Low Energy localization experiments conducted on the same hospital floor provide a physical-layer perspective on observation uncertainty. Filtering mitigates stochastic sensor noise but does not correct systematic calibration bias, mirroring the department-level setting. Together, the results provide empirical evidence that healthcare pathways can be effectively modeled as partially observed dynamical systems and demonstrate that probabilistic data assimilation offers a principled and computationally tractable framework for reconstructing latent institutional trajectories under uncertainty.

Keywords: Healthcare systems modeling · Data assimilation · Particle filtering

M. Paszynski et al. (Eds.): ICCS 2026 Workshops, LNCS 16788, pp. 136–150, 2026.
https://doi.org/10.1007/978-3-032-29915-4_12

1 Introduction

Many real-world systems are only partially observable: their underlying state evolves according to structured dynamics, while available measurements provide incomplete, delayed, or noisy information. Reconstructing latent trajectories from sparse observations is therefore a central problem in computational science, with established applications in geophysics, engineering, and biological systems [1–3]. In such settings, probabilistic state-space modeling provides a principled framework for integrating structural dynamics with uncertain data.

Organizational systems exhibit similar characteristics. Their evolution is governed by institutional rules, operational constraints, and resource allocation mechanisms, yet available data typically consist of irregular event logs rather than direct state measurements. Inferring structured dynamics from such event-level observations requires modeling under partial observability rather than direct sequence analysis.

Hospital care pathways provide a concrete and operationally critical example. Patients move between departments according to clinical workflows and capacity constraints, but hospital information systems (MIS) record only discrete medical events, often timestamped at administrative completion rather than at physical transition. Process mining approaches reconstruct and analyze observed activity sequences directly from event logs [4, 5]. While effective for workflow discovery and deviation analysis, such methods generally treat recorded events as complete representations of the process and do not explicitly reconstruct latent department-level trajectories evolving under hidden dynamics.

In contrast, this work treats department sequences as latent stochastic processes and focuses on reconstruction under partial and noisy observation. The contribution lies in formulating and evaluating a state-space approach that integrates transition modeling with probabilistic inference for healthcare pathways.

Stochastic modeling offers a complementary perspective. First-order Markov chains are widely used in healthcare pathway and decision modeling due to their interpretability and tractability [6]. Higher-order extensions allow transition probabilities to depend on recent history, relaxing the memoryless assumption and increasing expressive capacity [10]. However, Markov modeling alone describes transition tendencies and does not address inference under incomplete and noisy observation.

The reconstruction of latent trajectories from partial data is closely related to state-space modeling and sequential Bayesian filtering. The Kalman filter provides optimal inference for linear Gaussian systems [1], while Sequential Monte Carlo (SMC) methods—commonly referred to as particle filters—extend inference to nonlinear and non-Gaussian settings [3, 7]. These methods approximate posterior distributions using weighted particle ensembles and are widely applied in geosciences and tracking problems [2]. Their systematic application to institutional process reconstruction in healthcare remains comparatively limited.

A related line of research arises in indoor localization. RSSI-based Bluetooth Low Energy (BLE) fingerprinting methods provide fine-grained spatial observations but are sensitive to environmental calibration drift and measurement noise [8, 9]. Particle filtering has been used to stabilize localization trajectories under stochastic fluctuations, though filtering cannot compensate for systematic bias in the observation model. These findings illustrate a broader computational principle: structural dynamical constraints combined with probabilistic assimilation improve robustness under partial observability.

In this work, we integrate these strands by modeling daily ambulatory cardiology care pathways as partially observed stochastic dynamical systems within an agent-based representation. Each patient is represented as an agent whose latent state corresponds to the current department. State evolution follows a data-driven first- or second-order Markov transition model estimated from multi-year hospital data. Latent trajectories are reconstructed using a particle filter that assimilates sparse and noisy observations into the learned structural prior.

Although MIS event data and BLE localization data are analyzed separately, they represent complementary observational layers of the same institutional system. MIS records provide semantic but indirect information about departmental transitions, while BLE localization captures physical trajectories subject to sensor noise and calibration variability. By examining both layers, the study demonstrates that sequential probabilistic assimilation stabilizes inference under stochastic observation noise across semantic and physical representations of hospital processes.

The contributions of this paper are threefold:

1. A formulation of hospital care pathways as partially observed stochastic dynamical systems using data-driven first- and second-order Markov transition models within an agent-based representation.
2. A probabilistic data assimilation framework that integrates learned institutional transition dynamics with partial and noisy observational evidence to reconstruct latent department trajectories.
3. Quantitative in-sample and temporally held-out validation demonstrating substantial reconstruction gains over observation-only and model-only baselines, together with complementary physical-layer localization analysis illustrating the generality of the partial-observability principle.

The remainder of the paper presents the data sources and modeling framework, experimental results at both institutional and physical layers, and a discussion of implications for computational modeling of organizational systems.

2 Methods

We formulate hospital pathway reconstruction as a partially observed state-space model integrating structural transition dynamics with heterogeneous observational sources. Figure 1 provides an overview of the modeling architecture.

The following subsections detail the data sources, transition modeling, and sequential inference framework.

2.1 Institutional Event Data

MIS Event Structure. The empirical data originate from the hospital Medical Information System (MIS) and consist of timestamped medical process events linked to internal

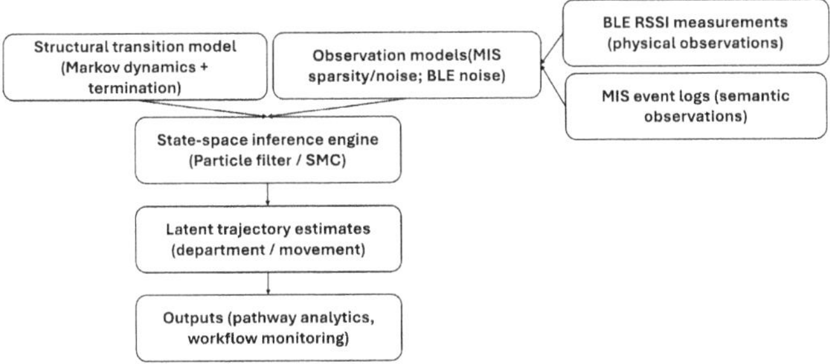

Fig. 1. State-Space Architecture for Hospital Pathway Reconstruction under Partial Observability.

patient identifiers. Each record contains the calendar date and time of event completion (CompletionDate and CompletionTime), the responsible Department, an ExecutionStatus flag (predominantly "completed"), and case-level boundaries (StartEpizode and EndEpizode).

Importantly, CompletionTime reflects administrative documentation rather than guaranteed physical transition time between departments. In routine clinical practice, events may be entered retrospectively or in batches, producing intra-day temporal compression and recording bias [5, 11]. For this reason, timestamps are treated as discrete observational markers rather than exact movement times.

The dataset spans 2015–2019 and includes ambulatory cardiology visits only.

Operational Episode Definition. An episode is defined as the ordered sequence of departments visited by a single patient during a single calendar day with cardiology-related activity.

Let i denote a visit identifier and d a calendar date. Let $E_{i,d}$ denote the set of MIS events associated with visit i on date d. Events are filtered to retain ambulatory admissions with completed status and valid department identifiers. The filtered events are sorted by CompletionTime. From the resulting ordered list, consecutive duplicate departments are removed to obtain a department trajectory

$$x_{i,d} = (x_1, x_2, \ldots, x_T),$$

where $x_t \in S$ denotes the department at position t, and T is the number of distinct department transitions observed during that calendar day.

Episodes are strictly day-bounded and independent of broader case-level boundaries. This operational definition aligns with outpatient workflow structure and avoids cross-day documentation artifacts [4].

After preprocessing, the dataset contains 5,308 episodes with a mean episode length of 3.66 departments over the period 2015–2019. Episodes of length one are retained for termination modeling but do not contribute to higher-order transition counts.

State Space Construction. Let S denote the department state space. Departments are ranked by frequency in the training period (2015–2018), and the 50 most frequent departments are retained explicitly. All remaining departments are aggregated into a residual state labeled OTHER, yielding $|S| = 51$.

This frequency-based truncation mitigates sparsity in higher-order transition estimation while preserving dominant cardiology care flows [10, 12].

Temporal Split. To evaluate temporal generalization, episodes are partitioned chronologically. Episodes from 2015–2018 (3,765 episodes) form the training set, and episodes from 2019 (1,543 episodes) form the test set. Transition probabilities and termination statistics are estimated exclusively from the training set, while the test set is reserved for out-of-sample reconstruction.

Chronological splitting avoids information leakage and reflects realistic deployment conditions in which historical institutional data are used to reconstruct future pathways [13].

Observational Characteristics. Two structural properties of the MIS data are central to modeling. First, completion-time bias may compress multiple events within short intervals, obscuring true temporal spacing [11]. Second, the MIS records medical actions rather than physical movement; department transitions are therefore inferred from successive event assignments rather than directly observed transfers [5].

These characteristics motivate modeling department sequences as latent stochastic trajectories observed through imperfect event-level proxies, rather than treating recorded event sequences as complete representations of patient movement.

2.2 Physical Localization Data (BLE)

To characterize the reliability of sensor-derived observations under realistic hospital conditions, Bluetooth Low Energy (BLE) indoor localization experiments were conducted on the second floor of the facility. The localization infrastructure consists of nine BLE access points (APs) and a predefined set of spatial key points (KPs) distributed across corridors and rooms.

Figure 2(a) illustrates the physical deployment of APs together with the dense grid of fingerprint KPs. The KPs serve as discrete reference locations for RSSI fingerprinting and define the measurement anchors for constructing the radio map. During a dedicated calibration session, RSSI measurements were collected at each KP to build a fingerprint-based radio map. This radio map specifies the observation model, providing the likelihood function that relates measured RSSI vectors to spatial hypotheses during inference.

In addition to the dense fingerprint grid, a reduced set of navigational waypoints defines the topological motion structure of the floor. As shown in Fig. 2(b), these waypoints are connected through a graph representation encoding feasible indoor movement paths. This graph is used to constrain particle propagation during localization, ensuring that motion respects architectural boundaries and navigable routes rather than unconstrained Euclidean transitions.

The deployment and calibration protocol follow prior experiments conducted on the same hospital floor [8, 9], but the present formulation explicitly separates the measurement layer (fingerprint KPs and RSSI likelihood) from the motion layer (waypoint graph and topology-aware constraints). The BLE dataset is analyzed independently from the MIS data and serves to quantify physical-layer observation uncertainty within the same institutional environment.

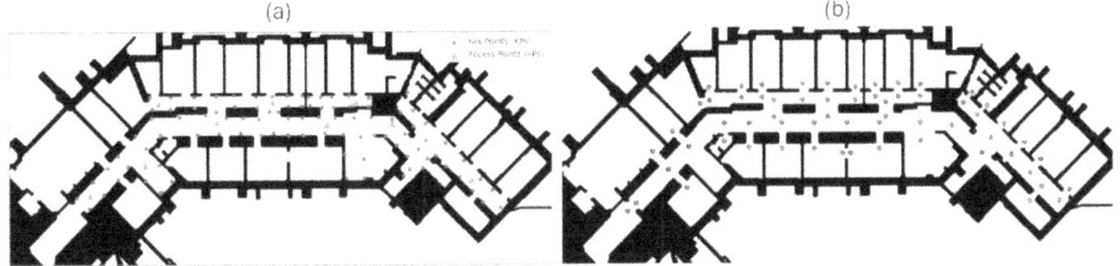

Fig. 2. BLE localization modeling components. (a) Access points (APs) and dense fingerprint key points (KPs) used for RSSI measurement modeling. (b) Reduced waypoint graph defining navigable indoor topology and constraining particle motion.

2.3 Markov Transition Modeling

Transition Structure. Let S denote the department state space with $|S| = 51$.
Each episode is represented as a sequence

$$x_{1:T}, x_t \in S.$$

Department transitions are modeled in discrete time using a Markov framework. As a baseline, we consider a first-order process

$$P(x_{t+1}|x_t),$$

which assumes that the next department depends only on the current department. First-order Markov models are widely used in healthcare pathway and decision modeling due to their interpretability and tractability [6, 14].

Transition probabilities are estimated from the training set using empirical maximum-likelihood estimation. Let $N(b, c)$ denote the number of observed transitions from department b to department c, and let

$$N(b) = \sum_{c \in S} N(b, c).$$

The first-order transition probability is then estimated as

$$\hat{P}(c|b) = \frac{N(b, c)}{N(b)}, \text{ for } N(b) > 0.$$

To capture short-term temporal dependencies beyond the memoryless assumption, we additionally evaluate a second-order extension [10]

$$P(x_{t+1}|x_t, x_{t-1}).$$

Let $N(a, b, c)$ denote the number of occurrences of the triplet.
$(x_{t-1} = a, x_t = b, x_{t+1} = c)$, and let

$$N(a, b) = \sum_{c \in S} N(a, b, c).$$

The second-order transition probability is estimated as

$$\hat{P}(c|a, b) = \frac{N(a, b, c)}{N(a, b)}, \text{ for } N(a, b) > 0.$$

When a second-order context (a, b) is unobserved, the model reverts to the first-order estimate $\hat{P}(c|b)$. All transition probabilities are computed via empirical maximum-likelihood estimation without additional smoothing or regularization, allowing the transition structure to reflect directly the observed institutional dynamics in the training data. Given the moderate state space ($|S| = 51$) and multi-year training corpus, sparsity effects were limited in practice.

The resulting transition model is time-homogeneous, i.e., transition probabilities are assumed to be stationary and do not vary over time within the modeled period. This assumption reflects aggregation of multi-year training data into a single empirical transition structure.

Empirical Termination Model. Episodes exhibit heterogeneous lengths. Rather than imposing a fixed stopping rule, termination probabilities are estimated empirically from training data.

For the first-order model, let $N_{\text{end}}(b)$ denote the number of times department b appears as the final state of an episode, and let $N_{\text{occ}}(b)$ denote the total number of occurrences of b in any position. The first-order termination probability is

$$\hat{P}_{\text{stop},1}(b) = \frac{N_{\text{end}}(b)}{N_{\text{occ}}(b)}.$$

For the second-order model, termination probabilities are defined analogously. Let $N_{\text{end}}(a, b)$ denote the number of times the ordered pair (a, b) occurs as the final two states of an episode, and let $N_{\text{occ}}(a, b)$ denote the total number of occurrences of this pair. The second-order termination probability is

$$\hat{P}_{\text{stop},2}(a, b) = \frac{N_{\text{end}}(a, b)}{N_{\text{occ}}(a, b)}.$$

During simulation or filtering, termination is sampled according to the corresponding empirical probability.

2.4   Particle Filter Assimilation Framework

State-Space Formulation. The reconstruction of department trajectories is formulated as a discrete-time state-space model. The latent state at time t is denoted by $x_t \in S$, where S is the department state space. State transitions follow either the first-order or second-order Markov dynamics previously introduced.

Observed medical events provide incomplete and potentially noisy information about the latent department sequence. Let y_t denote the observation at time t.

In the institutional setting, observations correspond to department-level proxies derived from recorded data sources. For MIS event data, each observation $y_t \in S$ is obtained from the department attribute associated with a recorded medical event, representing an administrative indication of patient presence rather than a direct measurement of physical location. For BLE localization data, observations originate from RSSI-based position estimates, which are mapped to the nearest department or spatial zone, yielding a discrete department-level proxy consistent with the state space S.

In both cases, y_t should be interpreted as a noisy and incomplete observation arising from delayed or aggregated MIS recording and measurement uncertainty in BLE localization, motivating the use of a probabilistic observation model.

The resulting model corresponds to a partially observed Markov process (POMP), or equivalently, a hidden Markov-type system [15, 16]. The objective is to infer the posterior distribution of the latent trajectory given the observations.

Observation Model. To evaluate robustness under controlled partial observability, we adopt a stochastic observation mechanism.

Observations are available every s time steps (stride). When an observation is available, it equals the true latent state with probability p_{correct}. With probability $1 - p_{\text{correct}}$, the observation is replaced by a uniformly sampled alternative state from $S \setminus \{x_t\}$.

The observation likelihood is therefore defined as

$$P(y_t|x_t) = \begin{cases} p_{\text{correct}} & \text{if } y_t = x_t \\ \frac{1 - p_{\text{correct}}}{|S| - 1} & \text{otherwise.} \end{cases}$$

This abstraction enables systematic evaluation of assimilation performance under varying observation sparsity and noise levels while keeping the structural transition model fixed.

Sequential Monte Carlo Approximation. We approximate the posterior distribution

$$P(x_{1:T}|y_{1:T}).$$

using a particle filter with $N = 500$ particles.

At each time step, particles are first propagated according to the chosen transition model. For the first-order model,

$$x_{t+1}^{(i)} \sim P(x_{t+1}|x_t^{(i)}),$$

and for the second-order model,

$$x_{t+1}^{(i)} \sim P(x_{t+1}|x_t^{(i)}, x_{t-1}^{(i)}).$$

Importance weights are then updated according to the observation likelihood,

$$w_{t+1}^{(i)} \propto w_t^{(i)} P(y_{t+1}|x_{t+1}^{(i)}).$$

Weights are normalized at each step. Multinomial resampling is performed when the effective sample size falls below a predefined threshold.

Sequential Monte Carlo methods provide flexible inference for nonlinear and non-Gaussian state-space models [17, 18]. In the present setting, they enable integration of institutional transition regularities with sparse and noisy observations. The particle filtering approach follows a standard bootstrap formulation and is used here as a general inference mechanism within the proposed modeling framework.

Reconstruction Output. The reconstructed trajectory is obtained using the maximum a posteriori (MAP) state estimate at each time step. At each time step, the estimated state corresponds to the department with the highest total posterior weight across the particle ensemble, effectively selecting the most probable state given the observations and transition dynamics. Formally,

$$\hat{x}_t = \underset{x \in S}{\operatorname{argmax}} \sum_{i=1}^{N} w_t^{(i)} 1\{x_t^{(i)} = x\},$$

where $1\{\cdot\}$ denotes the indicator function.

This corresponds to selecting, at each time step, the most probable department under the particle-based posterior approximation. Reconstruction accuracy is evaluated as the proportion of time steps for which the reconstructed department exactly matches the ground-truth department.

2.5   Experimental Design

MIS Part. Reconstruction performance is evaluated using per-time-step exact department match accuracy:

$$\text{Accuracy} = \frac{1}{\sum_i T_i} \sum_{i,t} \mathbf{1}\{\hat{x}_{i,t} = x_{i,t}\}$$

where $x_{i,t}$ denotes the true department at time t in episode i, $\hat{x}_{i,t}$ denotes the reconstructed estimate, and T_i is the episode length.

Transition probabilities are estimated from episodes in 2015–2018 (training set). Reconstruction is evaluated both in-sample (2015–2018) and out-of-sample (2019).

The primary experimental configuration uses stride $s = 4$, observation correctness $p_{correct} = 0.8$, and 500 particles. The parameter $p_{correct}$ represents the probability that an observed department label matches the true latent state and is used to control the level of observation noise.

In the absence of direct ground-truth estimates of observation reliability in MIS or BLE data, $p_{correct}$ was selected empirically to represent a moderate-noise regime. Values in the range 0.7–0.9 were explored during preliminary experiments and produced similar qualitative results, with 0.8 providing a representative balance between signal and noise. The reported performance trends were stable across this range, indicating that the conclusions are not sensitive to the exact choice of this parameter.

Sequential inference follows the particle filtering procedure described previously [16, 19]. Particle counts were selected to balance computational tractability and posterior stability; increasing particle number did not materially change accuracy estimates.

Reconstruction accuracy values are averaged over 500 randomly sampled evaluation episodes for each split. For particle filtering, results are further averaged over 10 independent runs with different random seeds. Reported means reflect aggregate performance across episodes; variability across episodes was comparable across models and did not affect relative performance ranking.

BLE Localization. Localization performance is evaluated on multiple controlled walking trajectories recorded on the same hospital floor. Ground truth is represented as a trajectory polyline aligned with the floor plan. Each evaluation trajectory was recorded using five independent devices, and reported errors correspond to averages across devices.

Two inference pipelines are compared. The baseline uses k-nearest neighbors (KNN) fingerprinting with $k = 6$, assigning positions based on similarity between observed RSSI vectors and the radio map. The sequential approach applies a particle filter with $N = 1000$ particles, sampling interval $\Delta t = 10$ s, and motion velocity parameter $v = 1.5$ m/s. Particle propagation follows a bounded-motion model, and importance weights are computed from RSSI consistency with the fingerprint radio map.

To ensure physically valid trajectories, topology constraints are incorporated into the particle filter. Particles are restricted to accessible indoor areas, preventing wall crossings, and motion feasibility is evaluated using shortest-path distances on the floor graph computed via Dijkstra's algorithm. Consequently, spatial propagation respects navigable indoor routes rather than straight-line Euclidean distances.

Localization accuracy is measured as the mean Euclidean distance between estimated positions and the ground-truth trajectory polyline at each timestamp, consistent with the evaluation protocol described in prior work [8, 9]. The objective of this experimental design is not to introduce a new localization algorithm, but to quantify observation variability and to evaluate the effect of sequential filtering under realistic sensor noise conditions.

3   Results

3.1   Department-Level Reconstruction

Baseline Comparison. Table 1 summarizes reconstruction accuracy under the primary configuration. The comparison isolates three effects: observation-only inference, structural modeling without assimilation, and sequential data assimilation. The largest improvement is obtained when structural transitions are combined with sequential particle filtering.

Table 1. Reconstruction accuracy (stride $= 4$, $p_{\text{correct}} = 0.8$)

Model	Train ($\leq$2018)	Test (2019)
OBS (observation only)	0.274	0.289
ABM (first-order rollout)	0.402	0.408
PF (first-order)	0.551	0.503
PF (second-order)	0.547	0.518

Comparing OBS and ABM isolates the effect of structural transition modeling without assimilation. Model-only rollout improves reconstruction accuracy from 0.274 to 0.402 in the training period and from 0.289 to 0.408 in the test period.

Sequential assimilation yields the largest gains. In training, first-order particle filtering improves accuracy from 0.402 to 0.551. Out-of-sample, accuracy increases from 0.408 to 0.503 (first-order) and to 0.518 (second-order). Gains grow with larger stride values.

The first- and second-order formulations show comparable performance in training, with a modest out-of-sample advantage for the second-order model (0.518 vs 0.503).

Variability across evaluation episodes was comparable across models (standard deviation approximately 0.23–0.25) and did not alter the observed performance ordering.

3.2 Localization Accuracy

Table 2 reports mean localization error (m) for representative trajectories.

Table 2. Mean localization error (meters)

Session	Path	KNN (mean)	PF (mean)
Eval A	1	0.82	0.76
Eval A	2	0.52	0.79
Eval A	3	1.20	1.18
Eval B	1	0.82	0.39
Eval B	2	1.00	0.81
Eval B	3	8.06	8.15

Two distinct behaviors emerge. For several trajectories (e.g., Eval B, Path 1), particle filtering substantially improves localization accuracy, reducing mean error from 0.82 m to 0.39 m by mitigating stochastic RSSI fluctuations and producing smoother, topology-consistent trajectories.

In contrast, in Eval B, Path 3, both KNN and PF exhibit large errors ($\approx$8 m), indicating systematic calibration mismatch rather than stochastic noise. In such cases, filtering does not yield improvement.

Figure 3 illustrates these behaviors: PF closely follows the ground truth in the improvement case, while both methods deviate substantially in the failure case, showing that filtering cannot compensate for structural bias in the observation model.

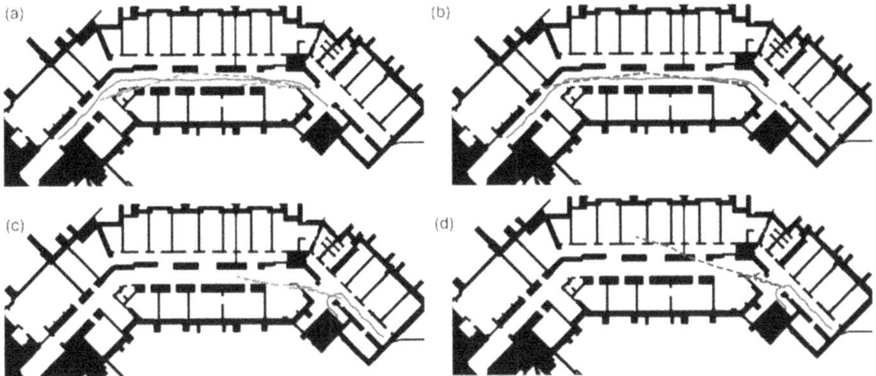

Fig. 3. Representative BLE localization trajectories. (a) KNN vs ground truth for the improvement case (Eval B, Path 1). (b) Particle filter vs ground truth for the same trajectory. (c) KNN vs ground truth for the failure case (Eval B, Path 3). (d) Particle filter vs ground truth for the same trajectory. Ground truth trajectories are shown in green; KNN estimates are shown as red dashed lines; particle filter estimates are shown in blue.

4   Discussion

This study models daily cardiology care pathways as partially observed dynamical systems. Instead of treating hospital event logs as complete representations of patient trajectories, department transitions are interpreted as latent states evolving under learned institutional transition regularities. The task therefore shifts from descriptive sequence analysis to probabilistic state inference under uncertainty.

The results indicate that structural transition modeling alone improves reconstruction relative to direct use of sparse and noisy observations, demonstrating that department flows exhibit statistically stable patterns rather than arbitrary sequencing. More importantly, sequential data assimilation yields the largest gains in both in-sample and temporally held-out evaluation. Together, these findings support modeling healthcare pathways as structured stochastic processes whose latent dynamics can be systematically exploited for probabilistic reconstruction. From a computational perspective, this illustrates that state-space modeling and sequential inference methods, traditionally applied in physical systems, transfer effectively to organizational settings characterized by discrete and partially informative observations.

Across all evaluated configurations, the principal improvement arises from sequential integration of observations with the learned transition prior. The particle filter combines institutional structure with partial evidence to approximate posterior trajectory distributions that consistently outperform both observation-only inference and model-only rollout. The persistence of gains in the temporally held-out 2019 data indicates that learned transition tendencies retain predictive value beyond the training period, suggesting gradual institutional evolution rather than rapid structural drift.

The comparison between first- and second-order transition models further clarifies the source of improvement. While incorporating short-term memory yields only modest additional benefit, the dominant effect stems from probabilistic state estimation itself. Assimilation—rather than increased transition order—constitutes the primary methodological mechanism driving reconstruction performance.

The BLE localization experiments provide a complementary perspective on observation reliability within the same institutional environment. Even under topology-aware particle propagation and graph-based motion constraints, localization accuracy varies across sessions. Sequential filtering reduces stochastic RSSI fluctuations but fails under systematic calibration mismatch, illustrating a general property of Bayesian state estimation: filtering mitigates random noise but cannot correct structural bias or misspecified likelihood models. This behavior parallels the department-level reconstruction problem. MIS event records, like RSSI measurements, provide indirect and imperfect proxies of the underlying state, potentially affected by delayed entries, aggregation effects, or partial transition visibility. Structural transition models combined with sequential assimilation stabilize inference when uncertainty is predominantly stochastic, yet remain sensitive to systematic distortions in the observation process. The BLE analysis therefore reinforces the broader modeling principle of this work: healthcare pathways can be treated as partially observed dynamical systems, and probabilistic assimilation yields measurable benefits when observational noise is stochastic rather than structurally biased.

From an operational perspective, improved reconstruction of care pathways enables more reliable analysis of patient flow from incomplete event data. By recovering latent department transitions, the approach supports identification of bottlenecks and atypical routing patterns, informing workflow optimization and resource allocation. It may also support online monitoring of patient trajectories under uncertainty.

4.1 Limitations and Future Work

Several limitations warrant consideration. First, the transition model is frequency-based and assumes stationarity over the training period. Although temporal holdout results indicate stability, substantial workflow changes could reduce predictive performance. Adaptive or time-varying transition estimation may address this limitation.

Second, the department-level observation model uses a controlled stride-based corruption mechanism. Real hospital event noise may exhibit structured temporal dependencies or department-specific biases not captured in this abstraction.

Third, BLE experiments were conducted on a single hospital floor and are intended to illustrate modeling principles rather than provide a comprehensive localization study.

Future work may explore adaptive transition modeling under evolving institutional dynamics, richer observation likelihoods derived directly from raw MIS event characteristics, and multi-scale assimilation frameworks that integrate physical localization and departmental state modeling within a unified inference architecture.

5 Conclusion

This study formulates daily ambulatory cardiology care pathways as partially observed stochastic processes and demonstrates that probabilistic data assimilation substantially improves reconstruction of department trajectories under sparse and noisy observations.

Department dynamics are modeled using data-driven first- and second-order Markov transitions learned from multi-year hospital data, and latent trajectories are inferred through particle filtering within a discrete-time state-space framework.

Across both in-sample and temporally held-out evaluation, sequential assimilation consistently outperforms observation-only inference and model-only rollout. Higher-order transition memory yields only modest additional benefit; the primary improvement arises from integrating structural transition priors with partial observations via Sequential Monte Carlo inference. Temporal holdout results further indicate that learned transition dynamics retain predictive value beyond the training period, supporting the interpretation of healthcare pathways as structured stochastic processes rather than arbitrary event sequences.

Complementary BLE localization experiments provide a physical-layer validation of the same principle. Filtering mitigates stochastic observation noise but cannot compensate for systematic calibration bias, mirroring the department-level setting. Assimilation therefore enhances reconstruction when uncertainty is primarily stochastic, while remaining sensitive to model misspecification.

Overall, the results show that state-space modeling and particle-based data assimilation extend naturally to institutional and healthcare systems characterized by partial observability. When structured transition dynamics are present, probabilistic assimilation provides a principled and computationally tractable framework for reconstructing latent process trajectories.

Future work may investigate adaptive transition estimation under evolving workflows, richer observation models derived directly from MIS event characteristics, and multi-scale assimilation strategies integrating physical and departmental state representations.

Acknowledgments. The research was supported by The Russian Science Foundation, agreement №24-11-00272, https://rscf.ru/project/24-11-00272/.

References

1. Kalman, R.E.: A new approach to linear filtering and prediction problems. J. Basic Eng. **82**(1), 35–45 (1960)
2. Evensen, G.: Data Assimilation: The Ensemble Kalman Filter. Springer, Cham (2009). https://doi.org/10.1007/978-3-642-03711-5
3. Doucet, A., de Freitas, N., Gordon, N. (eds.): Sequential Monte Carlo Methods in Practice. Springer, Cham (2001). https://doi.org/10.1007/978-1-4757-3437-9
4. van der Aalst, W.M.P.: Process Mining: Data Science in Action, 2nd edn. Springer, Cham (2016). https://doi.org/10.1007/978-3-662-49851-4
5. Rojas, E., Muñoz-Gama, J., Sepúlveda, M., Capurro, D.: Process mining in healthcare: a literature review. J. Biomed. Inform. **61**, 224–236 (2016)
6. Sonnenberg, F.A., Beck, J.R.: Markov models in medical decision making: a practical guide. Med. Decis. Making **13**(4), 322–338 (1993)
7. Arulampalam, M.S., Maskell, S., Gordon, N., Clapp, T.: A tutorial on particle filters for online nonlinear/non-gaussian bayesian tracking. IEEE Trans. Sig. Process. **50**(2), 174–188 (2002)

8. Prins, C.: Advancing healthcare navigation: indoor localization in hospitals using fingerprinting and particle filters. Master's thesis, University of Amsterdam (2024)
9. Vlasenko, V., Balakhontceva, M.: Implementation of indoor positioning methods: virtual hospital case. Procedia Comput. Sci. **193**, 183–189 (2021)
10. Ching, W.-K., Ng, M.K.: Markov Chains: Models, Algorithms and Applications. Springer, New York (2006). https://doi.org/10.1007/0-387-29337-X
11. Hripcsak, G., Albers, D.J.: Next-generation phenotyping of electronic health records. J. Am. Med. Inform. Assoc. **20**(1), 117–121 (2013)
12. Bishop, C.M.: Pattern Recognition and Machine Learning. Springer, New York (2006)
13. Bzdok, D., Meyer-Lindenberg, A.: Machine learning for precision psychiatry: opportunities and challenges. Biol. Psychiatr. Cogn. Neurosci. Neuroimaging **3**(3), 223–230 (2018)
14. Puterman, M.L.: Markov Decision Processes: Discrete Stochastic Dynamic Programming. Wiley, New York (1994)
15. Cappé, O., Moulines, E., Rydén, T.: Inference in Hidden Markov Models. Springer, New York (2005). https://doi.org/10.1007/0-387-28982-8
16. Doucet, A., Johansen, A.M.: A tutorial on particle filtering and smoothing: fifteen years later. J. Stat. Softw. **30**(12), 1–41 (2009)
17. Kantas, N., Doucet, A., Singh, S.S., Maciejowski, J., Chopin, N.: On particle methods for parameter estimation in state-space models. Stat. Sci. **30**(3), 328–351 (2015)
18. Naesseth, C.A., Lindsten, F., Schön, T.B.: Elements of sequential Monte Carlo. Found. Trends Mach. Learn. **12**(3), 307–392 (2019)
19. Chopin, N., Papaspiliopoulos, O.: An Introduction to Sequential Monte Carlo. Springer, Cham (2020). https://doi.org/10.1007/978-3-030-47845-2
20. Särkkä, S.: Bayesian Filtering and Smoothing. Cambridge University Press, Cambridge (2013)

Comparative Study of Linear Attention Architectures for Geopotential Height Forecasting

Varuni Sastry$^{(\boxtimes)}$ and Vishwas Rao

Argonne National Laboratory, Lemont, USA
`{vsastry,vhebbur}@anl.gov`

Abstract. Accurate forecasting of geopotential height is crucial for numerical weather prediction and climate modeling. While transformer-based models have shown promising results, their quadratic computational complexity in sequence length limits their scalability to long temporal contexts. In this work, we present a comprehensive comparison of linear attention architectures—including Gated Linear Attention (GLA), DeltaNet, Gated DeltaNet, Kimi Delta Attention (KDA), and Mamba2—for geopotential height forecasting on NCEP reanalysis data. We evaluate these architectures against full-attention transformers in terms of forecasting accuracy, computational efficiency, and memory usage. Our experiments demonstrate that linear attention mechanisms achieve competitive forecasting performance while offering significant computational advantages for processing long temporal sequences.

Keywords: Linear Attention · Weather Forecasting · Geopotential Height · State Space Models · Deep Learning

1 Introduction

Geopotential height, is a fundamental variable in atmospheric science, representing the height of a pressure surface above mean sea level and serving as a critical indicator for weather forecasting [6]. Accurate prediction of geopotential height fields enables identification of synoptic-scale features such as troughs, ridges, and jet streams, that influence surface weather. Traditional numerical weather prediction (NWP) solves complex partial differential equations governing atmospheric dynamics, requires substantial compute and careful parameterization of sub-grid processes [1].

Recent advances in deep learning have demonstrated that data-driven approaches can achieve competitive forecasting skill while significantly reducing computational costs at inference time [2,9,15]. Among these approaches, transformer architectures [20] have emerged as a powerful paradigm for modeling spatio-temporal dependencies in weather data. However, the self-attention mechanism's $\mathcal{O}(n^2)$ complexity with respect to sequence length poses significant

© The Author(s), under exclusive license to Springer Nature Switzerland AG 2026
M. Paszynski et al. (Eds.): ICCS 2026 Workshops, LNCS 16788, pp. 151–165, 2026.
https://doi.org/10.1007/978-3-032-29915-4_13

challenges for capturing long-range temporal dependencies inherent in atmospheric processes.

Linear attention mechanisms offer a promising solution to this scalability challenge by reducing the complexity to $\mathcal{O}(n)$, enabling efficient processing of longer sequences [8]. Recent innovations in this space include Gated Linear Attention (GLA) [22], which introduces data-dependent decay with gating mechanisms; DeltaNet [18] and its variant Gated-DeltaNet [21], which applies the delta rule from associative memory; Mamba-2 evolves from the original Mamba state space model by simplifying and restructuring the state dynamics computation introducing scalar identities and head dimensions, making it both algorithmically and hardware-efficient [3,4]. Most recently, Moonshot AI introduced Kimi Delta Attention (KDA) [27], which combines channel-wise gating with hardware-aware chunked recurrence for improved efficiency.

In this paper, we present a systematic comparison of the linear attention architectures-namely, GLA, DeltaNet, Gated-DeltaNet, Mamba2, and KDA architectures for geopotential height forecasting using NCEP reanalysis data, a standard benchmark for long-range atmospheric variability and forecast evaluation. Its temporal coverage (1948-present) and consistent data assimilation make it well-suited for training and comparing data-driven forecasting models. Our key contributions are:

1. A comprehensive benchmark comparing six attention based model architectures (Transformer, GLA, DeltaNet, Gated DeltaNet, Mamba2, and KDA) for geopotential height forecasting, including measuring forecasting skill (root mean square error), computational throughput, and memory consumption.
2. Adapting an open-source training framework, FLAME, built on Torchtitan [17] with specialized support for linear attention models, enabling reproducible research in weather forecasting.

The remainder of the paper is organized as follows. Section 2 reviews prior work in weather forecasting and efficient attention mechanisms. Section 3 describes the problem formulation, model architecture, and training objective. Section 4 details the dataset, training configurations, and evaluation metrics. Section 5 presents forecasting accuracy and computational scaling results, and Sect. 6 discusses the main findings and implications. We conclude in Sect. 7.

2   Related Work

2.1   Machine Learning for Weather Forecasting

The application of deep learning to weather forecasting has accelerated rapidly in recent years. FourCastNet [15] demonstrated that vision transformers with Fourier neural operators could achieve competitive global forecasts. A 3D Earth-specific transformer was introduced in Pangu-Weather [2] and GraphCast [9] formulated forecasting as message passing on a multi-scale mesh. GenCast [16] a diffusion-based probabilistic model is the current state-of-the-art in data-driven medium-range prediction. ClimaX [12], Stormer [13] are transformer based models used for weather forecasting research. Most of these approaches predominantly rely on transformer architectures with standard softmax attention. While effective, the quadratic complexity limits their ability to process very long temporal sequences or high-resolution spatial data without resorting to windowed attention or other approximations [10] [19]. Our work explores how linear attention mechanisms can maintain forecasting accuracy while overcoming these computational limitations.

2.2   Linear Attention Mechanisms

Linear attention replaces the softmax normalization in standard attention with feature maps, enabling a recurrent formulation with linear complexity [8]. Given queries Q, keys K, and values V, standard attention computes

$$\mathrm{Attn}(Q, K, V) = \mathrm{softmax}\left(\frac{QK^\top}{\sqrt{d}}\right) V, \tag{1}$$

whereas linear attention applies feature maps $\phi(\cdot)$ to obtain

$$\mathrm{LinAttn}(Q, K, V) = \phi(Q)\big(\phi(K)^\top V\big). \tag{2}$$

State Space Models (SSMs) provide an alternative linear-time formulation for sequence modeling [5]. Mamba introduces selective state updates with input-dependent parameters [4], and **Mamba2** further refines this formulation by establishing a duality between selective SSMs and structured attention [3]. Under this view, the state update can be written as

$$S_t = \alpha_t S_{t-1} + \beta_t k_t v_t^\top, \tag{3}$$

where past state information is selectively decayed and updated using current inputs.

Gated Linear Attention (GLA) [22] extends linear attention by introducing fine-grained, channel-wise decay. The recurrent state update is given by

$$S_t = \mathrm{Diag}(\alpha_t) S_{t-1} + k_t v_t^\top, \tag{4}$$

DeltaNet [18] introduces error-correcting learning via the classical delta rule. By minimizing the squared prediction error, the state update becomes

$$S_t = S_{t-1} + \beta_t k_t \big(v_t - S_{t-1}^\top k_t\big)^\top, \tag{5}$$

which improves stability and long-term credit assignment.

Gated DeltaNet (GDN) [21] combines the delta rule with selective decay inspired by Mamba-style updates, extending DeltaNet with input-dependent forgetting.. Performing stochastic gradient descent on a decayed state yields

$$S_t = \big(I - \beta_t k_t k_t^\top\big) \alpha_t S_{t-1} + \beta_t k_t v_t^\top, \tag{6}$$

integrating error correction with input-dependent forgetting.

Kimi Delta Attention (KDA) [27] further generalizes GDN by introducing channel-wise decay within the delta-rule framework. The resulting update is

$$S_t = (I - \beta_t k_t k_t^\top)\,\mathrm{Diag}(\alpha_t)S_{t-1} + \beta_t k_t v_t^\top, \tag{7}$$

providing a unified optimization-based perspective on linear attention, selective SSMs, and delta-rule learning.

2.3   Geopotential Height and Atmospheric Dynamics

Geopotential height measures the height of a constant-pressure surface above mean sea level, weighted by gravitational acceleration. It encodes the thermal structure of the atmosphere: warm columns expand and raise pressure surfaces, while cold columns contract and lower them. We focus on the $500\,\mathrm{hPa}$ level (Z500) because it is a standard benchmark for evaluating weather forecast quality. Unlike fields such as humidity or precipitation, Z500 exhibits smooth spatial gradients and is largely independent of local surface conditions such as topography, yet it retains the important global flow features—including midlatitude jets and the pole-to-equator geopotential gradient—that characterize large-scale atmospheric circulation [6,11].

3   Methods

3.1   Problem Formulation

We formulate geopotential height forecasting as a sequence-to-sequence regression problem. Given a sequence of T_{in} input frames $X = \{x_1, x_2, \ldots, x_{T_{in}}\}$ where each frame $x_t \in \mathbb{R}^{C \times H \times W}$ represents geopotential height at C pressure levels on a latitude-longitude grid of size $H \times W$, the goal is to predict the next T_{out} frames $Y = \{y_1, y_2, \ldots, y_{T_{out}}\}$.

3.2   Model Architecture

We adopt a unified architecture framework that wraps different attention backbones (Fig. 1). The architecture consists of three components:

Input Projection: Each input frame is flattened and projected to the model's hidden dimension:

$$h_t^{(0)} = W_{proj}[\mathrm{flatten}(x_t)] + b_{proj} \tag{8}$$

where $W_{proj} \in \mathbb{R}^{d_{model} \times (C \cdot H \cdot W)}$.

Sequence Backbone: The projected sequence is processed by L layers of the attention mechanism under evaluation (Transformer, GLA, Gated DeltaNet, KDA, Mamba2, or DeltaNet):

$$h^{(l)} = \mathrm{Layer}^{(l)}(h^{(l-1)}), \quad l = 1, \ldots, L \tag{9}$$

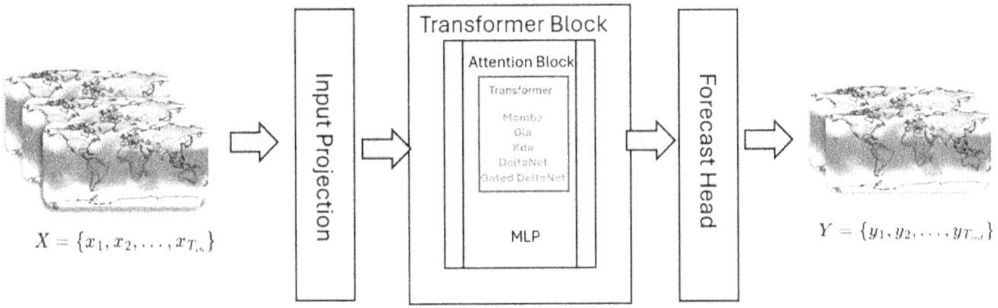

Fig. 1. Unified model architecture for geopotential height forecasting. The attention backbone is interchangeable, enabling fair comparison across mechanisms.

Forecast Head: The final hidden state is mapped to the output prediction:

$$\hat{Y} = \text{reshape}(W_{head}h_{T_{in}}^{(L)} + b_{head}) \tag{10}$$

where $W_{head} \in \mathbb{R}^{(T_{out} \cdot C \cdot H \cdot W) \times d_{model}}$.

3.3 Training Objective

We minimize the mean squared error between predictions and ground truth:

$$\mathcal{L} = \frac{1}{T_{out} \cdot C \cdot H \cdot W} \sum_{t=1}^{T_{out}} \|y_t - \hat{y}_t\|_2^2 \tag{11}$$

Data is normalized per-level using pre-computed statistics from the training set:

$$\tilde{x}_t^{(c)} = \frac{x_t^{(c)} - \mu^{(c)}}{\sigma^{(c)}} \tag{12}$$

where $\mu^{(c)}$ and $\sigma^{(c)}$ are the mean and standard deviation for pressure level c.

4 Experimental Setup

4.1 Dataset

We use NCEP/NCAR Reanalysis 1 geopotential height data [7], which provides 6-hourly global atmospheric fields from 1948 to present. The dataset is on a $2.5° \times 2.5°$ latitude–longitude grid (73×144 points) with 17 pressure levels spanning

Table 1. Normalization statistics for geopotential height at selected pressure levels.

Level (hPa)	Mean (m)	Std (m)	Min (m)	Max (m)
500	5,509.7	343.3	4,369.0	6,063.0

1000–10 hPa; unless otherwise stated, we report results at 500 hPa, a standard benchmark level in meteorology. We use 6-hourly snapshots with a chronological 90%/10% train–validation split. Table 1 summarizes the normalization statistics for selected pressure levels.

4.2   Model Configurations

To ensure a fair comparison, all models are configured to approximately 340M parameters (Table 2), with architecture-specific hyperparameters set following published recommendations; all configuration files are released in our GitHub repository. The transformer applies Rotary Position Embeddings (RoPE), while the linear attention variants do not use explicit positional encoding in their recurrent layers, and Mamba2 encodes ordering implicitly through its state-space recurrence. Unless otherwise noted, evaluations use a 48-hour lead time. For throughput and memory benchmarking, we report performance on a single-step output (6-hour lead). For baseline comparisons against persistence and climatology, we use a 24-hour horizon with $T_{out} = 4$ and report per-timestep errors at $t0$–$t3$ (corresponding to 6, 12, 18, and 24 h).

Table 2. Model configurations for the architecture comparison. All models have approximately 340M parameters.

Model	Layers	Hidden	Heads	Head Dim	Params
Transformer	24	1024	16	64	~340M
GLA	24	1024	4	256	~340M
Gated DeltaNet	21	1024	6	256	~340M
DeltaNet	24	1024	8	128	~340M
Mamba2	48	1024	–	64	~340M
KDA	21	1024	6	256	~340M

4.3   Training Configuration

All models are trained using the FLAME framework with consistent hyperparameters as listed in (Table 3). The model implementations are available in [24]. Training runs were executed on the Polaris system at the Argonne Leadership Computing Facility using 2 nodes. Each node provides 4 NVIDIA A100 GPUs (connected via NVLink) with 40 GB of HBM per GPU. We use all 8 GPUs in total for distributed training using the TorchTitan framework for each model. We flatten the spatial grid is flattened to a 10,512-dimensional feature vector $(C \times H \times W)$ per timestep, and the data is normalized with precomputed statistics for the pressure level considered.

Table 3. Training configuration for geopotential height forecasting.

Parameter	Value
Pressure level	500 hPa
Input length (T_{in})	8 timesteps (48 h)
Target length (T_{out})	1–4 timesteps (6–24 h)
Global batch size	256
Optimizer	AdamW with $\beta_1 = 0.9$, $\beta_2 = 0.999$, $\epsilon = 10^{-15}$
Learning rate	3×10^{-4} with cosine decay
Warmup steps	1,024
Total training steps	5,000
Gradient clipping	Max norm 1.0
Precision	Mixed precision (bfloat16)

4.4   Evaluation Metrics

Model Performance Metrics We evaluate model training and validation using standard meteorological metrics for a given batch of data. In all our analysis we average the metrics over a consistent batch of 256 samples: Root Mean Square Error (RMSE):

$$\text{RMSE} = \sqrt{\frac{1}{N} \sum_{i=1}^{N} (y_i - \hat{y}_i)^2} \tag{13}$$

where y_i is the true, observed value for the i-th data point in the dataset, and $\hat{y}_i$ is the value predicted by the model corresponding to the i-th data point.

Computational Metrics: We report training throughput in tokens/second, measured as the effective processed tokens per second across all GPUs, to capture end-to-end training efficiency. Peak GPU memory usage (GB) is recorded during the forward/backward pass to quantify the memory footprint at each sequence length. Inference latency is reported in milliseconds per sample and averaged over multiple batches with synchronized timing to reflect steady-state deployment performance.

Baselines Metrics: To contextualize model performance, we include two simple baselines that bracket short-term continuity and long-term mean behavior. Persistence predicts the last input frame and tests whether a model adds skill beyond trivial temporal extrapolation ($\hat{y}_t = x_{T_{in}}$); climatology predicts the per-batch mean field and provides a no-skill reference in anomaly space ($\hat{y}_t = \bar{y}$).

5   Results

We summarize forecasting performance, training dynamics, and efficiency across attention backbones. We present the accuracy comparison at 24-h lead time, analyze forecast-horizon behavior using per-timestep errors, and finally report throughput and memory scaling at long sequence lengths.

5.1   Model Comparison

Table 4 presents the forecasting performance of all architectures at 6-h lead time on 500 hPa geopotential height data. For model evaluation, we train each model for 5,000 steps and evaluate on the validation dataset every 20 steps. The early training curves (Fig. 2) indicate rapid convergence within the first 200–500 steps, with linear attention variants typically reaching lower evaluation loss earlier than the Transformer. By step 5,000, linear attention models achieve the strongest validation loss and ACC; GLA and DeltaNet yield the lowest validation losses (0.003550 and 0.003559) and the highest ACC values (0.920441 and 0.920416). Mamba2 and Gated DeltaNet remain competitive in training RMSE with slightly lower ACC. The Transformer shows earlier signs of overfitting, with its validation loss and ACC lagging behind despite continued training. Throughput and memory remain in the same operating regime across models at this step, with Gated DeltaNet and KDA exhibiting higher TFLOPS but also the largest memory footprints.

Figure 3 and 4 show GLA forecasts at step 5000 for training and validation samples. The predicted fields capture the large-scale geopotential height patterns with coherent gradients, and the validation example exhibits similar structure to the training case, suggesting good generalization at this training stage. Other models are show very comparable forecasts at this time step .

Table 4. Snapshot metrics at step 5000.

Model	Tr. RMSE	Val loss	Val ACC	Tokens/s	TFLOPS	Mem(GB)
Transformer	4.4e−2	6.3e−3	0.879579	31,980	95.19	4.28
GLA	4.1e−2	3.6e−3	0.920441	31,213	93.02	4.26
GDN	3.6e−2	4.2e−3	0.911715	29,313	109.32	5.91
DeltaNet	3.8e−2	3.6e−3	0.920416	31,875	94.97	4.31
Mamba2	3.6e−2	4.8e−3	0.903341	30,261	109.89	4.38
KDA	3.7e−2	3.8e−3	0.920187	26,247	98.74	5.92

5.2   Forecast Horizon Analysis

At a 24h lead time ($T_{out} = 4$), climatology yields $ACC \approx 0$ and high $RMSE \approx 118$m, reflecting its inability to capture day-scale variability once the mean field is removed. Persistence is substantially stronger at short horizons, achieving $RMSE \approx 63.6$m and $ACC \approx 0.826$, which is expected given the strong temporal autocorrelation of geopotential height. However, persistence

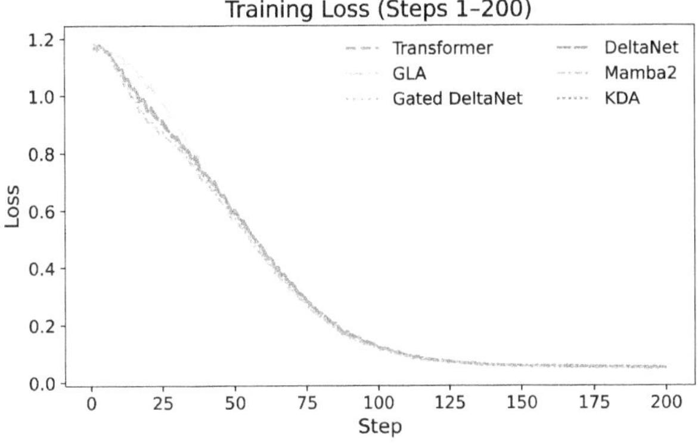

(a) Training loss (steps 1–200).

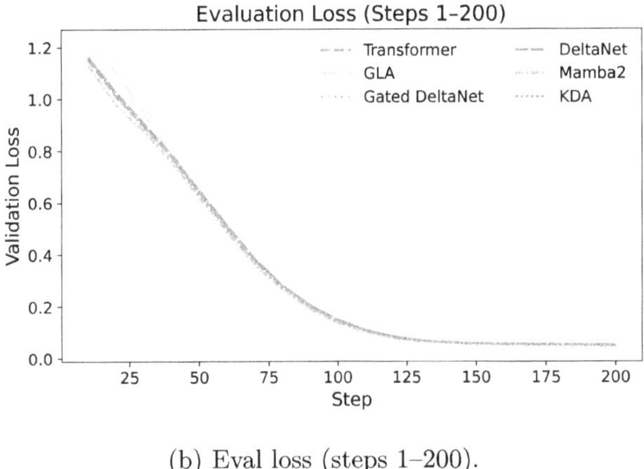

(b) Eval loss (steps 1–200).

Fig. 2. Training and evaluation loss on HGT over the first 200 steps for Transformer, GLA, DeltaNet, Gated DeltaNet, KDA, and Mamba2.

errors increase rapidly with forecast horizon. Per-timestep RMSE at step 5000 shows that persistence is best at the first step ($t0 = 31.6\,\mathrm{m}$) but degrades sharply by $t3 = 85.3\,\mathrm{m}$. In contrast, both the full-scale attention transformer model and linear attention models (shown with an example of GLA) maintain lower errors at longer horizons, with GLA consistently outperforming transformer across all four steps (e.g., $t3$: $59.2\,\mathrm{m}$ vs $66.6\,\mathrm{m}$) and exhibiting higher anomaly correlation ($ACC \approx 0.873$ vs 0.826). Together, these comparisons indicate that linear attention models—particularly GLA—learn temporal dynamics beyond last-frame copying, yielding improved multi-step forecasts at day-scale lead times Fig. 5.

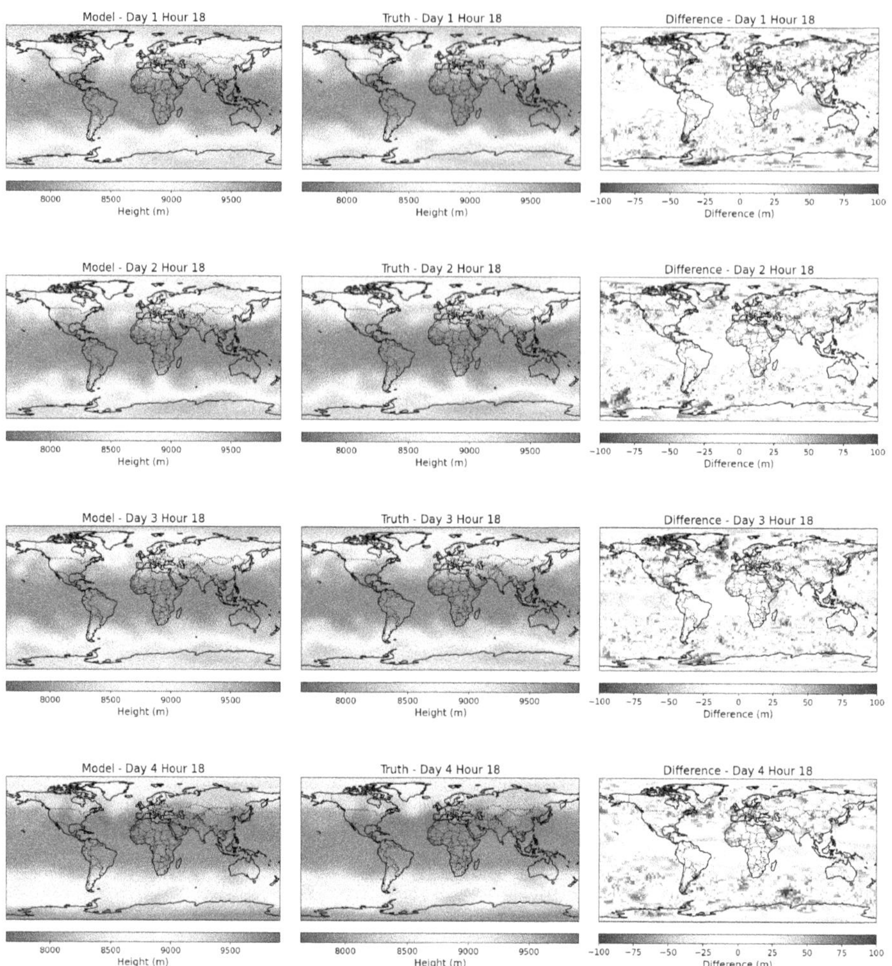

Fig. 3. Train forecast at step 5000.

5.3   Computational Efficiency

The throughput and memory scaling results as shown in Fig. 6 are measured at sequence lengths 16, 128, 1K, and 16K. Across all models, tokens/sec increases with sequence length, reflecting higher token throughput per optimization step as the sequence grows. At 16K, linear attention models such as GLA and DeltaNet show higher token throughput than the standard Transformer (21.1k vs 18.0k tokens/s, a 17% improvement), while Mamba2 is lower (15% below Transformer). Memory trends are more discriminative: at 16K, the Transformer reaches 16.28 GiB, whereas Mamba2 uses 11.35 GiB (about 30% lower), and DeltaNet remains similarly low at 11.87 GiB. These results indicate that linear attention variants can sustain higher long-sequence throughput while also

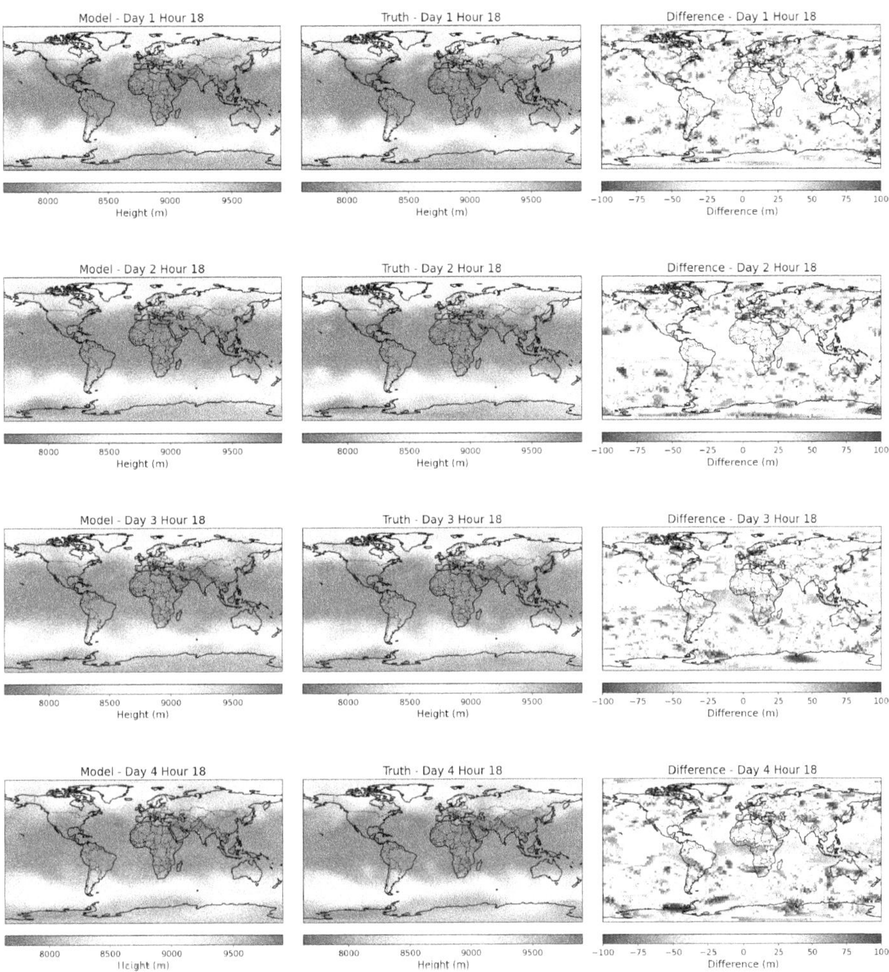

Fig. 4. Validation forecast at step 5000.

reducing peak memory at large context lengths.

At an extended context length of 131K with tensor parallelism $= 16$, GLA achieves higher throughput (2,030 vs 1,906 tokens/s) than the full-attention Transformer, with a modest increase in memory footprint (32.09 GiB vs 26.25 GiB), indicating that GLA sustains better long-context throughput. The higher memory usage stems from GLA's gated linear attention design, which adds extra projection and gating paths (e.g., additional $q/k/v/g$ projections and gating normalization), increasing activation and intermediate buffer memory. At moderate lengths, the Transformer's quadratic attention activations dominate total memory, so the extra GLA activations are comparatively less significant.

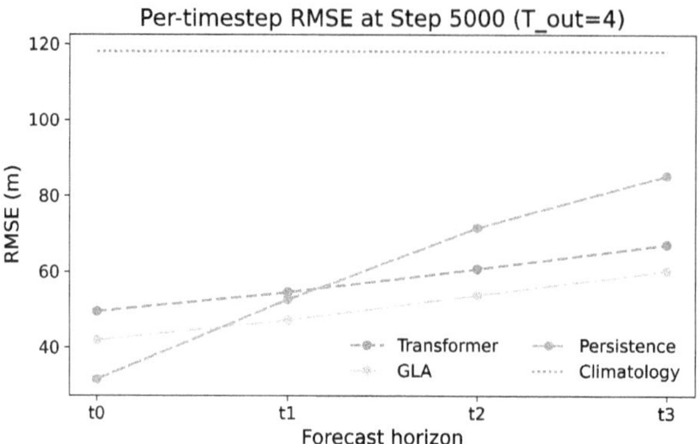

Fig. 5. Per-timestep RMSE at step 5000 for $T_{out} = 4$, comparing Transformer, GLA, persistence, and climatology.

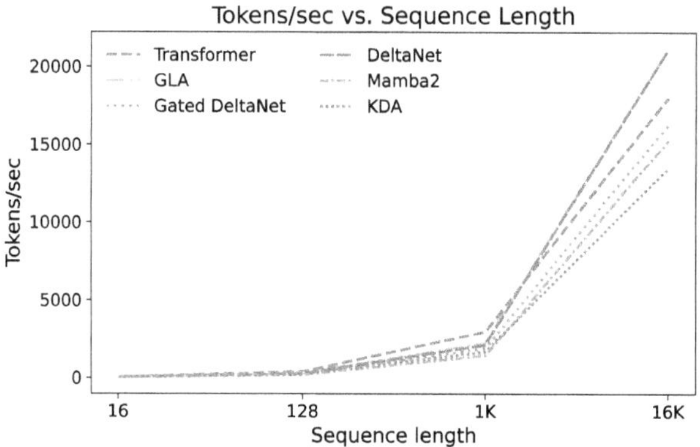

(a) Tokens/sec vs. sequence length.

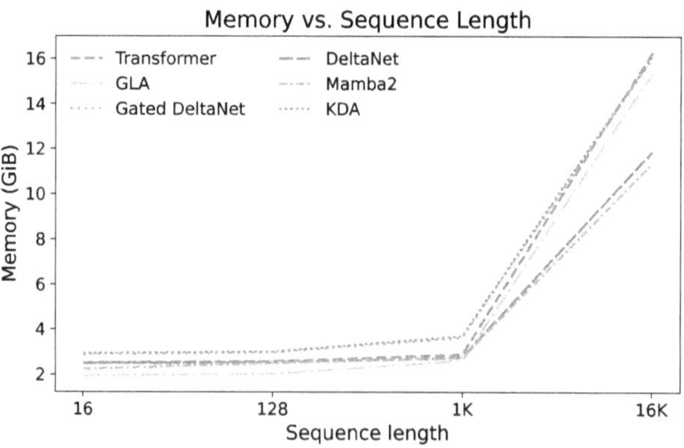

(b) Memory vs. sequence length.

Fig. 6. Throughput and memory scaling at sequence lengths 16, 128, 1K and 16K.

At extremely long sequences and high tensor parallel degree, however, those additional gating buffers—combined with a less-optimized TP implementation for GLA—can outweigh the Transformer's advantage, leading to higher measured memory. We expect this balance to shift with further sequence-length increases or with improved TP/fusion optimizations for GLA, revealing stronger memory advantages for linear attention at extreme contexts.

6 Discussion

Our results show that linear attention backbones can achieve competitive forecasting accuracy while scaling more effectively to long temporal contexts. The persistence baseline remains strong at short horizons, reflecting the inherent autocorrelation in geopotential height; nonetheless, linear attention models show clearer advantages as lead time increases, indicating learned dynamics beyond last-frame extrapolation. Among the linear variants, GLA consistently attains strong validation metrics, suggesting that gating and data-dependent decay help preserve useful long-range information. The scaling experiments reinforce that quadratic attention is the dominant bottleneck at long sequence lengths, whereas linear attention maintains higher throughput with a more gradual memory increase. At extreme contexts, some linear attention models still exhibit higher memory usage, which likely stems from model-parallel implementations that are not yet fully optimized. Overall, these trends support linear attention as a practical and scalable alternative to standard transformers for long-horizon atmospheric forecasting.

7 Conclusion

We presented a systematic comparison of linear attention architectures for geopotential height forecasting and bench-marked them against standard transformers on NCEP reanalysis data. The results indicate that linear attention models can match or improve forecasting quality while offering improved scalability at long sequence lengths, with GLA providing consistently strong validation performance. The FLAME framework enables reproducible training and evaluation of these models with distributed data parallelism and is released as open source to facilitate further research.

Limitations and Future Work: Our study focuses on single-variable forecasting at fixed spatial resolution and evaluates a limited set of lead times. Future work will extend to multivariate prediction, higher-resolution data, longer forecast horizons, and optimized parallel implementations for linear attention models.

Acknowledgments. This research used resources of the Argonne Leadership Computing Facility, which is a U.S. Department of Energy Office of Science User Facility operated under contract DE-AC02-06CH11357 and the work is supported by the Office of Science, U.S. Department of Energy, under contract DE-AC02-06CH11357.

References

1. Bauer, P., Thorpe, A., Brunet, G.: The quiet revolution of numerical weather prediction. Nature **525**(7567), 47–55 (2015)
2. Bi, K., Xie, L., Zhang, H., Chen, X., Gu, X., Tian, Q.: Accurate medium-range global weather forecasting with 3D neural networks. Nature **619**(7970) (2023)
3. Dao, T., Gu, A.: Transformers are SSMs: generalized models and efficient algorithms through structured state space duality (2024)
4. Gu, A., Dao, T.: Mamba: linear-time sequence modeling with selective state spaces. arXiv preprint arXiv:2312.00752 (2024)
5. Gu, A., Goel, K., Ré, C.: Efficiently modeling long sequences with structured state spaces. In: International Conference on Learning Representations (2022)
6. Holton, J.R., Hakim, G.J.: An Introduction to Dynamic Meteorology, 5th edn. Academic Press (2013)
7. Kalnay, E., et al.: The NCEP/NCAR 40-year reanalysis project. Bull. Am. Meteor. Soc. **77**(3), 437–472 (1996)
8. Katharopoulos, A., Vyas, A., Pappas, N., Fleuret, F.: Transformers are RNNs: Fast autoregressive transformers with linear attention. In: ICML. PMLR (2020)
9. Lam, R., et al.: Learning skillful medium-range global weather forecasting. Science **382**(6677), 1416–1421 (2023)
10. Liu, Z., et al.: Swin transformer: hierarchical vision transformer using shifted windows. In: Proceedings of the IEEE/CVF International Conference on Computer Vision (2021)
11. Maulik, R., et al.: Efficient high-dimensional variational data assimilation with machine-learned reduced-order models. Geosci. Model Dev. **15**(8), 3433–3445 (2022)
12. Nguyen, T., Brandstetter, J., Kapoor, A., Gupta, J.K., Grover, A.: ClimaX: a foundation model for weather and climate. In: ICML, PMLR (2023)
13. Nguyen, T., et al.: Scaling transformer neural networks for skillful and reliable medium-range weather forecasting (2024). https://arxiv.org/abs/2312.03876
14. Paszke, A., et al.: PyTorch: an imperative style, high-performance deep learning library. Adv. Neural. Inf. Process. Syst. **32** (2019)
15. Pathak, J., et al.: FourCastNet: a global data-driven high-resolution weather model using adaptive Fourier neural operators. arXiv preprint arXiv:2202.11214 (2022)
16. Price, I., etal.: Gencast: diffusion-based ensemble forecasting for medium-range weather (2024). https://arxiv.org/abs/2312.15796
17. PyTorch Team: TorchTitan: A native PyTorch library for large model training (2024). https://github.com/pytorch/torchtitan
18. Schlag, I., Irie, K., Schmidhuber, J.: Linear transformers are secretly fast weight programmers. In: ICML, pp. 9355–9366. PMLR (2021)
19. V., H., et al.: Aeris: argonne earth systems model for reliable and skillful predictions (2025). https://arxiv.org/abs/2509.13523
20. Vaswani, A., et al.: Attention is all you need. Adv. Neural Inf. Process. Syst. **30** (2017)
21. Yang, S., Kautz, J., Hatamizadeh, A.: Gated delta networks: improving mamba2 with delta rule. In: Proceedings of ICLR (2025)
22. Yang, S., Wang, B., Shen, Y., Panda, R., Kim, Y.: Gated linear attention transformers with hardware-efficient training. In: Proceedings of ICML (2024)
23. Yang, S., Wang, B., Zhang, Y., Shen, Y., Kim, Y.: Parallelizing linear transformers with the delta rule over sequence length. In: Proceedings of NeurIPS (2024)

24. Yang, S., Zhang, Y.: Fla: a triton-based library for hardware-efficient implementations of linear attention mechanism (2024). https://github.com/fla-org/flash-linear-attention
25. Zhang, Y., Yang, S.: Flame: flash language modeling made easy (2025). https://github.com/fla-org/flame
26. Zhang, Y., et al.: Gated slot attention for efficient linear-time sequence modeling. In: Proceedings of NeurIPS (2024)
27. Zhang, Y., et al.: Kimi linear: an expressive, efficient attention architecture (2025)

Data Assimilation with Surrogate Measurement Equations

Marco Arzeo[2] , Stefano Chessa[2] , Fabio Marcuzzi[1]([✉]) ,
Pietro Paglierani[2] , and Joao Alves[2]

[1] Department of Mathematics "Tullio Levi Civita", University of Padova,
Via Trieste 63, 35121 Padova, Italy
`marcuzzi@math.unipd.it`
[2] NATO STO Centre for Maritime Research and Experimentation, La Spezia, Italy
`pietro.paglierani@cmre.nato.int`

Abstract. Classical data-assimilation methods, like the Kalman Filter, and even most recent formulations, are model-based methods where it is assumed that the relation between the state-vector and the measurements can be expressed analytically up to a random error component. Here we refer to situations where the available analytical expression for the measurement equation is a surrogate of the true one, in the sense that the former approximates the latter with not negligible deterministic discrepancies. Moreover, the analytic expression of these discrepancies, if it exists, is presumed to be very unlikely to be found at a reasonable cost. We also assume that an accurate measurement equation exists for measurements that can be done only in laboratory experiments. The aim of this paper is to show that a Deep Kalman Filter can use a surrogate measurement equation to form the innovations and optimally estimate the state-vector, when the supervised learning of the corrector-gain matrices has been done using an accurate measurement equation (and corresponding data). The resulting method is trajectory-dependent, in principle, but can generalize to multiple trajectories. As a general test, we show some results with multiple abstract dynamical systems and measurement equations with additive piecewise-polynomial and/or trigonometric biases.

Keywords: Kalman filtering · Deep unfolding · surrogate measurements

1 Introduction

A current trend is the incorporation of machine learning (ML) in data assimilation, in various forms, see e.g. the recent review [5].

There is a common assumption in data-assimilation methods, i.e. that the measurement equation is accurate, and the ML effort is more concentrated, e.g. on using machine learning to map the joint predicted state and observation to the updated state estimate [3], to learn the dynamical error in the predictor [6,12] and/or to learn compression mechanisms for high-dimensional measurements [4].

M. Paszynski et al. (Eds.): ICCS 2026 Workshops, LNCS 16788, pp. 166–180, 2026.
https://doi.org/10.1007/978-3-032-29915-4_14

Here, instead, we leverage machine learning for adapting the data-assimilation algorithm to work with surrogate measurement equations that, otherwise, would deviate the state-trajectory estimate far from the real one. We will study this adaptation in the context of the Deep Kalman Filter (DKF) [6], which implements a predictor-corrector scheme similar to the Kalman Filter (KF), but the corrector gains are learned from data. Related approaches that combine Kalman-type filters with learned or surrogate observation operators have recently appeared in several application domains. For instance, in satellite data assimilation, machine-learning-based observation operators have been trained to emulate complex radiative-transfer models and associated bias-correction schemes, and then used within an ensemble Kalman filter without explicit access to the underlying physical measurement equation [13]. In robotics, the Koopman-Inspired Learned Observations Extended Kalman Filter (KILO-EKF) learns a measurement model for complex or poorly calibrated sensors by lifting raw measurements into a feature space where they are linearly related to the state, thereby enabling an EKF correction step driven by a data-driven observation operator rather than an analytic sensor model [10]. In environmental monitoring, deep neural surrogates of high-fidelity forward models have been embedded in sequential Monte Carlo schemes to perform real-time Bayesian inversion of gas emissions, effectively replacing an expensive but accurate measurement equation with a learned surrogate while preserving the recursive Bayesian estimation structure [16]. In a similar spirit, Latent Assimilation combines a convolutional autoencoder, a recurrent neural network surrogate of the dynamics, and an Optimal Interpolated Kalman Filter in the latent space, so that the effective observation mapping is mediated by a learned encoder–decoder rather than a simple analytic operator on the full physical state [1]. In structural health monitoring, Neural Extended Kalman Filters parameterize both the process dynamics and the sensory observation mapping with neural networks and train them end-to-end under a variational-inference framework, yielding an EKF-like architecture with a learned measurement model that can predict structural responses on simulated and real datasets [14]. In oceanography, LSTM-based Kalman filters have been proposed for data assimilation of spatio-temporal ocean currents, combining LSTM-derived state dynamics with glider and radar observations to produce short-term forecasts for path planning [18]. In parallel, several "deep Kalman" formulations have been proposed in which the predictor–corrector structure of the Kalman filter is retained, but the correction step is parametrized by neural networks trained from data, as in Neural Assimilation [2] and Recursive KalmanNet [15]. These works collectively demonstrate that it is possible either to learn surrogate measurement equations or to learn data-driven correctors that compensate for nonideal measurement models. However, they typically assume that the observation model used in training and in operation coincide, or do not explicitly address the case where only a biased surrogate measurement equation is available in the field while a more accurate measurement equation exists only in laboratory conditions. In contrast, the present work considers precisely this scenario and shows that a Deep Kalman Filter can be trained, using laboratory data and an accurate measurement equation, to compute trajectory-dependent gains that optimally exploit innovations formed with a surrogate measurement equation, thereby mitigating its deterministic discrepancies and recovering accurate state estimates even when the operational observation operator is structurally imperfect.

2 Model Problem

The *reference model*, used by the Deep Kalman Filter as (deterministic) predictor, is a general, discrete-time, nonlinear state-space model (SSM) of the form:

$$\begin{aligned} x(k+1) &= f(\ x(k),\ p,\ u(k) + w_u(k)\ ) + w_m(k) \\ y(k) &= h(\ x(k)\ ) + w_y(k) \end{aligned} \tag{1}$$

where $f = f(x, p, u)$ is a p-parametric transition map acting on both current input $u(k) \in R^{n_u}$ and state $x(k) \in R^{n_x}$ vectors; $w_u(k)$ is input measurement noise and $w_m(k) \in R^{n_x}$ is model noise; $y(k) \in R^{n_y}$ is current output and $w_y(k) \in R^{n_y}$ is output measurement noise. Note that in classic Kalman filtering the input is assumed to be known exactly and input noise is eventually incorporated in the model noise, while here we assume both that we can simulate our reference model only with noisy inputs, and that the true model is driven by the exact, noiseless inputs, i.e. we have an input-measurement noise. A common choice is $w_m(k) \sim \mathcal{N}(0, Q)$, $w_y(k) \sim \mathcal{N}(0, R)$ and $w_u(k) \sim \mathcal{N}(0, Z)$, but not the only possible. The measurement equation $h(x(k))$ is a general nonlinear function of the states, with an important special case $h(x(k)) = C\,x(k)$, i.e. a linear relation between measurements and state variables. For an assumed optimal choice of the map f, the parameters and the noise models, this reference model approximates a true, at least partially unknown, state-transition model, which is supposed of the form:

$$\begin{aligned} x(k+1) &= f^*(x(k), u(k) + w_u^*(k)) + w_m^*(k) \\ y(k) &= h^*(x(k)) + w_y^*(k) \end{aligned} \tag{2}$$

where a classic case is $w_m^*(k) \sim \mathcal{N}(0, Q^*)$, $w_y^*(k) \sim \mathcal{N}(0, R^*)$ and $w_u^*(k) \sim \mathcal{N}(0, Z^*)$, but not the only possible here. This true model is intended to generate the measurement data. For simplicity, without loss of generality here we concentrate on a model problem without a deterministic model error in the predictor (see e.g. [12] for a clarification of this concept). Instead, we consider the presence of a deterministic model error in the measurement equation. Precisely, if the sensor data are defined as $\tilde{y}(k) = \tilde{h}(x(k)) + \tilde{\omega}(k)$, where $\tilde{h}(x(k))$ is analytically unknown, we assume that in laboratory tests it holds that:

$$\tilde{h}(x(k)) = h(x(k)) = h^*(x(k))\quad, \tag{3}$$

while in general operating conditions there is available only a *surrogate* measurement equation $h_s(x(k))$, i.e.

$$h_s(x(k)) = h^*(x(k)) + m_h(x(k)) + \omega_h(x(k)) \tag{4}$$

with $m_h(x(k))$ a deterministic error component and $\omega_h(x(k))$ a stochastic error component. The notation adopted for the different introduced measurement equations is listed in Table 1.

Table 1. Notation used in the text for the measurement equations.

h^*	the measurement equation of the true model
$\tilde{h}$	the measurement equation of the sensor
h	the measurement equation used by the Deep Kalman Filter
h_s	the surrogate measurement equation available in field operations

In the numerical experiments (see Sect. 4), we will refer to the following three case studies:

1. $\tilde{h}(x(k)) = h^*(x(k))$ and $h(x(k)) = h_s(x(k))$, where we are able to do very good measurements but we don't have an accurate analytical expression of the measurements as a function of the state vector;
2. $\tilde{h}(x(k)) = h_s(x(k))$ and $h(x(k)) = h^*(x(k))$, where we know an accurate analytical description of the measurements as a function of the state vector, but we have actual measurements that are surrogates of the real ones;
3. $\tilde{h}(x(k)) = h'_s(x(k))$ and $h(x(k)) = h''_s(x(k))$, where both the measurements and the measurement equation are surrogate, but not the same.

3   The Deep Kalman Filter for Surrogate Measurement Equations

In this section we briefly present the Deep Kalman Filter equations in a schematic form. Given a measurable final state $x(N)$ we consider the following loss function:

$$\mathcal{L} = \frac{\lambda_N}{2}\|\hat{x}(N) - x(N)\|_2^2 + \frac{1}{2}\sum_{l=1}^{N}\|y(l) - C\hat{x}(l)\|_{R_l^{-1}}^2 +$$

$$+ \frac{1}{2}\sum_{l=1}^{N}\|\mathcal{K}_G^{(l)}\left(y(l) - C\hat{x}(l\,|\,l-1)\right)\|_{P_l^{-1}}^2 + \frac{\lambda_D}{2}\sum_{i,j=1}^{m,n}\|Dv^{ij}\|_2^2 = \qquad (5)$$

$$= \mathcal{E}_{\lambda_N} + \sum_{l=1}^{N}\mathcal{F}^l + \sum_{l=1}^{N}\mathcal{G}^l + \mathcal{H}_{\lambda_D}.$$

where R_l, P_l are symmetric weight matrices, D is the second order finite differences matrix and $v^{ij} = \left[(\mathcal{K}_G^{(1)})_{ij} \ldots (\mathcal{K}_G^{(N)})_{ij}\right]^\top$. For a in-depth description of the contribution given by each term and its computational involvement in the optimization process, see [6]. In this paper we present the modification from the

a) DKF standard formulation [6]:

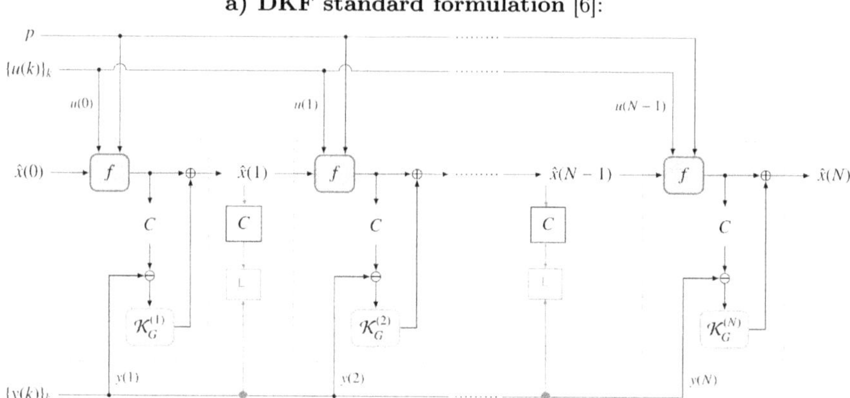

b) DKF evolved formulation for surrogate measurement equations:

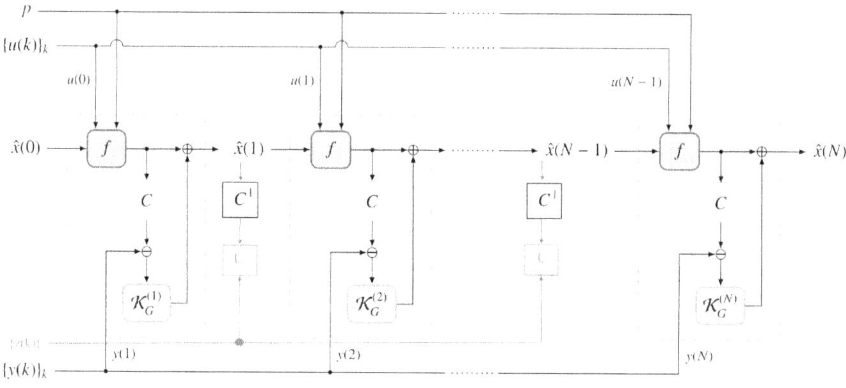

Fig. 1. At the top part ("a)") is shown the structure of the standard Deep Kalman Filter network. Each layer is contained in a gray box. The l-th layer receives a state estimate $\hat{x}(l-1)$, measurement $y(l)$, input $u(l-1)$, parameter p, and outputs the new estimated state $\hat{x}(l)$. The predictor component f (blue box) receives $u(l-1)$ and p to form the predicted state $\hat{x}(l\,|\,l-1)$. The corrector component, composed of the observation matrix C (yellow box), or of an arbitrary measurement equation h, and gain matrix $\mathcal{K}_G^{(l)}$ (orange box), receives $y(l)$ and computes the correction $\mathcal{K}_G^{(l)} e_{\hat{y}}(k)$. Predicted-state and correction are then summed to form the new state estimate. The learnable weights are the gains $\{\mathcal{K}_G^{(l)}\}_{l=1,\dots,N}$ and parameters p. The loss-function "L" (in red) (5) of back-propagation learning uses the same measurements and the same measurement equation used by the filter. At the bottom part ("b)") is shown the evolved formulation for surrogate measurement equations: the difference is that here the loss-function "L" (in red) 5 uses different measurements and measurement-equation than those used by the filter. (Color figure online)

standard form of the DKF, schematically depicted in Fig. 1a, to the evolved form that can exploit surrogate measurement functions, depicted in Fig. 1b.

The standard form of the DKF is derived adopting a common assumption in data-assimilation methods, i.e. that the measurement equation is accurate. The DKF aims at estimating the state-vector of a dynamical system by using a deterministic predictor (the function f in (1) and shown in Fig. 1) and a correction scheme based on the product between learned gain matrices and vectors containing the output prediction error (see Fig. 1). This error, called *innovation*, is the comparison between measurements and their prediction obtained through the state-prediction and a measurement equation. For situations where measurements corresponding to a precise measurement equation are available only during laboratory tests, we show in this section how the information produced in these tests can be used by the DKF also in an operational context where a less precise measurement equation is applicable, i.e. a surrogate measurement function.

In Fig. 1a it is shown the standard situation depicted so far, where we can notice in black color the *forward path*, where the output prediction errors are multiplied by the gains matrix $\mathcal{K}_G^{(l)}$ to correct the state-prediction. In red color there is the *backward path*, existing only during the learning process, that uses also the output filter errors to compute the loss function L (5) and then update the matrices $\mathcal{K}_G^{(l)}$ by backpropagation learning. Note that here the measurement equations are the same, i.e. the matrix C (but it could be an arbitrary nonlinear function h, as said before). Then, when the learning process is finished, the red part is removed and the DKF behaves like has been described in the previous sections.

If in the operational context only a surrogate measurement function can be used, the evolved scheme here presented, shown in Fig. 1b, has a modified backward path. Indeed, here we assume that $y(k)$ is the measurement data comparable with the output of the surrogate measurement equation (C in the Figure), that the filter can use, but for backpropagation learning we introduce into the loss function $\mathcal{L}$ the high-precision measurements $z(k)$ and the comparison with the corresponding measurement equation (C' in the Figure). In this way, the DKF learns how to accurately track the state-vector even when it uses a measurement function which is not accurate. When the learning process is finished, the red part is removed and the learned filter (black part) is able to repeat the same trajectory by using a surrogate measurement function. Note that the optimization given by this learning method is in principle trajectory-dependent, but has the ability to generalize, as we will see in the following sections.

4   Numerical Experiments

Here we assume that in lab experiments we have a trivial linear measurement equation, i.e. the identity $h(x(k)) = C\,x = I\,x = x$, where I is the identity matrix, whereas in the field operation we will consider the three cases defined in Sect. 2. The surrogate nonlinear map $h_s(x)$ is described in the next subsection.

The experiment consists in estimating a trajectory in either a bi-dimensional or a tri-dimensional state-space.

4.1   The Surrogate Measurement Equation $h_s(x)$

Let $x \in \mathbb{R}^d$ be the state vector. The surrogate measurement equation is defined as:

$$h_s(x) = x + \alpha_0 h_0 + \alpha_1 H_1 x + \alpha_2 \underbrace{x \cdot e^{x^T \Sigma x}}_{\text{Exp. Scaling}} + \alpha_3 \sin(kx) . \tag{6}$$

The function relies on the following parameters:

- **Bias Vector** (h_0): A constant offset vector in $\mathbb{R}^d$.
- **Linear Matrix** (H_1): A transformation matrix in $\mathbb{R}^{d \times d}$.
- **Quadratic Matrix** (Σ): A symmetric matrix in $\mathbb{R}^{d \times d}$ (often positive semi-definite) representing the covariance or metric of the quadratic form.
- **Wave vector** (k): A vector determining the frequency of the oscillatory cosine term in the state space.
- **Noise attenuation** (α_i): Scalar parameters that allow us to "tune" the noise contribution of each component in the function.

The function is composed of four distinct structural components. At this stage, we did not enforce any specific meaning to the shape (and incidentally to the components) of the function. We added terms that could be interpreted as "representatives" of the typical basis employed for function approximation, e.g. polynomial, harmonic, (exponential) kernel functions in order to have a superficial understanding of the flexibility of our approach in this sense. Nevertheless, the considered measurement equation is also thought to capture possible noise contributions when sensing inertial and/or geophysical quantities. First, sensors often introduce a persistent offset (here represented as $\alpha_0 h_0$) that can rapidly result in large errors when performing state estimations. In real-scenarios this bias is rarely constant, but rather a stochastic process often modeled as a first-order Gauss-Markov process or a random walk (bias drift) [8]. In conventional data-assimilation methods, such as the Kalman filter, the detrimental effect of a bias term is typically mitigated by accounting it as an additional state variable (state augmentation) [7]. Additionally, measurement errors can also evolve through complex polynomial (here limited to a linear component $\alpha_1 H_1 x$) and periodic dynamics (here expressed as $\alpha_3 \sin(kx)$). While polynomial terms typically reflect sensor non-linearities, aging, and scale-factor instabilities, periodic errors represent platform resonances and environmental coupling such as mechanical vibrations, thermal cycling [17], or cyclic satellite signal multipath [9] in integrated systems. Finally, the exponential magnitude scaling is included to capture possible correlations between state variables. Other transient effects characterized by exponential decay could also appear due to abrupt variations of the external environment conditions (e.g. temperature, powering, etc.). Functionally speaking, the components are:

Linear Component

$$L(x) = x + h_0 + H_1 x$$

This represents the affine transformation of the input, preserving the baseline geometry and orientation.

Exponential Magnitude Scaling

$$E(x) = x \cdot e^{x^T \Sigma x}$$

The term $x^T \Sigma x$ computes a scalar quadratic form (representing the "energy" or Mahalanobis distance of the vector). Note that:

- Since the exponent is a scalar, it acts as a non-linear gain.
- The original vector direction x is preserved, but its magnitude is scaled exponentially based on its alignment with Σ.

Due to the rapid growth of the exponential function, the term $e^{x^T \Sigma x}$ can dominate the output or cause numerical overflow. To mitigate this, a temperature scaling parameter τ is often introduced. The stabilized exponential term is written as:

$$E_{\text{stable}}(x) = x \cdot e^{\frac{1}{\tau} x^T \Sigma x}, \tag{7}$$

where $\tau > 0$ acts as a dampening factor. This is mathematically equivalent to scaling the matrix Σ by $1/\tau$.

Periodic Component

$$P(x) = \cos(kx)$$

This term introduces (possibly) periodic non-linearities. The cosine function is applied element-wise to the vector kx.

In Fig. 2 we see the effect of each term in the function $h_s(k)$, i.e. only one α_i different from zero.

4.2 ML Contribution to the Data Assimilation

Let us consider an example, where the model problem is simplified to avoid unnecessary phenomena (in accordance with the Occam's razor): $f^*(x, p, u) = A\,x + B\,u$, where $A = \begin{bmatrix} 1 & 0 \\ 0 & 1 \end{bmatrix}$ and $B = \begin{bmatrix} 1 & 0 \\ 0 & 1 \end{bmatrix}$, i.e. there is no model error $(Q^* \approx 0)$.

A more complex dynamical system would add observability issues that are per-se well studied in data assimilation methods. Therefore, here, we primarily focus on the effects of a misleading measurement equation. Nevertheless, in Sect. 4.4 we will see that the obtained results hold also with a nonlinear dynamical system. In all cases we will assume that $f(x, p, u) = f^*(x, p, u)$.

The true measurement function is simply $h^*(x(k)) = C\,x = \begin{bmatrix} 1 & 0 \\ 0 & 1 \end{bmatrix} x = x$, i.e. there is no measurement error $(R^* \approx 0)$. In the lab tests, we assume

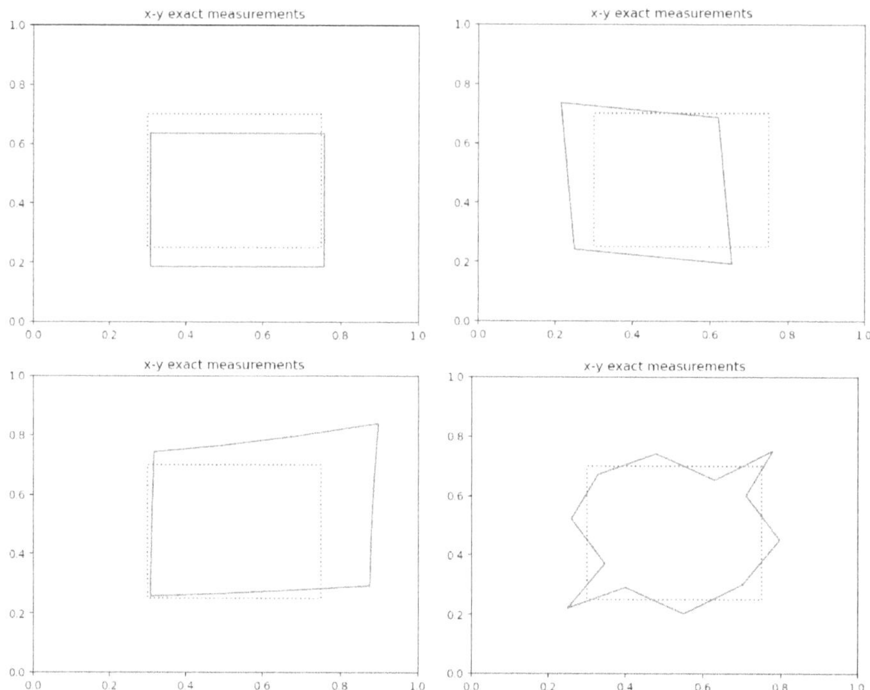

Fig. 2. The effect of each single term in the function $h_s(k)$, i.e. only one α_i different from zero, is shown. Top-left: the constant term (α_0); top-right: the linear term (α_1); bottom-left: the exponential magnitude scaling term (α_2); bottom-right: the periodic component (α_3).

that $\tilde{h}(x(k)) = h^*(x(k))$, while for the data assimilation we consider the three case studies listed in Sect. 2. The relative results are presented in the following subsections.

Case Study 1. Here $\tilde{h}(x(k)) = h^*(x(k))$ and $h(x(k)) = h_s(x(k))$ defined in Sect. 4.1. In particular, for the experiment presented in Fig. 4, $\alpha_0 = \alpha_1 = 0$ and $\alpha_2 = \alpha_3 \neq 0$ for $h_s(x(k))$. The trajectory estimates obtained with the KF and the DKF are respectively shown in Fig. 3 (a) and (b).

Case Study 2. Here $\tilde{h}(x(k)) = h_s(x(k))$ defined in Sect. 4.1 and $h(x(k)) = h^*(x(k))$. In particular, for the experiment presented in Fig. 4, $\alpha_0 = \alpha_1 = 0$ and $\alpha_2 = \alpha_3 \neq 0$ for $h_s(x(k))$. The trajectory estimates obtained with the KF and the DKF are respectively shown in Fig. 4 (a) and (b).

Case Study 3. Here $\tilde{h}(x(k)) = h_s^{'}(x(k))$ and $h(x(k)) = h_s^{''}(x(k))$, both defined in Sect. 4.1 but with different values of the coefficients α_0, α_1, α_2 and α_3. More

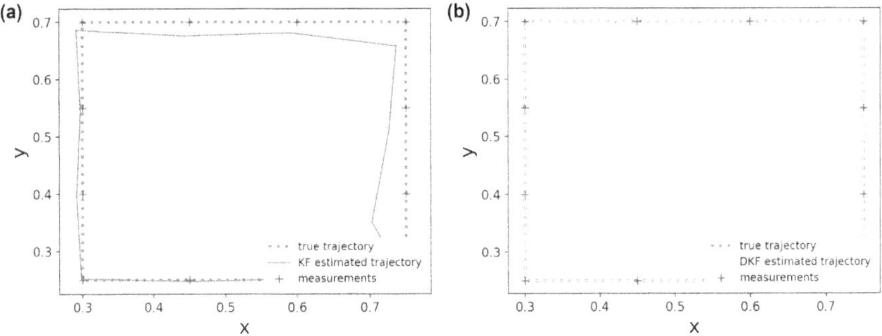

Fig. 3. True trajectory (magenta dotted line) and measurement points (blue cross) for case 1. The estimated trajectories via KF (a) and DKF (b) are respectively plotted as green and orange solid lines. (Color figure online)

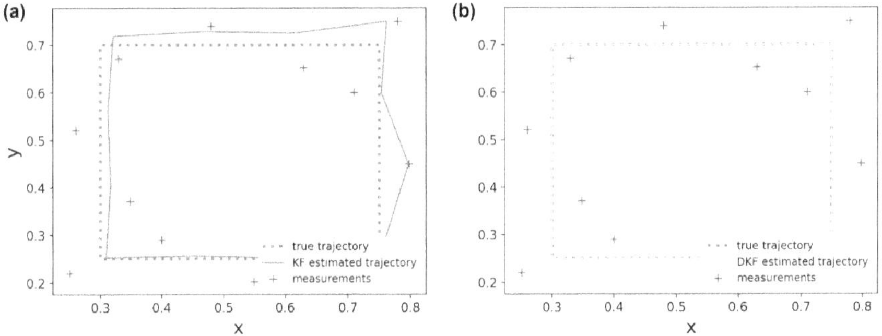

Fig. 4. True trajectory (magenta dotted line) and measurement points (blue cross) for case 2. The estimated trajectories via KF (a) and DKF (b) are respectively plotted as green and orange solid lines. (Color figure online)

specifically, for the experiment presented in Fig. 5, $\alpha_0 = \alpha_1 = 0$ and $\alpha_2 = \alpha_3 \neq 0$ for $h_s'(x(k))$, whereas $\alpha_0 \neq 0$ and $\alpha_1 = \alpha_2 = \alpha_3 = 0$ for $h_s''(x(k))$. The trajectory estimates obtained with the KF and the DKF are respectively shown in Fig. 5 (a) and (b).

In all the three studied cases, despite the use of surrogate measurements and/or measurement equation, the DKF provides an estimate of the state-trajectory that accurately reproduce the considered true-trajectory. By comparison, the KF does not result in an accurate estimate.

4.3   Generalization

In Sect. 4.2 we have seen that the gain-learning process operated by the DKF is able to accurately estimate the state-trajectory in all the three case-studies. In those experiments the learning was performed on a single trajectory. Here we see that the DKF is able to generalize to multiple trajectories, and we give an

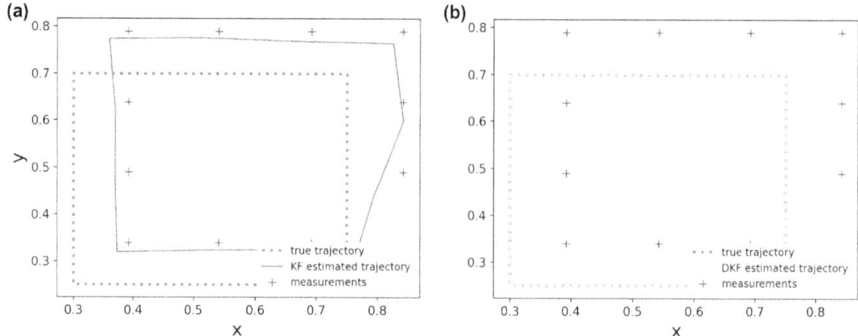

Fig. 5. True trajectory (magenta dotted line) and measurement points (blue cross) for case 3. The estimated trajectories via KF (a) and DKF (b) are respectively plotted as green and orange solid lines. (Color figure online)

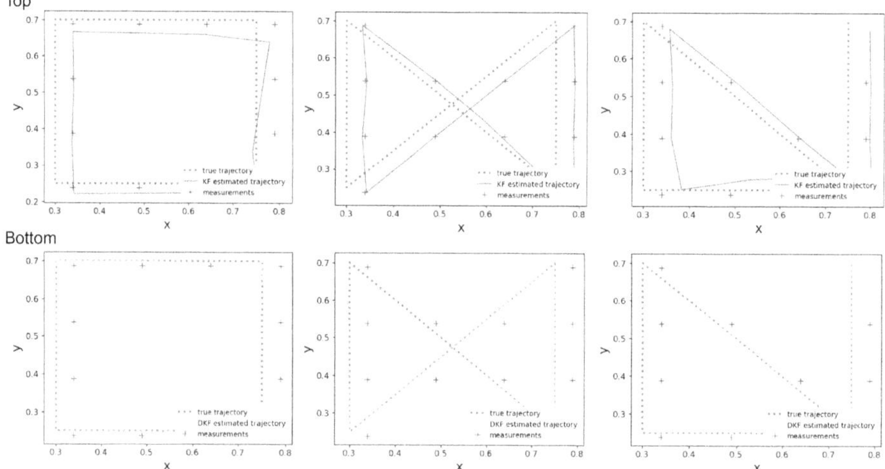

Fig. 6. True trajectory (magenta dotted line) and measurement points (blue cross) for Simultaneous learning of multiple trajectories in the "Case 3" settings. The estimated trajectories via KF (top row) and DKF (bottom row) are respectively plotted as green and orange solid lines. (Color figure online)

explanation. In Fig. 6 we see the simultaneous learning of multiple trajectories in the "Case 3" settings (the most difficult, since both the measurements and the measurement equation are surrogate). The plots in the top row display the behavior of the KF (solid green lines), whereas in the bottom row the corresponding responses of the DKF are shown (solid orange line). The presented results indicate that a single DKF is able to learn multiple different trajectories.

The example made in this section allows us to do a precise statement about the capacity limit. Since the predictor is exact, $f(x, p, u) = f^*(x, p, u)$, and there are no model nor measurement errors, the optimal correction made by the learned gain matrices $\mathcal{K}_G^{(l)}$ at each layer l should be zero, i.e.

$$\mathcal{K}_G^{(l)} \, e_{\hat{y}}(l) = 0 \tag{8}$$

and this can happen if the DKF learns gain matrices $\mathcal{K}_G^{(l)}$ whose kernel is aligned with the output prediction error $e_{\hat{y}}(l) = y(l) - h\left(\hat{x}(l \mid l - 1)\right)$.

At each layer l we will have a number of output prediction errors (vectors) equal to the number of trajectories. If these vectors span a subspace of dimension not bigger than that of the biggest possible kernel of the matrices $\mathcal{K}_G^{(l)}$, than the DKF can learn gain matrices satisfying this property, otherwise not. This statement holds also in more general settings: the gain matrices $\mathcal{K}_G^{(l)}$ must be able to filter out the deterministic output error created by the surrogate measurement equations and the DKF make this by shaping their kernels during the learning process.

4.4 Nonlinear Dynamics

To further validate the presented method, we tested it against four different examples of nonlinear dynamics: Duffing, Hindmarsh–Rose, Lorenz and van der Pol, two of which are in a tridimensional state. In Fig. 7, the tridimensional true trajectory (magenta dotted line) and the measurements points (blue cross) from an Hindmarsh–Rose model [11] are plotted in the "Case 3" settings. In particular, Fig. 7a shows the DKF estimates (green solid line) in the standard form (see Fig. 1a), i.e. when the learning is carried out on the corrupted measurement equation, which is assumed accurate. In comparison, Fig. 7b shows the DKF

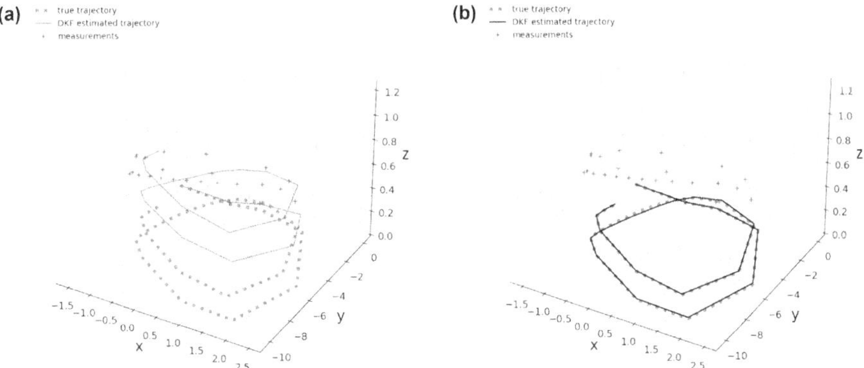

Fig. 7. Comparison between trajectory estimates obtained with the standard form of the DKF (a) and the evolved DKF (b) for an Hindmarsh–Rose nonlinear dynamics example. The magenta dotted line indicate the true trajectory, the blue cross the measurement points, the green and black solid lines are the trajectory estimates respectively for the two different approaches. The evolved DKF provides a much more accurate estimate. (Color figure online)

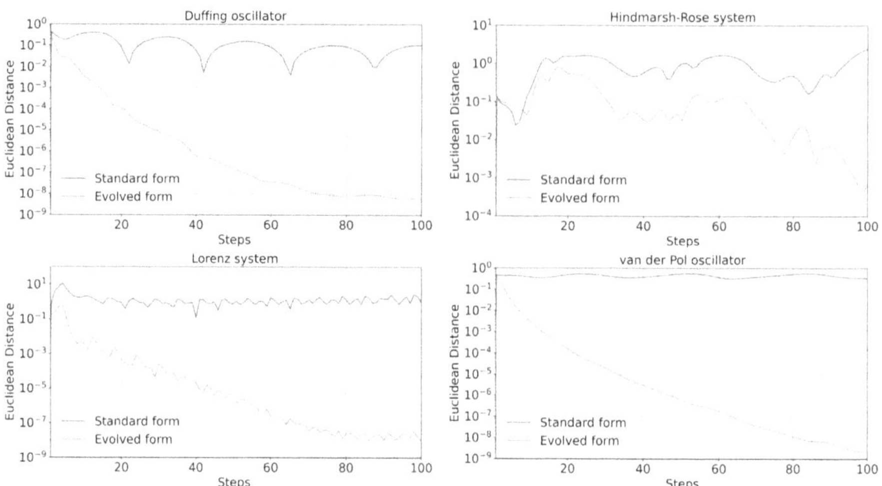

Fig. 8. Performance comparison between standard and evolved form of the DKF for four instances of nonlinear model dynamics.

estimates (green solid line) in the evolved form (see Fig. 1b), i.e. when instead a surrogate not accurate measurement equation is taken into account.

The results for all the four tested nonlinear dynamics are summarized in Fig. 8, where the euclidean norm is used as a metric to compare the two DKF approaches described in Sect. 3.

The obtained results indicate that the evolved DKF can provide an accurate estimate of the true-trajectory when the standard form fails due to a not accurate measurement equation, even in more complex nonlinear dynamics (Table 2).

Table 2. Performance comparison between standard and evolved form of the DKF for four instances of nonlinear model dynamics.

Nonlinear model	Standard DKF 2-norm	Evolved DKF 2-norm
Duffing	10^{-1}	10^{-8}
Hindmarsh–Rose	10^{0}	10^{-3}
Lorenz	10^{0}	10^{-7}
van der Pol	10^{-1}	10^{-9}

4.5   Comparison with Other Methods

The key point of the method proposed here is that it uses two measurement equations during filter design: one is used to optimize the state trajectory tracking and the other to tune the corrector gains for this purpose. We have seen in Sect. 4.4 that if the DKF learns the gain matrices on accurate measurements but with a surrogate measurement equation, the estimated trajectory is intrinsically poor. The same occurs in principle to other methods, and an evolution analogous to that presented here does not appear to exist in the literature for other methods, as we know. What we can say is that the effort to modify the existing methods, be analytical like the (Extended) Kalman Filter, or based on the statistical ensemble like the EnKF or learning-enhanced like KalmanNet [4] would be not immediate and, probably, not trivial.

5   Conclusions

We are devising a strategy to tackle with surrogate measurements and/or measurement equations, in data assimilation procedures. The proposed method shows potentials in learning corrector gains, during over-instrumented laboratory experiments, that allow a field-operational surrogate measurement process to be accurate in state estimation.

Acknowledgments. This work was supported by the NATO Science and Technology Organization, NATO Office of the Chief Scientist, Bruxelles, Belgium.

Disclosure of Interests. The authors have no competing interests to declare that are relevant to the content of this article.

References

1. Amendola, M., et al.: Data assimilation in the latent space of a neural network. In: arXiv preprint arXiv:2012.12056 (2020). https://doi.org/10.48550/arXiv.2012.12056
2. Arcucci, R., Moutiq, L., Guo, Y.-K.: Neural assimilation. In: Krzhizhanovskaya, V.V., et al. (eds.) ICCS 2020. LNCS, vol. 12142, pp. 155–168. Springer, Cham (2020). https://doi.org/10.1007/978-3-030-50433-5_13
3. Bach, E., Baptista, R., Calvello, E., Chen, B., Stuart, A.: Learning enhanced ensemble filters. J. Comput. Phys. **547** (2026). https://doi.org/10.1016/j.jcp.2025.114550
4. Buchnik, I., Revach, G., Steger, D., Van Sloun, R.J.G., Routtenberg, T., Shlezinger, N.: Latent-Kalmannet: learned Kalman filtering for tracking from high-dimensional signals. IEEE Trans. Sig. Process. **72**, 352–367 (2024). https://doi.org/10.1109/TSP.2023.3344360
5. Cheng, S.: Machine learning with data assimilation and uncertainty quantification for dynamical systems: a review. IEEE/CAA J. Automatica Sinica **10** (2023). https://doi.org/10.1109/JAS.2023.123537
6. Chinellato, E., Marcuzzi, F.: State, parameters and hidden dynamics estimation with the deep Kalman filter: regularization strategies. J. Comput. Sci. **87**, 102569 (2025). https://doi.org/10.1007/978-3-031-63775-9
7. Farrell, J.: Aided Navigation: GPS with High Rate Sensors. McGraw-Hill professional engineering: Electronic engineering, McGraw Hill LLC (2008). https://books.google.it/books?id=yNujEvIMszYC

8. Groves, P.: Principles of GNSS, Inertial, and Multisensor Integrated Navigation Systems, 2nd edn (2013)
9. Guo, H., Liu, X., Jin, X., Wang, G., Jiang, Y., Guo, J.: GNSS standard point positioning method based on spherical harmonic expansion of signal propagation path relating errors. Adv. Space Res. **72**(4), 1153–1171 (2023). https://doi.org/10.1016/j.asr.2023.04.003
10. Guo, Z.C., Forbes, J.R., Barfoot, T.D.: KILO-EKF: Koopman-inspired learned observations extended Kalman filter. arXiv preprint arXiv:2601.12463 (2026). https://doi.org/10.48550/arXiv.2601.12463, submitted to IEEE Robotics and Automation Letters
11. Hindmarsh, J.L., Rose, R.M.: A model of neuronal bursting using three coupled first order differential equations. Proc. Roy. Soc. Lond. B. Biol. Sci. **221**(1222), 87–102 (1984). https://doi.org/10.1098/rspb.1984.0024
12. Levine, M.E., Stuart, A.M.: A framework for machine learning of model error in dynamical systems (2022)
13. Liang, J., Terasaki, K., Miyoshi, T.: A machine learning approach to the observation operator for satellite radiance data assimilation. J. Meteorol. Soc. Jpn. Ser. II **101**(1), 79–95 (2023). https://doi.org/10.2151/jmsj.2023-005
14. Liu, W., Lai, Z., Bacsa, K., Chatzi, E.: Neural extended Kalman filters for learning and predicting dynamics of structural systems. Struct. Health Monit. **23**(2), 1037–1052 (2024). https://doi.org/10.1177/14759217231179912
15. Mortada, H., Falcon, C., Kahil, Y., Clavaud, M., Michel, J.P.: Recursive Kalman-net: deep learning-augmented Kalman filtering for state estimation with consistent uncertainty quantification. In: 2025 33rd European Signal Processing Conference (EUSIPCO), pp. 885–889 (2025). https://doi.org/10.23919/EUSIPCO63237.2025.11226444
16. Newman, T., Nemeth, C., Jones, M., Jonathan, P.: Deep learning surrogates for real-time gas emission inversion. arXiv preprint arXiv:2506.14597 (2025). https://doi.org/10.48550/arXiv.2506.14597
17. Titterton, D., Weston, J.: Strapdown Inertial Navigation Technology, 2nd edn. The Institution of Engineering and Technology (2004). https://doi.org/10.1049/PBRA017E
18. Zhang, Z., Hou, M., Zhang, F., Edwards, C.R.: An LSTM based Kalman filter for spatio-temporal ocean currents assimilation. In: Proceedings of the 14th International Conference on Underwater Networks and Systems. WUWNet '19. Association for Computing Machinery, New York, NY, USA (2020). https://doi.org/10.1145/3366486.3366522

Latent Attention on Masked Patches for Flow Reconstruction

Ben Eze[1] , Luca Magri[1,2] , and Andrea Nóvoa[1,3]( )

[1] Aeronautics Department, Imperial College London, Exhibition Road, London SW7 2BX, UK
{ben.eze21,l.magri,a.novoa}@imperial.ac.uk
[2] DIMEAS, Politecnico di Torino, Corso Duca degli Abruzzi, 24, Torino 10129, Italy
[3] I-X, Imperial College London, 84 Wood Lane, London W12 0BZ, UK

Abstract. Vision transformers have shown outstanding performance in image generation, yet their adoption in fluid dynamics remains limited. We introduce the *Latent Attention on Masked Patches* (LAMP) model, an interpretable regression-based modified vision transformer designed for masked flow reconstruction. LAMP follows a three-fold strategy: (i) partition of each flow snapshot into patches, (ii) patch-wise dimensionality reduction via proper orthogonal decomposition, and (iii) reconstruction of the full field from a masked input using a single-layer transformer trained via closed-form linear regression. We test the method on two canonical 2D unsteady wakes: a laminar wake past a bluff body, and a chaotic wake past two cylinders. On the laminar case, LAMP accurately reconstructs the full flow field from a 90%-masked and noisy input, across signal-to-noise ratios between 10 and 30 dB. Further, the learned attention matrix yields interpretable multi-fidelity optimal sensor-placement maps. LAMP's performance on the chaotic wake is limited, but outperforms other regression methods such as gappy POD. The modularity of the framework, however, naturally accommodates nonlinear compression and deep attention blocks, thereby providing an efficient baseline for nonlinear, high-dimensional masked flow reconstruction.

Keywords: Flow reconstruction · Vision Transformers · POD

1 Introduction

Reconstructing high-dimensional fields from sparse, noisy, and masked measurements is a central challenge in scientific machine learning and fluid mechanics [8,10,19]. In experimental settings, particle image velocimetry (PIV) measurements cover only a subset of the domain, and, since each run captures an independent realisation of the flow, PIV is often limited to mean-flow analyses rather than time-resolved full-field measurements in high-dimensional settings, e.g., [1]. To reconstruct full flow fields, data-driven approaches have been employed, such as convolutional neural networks [9,11], generative adversarial networks [12], or graph neural networks [15], among many others. However, these

© The Author(s), under exclusive license to Springer Nature Switzerland AG 2026
M. Paszynski et al. (Eds.): ICCS 2026 Workshops, LNCS 16788, pp. 181–188, 2026.
https://doi.org/10.1007/978-3-032-29915-4_15

methods typically assume that a large fraction of the field is observed and are primarily designed for super-resolution, in-painting, or mean-flow reconstruction tasks. Real-time full-field reconstruction from sparse measurements can alternatively be achieved by coupling reduced-order models with data assimilation [3,13]. Vision Transformers (ViTs) [4], in particular, have become the state-of-the-art backbone for image generation and large language models [14], but have not been fully adopted yet in the fluid dynamics community. Here, we introduce the *Latent Attention on Masked Patches* (LAMP) model, inspired by ViTs and masked autoencoders [7]. The key idea is to (i) partition each flow snapshot into non-overlapping patches; (ii) compress each patch into a low-dimensional latent representation; here, patch-wise Proper Orthogonal Decomposition (POD) [2]; and (iii) reconstruct the full field from a subset of the patches, i.e., a masked input, using an attention-based patch-to-patch prediction mechanism; here, implemented as a single-layer transformer trained via closed-form linear regression. This design guarantees convergence to a global minimum, eliminates dependence on learning-rate schedules and random weight initialisation, and yields fast, reproducible and physically interpretable results. Further, the modular architecture allows expressive components to be incorporated where performance demands it—such as nonlinear autoencoders [6,16] or multi-layer transformers. The paper is structured as follows. Section 2 details the proposed LAMP. Section 3 demonstrates LAMP on two canonical unsteady wakes: a laminar bluff-body wake and a chaotic wake over two adjacent cylinders. Section 4 closes the paper with conclusions and future work directions.

2   Latent Attention on Masked Patches (LAMP)

As illustrated in Fig. 1, LAMP consists of three stages: (i) data patching and reshaping; (ii) patch-wise dimensionality reduction via linear autoencoding with proper orthogonal decomposition (POD);   and (iii) attention-based patch-to-patch prediction in the latent space.

Patching. First, we divide the normalized input 2D data (of height H, width W and C components) $\mathbf{X}_{\mathrm{in}} \in \mathbb{R}^{H \times W \times C}$ into N size-P square patches of dimension $D := CP^2$, which are flattened to obtain the patched data $\mathbf{X} \in \mathbb{R}^{N \times D}$ (see [4]).

Patch-Wise POD. We apply dimensionality reduction to compress $\mathbf{X}$ into $\mathbf{Z} \in \mathbb{R}^{N \times N_e}$, with embedding (latent) dimension $N_e \ll D$. Each patch vector $\mathbf{x}_n \in \mathbb{R}^D$ is compressed into $\mathbf{z}_n \in \mathbb{R}^{N_e}$ by minimizing

$$\mathcal{L}^{\mathrm{AE}} = \sum_{n=1}^{N} \|\tilde{\mathbf{x}}_n - \mathbf{x}_n\|_2^2, \quad \text{subject to} \quad \tilde{\mathbf{x}}_n = \mathbf{U}_n \mathbf{U}_n^\top \mathbf{x}_n. \tag{1}$$

The patch-wise optimal orthonormal bases $\mathbf{U}_n \in \mathbb{R}^{D \times N_e}$ are obtained from the training time series as $\mathbf{X}_n^{\mathrm{train}} \approx \mathbf{U}_n \mathbf{\Sigma} (\mathbf{V}_n^{\mathrm{train}})^\top$, where the approximation arises as we retain only the first N_e leading singular vectors. Finally, we construct the

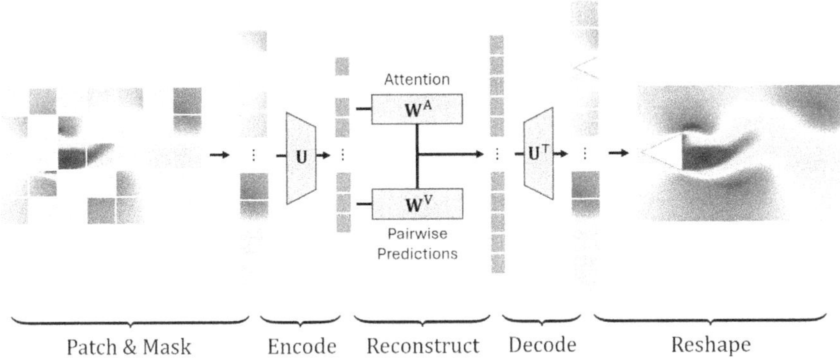

Fig. 1. Pictorial illustration of the patch-wise latent attention model (LAMP). A linear autoencoder embeds the input in a lower-dimensional latent space, where predictions can be made efficiently. The predictions are pair-wise (i.e. each patch predicts every other patch) and weighted with a confidence score.

encoding and decoding operators, $\mathbf{E}$ and $\mathbf{D}$, as block-diagonal matrices composed of the patch-wise bases $\{\mathbf{U}_n\}_{n=1}^{N}$ such that

$$\mathbf{Z} = \mathbf{EX}, \quad \text{and} \quad \tilde{\mathbf{X}} = \mathbf{DZ}, \tag{2}$$

where the n-th block in $\mathbf{E}$ and $\mathbf{D}$ contain $\mathbf{U}_n^{\top}$ and $\mathbf{U}_n$, respectively. The patched latent data $\mathbf{Z}$ is then passed to the transformer. A low reconstruction loss $\mathcal{L}^{\mathrm{AE}}$ is a prerequisite for accurate masked predictions.

Masked Prediction. We modify the attention equation presented in [18] for the task of single-layer reconstruction. The aim is to predict the full latent snapshot $\mathbf{Z}^{\star}$ from a masked input $\mathbf{Z}^{\mathrm{masked}}$, where $Z_n^{\mathrm{masked}} = 0$ for all masked indices $n \in \mathcal{N}_{masked}$. Each component in $\mathbf{Z}^{\star}$ is

$$Z_{me}^{\star} = \sum_{n=1}^{N} \mathrm{softmax}(\mathbf{a}_m)_n V_{mne}, \quad \text{for} \begin{cases} m = 1, \ldots, N, \\ e = 1, \ldots, N_e \end{cases} \tag{3}$$

where $\mathbf{a}_m$ is the m-th row of the log-attention matrix $\mathbf{A} \in \mathbb{R}^{N \times N}$, and $\mathbf{V} \in \mathbb{R}^{N \times N \times N_e}$ is the value tensor; these are defined as

$$A_{mn} = \sum_{e=1}^{N_e} W_{mne}^{\mathrm{A}} Z_{ne}^{\mathrm{masked}}, \quad \text{and} \quad V_{mne} = \sum_{f=1}^{N_e} W_{mnef}^{\mathrm{V}} Z_{nf}^{\mathrm{masked}}, \tag{4}$$

where $\mathbf{W}^{\mathrm{V}} \in \mathbb{R}^{N \times N \times N_e \times N_e}$ and $\mathbf{W}^{\mathrm{A}} \in \mathbb{R}^{N \times N \times N_e}$ are the value and attention weight-tensors, which are trained on *unmasked* data with a two-step approach:

1. The value tensor $\mathbf{W}^{\mathrm{V}}$ can be viewed as an $N \times N$ grid of matrices: each block $\mathbf{W}_{mn}^{\mathrm{V}} \in \mathbb{R}^{N_e \times N_e}$ defines a linear map that predicts patch $\mathbf{z}_m$ from patch $\mathbf{z}_n$. These blocks are obtained by least-squares regression,

$$(\mathbf{Z}^{\mathrm{train}})_m \approx \mathbf{W}_{mn}^{\mathrm{V}} (\mathbf{Z}^{\mathrm{train}})_n, \tag{5a}$$

where the corresponding linear prediction error is

$$\mathcal{L}^{\text{lin}}_{mn} = \left\| (\mathbf{Z}^{\text{train}})_m - \mathbf{W}^{\text{V}}_{mn}(\mathbf{Z}^{\text{train}})_n \right\|^2_2 . \tag{5b}$$

2. The attention tensor $\mathbf{W}^A$ is learned in a second stage and can be decomposed analogously, as a $N \times N$ grid of vectors $w^A_{mn} \in \mathbb{R}^{N_e}$. The error $\mathcal{L}^{\text{lin}}_{mn}$ provides a prediction uncertainty measure, so that predictions with lower $\mathcal{L}^{\text{lin}}_{mn}$ are assigned higher attention weights. In practice, we regress the *log-error*,

$$-\log(\mathcal{L}^{\text{lin}}_{mn}) \approx \mathbf{W}^A_{mn}(\mathbf{Z}^{\text{train}})_n . \tag{6}$$

At inference, the log-error is set to $-\infty$ for masked patches, so that softmax assigns them zero attention weight. The model is then evaluated on unseen test data $\mathbf{X}^{\text{test}}$. The overall prediction error is defined as

$$\mathcal{L}^{\text{pred}} = \left\| \tilde{\mathbf{X}}^\star - \mathbf{X}^{\text{test}} \right\|^2_2 = \left\| \mathbf{D}\mathbf{Z}^\star - \mathbf{X}^{\text{test}} \right\|^2_2 . \tag{7}$$

3   Results

We deploy LAMP to reconstruct the streamwise u and spanwise v velocity fields of two 2D unsteady wakes. First, we test LAMP on the laminar wake of a triangular bluff body at Reynolds number $Re = 100$ [11] in Sect. 3.1 and analyse the effect of varying latent-space dimension, noise intensity, and patch placement. We use 100 snapshots for training and 60 for testing (one shedding period is 32 snapshots). Second, Sect. 3.2 showcases LAMP on a chaotic wake past two cylinders of diameter d with centres spaced $1.5d$ apart vertically. The flow has $Re = 200$, Mach number $M = 0.1$, uniform inlet velocity, convective outflow, and periodic side boundary conditions. After discarding transients, 7000 snapshots ($\Delta t = 1.39$) are split 75%/20% for training and testing, discarding the intermediate 5% to reduce temporal leakage. Both datasets are standardized to zero mean and unit variance for a fair comparison between them.

3.1   Laminar Wake Results

First, we validate the patch-wise POD and examine the loss $\mathcal{L}^{\text{AE}}$ (1), which sets the lower bound for the masked reconstruction error. Figure 2 shows that (i) $\mathcal{L}^{\text{AE}}$ saturates rapidly with N_e, which is consistent with the well-known energy concentration of laminar bluff-body wakes into a few dominant POD modes; and (ii) larger patches reach the same $\mathcal{L}^{\text{AE}}$ at higher compression factors, which indicates that using very small patches may fragment the coherent vortex structures into features that carry little dynamical information.

Figure 3 shows the LAMP masked flow reconstruction results from randomly unmasked patches covering 10% of the domain for noise-free (Fig. 3a) and noisy

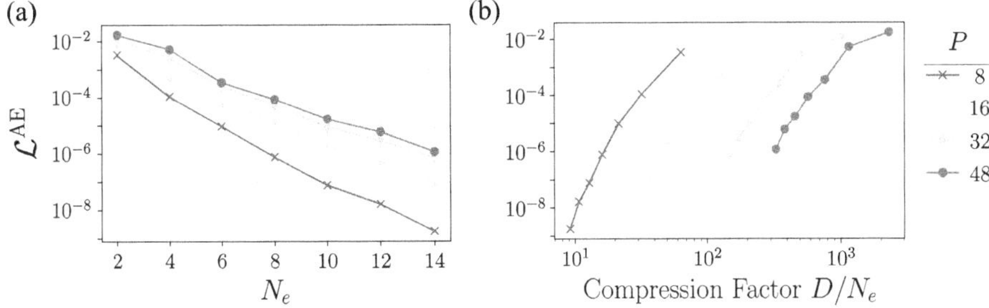

Fig. 2. Patch-wise POD reconstruction performance for varying patch size P. Loss $\mathcal{L}^{\mathrm{AE}}$ versus (a) latent dimension N_e and (b) compression factor D/N_e.

input (Fig. 3b–c). Noise is added to the input as $\tilde{\mathbf{X}}^{\mathrm{noisy}} = \tilde{\mathbf{X}}^{\mathrm{masked}} + \varepsilon$, where $(\tilde{\cdot})$ denotes unnormalized data, $\varepsilon \sim \mathcal{N}(0, \boldsymbol{\Sigma})$, and $\boldsymbol{\Sigma} = \mathbb{E}[\tilde{\mathbf{X}}^{\mathrm{masked}}]10^{-\mathrm{SNR}/10}$.

In the noisy cases, the LAMP provides flow-field reconstructions with prediction errors $\mathcal{L}^{\mathrm{pred}}$ consistently lower than the variance of the added noise. Increasing the latent dimension N_e reduces $\mathcal{L}^{\mathrm{pred}}$ (Fig. 3a), with larger patches outperforming smaller ones once sufficient modes are retained to resolve the coherent shedding. However, adding Gaussian noise shifts the $\mathcal{L}^{\mathrm{pred}}$ minima toward lower N_e (Fig. 3b–d). Small patches are less robust because their local POD bases amplify sub-patch-scale noise. In contrast, larger patches act as spatial filters that preserve the dominant flow structures. Notably, for moderate SNR a broad range of (P, N_e) yields $\mathcal{L}^{\mathrm{pred}}$ below the noise variance $\sigma_{\mathrm{noise}}^2$ (horizontal dashed lines). Therefore, the proposed LAMP successfully achieves simultaneous noise removal and flow reconstruction from masked data.

Next, we focus on the attention matrix, which yields as a by-product an interpretable method for informing sensor placement: the predictive-power maps shown in Fig. 4, which are computed by averaging the columns of $- \log \mathcal{L}^{\mathrm{lin}}_{mn}$ (6) and reshaping into the physical space. Patches with highest predictive power are those whose local dynamics most accurately predict the rest of the field, i.e., the optimal sensor placement for reconstruction. Beyond reducing the resolution, increasing the patch size predominantly reduces the range of values in the attention map. By contrast, as N_e increases, high-power regions multiply from 1–2 near-body patches to distributed coverage across shear layers and far wake, mirroring the POD hierarchy. Placing sensors at persistent predictive-power peaks across N_e thus provides optimal multi-fidelity sensor layouts for both coarse and fine robust reconstructions.

3.2   Chaotic Wake Results

Because of the chaotic nature of the flow, the two-cylinder wake requires larger patches and more POD modes compared to the laminar case, as reflected in the prediction loss in Fig. 5a. The requirement for larger patches to minimise $\mathcal{L}^{\mathrm{pred}}$ indicates that each patch must span a sufficient spatial extent to capture

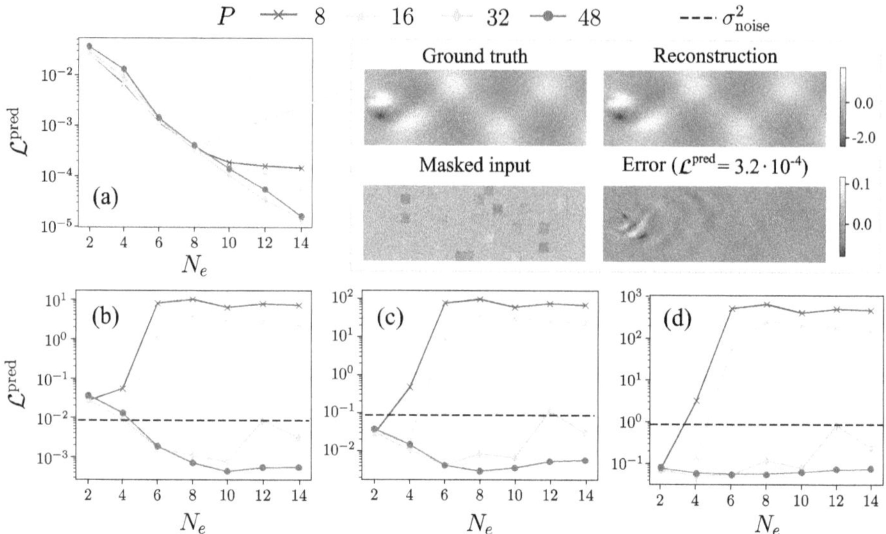

Fig. 3. Reconstruction error $\mathcal{L}^{\mathrm{pred}}$ for varying noise levels, patch size P and latent dimension N_e, all with 10% patches unmasked. The input is noisy masked data with SNR = (a) ∞ (noise-free), (b) 30 dB, (c) 20 dB, (d) 10 dB. The loss is computed against the noise-free target $\mathbf{X}^{\mathrm{test}}$ and the model is trained on noise-free data. Horizontal dashed lines show the noise variance. $\mathcal{L}^{\mathrm{pred}}$ is calculated for 25 random patch arrangements and the *median* is plotted. An example reconstruction for the noise-free case with $P = 16$, $N_e = 8$ is shown.

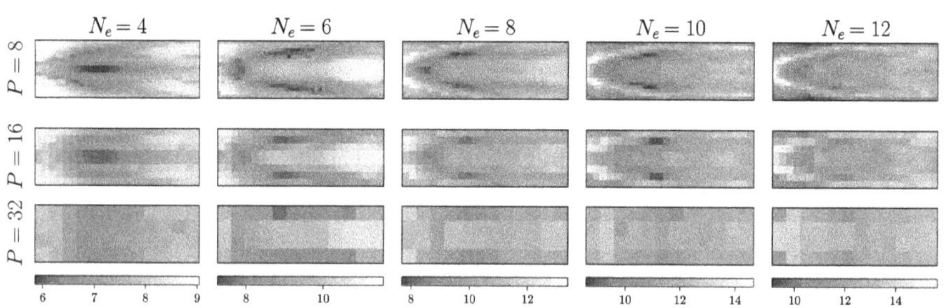

Fig. 4. Predictive-power maps for varying P and N_e. Patches with higher predictive power predict the rest of the patches with lower average loss.

the dominant coherent structures because the relevant dynamical correlations operate over larger spatial scales than in the laminar case.

Despite the increased reconstruction loss compared to dataset 1, LAMP achieves a 26% lower reconstruction error $\mathcal{L}^{\mathrm{pred}}$ than gappy POD [5] on identical inputs (results not shown for brevity). Qualitatively, gappy POD tends to overestimate velocity fluctuations in regions of greater uncertainty further downstream, whereas LAMP produces smoother reconstructions. LAMP's prediction

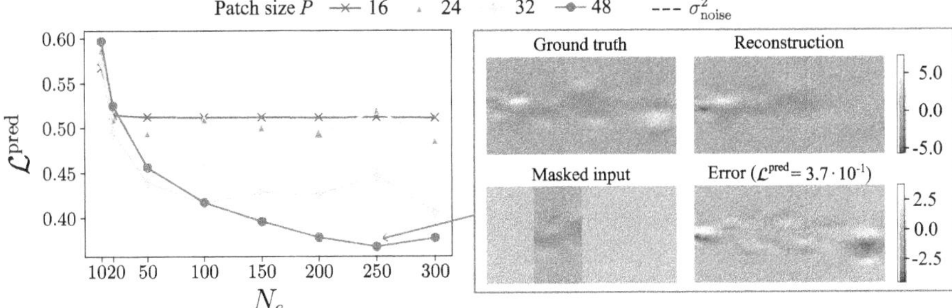

Fig. 5. Masked reconstruction of the chaotic wake from 25% unmasked patches, patches placed at the locations of highest predictive power. The reconstruction of one snapshot with the best model ($P = 48$, $N_e = 250$) is shown on the right.

accuracy is highest immediately downstream of unmasked patches and degrades further away. This is due to the spatio-temporally chaotic nature of the flow; two patches become less correlated with each other the further apart they are. Extending to LAMP with *multi-layer* transformers is required to predict nonlinear relationships between multiple patches. Additionally, time-delay embedding [17] could improve accuracy by exploiting temporal correlations.

4   Conclusion and Future Work

We introduce the *Latent Attention on Masked Patches* (LAMP) model, which consists of a regression-based architecture inspired by Vision Transformers. LAMP is designed to reconstruct high-dimensional flow fields from noisy and masked measurements. By integrating patch-wise POD with a linearly decomposable attention mechanism, we provide a framework that avoids extensive hyperparameter tuning and back-propagation. We showcase the LAMP on two test cases: a laminar wake past a triangular bluff body and a chaotic wake past two cylinders. On the laminar wake, LAMP successfully reconstructs flow fields from only 10% unmasked patches even when the input patches are corrupted by noise levels up to SNR = 10 dB. The reconstruction error remains an order of magnitude lower than the input noise variance, which shows that LAMP is both a reconstruction and de-noising tool. Beyond reconstruction, the attention maps from the LAMP provide an interpretable multi-fidelity sensor placement approach, which identifies the patches of highest importance for reconstruction. On the two-cylinder wake, LAMP outperforms gappy POD with 26% lower $\mathcal{L}^{\text{pred}}$. The overall error is, however, larger than the laminar case, suggesting that multi-layer attention blocks and nonlinear autoencoding might be required to reconstruct higher-dimensional, spatio-temporally chaotic flows. The modular architecture of the framework provides a natural pathway to more expressive extensions.

Acknowledgments. LM acknowledges funding from ERC Starting Grant PhyCo 949388. AN is supported by the Eric and Wendy Schmidt AI in Science Fellowship.

References

1. Bekoglu, E., Bempedelis, N., Steiros, K.: Formation of turbulent secondary vortex street in absence of vortex shedding instability. J. Fluid Mech. **1024**, A7 (2025)
2. Berkooz, G., et al.: The proper orthogonal decomposition in the analysis of turbulent flows. Annu. Rev. Fluid Mech. **25**, 539–575 (1993)
3. Cheng, S., Liu, C., Guo, Y., Arcucci, R.: Efficient deep data assimilation with sparse observations and time-varying sensors. J. Comput. Phys. **496**, 112581 (2024)
4. Dosovitskiy, A.: An image is worth 16×16 words: transformers for image recognition at scale. In: Proceedings of IEEE/CVF CVPR, pp. 45–67 (2021)
5. Everson, R., Sirovich, L.: Karhunen-loève procedure for gappy data. J. Opt. Soc. Am. A **12**(8), 1657–1664 (1995)
6. Fukami, K., Fukagata, K., Taira, K.: Super-resolution reconstruction of turbulent flows with machine learning. J. Fluid Mech. **870**, 106–120 (2019)
7. He, K., Chen, X., Xie, S., Li, Y., Dollár, P., Girshick, R.: Masked autoencoders are scalable vision learners. In: Proceedings of IEEE/CVF CVPR, pp. 16000–16009 (2022)
8. Lam, R., et al.: Learning skillful medium-range global weather forecasting. Science **382**(6677), 1416–1421 (2023)
9. Lee, Y., Yang, H., Yin, Z.: Piv-DCNN: cascaded deep convolutional neural networks for particle image velocimetry. Exp. Fluids **58**(12), 171 (2017)
10. Mo, Y., Magri, L.: Reconstruction of three-dimensional turbulent flows from sparse and noisy planar measurements: a weight-sharing neural network approach. Data-Centric Eng. **7**, e5 (2026)
11. Mo, Y., Traverso, T., Magri, L.: Decoder decomposition for the analysis of the latent space of nonlinear autoencoders with wind-tunnel experimental data. Data-Centric Eng. **5**, e38 (2024)
12. Nista, L., et al.: Influence of adversarial training on super-resolution turbulence reconstruction. Phys. Rev. Fluids **9**(6), 064601 (2024)
13. Özalp, E., Nóvoa, A., Magri, L.: Real-time forecasting of chaotic dynamics from sparse data and autoencoders. Comput. Methods Appl. Mech. Eng. **450**, 118600 (2026)
14. Peebles, W., Xie, S.: Scalable diffusion models with transformers. In: Proceedings of IEEE/CVF ICCV, pp. 4172–4182 (2023)
15. Quattromini, M., Bucci, M.A., Cherubini, S., Semeraro, O.: Mean flow data assimilation using physics-constrained graph neural networks. Data-Centric Eng. **6**, e48 (2025)
16. Racca, A., Doan, N.A.K., Magri, L.: Predicting turbulent dynamics with the convolutional autoencoder echo state network. J. Fluid Mech. **975**, A2 (2023)
17. Sauer, T., Yorke, J.A., Casdagli, M.: Embedology. J. Stat. Phys. **65**(3–4), 579–616 (1991)
18. Vaswani, A., et al.: Attention is all you need. In: Advances in Neural Information Processing Systems, vol. 30 (2017)
19. Xia, C., Zhang, J., Kerrigan, E.C., Rigas, G.: Active flow control for bluff body drag reduction using reinforcement learning with partial measurements. J. Fluid Mech. **981**, A17 (2024)

Multi-Criteria Decision-Making: Methods, Applications, and Innovations

Attribute Importance in Conflict Models: Using Clustering Metrics and Bi-coalitions for Issue Evaluation

Małgorzata Przybyła-Kasperek[1,2]($\boxtimes$) (iD) and Rafał Deja[3] (iD)

[1] Institute of Computer Science, University of Silesia, ul. Bedzinska 39, Sosnowiec, Poland
malgorzata.przybyla-kasperek@us.edu.pl
[2] Constantine the Philosopher University in Nitra, 949 01 Nitra, Slovakia
[3] Department of Computer Science, WSB University, ul. Cieplaka 1c, 41-300 Dabrowa Gornicza, Poland
rdeja@wsb.edu.pl

Abstract. This paper introduces a new approach to assessing attribute importance in conflict situations to better support negotiation processes. Building on Pawlak's conflict model, it proposes a bi-coalition-based measure that identifies issues enabling unanimous agreement and examines their impact on coalition formation. This qualitative perspective is contrasted with a quantitative method based on clustering metrics, revealing complementary dimensions of conflict dynamics. Applied to the Russia-Ukraine case, the framework highlights territorial integrity as the central dividing issue and shows how the bi-coalition-based measure helps pinpoint factors that hinder or facilitate consensus, offering practical insights for dispute mediation.

Keywords: Conflict analysis · Bi-coalitions · Attribute importance · Consensus · Multi-Agent Decision-Making

1 Introduction

Understanding contemporary geopolitical conflicts requires analytical tools capable of representing divergent interests, asymmetric dependencies, and multidimensional issue interactions. A foundational approach in this domain is Pawlak's conflict model, which encodes disagreements through ternary evaluations and rough-set-based relational structures [6]. Its subsequent developments – covering extended distance functions, Boolean reasoning, and negotiation-oriented perspectives – demonstrate how structured opinion data can be used to derive coalition patterns, conflict intensity, and consensus conditions [2,7,9]. The tri-valued representation of actor positions is further supported by the theory of three-way decisions, which generalizes classical rough-set partitions into positive, boundary, and negative regions and offers a decision-theoretic semantics

M. Paszynski et al. (Eds.): ICCS 2026 Workshops, LNCS 16788, pp. 191–199, 2026.
https://doi.org/10.1007/978-3-032-29915-4_16

for interpreting support, neutrality, and opposition [12,13]. This framework provides a principled foundation for the threshold-controlled aggregations employed in our analysis. Complementary insights arise from quantitative measures used to evaluate structural groupings. Cluster validity indices – the Dunn [5], Silhouette [4], and Davies-Bouldin [11] measures – originally designed to assess cluster compactness and separability, have recently been applied to coalition analysis, where relational structures between actors resemble distance-based clustering [8]. Parallel research in network science highlights how densely connected actors tend to form coherent communities, whereas game-theoretic approaches illuminate strategic incentives, externalities, and stability properties underlying coalition formation [1,10]. These perspectives jointly broaden the conceptual background for analysing coalitional structures within formal conflict-modelling frameworks. Building on these methodological foundations, this study introduces an integrated approach that: (i) employs clustering-inspired quality indices to quantify coalition cohesion and separability; (ii) advances attribute-importance analysis through a dual perspective combining removal-based coalition-quality degradation with a qualitative evaluation using Pareto-optimal bi-coalitions; and (iii) applies this framework to analyse the Russia-Ukraine conflict. The results consistently identify the restoration of Ukraine's territorial integrity as the dominant axis of disagreement shaping coalition stability, while distinguishing between issues that restrict coalition expansion and those that enable broader consensus. Overall, the proposed methodology contributes both a refined theoretical extension of conflict-modelling techniques and a practical toolset for interpreting complex international disputes.

2   Conflict Model Preliminaries

The present paper builds on Pawlak's conflict model [6], in which a conflict between agents is represented through discrepancies in their ternary evaluations of a set of issues. Each agent assigns to every issue a value from $V = \{-1, 0, +1\}$, corresponding to opposition, neutrality, and support, forming an information table with agents as rows and issues as columns.

Definition 1 (Conflict model). *Let $X = \{x_1, \ldots, x_m\}$ be a finite set of agents and $I = \{i_1, \ldots, i_n\}$ a finite set of issues. A conflict situation is a quadruple (X, I, V, r), where $V = \{-1, 0, +1\}$ and $r : X \times I \to V$ assigns a ternary rating to each agent–issue pair.*

For each issue i, the value space induces the classes $X_i^{+1} = \{x \mid r(x,i) = 1\}$, $X_i^0 = \{x \mid r(x,i) = 0\}$, $X_i^{-1} = \{x \mid r(x,i) = -1\}$, representing support, neutrality, and opposition. These partitions serve as the basic components for multi-issue aggregation.

For any subset $B \subseteq I$, aggregated opinions are defined by $r(x,B) = \frac{\sum_{i \in B} r(x,i)}{|B|}$, which induces the three-way split (with thresholds $-1 \leq l_1 < 0 < h_1 \leq 1$):

$$X_B^+ = \{x \mid r(x,B) \geq h_1\}, X_B^0 = \{x \mid l_1 < r(x,B) < h_1\}, X_B^- = \{x \mid r(x,B) \leq l_1\}.$$

Disagreement between agents x_j and x_k is quantified by the distance

$$d(x_j, x_k) = \frac{\sum_{i \in I} \varphi_i(x_j, x_k)}{|I|},$$

where

$$\varphi_i(x_j, x_k) = \begin{cases} 0, & r(x_j, i) = r(x_k, i), \\ 0.5, & r(x_j, i) \cdot r(x_k, i) = 0 \text{ and } r(x_j, i) \neq r(x_k, i), \\ 1, & r(x_j, i) = -r(x_k, i). \end{cases}$$

Using thresholds $0 \leq l_2 < h_2 \leq 1$, agent pairs are classified as $R^= = \{(x_j, x_k) \mid d(x_j, x_k) \leq l_2\}$, $R^\approx = \{(x_j, x_k) \mid l_2 < d(x_j, x_k) < h_2\}$, $R^{\neq} = \{(x_j, x_k) \mid d(x_j, x_k) \geq h_2\}$.

This relational tri-partition distinguishes aligned, neutral, and conflicting pairs. By symmetry, analogous partitions may be defined for subsets of agents to determine the issues they predominantly support, oppose, or treat neutrally.

3 Coalition Strength Recognition Through Clustering-Inspired Quality Measures

Coalition strength reflects how cohesive a group of agents is and how clearly it stands apart from other groups. In Pawlak's conflict model, alliances are determined through pairwise agreement thresholds, but the model itself does not evaluate how compact or well-separated these coalitions are. To address this limitation, we extend the framework with clustering-based quality measures that assess coalition cohesion and distinctness, following the approach in [8]. We employ three widely used indices: the Dunn index (separation vs. compactness), the Silhouette index (individual fit within coalitions), and the Davies–Bouldin index (average compactness relative to inter-group distance).

Coalitions are defined as maximal subsets $C \subseteq X$ such that for all $x, y \in C$ the allied condition $d(x, y) < 0.5$ holds. Since some agents may be close to multiple groups, coalitions may overlap. Let $\mathcal{C} = \{C_1, \ldots, C_K\}$ denote the resulting structure.

Dunn index. $D = \dfrac{\min\limits_{p \neq q} \min\limits_{x \in C_p,\, y \in C_q} d(x, y)}{\max\limits_{k} \max\limits_{x, y \in C_k} d(x, y)}.$

Silhouette index. Let $a(x)$ be the average distance between x and members of its coalition, and $b(x)$ the minimum average distance to another coalition.

$$s(x) = \frac{b(x) - a(x)}{\max\{a(x), b(x)\}}, \quad S = \frac{1}{|X|} \sum_{x \in X} s(x).$$

Davies–Bouldin index. Let S_k denote the mean intra-coalition distance in C_k, and M_{kj} the mean pairwise distance between C_k and C_j:

$$DB = \frac{1}{K} \sum_{k=1}^{K} \max_{j \neq k} \frac{S_k + S_j}{M_{kj}}.$$

Together, these metrics provide a complementary evaluation: Dunn emphasizes global separation, Silhouette measures how well individual agents fit their coalitions, and Davies–Bouldin captures average compactness relative to inter-coalition similarity. High-quality coalition structures thus exhibit high D and S, and low DB. To summarize these criteria, we define a normalized combined quality measure $Q = w_D\,D^{norm} + w_S\,S^{norm} - w_{DB}\,DB^{norm}$, where each index is normalized to $[0,1]$ based on its minimum and maximum values obtained across all attribute-removal variants. Since distances between agents are calculated directly from issue evaluations, each issue contributes differently to coalition formation and stability. Attribute-importance analysis therefore examines how the coalition structure and quality change when an issue is removed.

Definition 2. *For each issue $a \in I$, let Q_a denote the quality of the coalition structure obtained from the reduced system $IS_a = (X, I \setminus \{a\})$. A higher value of Q_a indicates that removing issue a increases coalition coherence and separation, meaning that a plays a critical role in shaping the original conflict. The most influential issue is identified by $\arg\max_{a \in I} Q_a$.*

This measure provides a practical tool for analysing conflict drivers: issues whose removal improves coalition quality act as major sources of disagreement, while those whose removal weakens coalition clarity support internal cohesion or maintain boundaries between groups. The attribute-ranking procedure follows the hierarchical evaluation scheme introduced in [8], where successive removals reveal the relative strategic importance of each issue.

4   Qualitative Conflict Analysis

We analyse qualitative agreement structures using the concept of bi–coalitions, introduced in [3], which extends Pawlak's conflict model by identifying groups of agents who unanimously agree on a subset of issues. A bi–coalition is a pair (Y, B) with $Y \subseteq X$ and $B \subseteq I$ such that all agents in Y assign identical values to all issues in B. Formally, $\sigma_B(x_j, x_k) = \{\, i \in B \mid r(x_j, i) = r(x_k, i)\,\}$, and (Y, B) is a bi–coalition if

$$B = \bigcap_{x_j, x_k \in Y} \sigma_B(x_j, x_k) \neq \emptyset.$$

Its strength may be evaluated by

$$\mathrm{str}_1(Y, B) = \frac{|Y|}{|X|} \cdot \frac{|B|}{|I|} \quad \text{or} \quad \mathrm{str}_2(Y, B) = \frac{|Y| + |B|}{|X| + |I|},$$

which measure the extent of consensus. A relaxed version that treats neutrality as compatible replaces σ_B with $\sigma_B^*(x_j, x_k) = \{\, i \in B \mid r(x_j, i) = r(x_k, i) \ \lor\ r(x_j, i) = 0 \ \lor\ r(x_k, i) = 0\,\}$.

We focus on Pareto–optimal bi–coalitions (denoted BIC^{max}), defined as those (Y, B) for which no enlargement of Y or B is possible without violating unanimity: $(Y', B') \succ (Y, B) \Rightarrow (Y, B)$ not Pareto–optimal.

Bi–coalitions provide a direct constraint-based view of agreement formation and enable issue-level importance assessment. Since each (Y, B) is characterised by the issues enabling unanimous agreement, the presence and strength of bi–coalitions reveal which issues support broad consensus and which restrict coalition expansion.

For each issue $i \in I$, we define its importance based on Pareto-optimal bi–coalitions as

$$Imp_{BIC}(i) = \sum_{(Y,B) \in BIC^{\mathrm{max}}, \; i \in B} \mathrm{str}(Y, B),$$

where str denotes any chosen strength measure. A high value indicates that many agents can jointly agree on i, meaning that the issue is non-obstructive in coalition building. A low value reflects that only small groups can reach unanimity on i, identifying it as a significant barrier to consensus.

To align the bi–coalition framework with the removal-based approach used for distance-based coalitions, we define a complementary importance measure. For each issue i, consider the reduced system $IS_{-i} = (X, I \setminus \{i\}, V, r|_{I \setminus \{i\}})$, recompute its set of Pareto-optimal bi–coalitions BIC^{max}_{-i}, and evaluate their total quality

$$Q = \sum_{(Y,B) \in BIC^{\mathrm{max}}} \mathrm{str}(Y, B), \qquad Q_{-i} = \sum_{(Y,B) \in BIC^{\mathrm{max}}_{-i}} \mathrm{str}(Y, B).$$

The importance of issue i is defined by $Imp_{rem}(i) = Q - Q_{-i}$.

A larger value of $Imp_{rem}(i)$ means that the removal of issue i significantly weakens the structure of unanimous-agreement groups, identifying it as essential for maintaining stable agreement patterns. Issues with low values play a minor role and do not substantially influence the qualitative coalition landscape.

5 Russia–Ukraine Conflict

To illustrate the proposed methodology, we analyse the Russia–Ukraine conflict, one of the most consequential and persistent geopolitical crises of recent years. The conflict is represented by six key agents (Ukraine, Russia, United States, European Union, NATO, China) and seven issues covering territorial, military, political, and economic dimensions. Belarus is excluded, as its evaluations coincide with Russia's. The resulting conflict situation is shown in Table 1. The issues encode: i_1 territorial restoration; i_2 NATO membership; i_3 Western military aid; i_4 recognition of Russian annexations; i_5 ceasefire on current lines; i_6 non-NATO security guarantees; i_7 Western sanctions on Russia.

Using the distance measure from Sect. 3, the agents form two coalitions: $C_1 = \{x_1, x_3, x_4, x_5\}, C_2 = \{x_2, x_6\}$, corresponding respectively to a Western-aligned group and a Russia-aligned bloc.

Applying the Dunn, Silhouette and Davies–Bouldin indices produces: $D = 2.0$, $S = 0.728$, $DB = 0.553$, indicating that these coalitions are internally coherent and clearly separated.

Table 1. Agents × Issues: Russia–Ukraine conflict

A \ I	i_1	i_2	i_3	i_4	i_5	i_6	i_7
Ukraine (x_1)	+1	+1	+1	−1	−1	+1	+1
Russia (x_2)	−1	−1	−1	+1	+1	−1	−1
United States (x_3)	−1	0	+1	−1	0	+1	+1
European Union (x_4)	0	+1	+1	−1	0	0	+1
NATO (x_5)	0	0	+1	−1	0	+1	+1
China (x_6)	0	−1	−1	0	+1	0	−1

To evaluate issue importance, each issue is removed in turn, coalition structures are recomputed, and the resulting quality indices are normalized to obtain: $Q_a = \frac{1}{3}D_a^{norm} + \frac{1}{3}S_a^{norm} - \frac{1}{3}DB_a^{norm}$. The values Q_a (summarized in Table 2) show that issue i_1 (territorial integrity) is the strongest driver of the coalition split. Issues such as i_3 (military aid) and i_7 (sanctions) have low or negative Q_a, meaning that their removal does not substantially alter the coalition structure and they play a secondary role.

Table 2. Quality indices and issue quality Q_a after removing issue i_a.

Issue removed	D_a	S_a	DB_a	D_a^{norm}	S_a^{norm}	DB_a^{norm}	Q_a
i_1	4	0.81	0.39	1	1	0	0.67
i_2	2	0.73	0.57	0.2	0.47	0.6	0.02
i_3	1.5	0.66	0.69	0	0	1	−0.33
i_4	1.75	0.72	0.53	0.1	0.4	0.47	0.01
i_5	2.33	0.73	0.57	0.33	0.47	0.6	0.07
i_6	1.75	0.77	0.46	0.1	0.73	0.23	0.2
i_7	1.5	0.66	0.69	0	0	1	−0.33

We now illustrate the two previously defined importance measures: the participation based $Imp_{BIC}(i)$ and the removal-based $Imp_{rem}(i)$. In this example, we use the str_1 strength measure. Using the full conflict table, we compute all Pareto-optimal bi–coalitions (Y, B); their sets and strengths are listed in Table 3. Based on these values, the participation-based importance measure $Imp_{BIC}(i)$ is reported in Table 4. Issues i_3 and i_7 obtain the highest scores, indicating frequent participation in strong unanimity groups. Issues i_4 and i_5 play a moderate role, while i_1, i_2, and i_6 appear mostly in small coalitions and therefore show low importance.

The total bi–coalition quality for the full system equals $Q = 2.9762$. To compute the removal-based measure, we remove each issue in turn, recompute all Pareto-optimal bi–coalitions, and obtain $Imp_{rem}(i) = Q - Q_{-i}$, where Q_{-i}

Table 3. Pareto-optimal bi-coalitions in the full system.

Bi–coalition (Y,B), str_1	Bi–coalition (Y,B), str_1
$(\{x_1\}, \{i_1, \ldots, i_7\})$, 0.1667	$(\{x_5\}, \{i_1, \ldots, i_7\})$, 0.1667
$(\{x_2\}, \{i_1, \ldots, i_7\})$, 0.1667	$(\{x_6\}, \{i_1, \ldots, i_7\})$, 0.1667
$(\{x_3\}, \{i_1, \ldots, i_7\})$, 0.1667	$(\{x_1, x_4\}, \{i_2, i_3, i_4, i_7\})$, 0.1905
$(\{x_4\}, \{i_1, \ldots, i_7\})$, 0.1667	$(\{x_2, x_3\}, \{i_1\})$, 0.0476
$(\{x_2, x_6\}, \{i_2, i_3, i_5, i_7\})$, 0.1905	$(\{x_4, x_6\}, \{i_1, i_6\})$, 0.0952
$(\{x_3, x_5\}, \{i_2, i_3, i_4, i_5, i_6, i_7\})$, 0.2857	$(\{x_1, x_3, x_5\}, \{i_3, i_4, i_6, i_7\})$, 0.2857
$(\{x_4, x_5\}, \{i_1, i_3, i_4, i_5, i_7\})$, 0.2381	$(\{x_3, x_4, x_5\}, \{i_3, i_4, i_5, i_7\})$, 0.2857
$(\{x_4, x_5, x_6\}, \{i_1\})$, 0.0714	$(\{x_1, x_3, x_4, x_5\}, \{i_3, i_4, i_7\})$, 0.2857

Table 4. Issue importance $Imp_{BiC}(i)$.

Issue i	i_1	i_2	i_3	i_4	i_5	i_6	i_7
$\mathrm{Imp}_{\mathrm{BiC}}(i)$	1.4524	1.6667	2.7619	2.5714	2.0000	1.6667	2.7619

is the total strength in the reduced system. These values are summarized in Table 5. Removing issue i_1 produces the largest drop (0.4762), confirming that it is the most restrictive and structurally significant dimension. Issues i_3, i_5, i_6, and i_7 show moderate influence, while issue i_2 has only marginal effect.

Table 5. Values of Q_{-i} and removal-based issue importance $Imp_{rem}(i)$.

Issue i	i_1	i_2	i_3	i_4	i_5	i_6	i_7
Q_{-i}	2.5	2.9722	2.8056	2.8611	2.8056	2.8056	2.8056
$\mathrm{Imp}_{\mathrm{rem}}(i)$	0.4762	0.004	0.1706	0.1151	0.1706	0.1706	0.1706

Both measures consistently indicate that i_1 is the key point of disagreement, while i_3, i_7, and partially i_4 correspond to issues with relatively broad agreement and lower restrictiveness.

6 Discussion and Conclusion

This study presents an integrated framework for analysing coalition structures and assessing attribute importance in conflict situations, combining clustering-based metrics with a qualitative bi-coalition approach. Building on Pawlak's conflict model, we introduced a unanimity-focused measure and compared it with a quantitative distance-based assessment. The Russia–Ukraine case study showed that both measures consistently identify territorial integrity as the principal factor shaping coalition divisions, while other issues display varying levels of flexibility. The bi-coalition measure reveals negotiation-relevant agreement patterns, complementing the structural perspective provided by clustering indices.

The proposed dual-perspective approach offers concrete analytical support for negotiation and mediation processes. The clustering-based component highlights structural divisions and identifies issues that most strongly shape coalition boundaries, while the bi–coalition analysis pinpoints where unanimous agreement is feasible and where it is structurally constrained. Together, these insights help practitioners prioritise negotiation topics and estimate the room for possible consensus. While the current study focuses on a representative medium-sized conflict scenario, the methodological design allows for straightforward application to larger multi-agent or multi-issue environments. As the number of potential bi–coalitions may grow with system complexity, future work may explore efficient pruning strategies or approximate evaluation schemes to enhance scalability without reducing interpretability. Thresholds and weights used in the clustering-based measure follow conventions from earlier conflict-modelling studies and standard clustering literature; however, their robustness and sensitivity would benefit from a separate parametrical analysis. This suggests an additional avenue for future research.

Overall, the results demonstrate that analysing attribute importance is essential for understanding conflict dynamics and supporting negotiation processes.

References

1. Amirkhani, A., Barshooi, A.H.: Consensus in multi-agent systems: a review. Artif. Intell. Rev. **55**(5), 3897–3935 (2022)
2. Deja, R.: Conflict analysis. Int. J. Intell. Syst. **17**(2), 235–253 (2002)
3. Deja, R., Przybyła-Kasperek, M.: Bi-coalitions analysis in the rough sets conflict model. Inf. Sci. 122746 (2025)
4. Dudek, A.: Silhouette index as clustering evaluation tool. In: Jajuga, K., Batóg, J., Walesiak, M. (eds.) SKAD 2019. SCDAKO, pp. 19–33. Springer, Cham (2020). https://doi.org/10.1007/978-3-030-52348-0_2
5. Gupta, T., Panda, S.P.: Clustering validation of Clara and k-means using silhouette & Dunn measures on iris dataset. In: 2019 COMITCon, pp. 10–13. IEEE (2019)
6. Pawlak, Z.: Some remarks on conflict analysis. Eur. J. Oper. Res. **166**(3), 649–654 (2005)
7. Przybyła-Kasperek, M.: Coalitions' weights in a dispersed system with Pawlak conflict model. Group Decis. Negot. **29**(3), 549–591 (2020)
8. Przybyła-Kasperek, M., Deja, R., Wakulicz-Deja, A.: Hierarchical system in conflict scenarios constructed based on cluster analysis-inspired method for attribute significance determination. Appl. Soft Comput. **167**, 112304 (2024)
9. Skowron, A., Ramanna, S., Peters, J.F.: Conflict analysis and information systems: a rough set approach. In: Wang, G.-Y., Peters, J.F., Skowron, A., Yao, Y. (eds.) RSKT 2006. LNCS (LNAI), vol. 4062, pp. 233–240. Springer, Heidelberg (2006). https://doi.org/10.1007/11795131_34
10. Tran, T.N.T., Felfernig, A., Le, V.M.: An overview of consensus models for group decision-making and group recommender systems. User Model. User-Adap. Inter. (2023)

11. Xiao, J., Lu, J., Li, X.: Davies Bouldin index based hierarchical initialization k-means. Intell. Data Anal. **21**(6), 1327–1338 (2017)
12. Yao, J., Medina, J., Zhang, Y., Ślęzak, D.: Formal concept analysis, rough sets, and three-way decisions. Int. J. Approx. Reason. **140**, 1–6 (2022)
13. Yao, Y.: Three-way decisions with probabilistic rough sets. Inf. Sci. **180**(3), 341–353 (2010)

Designing Form-Based Interaction in Virtual Reality: A Multidimensional Usability Evaluation Using Eye-Tracking and MCDA

Agnieszka Olejnik-Krugły$^{(\boxtimes)}$, Kamil Bortko ,
and Krzysztof Warpachowicz

Faculty of Computer Science and Information Technology, West Pomeranian
University of Technology in Szczecin, Szczecin, Poland
`{aolejnik,kbortko,kwarpachowicz}@zut.edu.pl`
`http://www.zut.edu.pl`

Abstract. The increasing use of virtual reality (VR) beyond entertainment raises questions about the evaluation of task-oriented immersive applications. This paper presents form-based interaction in VR as a multi-criteria decision-making problem. An experimental study was conducted in a three-dimensional virtual travel agency, where users performed a trip reservation task using interactive forms. The analysis focused on eye-tracking-based criteria related to visual attention allocation, exploration dynamics, and selected indicators of cognitive load, integrated within a multi-criteria framework to support a structured and interpretable evaluation of interaction quality. The results indicate that the proposed approach helps identify key factors influencing VR form usability and provides a systematic basis for evaluating immersive applications.

Keywords: Multi-Criteria Decision Analysis · Forms · VR · UX/UI

1 Introduction

Virtual reality is increasingly used in education, healthcare, e-commerce, and professional training, making the design and evaluation of immersive user interfaces an important research challenge [15]. However, classical usability and user experience approaches, including Nielsen's heuristics [9], Norman's interaction design principles [10], and ISO human-centred design standards [5], were developed primarily for two-dimensional interfaces and do not fully reflect the spatial, perceptual, and motor characteristics of VR. This limitation is especially relevant to form-based interactions, which remain essential in transactional systems but require different design assumptions in immersive environments.

VR interface evaluation often relies on isolated metrics or subjective opinions, limiting comparability and practical usefulness. This paper proposes a structured framework for evaluating form-based interaction in immersive environments, focusing on eye-tracking-derived measures interpreted through multi-criteria decision analysis. The framework was applied in an experimental study conducted in a three-dimensional virtual travel agency, where participants completed a trip reservation task using interactive forms. The collected eye-tracking data were analysed with PROMETHEE II to compare weighting scenarios and identify the criteria most influential for interaction quality.

2 Literature Review

Literature increasingly describes VR as a platform supporting task-oriented activities rather than entertainment alone, with applications spanning domains such as education, e-commerce, healthcare, and professional settings [3,8]. As VR adoption expands, immersive interfaces are expected to meet requirements similar to those of conventional information systems, including efficiency, clarity, and low error rates. However, established usability and UX approaches [5,9,10] were developed primarily for two-dimensional interfaces and do not fully capture key characteristics of immersive interaction, such as depth perception, viewpoint variability, physical effort, and increased cognitive load [2]. This limitation becomes especially relevant in the case of form-based interaction, where users must process textual information, identify labels, and select interface elements within a three-dimensional space.

A particularly important issue in this context concerns the perceptual and ergonomic constraints affecting form-based interaction in VR. Recent studies indicate that interaction quality in immersive environments is shaped not only by layout and information structure, but also by perceptual constraints, pointing accuracy, visual stability, and muscular fatigue [1,7]. Unlike two-dimensional interfaces, where forms rely on relatively stable visual conventions and predictable layouts, VR introduces additional variability resulting from user movement, changing viewpoints, and field-of-view limitations. Consequently, forms in immersive environments cannot be treated as direct counterparts of their 2D equivalents and require dedicated evaluation approaches.

Against this background, the contribution of the present study lies in proposing a structured evaluation framework for form-based interaction in VR that integrates eye-tracking and interaction-based evidence within a multi-criteria analytical perspective. Rather than introducing a standalone formal model, the study develops an integrated evaluation approach that treats form interaction as a complex process involving information processing, spatial presentation, and interaction ergonomics. Unlike prior studies that often rely on isolated indicators such as task completion time or error rate, the proposed perspective supports the joint interpretation of heterogeneous criteria relevant to immersive interaction.

This approach is further motivated by the fact that eye-tracking metrics may provide indirect evidence of visual attention allocation, search efficiency, and processing effort, while interaction-based indicators complement them in the assessment of usability-related aspects associated with cognitive load and interaction quality [1,2]. However, the literature still lacks coherent approaches that combine such heterogeneous indicators within a structured evaluation framework specifically for VR forms. Existing work on text entry and interaction in immersive environments has largely focused on individual techniques, such as virtual keyboards, raycasting, gaze-based input, or controller-based interaction, rather than on forms as complete interaction processes [4,14].

More recent literature also highlights the need for evaluation approaches that are not only methodologically rigorous but also practically applicable in domains where VR supports structured user processes rather than exploratory experiences alone [8,11,13]. In this context, the framework proposed in this paper aims to provide a systematic basis for comparing alternative analytical perspectives and identifying the criteria that matter most for form usability in immersive environments. This gap motivates the conceptual framework introduced in the following section.

3   Conceptual Framework and Methods

The study was designed as a multidimensional evaluation of form-based interaction in a proprietary VR travel agency prototype. The choice of participants, task scenarios, and evaluation metrics was guided by the aim of reproducing a realistic booking process as a representative stress-test for spatial user interfaces. Following prior work indicating that form-based interaction in VR cannot be reliably assessed using isolated measures alone [12], the study focused primarily on eye-tracking-derived indicators related to visual attention, exploration dynamics, and selected aspects of cognitive load [6]. In this perspective, usability was examined through the joint interpretation of these heterogeneous measures under controlled laboratory conditions, while MCDA supported a structured analysis of trade-offs between different interaction dimensions. Although the study used a single application scenario, the selected participants, task sequence, and evaluation dimensions were intended to reflect common challenges of form-based interaction in immersive environments, thereby supporting cautious transferability of the findings to other task-oriented VR systems.

As illustrated in Fig. 1, the user was positioned at the center of a 360° environment, with the form located in the central visual field to support precise data entry and peripheral regions (45–60°) supporting exploration. Behavioral data, derived primarily from eye-tracking, were analysed in relation to visual attention, exploration dynamics, and cognitive load, allowing the effects of locomotion and spatial layout on psychophysical comfort to be examined in an integrated manner.

The experiment used an HTC Vive Pro 2 headset to ensure sufficient text legibility and visual clarity in a task requiring participants to read hotel descriptions and price lists. Its resolution (4896×2448) reduced the screen-door effect known from earlier head-mounted displays, while 120 Hz refresh rate helped minimize motion-to-photon latency and reduce the risk of motion sickness. To improve ecological validity and eliminate movement constraints, the setup also included the VIVE Wireless Adapter based on WiGig technology, enabling unrestricted

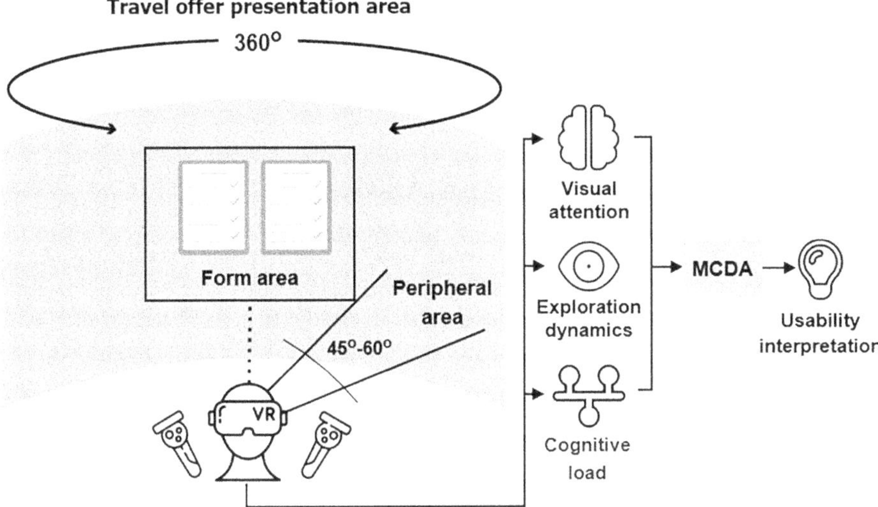

Fig. 1. Conceptual diagram of form-based interaction in a virtual travel agency, illustrating the central form area, peripheral exploration regions, and the integration of interaction data across visual attention, exploration dynamics, and cognitive load using MCDA.

360° exploration. The software environment integrated SteamVR with the Cognitive3D analytics platform, which enabled unobtrusive collection of gaze paths and heatmaps.

The study involved $N = 45$ participants (24 women and 21 men) aged 17–46 ($\bar{x} = 27.2$). The sample deliberately included both experienced VR users ($n = 33$) and novices ($n = 12$), allowing the evaluation to capture both learned and intuitive interaction patterns. In addition, 40% of participants ($n = 18$) had diagnosed vision impairments, including astigmatism, which supported an accessibility-oriented assessment of text legibility and interface sizing. The experiment was conducted in a dedicated laboratory room with a safe interaction area of 3 m × 3 m. Lighthouse base stations were positioned to minimize controller occlusion, and the researcher acted as a spotter throughout the session.

The procedure followed a structured protocol. After screening for health contraindications and completing a short introductory interview, each participant underwent headset calibration, including individual adjustment of interpupillary distance and headset position. A three-minute training session in a neutral virtual environment was then used to familiarize participants with the controls: parabolic teleportation with the left controller and interaction with interface elements using the right controller. The main experimental phase comprised four tasks with different cognitive demands: (1) a guided task verifying interface logic, (2) a free task assessing autonomous decision-making during trip selection, (3) a readability task requiring participants to locate and report specific pricing information, and (4) a time-constrained task (120 s) evaluating performance under stress. This task sequence was intended to cover a range of interaction conditions relevant to form use in VR, from guided completion to autonomous exploration and time pressure. The procedure concluded with a post-experimental questionnaire completed immediately after immersion.

4   Experimental Results and Analysis

The eye-tracking analysis revealed consistent visual behavior typical of cognitively demanding tasks. Users spent approximately 75–85% of samples in fixations, indicating strong sustained attention, in line with prior literature.

Fixation duration varied from about 295 ms to 1380 ms, suggesting two dominant strategies: rapid scanning (300–500 ms) and deeper analytical processing (600–1400 ms). Despite this, fixation rates remained stable (0.09–0.13 fixations/s), indicating moderate interaction tempo without time pressure. This supports the conclusion that the interface promotes analytical rather than exploratory behavior.

The proportion of fixation time differed across users (3–18%), reflecting individual exploration styles. A one-way ANOVA confirmed significant differences in mean fixation duration: $F(9, 500000) = 14.23$, $p < 0.001$, which was supported by the Kruskal–Wallis test: $H = 112.8$, $p < 0.001$.

Spearman correlation analysis showed strong relationships between key metrics. Mean fixation duration correlated with fixation time proportion ($\rho = 0.82$), fixation count with recording duration ($\rho = 0.91$), and fixation rate moderately with fixation proportion ($\rho = 0.67$), indicating consistent viewing behavior.

Overall, the interface supports sustained analytical attention without excessive cognitive load, while significant inter-user differences emphasize the need for adaptive design approaches.

4.1   Multi-criteria Decision Analysis Using PROMETHEE II

Multi-Criteria Decision Analysis (MCDA) enables evaluation of complex phenomena described by multiple criteria. In eye-tracking studies, it allows integration of heterogeneous metrics into a unified and interpretable framework, emphasizing trade-offs rather than a single optimal solution.

In this study, the PROMETHEE II method was applied. It is an outranking approach providing a complete ranking based on pairwise comparisons and preference functions, well-suited for behavioral data due to its transparency and robustness.

Five eye-tracking criteria were used: fixation ratio [%] (C_1, max), average fixation duration [ms] (C_2, min), exploration rate (fixations/s) (C_3, max), fixation time proportion [%] (C_4, max), and spatial dispersion (std. dev. in X,Y) (C_5, min). Criteria C_1 and C_4 reflect fixation dominance, C_3 captures exploration dynamics, whereas C_2 and C_5 relate to cognitive load and stability.

PROMETHEE II was applied to compare weighting scenarios as preference profiles, where Φ denotes net dominance. Four scenarios were defined to reflect different analytical priorities: fixation stability (S1), exploration (S2), cognitive load minimization (S3), and balanced weighting (S4) (Table 1).

Table 1. Weighting scenarios and PROMETHEE II results

Scenario	C_1	C_2	C_3	C_4	C_5
S1	0.35	0.10	0.10	0.35	0.10
S2	0.20	0.10	0.40	0.20	0.10
S3	0.10	0.50	0.10	0.20	0.10
S4	0.20	0.20	0.20	0.20	0.20

Scenario	Φ^+	Φ^-	Φ	Rank
S3	0.320	0.180	**0.140**	1
S1	0.295	0.205	**0.090**	2
S2	0.270	0.230	**0.040**	3
S4	0.200	0.300	**-0.100**	4

Scenario S3 achieved the highest dominance, whereas S4 served as a neutral baseline. Using average weights, the criteria were ranked as follows: C_4 ($\Phi = 0.090$), C_2 ($\Phi = 0.070$), C_1 ($\Phi = 0.050$), C_3 ($\Phi = 0.020$), and C_5 ($\Phi = -0.100$). Thus, temporal fixation measures (C_4, C_2) were the most influential, whereas spatial dispersion (C_5) played a minor role.

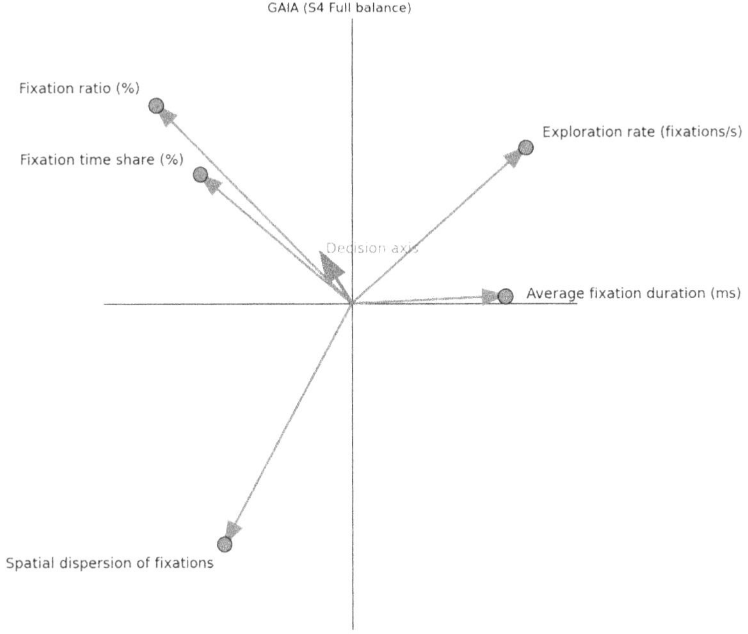

Fig. 2. S4: Full balance.

GAIA plane (Fig. 2) provides a geometric interpretation of criteria relationships. While criteria positions remain stable, the decision axis varies with weighting. S1 emphasizes fixation dominance, S2 favors exploration (C_3), and S3 highlights fixation duration (C_2) as a proxy for cognitive load. S4 represents a balanced configuration without strong alignment.

The GAIA analysis for the full balance scenario illustrates the trade-off between stability and exploration criteria within a single, representative configuration. This example demonstrates how the balanced weighting scheme captures a compromise between competing objectives, providing an interpretable and holistic view of the decision space.

The PROMETHEE II results indicate that S3 (cognitive load minimization) is the dominant preference profile, followed by S1 and S2, while S4 acts as a neutral reference. Among criteria, fixation time proportion (C_4) and duration (C_2) are most influential, while C_1 and C_3 are moderate, and C_5 remains least significant. The consistency of rankings confirms the robustness of the MCDA framework for eye-tracking analysis.

5   Conclusions

This paper presented a multidimensional evaluation of form-based interaction in virtual reality using a proprietary virtual travel agency prototype as a case study. The findings indicate that the usability of VR forms cannot be captured by isolated performance measures alone, as interaction quality emerges from the interplay of perceptual, cognitive, and behavioral factors.

Eye-tracking results suggest that form completion in VR is associated with an analytical visual processing strategy, reflected in longer fixations and structured allocation of attention. This implies that VR form interfaces should prioritise visual stability, clear information hierarchy, limited numbers of simultaneously displayed elements, and high typographic legibility. At the same time, the observed inter-user variability indicates that effective solutions should also accommodate differences in prior experience and individual interaction strategies through guidance, feedback, and error-prevention mechanisms.

The study also demonstrated the usefulness of MCDA (PROMETHEE II) as a tool for interpreting heterogeneous interaction data. The analysis showed that temporal fixation measures, such as fixation time proportion and average fixation duration, had a stronger effect on the overall preference structure than spatial dispersion measures. Rather than reducing usability to a single score, the MCDA approach made it possible to expose trade-offs between interaction stability, exploration, and cognitive efficiency, thus providing a more informative basis for design decisions in immersive environments.

The study has several limitations. It was conducted under controlled laboratory conditions, within a single application scenario, and with a limited set of form-related tasks, which constrains generalizability. Future research should therefore extend the framework to other VR form types, interaction techniques, and application domains, as well as explore adaptive solutions responsive to individual user differences.

In conclusion, the proposed approach contributes to immersive interface research by offering a structured perspective on VR form usability and by showing how MCDA can support the interpretation of complex behavioral data and more informed VR interface design.

References

1. Bhowmik, A.K.: Virtual and augmented reality: human sensory-perceptual requirements and trends for immersive spatial computing experiences. J. Soc. Inform. Display **32**(8), 605–646 (2024)
2. Chen, M.X., Hu, H., Yao, R., Qiu, L., Li, D.: A survey on the design of virtual reality interaction interfaces. Sensors **24**(19) (2024). https://doi.org/10.3390/s24196204
3. Choudhery, H., Kesharwani, S.: The role of AR and VR in shaping e-commerce: a literature review. Glob. J. Enterp. Inf. Syst. **16**(2), 83–90 (2024)
4. Dube, T.J., Arif, A.S.: Text entry in virtual reality: a comprehensive review of the literature. In: Kurosu, M. (ed.) HCII 2019. LNCS, vol. 11567, pp. 419–437. Springer, Cham (2019). https://doi.org/10.1007/978-3-030-22643-5_33
5. ISO: Ergonomics of human-system interaction – part 9241-210: Human-centred design for interactive systems (2019). https://www.iso.org/standard/77520.html
6. Makransky, G., Petersen, G.B.: The cognitive affective model of immersive learning (camil): a theoretical research-based model of learning in immersive virtual reality. Educ. Psychol. Rev. **33**(3), 937–958 (2021)
7. Mimnaugh, K.J., et al.: Virtual reality sickness reduces attention during immersive experiences. IEEE Trans. Vis. Comput. Graph. **29**(11), 4394–4404 (2023)
8. Moskala, K., Frankowski, M., Igras-Cybulska, M., Bohné, T., Witoszek-Kubicka, A., Tadeja, S.: A novel approach to enhance VR user awareness of nearby non-virtual hazards through adaptive visual alerts. In: 2024 IEEE International Symposium on Mixed and Augmented Reality Adjunct (ISMAR-Adjunct), pp. 252–255. IEEE (2024)
9. Nielsen, J.: Usability Engineering. Morgan Kaufmann Publishers Inc., San Francisco, CA, USA (1994)
10. Norman, D.A.: The Design of Everyday Things. The MIT Press. Cambridge, Mass. (2013)
11. Olejnik-Krugły, A., Bortko, K., Jankowski, J., Bródka, J.: Towards effective visual alerts in immersive VR environments: balancing visibility and user experience. In: Proceedings of the 59th Hawaii International Conference on System Sciences (HICSS-59), p. 299 (2026). https://hdl.handle.net/10125/111428
12. Radianti, J., Majchrzak, T.A., Fromm, J., Wohlgenannt, I.: A systematic review of immersive virtual reality applications for higher education: design elements, lessons learned, and research agenda. Comput. Educ. **147**, 103778 (2020)
13. Sharma, G., Mishra, S.: Alert modalities in connected and smart work zones to enhance workers' safety from traffic accidents using virtual reality (VR) experiments. Transp. Res. Part C: Emerg. Technol. **174**, 105085 (2025)

14. Speicher, M., Feit, A.M., Ziegler, P., Krüger, A.: Selection-based text entry in virtual reality. In: Proceedings of the 2018 CHI Conference on Human Factors in Computing Systems. CHI '18, pp. 1–13. Association for Computing Machinery, New York, NY, USA (2018). https://doi.org/10.1145/3173574.3174221
15. Sung, H., Kim, M., Park, J., Shin, N., Han, Y.: Effectiveness of virtual reality in healthcare education: systematic review and meta-analysis. Sustainability **16**(19), 8520 (2024)

Simulating Decision-Makers' Behaviour in Risk Management Problems Using Prospect Theory

Jakub Więckowski[1]($\boxtimes$) iD and Mariusz Sołtysik[2] iD

[1] National Institute of Telecommunications, ul. Szachowa 1, 04-894 Warsaw, Poland
J.Wieckowski@il-pib.pl
[2] Cracow University of Economics, ul. Rakowicka 27, 31-510 Cracow, Poland
soltysik@uek.krakow.pl

Abstract. Risk management plays a crucial role in multi-criteria decision analysis, as decision-makers must balance the attractiveness of alternatives with the uncertainty and risk associated with their selection. Behavioural aspects such as sensitivity to gains and losses and loss aversion significantly influence how risk is perceived and processed, yet their impact on the stability of decision-support outcomes remains insufficiently explored. This study provides a systematic analysis of recommendation robustness under structured behavioural perturbations using the Risk-Informed Decision Making (RIDM) method. A large-scale simulation framework is proposed to model decision-makers' behavior through systematic modifications of prospect-theory parameters representing gain sensitivity, loss sensitivity, and loss aversion. Three complementary experimental approaches are considered: directional behavioural profiles reflecting rational, emotional, and asymmetric attitudes; unequal responsiveness of risk parameters; and isolated single-parameter modifications. The experiments examine how changes in risk perception affect local ranking stability, measured as one-position shifts in the ordering of alternatives. The results indicate that asymmetric and gain-oriented behaviors lead to less stable rankings, requiring smaller behavioural changes to alter outcomes, while more balanced profiles exhibit higher robustness. These findings provide behavioural insight into the sensitivity of RIDM-based recommendations and support their interpretation in risk-aware decision-support applications.

Keywords: risk management · multi-criteria decision analysis · prospect theory · RIDM method

1 Introduction

Decision-makers facing Multi-Criteria Decision Analysis (MCDA) problems frequently rely on various analytical tools to support their choices [15]. With rapid technological development in recent years, a wide range of decision support techniques has emerged to address increasingly complex decision environments [5, 7].

M. Paszynski et al. (Eds.): ICCS 2026 Workshops, LNCS 16788, pp. 209–223, 2026.
https://doi.org/10.1007/978-3-032-29915-4_18

A key challenge in such problems is the rational handling of both the attractiveness and the risk associated with selecting particular decision alternatives [11]. Appropriately accounting for risk, in line with a decision-maker's preferences and risk aversion, can lead to more informed, justified, and expectation-consistent decisions [9,10]. One theoretical framework that enables a nuanced representation of decision-makers' attitudes toward risk is prospect theory, which captures behavioral responses to gains and losses and allows for asymmetric risk perception [6,8].

Supporting decision-makers in managing risk within multi-criteria decision problems is an important area of development for decision support systems [13]. One recently proposed approach addressing this challenge is the Risk-Informed Decision Making (RIDM) method. RIDM extends traditional MCDA assessments by complementing attractiveness-based evaluations with an explicit assessment of the risk-taking tendencies associated with selecting particular alternatives. In this way, RIDM brings a second evaluation dimension, enabling decision-makers to balance attractiveness and risk when forming final recommendations. The method is grounded in prospect theory and employs its value function, parameterized by α, β, and λ, which jointly represent the decision-maker's attitudes toward risk, gains, and losses [14]. Additionally, decision-makers specify neutral reference points for each criterion, representing performance levels at which neither gains nor losses are perceived.

Reliable recommendations regarding the risk-taking tendencies associated with alternatives depend strongly on accurate specification of these parameters. However, despite their importance, the effects of modifying them, reflecting changes in the decision-maker's risk preferences and attitudes, have not yet been systematically examined. In practice, decisions under risk often change not because of new data, but due to shifts in the perception of gains, losses, and risks. Many decision support methods, however, assume stable managerial preferences and overlook the resilience of recommendations to behavioral fluctuations. This motivates research into the sensitivity of decision outcomes to changes in decision-makers' behavior and justifies the present study, which investigates how variations in RIDM parameters affect the stability of resulting recommendations.

To address this objective, the study proposes a simulation-based experiment that evaluates how changes in decision-maker parameters influence RIDM outcomes. The key novelty lies in the systematic analysis of recommendation robustness under structured behavioural perturbations. The experiments rely on synthetically generated decision problems and simulated representations of decision-makers' risk attitudes, allowing systematic control of the prospect-theory-based parameters α, β, and λ. The simulation framework is organized into three complementary experimental approaches. The first approach examines directional attitudes toward gains and losses, represented by four decision-maker profiles: rational, emotional, gain-oriented, and loss-aversion-oriented. These profiles are implemented through coherent and asymmetric perturbations of the parameters α and β, capturing both theoretically consistent behaviors and departures from symmetry between gains and losses. The second approach focuses on parameter responsiveness, considering scenarios in which α and β change at unequal rates, reflecting differences in how quickly specific aspects of risk perception evolve. The third approach investigates single-parameter modifications, analyzing cases in which only one of the parameters α or β is altered while the remaining parameters are held constant.

The analysis focuses on local ranking disturbances, examining how sensitive specific positions in the ranking are to parameter changes. In particular, the study quantifies the mean magnitude of parameter modifications required to induce a one-position shift (upward or downward) for a given alternative in the ranking. This perspective enables a direct interpretation of stability in terms of decision-maker behaviour: how substantial a change in risk perception or preference structure is necessary to achieve a desired change in the ranking outcome. In this way, the study directly operationalizes and measures recommendation robustness within the RIDM framework, linking behavioural parameter changes to observable effects on ranking stability. By examining how local ranking changes emerge under structured perturbations, the proposed approach provides new insights into the interdependencies between behavioural parameters and the robustness of recommendations, strengthening the interpretability and practical applicability of RIDM as a risk-aware decision support tool.

The rest of the paper is organized as follows. Section 2 presents the preliminaries of the RIDM method. Section 3 describes the methodology used to perform simulation experiments. Section 4 shows the results of those experiments, including different behaviors of decision-makers. Finally, Sect. 5 draws conclusions from the research and indicates future directions

2 Preliminaries

2.1 The Risk-Informed Decision Making Method

The RIDM method incorporates a behavioural perspective into multi-criteria evaluation by focusing on decision-makers' risk attitudes. It assesses how alternatives relate to neutral reference points and whether they induce risk-seeking or risk-averse behaviour, complementing traditional MCDA with a two-dimensional analysis of attractiveness and behavioural response. The approach is grounded in prospect theory, particularly the evaluation of outcomes relative to reference points and the asymmetric perception of gains and losses. Following Audia and Greve [2], risk is interpreted as attitudes toward deviations from aspiration levels rather than the likelihood of adverse outcomes. Thus, RIDM captures behavioural responses to known outcomes and is especially useful in contexts where such effects influence decision-making.

Decision Problem Formulation. The RIDM method builds on standard MCDA input data. When used alongside MCDA methods, it directly adopts the set of alternatives, the set of criteria, the performance values from the decision matrix, and the criteria weights, acting as a complementary extension without requiring data modification. When applied independently, the same elements must be defined explicitly. In both cases, these inputs form the basis for the behavioural analysis conducted within the RIDM framework.

Definition of Neutral Reference Points. In the context of the RIDM method, neutral reference points represent criterion-specific performance levels at which decision-makers perceive neither gains nor losses. They provide a behavioural baseline that defines the threshold between outcomes that are likely to trigger risk-averse responses and those that may encourage risk-seeking behavior, thus serving as a key element in assessing risk-taking tendencies. The vector of neutral reference points is defined as (1):

$$P = [p_1, p_2, \ldots, p_j, \ldots, p_n], \quad j = 1, \ldots, n, \tag{1}$$

where p_j denotes the neutral performance level for criterion C_j.

Behavioural Value Transformation. To capture the asymmetric perception of gains and losses in RIDM, each performance value x_{ij} is transformed relative to the neutral reference point p_j for criterion C_j using value functions inspired by prospect theory. It reflects behavioural responses to deviations from the neutral performance level, enabling evaluation of risk-taking tendencies at the criterion level.

Two types of criterion-specific value functions are applied depending on the preference direction of the criterion:

- Increasing value function (for criteria where higher values lead to gains and smaller to losses) as (2):

$$v(x_{ij}) = \begin{cases} (x_{ij} - p_j)^\alpha, & x_{ij} \geq p_j, \\ -\lambda(-(x_{ij} - p_j))^\beta, & x_{ij} < p_j, \end{cases} \tag{2}$$

- Decreasing value function (for criteria where lower values lead to gains and higher to losses) as (3):

$$v(x_{ij}) = \begin{cases} (-(x_{ij} - p_j))^\alpha, & x_{ij} \leq p_j, \\ -\lambda((x_{ij} - p_j))^\beta, & x_{ij} > p_j. \end{cases} \tag{3}$$

The parameters α and β control the sensitivity to gains and losses, respectively, while λ captures decision-makers' loss aversion. Applying these transformations to all elements of the decision matrix X produces the behavioural value matrix V defined as (4):

$$V = \begin{bmatrix} v_{11} & v_{12} & \cdots & v_{1j} & \cdots & v_{1n} \\ v_{21} & v_{22} & \cdots & v_{2j} & \cdots & v_{2n} \\ \vdots & \vdots & \cdots & \vdots & \cdots & \vdots \\ v_{i1} & v_{i2} & \cdots & v_{ij} & \cdots & v_{in} \\ \vdots & \vdots & \cdots & \vdots & \cdots & \vdots \\ v_{m1} & v_{m2} & \cdots & v_{mj} & \cdots & v_{mn} \end{bmatrix} \tag{4}$$

where each entry v_{ij} quantifies the potential risk-taking or risk-averse response of decision-makers to deviations from the neutral reference point at the criterion level.

Behavioural Value Standardization. To ensure comparability across criteria, values in the behavioral matrix V are standardized using absolute maximum scaling [3]. For each criterion C_j, all values are divided by the maximum absolute value in the column, standardizing gains and losses to $[-1, 1]$ while preserving their relative magnitudes. Formally, the standardized value $\bar{v}_{ij}$ is given by (5):

$$\bar{v}_{ij} = \frac{v_{ij}}{\max |v_j|}, \quad i = 1, \ldots, m, \quad j = 1, \ldots, n. \tag{5}$$

Aggregation and Construction of Risk-Taking Tendency Indicator. The normalized values are aggregated across criteria to obtain an overall indicator of risk-taking tendency for each alternative with (6):

$$R_i = \sum_{j=1}^{n} \bar{v}_{ij} \cdot w_j, \tag{6}$$

where w_j denotes the weight of criterion C_j. The resulting measure R_i reflects the extent to which a given alternative may be associated with potential risk-seeking or risk-averse tendencies relative to the defined neutral reference points.

3   Methodology

This section presents a simulation-based methodology for modeling decision-makers' behavior in risk management using the RIDM method to evaluate the risk of selecting alternatives in MCDA problems. The main objective is to assess the stability of RIDM-based recommendations, focusing on local ranking shifts at specific positions.

The approach examines how changes in decision-makers' preferences and risk attitudes, represented by RIDM's prospect-theory parameters, affect rankings. It quantifies the parameter modifications needed to induce one-position promotions or demotions, providing a behavioural interpretation of ranking stability. The methodology combines simulated decision-makers with varying risk attitudes, synthetic decision problems, and controlled incremental parameter perturbations.

3.1   Decision-Makers Behavior

The simulation experiment considers several decision-maker profiles reflecting different risk attitudes as described by prospect theory [13], including (a) rational, (b) emotional, (c) gain-oriented, and (d) loss-aversion-oriented types. It also models parameter changes with unequal rates or single-parameter modifications. All profiles are represented through controlled variations of RIDM parameters α, β, and λ, capturing sensitivities to gains, losses, and loss aversion.

A baseline decision-maker is generated by sampling the parameters $(\alpha_0, \beta_0, \lambda_0)$ from predefined distributions. The gain-related parameter α_0 is drawn from a uniform distribution as (7):

$$\alpha_0 \sim \mathcal{U}(0.6, 1.0). \tag{7}$$

The loss-related parameter β_0 is sampled in relation to α_0 with (8):

$$\beta_0 = \alpha_0 + \varepsilon, \qquad \varepsilon \sim \mathcal{N}(0, 0.05), \tag{8}$$

and clipped to the interval $[0.5, 1.2]$ to ensure behavioural credibility. The loss-aversion parameter λ_0 is drawn from (9)

$$\lambda_0 \sim \mathcal{U}(1.5, 3.0), \tag{9}$$

and adjusted to account for interdependence with gain sensitivity with (10):

$$\lambda_0 \leftarrow \max\big(\lambda_0 \cdot \big(1 - 0.3(\alpha_0 - 0.8)\big), 1.0\big). \tag{10}$$

This adjustment reflects a stylized behavioural assumption that higher sensitivity to gains is typically associated with lower relative loss aversion. While this relationship is model-driven rather than empirically derived, it ensures consistency between parameters and prevents unrealistic combinations of high gain sensitivity and strong loss aversion.

To model changes in decision-makers' attitudes, controlled perturbations of the prospect-theory parameters are applied. Three complementary experimental approaches are considered, each defined by a specific set of directional perturbations of the parameters (α, β). In general, directional changes are represented by vectors (11):

$$(\Delta\alpha, \Delta\beta) = (s_\alpha, s_\beta), \tag{11}$$

where (s_α, s_β) denotes the direction of change applied to the gain- and loss-sensitivity parameters, respectively. The first set D_1 represents coherent and asymmetric attitudes toward gains and losses, corresponding to increasingly rational behavior, increasingly emotional behavior, gain-oriented asymmetry, and loss-oriented asymmetry. It is defined as (12):

$$D_1 = \{(+1, +1), (-1, -1), (+1, -1), (-1, +1)\}, \tag{12}$$

The second set D_2 models unequal responsiveness of α and β, allowing one parameter to vary more slowly than the other. It is determined as follows (13):

$$D_2 = \{(+0.5, +1), (-0.5, -1), (+1, +0.5), (-1, -0.5)\}, \tag{13}$$

The third set D_3 isolates single-parameter effects by modifying only one sensitivity parameter at a time. It is defined as (14):

$$D_3 = \{(+1, 0), (-1, 0), (0, +1), (0, -1)\}. \tag{14}$$

For a selected direction (s_α, s_β), parameters are modified incrementally according to (15):

$$\alpha = \alpha_0 + s_\alpha \cdot t, \qquad \beta = \beta_0 + s_\beta \cdot t, \tag{15}$$

where t denotes the perturbation magnitude expressed in direction sets. The maximum deviation is constrained by (16)

$$|\alpha - \alpha_0| \leq 0.5, \qquad |\beta - \beta_0| \leq 0.5, \tag{16}$$

ensuring that simulated behavioural changes remain within realistic bounds.

The loss-aversion parameter λ is updated consistently with changes in α according to

$$\lambda = \begin{cases} \lambda_0 \cdot \left(1 - 0.3(\alpha - 0.8)\right) & \text{if } s_\alpha \neq 0, \\ \lambda_0 \cdot \left(1 - 0.3(\beta - 0.8)\right) & \text{otherwise} \end{cases} \tag{17}$$

This functional form operationalizes a controlled dependency between sensitivity parameters and loss aversion, enabling systematic analysis of behavioural perturbations while preserving interpretable parameter relationships. However, it should be noted, that this specification is a modelling assumption introduced for experimental tractability; alternative formulations of this dependency may lead to quantitatively different results, although the qualitative patterns of robustness are expected to remain comparable.

3.2   Input Data

The simulation experiments are based on synthetically generated multi-criteria decision problems. For each experiment, a decision matrix $\mathbf{X} = [x_{ij}]$ of size 5×5 is generated, where i denotes decision alternatives and j denotes evaluation criteria. Each matrix element represents the performance of alternative i with respect to criterion j and is sampled from a uniform distribution as (18):

$$x_{ij} \sim \mathcal{U}(0, 100) \tag{18}$$

For each criterion j, a neutral reference point N_j is defined, representing a reference level at which neither gains nor losses are perceived. Neutral points are independently sampled from the same bounded range as the decision matrix values described as (19):

$$N_j \sim \mathcal{U}(\min x_i, \max x_i), \quad j = 1, \ldots, 5. \tag{19}$$

This assumption ensures that neutral reference points lie within the feasible performance space of the analyzed decision problem. Criteria types are defined to reflect both profit-type and cost-type evaluations. The set of criteria types is specified by a vector $\mathbf{ct} = (ct_1, \ldots, ct_5)$, where (20):

$$ct_j = \begin{cases} \text{profit}, & \text{if } j \text{ is odd}, \\ \text{cost}, & \text{if } j \text{ is even}. \end{cases} \tag{20}$$

This alternating structure ensures a balanced representation of gain-oriented and loss-oriented criteria within each simulated decision problem. The equal weighting scheme was applied to model the importance of the criteria weights. All input data components are generated independently for each iteration of the simulation experiment, allowing for a diverse and unbiased exploration of decision-making scenarios.

3.3 Evaluation Flow

The evaluation follows a simulation-based procedure repeated independently for each iteration. At the start, a decision matrix, criteria types, and neutral reference points are generated according to the input specification, and a decision-maker is sampled by drawing RIDM parameters α_0, β_0, and λ_0.

The RIDM method is applied to obtain reference scores and a baseline ranking, which serves as a benchmark for assessing stability under parameter perturbations. For each decision-maker profile, α and β are incrementally modified in the prescribed direction up to a maximum deviation of $\Delta_{\max} = 0.5$, updating λ accordingly, and RIDM is reapplied. A change that alters the relative ordering of the two alternatives defining a ranking position is recorded as a successful ranking shift.

Within each iteration, all directions and experimental approaches are applied across behavioural profiles. A total of 20,000 iterations are performed to enable statistical analysis of ranking stability and sensitivity to risk-related preference changes.

4 Results

This section presents the results of the simulation experiments conducted for the considered approaches to modelling decision-makers' behavior. As a first step, the distributions of the simulated parameters are analyzed to illustrate the characteristics of the generated decision-maker profiles and to verify the correctness of the simulation setup.

Figure 1 shows the joint distributions of the prospect-theory parameters α, β, and λ for 1,000 randomly selected iterations from the full set of simulation experiments. The relationships are presented in three parameter pairs, allowing direct comparison of their mutual dependencies. The parameters α and β exhibit similar distributions, with α ranging from 0.6 to 1.0 and β from 0.5 to approximately 1.1.

The (α, λ) and (β, λ) pairs show a wide spread, with λ values ranging from about 1.3 to 3.2. The (α, λ) distribution is relatively uniform, while (β, λ) is more concentrated, especially for β between 0.65 and 0.95, indicating that sensitivities

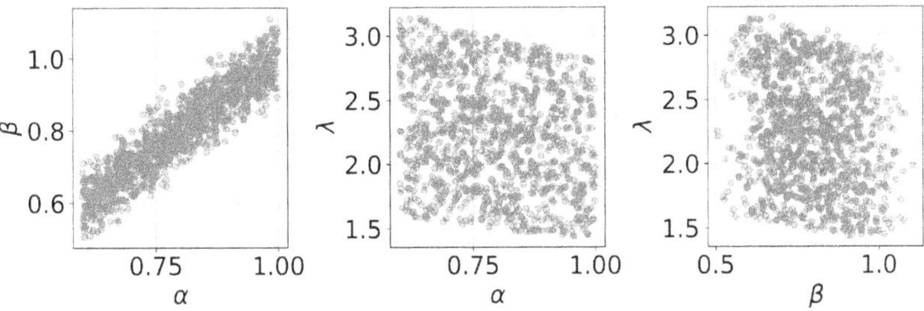

Fig. 1. Distribution of generated α, β, and λ parameters representing simulated decision-makers' attitudes toward risk across 1,000 selected iterations.

to gains and losses are balanced but loss aversion varies substantially. The simulated parameters cover a broad spectrum of risk attitudes, from risk-tolerant to strongly risk-averse.

Figure 2 shows the distribution of neutral reference points. Although sampled uniformly, their bounds vary across iterations and criteria based on observed performance values, producing higher density near the center of the scale and ensuring all reference points remain feasible within the generated decision problems.

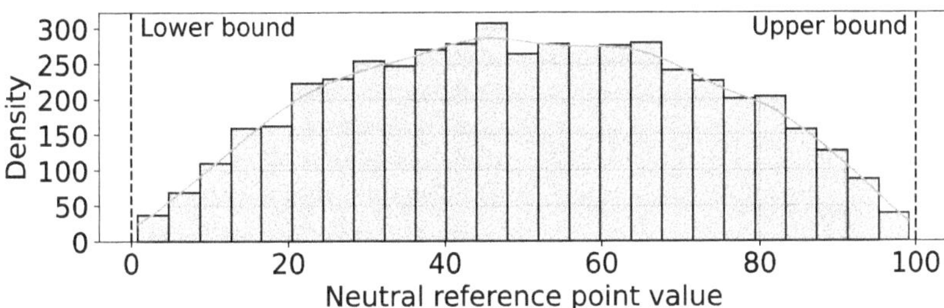

Fig. 2. Histogram of generated neutral reference points based on a uniform distribution across 1,000 selected iterations.

4.1 Different Profiles of Decision-Makers

Figure 3 presents the percentage shares of successful and unsuccessful simulation runs for the four considered decision-maker profiles: (a) rational, (b) emotional, (c) gain-oriented, and (d) loss-aversion-oriented, based on 20,000 iterations. The results indicate substantial differences in ranking sensitivity across behavioural types. In particular, the gain-oriented attitude allows the highest percentage share of successful ranking shifts, reaching 37.1% of all runs. In contrast, the rational decision-maker profile exhibits the lowest share of successful outcomes at 14.9%, which is 2.8% lower than in the case of the emotional decision-maker. This observation suggests that asymmetric sensitivity to gains substantially increases the likelihood of inducing local ranking disturbances, whereas symmetric and theory-consistent attitudes lead to more stable rankings.

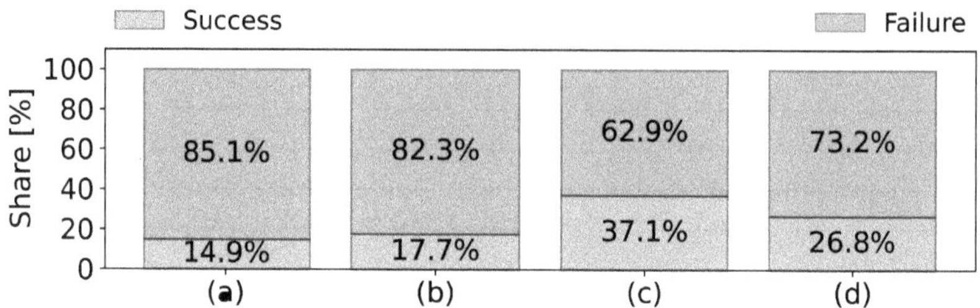

Fig. 3. Percentage share distributions of performed experiments with 20,000 iterations comparing successful and failed runs regarding obtaining shifts in ranking positions for four considered decision-maker behaviors: (a) rational, (b) emotional, (c) gain-oriented, and (d) loss-aversion-oriented.

In all scenarios, α and β were modified with equal magnitudes ($t = 1$) and bounded as described in Sect. 3. After each change, the loss-aversion parameter λ was recalculated according to Eq. 17 to maintain consistency between sensitivities to gains and losses and overall loss aversion. This ensures that differences in ranking stability reflect the assumed decision-maker profiles rather than unequal parameter scaling.

Table 1. Comparison of mean difference (Δ) required to notice ranking shifts between particular positions according to modeled decision-makers' behavior: (a) rational, (b) emotional, (c) gain-oriented, and (d) loss-aversion-oriented.

Rank shift	(a)			(b)			(c)			(d)		
	$\Delta\alpha$	$\Delta\beta$	$\Delta\lambda$	$\Delta\alpha$	$\Delta\beta$	$\Delta\lambda$	$\Delta\alpha$	$\Delta\beta$	$\Delta\lambda$	$\Delta\alpha$	$\Delta\beta$	$\Delta\lambda$
$1 \leftrightarrow 2$	0.22	0.22	−0.14	−0.23	−0.23	0.16	0.18	−0.18	−0.12	−0.17	0.15	0.11
$2 \leftrightarrow 3$	0.22	0.22	−0.14	−0.22	−0.22	0.15	0.17	−0.17	−0.11	−0.15	0.15	0.10
$3 \leftrightarrow 4$	0.22	0.22	−0.14	−0.22	−0.22	0.15	0.16	−0.16	−0.11	−0.15	0.15	0.10
$4 \leftrightarrow 5$	0.23	0.23	−0.15	−0.23	−0.23	0.15	0.18	−0.18	−0.12	−0.16	0.16	0.11

Table 1 summarizes the average parameter changes needed to induce a one-position shift between adjacent alternatives, reported by decision-maker profile and rank pair. For rational and emotional profiles, $\Delta\alpha$ and $\Delta\beta$ are comparable across ranks, while λ changes in opposite directions. Gain- and loss-aversion-oriented profiles require smaller changes in one parameter relative to the other, indicating that asymmetric attitudes reduce resistance to local ranking disturbances.

Across all profiles, the changes of examined parameters are relatively consistent across different rank positions, indicating that local ranking stability is primarily driven by behavioural characteristics rather than by the absolute position in the ranking.

4.2   Unequal Rates of Parameter Changes

Results of the second experimental approach, which focuses on unequal responsiveness of the parameters α and β, are presented below. In this approach, the parameters are modified with different rates of change, modeling scenarios in which decision-makers adjust their sensitivity to gains and losses at different speeds. Figure 4 indicates that the success rates of inducing ranking shifts are more homogeneous than in the first experimental approach. The share of successful runs varies from 12.9% for scenarios with slower decreases in α to 21.4% for scenarios with slower decreases in β, resulting in a narrower range of outcomes compared to the directional attitude experiment. Unequal changes in α and β represent decision-makers who adapt asymmetrically to changes in gains and losses, reflecting differences in behavioural responsiveness rather than purely directional preferences.

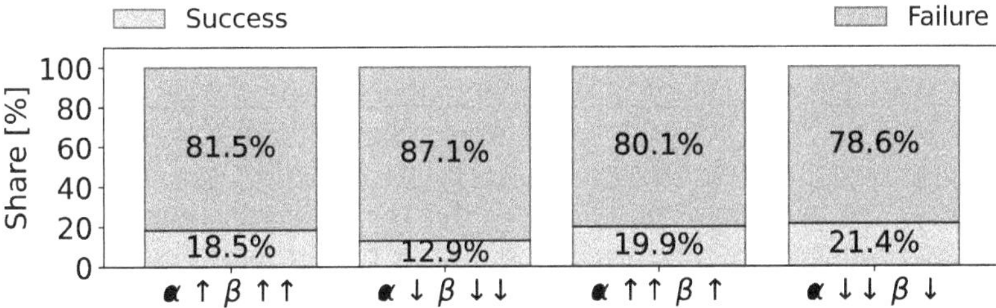

Fig. 4. Percentage share distributions of successful and unsuccessful simulation runs across 20,000 iterations for the second experimental approach, comparing scenarios with unequal rates of change in the parameters α and β.

Furthermore, Table 2 reports the mean magnitudes of parameter changes required to induce ranking shifts between adjacent positions. The results show comparable changes required for increasing and decreasing trends for both parameters. For scenarios in which α changes more slowly than β, decreasing trends require 0.01–0.03 higher parameter changes than increasing trends. Conversely, when β changes more slowly than α, increasing trends require changes larger by 0.01–0.02 than decreasing trends. It suggests that delayed adjustment of sensitivity to losses or gains may either weaken or strengthen ranking instability, depending on which element of behavior is less responsive.

Table 2. Comparison of mean difference (Δ) required to notice ranking shifts between particular positions according to modeled decision-makers' behavior with unequal rates of changes in α and β.

Rank shift	$\alpha \uparrow \beta \uparrow\uparrow$			$\alpha \downarrow \beta \downarrow\downarrow$			$\alpha \uparrow\uparrow \beta \uparrow$			$\alpha \downarrow\downarrow \beta \downarrow$		
	$\Delta\alpha$	$\Delta\beta$	$\Delta\lambda$	$\Delta\alpha$	$\Delta\beta$	$\Delta\lambda$	$\Delta\alpha$	$\Delta\beta$	$\Delta\lambda$	$\Delta\alpha$	$\Delta\beta$	$\Delta\lambda$
$1 \leftrightarrow 2$	0.11	0.22	−0.07	−0.13	−0.25	0.09	0.22	0.11	−0.14	−0.22	−0.11	0.15
$2 \leftrightarrow 3$	0.11	0.22	−0.07	−0.12	−0.25	0.09	0.21	0.11	−0.14	−0.21	−0.10	0.14
$3 \leftrightarrow 4$	0.11	0.21	−0.06	−0.12	−0.24	0.08	0.21	0.11	−0.14	−0.20	−0.10	0.14
$4 \leftrightarrow 5$	0.11	0.22	−0.07	−0.13	−0.25	0.09	0.22	0.11	−0.14	−0.20	−0.10	0.13

4.3   Modifications of a Single Parameter

The third experimental approach focuses on scenarios in which only one parameter, either α or β, is modified, while the other is held constant. This setup models decision-makers whose sensitivity to either gains or losses changes independently, without a simultaneous adjustment of the complementary component. As in the previous experiments, the loss-aversion parameter λ is recalculated after each modification, reflecting the assumed interdependence between sensitivity to gains and overall loss aversion in decision-makers' behavior.

The observed success rates are more diverse than in the second experimental approach and closer to those obtained for distinct decision-maker profiles in the first approach. The percentage of successful ranking shifts ranges from 18.8% for decreases in β to 28.7% for decreases in α, as illustrated in Fig. 5. Furthermore, the scenario involving the increase of β exhibits a slightly smaller success rate, compared to the increase of α. This indicates that isolated changes in gain sensitivity can influence ranking stability slightly stronger than isolated changes in loss sensitivity.

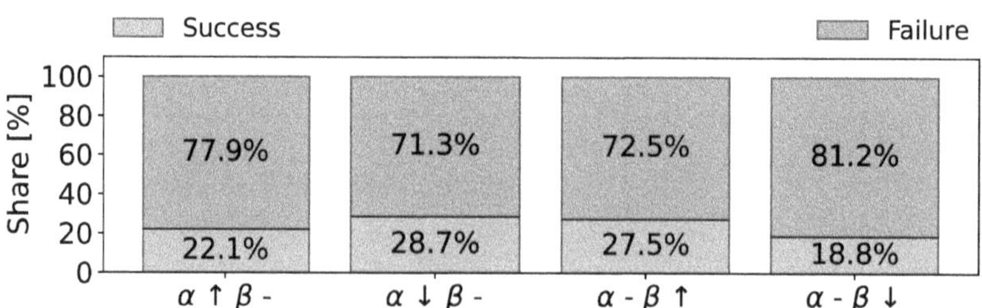

Fig. 5. Percentage share distributions of performed experiments with 20,000 iterations comparing successful and failed runs regarding obtaining shifts in ranking positions with changes introduced in only a single parameter (α or β).

The mean magnitudes of parameter changes required to induce ranking shifts for this experimental approach are reported in Table 3. The smallest required

Table 3. Comparison of mean difference (Δ) required to notice ranking shifts between particular positions according to modeled decision-makers' behavior with changes introduced in only a single parameter (α or β).

Rank shift	$\alpha\uparrow\beta$—			$\alpha\downarrow\beta$—			α—$\beta\uparrow$			α—$\beta\downarrow$		
	$\Delta\alpha$	$\Delta\beta$	$\Delta\lambda$	$\Delta\alpha$	$\Delta\beta$	$\Delta\lambda$	$\Delta\alpha$	$\Delta\beta$	$\Delta\lambda$	$\Delta\alpha$	$\Delta\beta$	$\Delta\lambda$
$1 \leftrightarrow 2$	0.21	—	-0.14	-0.19	—	0.13	—	0.21	-0.14	—	-0.24	0.16
$2 \leftrightarrow 3$	0.20	—	-0.13	-0.18	—	0.12	—	0.20	-0.13	—	-0.22	0.16
$3 \leftrightarrow 4$	0.20	—	-0.13	-0.18	—	0.12	—	0.19	-0.13	—	-0.22	0.15
$4 \leftrightarrow 5$	0.21	—	-0.14	-0.18	—	0.12	—	0.20	-0.13	—	-0.23	0.16

change is observed for decreasing values of α, with an average magnitude of approximately -0.18 relative to the baseline. The remaining scenarios exhibit comparable absolute changes, ranging from 0.19 to 0.2, with slightly higher changes for decreasing β. Also, increases in β are associated with slightly larger mean changes in the λ parameter compared to other cases, indicating that stronger adjustments in loss aversion are needed when decreasing sensitivity to losses in order to induce a ranking shift. This suggests a higher behavioural resistance to ranking changes driven solely by decreasing loss sensitivity than by increasing it.

4.4   Discussion

The findings have important managerial implications for the design of management information systems and decision-making under risk. By incorporating a behavioral component through prospect-theory parameters (α, β, λ), the proposed approach enables a more realistic representation of managerial decision processes. It allows for assessing the stability of recommendations under changes in risk perception and identifying behavioral thresholds at which preferred alternatives change, improving transparency and supporting more informed decisions.

From a strategic perspective, the approach enables behavioral robustness analysis by simulating different decision-maker profiles and evaluating their impact on the stability of choices. This is particularly relevant for investment decisions, resource allocation, and strategic planning, where sensitivity to managerial preferences may affect outcomes [1, 12]. The results also highlight the importance of accounting for cognitive diversity, supporting the integration of individualized decision profiles into decision support and business intelligence systems.

At the same time, the high sensitivity of results to behavioral parameters underscores the need for appropriate governance mechanisms. In particular, this justifies the need to introduce mechanisms that limit excessive subjectivity in decisions, such as collegial procedures, the aggregation of assessments from multiple decision-makers, or the formalization of assumptions regarding risk perception within decision-making processes [4]. From an organizational management perspective, the proposed approach supports the development of more advanced, hybrid decision support systems that integrate multi-criteria analytical methods with a behavioral approach. Consequently, the research findings contribute to the development of management practices based on a deeper reflection on the role of risk perception in decision-making processes, strengthening the organization's ability to make accurate and stable decisions under conditions of uncertainty.

5   Conclusion

This study analyzed the stability of RIDM-based rankings under systematic modifications of decision-makers' risk preferences modeled by using prospect-theory parameters. Large-scale simulations examined directional attitudes toward gains and losses, unequal parameter responsiveness, and isolated single-parameter changes. Ranking stability strongly depended on both the direction and structure of behavioural modifications: gain-oriented and asymmetric attitudes induced shifts more easily than rational or emotionally consistent behaviors, and changes in gain sensitivity had a stronger impact than comparable changes in loss sensitivity. Managerial decisions under risk proved highly sensitive to decision-makers' behavioural characteristics, particularly asymmetric sensitivity to gains and losses, with profit-oriented profiles showing greater instability than more balanced ones. The findings highlight the importance of accounting for behaviour in decision processes and using prospect-theory-based tools as reflective support, while noting that results are conditioned by the assumed functional dependency between sensitivity parameters and loss aversion, which may affect quantitative outcomes.

Despite its contributions, the study has several limitations. The experiments were conducted on fixed-size, synthetic decision problems and relied on simulated behavioural profiles, which may affect the generalizability of the results to real-world settings. The fixed number of alternatives and criteria further limits applicability to larger or structurally different problems. Neutral reference points were generated using uniform distributions within decision-space bounds, which may not fully reflect actual preference structures. Moreover, the loss-aversion parameter λ was updated using a predefined functional relationship, whereas real behavioural interactions between gains, losses, and loss aversion may be more complex. Consequently, the results should be interpreted as indicative rather than definitive.

Future research should address these limitations by extending the analysis to decision problems with varying sizes and structures, exploring other distributions and elicitation methods for neutral reference points, and investigating more flexible or data-driven relationships between prospect-theory parameters. Incorporating empirical data from surveys or controlled experiments with decision-makers would be particularly valuable for validating the behavioural assumptions and strengthening the practical relevance of the findings.

Acknowledgments. The work was supported by the National Science Centre 2024/55/B/HS4/00426.

References

1. Almansour, B.Y., Elkrghli, S., Almansour, A.Y.: Behavioral finance factors and investment decisions: a mediating role of risk perception. Cogent Econ. Finance **11**(2), 2239032 (2023)
2. Audia, P.G., Greve, H.R.: Less likely to fail: low performance, firm size, and factory expansion in the shipbuilding industry. Manage. Sci. **52**(1), 83–94 (2006)
3. Cabello-Solorzano, K., Ortigosa de Araujo, I., Peña, M., Correia, L., J. Tallón-Ballesteros, A.: The impact of data normalization on the accuracy of machine learning algorithms: A comparative analysis. In: International Conference on Soft Computing Models in Industrial and Environmental Applications, pp. 344–353. Springer (2023). https://doi.org/10.1007/978-3-031-42536-3_33
4. Develaki, M.: Uncertainty, risk, and decision-making: concepts, guidelines, and educational implications. Science & Educ., 1–32 (2024)
5. Digkoglou, P., Papathanasiou, J.: Application of multiple criteria decision aiding in environmental policy-making processes. Int. J. Environ. Sci. Technol. **22**(8), 6967–6982 (2025)
6. Ding, J., Zhang, C., Li, D., Li, W., Zhan, J.: A three-way large-scale group decision-making method integrating sentiment analysis and quantum interference-based prospect theory for the selection of new energy vehicles. Expert Syst. Appl. **275**, 126940 (2025)
7. Gaievskyi, S., Delfrate, N., Ragazzoni, L., Bahattab, A.: Use of multi-criteria decision analysis (MCDA) to support decision-making during health emergencies: a scoping review. Front. Public Health **13**, 1584026 (2025)
8. Ladrón de Guevara Cortés, R., Tolosa, L.E., Rojo, M.P.: Prospect theory in the financial decision-making process: an empirical study of two Argentine universities. J. Econ. Finance Administrative Sci. **28**(55), 116–133 (2023)
9. Kheybari, S., Mehrpour, M.R., Bauer, P., Ishizaka, A.: How can risk-averse and risk-taking approaches be considered in a group multi-criteria decision-making problem? Group Decis. Negot. **33**(4), 883–909 (2024)
10. Liao, N., Gao, H., Lin, R., Wei, G., Chen, X.: An extended EDAS approach based on cumulative prospect theory for multiple attributes group decision making with probabilistic hesitant fuzzy information. Artif. Intell. Rev. **56**(4), 2971–3003 (2023)
11. Paté-Cornell, E.: Preferences in AI algorithms: the need for relevant risk attitudes in automated decisions under uncertainties. Risk Anal. **44**(10), 2317–2323 (2024)
12. Sinnaiah, T., Adam, S., Mahadi, B.: A strategic management process: the role of decision-making style and organisational performance. J. Work-Appli. Manag. **15**(1), 37–50 (2023)
13. Tian, X., Ma, J., Li, L., Xu, Z., Tang, M.: Development of prospect theory in decision making with different types of fuzzy sets: a state-of-the-art literature review. Inf. Sci. **615**, 504–528 (2022)
14. Wang, J., Ma, X., Xu, Z., Pedrycz, W., Zhan, J.: A three-way decision method with prospect theory to multi-attribute decision-making and its applications under hesitant fuzzy environments. Appl. Soft Comput. **126**, 109283 (2022)
15. Wulf, C., Mesa Estrada, L.S., Haase, M., Tippe, M., Wigger, H., Brand-Daniels, U.: MCDA for the sustainability assessment of energy technologies and systems: identifying challenges and opportunities. Energy, Sust. Soc. **15**(1), 45 (2025)

When Decisions Are Blocked: Inhibitory Rules Induced from Tree Ensembles

Beata Zielosko[1]([✉])(iD), Anton Dmytrenko[1](iD), Azimkhon Ostonov[2](iD),
and Mikhail Moshkov[2](iD)

[1] Institute of Computer Science, University of Silesia in Katowice, Będzińska 39,
41-200 Sosnowiec, Poland
{beata.zielosko,anton.dmytrenko}@us.edu.pl
[2] Computer, Electrical and Mathematical Sciences and Engineering Division,
King Abdullah University of Science and Technology (KAUST),
Thuwal 23955-6900, Saudi Arabia
{azimkhon.ostonov,mikhail.moshkov}@kaust.edu.sa

Abstract. Decision trees and rule-based systems are widely used in various data mining tasks. Their great advantage is the ability to describe decision-making processes in a transparent manner. Unlike standard decision rules "if-then", inhibitory rules have in their successor form: "attribute $\neq$ decision". In the paper, two types of inhibitory rules have been defined: inner and general. Inner inhibitory rules are derived from complete paths in individual decision trees (path from the root to leaf of the tree), whereas general inhibitory rules are constructed using any attributes present across the trees. This work explores the problem of extracting both inner and general inhibitory rules that are valid for the largest possible number of decision trees within a given set. We introduce a polynomial-time algorithm to solve the inner inhibitory rule optimization problem, establish that optimizing general inhibitory rules is NP-hard, and propose a heuristic approach to approximate its solution. Experimental evaluations are conducted using synthetically generated decision tree sets to compare the performance of the proposed algorithms, taking into account the number of trees for which the constructed rules are true, and their length.

Keywords: Inhibitory Rules · Inner Rules · General Rules · Decision Trees · Distributed Data

1 Introduction

Decision trees and rule-based systems are widely used in various tasks related to classification and knowledge representation [8,11,14]. Their great advantage is the interpretable and structured way of modelling decision-making processes [7, 15,16]. Decision trees represent knowledge that can be expressed in the form of 'if-then' decision rules. Each internal node of a decision tree corresponds to an attribute test, the branches represent possible test results, and the terminal

M. Paszynski et al. (Eds.): ICCS 2026 Workshops, LNCS 16788, pp. 224–239, 2026.
https://doi.org/10.1007/978-3-032-29915-4_19

nodes (tree leaves) define decisions (class labels). This structure facilitates the representation of knowledge in the form of rules, making it easy to understand, analyze, and explain, even for those without expertise in a particular field.

Inhibitory rules complement this approach by explicitly modelling constraints or exceptions that prevent certain conclusions from being drawn when specific conditions are met. Unlike standard decision rules, inhibitory rules have a consequent in the form of: "attribute $\neq$ decision" and often suggest insights not captured by traditional decision rules [1,2,6]. Previous studies [9] demonstrated that for some information systems, ordinary (decision) rules cannot describe the whole information contained in the system. However, inhibitory rules describe the whole information for every information system. It means that inhibitory rules can express more information encoded in data than decision rules. Moreover, classifiers based on inhibitory rules often have better accuracy than classifiers based on decision rules [5].

The rationale for using inhibitory rules can be explained by highlighting their role as safeguards and a kind of filter in real-world decision support systems. While models based on ordinary decision rules suggest a positive decision during the classification process, inhibitory rules allow for the identification of conditions under which certain decisions should be suspended or reconsidered.

This study addresses the challenging problems of extracting inhibitory rules from a set of decision trees. A framework for decision rules was developed in [17]. However, existing research on pattern discovery from distributed data has not considered the use of inhibitory rules. This paper addresses this gap by proposing their first application in this context.

The proposed method can be applied in scenarios involving multiple local and distributed data sources represented as decision trees, where the goal is to extract knowledge that is important for all these sources and can be used both locally and globally. The main objective is to identify patterns that reflect knowledge common to most data sources, while also being applicable at the level of individual sources. One example of the proposed approach's application is in the field of medicine, where patient data is scattered across various departments and facilities. Integrating this data provides a more comprehensive picture of a patient's health, which supports more accurate diagnoses, ensures better treatment selection, and enables more efficient resource management.

Given a finite set S of decision trees, we investigate two types of inhibitory rules: *general inhibitory rules*, formed using any attributes occurring across the trees in S, and *inner inhibitory rules*, which are derived from complete root-to-leaf paths within individual trees. An inhibitory rule r is considered *true* for a tree $\Gamma \in S$ if an inner inhibitory rule r' exists in Γ such that the elementary conditions in r' are a subset of those in r, and both rules share the same conclusion.

This work addresses two key optimization problems: (i) identifying an inner inhibitory rule that holds for the maximum number of trees in S, and (ii) determining a general inhibitory rule that is valid for the largest subset of trees in S. These problems are particularly relevant in distributed learning environments, where multiple agents independently generate datasets using overlapping condition attributes and a shared decision attribute, producing separate decision trees. In this context, inhibitory rules that are valid across many trees can represent common knowledge.

We present a polynomial-time algorithm, denoted $\mathcal{A}^{inh}$, that solves the inner inhibitory rule optimization problem. We show also that optimizing general inhibitory rules is an NP-hard problem. To address this, we propose a heuristic algorithm $\mathcal{H}_1^{inh}$, which is an iterative method derived from $\mathcal{A}^{inh}$.

The main contribution of this work is a new approach to the problem of inducing inhibitory rules in a distributed data environment. The paper formalizes the problems of optimization of inner and general rules, and proposes dedicated algorithms for solving them. The effectiveness of the proposed methods was assessed in an experimental analysis on artificially generated datasets, aimed at comparing the number of induced inhibitory rules which are true for the maximum number of trees in the set. The experimental results showed that heuristic $\mathcal{H}_1^{inh}$ constructs rules that are true for a larger number of decision trees than the rules constructed by algorithm $\mathcal{A}^{inh}$.

The paper is organized as follows: Sect. 2 presents information related to decision trees. Section 3 contains the core definitions and preliminaries related to the considered problems. Optimization of inner and general inhibitory rules and algorithms proposed in this context is described. It was also shown that the general inhibitory optimization problem is NP-hard. Section 4 presents the experimental setup and discusses experimental results devoted to quality of algorithms $\mathcal{A}^{inh}$ and $\mathcal{H}_1^{inh}$. Section 5 concludes the paper.

2   Decision Modelling in the Form of Trees

Decision trees are hierarchical structures used to model classification and regression problems in machine learning. In the context of classification, a decision tree recursively partitions the feature space into regions, each associated with a class label. Due to their explicit, rule-based nature, decision trees offer a significant advantage over many other classification methods: interpretability. Unlike neural networks or ensemble methods that often function as opaque models, a decision tree provides a transparent reasoning process that can be examined and understood by domain experts [4,12].

Structurally, a decision tree consists of three types of elements. Internal nodes (including the root node) represent tests on attribute values, where each node evaluates a condition involving a single attribute. Branches emanating from an internal node correspond to the possible outcomes of the test: in binary trees, these are typically "yes" and "no" branches, while multi-way splits allow features to take multiple discrete values. Leaf nodes, also called terminal nodes, represent the final classification decision and are labeled with a class. The path from the root node to any leaf node traverses a sequence of tests on conditional attributes, and this sequence determines the outcome of classification of a particular entity being processed. The depth of a tree, defined as the length of the longest root-to-leaf path, directly influences both the complexity of the model and its capacity to capture intricate decision boundaries.

Each root-to-leaf path in a decision tree corresponds to a decision rule of the form: *if $c_1 \wedge c_2 \wedge \ldots \wedge c_n$ then $d = k$*, where c_i are conditions on attribute values and $d = k$ denotes a decision, namely assignment to class k. These rules are mutually exclusive (any given instance satisfies exactly one path) and collectively exhaustive, covering all possible instances in the feature space. The length of a rule, measured by the number of conditions it contains, corresponds to the depth of the associated leaf in the tree. Shorter rules are generally preferred as they tend to generalize better to unseen data and are less prone to overfitting.

The construction of decision trees typically follows a top-down inductive approach, commonly referred to as Top-Down Induction of Decision Trees [12]. Starting from the root node, an algorithm selects an attribute to partition the training data, creating child nodes for each split. This process continues recursively until a stopping criterion is met, such as reaching pure leaf nodes or a maximum depth. The selection of attributes at each step is guided by heuristic measures that quantify the quality of a split. Information gain, based on entropy reduction, is employed by the ID3 and C4.5 algorithms [13], while the Gini impurity criterion is used by CART [4]. These algorithms are greedy in nature: they make locally optimal choices at each node without backtracking, which means that different attribute orderings or tie-breaking strategies can produce substantially different trees from the same training data.

This sensitivity to attribute ordering and changes in the data is a well-known limitation of decision trees. Small changes in the training set—such as the addition or removal of a few entries—can lead to significantly different tree structures [3]. Moreover, for any given dataset, multiple valid trees may exist that achieve comparable classification results. This inherent variability motivates the examination of decision rules not only within a single tree, but across a set of trees induced from the same data. By analyzing which rules appear consistently across multiple trees, one can identify more robust classification knowledge [3,10]. Furthermore, this perspective opens the possibility of extracting rules that describe what an instance is *not* (inhibitory rules that specify class exclusion rather than class membership) providing an alternative representation of the classification knowledge embedded in decision trees.

3   Learning Inhibitory Rules from Sets of Decision Trees

This section presents the main notions related to the induction of inhibitory rules from sets of decision trees. Concepts related to general and inner inhibitory rules are defined along with proposed algorithms for defined problems of their optimization.

3.1   Main Notions

Let $\omega = \{0, 1, 2, \ldots\}$ denote the set of nonnegative integers, and let F be a set of binary attributes taking values in $\{0, 1\}$.

An *inhibitory rule* r over the attribute set F is an expression of the form:

$$(f_1 = \delta_1) \wedge \cdots \wedge (f_m = \delta_m) \rightarrow \neq t, \tag{1}$$

where $m \in \omega$, the attributes $f_1, \ldots, f_m$ are pairwise distinct elements of F, each $\delta_j \in \{0,1\}$ for $1 \leq j \leq m$, and $t \in \omega$ denotes a decision value. The conjunction on the left-hand side is referred to as the set of elementary conditions, denoted $C(r)$, while the right-hand side expresses that the decision is different from t, written as $\neq t$, where $t(r)$ denotes the decision t.

Two inhibitory rules r_1 and r_2 are said to be *incompatible* if there exists an attribute f and a value δ such that the condition $f = \delta$ appears in $C(r_1)$, and $f = \neg\delta$ appears in $C(r_2)$, with $\neg 0 = 1$ and $\neg 1 = 0$.

A *decision tree* over the attribute set F is a labeled, directed tree with a root node, satisfying the following properties:

- Each leaf (terminal node) is labeled with a decision value from ω.
- Each internal (non-terminal) node is labeled with an attribute from F and has exactly two outgoing edges labeled 0 and 1.
- Along any root-to-leaf (complete) path, the internal node attributes are pairwise distinct.

Let S be a non-empty finite set of decision trees. Define $D(S)$ as the set of all decision values that appear at the leaves across the trees in S. For any tree $\Gamma \in S$, the number of leaves equals the number of internal nodes plus one. Each complete root-to-leaf path corresponds uniquely to a leaf.

Let ξ be a complete path in a tree Γ with m internal nodes. Denote by $d(\xi)$ the decision value at the leaf node at the end of ξ. For every $t \in D(S) \setminus \{d(\xi)\}$, we define the associated inhibitory rule $rule(\xi, t)$. If $m = 0$, then the rule $rule(\xi, t)$ has the form of Eq. (2).

$$\rightarrow \neq t. \tag{2}$$

Otherwise, if the attributes $f_1, \ldots, f_m$ label the internal nodes along ξ, and $\delta_1, \ldots, \delta_m$ are the corresponding edge labels (0 or 1), then the rule $rule(\xi, t)$ has the form of Eq. (3). The number m denotes the length of the rule.

$$(f_1 = \delta_1) \wedge \cdots \wedge (f_m = \delta_m) \rightarrow \neq t. \tag{3}$$

Let $\Xi(\Gamma)$ denote the set of all complete paths in Γ. The set of *inner inhibitory rules* for Γ is then defined as presented by eq. (4):

$$IIR(\Gamma) = \{rule(\xi, t) : \xi \in \Xi(\Gamma),\ t \in D(S) \setminus \{d(\xi)\}\}. \tag{4}$$

We further define:

- $IIR(S) = \bigcup_{\Gamma \in S} IIR(\Gamma)$ – the set of all inner inhibitory rules extracted from trees in S.
- $F(S)$ – the set of all attributes used in the internal nodes of trees in S.
- $GIR(S)$ – the set of all inhibitory rules over the attribute set $F(S)$ with right-hand side of the form $\neq t$ for some $t \in D(S)$.

We refer to elements of $IIR(S)$ as *inner inhibitory rules over S*, and elements of $GIR(S)$ as *general inhibitory rules over S*. Clearly, the inclusion holds, see Eq. (5).

$$IIR(S) \subseteq GIR(S). \tag{5}$$

Given a tree $\Gamma \in S$ and a rule $r \in GIR(S)$, we say that r is *true* for Γ if there exists a rule $r' \in IIR(\Gamma)$ such that $t(r') = t(r)$ and $C(r') \subseteq C(r)$.

3.2   Optimization of Inner Inhibitory Rules

This section focuses on the *Inner Inhibitory Optimization Problem* (IIOP), defined as follows: Given a set of decision trees S, identify an inner inhibitory rule that holds for the maximum number of trees in S.

Let $T(S)$ denote the total number of nodes–both internal and terminal–across all trees in S. The total number of inner inhibitory rules in $IIR(S)$ is upper-bounded by $T(S)^2$. Furthermore, the number of conditions on the left-hand side of any rule in $IIR(S)$ is at most $T(S)$. As a result, the entire set $IIR(S)$ can be generated in time polynomial in $T(S)$.

We begin by presenting algorithm $\mathcal{A}_0^{inh}$, which verifies whether a given rule $r \in IIR(S)$ is valid for a specific tree $\Gamma \in S$. This algorithm operates in polynomial time relative to $T(S)$.

Algorithm $\mathcal{A}_0^{inh}$

For each rule $r' \in IIR(\Gamma)$, check whether $t(r') = t(r)$ and $C(r') \subseteq C(r)$. If such a rule r' exists, then r is considered true for Γ; otherwise, it is not.

We now introduce the main algorithm, $\mathcal{A}^{inh}$, which solves the IIOP by searching for the optimal rule within a specified subset $I \subseteq IIR(S)$. This algorithm identifies, in polynomial time with respect to $T(S)$, a rule from I that is valid for the largest number of trees in S.

Algorithm $\mathcal{A}^{inh}$

For each rule $r \in I$ and each tree $\Gamma \in S$, apply algorithm $\mathcal{A}_0^{inh}$ to determine whether r is true for Γ. After evaluating all rules, return the one that is valid for the greatest number of trees in S.

3.3   Optimization of General Inhibitory Rules

In this section, we consider the *General Inhibitory Optimization Problem* (GIOP), which aims to find, for a given set of decision trees S, a general inhibitory rule over S that is valid for the largest number of trees in S.

Let $F(S) = \{f_1, \ldots, f_m\}$ represent the set of attributes appearing in the trees of S. It can be shown that an optimal solution to GIOP always exists among the so-called *complete inhibitory rules over S*, defined as in eq. (6),

$$(f_1 = \delta_1) \wedge \cdots \wedge (f_m = \delta_m) \to \neq t, \tag{6}$$

where each $\delta_i \in \{0, 1\}$ and $t \in D(S)$.

We now demonstrate that solving GIOP is an NP-hard problem. This is proven via a polynomial-time reduction from the classical NP-complete problem 3-SAT.

A Boolean formula known as 3-conjunctive normal form (3-CNF) has the structure $N(x_1, \ldots, x_n) = C_1 \wedge \cdots \wedge C_k$, where each clause C_j $(1 \leq j \leq k)$ consists of exactly three distinct literals connected by logical OR. Each literal is either a Boolean variable from $\{x_1, \ldots, x_n\}$ or its negation, and every variable from $\{x_1, \ldots, x_n\}$ appears in at least one clause.

3-SAT Problem: Given a 3-CNF formula $N(x_1, \ldots, x_n)$, determine whether there exists a truth assignment $(a_1, \ldots, a_n) \in \{0, 1\}^n$ such that $N(a_1, \ldots, a_n) = 1$.

To reduce 3-SAT to GIOP, we construct a set of decision trees $S_N = \{\Gamma_0, \Gamma_1, \ldots, \Gamma_k\}$ based on the formula $N = C_1 \wedge \cdots \wedge C_k$. Each clause $C_i = x_{t(i,1)}^{b_{i1}} \vee x_{t(i,2)}^{b_{i2}} \vee x_{t(i,3)}^{b_{i3}}$ (where $b_{ij} \in \{0, 1\}$, with $x^0 = \neg x$ and $x^1 = x$) corresponds to a decision tree Γ_i.

Note that the condition $x^b = 1$ is satisfied precisely when $x = b$. The tree Γ_0 plays an auxiliary role, while each Γ_i encodes a specific clause. Figure 1 illustrates the structure of Γ_0 and a representative clause tree Γ_i. All decision trees in S_N use decisions from the set $D(S_N) = \{0, 1\}$.

We now prove the equivalence between the satisfiability of the formula N and the existence of a complete inhibitory rule over S_N that is valid for every tree in S_N.

Assume there exists a truth assignment $(a_1, \ldots, a_n) \in \{0, 1\}^n$ such that $N(a_1, \ldots, a_n) = 1$. Then each clause C_i evaluates to true under this assignment. That is, for every $i \in \{1, \ldots, k\}$, there exists an index $p_i \in \{1, 2, 3\}$ such that $a_{t(i,p_i)} = b_{ip_i}$.

Using this assignment, we define the following complete inhibitory rule:

$$(x_1 = a_1) \wedge \cdots \wedge (x_n = a_n) \to \neq 1.$$

This rule can be verified to be valid for all trees in S_N.

Conversely, suppose there exists a complete inhibitory rule r over S_N that is true for every tree in the set. Then r must have the form:

$$(x_1 = a_1) \wedge \cdots \wedge (x_n = a_n) \to \neq 1.$$

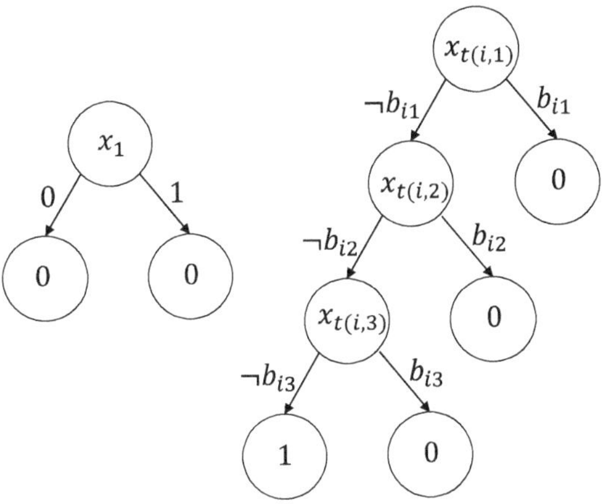

Fig. 1. Decision trees Γ_0 and Γ_i, $i = 1, \ldots, k$.

Since r holds for each tree Γ_i, the corresponding clause C_i must be satisfied under the assignment $(a_1, \ldots, a_n)$. Hence, the entire formula N is satisfied.

This shows a polynomial-time reduction from 3-SAT to GIOP: Given a 3-CNF formula N, we construct the associated decision tree set S_N in polynomial time. Solving GIOP on S_N involves finding a general inhibitory rule that is valid for the maximum number of trees. We then verify in polynomial time whether the rule is valid for all trees.

If the considered rule is not valid for all trees, then N is unsatisfiable. If this rule holds for every tree, then it can be extended to a complete inhibitory rule over S that is valid for every tree from S_N. Thus, N is satisfiable.

Therefore, GIOP is NP-hard.

3.4   Heuristic for General Inhibitory Rule Optimization

As established earlier, the general inhibitory rule optimization problem (GIOP) is NP-hard. Consequently, this section introduces heuristic approach designed to approximate solutions to GIOP in polynomial time.

The heuristic, denoted $\mathcal{H}_1^{inh}$, extends the inner inhibitory optimization algorithm $\mathcal{A}^{inh}$ and relies on a supporting procedure $\mathcal{B}^{inh}$, described below. This method runs in time polynomial with respect to $T(S)$.

Heuristic $\mathcal{H}_1^{inh}$

For each decision value $t \in D(S)$, execute algorithm $\mathcal{B}^{inh}$ on the decision tree set S. Among all rules generated for different values of t, select the one that is valid for the largest number of trees in S.

Algorithm $\mathcal{B}^{inh}$

Step 0. Construct the initial set I_0 containing all rules from $IIR(S)$ with right-hand side $\neq t$ and a non-empty left-hand side. Initialize rule r_0 with an empty left-hand side and right-hand side $\neq t$.

Assume that step i ($i \geq 0$) produces a rule r_i and a corresponding rule set I_i.

Step $i+1$. Apply algorithm $\mathcal{A}^{inh}$ to the current set I_i to identify a rule ρ_{i+1} that holds for the largest number of trees in S. Define the new rule r_{i+1} with right-hand side $\neq t$ and left-hand side $C(r_{i+1}) = C(r_i) \cup C(\rho_{i+1})$.

Remove from I_i all rules that are either:

- incompatible with r_{i+1}, or
- have condition sets that are subsets of $C(r_{i+1})$.

Let I_{i+1} denote the resulting rule set.

If I_{i+1} is empty, terminate and return r_{i+1}; otherwise, proceed to the next step.

4   Experiments

This section presents a comparative experimental evaluation of the algorithm $\mathcal{A}^{inh}$ and the heuristic $\mathcal{H}_1^{inh}$, using synthetically generated sets of decision trees induced with the ID3 algorithm and entropy as attribute selection criterion. The aim is to compare the number of trees for which the constructed rules are true and their length.

4.1   Experimental Setup

We recall the main interpretation of the problem addressed in the paper. We consider t agents working on similar tasks who utilize attributes drawn from a common set of a attributes. Each agent constructs its own decision table and produces a decision tree based on it. Consequently, we obtain a collection S consisting of t decision trees. The objective is to identify rules that hold for as many trees in S as possible. Considering that the length of a rule plays a significant role in assessing its quality and interpretability, additional experiments and analyses were also conducted concerning the length of rules induced by the compared algorithms.

The study involved two groups of experiments. The key distinction between them lies in the selection of attributes in the decision tables for each agent. In the first group, all attributes from the common set are used, whereas in the second one, only 50% of attributes from the common set is selected. Denote

- $T = \{10, 20, 30, 40, 50\}$,
- $A_1 = \{10, 20, 30, 40, 50\}$,
- $A_2 = \{20, 40, 60, 80, 100\}$.

The First Group of Experiments

Fix $t \in T$ and $a \in A_1$. Construct a decision table with a columns labeled with the attributes $\{f_1, \ldots, f_a\}$ and $2a$ pairwise different rows chosen randomly. Rows are filled with numbers from the set $\{0, 1\}$. They are labeled with decisions chosen randomly from the set $\{1, 2, 3, 4\}$.

Construct a decision tree for this table. Repeat the described step t times (each time, a new table is constructed). As a result, a set S_1 of t decision trees is obtained.

After repeating the whole procedure 5 times, we obtain ensembles $S_1, \ldots, S_5$ of decision trees. Specifically, this results in five ensembles with 10 trees, five with 20 trees, and so on, up to five ensembles with 50 trees.

For $i = 1, \ldots, 5$, apply the algorithm $\mathcal{A}^{inh}$ to S_i. As a result, we obtain a decision rule r_i. Let $true_i$ be the number of trees from S_i for which the rule r_i is true. Let $length_i$ be the length of this rule. For the fixed a and t, the quality of the algorithm $\mathcal{A}^{inh}$ is the number defined by eq. (7).

$$\frac{true_1 + \cdots + true_5}{5t}. \tag{7}$$

For the fixed a and t, the quality of the heuristic $\mathcal{H}_1^{inh}$ is obtained similarly. We find the quality of $\mathcal{A}^{inh}$ and $\mathcal{H}_1^{inh}$ for each $t \in T$ and $a \in A_1$.

Considering the length of the rule r_i, for the fixed a and t, the quality of the algorithm $\mathcal{A}^{inh}$ and heuristic $\mathcal{H}_1^{inh}$ in this context, is the number defined by eq. (8).

$$\frac{length_1 + \cdots + length_5}{5}. \tag{8}$$

The Second Group of Experiments

This collection of experiments differs from the first one in the way how the decision tables are constructed. Fix $t \in T$ and $a \subset A_2$. Construct a decision table with $a/2$ columns labeled with the pairwise different attributes chosen randomly from the set $\{f_1, \ldots, f_a\}$ and a pairwise different rows chosen randomly. Rows are filled with numbers from the set $\{0, 1\}$. They are labeled with decisions chosen randomly from the set $\{1, 2, 3, 4\}$. The remaining steps of the procedure are the same as in the first group of experiments.

4.2   Results of Experiments

Tables 1a and 1b present results for the first group of experiments. At the intersection of row $a \in A_1$ and column $t \in T$ we have two numbers. The top one is the quality of $\mathcal{A}^{inh}$ and the bottom one is the quality of $\mathcal{H}_1^{inh}$ for a and t. The column Avg contains average values of qualities $\mathcal{A}^{inh}$ and $\mathcal{H}_1^{inh}$ for given a. The row Avg contains average values of qualities $\mathcal{A}^{inh}$ and $\mathcal{H}_1^{inh}$ for given t. At the intersection of the row Avg and the column Avg, we have average values of qualities $\mathcal{A}^{inh}$ and $\mathcal{H}_1^{inh}$ for all a and t.

Table 1a presents the results concerning the number of trees, for which the constructed rule is true (see Eq. (7), Table 1b – results related to the length of such rule (see eq. (8)).

Table 1. Quality of algorithms $\mathcal{A}^{inh}$ and $\mathcal{H}_1^{inh}$ related to the first group of experiments.

(a) Results related to the number of trees for which the constructed rules are true.

		t					Avg
		10	20	30	40	50	
	10	0.360	0.380	0.327	0.365	0.348	0.356
		1.000	0.910	0.893	0.865	0.848	0.903
	20	0.200	0.110	0.107	0.080	0.068	0.113
		1.000	0.920	0.867	0.845	0.860	0.898
a	30	0.140	0.090	0.073	0.055	0.044	0.080
		1.000	0.950	0.913	0.885	0.860	0.922
	40	0.100	0.070	0.067	0.055	0.044	0.067
		1.000	0.960	0.913	0.870	0.872	0.923
	50	0.120	0.060	0.040	0.040	0.036	0.059
		1.000	0.990	0.947	0.905	0.876	0.944
Avg		0.184	0.142	0.123	0.119	0.108	0.135
		1.000	0.946	0.907	0.874	0.863	0.918

(b) Results related to the length of constructed rules.

		t					Avg
		10	20	30	40	50	
	10	5.8	6.4	6.6	7.0	7.0	6.56
		10.0	10.0	10.0	10.0	10.0	10.00
	20	5.4	5.0	6.4	6.4	6.0	5.84
		18.6	20.0	19.8	20.0	20.0	19.68
a	30	5.4	5.6	5.4	5.4	5.0	5.36
		27.2	28.6	30.0	30.0	30.0	29.16
	40	5.2	5.8	5.8	6.2	5.4	5.68
		31.0	37.6	39.6	40.0	49.4	39.52
	50	5.6	5.8	6.0	5.8	6.0	5.84
		36.8	46.6	48.4	49.4	50.0	46.24
Avg		5.48	5.72	6.04	6.16	5.88	5.86
		24.72	28.56	29.56	29.88	31.88	28.92

Tables 2a and 2b present results for the second group of experiments. At the intersection of row $a \in A_1$ and column $t \in T$ we have two numbers. The top one is the quality of $\mathcal{A}^{inh}$ and the bottom one is the quality of $\mathcal{H}_1^{inh}$ for a and t. The column Avg contains average values of qualities $\mathcal{A}^{inh}$ and $\mathcal{H}_1^{inh}$ for given a. The row Avg contains average values of qualities $\mathcal{A}^{inh}$ and $\mathcal{H}_1^{inh}$ for given t. At the intersection of the row Avg and the column Avg, we have average values of qualities $\mathcal{A}^{inh}$ and $\mathcal{H}_1^{inh}$ for all a and t.

Table 2a presents the results concerning the number of trees, for which the constructed rule is true (see eq. (7), Table 2b – results related to the length of such rule (see eq. (8)).

All experiments were conducted on a system equipped with an ARM-based processor featuring 8 cores (6 performance cores at 3.2 GHz and 2 efficiency cores at 2.0 GHz) and 16 GB of LPDDR5 unified memory. The implementation was developed in Python 3.13.8 using Jupyter notebooks for organization of experiments and core Python code for implementing core structures and modules, with NumPy 2.3.3 for numerical computations and Pandas 2.3.2 for data manipulation, and Plotly 6.5.1 for 3D visualizations.

Based on the obtained results, it is possible to see that heuristics $\mathcal{H}_1^{inh}$ produces rules that are true for more trees than rules produced by algorithm $\mathcal{A}^{inh}$, for both groups of experiments (see Tables 1a and 2a). It can also be seen that

Table 2. Quality of algorithms $\mathcal{A}^{inh}$ and $\mathcal{H}_1^{inh}$ related to the second group of experiments.

(a) Results related to the number of trees for which the constructed rules are true.

		t				Avg
	10	20	30	40	50	
20	0.200	0.150	0.133	0.110	0.096	0.138
	1.000	0.980	0.913	0.870	0.868	0.926
40	0.160	0.080	0.067	0.050	0.040	0.079
	1.000	0.980	0.933	0.915	0.888	0.943
a 60	0.100	0.060	0.060	0.050	0.040	0.062
	1.000	1.000	0.960	0.925	0.908	0.959
80	0.100	0.050	0.040	0.030	0.024	0.049
	1.000	0.990	0.987	0.930	0.920	0.965
100	0.100	0.050	0.040	0.030	0.024	0.049
	1.000	1.000	0.987	0.960	0.928	0.975
Avg	0.132	0.078	0.068	0.054	0.045	0.075
	1.000	0.990	0.956	0.920	0.902	0.954

(b) Results related to the length of constructed rules.

		t				Avg
	10	20	30	40	50	
20	5.0	5.6	5.8	6.0	6.2	5.72
	17.4	19.8	20.0	20.0	20.0	19.44
40	5.0	5.2	6.2	5.2	5.0	5.32
	28.8	36.2	38.0	39.6	40.0	36.52
a 60	4.6	5.0	5.4	5.4	5.2	5.12
	37.4	51.0	56.4	57.6	58.6	52.20
80	5.2	5.4	5.6	5.4	5.4	5.40
	42.8	60.0	71.6	75.2	77.8	65.48
100	5.8	5.6	6.4	5.8	6.0	5.92
	42.8	73.0	83.8	89.0	95.6	76.84
Avg	5.12	5.36	5.88	5.56	5.56	5.50
	33.84	48.00	53.96	56.28	58.40	50.10

the length of the rules induced by algorithm $\mathcal{A}^{inh}$ is significantly shorter than in the case of algorithm $\mathcal{H}_1^{inh}$.

Considering the length of the rules, it can be observed that it increases with the number of attributes and the number of trees in the case of heuristic $\mathcal{H}_1^{inh}$. Often, the length of a constructed rule reaches a value equal to or close to the number of attributes in the set. Although algorithm $\mathcal{A}^{inh}$ produces rules that are true for less number of trees in set S, it should be emphasized that they are relatively short and do not change significantly with an increase in the number of trees and attributes in the set. Determining what rule length is acceptable in terms of interpretability depends on the specific application. It should also be noted that algorithm $\mathcal{A}^{inh}$ and heuristic $\mathcal{H}_1^{inh}$ are used for different optimization problems.

The figures, Fig. 2 and Fig. 3, provide a visualization of the results presented in the Tables 1a and 2a, respectively.

In the case of Fig. 2 on the left-hand side, results related to the quality of algorithm $\mathcal{A}^{inh}$ are presented, on the right-hand side – results related to heuristic $\mathcal{H}_1^{inh}$, for the first group of experiments where 100% of attributes is considered during construction of decision tress.

Figure 3 presents on the left-hand side results related to the quality of algorithm $\mathcal{A}^{inh}$, on the right-hand side – results related to heuristic $\mathcal{H}_1^{inh}$, for the second group of experiments where 50% of attributes is considered during construction of decision trees.

Based on graphical representation of results on Figs. 2 and 3, it is possible to note that the results obtained by algorithm $\mathcal{A}^{inh}$ mostly demonstrate a rapid

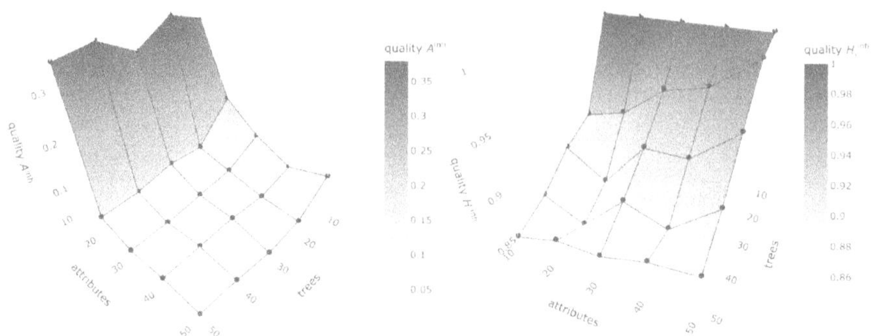

Fig. 2. The number of trees for which the constructed rules are true: for rules obtained by algorithm $\mathcal{A}^{inh}$ (the left-hand side) and heuristics $\mathcal{H}_1^{inh}$ (the right-hand side), for selection of 100% of attributes from the set.

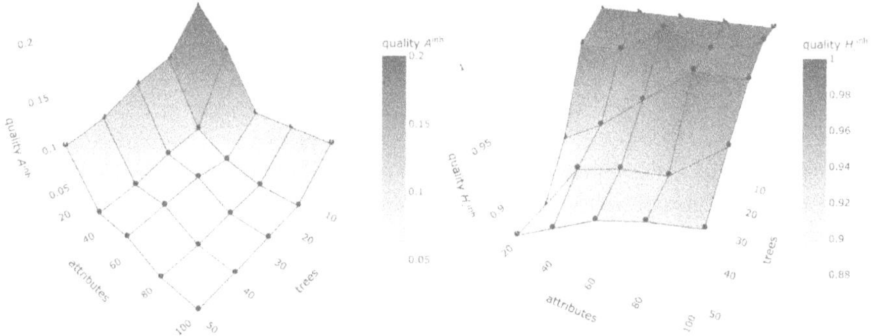

Fig. 3. The number of trees for which the constructed rules are true: for rules obtained by algorithm $\mathcal{A}^{inh}$ (the left-hand side) and heuristics $\mathcal{H}_1^{inh}$ (the right-hand side), for selection of 50% of attributes from the set.

decline in quality measure as a (the number of attributes) increases as well as a much more moderate decline in quality as t (the number of trees) increases. It appears to be more exaggerated on the left hand side of Fig. 2, whereas on Fig. 3 the relation of quality to these parameters looks more uniform. As it has been mentioned above, algorithm $\mathcal{H}_1^{inh}$ produces significantly higher quality metric values which can also be derived from the scale of the Z-axis on Figs. 2 and 3. On the contrary, the obtained values represent different trends in relation of quality to number of attributes and trees, where there is an overall increase in quality measure with the increase of a and a noticeable decrease of quality as the number of trees t increases, that can be observed on both right side graphs of Figs. 2 and 3, leading to a conclusion that algorithm $\mathcal{H}_1^{inh}$ produces results with higher number of attributes.

5 Conclusions

Inhibitory rules and decision trees play an important role in decision-making systems and data analysis because they enable transparent and interpretable representation of knowledge. Decision trees provide a hierarchical decision structure in which each path from the root to the leaf can be written as a decision rule. Inhibitory rules are particularly important in situations where is a need to clearly define the conditions under which a decision should not be made. They enable the formal expression of restrictions or exceptions, which increases the precision and reliability of decision models.

The length of inhibitory rules, understood as the number of conditions in their premise, is an important factor affecting both the interpretability and quality of decision models. Shorter rules are usually easier to understand and analyze, which increases their usefulness in practical applications requiring transparency of the decision-making process. On the other hand, longer rules, although potentially more precise, can lead to excessive complexity and make it difficult to interpret the results.

In this paper, we defined and investigated the problem of learning inner and general inhibitory rules valid for the maximum number of decision trees in a given set. The novelty of the paper is related to the first application of inhibitory rules for discovering pattern from distributed data. It has been shown that the problem of optimizing general inhibitory rules is NP-hard, and a heuristic $\mathcal{H}_1^{inh}$ for inducing such rules has been proposed. In the case of the problem of optimization of inner rules, algorithm $\mathcal{A}^{inh}$ has been proposed. Both algorithms were compared, taking into account the maximum number of trees for which the induced rules are true, and their length, for different numbers of trees in the set S and different numbers of attributes. Moreover, performed experiments were related to two scenarios, where decision trees are constructed using the full set of attributes, and where only 50% of attributes from the entire set is available. The results obtained show that the algorithm $\mathcal{A}^{inh}$ induces significantly shorter rules than the heuristic $\mathcal{H}_1^{inh}$ however, taking into account the number of trees for which rules are true, the heuristic $\mathcal{H}_1^{inh}$ gives better results.

The proposed approach can be applied in organizations with a distributed structure, such as hospitals, where individual units operate based on their own knowledge resources. The knowledge accumulated in each of these units is represented in the form of decision trees. The aim is to identify patterns common to a significant proportion of the units that reflect the knowledge characteristic of the entire organization.

In the future, we plan to consider the problem of learning not just a single inhibitory rule (inner or general) valid for the maximum number of decision trees in a given set, but a group of rules, each valid for a number of trees close to the maximum. The proposed methods will be generalized to handle k-valued attributes for any $k \geq 3$. Future work will include also empirical validation using real-world datasets and comparison with other approaches for inducing rules.

Acknowledgments. Research reported in this publication was supported by the Remote Working Individual Consultancy Agreement No. KAUST-2025-C0148, and King Abdullah University of Science and Technology (KAUST) and the Institute of Computer Science, University of Silesia in Katowice, Poland. The research activities co-financed by the funds granted under the Research Excellence Initiative of the University of Silesia in Katowice.

References

1. Alsolami, F., Azad, M., Chikalov, I., Moshkov, M.: Decision and Inhibitory Trees and Rules for Decision Tables with Many-valued Decisions. ISRL, vol. 156. Springer, Cham (2020). https://doi.org/10.1007/978-3-030-12854-8
2. Alsolami, F., Chikalov, I., Moshkov, M., Zielosko, B.: Optimization of approximate inhibitory rules relative to number of misclassifications. In: Watada, J., Jain, L.C., Howlett, R.J., Mukai, N., Asakura, K. (eds.) 17th International Conference in Knowledge Based and Intelligent Information and Engineering Systems, KES 2013, Kitakyushu, Japan, 9-11 September 2013. Procedia Computer Science, vol. 22, pp. 295–302. Elsevier (2013)
3. Breiman, L.: Bagging predictors. Mach. Learn. **24**(2), 123–140 (1996)
4. Breiman, L., Friedman, J., Stone, C.J., Olshen, R.A.: Classification and Regression Trees. Chapman and Hall/CRC (1984)
5. Delimata, P., Moshkov, M., Skowron, A., Suraj, Z.: Comparison of lazy classification algorithms based on deterministic and inhibitory decision rules. In: Wang, G., Li, T., Grzymala-Busse, J.W., Miao, D., Skowron, A., Yao, Y. (eds.) RSKT 2008. LNCS (LNAI), vol. 5009, pp. 55–62. Springer, Heidelberg (2008). https://doi.org/10.1007/978-3-540-79721-0_13
6. Delimata, P., Moshkov, M.J., Skowron, A., Suraj, Z.: Inhibitory Rules in Data Analysis: A Rough Set Approach, SCI, vol. 163. Springer (2009). https://doi.org/10.1007/978-3-540-85638-2
7. Kozielski, M., Sikora, M., Wawrowski, L.: Towards consistency of rule-based explainer and black box model - fusion of rule induction and xai-based feature importance. Knowl. Based Syst. **311**, 113092 (2025). https://doi.org/10.1016/J.KNOSYS.2025.113092
8. Moshkov, M.J.: Time complexity of decision trees. In: Peters, J.F., Skowron, A. (eds.) Transactions on Rough Sets III. LNCS, vol. 3400, pp. 244–459. Springer, Heidelberg (2005). https://doi.org/10.1007/11427834_12
9. Moshkov, M., Skowron, A., Suraj, Z.: Maximal consistent extensions of information systems relative to their theories. Inf. Sci. **178**(12), 2600–2620 (2008). https://doi.org/10.1016/J.INS.2008.01.018
10. Moshkov, M., Zielosko, B.: Combinatorial Machine Learning: A Rough Set Approach. SCI, vol. 360. Springer (2011). https://doi.org/10.1007/978-3-642-20995-6
11. Pawlak, Z., Skowron, A.: Rudiments of rough sets. Inf. Sci. **177**(1), 3–27 (2007). https://doi.org/10.1016/J.INS.2006.06.003
12. Quinlan, J.R.: Induction of decision trees. Mach. Learn. **1**(1), 81–106 (1986)
13. Quinlan, J.R.: C4.5: Programs for Machine Learning. Morgan Kaufmann, San Mateo, CA (1993)

14. Sakai, H., Nakata, M., Slezak, D., Watada, J.: Rule generation in rough set non-deterministic information analysis (RNIA) and some applications of the obtained rules. Appl. Soft Comput. **172**, 112842 (2025). https://doi.org/10.1016/J.ASOC.2025.112842
15. Yao, J., Cornelis, C., Wang, G., Yao, Y.: Uncertainty and three-way decision in data science. Int. J. Approx. Reason. **162**, 109024 (2023). https://doi.org/10.1016/J.IJAR.2023.109024
16. Zielosko, B.: Application of dynamic programming approach to optimization of association rules relative to coverage and length. Fundam. Inform. **148**(1–2), 87–105 (2016). https://doi.org/10.3233/FI-2016-1424
17. Zielosko, B., Moshkov, M., Tetteh, E.T.: Optimization of inner and general rules. Inf. Sci. **719**, 122466 (2025)

An Ensemble CNN Transfer Learning Model for Wheat Grain Classification

Małgorzata Charytanowicz[1,3] (iD), Urszula Kużelewska[2(✉)] (iD), and Rafał Stęgierski[1] (iD)

[1] Department of Computer Science, Lublin University of Technology, Nadbystrzycka 36B, 20-618 Lublin, Poland

[2] Department of Information Systems and Computer Networks, Bialystok University of Technology, Wiejska 45a, 15-351 Bialystok, Poland
u.kuzelewska@pb.edu.pl

[3] Systems Research Institute, Polish Academy of Sciences, Newelska 6, 01-447 Warsaw, Poland

Abstract. Automated image classification is a fundamental task in computer vision. One of the most powerful deep learning (DL) models employed in image classification is the Convolutional Neural Network (CNN). Its key strength is the automatic extraction of features during direct raw image processing. This work proposes an ensemble transfer learning model based on CNNs to classify wheat grains. The dataset consists of 288 images of the kernels of three wheat grain varieties. In order to build the ensemble model, VGG16, InceptionV3, DenseNet201-V1, DenseNet201-V2, and NASNetMobile were evaluated and compared on the basis of the performance metrics including accuracy, Cohen's Kappa, precision, recall and F1 score. The ensemble CNN model demonstrated a higher level of performance than its base models achieving an accuracy of 96.48% and F1 score of 97%. Despite the limited amount of data available, the study's findings indicate that the proposed approach is an effective means of enhancing wheat grain classification.

Keywords: Computer Vision · Convolutional Neural Networks · Ensemble Learning · Wheat Grain · Shapley Values

1 Introduction

Wheat is the most extensively cultivated crop in the world, and for the world's population, it is a fundamental source of essential nutrients. The number of wheat varieties is constantly increasing. Therefore, the proper selection of the wheat variety is a key factor in determining yield, as well as in marketing the commodity. With the rapid advancement of computer-aided methods, object detection and recognition have achieved tremendous progress. These are widely used in many fields, including their application in agriculture [1, 2].

With the advent of automatic image processing and artificial intelligence, classification of wheat grains can be carried out on an industrial scale. It should be noted that this is more effective, cheaper and faster than expert judgement [3]. For these reasons,

M. Paszynski et al. (Eds.): ICCS 2026 Workshops, LNCS 16788, pp. 240–247, 2026.
https://doi.org/10.1007/978-3-032-29915-4_20

effective classification methods based on visual features of wheat kernels are still being developed [3, 4].

Nowadays, convolutional neural networks (CNNs) and other forms of deep learning (DL) have been employed in digital image processing with the objective of enhancing prediction performance. In comparison to the outcomes yielded by traditional machine learning, these DL methods have demonstrated notable improvements. One of the first experiments using neural networks for classifying texture images was carried out in 1999 [5]. The results obtained for pollen images showed that the neural network was superior to some previously published statistical classifiers. Indeed, 100% accuracy was evidenced. Daood et al. [6] also developed a CNN model for pollen grain classification. In this case, achieving 94% classification rate on a dataset of 30 pollen types with a database containing 1000 images.

Recently, Agarwal and Bachan [3] proposed a computer vision based system for automatic quality grading of wheat grains. The authors obtained accuracy of 93%. In related work, Koklu et al. [7] developed a method for classifying rice varieties. The features dataset and the image dataset were used as inputs. The classification success rate was found to be 99.95% for Deep Neural Networks (DNNs) and 100% for CNN.

Brahimi et al. [8] reached 99.18% of accuracy and demonstrated that CNNs outperformed SVM and RF in tomato diseases classification. Yang et al. proposed a novel method for peanut variety identification and classification by improving VGG16 [9]. The average accuracy of the improved model was 96.7%, which was 1.6–12.3% higher than that of other classical models. The identification of grain diseases was successfully achieved using one of the transfer learning methods, DenseNet201, which resulted in the highest accuracy of 96.8% [10]. The recent article [11] is devoted to the diagnosis of tomato leaf diseases. The authors performed experiments with YOLOv5, MobileNetV2, ResNet18, and a custom CNN model. The dedicated CNN model demonstrated superior performance, attaining an accuracy of 95.2%.

In summary, despite great progress in the field of wheat grain classification, there are still challenges in achieving more efficient classifiers. Therefore, the aim of our paper is to propose an ensemble classifier based on CNNs for multiclass classification of wheat grain. A further challenge is posed by the limited amount of data available, which frequently proves to be a significant problem for CNN-based solutions. Analysis was performed in order to provide a model interpretation based on Shapley values.

2   Materials and Methods

2.1   Characteristics of the Study Material

The experimental material comprised cleaned wheat grain of three varieties: Canadian, Kama and Rosa. The study covered X-ray photograms containing 10 to 12 grain kernels groove down positioned. The photograms were then scanned by an Epson Perfection V700 table photo-scanner with 600 dpi scanning resolution and 8 bit gray scale image digitization [12]. This X-raying and photo-scanning procedure provided resolution images of sufficient quality for extracting distinct features important for accurate kernel characterization. Finally a randomly selected sample of 288 kernels was studied. Figure 1 presents an exemplary images of wheat kernels.

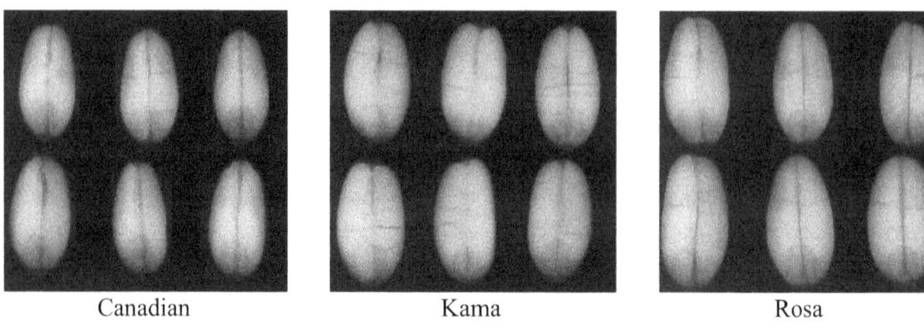

Canadian   Kama   Rosa

Fig. 1. X-ray image of kernels of three wheat varieties: Canadian, Kama and Rosa.

2.2 Deep Learning Models

In our study, a transfer learning approach was used that is rooted in pre-trained CNN models. This approach enables the application of pre-existing models to successfully adjust and tune to new domains and tasks. The growing number of studies on transfer learning models confirms their high adaptability and versatility [13]. The following CNN models were investigated: VGG16 [14], InceptionV3 [15], DenseNet201 [16] and NASNetMobile [17]. Combining a diverse set of individual CNN models can improve the stability of the overall model, resulting in more accurate predictions. Thus, ensemble learning was applied to produce one optimal and more robust predictive model [18, 19].

2.3 Model Evaluation and Interpretation

The evaluation of the proposed models was carried out using a multi-class confusion matrix and the performance metrics: accuracy, Cohen's Kappa, precision, recall and F1 score [20]. Five-fold cross-validation was applied to estimate the effectiveness of a classifier model in predicting the class of an unseen data. At the end, the error in cross-validating the data is determined as an average of all computed errors.

A game theory-based framework known as SHapley Additive exPlanations (SHAP) is applied to explain the CNN models [21]. The idea used for explanations of model predictions is to treat features that explain the prediction models as players and the prediction as the total payout [22]. A CNN model for image classification is to be trained and the final model is used to predict classifications of images in the test set. In the context of an image, each pixel is treated as a feature, therefore, Shapley value can be used to determine the pixel level importance in classifying images. The interpretation of visualization of the images shows highlighted parts in shades of red and blue. Red pixels represent positive SHAP values that increase the probability of the class, while blue pixels represent negative SHAP values that reduce the probability of the class.

2.4 Proposed Ensemble Approach

In our work, five machine learning classification models, namely, VGG16, InceptionV3, DenseNet201-V1, DenseNet201-V2, NASNetMobile were built. All classifiers were trained from a total of 288 kernel images of three classes (Canadian – 108, Kama – 72,

Rosa – 108). All input images were augmented with the following operations: rotation with angle 0–5, width shift 0–2%, height shift 0–0.5% [23].

The architectures and their optimal parameter values were selected based on prior experiments, which were then hypertuned. The final parameter specification of the employed models are presented in Table 1.

Table 1. Model parameters.

Parameter	Specification
Image size	$200 \times 150 \times 3$
Optimizer	Adam
Learning rate	0.001
Epochs	30
Dense Layer activation function	ReLU
Dropout	0.5
Output Layer activation function	Softmax
Loss function	Categorical Cross-entropy

The models were executed apportioning 80% of the data to train and 20% to test. Three best models were combined to build the soft voting ensemble CNN classifier.

3 Experimental Results and Discussion

3.1 Classification Results

This section presents the results of the study. Tables 2 and 3 display the outcomes of our study. The three best results for the Kappa, accuracy and weighted-average indicators of the individual CNN models are in bold.

As shown in Table 2, the VGG16 and InceptionV3 models achieved the lowest global accuracy of 91.97% and 88.89%. The DenseNet201-V1 and DenseNet201-V2 models demonstrated a 94.78% and 95.47% success rate in classification, respectively. The DenseNet201-V2 model displayed the highest level of efficiency in identifying the Canadian variety (98.2%) while DenseNet201-V1 achieved the highest result for the Kama variety (91.7%). The NASNetMobile model achieves an accuracy of 94.78% and a Cohen's Kappa score of 87%. However, this model was particularly effective in the recognition of the Rosa variety (99.1%). The three models with the highest Cohen's Kappa and global accuracy were included in the ensemble model. In addition, the base models differed in their ability to identify specific wheat varieties.

Table 2. Classification results with CNN models.

VGG16				InceptionV3			
Accuracy	91.97%			Accuracy	88.89%		
Kappa	86.00%			Kappa	82.00%		
	Precision	Recall	F1 score	Class	Precision	Recall	F1 score
Canadian	0.88	0.94	0.91	Canadian	0.89	0.92	0.90
Kama	0.94	0.89	0.91	Kama	0.86	0.82	0.84
Rosa	0.95	0.92	0.93	Rosa	0.91	0.91	0.91
Average	0.92	0.92	0.92	Average	0.89	0.89	0.89
DenseNet201-V1				DenseNet201-V2			
Accuracy	**94.78%**			Accuracy	**95.47%**		
Kappa	**91.00%**			Kappa	**93.00%**		
	Precision	Recall	F1 score	Class	Precision	Recall	F1 score
Canadian	0.95	0.97	0.96	Canadian	0.97	0.98	0.98
Kama	0.96	0.92	0.94	Kama	0.97	0.90	0.94
Rosa	0.93	0.94	0.93	Rosa	0.93	0.96	0.95
Average	**0.95**	**0.95**	**0.94**	Average	**0.96**	**0.95**	**0.96**
NASNetMobile				**Ensemble model**			
Accuracy	**94.78%**			Accuracy	**96.48%**		
Kappa	**87.00%**			Kappa	**94.00%**		
	Precision	Recall	F1 score	Class	Precision	Recall	F1 score
Canadian	0.96	0.92	0.94	Canadian	0.96	0.98	0.97
Kama	0.89	0.89	0.89	Kama	0.97	0.94	0.96
Rosa	0.95	0.99	0.97	Rosa	0.96	0.97	0.97
Average	**0.94**	**0.94**	**0.94**	Average	**0.96**	**0.97**	**0.97**

The ensemble model used DenseNet201-V1, DenseNet201-V2 and NASNetMobile as base learners. The experimental settings remained constant. The ensembles were trained separately, and an average of all predictions was combined as the final result.

Table 3. The confusion matrix obtained from the ensemble model (5-fold cross validation).

		Predicted Class		
		Canadian	Kama	Rosa
Actual Class	Canadian	**104 (96.2%)**	2 (1.9%)	2 (1.9%)
	Kama	1 (1.4%)	**68 (94.4%)**	3 (4.2%)
	Rosa	3 (2.8%)	0 (0.0%)	**105 (97.2%)**

The confusion matrix can be found in Table 3. There was a significant improvement for the Kama variety (94.4%), and a deterioration for the Canadian (96.2%) and Rosa varieties (97.2%). However, weighted-average precision value, as well as the efficiency of this model and F1 score had the highest rate of 0.96, 0.97 and 0.97. The ensemble classifier gave the highest global accuracy (96.48%) and Kappa (94%).

3.2 Features Importance Analysis

For the interpretation of the CNN models, the Deep SHAP algorithm was applied to generate an explaining module. Figure 2 presents the results of DenseNet201-V2 model's SHAP generated for three inputs on the leftmost column.

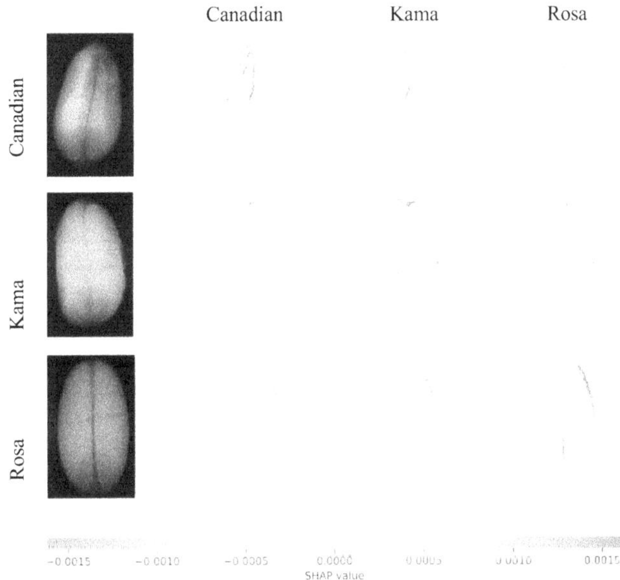

Fig. 2. DenseNet201-V2 model's SHAP values for wheat variety kernel images.

In the case of the image with the Rosa wheat variety, red pixels are presented mainly in the kernel groove. Here, the kernel groove is the longest. This region is also presented for the Kama and Canadian variety kernels. The average kernel groove length was significantly higher for Rosa, in comparison with the two other varieties [24]. Thus, the most discriminatory feature for the Rosa variety is kernel groove length.

In addition, red pixels emphasized regions of interest at the edges of the Kama and Rosa kernels, which contributed to the correct classification. This is consistent with the fact that according to the SHAP values, kernel perimeter is the second most discriminatory feature. The results for the Canadian and Kama variety kernels show red pixels concentrated in specific large internal kernel parts. It is evident that there is a substantial disparity between the average kernel area and the average kernel perimeter of the Rosa variety and those of the other varieties [24].

3.3 Discussion

The classification of small datasets is a challenging task, especially in the context of computer vision approaches. However, it is an area of interest for many researchers [25]. The issue of having a limited number of grain images by an ensemble of CNN models for image classification is addressed in our study.

The outcomes of almost all transfer learning methods were excellent, with accuracy, Kappa, precision, recall and F1 score exceeding 90%. In comparison, only InceptionV3 demonstrated slightly lower performance, achieving an accuracy of 88.89%, a Kappa of 82%, a precision of 0.89, a recall of 0.89, and an F1 score of 0.89. The DenseNet201-V2 model demonstrated a very high accuracy of 95.47%. The remaining outcomes, i.e. Kappa, precision, recall and F1 score, confirmed the accuracy. The Kappa score was 93%, the precision rate was 0.96, the recall rate was 0.95 and the F1 score was 0.96. The proposed soft-voting ensemble CNN model outperformed single classifiers achieving an accuracy of 96.48%, a Cohen Kappa of 94% and an F1 score of 97%. It also outperformed traditional ML models based on the main shape features as extracted from the same X-ray wheat kernel images, achieving an improvement in F1 score of 3% [24]. Furthermore, the feature importance analysis of the CNN models was consistent with the SHAP values of traditional models.

4 Limitations and Future Works

This study presented a soft-voting ensemble CNN approach for classifying X-ray images of wheat grains. A key limitation of this study is the relatively small size of the dataset, which may restrict the model's ability to generalize. However, the dataset is unique and challenging to obtain, which enhances the value of this work despite its limited scale. Future work will focus on more advanced ensemble techniques to improve the performance and robustness of the model using larger and more diverse datasets. The results demonstrate that the proposed approach effectively enhances wheat grain classification even when the size of the dataset is limited.

Acknowledgments. The research was partly carried out within project no. WZ/WI-IIT/3/2023 at Bialystok University of Technology and financed from the research subsidy of Bialystok University of Technology.

Disclosure of Interests. The authors have no competing interests to declare that are relevant to the content of this article.

References

1. Utku, H.: Application of the feature selection method to discriminate digitized wheat varieties. J Food Eng (46), 211216 (2016)
2. Zhang, Q., Liu, Y., Gong, C., Chen, Y., Yu, H.: Applications of deep learning for dense scenes analysis in agriculture: a review. Sensors **20**(5), 1520 (2020)
3. Agarwal, D., Bachan, S.P.: Machine learning approach for the classification of wheat grains. Smart Agricult. Technol. **3**, 100136 (2023)

4. O'Mahony, N., et al.: Deep learning vs. traditional computer vision. In: Arai, K., Kapoor, S. (eds.) CVC 2019. AISC, vol. 943, pp. 128–144. Springer, Cham (2020). https://doi.org/10.1007/978-3-030-17795-9_10

5. Li, P., Flenley, J.R.: Pollen texture identification using neural networks. Grana **38**(1), 59–64 (1999)

6. Daood, A., Ribeiro, E., Bush, M.: Pollen grain recognition using deep learning. In: Bebis, G., et al. Advances in Visual Computing. ISVC 2016. LNCS, vol. 10072. Springer, Cham (2016).https://doi.org/10.1007/978-3-319-50835-1_30

7. Koklu, M., Cinar, I., Taspinar, Y.S.: Classification of rice varieties with deep learning methods. Comput. Electron. Agric. **187**(3), 106285 (2021)

8. Brahimi, M., Boukhalfa, K., Moussaoui, A.: Deep learning for tomato diseases: classification and symptoms visualization. Appl. Artif. Intell. **31**(4), 299–315 (2017)

9. Yang, H., Ni, J., Gao, J., Han, Z., Luan, T.: A novel method for peanut variety identification and classification by Improved VGG16. Sci. Rep. **11**(1), 1–17 (2021)

10. Adimas, A.K., et al.: Soybean leaf disease detection and classification using deep learning approach. Bull. Electr. Eng. Inform. **14**(4), 2697–2704 (2025)

11. Prama, T.T., Oni, M.K.: Optimized custom CNN for Real-time tomato leaf disease detection. In: Paszynski, M., Barnard, A.S., Zhang, Y.J. (eds.) ICCS 2025. LNCS, vol 15909. Springer, Cham (2025). https://doi.org/10.1007/978-3-031-97564-6_6

12. Charytanowicz, M., et al.: An evaluation of utilizing geometric features for wheat grain classification using X-ray images. Comput. Electron. Agric. **144**, 260–268 (2018)

13. Rostami, M.A., et al.: Efficient pollen grain classification using pre-trained convolutional neural networks: a comprehensive study. J. Big Data **10**(1), 151 (2023)

14. Simonyan, K., Zisserman, A.: Very deep convolutional networks for large-scale image recognition. Comput. Vis. Pattern Recogn. (2014)

15. Szegedy, C., Vanhoucke, V., Ioffe, S., Shlens, J., Wojna, Z.: Rethinking the Inception Architecture for Computer Vision (2015)

16. Zoph, B., Vasudevan, V., Shlens, J., Le, Q.V.: Learning transferable architectures for scalable image recognition. Comput. Vis. Pattern Recogn. (2017)

17. Ganaie, M.A., Hu, M., Malik, A.K., Tanveer, M., Suganthan, P.N.: Ensemble deep learning: a review. Eng. Appl. Artif. Intell. **115**, 105151 (2022)

18. Pudumalar, S., Muthuramalingam, S.: An ensemble deep learning recognition model for plant diseases. J. Eng. Res. (2023)

19. Iqbal, M.S., et al.: An adaptive ensemble deep learning framework for reliable detection of pandemic patients. Comput. Biol. Med. **168**, 107836 (2024)

20. Yilmaz, A., Demircali, A.A., Kocaman, S., Uvet, H.: Comparison of deep learning and traditional machine learning techniques for classification of pap smear images. Image Video Process. (2020)

21. Lundberg, S.M., Lee, S.-I.: A unified approach to interpreting model predictions. Adv. Neural. Inf. Process. Syst. **30**, 4765–4774 (2017)

22. Pitts, O.et al.: SHAP-prioritised machine learning for diagnostic-grade prediction of lung function. In: Paszynski, M., Barnard, A.S., Zhang, Y.J. (eds) ICCS 2025. LNCS, vol. 15910. Springer, Cham. (2025). https://doi.org/10.1007/978-3-031-97567-7_7

23. Arora, J., Agrawal, U.: Systems. Classification of Maize leaf diseases from healthy leaves using Deep Forest. J. Artif. Intell. Syst. 2, 14–26 (2020)

24. Charytanowicz, M.: Explainable ensemble machine learning for wheat grain identification. In: The 23rd IEEE International Conference on Data Mining (ICDM), pp. 1–9. IEEE, (2023)

25. Dong, L., Shu, H., Tang, Z., Yan, X.: Microseismic event waveform classification using CNN-based transfer learning models. Int. J. Min. Sci. Technol. **33**(10), 1203–1216 (2023)

Boredom-Decay Multi-armed Bandits as a Sequential Multi-criteria Decision-Making Framework

Kamil Bortko[(✉)] [iD], Kacper Fornalczyk [iD], and Jarosław Jankowski [iD]

Faculty of Computer Science and Information Technology, West Pomeranian University of Technology in Szczecin, Szczecin, Poland
{kbortko,kfornalczyk,jjankowski}@zut.edu.pl
http://www.zut.edu.pl

Abstract. In this paper, we introduce Boredom-Decay Multi-Armed Bandits (BD-MAB), a novel extension of the Multi-Armed Bandit (MAB) framework that models boredom as a perceptualâĂŞcognitive factor in sequential decision-making. The approach incorporates a boredom-decay mechanism that reduces the perceived value of frequently selected options, capturing habituation and loss of novelty in user-facing systems. From a decision-theoretic perspective, BD-MAB can be viewed as a sequential multi-criteria decision-making (MCDM) framework, combining reward maximization with a dynamic novelty-oriented criterion. Unlike classical MCDM methods with static weights, preference adaptation is embedded implicitly in the decision process. Experimental results show that BD-MAB increases selection diversity (entropy) while maintaining competitive cumulative rewards, supporting the integration of cognitive-inspired mechanisms into bandit algorithms for human-centered systems.

Keywords: multi-armed bandit · multi-criteria decision-making · boredom decay · temporal decision-making · user engagement

1 Introduction

The Multi-Armed Bandit (MAB) problem is a well-known framework for modeling decision-making under uncertainty, balancing exploration and exploitation. Classical MAB algorithms assume stationary rewards determined solely by environmental factors, without considering user perception. In practice, users may experience boredom or perceptual fatigue when repeatedly exposed to the same options [12]. This habituation effect reduces the perceived value of even high-reward options, which is critical in user-facing systems where engagement and satisfaction matter. However, most MAB approaches do not account for such perceptual decay. This motivates incorporating a boredom-aware mechanism into decision-making. In this paper, we use the terms perceptual boredom and boredom-driven perceptual decay interchangeably.

M. Paszynski et al. (Eds.): ICCS 2026 Workshops, LNCS 16788, pp. 248–255, 2026.
https://doi.org/10.1007/978-3-032-29915-4_21

Recent studies [5] show that repeated exposure can lead to user disengagement. While extensions such as rotting bandits model declining rewards [11,14], they focus on environmental changes rather than internal cognitive effects. Few approaches explicitly incorporate perceptual boredom as an independent factor, highlighting the need for lightweight, boredom-aware strategies.

The main objective of this work is to introduce the Boredom-Decay MAB (BD-MAB), which penalizes frequently selected arms to simulate declining perceived reward. This encourages exploration and prevents premature convergence, improving diversity while maintaining competitive cumulative rewards. We hypothesize that boredom-driven decay increases long-term engagement without significant performance loss.

From a decision-theoretic perspective, real-world systems often involve multiple criteria such as reward, diversity, and user engagement. We interpret BD-MAB within the Multi-Criteria Decision-Making (MCDM) paradigm, where each decision aggregates reward maximization with boredom minimization. Unlike classical MCDM with static weights, BD-MAB adapts criteria dynamically over time, embedding preference evolution implicitly. This positions BD-MAB as a temporal, adaptive MCDM framework bridging reinforcement learning and multi-criteria decision-making.

By modeling boredom as an intrinsic criterion, this work contributes to hybrid MAB–MCDM approaches and demonstrates how cognitive factors can be integrated into sequential decision-making algorithms.

2 Literature Review

The Multi-Armed Bandit (MAB) problem is a fundamental framework for sequential decision-making under uncertainty. Classical algorithms such as ε-greedy, UCB1, and Thompson Sampling balance exploration and exploitation through randomization, confidence bounds, or Bayesian inference [1,2].

Recent research extends MAB to more complex settings, including adaptive exploration [6], non-stationary environments [13], and contextual or action-centric approaches [7]. Studies have also explored perceptual and behavioral aspects of decision-making [3,4,9], highlighting the importance of adapting to user preferences and engagement dynamics [15].

Non-stationary bandit models, such as rotting bandits, explicitly account for reward decay over time [11,14], encouraging adaptive exploration in dynamic environments. These approaches model changes in environmental rewards but do not capture internal cognitive effects.

In parallel, research in human-computer interaction and cognitive psychology has demonstrated that repeated exposure leads to perceptual habituation and reduced engagement [8]. This phenomenon is critical in user-facing systems, where novelty and diversity influence long-term satisfaction.

Although no prior work explicitly defines the Boredom-Decay MAB (BD-MAB), related approaches address reward decay or large-scale arm spaces [10].

However, these methods typically focus on external reward dynamics or contextual adaptation rather than internal perceptual effects. Importantly, none model boredom as an independent cognitive penalty applied to arm selection.

To address this gap, we propose BD-MAB, which introduces an intrinsic boredom penalty that increases with repeated selections while preserving the underlying reward distribution. Unlike rotting bandits, the decay is purely perceptual rather than environmental, enabling sustained exploration even in stationary settings.

By integrating perceptual boredom into the MAB framework, this work bridges insights from cognitive science and reinforcement learning, contributing to more human-centered and adaptive decision-making systems.

3   Proposed Method: The Boredom-Decay MAB Algorithm

In this section, we outline the conceptual and mathematical foundations of our proposed algorithm and describe how it differs from classical MAB strategies.

3.1   Classical MAB Strategies

The classical ε-greedy algorithm balances exploration and exploitation by selecting a random arm with probability ε, and otherwise choosing the arm with the highest empirical mean reward. UCB1, on the other hand, uses an optimism-based approach, adding a confidence interval to the estimated rewards to encourage exploration of less frequently chosen arms.

Both of these algorithms treat the reward structure as stationary and do not consider perceptual or behavioral effects that might reduce the subjective value of repeatedly chosen options.

3.2   The Boredom-Decay MAB (BD-MAB) Algorithm

The BD-MAB algorithm extends the ε-greedy framework by introducing a boredom penalty term, $B_k(t)$, which is dynamically updated based on the frequency of choosing arm k. The adjusted expected reward for each arm is calculated as:

$$\tilde{\mu}_k(t) = \hat{\mu}_k(t) - B_k(t),$$

where $\hat{\mu}_k(t)$ is the empirical mean reward for arm k at time t, and $B_k(t)$ represents the boredom penalty, growing with each repeated choice and decaying for unchosen arms:

$$B_k(t+1) = \begin{cases} B_k(t) + \beta, & \text{if } k = a_t \\ \gamma \cdot B_k(t), & \text{otherwise} \end{cases}$$

Here, β is the boredom growth rate, and $\gamma \in (0, 1)$ is the boredom dissipation factor.

This boredom-aware adjustment encourages the algorithm to diversify its selections, reflecting the perceptual reality that repeated exposure to the same option can diminish its perceived attractiveness.

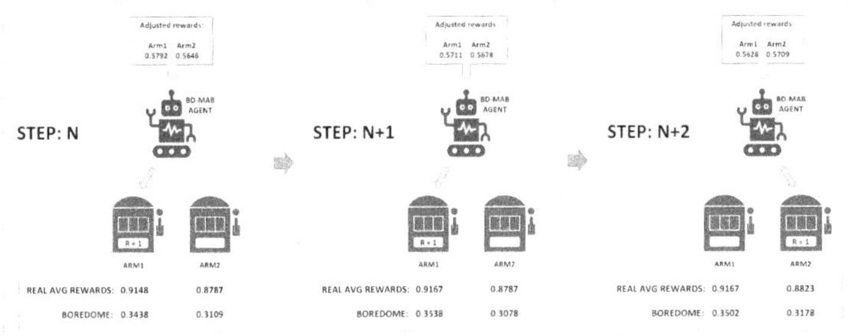

Fig. 1. Conceptual drawing of the algorithm's operation.

To facilitate understanding, Fig. 1 presents a simplified example with two arms over three steps. At each step, the agent selects the arm with the highest adjusted reward, defined as the empirical mean minus the boredom penalty. In round 1, arm 1 is selected due to a higher adjusted reward, yielding reward $R = 1$. The mean reward and boredom vector are then updated. In round 2, arm 1 is chosen again, but its increasing penalty and the decreasing penalty of arm 2 shift the balance. By round 3, arm 2 becomes more favorable and is selected. Importantly, BD-MAB is a lightweight extension that requires only minimal modifications to the classical ε-greedy algorithm and does not rely on external data or user feedback beyond selection history, making it practical and scalable.

3.3   Mapping BD-MAB to Classical MCDM Concepts

From a multi-criteria decision-making (MCDM) perspective, the Boredom-Decay Multi-Armed Bandit (BD-MAB) can be interpreted as a sequential framework where actions are evaluated based on dynamically evolving criteria. While classical MAB focuses on reward maximization, BD-MAB introduces an additional perceptual criterion related to boredom and diversity.

Each arm represents a decision alternative with two implicit criteria: exploitation, modeled by empirical mean reward, and novelty, captured by a boredom penalty that increases with repeated selections and decays over time. Unlike rotting bandits, this penalty reflects a perceptual effect rather than environmental reward changes. BD-MAB operates in a sequential, adaptive setting, where preferences emerge from interaction history. This positions it as a temporal MCDM framework that bridges reinforcement learning with multi-criteria decision analysis in dynamic, human-centered environments.

4   Experimental Setup

To evaluate BD-MAB, experiments were conducted in a stationary MAB environment with 10 arms, each assigned a fixed reward probability sampled from $\mathcal{U}(0,1)$. The focus was on algorithmic behavior and the diversityâĂŞreward trade-off.

Algorithm 1: Boredom-Decay Multi-Armed Bandit (BD-MAB)

Input: number of arms n, exploration probability ε, boredom growth rate β, dissipation factor γ

Output: selected arm a_t at each time step

for $i \leftarrow 1$ **to** n **do**
   $\hat{\mu}_i \leftarrow 0$;
   $N_i \leftarrow 0$;
   $B_i \leftarrow 0$;

for *each time step* $t = 1, 2, \ldots$ **do**
   if $rand(0,1) < \varepsilon$ **then**
     Select arm a_t uniformly at random;
   else
     for $i \leftarrow 1$ **to** n **do**
       $\tilde{\mu}_i \leftarrow \hat{\mu}_i - B_i$;
     $a_t \leftarrow \arg\max_i \tilde{\mu}_i$;
   Observe reward r_t;
   $N_{a_t} \leftarrow N_{a_t} + 1$;
   $\hat{\mu}_{a_t} \leftarrow \hat{\mu}_{a_t} + \frac{1}{N_{a_t}}(r_t - \hat{\mu}_{a_t})$;
   $B_{a_t} \leftarrow B_{a_t} + \beta$;
   for $j \leftarrow 1$ **to** n **do**
     if $j \neq a_t$ **then**
       $B_j \leftarrow \gamma \cdot B_j$;

Algorithm 1 extends ε-greedy by introducing a boredom penalty that reduces perceived rewards of frequently selected arms, promoting exploration. The penalty increases for the chosen arm and decays for others, enabling dynamic balance without modifying true rewards.

Experiments used $\varepsilon = 0.1$, $\beta = 0.01$, and $\gamma = 0.99$. Simulations ran for 5000 steps and were repeated 20 times. Performance was evaluated using cumulative reward, moving average reward, and entropy to assess diversity, with ε-greedy as a baseline.

5   Results

Figure 2 shows the cumulative rewards accumulated by BD-MAB and ε-greedy over 5000 time steps. As expected, the ε-greedy algorithm exhibits a slightly faster convergence to a higher cumulative reward in these stationary environments. This is due to its direct focus on exploiting the arm with the highest empirical reward without any penalization for repeated choices.

However, achieves competitive cumulative rewards despite its built-in boredom penalty. This indicates that while algorithm encourages exploration, it does not significantly compromise long-term performance in stable scenarios.

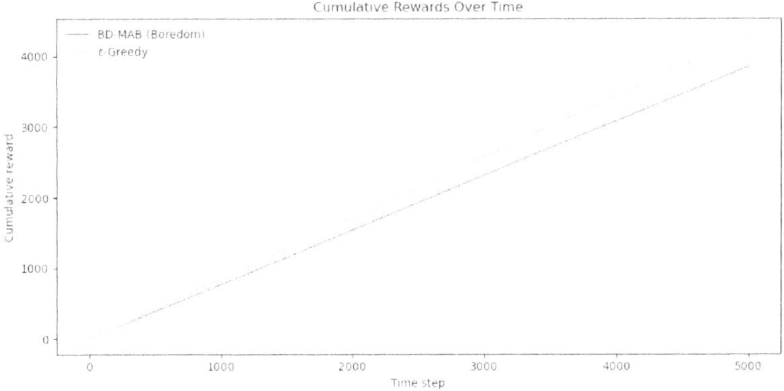

Fig. 2. Cumulative rewards over time for BD-MAB and ε-greedy.

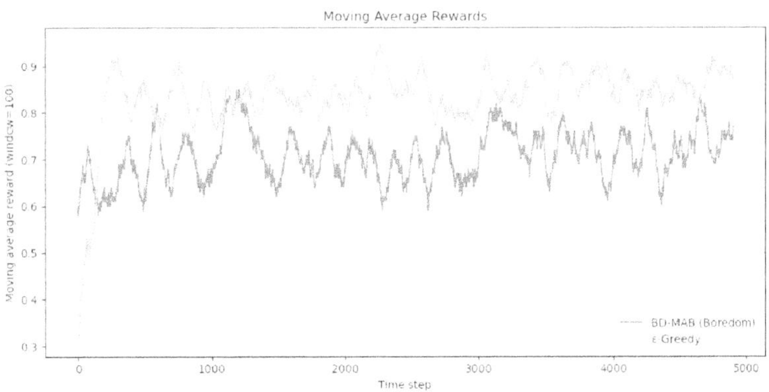

Fig. 3. Moving average of rewards with a window size of 100 time steps. BD-MAB exhibits more fluctuation due to its periodic exploration, stabilizing at competitive performance levels.

Figure 3 presents the moving average of rewards, computed with a window size of 100 time steps. The curves demonstrate that after an initial period of increased exploration, BD-MAB stabilizes to a similar moving average as ε-greedy. This suggests that our boredom decay mechanism short-term penalty for repeated choices is gradually balanced out by its adaptive exploration, leading to stable performance in the long run.

To measure the diversity of the arm selections, we compute the entropy of the choice distribution at each time step. Figure 4 reveals that algorithm maintains consistently higher entropy compared to ε-greedy. This confirms that BD-MAB promotes greater diversity in its choices over time.

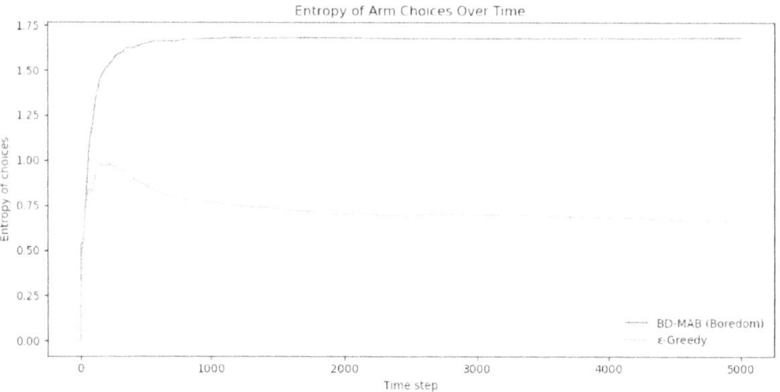

Fig. 4. Entropy of arm choices over time. BD-MAB maintains higher entropy, confirming its ability to sustain selection diversity, which is crucial for user-facing applications.

6   Conclusions

The results demonstrate that BD-MAB consistently achieves higher entropy than the ε-greedy baseline, confirming that the boredom mechanism promotes broader exploration and mitigates premature convergence. This is particularly relevant in user-facing systems, where repeated exposure can reduce engagement. Although BD-MAB attains slightly lower cumulative rewards in stationary environments, this reflects a trade-off between exploration and exploitation, with diversification offering advantages in dynamic settings.

From a decision-theoretic perspective, BD-MAB can be interpreted as a lightweight sequential multi-criteria decision-making framework, combining reward maximization with a dynamic, diversity-oriented boredom criterion. Unlike classical MCDM approaches, criteria are aggregated over time, enabling implicit adaptation without predefined weights.

The method is computationally simple and practical but depends on parameters such as the boredom growth rate β and dissipation factor γ, which influence the balance between exploration and exploitation. While effective, the approach may slow convergence in purely stationary scenarios.

Future work will focus on adaptive parameter tuning, evaluation in non-stationary and user-driven environments, and extensions to contextual and Bayesian bandits, further enhancing the applicability of boredom-aware decision frameworks.

References

1. Agrawal, S., Goyal, N.: Analysis of thompson sampling for the multi-armed bandit problem. In: Conference on Learning Theory (2012)
2. Auer, P., Cesa-Bianchi, N., Fischer, P.: Finite-time analysis of the multiarmed bandit problem. Mach. Learn. **47**(2–3), 235–256 (2002)
3. Bortko, K., Bartków, P., Jankowski, J.: Modeling the impact of habituation and breaks in exploitation process on multi-armed bandits performance. Proc. Comput. Sci. **225**, 4730–4739 (2023)
4. Bortko, K., Fornalczyk, K., Jankowski, J.: Integrating habituation effects with ucb and softmax multi-armed bandit algorithms for optimized digital content delivery. In: International Conference on Computational Science, pp. 153–166. Springer (2025). https://doi.org/10.1007/978-3-031-97567-7_1
5. Camerini, A.L., Morlino, S., Marciano, L.: Boredom and digital media use: a systematic review and meta-analysis. Comput. Human Behav. Rep. **11**, 100313 (2023)
6. Dubey, R., Griffiths, T.L., Dayan, P.: The pursuit of happiness: A reinforcement learning perspective on habituation and comparisons. PLoS Comput. Biol. **18**(8), e1010316 (2022)
7. Greenewald, K., Tewari, A., Murphy, S., Klasnja, P.: Action centered contextual bandits. Adv. Neural. Inf. Process. Syst. **30** (2017)
8. Hollebeek, L.D., Maslowska, E., Malthouse, E.C.: The role of recommender systems in fostering consumers' long-term platform engagement. J. Serv. Manag. **33**(4/5), 721–732 (2022)
9. Killian, J., Lalan, A., Mate, A., Jain, M., Taneja, A., Tambe, M.: Adherence bandits (2023)
10. Kim, Y., Jun, K.S., Nowak, R.: Rotting bandits are no harder than stochastic ones. In: Proceedings of the 39th International Conference on Machine Learning (ICML) (2022)
11. Levine, N., Crammer, K., Mannor, S.: Rotting bandits. Adv. Neural. Inf. Process. Syst. **30**, 3077–3086 (2017)
12. Ma, H., Liu, X., Shen, Z.: User fatigue in online news recommendation. In: Proceedings of the 25th International Conference on World Wide Web, pp. 1363–1372 (2016)
13. Mintz, Y., Aswani, A., Kaminsky, P., Flowers, E., Fukuoka, Y.: Nonstationary bandits with habituation and recovery dynamics. Oper. Res. **68**(5), 1493–1516 (2020)
14. Seznec, J., Menard, P., Lazaric, A., Valko, M.: A single algorithm for both restless and rested rotting bandits. In: Proceedings of the 23rd International Conference on Artificial Intelligence and Statistics, pp. 3784–3794 (2020)
15. Slivkins, A., et al.: Introduction to multi-armed bandits. Foundat. Trends Mach. Learn. **12**(1–2), 1–286 (2019)

Strategic Performance Monitoring in Higher Education: An Analytic Hierarchy Process Approach

Łukasz Wiechetek[(✉)] [iD], Marek Mędrek [iD], and Zbigniew Pastuszak [iD]

Maria Curie-Skłodowska University, Pl. M. Curie-Skłodowskiej 5, 20-031 Lublin, Poland
{lukasz.wiechetek,marek.medrek,zbigniew.pastuszak}@umcs.pl

Abstract. This article explores the application of Analytic Hierarchy Process (AHP) to strategic performance monitoring in university strategy implementation, proposing an integrated approach that enhances clarity, alignment, and managerial effectiveness. The research chapter develops and applies a three-level measurement and aggregation framework for computing an Integrated Strategy Monitoring Index (ISMI) for a university. Results from two-phase AHP show consistent strategic weights. Operational priorities vary by stakeholder, with moderate but acceptable inconsistency ($CR \approx 0.16$–0.18), supporting reliable, stratified KPI prioritization.

Keywords: AHP · Strategy Monitoring · MCDA Framework · Multi-Criteria Decision · University Management

1 Introduction

Traditional performance measurement systems in higher education have many limitations [1] and often rely on fragmented indicators that fail to provide a comprehensive view of strategy implementation. While key performance indicators (KPIs) are widely used, institutions frequently struggle to integrate them into a coherent framework that reflects strategic priorities and supports informed decision-making [2]. This challenge highlights the need for methodologies that enable systematic aggregation, prioritization, and evaluation of multiple performance dimensions [3].

This article explores the application of AHP to strategic performance monitoring in university strategy implementation, proposing an integrated approach that enhances clarity, alignment, and managerial effectiveness.

The article introduces a novel integrated three-level ISMI framework using two-phase AHP for university strategy monitoring. In the next parts of the article the authors present the literature background, construction of the three-level ISMI framework, research design and data collection, AHP-based weighting procedure, aggregation methodology, empirical results, consistency analysis, and concluding implications.

M. Paszynski et al. (Eds.): ICCS 2026 Workshops, LNCS 16788, pp. 256–264, 2026.
https://doi.org/10.1007/978-3-032-29915-4_22

2 Literature Review

Universities increasingly treat strategy not as a static document but as something continuously monitored, evaluated, and adjusted. Strategic monitoring focuses on translating goals into indicators across domains such as teaching, research, infrastructure, and internationalization, then tracking progress [4]. Performance measurement in organizations must capture multiple goals, long causal chains, and intangible social outcomes, while satisfying diverse stakeholders and accountability demands [2].

KPIs in universities span academic outcomes, research productivity, efficiency, and quality dimensions, grouped into academic, research, financial, and stakeholder categories [5]. Common limitations include data reliability, and difficulty capturing qualitative teaching–learning quality and complex educational processes [6].

AHP has been applied in higher education for evaluation, resource allocation, and strategic assessment. It supports group evaluation of research outputs and institution-wide strategic planning [7]. Literature shows dominant use in quality measurement, faculty evaluation, performance assessment, and strategic planning [8].

3 Research Method

3.1 Overview of the Research Design

This study develops a three-level measurement and aggregation framework for computing an Integrated Strategy Monitoring Index (ISMI) for the university. The framework follows the logic of composite indicators, in which a top-level index is derived from a structured hierarchy of lower-level components [9].

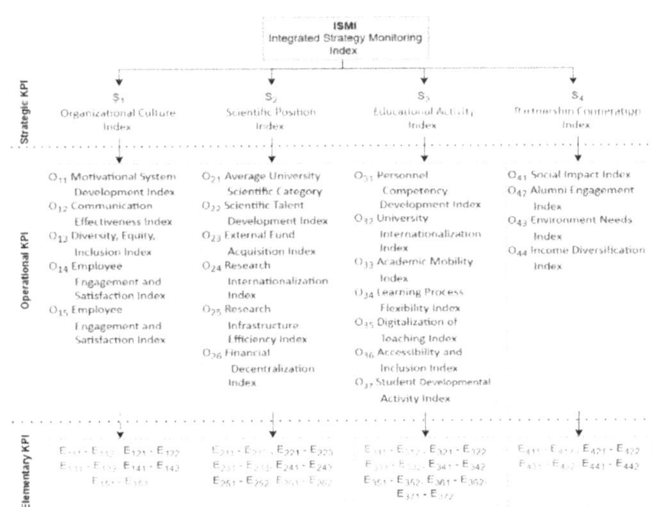

Fig. 1. Research model integrating expert-based AHP weighting of first level hierarchy strategic goals $S_1 S_4$ with second level operational goals $O_{11} O_{44}$ (for elementary KPI definition see Appendix 1).

Figure 1 shows the hierarchy of the research model. At the first level, the model defines four strategic KPI indices (S_1-S_4). The key strategic dimensions of the university strategy: S_1 (organizational culture), S_2 (scientific position), S_3 (educational activity), and S_4 (partnership cooperation). The second level decomposes each strategic dimension into synthetic operational KPI indices, O_{ij}, where i is the strategic index number and j corresponds to the synthetic index number within each first-level KPI. These indices reflect actionable, monitorable operational goals. The third level operationalizes each synthetic operational index (O_{ij}) as a set of elementary KPIs (E), typically two or three per operational goal. These KPIs are measured from administrative/IT data sources or elicited through stakeholder surveys using Likert-type scales. This design explicitly separates (i) the conceptual structure of the strategy, (ii) the operational monitoring layer, and (iii) the measurement layer, where raw evidence is collected. This improves transparency and traceability in monitoring [10].

Aggregation proceeds bottom-up: elementary KPIs are combined to compute each O_{ij}, operational indices are aggregated into strategic indices S_i, and finally the overall ISMI is computed as a weighted aggregation of $S_1 - S_4$. This enables "drill-down" managerial diagnostics rather than purely descriptive reporting [11].

3.2   Data Sources and Tools

Expert Weighting Instrument (AHP Survey)

Weights are obtained using a web-based, AHP-aligned pairwise comparison questionnaire. Experts provide comparisons on a symmetric scale ranging. The form was prepared in LimeSurvey, the questionnaire had five questions (one related to strategic goals and four related to operational goals). The link to the questionnaire was sent to 90 experts (66 completed). The instrument is applied at two levels: the strategic level, and the operational level associated with each strategic goal (see Fig. 1).

KPI Measurement Tools and Data Sources

Elementary KPIs (E) that feed the operational indices (O_{ij}) are obtained through two channels, as defined in the KPI catalog: administrative/IT data and structured surveys conducted periodically. Administrative data cover indicators that can be measured directly in institutional systems. Survey data cover perception-based or experience-based evidence measured using Likert-type items or threshold questions. All elementary KPIs are harmonized to a common reporting range prior to aggregation through KPI-specific normalization rules.

4   Data Collection

The weighting stage was based on an expert survey designed to elicit pairwise comparisons required by the AHP model. The expert panel represented the leading stakeholder roles involved in strategy governance and execution at the University. The questionnaire was distributed online in December 2025 and contained two sections of pairwise comparisons corresponding to the two weighted levels of the hierarchy (see Fig. 1.). Research model integrates expert-based AHP weighting of first level hierarchy strategic goals S_1-S_4 with second level operational goals O_{11}-O_{44} (for elementary KPI definition see Appendix 1).

5   Results

5.1   Weights for the Strategic KPI Level

From the aggregated expert answers, we obtained corresponding consistency measures:

$$\lambda_{max} = 4.023, \quad CI = 0.008, \quad CR = 0.008 \tag{1}$$

which indicate good coherence of expert judgments ($CR \ll 0.10$). The resulting consensus matrix $\overline{A}$ for strategic KPIs is

$$\overline{A} = \begin{bmatrix} 1 & 0.495 & 0.961 & 1.159 \\ 2.019 & 1 & 2.453 & 2.595 \\ 1.041 & 0.408 & 1 & 1.651 \\ 0.863 & 0.385 & 0.606 & 1 \end{bmatrix}. \tag{2}$$

The eigenvector method of matrix $\overline{A}$ yields the normalized weight vector for strategic KPIs:

$$w_S = (0.198, 0.436, \ 0.211, 0.154). \tag{3}$$

5.2   Weights for the Operational KPI Level

Table 2 reports the AHP consistency diagnostics λ_{max}, CI, and CR for the operational-level comparisons within each strategic dimension ($S_1 - S_4$)..

In classical AHP, the commonly used rule-of-thumb is $CR \leq 0.10$,, which indicates that pairwise judgements are sufficiently transitive and logically coherent (e.g., if $A > B$ and $B > C$, then $A > C$). In our survey-based setting, the observed group-average CR values are generally above this strict threshold. For the full sample, CR ranges from 0.161

Table 1. The AHP weights with SEM for operational KPIs for different respondent groups.

Strategic KPI	Operational KPI	AHP Weights for respondent groups				
		All (n = 66)	Research (n = 42)	Administrative (n = 13)	Educational (n = 8)	Student (n = 2)
S_1	O_{11}	0.228 ± 0.017	0.223 ± 0.020	0.228 ± 0.047	0.248 ± 0.044	0.335 ± 0.086
	O_{12}	0.210 ± 0.017	0.198 ± 0.021	0.244 ± 0.047	0.198 ± 0.040	0.247 ± 0.054
	O_{13}	0.086 ± 0.008	0.088 ± 0.012	0.065 ± 0.014	0.114 ± 0.022	0.068 ± 0.034
	O_{14}	0.247 ± 0.014	0.247 ± 0.018	0.235 ± 0.037	0.263 ± 0.035	0.237 ± 0.128
	O_{15}	0.228 ± 0.019	0.244 ± 0.025	0.229 ± 0.038	0.178 ± 0.051	0.114 ± 0.023

(continued)

Table 1. (*continued*)

Strategic KPI	Operational KPI	AHP Weights for respondent groups				
		All (n = 66)	Research (n = 42)	Administrative (n = 13)	Educational (n = 8)	Student (n = 2)
S_2	O_{21}	0.213 ± 0.018	0.219 ± 0.024	0.209 ± 0.038	0.207 ± 0.048	0.104 ± 0.044
	O_{22}	0.154 ± 0.016	0.138 ± 0.017	0.259 ± 0.049	0.100 ± 0.031	0.063 ± 0.037
	O_{23}	0.179 ± 0.009	0.172 ± 0.012	0.184 ± 0.018	0.182 ± 0.009	0.232 ± 0.078
	O_{24}	0.175 ± 0.011	0.170 ± 0.013	0.171 ± 0.028	0.170 ± 0.015	0.327 ± 0.034
	O_{25}	0.123 ± 0.009	0.120 ± 0.012	0.109 ± 0.018	0.147 ± 0.025	0.194 ± 0.011
	O_{26}	0.155 ± 0.017	0.181 ± 0.023	0.067 ± 0.016	0.194 ± 0.058	0.080 ± 0.020
$S3$	O_{31}	0.158 ± 0.012	0.157 ± 0.016	0.183 ± 0.031	0.117 ± 0.025	0.144 ± 0.086
	O_{32}	0.157 ± 0.012	0.164 ± 0.016	0.140 ± 0.023	0.163 ± 0.037	0.097 ± 0.051
	O_{33}	0.169 ± 0.013	0.173 ± 0.014	0.143 ± 0.034	0.169 ± 0.035	0.287 ± 0.183
	O_{34}	0.137 ± 0.009	0.126 ± 0.011	0.156 ± 0.021	0.162 ± 0.037	0.102 ± 0.083
	O_{35}	0.137 ± 0.008	0.137 ± 0.010	0.149 ± 0.023	0.129 ± 0.012	0.115 ± 0.048
	O_{36}	0.109 ± 0.008	0.112 ± 0.010	0.091 ± 0.014	0.119 ± 0.015	0.116 ± 0.096
	O_{37}	0.133 ± 0.013	0.130 ± 0.016	0.137 ± 0.039	0.140 ± 0.029	0.138 ± 0.094
$S4$	O_{41}	0.211 ± 0.013	0.201 ± 0.017	0.180 ± 0.028	0.290 ± 0.026	0.264 ± 0.142
	O_{42}	0.184 ± 0.015	0.190 ± 0.019	0.178 ± 0.033	0.172 ± 0.025	0.189 ± 0.137
	O_{43}	0.274 ± 0.019	0.289 ± 0.026	0.255 ± 0.045	0.245 ± 0.046	0.181 ± 0.010
	O_{44}	0.331 ± 0.024	0.319 ± 0.028	0.387 ± 0.068	0.292 ± 0.047	0.366 ± 0.269

to 0.177 across the four strategic blocks (S_1: 0.169, S_2: 0.172, S_3: 0.161, S_4: 0.177), indicating moderate inconsistency in operational-level judgements.

Although the strict $CR \leq 0.10$ criterion is exceeded in most cases, such levels are frequently observed in large-sample, online survey AHP applications and can be considered acceptable when the goal is to capture robust priority patterns.

Table 2. The AHP consistency measures for operational KPIs (In the table with consistency measures, groups with size n < 3 (Student, Other) were omitted due to the low representativeness of the statistical mean).

Strategic KPI	Operational KPI	Respondent group	No. of respondents	λ_{max}	CI	CR
S1	O_{11}-O_{15}	All	66	5.756	0.189	0.169
		Research	42	5.822	0.206	0.184
		Administrative	13	5.686	0.171	0.153
		Educational	8	5.458	0.115	0.102
S2	O_{21}-O_{26}	All	66	7.064	0.213	0.172
		Research	42	7.051	0.210	0.170
		Administrative	13	7.353	0.271	0.218
		Educational	8	6.610	0.122	0.098
S3	O_{31}-O_{37}	All	66	8.272	0.212	0.161
		Research	42	8.197	0.200	0.151
		Administrative	13	8.613	0.269	0.204
		Educational	8	7.868	0.145	0.110
S4	O_{41}-O_{44}	All	66	4.478	0.159	0.177
		Research	42	4.544	0.181	0.201
		Administrative	13	4.434	0.145	0.161
		Educational	8	4.292	0.097	0.108

6 Conclusions

The strategic-level weighting indicates that experts prioritize Scientific Position (S_2) most strongly (0.436 ± 0.023), followed by Educational Activity (S_3) (0.211 ± 0.015) and Organizational Culture (S_1) (0.198 ± 0.022), with Partnership Cooperation (S_4) receiving the lowest weight (0.154 ± 0.016).

The researchers show the strongest polarization, clearly prioritizing scientific position over other goals. The education group gives highest priority to educational activity. Administration is balanced, emphasizing both organizational culture and science.

At the operational level, priorities concentrate on a small subset of levers within each strategic area—e.g., for S_4 the largest weight is assigned to Income Diversification (O_{44}) (0.331 ± 0.024), while in S_1 the highest operational weight is Employee Engagement and Satisfaction (O_{14}) (0.247 ± 0.014).

Consistency diagnostics for operational comparisons show moderate inconsistency (typical $CR \approx 0.16 - 0.18$ across blocks), which is commonly encountered in survey-based AHP with abstract criteria; in comparable applications, thresholds up to $CR \leq 0.2$ are often treated as acceptable for retaining judgements [12].

Limitations include stakeholder variability, moderate inconsistency, and context specificity. Future research should validate ISMI across other institutions.

Appendix 1 - The Elementary Indicators Definition

Op. KPI	El. KPI	Definition (for strategic and operational goals definition see Fig. 1)
Organizational Culture Index (S_1)		
O_{11}	E_{111}	Number of employees covered by the incentive system / Total number of employees
	E_{112}	Number of survey ratings > = 4 (scale 1–5) / Number of completed surveys
O_{12}	E_{121}	Number of employees using the newsletter / Number of all employees
	E_{122}	Number of survey ratings > = 4 (scale 1–5) / Number of completed surveys
O_{13}	E_{131}	Min (Number of women in managerial positions, Number of men in managerial positions) / 0.5 x Total number of managerial positions
	E_{132}	Number of fully accessible buildings / Total number of buildings
O_{14}	E_{141}	1 – (Number of people leaving work / Average annual employment)
	E_{142}	Average survey score / Maximum possible score
O_{15}	E_{151}	Number of fully digital processes / Number of admin processes
	E_{152}	Value of completed investments / Planned investment budget at the beginning of the year
Scientific Position Index (S_2)		
O_{21}	E_{211}	Number of disciplines A + or A / Number of disciplines evaluated
	E_{212}	Number of publications for ≥ 100 points / Total number of publications
O_{22}	E_{221}	Number of employees who have obtained an academic degree or title / Number of planned promotions
	E_{222}	Number of academic teachers from abroad / Total number of teachers
	E_{223}	Number of employed young scientists / Total number of employed
O_{23}	E_{231}	Number of applications with a funding agreement / Number of applications submitted
	E_{232}	Value of funds obtained / Value of applications submitted
	E_{233}	Value of funds obtained in projects / Budget for science
O_{24}	E_{241}	Number of pub. With a co-author with foreign affiliation / Number of all publications
	E_{242}	Number of projects with foreign partners / Total number of projects
	E_{243}	Number of international conferences organized with the participation of university / Number of conferences organized with the participation of university
O_{25}	E_{251}	Number of articles for above 100 p. prepared using equipment / Number of all publications
	E_{252}	Research Services Revenue / Operating Costs
O_{26}	E_{261}	Funds at the disposal of units / General budget
	E_{262}	Non-administrative employees / Number of employees
Educational Activity Index (S_3)		
O_{31}	E_{311}	Number of teachers participating in training / Total number of teachers
	E_{312}	Number of student grades > 5.0 (in: 2.0–6.0 scale)/ Number of all grades
O_{32}	E_{321}	Number of foreign students / Total number of students
	E_{322}	Number of foreign language courses / Total number of courses
O_{33}	E_{331}	Number of students leaving (min. 5 days) / Total number of students
	E_{332}	Number of employees using mobility / Total number of employees
O_{34}	E_{341}	Number of working graduates /Total number of graduates
	E_{342}	Number of subjects in remote, hybrid form / Total number of subjects

(continued)

(continued)

Op. KPI	El. KPI	Definition (for strategic and operational goals definition see Fig. 1)
O_{35}	E_{351}	Number of subjects on the LMS platform / Number of all subjects
	E_{352}	Number of teaching rooms with projector and Wi-Fi / Number of all teaching rooms
O_{36}	E_{361}	Number of students with disabilities receiving support / Number of students with disabilities
	E_{362}	WCAG -compliant resources / Number of all online resources
O_{37}	E_{371}	Number of students in student clubs and organizations / Total number of students
	E_{372}	Number of students on internships and traineeships / Total number of students
	E_{373}	Number of people pursuing individual study programs / Total number of students
Partners Cooperation Index (S_4)		
O_{41}	E_{411}	Number of active partnership agreements / Number of all signed agreements
	E_{412}	Number of positive responses / Number of all surveys
O_{42}	E_{421}	Number of alumni in the BPA contact database / Number of alumni from the last 5 years
	E_{422}	Number of people with alumni cards participating in events at university / Number of alumni cards
O_{43}	E_{431}	Number of programs consulted with external organizations / Number of all programs
	E_{432}	Number of diploma theses and projects carried out in cooperation with the environment / Number of all theses
O_{44}	E_{441}	Non-subsidy revenues / Value of total revenues
	E_{442}	Commercialization revenue value / Total revenue value

References

1. Micheli, P., Manzoni, J.-F.: Strategic performance measurement: benefits. Limit. Paradoxes. Long Range Plann. **43**, 465–476 (2010). https://doi.org/10.1016/j.lrp.2009.12.004
2. Ahearn, E., Mai, C.: The nature of measurement across the hybridised social sector: a systematic review of reviews. Aust. J. Public Adm. **84**, 210–229 (2025). https://doi.org/10.1111/1467-8500.12616
3. Boix-Cots, D., Pardo-Bosch, F., Pujadas, P.: A systematic review on multi-criteria group decision-making methods based on weights: analysis and classification scheme. Inform. Fusion. **96**, 16–36 (2023). https://doi.org/10.1016/j.inffus.2023.03.004
4. Biondi, L., Russo, S.: Integrating strategic planning and performance management in universities: a multiple case-study analysis. J. Manage. Governance **26**, 417–448 (2022). https://doi.org/10.1007/s10997-022-09628-7
5. Ghulam, M.G.A.: Introducing and evaluating key performance indicators and generating awareness of competence among inter-departments for quality performance in large academic and research institutions. Inter. J. Educ. Res. Rev. **10**, 20–28 (2025). https://doi.org/10.24331/ijere.1535062
6. Sarrico, C.S.: Quality management, performance measurement and indicators in higher education institutions: between burden, inspiration and innovation. Qual. High. Educ. **28**, 11–28 (2022). https://doi.org/10.1080/13538322.2021.1951445
7. Liberatore, M.J., Nydick, R.L.: Group decision making in higher education using the analytic hierarchy process. Res. High. Educ. **38**, 593–614 (1997). https://doi.org/10.1023/A:1024948630255
8. Anis, A., Islam, R.: The application of analytic hierarchy process in higher-learning institutions: a literature review. J. Inter. Bus. Entreprencurship Develop. **8**, 166 (2015). https://doi.org/10.1504/JIBED.2015.070446

9. Nardo, M., et al.: Handbook on Constructing Composite Indicators: Methodology and User Guide. OECD Statistics Working Papers, 2005/03. OECD Publishing, Paris (2005). https://doi.org/10.1787/533411815016
10. Kaplan, R., Norton, D.: The Balanced Scorecard: Translating Strategy into Action. Harvard Business School Press, (1996)
11. Belton, V., Stewart, T.J.: Multiple Criteria Decision Analysis. Springer, US, Boston, MA (2002)
12. Pauer, F., Schmidt, K., Babac, A., Damm, K., Frank, M., von der Schulenburg, J.-M.G.: Comparison of different approaches applied in analytic hierarchy process – an example of information needs of patients with rare diseases. BMC Med. Inform. Decis. Mak. **16**, 117 (2016). https://doi.org/10.1186/s12911-016-0346-8

Computing Wasserstein Distances Between Asymmetric Interval Numbers

Andrii Shekhovtsov[1,2]($\boxtimes$) and Wojciech Sałabun[1,2]

[1] National Institute of Telecommunications, Szachowa 1, 04-894 Warsaw, Poland
{a.shekhovtsov,w.salabun}@il-pib.pl
[2] West Pomeranian University of Technology in Szczecin, Żołnierska 49, 71-210 Szczecin, Poland

Abstract. Asymmetric interval numbers (AINs) extend classical intervals by incorporating an expected value. Each AIN is associated with a canonical probabilistic representation in the form of a piecewise-constant approximating distribution composed of two uniform distributions, uniquely determined so that the normalization condition holds, reflecting the distributional asymmetry. However, classical interval distances, such as the Hausdorff distance, depend only on interval endpoints and assign distance zero to AINs sharing the same support but differing in expected value. In this paper, we derive closed-form analytical formulas for the Wasserstein distances W_1, W_2, and W_∞ between AINs, exploiting the piecewise-linear structure of the quantile functions of the associated distributions. All three formulas are evaluated in constant time $\mathcal{O}(1)$, eliminating the need for numerical integration $\mathcal{O}(n)$. We prove that the proposed distances are proper metrics and establish their key structural properties, including translation invariance, positive homogeneity, continuity, and ordering $W_1 \leq W_2 \leq W_\infty$. We further demonstrate that these distances are sensitive to distributional asymmetry, making them strictly more informative than classical interval metrics.

Keywords: Asymmetric Interval Numbers · AIN · Metric · Distance

1 Introduction

In many scientific problems, numerical quantities are not known precisely but are specified with uncertainty. Such situations arise when values are obtained from imprecise measurements, aggregated expert assessments, or incomplete data [5]. A fundamental task is then the comparison of two uncertain quantities and the quantification of their dissimilarity. The natural mathematical formalization of this task is a metric, that is, a distance function satisfying non-negativity, identity of indiscernibles, symmetry, and the triangle inequality [3,9].

A common representation of uncertain quantities is an interval defined by its lower and upper bounds. However, distances defined only in terms of interval bounds capture merely the support of the uncertainty [4]. In particular, interval-based metrics such as the Hausdorff distance assign distance zero to any two intervals with identical endpoints [1]. Consequently, two quantities that differ substantially in the location of their probability mass may be considered identical from the metric perspective. This limitation becomes evident when considering two uncertain quantities defined on the same interval but with different expected values. One quantity may concentrate probability near the lower bound, while the other concentrates near the upper bound. Despite representing substantially different uncertainty patterns, classical interval distances evaluate them as equal. Interval metrics therefore ignore the internal structure of uncertainty and cannot distinguish distributions sharing the same support.

Asymmetric Interval Numbers (AINs) address this limitation by augmenting an interval with an additional parameter representing the expected value [7]. Formally, an AIN is defined as a triple consisting of a lower bound, an upper bound, and an expected value. This representation can be interpreted as a parametric encoding of a probability distribution on the real line within a class of distributions with piecewise constant density with two levels. In this class, the density is uniquely determined by the normalization and expectation constraints.

Existing interval distance measures can formally be applied to AINs, yet they depend only on the interval endpoints. Consequently, they remain insensitive to the expected value and therefore to the distributional asymmetry encoded by AINs. Two AINs with identical support but different expectations are assigned distance zero by all classical interval metrics, despite representing different probability distributions.

To compare probability distributions rather than only their supports, a distribution-sensitive metric is required. Wasserstein metrics, originating from optimal transport theory [11], provide a natural framework for this purpose. For probability measures on the real line, the Wasserstein distance admits an equivalent formulation in terms of quantile functions, which makes it particularly suitable when quantile functions are known analytically. Moreover, unlike divergences such as the Kullback–Leibler divergence, Wasserstein distances remain well defined for distributions with non-overlapping supports [2].

The aim of this work is to construct mathematically rigorous and computationally efficient distance measures between asymmetric interval numbers based on Wasserstein metrics. We derive explicit analytical formulas for the distances W_1, W_2, and W_∞ and investigate their structural and metric properties in the space of AINs.

In particular, we address the following research questions:

RQ1: Can explicit closed-form formulas for the Wasserstein distances W_1, W_2, and W_∞ between two AINs be derived from the piecewise-linear structure of their quantile functions?

RQ2: Do the Wasserstein distances W_1, W_2, and W_∞, when restricted to the space of AINs, define proper metrics and preserve key structural properties required in practical use, such as consistency with real numbers, translation invariance, positive homogeneity, and the ordering relation $W_1 \leq W_2 \leq W_\infty$?

RQ3: Can Wasserstein distances distinguish between AINs that share the same support interval but differ in the location of the expected value, in contrast to classical interval distances?

An additional consequence of the analytical formulas is computational simplicity. The distances W_1, W_2, and W_∞ can be evaluated directly from the three parameters of each AIN, without discretization of the underlying distributions or numerical integration of quantile functions. In contrast to numerical approximation schemes based on discretization, which incur computational cost $\mathcal{O}(n)$ in the number of sampling points, the proposed formulas compute all three distances in constant time $\mathcal{O}(1)$.

The remainder of the paper is organized as follows. Section 2 recalls the definition and probabilistic interpretation of asymmetric interval numbers. Section 3 introduces the Wasserstein distances and derives closed-form expressions for W_1, W_2, and W_∞ for AINs. Section 4 establishes the metric and structural properties of the proposed distances. Section 5 provides illustrative examples and comparisons. Finally, Sect. 6 concludes the paper.

2   Asymmetric Interval Numbers

This section recalls the definition and probabilistic interpretation of asymmetric interval numbers following [7].

Definition 1 (Asymmetric interval number).   *An asymmetric interval number (AIN) is a triple $X = [a, b]_c$, where $a, b, c \in \mathbb{R}$ satisfy $a \leq c \leq b$, with $a < b$ for a non-degenerate AIN. The parameter c represents the expected value of the probability distribution induced by the AIN. When $a = b = c$, the AIN is called degenerate and corresponds to a real number.*

Every non-degenerate AIN $X = [a, b]_c$ induces a probability distribution on $[a, b]$ with a piecewise-constant density function:

$$f(x) = \begin{cases} \alpha, & a \leq x < c, \\ \beta, & c \leq x \leq b, \\ 0, & \text{otherwise,} \end{cases} \tag{1}$$

where α and β are uniquely determined by the normalization condition $\int_a^b f(x)\, \mathrm{d}x = 1$ and the expectation constraint $\int_a^b x f(x)\, \mathrm{d}x = c$. Solving this system yields:

$$\alpha = \frac{b - c}{(b - a)(c - a)}, \qquad \beta = \frac{c - a}{(b - a)(b - c)}. \tag{2}$$

The cumulative distribution function of an AIN is given by:

$$F(x) = \begin{cases} 0, & x < a, \\ \alpha(x - a), & a \le x < c, \\ \alpha(c - a) + \beta(x - c), & c \le x \le b, \\ 1, & x > b. \end{cases} \tag{3}$$

The quantile function (inverse CDF) of an AIN $[a, b]_c$ is piecewise linear with a single breakpoint at $t = \alpha(c - a)$:

$$Q(q) = \begin{cases} a + \dfrac{q}{\alpha}, & 0 \le q \le t, \\ c + \dfrac{q - t}{\beta}, & t \le q \le 1. \end{cases} \tag{4}$$

Remark 1. When $c = (a + b)/2$, the density satisfies $\alpha = \beta = 1/(b - a)$, and the AIN reduces to a classical interval number with a uniform distribution. In this sense, classical interval numbers form a symmetric subclass of AINs.

3   Wasserstein Distances for AINs

This section introduces the Wasserstein distances and derives closed-form expressions for W_1, W_2, and W_∞ between two asymmetric interval numbers.

3.1   Wasserstein Distances

Let $\mathcal{P}(\mathbb{R})$ denote the set of all Borel probability measures on $\mathbb{R}$. For $p \ge 1$, the Wasserstein space of order p is defined as [10]:

$$\mathcal{P}_p(\mathbb{R}) = \left\{ P \in \mathcal{P}(\mathbb{R}) : \int_\mathbb{R} |x|^p \, \mathrm{d}P(x) < \infty \right\}. \tag{5}$$

For a probability measure $P \in \mathcal{P}_p(\mathbb{R})$, let F_P denote its cumulative distribution function and let Q_P denote its quantile function (generalized inverse):

$$Q_P(u) = \inf\{x \in \mathbb{R} : \ F_P(x) \ge u\}, \qquad u \in [0, 1]. \tag{6}$$

The Wasserstein distance of order p between two distributions in $\mathcal{P}_p(\mathbb{R})$ is given by [10, 11]:

$$W_p(X, Y) = \left(\int_0^1 |Q_X(u) - Q_Y(u)|^p \, \mathrm{d}u \right)^{\frac{1}{p}}. \tag{7}$$

The Wasserstein distance of order ∞, also called the Chebyshev–Wasserstein distance, is defined as:

$$W_\infty(X, Y) = \sup_{u \in [0, 1]} |Q_X(u) - Q_Y(u)|. \tag{8}$$

Remark 2. Since every AIN induces a probability measure supported on the bounded interval $[a, b]$, the condition $\int_\mathbb{R} |x|^p \, \mathrm{d}P(x) < \infty$ is automatically satisfied for all $p \ge 1$. Therefore, AIN-induced distributions belong to $\mathcal{P}_p(\mathbb{R})$ for any $p \ge 1$, and the Wasserstein distances W_1, W_2, and W_∞ are well defined for all pairs of AINs.

3.2   Setup and Notation

Let $X = [a_1, b_1]_{c_1}$ and $Y = [a_2, b_2]_{c_2}$ be two AINs with distribution parameters α_i, β_i for $i = 1, 2$, as defined in (2). The quantile functions Q_X and Q_Y are piecewise linear with breakpoints at:

$$t_1 = \alpha_1(c_1 - a_1), \qquad t_2 = \alpha_2(c_2 - a_2). \tag{9}$$

Without loss of generality, assume $t_1 \leq t_2$. This can always be ensured by relabeling, since the Wasserstein distances are symmetric. The breakpoints partition the interval $[0, 1]$ into three subintervals:

$$[0, t_1], \quad [t_1, t_2], \quad [t_2, 1]. \tag{10}$$

On each subinterval, both quantile functions are linear, so their difference $D(q) = Q_X(q) - Q_Y(q)$ is also linear and can be written as $D_i(q) = A_i + B_i q$ for each subinterval, where the coefficients are:

Subinterval 1: $q \in [0, t_1]$, both quantiles in their left segment:

$$A_1 = a_1 - a_2, \qquad B_1 = \frac{1}{\alpha_1} - \frac{1}{\alpha_2}. \tag{11}$$

Subinterval 2: $q \in [t_1, t_2]$, Q_X in its right segment, Q_Y still in its left segment:

$$A_2 = c_1 - a_2 - \frac{t_1}{\beta_1}, \qquad B_2 = \frac{1}{\beta_1} - \frac{1}{\alpha_2}. \tag{12}$$

Subinterval 3: $q \in [t_2, 1]$, both quantiles in their right segment:

$$A_3 = c_1 - c_2 - \frac{t_1}{\beta_1} + \frac{t_2}{\beta_2}, \qquad B_3 = \frac{1}{\beta_1} - \frac{1}{\beta_2}. \tag{13}$$

3.3   Closed-Form Formula for W_1

Substituting $p = 1$ into (7):

$$W_1(X, Y) = \int_0^1 |Q_X(q) - Q_Y(q)|\, dq = \sum_{i=1}^{3} \int_{p_i}^{r_i} |D_i(q)|\, dq. \tag{14}$$

Since $D_i(q) = A_i + B_i q$ is linear on each subinterval $[p_i, r_i]$, it can change sign at most once. A sign change occurs if and only if:

$$\sigma_i = D_i(p_i) \cdot D_i(r_i) = (A_i + B_i p_i)(A_i + B_i r_i) < 0. \tag{15}$$

We denote the subinterval boundaries as:

$$p_1 = 0, \; r_1 = t_1, \qquad p_2 = t_1, \; r_2 = t_2, \qquad p_3 = t_2, \; r_3 = 1. \tag{16}$$

Case 1: No sign change ($\sigma_i \geq 0$). The function D_i does not change sign on $[p_i, r_i]$, and:

$$I_i = \left| A_i(r_i - p_i) + \frac{B_i}{2}(r_i^2 - p_i^2) \right|. \tag{17}$$

Case 2: Sign change ($\sigma_i < 0$). The function D_i changes sign at:

$$q_{0,i} = -\frac{A_i}{B_i}, \tag{18}$$

and the integral splits into two parts:

$$I_i = \left| A_i(q_{0,i} - p_i) + \frac{B_i}{2}(q_{0,i}^2 - p_i^2) \right| + \left| A_i(r_i - q_{0,i}) + \frac{B_i}{2}(r_i^2 - q_{0,i}^2) \right|. \tag{19}$$

The W_1 distance is then:

$$W_1(X, Y) = I_1 + I_2 + I_3. \tag{20}$$

3.4   Closed-Form Formula for W_2

Substituting $p = 2$ into (7) and noting that $|D(q)|^2 = D(q)^2$:

$$W_2(X, Y) = \left(\int_0^1 (Q_X(q) - Q_Y(q))^2 \, dq \right)^{\frac{1}{2}}. \tag{21}$$

The squaring operation eliminates the absolute value, so no sign-change analysis is required. The squared distance decomposes as:

$$W_2^2(X, Y) = \sum_{i=1}^{3} \int_{p_i}^{r_i} (A_i + B_i q)^2 \, dq = \sum_{i=1}^{3} J_i, \tag{22}$$

where each term is evaluated by expanding $(A_i + B_i q)^2 = A_i^2 + 2A_i B_i q + B_i^2 q^2$ and integrating:

$$J_i = A_i^2(r_i - p_i) + A_i B_i(r_i^2 - p_i^2) + \frac{B_i^2}{3}(r_i^3 - p_i^3). \tag{23}$$

The W_2 distance is then:

$$W_2(X, Y) = \sqrt{J_1 + J_2 + J_3}. \tag{24}$$

Remark 3. In contrast to W_1, the formula for W_2 does not require sign-change analysis of the quantile difference $D(q)$, making it simpler both in formulation and in implementation.

3.5   Closed-Form Formula for W_∞

The Chebyshev–Wasserstein distance is defined as:

$$W_\infty(X,Y) = \sup_{q\in[0,1]} |Q_X(q) - Q_Y(q)| = \sup_{q\in[0,1]} |D(q)|. \tag{25}$$

Since $D(q) = A_i + B_i q$ is linear on each subinterval $[p_i, r_i]$, and a linear function attains its extrema at the endpoints of its domain, the supremum of $|D(q)|$ over $[0,1]$ is attained at one of the subinterval boundaries. Therefore:

$$W_\infty(X,Y) = \max\left\{|D(0)|,\ |D(t_1)|,\ |D(t_2)|,\ |D(1)|\right\}, \tag{26}$$

where the values are computed directly from the coefficients:

$$D(0) = A_1 + B_1 \cdot 0 = a_1 - a_2, \tag{27}$$
$$D(t_1) = A_1 + B_1\,t_1 = A_2 + B_2\,t_1, \tag{28}$$
$$D(t_2) = A_2 + B_2\,t_2 = A_3 + B_3\,t_2, \tag{29}$$
$$D(1) = A_3 + B_3 \cdot 1 = b_1 - b_2. \tag{30}$$

Remark 4. The formula for W_∞ is the simplest among the three distances considered. It requires only four evaluations and no integration. The computational cost is $\mathcal{O}(1)$, as for W_1 and W_2.

Remark 5. The distance W_∞ measures the maximum pointwise difference between quantile functions, making it sensitive to local discrepancies between distributions. While W_1 and W_2 average the differences (without and with quadratic weighting, respectively), W_∞ is dominated by the worst-case quantile divergence. This property makes W_∞ particularly useful in applications where bounding the maximum comparison error is important.

4   Properties of W_1, W_2, and W_∞ for AINs

In this section, we investigate the fundamental properties of the Wasserstein distances W_1, W_2, and W_∞ defined on asymmetric interval numbers. We demonstrate that these distances inherit the metric axioms from the general theory of optimal transport, and we establish several additional properties relevant to their application in multi-criteria decision analysis.

Theorem 1 (Metric property). *The Wasserstein distances W_1, W_2, and W_∞ are proper metrics on the space of AINs, i.e., for any AINs X, Y, Z, the following axioms hold:*

1. Non-negativity: $W_p(X,Y) \geq 0$,
2. Identity of indiscernibles: $W_p(X,Y) = 0 \iff X = Y$,
3. Symmetry: $W_p(X,Y) = W_p(Y,X)$,
4. Triangle inequality: $W_p(X,Z) \leq W_p(X,Y) + W_p(Y,Z)$,

where $p \in \{1, 2, \infty\}$.

Proof. Every AIN $X = [a, b]_c$ induces a well-defined probability distribution μ_X on $\mathbb{R}$ with a piecewise-constant density function supported on the bounded interval $[a, b]$. The normalization condition $\int_a^b f(x)\,\mathrm{d}x = 1$ is satisfied by construction, and the boundedness of the support guarantees that $\mu_X \in \mathcal{P}_p(\mathbb{R})$ for all $p \geq 1$.

By the Kantorovich–Rubinstein theorem [11], the Wasserstein distance W_1 is a metric on $\mathcal{P}_1(\mathbb{R})$. More generally, for $p \geq 1$, the distance W_p is a metric on $\mathcal{P}_p(\mathbb{R})$ [11]. The distance W_∞ is a metric on the space of probability measures with bounded support [11]. Since the set of AIN-induced distributions forms a subset of these spaces, the restriction of W_p to this subset inherits all four metric axioms for $p \in \{1, 2, \infty\}$. $\qquad\square$

Proposition 1 (Compatibility with real numbers). *If AINs degenerate to real numbers $X = [x, x]_x$ and $Y = [y, y]_y$, then*

$$W_1(X, Y) = W_2(X, Y) = W_\infty(X, Y) = |x - y|.$$

Proof. For a degenerate AIN $[x, x]_x$, the quantile function is constant: $Q_X(q) = x$ for all $q \in [0, 1]$. Therefore,

$$W_1(X, Y) = \int_0^1 |x - y|\,\mathrm{d}q = |x - y|,$$

$$W_2(X, Y) = \sqrt{\int_0^1 (x - y)^2\,\mathrm{d}q} = |x - y|,$$

$$W_\infty(X, Y) = \sup_{q \in [0,1]} |x - y| = |x - y|.$$

$\qquad\square$

Remark 6. Proposition 1 confirms that the Wasserstein distances on AINs are consistent extensions of the standard Euclidean metric on $\mathbb{R}$.

Remark 7. More generally, the closed-form formulas derived in Sect. 3 remain valid when only one of the two AINs degenerates to a real number. Although the density-based representation from Sect. 2 requires $a < b$, the quantile formulation (7) extends naturally to all degenerate cases, where $Q_X(q) = x$ for all $q \in [0, 1]$.

Proposition 2 (Translation invariance). *For any AINs X, Y and any $t \in \mathbb{R}$,*

$$W_p(X + t, Y + t) = W_p(X, Y), \qquad p \in \{1, 2, \infty\}.$$

Proof. Translation shifts the quantile functions by a constant: $Q_{X+t}(q) = Q_X(q) + t$. The constants cancel in the difference:

$$Q_{X+t}(q) - Q_{Y+t}(q) = Q_X(q) - Q_Y(q).$$

Therefore, the integrals defining W_1 and W_2, as well as the supremum defining W_∞, remain unchanged. $\qquad\square$

Proposition 3 (Positive homogeneity). *For any AINs X, Y and any $k > 0$,*

$$W_p(kX, kY) = k\, W_p(X, Y), \qquad p \in \{1, 2, \infty\}.$$

Proof. Scaling an AIN by $k > 0$ scales the quantile function: $Q_{kX}(q) = k \cdot Q_X(q)$. For W_1:

$$W_1(kX, kY) = \int_0^1 |k \cdot Q_X(q) - k \cdot Q_Y(q)|\, dq = k \int_0^1 |Q_X(q) - Q_Y(q)|\, dq = k\, W_1(X, Y).$$

For W_2, the factor k exits the square root:

$$W_2(kX, kY) = \sqrt{\int_0^1 k^2 (Q_X(q) - Q_Y(q))^2\, dq} = k\, W_2(X, Y).$$

For W_∞, the factor k exits the supremum:

$$W_\infty(kX, kY) = \sup_{q \in [0,1]} |k \cdot Q_X(q) - k \cdot Q_Y(q)|$$

$$= k \sup_{q \in [0,1]} |Q_X(q) - Q_Y(q)| = k\, W_\infty(X, Y).$$

$\square$

Proposition 4 (Sensitivity to uncertainty width). *If two AINs share the same expected value $c_1 = c_2$ but have different supports $(a_1, b_1) \neq (a_2, b_2)$, then*

$$W_p(X, Y) > 0, \qquad p \in \{1, 2, \infty\}.$$

Proof. Without loss of generality, assume $a_1 \neq a_2$. Since $Q_X(0) = a_1$ and $Q_Y(0) = a_2$, we have $D(0) = a_1 - a_2 \neq 0$. Therefore,

$$W_\infty(X, Y) \geq |D(0)| = |a_1 - a_2| > 0.$$

By continuity of the quantile functions, $D(q) \neq 0$ on a neighborhood of $q = 0$ of positive Lebesgue measure, so $W_1(X, Y) > 0$. The result for W_2 follows from the ordering $W_1 \leq W_2$ (Proposition 7). $\square$

Proposition 5 (Sensitivity to asymmetry). *If two AINs have identical supports $(a_1, b_1) = (a_2, b_2)$ but different expected values $c_1 \neq c_2$, then*

$$W_p(X, Y) > 0, \qquad p \in \{1, 2, \infty\}.$$

Proof. Let $a_1 = a_2 = a$ and $b_1 = b_2 = b$. Since $c_1 \neq c_2$, the distribution parameters satisfy $\alpha_1 \neq \alpha_2$. On the subinterval $[0, \min\{t_1, t_2\}]$, both quantile functions are in their left segments, and

$$D(q) = q \left(\frac{1}{\alpha_1} - \frac{1}{\alpha_2} \right).$$

Since $\alpha_1 \neq \alpha_2$, we have $D(q) \neq 0$ for all $q > 0$ in this subinterval. The integral of $|D(q)|$ over a set of positive measure is strictly positive, hence $W_1(X, Y) > 0$. The results for W_2 and W_∞ follow from the ordering $W_1 \leq W_2 \leq W_\infty$ (Proposition 7). $\square$

Remark 8. Proposition 5 highlights a fundamental advantage of the Wasserstein distances over classical interval metrics. For two AINs with identical supports but different expected values, the Hausdorff distance yields $d_H(X, Y) = 0$, the width distance gives $|w(X) - w(Y)| = 0$, and the midpoint distance gives $|m(X) - m(Y)| = 0$. All of these classical measures operate solely on the interval endpoints, disregarding the internal distribution structure. The Wasserstein distances, by contrast, are sensitive to the shape of the distribution, and in particular to the asymmetry encoded by the expected value c.

Proposition 6 (Continuity). *If $(a_n, b_n, c_n) \to (a, b, c)$, then*

$$W_p([a_n, b_n]_{c_n}, [a, b]_c) \to 0, \qquad p \in \{1, 2, \infty\}.$$

Proof. The quantile function $Q_{[a,b]_c}(q)$ is continuous in the parameters (a, b, c) for non-degenerate AINs, since the distribution parameters α and β are continuous functions of (a, b, c), and the quantile formula (4) is continuous in α, β, a, b, and c.

Therefore, $Q_{[a_n, b_n]_{c_n}}(q) \to Q_{[a,b]_c}(q)$ pointwise for all $q \in [0, 1]$. Moreover, for sufficiently large n, all quantile functions are uniformly bounded:

$$|Q_n(q) - Q(q)| \leq M \quad \text{for all } q \in [0, 1],$$

where M is a constant depending on the convergent sequences. By the Lebesgue dominated convergence theorem,

$$W_1 = \int_0^1 |Q_n(q) - Q(q)| \, dq \to 0,$$

and analogously $W_2^2 \to 0$. For W_∞, the convergence $Q_n \to Q$ is in fact uniform on the compact set $[0, 1]$, since the quantile functions are piecewise linear and their slopes and intercepts converge. Therefore,

$$W_\infty = \sup_{q \in [0,1]} |Q_n(q) - Q(q)| \to 0.$$

$\square$

Remark 9. The continuity property has important practical implications. In multi-criteria decision analysis, where AIN parameters are elicited from expert judgments subject to natural imprecision, continuity guarantees that small perturbations in the input parameters (a, b, c) lead to proportionally small changes in the computed distances. This ensures the stability of resulting decision rankings. Furthermore, from a numerical standpoint, continuity guarantees robustness of the computations against floating-point rounding errors.

Theorem 2 (Symmetry of W_1 under symmetric shifts). *Let $X = [a, b]_c$ be an AIN with $a < c < b$, and let $\delta \in (0, \min\{c - a, b - c\})$. Define $Y_- = [a, b]_{c-\delta}$ and $Y_+ = [a, b]_{c+\delta}$. Then*

$$W_1(X, Y_-) = W_1(X, Y_+) = \delta.$$

Proof. Since X, Y_-, and Y_+ share the same support $[a, b]$, we have $D(0) = 0$ and $D(1) = 0$ in all cases. The difference $D(q) = Q_X(q) - Q_Y(q)$ is a piecewise-linear function that starts and ends at zero. Its integral equals the difference of expected values:

$$\int_0^1 D(q)\, dq = E(X) - E(Y).$$

We claim that when two AINs share the same support, $D(q)$ does not change sign on $[0, 1]$. Indeed, $D(0) = 0$ and, by the structure of AIN quantile functions, D is piecewise linear with at most three segments. Since $D(0) = 0$ and $D(1) = 0$, a sign change would require D to cross zero in the interior, which would imply the existence of a quantile q^* at which $Q_X(q^*) = Q_Y(q^*)$. However, for AINs with identical supports but $c_1 \neq c_2$, the quantile functions intersect only at the endpoints $q = 0$ and $q = 1$.

Therefore, $|D(q)| = D(q)$ or $|D(q)| = -D(q)$ throughout $[0, 1]$, and

$$W_1(X, Y) = \left| \int_0^1 D(q)\, dq \right| = |c_1 - c_2|.$$

Applying this to Y_- and Y_+:

$$W_1(X, Y_-) = |c - (c - \delta)| = \delta = |c - (c + \delta)| = W_1(X, Y_+).$$

$\square$

Theorem 3 (Symmetry condition for W_2). *Let $X = [a, b]_c$ with $c = \frac{a+b}{2}$ (i.e., X is a symmetric AIN), and let $\delta \in (0, \frac{b-a}{2})$. Define $Y_- = [a, b]_{c-\delta}$ and $Y_+ = [a, b]_{c+\delta}$. Then*

$$W_2(X, Y_-) = W_2(X, Y_+).$$

In general, for $c \neq \frac{a+b}{2}$, this equality does not hold.

Proof. When $c = \frac{a+b}{2}$, the AIN X has a symmetric distribution with $\alpha = \beta = \frac{2}{b-a}$. The quantile function Q_X is then symmetric about $q = \frac{1}{2}$ in the sense that $Q_X(q) + Q_X(1 - q) = a + b$ for all $q \in [0, 1]$.

Consider the substitution $u = 1 - q$. Under this transformation, the symmetry of Q_X and the mirror relationship between Q_{Y_-} and Q_{Y_+} yield

$$(Q_X(q) - Q_{Y_-}(q))^2 \big|_{q \to 1-u} = (Q_X(u) - Q_{Y_+}(u))^2,$$

and therefore

$$W_2^2(X, Y_-) = \int_0^1 (Q_X(q) - Q_{Y_-}(q))^2\, dq = \int_0^1 (Q_X(u) - Q_{Y_+}(u))^2\, du = W_2^2(X, Y_+).$$

For $c \neq \frac{a+b}{2}$, the symmetry argument fails, and numerical counterexamples confirm that the equality does not hold in general (e.g., $X = [0, 10]_3$, $\delta = 1$: $W_2(X, Y_-) \neq W_2(X, Y_+)$). $\square$

Theorem 4 (Symmetry condition for W_∞). *Let $X = [a, b]_c$ with $c = \frac{a+b}{2}$, and let $\delta \in (0, \frac{b-a}{2})$. Define $Y_- = [a, b]_{c-\delta}$ and $Y_+ = [a, b]_{c+\delta}$. Then*

$$W_\infty(X, Y_-) = W_\infty(X, Y_+).$$

In general, for $c \neq \frac{a+b}{2}$, this equality does not hold.

Proof. When $c = \frac{a+b}{2}$, the quantile function Q_X is symmetric about $q = \frac{1}{2}$. By the same substitution $u = 1 - q$ as in the proof of Theorem 3:

$$\left|Q_X(q) - Q_{Y_-}(q)\right|\big|_{q \to 1-u} = |Q_X(u) - Q_{Y_+}(u)|.$$

Since the substitution $q \mapsto 1 - q$ is a bijection on $[0, 1]$, the suprema coincide:

$$W_\infty(X, Y_-) = \sup_{q \in [0,1]} |Q_X(q) - Q_{Y_-}(q)| = \sup_{u \in [0,1]} |Q_X(u) - Q_{Y_+}(u)| = W_\infty(X, Y_+).$$

For $c \neq \frac{a+b}{2}$, the symmetry of Q_X does not hold, and the equality fails in general. $\qquad\square$

Remark 10. The difference between W_1 on the one hand and W_2, W_∞ on the other in the context of symmetric shifts arises from the following observation. The distance W_1 depends only on the integral of $|D(q)|$, which for AINs with identical supports reduces to $|c_1 - c_2|$ regardless of the distribution shape. By contrast, W_2 involves the integral of $D(q)^2$ and W_∞ involves the supremum of $|D(q)|$, both of which are sensitive to the pointwise magnitude of the quantile difference and thus to the asymmetry of the reference distribution.

Proposition 7 (Magnitude bound). *For any AINs $X = [a_1, b_1]_{c_1}$ and $Y = [a_2, b_2]_{c_2}$,*

$$|c_1 - c_2| \leq W_1(X, Y) \leq W_2(X, Y) \leq W_\infty(X, Y) \leq d_H(X, Y),$$

where $d_H(X, Y) = \max\{|a_1 - a_2|, |b_1 - b_2|\}$ denotes the Hausdorff distance between the supports.

Proof. *Lower bound.* By Jensen's inequality applied to the convex function $|\cdot|$:

$$W_1(X, Y) = \int_0^1 |Q_X(q) - Q_Y(q)| \, dq \geq \left|\int_0^1 (Q_X(q) - Q_Y(q)) \, dq\right|$$

$$= |E(X) - E(Y)| = |c_1 - c_2|.$$

Ordering $W_1 \leq W_2$. By Jensen's inequality applied to the convex function $\varphi(t) = t^2$:

$$\left(\int_0^1 |Q_X(q) - Q_Y(q)| \, dq\right)^2 \leq \int_0^1 (Q_X(q) - Q_Y(q))^2 \, dq,$$

which yields $W_1(X, Y)^2 \leq W_2(X, Y)^2$. Since both sides are non-negative, $W_1(X, Y) \leq W_2(X, Y)$.

Ordering $W_2 \leq W_\infty$. Since $|Q_X(q) - Q_Y(q)| \leq W_\infty(X,Y)$ for all $q \in [0,1]$:

$$W_2(X,Y) = \sqrt{\int_0^1 (Q_X(q) - Q_Y(q))^2 \, dq} \leq \sqrt{W_\infty(X,Y)^2 \int_0^1 dq} = W_\infty(X,Y).$$

Upper bound $W_\infty \leq d_H$. Since $Q_X(q) \in [a_1, b_1]$ and $Q_Y(q) \in [a_2, b_2]$ for all $q \in [0,1]$:

$$|Q_X(q) - Q_Y(q)| \leq \max\{|a_1 - a_2|, |b_1 - b_2|\} = d_H(X,Y).$$

Taking the supremum over q yields $W_\infty(X,Y) \leq d_H(X,Y)$. $\square$

Remark 11. The chain of inequalities $|c_1 - c_2| \leq W_1 \leq W_2 \leq W_\infty \leq d_H$ provides a complete hierarchy of distances between AINs. The Wasserstein distances occupy intermediate positions between the difference in expected values and the Hausdorff distance on the supports, combining information about the location of the distribution with information about its shape. The lower bound becomes an equality when the supports are identical (Theorem 2), while the upper bound is attained in the degenerate case.

5   Illustrative Examples

We present three examples illustrating the behavior of the derived Wasserstein distances. All values are computed directly from the closed-form formulas of Sect. 3.

Example 1. Identical support, different asymmetry. Let $X = [0,10]_3$ and $Y = [0,10]_7$. Since the supports coincide, the Hausdorff distance equals zero: $d_H = 0$. Yet the two AINs represent qualitatively different uncertainty patterns, where X concentrates mass near the lower bound, Y near the upper. The Wasserstein distances capture this distinction: $W_1 = 1.00$, $W_2 \approx 4.43$, $W_\infty \approx 5.71$. The increasing values reflect a general property: W_1 measures the average quantile displacement, W_2 penalizes larger local deviations more heavily, and W_∞ reports the worst-case quantile divergence. In this example, the quantile functions diverge most near $q = 0$ and $q = 1$, which amplifies W_∞ relative to W_1.

Example 2. Full hierarchy on a mixed pair. Let $X = [1,8]_3$ and $Y = [2,6]_4$. Here the AINs differ in both support and asymmetry. The five quantities from Proposition 7 evaluate to:

$$|c_1 - c_2| = 1.00 \leq W_1 \approx 1.30 \leq W_2 \approx 1.36 \leq W_\infty = 2.00 \leq d_H = 2.00.$$

The gap between $|c_1 - c_2| = 1.00$ and $W_1 \approx 1.30$ shows that the distributional shape contributes to the distance beyond the shift in expected values alone. The equality $W_\infty = d_H = 2.00$ occurs because the maximum quantile divergence is attained at the endpoints ($|a_1 - a_2| = 1$, $|b_1 - b_2| = 2.00$), where the Wasserstein and Hausdorff distances coincide.

Example 3. Symmetric vs. asymmetric reference. Let $\delta = 2$. We compare two reference AINs defined on $[0, 10]$ with different symmetry properties.

Symmetric Reference. Let $X = [0, 10]_5$, $Y_1 = [0, 10]_3$, and $Y_2 = [0, 10]_7$. Both Y_1 and Y_2 are obtained by shifting the representative value by $\delta = 2$ in opposite directions. By Theorem 2, $W_1(X, Y_1) = W_1(X, Y_2) = 2.00$. Since X is symmetric ($c = (a + b)/2$), Theorem 3 further yields $W_2(X, Y_1) = W_2(X, Y_2) = 2.34$. The symmetric density treats both tails identically, so equal shifts produce equal distances under all three metrics.

Asymmetric Reference. Let $X' = [0, 10]_3$, $Y'_1 = [0, 10]_1$, and $Y'_2 = [0, 10]_5$. Again, both are shifts of the representative value by $\delta = 2$. By Theorem 2, $W_1(X', Y'_1) = W_1(X', Y'_2) = 2.00$. However, since X' is asymmetric ($c \neq (a + b)/2$), the symmetry condition of Theorem 3 does not hold, and $W_2(X', Y'_1) \neq W_2(X', Y'_2)$. The shift toward the already-concentrated left tail ($c = 1$) produces a larger W_2 than the shift toward the sparser right tail ($c = 5$), because the quantile displacement is distributed less uniformly. This asymmetric response is invisible to W_1, which depends only on the total integral of the quantile difference, but is detected by W_2 through its sensitivity to the pointwise magnitude of the displacement.

6   Conclusion

This paper addressed the problem of measuring distances between asymmetric interval numbers using Wasserstein metrics. We now summarize the answers to the research questions posed in the introduction.

Regarding RQ1, we derived explicit closed-form analytical formulas for the Wasserstein distances W_1, W_2, and W_∞ between two AINs. The derivation exploits the piecewise-linear structure of the AIN quantile functions, which partitions the unit interval into at most three subintervals on each of which the quantile difference is linear. For W_1, the formula requires a sign-change analysis on each subinterval. For W_2, the squaring operation eliminates the absolute value, yielding a simpler expression. For W_∞, the distance reduces to the maximum of four point evaluations, requiring no integration at all. All three formulas are expressed directly in terms of the AIN parameters (a, b, c) and evaluate in constant time $\mathcal{O}(1)$.

Regarding RQ2, we proved that W_1, W_2, and W_∞ are proper metrics on the space of AINs, inheriting the metric axioms from the general theory of optimal transport. We further established compatibility with the Euclidean metric on real numbers, translation invariance, positive homogeneity, continuity with respect to AIN parameters, and the ordering relation $W_1 \leq W_2 \leq W_\infty$. The magnitude bound $|c_1 - c_2| \leq W_1 \leq W_2 \leq W_\infty \leq d_H$ places the Wasserstein distances within a complete hierarchy between the difference in expected values and the Hausdorff distance.

Regarding RQ3, we demonstrated that the Wasserstein distances are sensitive to distributional asymmetry. Two AINs with identical support but different expected values are assigned strictly positive distance by W_1, W_2, and

W_∞, whereas the classical Hausdorff interval metric assigns distance zero. The Wasserstein distances are therefore more informative than the Hausdorff interval distance when comparing uncertain quantities represented as AINs.

The results presented in this work open several directions for future research. First, analogous closed-form formulas may be derivable for other distribution-sensitive distances, such as the Cramér distance and the Hellinger distance, exploiting the piecewise-constant density and piecewise-linear quantile structure of AINs. Second, the proposed Wasserstein distances can be integrated into multi-criteria decision analysis methods that require distance or dissimilarity measures between uncertain evaluations [8]. Third, the derived formulas can be implemented in the open-source Python library `asymintervals` [6], enabling their immediate use in scientific and engineering computations.

Acknowledgments. This work was supported by the National Science Centre, Poland, under Grant No. 2024/55/D/ST6/01627.

References

1. Chen, Y., Billard, L.: A study of divisive clustering with hausdorff distances for interval data. Pattern Recogn **96**, 106969 (2019)
2. Csiszár, I.: I-divergence geometry of probability distributions and minimization problems. Annals Probability, 146–158 (1975)
3. Deza, M.M., Deza, E.: Encyclopedia of Distances, pp. 1–583. Springer, Berlin (2009). https://doi.org/10.1007/978-3-642-00234-2_1
4. Di Caprio, D., Santos-Arteaga, F.J.: Uncertain interval topsis and potentially regrettable decisions within ict evaluation environments. Appl. Soft Comput. **142**, 110301 (2023)
5. Kovalerchuk, B., Kreinovich, V.: Concepts of solutions of uncertain equations with intervals, probabilities and fuzzy sets for applied tasks. Granular Comput. **2**(3), 121 130 (2017)
6. Sałabun, W.: Asymintervals: a python library for uncertainty modeling with asymmetric interval numbers. SoftwareX **32**, 102380 (2025)
7. Sałabun, W.: Asymmetric interval numbers: a new approach to modeling uncertainty. Fuzzy Sets Syst. **499**, 109169 (2025)
8. Shekhovtsov, A., Kizielewicz, B., Sałabun, W.: New rank-reversal free approach to handle interval data in MCDA problems. In: Paszynski, M., Kranzlmüller, D., Krzhizhanovskaya, V.V., Dongarra, J.J., Sloot, P.M.A. (eds.) ICCS 2021. LNCS, vol. 12747, pp. 458–472. Springer, Cham (2021). https://doi.org/10.1007/978-3-030-77980-1_35
9. Tran, L., Duckstein, L.: Comparison of fuzzy numbers using a fuzzy distance measure. Fuzzy Sets Syst. **130**(3), 331–341 (2002)
10. Vallender, S.: Calculation of the wasserstein distance between probability distributions on the line. Theory Probability Appli. **18**(4), 784–786 (1974)
11. Villani, C., et al.: Optimal transport: old and new, vol. 338. Springer (2009). https://doi.org/10.1007/978-3-540-71050-9

On Effectiveness of Rule Classifiers Under Transformations of Input Domain

Urszula Stańczyk[(✉)] and Grzegorz Baron

Department of Computer Graphics, Vision and Digital Systems, Silesian University of Technology, Akademicka 2A, 44-100 Gliwice, Poland
`{urszula.stanczyk,grzegorz.baron}@polsl.pl`

Abstract. Decision support systems often rely on the induction of decision rules, which results from the explicit presentation of premises that provide a basis on which decisions are made, improving the interpretability of the process. Algorithms for inferring rules can vary in effectiveness and in the forms in which the rule conditions are expressed. Any modifications of representation affect knowledge patterns present, therefore, they reflect also on data mining processes. The paper presents research on performance of rule classifiers constructed by the MODLEM algorithm that is capable of inducing rules from continuous data due to inherent discretisation-like processing of attribute domains. This mechanism was combined with discretisation of the input space, and the results were investigated. The experiments carried out on the task of authorship attribution led to the conclusion that a partial transformation of the input datasets can return representations of attributes that improve accuracy.

Keywords: Rule-based classifier · Rule induction · MODLEM · Discretisation · Ranking · Stylometry

1 Introduction

High effectiveness belongs to primary objectives when decision support systems are designed and various data sources and forms are explored in search of representations advantageous to knowledge discovery approaches. When the process is characterised by transparency, it supports understanding and generalisation of learnt patterns, adaptation to changing conditions. These properties can play an important role, in particular, when many criteria are taken into account [11].

When learning from examples is performed, a closer study of the input space and characteristics of features [6], can result in improved accuracy, which is a frequent aim of investigations. Transformations such as discretisation [1] enable a wider scope of data mining techniques because not all algorithms can operate on continuous-valued attributes. Even when they can, translation into discrete type leads to simplification, which can prove to be favourable for performance.

MODLEM is a decision rule induction algorithm [10] that can work directly in continuous space. This is possible due to processing of attribute domains that closely follows discretisation principles by locating threshold values partitioning the space [3], used to formulate rule descriptors. In the research presented in the paper, the effectiveness of MODLEM was studied under changing representation of space, caused by sequential discretisation by selected methods.

The experiments were conducted on the datasets prepared for the stylometric task of authorship attribution [5]. The nature of stylometric space explored with style markers resulted in continuous values of attributes based on text samples labelled by their authors. With uncertainty of knowledge, the data were suitable for the application of rough set approaches and the MODLEM algorithm. Observations of the results led to the conclusion that, despite the operation mode of MODLEM, direct discretisation of space can be beneficial for performance, which confirmed the merits of the methodology illustrated in the paper.

The content of the paper is organised as follows. Section 2 presents the research background. Section 3 details the experimental setup. Section 4 is dedicated to the results obtained. Conclusions are given in Sect. 5.

2 Background and Related Works

The reported research involved feature selection mechanisms driving the transformation of the input domain, and their influence on the performance of constructed rule classifiers. The section presents the elements of this background.

2.1 Algorithms for Induction of Decision Rules

The MODLEM algorithm infers a minimal set of rules for every class by sequential covering. Its specific mode of operation lies in direct handling of attribute domains, in the processing similar to discretisation, without the transformation taking place. Rule induction starts with sorting values of attributes in non-decreasing order. For each condition attribute, its values are analysed to find a cut-point located in the middle between two successive values characterising examples with different class labels. The quality of this threshold is evaluated by the chosen measure [3], which can be the class entropy or the Laplacian accuracy Acc_L:

$$Acc_L = (N_C + 1)/N_{tot} + k. \tag{1}$$

Here, N_C stands for the number of positive examples covered by the condition, N_{tot} is the total number of examples covered, and k is the number of decision classes. In evaluation, higher accuracy values are preferred. Once the optimal value v_a is chosen, it is used as a condition in the premise of the rule.

The premise of a decision rule includes a conjunction of P elementary conditions (rule descriptors) listing the threshold values v_{a_i} of attributes a_i:

$$If\,(a_{i_1}(x)\; rel_1\; v_{a_{i_1}}) \wedge \ldots \wedge (a_{i_P}(x)\; rel_P\; v_{a_{i_P}})\; then\; v_d, \tag{2}$$

and v_d is the label of the class to which an example should be assigned when all conditions are met. The forms used for the conditions depend on a relational operator *rel*. The selected v_a is incorporated in a condition on a as either $(a < v_a)$ or $(a \geq v_a)$, depending on which relation covers more examples. For a rule, some attribute can be chosen with two threshold points v_1 and v_2, leading to a condition $a = [v_1, v_2)$. This descriptor is a consequence of forming an intersection of conditions $(a < v_2)$ or $(a \geq v_1)$ for $v_1 < v_2$. The simplest descriptors are defined for nominal or discrete attributes because then $(a = v_a)$ can be used.

2.2   Characteristics of the Input Space and Transformations

Data are at the centre of any exploration procedures applied. The type and amount available determine how it can be processed. Understanding domain characteristics is one of the key elements in the construction of an effective classification system. Recognition of the importance of features is another factor of such an impact. Relevance assessment begins with expert domain knowledge, but feature selection techniques can support the process [6]. One of such mechanisms is ranking, which orders the attributes from most to least relevant.

When the input domain is transformed, the patterns and characteristics of the attributes also undergo some changes. Discretisation procedure is responsible for replacing continuous values of features with categorical representations [1]. The domains of the variables are partitioned into intervals, and for each a nominal value is defined. Two main groups of algorithms are distinguished: supervised and unsupervised [7]. In supervised discretisation, information on classes is relevant to the interval construction problem. Unsupervised methods focus exclusively on the transformed domain and observed attribute values.

Discretisation is commonly included in the pre-processing stage. So, the data are first transformed and then explored. If the learnt knowledge patterns can be directly accessible (as in the case of decision rules), the order of proceeding can be reversed, and the knowledge discovered first and then discretised [9]. Typically, one algorithm is applied to all domains, transformed at the same time.

2.3   Motivation

The MODLEM algorithm does not need discrete data to operate. However, it does not imply that it is impervious to transformation of the input domain. The observed degree of sensitivity to data processing depends on the type of processing and the specific characteristics of the input space under investigation. This line of reasoning was the primary motivation for the presented research.

Furthermore, no single discretisation algorithm is optimal for all conditions. Supervised approaches are often considered superior to unsupervised ones due to their support for class distinction. For both categories of methods, several variants were developed, making the choice not trivial and suggesting a study in search of advantageous representation, focused on properties of a specific domain.

3   Experimental Setup

In the investigations, WEKA software [4] was applied for data transformations and knowledge discovery. The section details the scope of the experiments.

3.1   Application Domain and Input Features

The task chosen for the experiments was binary authorship attribution, from the domain of stylometric analysis of texts, based on writing styles [5]. The authors studied were two pairs of known writers, Edith Wharton and Mary Johnston, and Henry James and Thomas Hardy. Their literary works, divided into smaller text blocks of comparable size, provided the text corpus for analysis.

The selected attributes reflected the frequency of occurrence of 12 function words [12]. This made the features continuous. They were calculated over text samples and grouped into three sets included in each of the two datasets (the female writer dataset, F-writers, and the male writer dataset, M-writers): one training set and two test sets. In all sets, the data was balanced.

Three orderings of attributes were obtained, shown in Table 1. Two were returned from the ranking mechanism: WrapB which belongs to the wrapper category and Relief, which is instance-based [6]. In addition, over the samples included in the train sets, the average values of all features were calculated, and then the attributes were sorted by this value, resulting in the third ordering. The three orders were used to control sequential discretisation of space.

Table 1. Relief and WrapB ranking and average-based ordering of attributes

	F-writers													M-writers											
Position	1	2	3	4	5	6	7	8	9	10	11	12	Order	1	2	3	4	5	6	7	8	9	10	11	12 Position
	on	to	of	as	by	if	or	up	at	in	so	no	Relief	by	if	so	or	in	as	at	on	no	of	up	to
	to	on	of	no	at	if	so	up	in	or	by	as	WrapB	by	if	to	in	so	no	at	of	as	on	up	or
	of	to	in	as	at	on	by	so	no	if	or	up	Average	to	of	in	as	at	on	so	by	if	no	up	or

3.2   Discretisation Approaches and Methodology of Transformations

Four main discretisation methods were applied to the data. Unsupervised equal width (duw) binning defines the required number of bins with equal width. Unsupervised equal frequency (duf) binning constructs such intervals that represent the same number of original datapoints. For both methods, the number of bins ranged from two to ten. Fayyad and Irani (dsF) [2] and Kononenko (dsK) [7] are supervised algorithms that refer to the Minimum Description Length principle. All in all, the total number of discretisation approaches was 20, but more data versions were obtained due to the methodology of transformations implemented.

The input data was processed gradually, one attribute at a time. The feature to be translated was selected on the basis of an ordering provided as the input parameter to the procedure, starting with the highest positions in the ordering and then sequentially proceeding down the list of variables. With three orderings used and 12 features, the total number of data variants studied was equal to

1 continuous $+(11 \times 3) \times 20$ partially discrete $+20$ entirely discrete $= 681$

All data variants were explored and decision rules inferred from the training sets by the MODLEM algorithm with Laplacian accuracy used as a measure when conditions were evaluated. The performance was then verified by classifying samples from the corresponding test sets. The test sets were discretised using definitions of intervals formed in transformations of the training sets [8].

4   Results From Experiments

The investigations began with establishing inducer effectiveness in the continuous domain, expressed by the classification accuracy averaged over the test sets. For the female writer dataset, the accuracy was 92.08% and for the male writer dataset it was 79.31%. These two values were treated as reference points.

The results of the subsequent rule induction under changing conditions are shown in Table 2 by differences, with the reference classification accuracy subtracted from the performance reported in each case. Positive values correspond to improvement, and negative values indicate the degraded power of the classifiers.

For the F-writer dataset, when a few bins were constructed by unsupervised methods, a noticeable drop in performance was noted. With increasing numbers of discretised features, the predictions were closer to the reference point. duw presented fewer cases of improved accuracy than duf. Supervised discretisation methods returned observations mostly to the disadvantage. The highest number of favourable cases occurred for the average-based order of variables. The rankings produced close results, with a slight superiority of WrapB over Relief.

For M-writers, when two bins were defined by two unsupervised approaches and WrapB or Relief directed the processing, only degraded powers of classifiers were noted. In other processing paths, for some number of discretised features, such classification accuracy was recorded which was an improvement over the reference point in the continuous domain. Supervised discretisation resulted in more cases of enhanced predictions than for F-writers. With the exception of a pairing Relief with duf, equal width binning gave better results than following distributions when WrapB or average-based orders were involved in processing.

For all transformations paths, the statistics were calculated, referring to the entire sequential discretisation path (from a single categorised variable to the entirely discrete space). They are provided by Table 3 and include the average classification accuracy with the standard deviation and the minimum and maximum accuracy. Among all discrete variants, in each row the preferred best values (highest for classification accuracy, lowest for std) are marked in bold font.

In general, the values of std were higher mainly when a low number of bins was constructed for variables by unsupervised approaches. The lowest values were reported for more bins defined for attributes. For the three orderings controlling transformations, the statistics for two supervised algorithms were relatively close and inferior to those for unsupervised discretisation.

For F-writers, the best scenario for rule induction was for equal frequency binning with six bins and following WrapB ranking. For M-writers, the same ordering and discretisation approach worked the best, but for ten bins. For both

Table 2. Difference in performance of rule classifiers observed in sequential discretisation following *Order*, with P giving the number of transformed features. The discretisation approaches included supervised methods (dsF for Fayyad and Irani, and dsK for Kononenko), and unsupervised equal frequency (duf) and equal width (duw) binning.

Order	P	Supervised		Unsupervised duf									Unsupervised duw								
		dsF	dsK	2	3	4	5	6	7	8	9	10	2	3	4	5	6	7	8	9	10
F-writers																					
WrapB	1	-1.667	-1.667	-2.222	1.875	0.833	0.208	-0.347	-1.111	0.833	0.833	0.278	0.764	-2.847	-0.972	-0.833	1.389	-2.153	-0.417	-0.972	0.278
	2	0.139	0.139	-12.153	2.014	-0.278	-2.361	1.389	-0.486	-0.347	-0.486	-0.833	-5.833	-3.403	-1.042	-2.778	-0.556	0.278	-2.153	0.208	-2.847
	3	-6.250	-3.264	-8.472	-0.972	-0.347	1.181	1.944	0.694	-1.042	2.569	-2.014	-5.764	-3.125	0.069	-6.250	-1.597	1.458	1.389	2.014	-1.042
	4	-8.681	-3.889	-8.472	-0.417	1.389	1.875	1.319	0.694	0.000	2.500	-1.458	-5.764	-2.639	0.069	-6.250	-1.597	1.528	0.833	2.014	-1.042
	5	-1.528	-1.667	-4.583	-2.292	-0.278	1.875	3.125	-1.597	0.069	1.250	-1.458	-5.139	-5.486	-1.111	-2.708	-3.403	-0.278	0.833	2.014	-0.417
	6	-1.528	-1.667	-4.028	-1.736	-0.833	2.500	3.125	-1.597	-0.486	1.875	-1.458	-5.833	-5.486	-0.486	-3.333	-2.778	0.278	0.833	2.014	-0.417
	7	-0.347	0.139	-4.514	-1.667	1.875	0.694	3.750	-1.597	-1.042	1.875	-2.083	-5.833	-4.931	-1.042	-4.444	-2.778	-1.528	-0.903	1.458	-0.417
	8	-0.972	-0.417	-2.153	-1.667	1.875	0.069	1.944	-1.042	1.250	1.875	-3.264	-5.833	-8.681	-1.042	0.278	-2.778	-1.528	0.208	1.458	0.139
	9	-0.347	-1.042	-3.333	-1.597	1.250	2.986	1.944	0.694	1.250	2.500	-3.264	-5.208	-3.333	-1.736	0.278	-2.153	-2.083	-0.972	0.833	-0.972
	10	-2.708	-4.583	-0.903	-2.847	0.139	1.875	1.319	-0.486	1.250	1.944	-3.264	-6.944	-3.958	-0.486	-0.903	-2.153	-2.708	-0.972	-0.347	-0.972
	11	-6.250	-3.889	-3.333	-2.292	-1.111	2.500	0.139	0.139	1.250	1.875	-5.139	-4.722	-5.000	0.139	-2.917	-1.597	0.278	-0.972	0.833	-1.042
	12	-1.181	-2.361	-5.694	-0.556	2.500	0.069	1.806	3.681	-0.486	-0.417	2.014	-7.014	-2.847	-4.028	1.389	-1.667	-0.486	-1.042	-1.528	-1.597
Relief	1	-1.111	-1.111	-3.333	0.764	-1.528	0.694	-2.014	-1.042	-0.486	-1.597	-0.903	-1.667	-4.097	-1.042	-1.042	-3.958	-0.417	-2.639	-1.597	-2.153
	2	0.139	0.139	-12.153	2.014	-0.278	-2.361	1.389	-0.486	-0.347	-0.486	-0.833	-5.833	-3.403	-1.042	-2.778	-0.556	0.278	-2.153	0.208	-2.847
	3	-6.250	-3.264	-8.472	-0.972	-0.347	1.181	1.944	0.694	-1.042	2.569	-2.014	-5.764	-3.125	0.069	-6.250	-1.597	1.458	1.389	2.014	-1.042
	4	-8.194	-7.500	-8.542	-0.347	2.014	0.694	0.833	1.875	1.389	-2.014	0.278	-12.361	-4.931	1.458	-2.153	-3.264	0.208	-0.972	-0.417	-0.556
	5	-6.944	-4.028	-4.444	0.139	1.458	2.500	0.833	1.875	1.389	-2.639	-0.278	-7.083	-1.528	-2.292	-1.597	0.139	-0.347	-0.417	-0.417	-1.181
	6	-7.569	-4.653	-4.097	0.764	0.903	3.681	1.389	1.875	0.833	0.903	-0.278	-8.750	-1.528	-1.250	-2.847	0.139	-0.347	-0.417	-0.417	0.556
	7	-6.528	-3.611	-6.875	-1.042	-0.903	3.125	1.250	1.875	0.833	0.903	1.389	-8.681	-0.903	-1.181	-1.042	-0.417	-0.417	-0.417	-0.417	0.556
	8	-7.153	-4.167	-5.278	-0.417	-0.903	2.431	1.250	0.833	1.389	0.903	1.389	-4.653	-1.528	-1.181	-0.417	-2.778	0.139	1.319	-0.417	0.556
	9	-6.458	-2.917	-5.208	-1.181	-0.417	1.250	1.806	-4.028	0.208	-1.458	1.389	-5.625	-5.000	-1.806	-0.417	-3.333	-1.597	1.319	-0.972	0.000
	10	-1.111	0.625	-2.292	-1.181	0.139	1.250	0.694	1.181	-0.417	1.319	1.389	-4.444	-0.417	-2.431	0.764	-0.417	-1.597	-0.417	-0.972	-1.597
	11	-2.986	-3.542	-5.833	0.069	1.389	1.875	0.694	2.431	1.944	0.764	1.389	-4.583	-0.486	-4.028	0.764	-1.042	-0.486	-1.042	-1.528	-1.042
	12	-1.181	-2.361	-5.694	-0.556	2.500	0.069	1.806	3.681	-0.486	-0.417	2.014	-7.014	-2.847	-4.028	1.389	-1.667	-0.486	-1.042	-1.528	-1.597
Average	1	3.056	3.125	2.014	-0.417	1.389	1.319	3.056	1.250	0.764	0.139	-0.972	2.569	2.431	1.458	0.903	1.458	2.500	3.750	3.194	-0.278
	2	-3.889	-0.903	-5.139	-0.486	0.278	1.319	3.056	0.764	1.389	0.139	0.208	0.139	-0.903	1.250	-2.014	2.569	2.014	3.056	2.639	-2.639
	3	-2.153	-1.528	-4.653	-2.153	0.278	0.278	2.500	1.319	-1.458	-2.153	-2.708	-1.667	0.833	0.625	-2.708	2.569	2.014	2.431	2.639	-2.083
	4	-6.319	-3.958	-1.389	-3.333	0.903	0.903	2.500	-0.903	-0.347	1.319	-2.708	-3.403	-1.528	-1.111	-1.528	-0.972	1.389	1.250	1.389	-2.153
	5	-5.833	-3.472	0.833	-3.958	0.903	0.278	1.319	0.139	0.208	0.139	-2.708	-1.597	-1.458	-0.486	-0.278	-1.597	0.833	-0.486	1.389	-2.153
	6	-4.653	-4.028	-5.625	-1.181	1.389	-1.528	0.833	-0.417	0.208	-2.708	0.278	-9.931	-1.597	-0.972	0.139	-1.597	-1.597	-1.528	-0.347	-3.403
	7	-1.181	-0.069	-4.583	-0.556	0.764	1.875	0.208	0.694	0.764	-2.153	-0.278	-10.347	-0.278	0.139	0.139	-1.111	-2.153	-2.153	-0.347	-2.222
	8	-0.556	0.139	-5.625	-1.111	0.208	1.319	0.208	0.694	1.389	-2.778	-0.278	-9.722	-2.222	-2.917	2.569	-2.292	-1.042	-2.153	-0.347	-2.222
	9	-2.222	-1.597	0.278	0.069	1.458	1.875	0.625	1.250	0.833	-1.111	0.903	-7.431	-6.250	-4.653	2.569	-2.292	-1.042	-2.153	-0.347	-4.028
	10	-2.292	-1.736	-3.194	0.069	0.764	1.944	1.806	1.250	1.389	0.764	0.903	-8.542	-1.597	-4.722	0.764	-2.292	-1.597	-2.153	-0.347	-3.472
	11	-4.028	-2.847	-2.778	-8.542	1.944	1.319	1.806	3.056	-0.486	0.764	1.389	-5.625	-1.042	-5.278	1.389	-2.292	-1.042	-2.778	-1.528	-3.472
	12	-1.181	-2.361	-5.694	-0.556	2.500	0.069	1.806	3.681	-0.486	-0.417	2.014	-7.014	-2.847	-4.028	1.389	-1.667	-0.486	-1.042	-1.528	-1.597
M-writers																					
WrapB	1	-2.222	-2.222	-0.069	-3.542	-2.500	-1.944	-2.153	-4.653	-5.556	-0.556	-0.417	-5.764	-1.042	-5.208	-3.056	-2.083	-2.292	-2.847	-2.431	-2.431
	2	-0.972	-0.972	-4.444	-1.736	-0.139	-0.278	1.319	-2.778	-4.306	0.069	0.625	-4.722	-0.903	-4.375	-3.472	0.694	-1.667	-3.403	-1.806	-1.181
	3	-3.472	-3.472	-3.194	-8.056	-2.292	-1.319	0.694	-2.222	-3.542	-0.556	-0.417	-5.833	1.458	-3.125	-2.361	-1.042	-3.958	-2.083	-3.403	-1.181
	4	-2.708	-2.708	-4.514	-2.708	1.111	-1.250	3.125	-1.667	-1.875	-0.972	1.875	-5.000	-0.278	-1.597	-1.111	1.250	0.208	-0.972	-1.111	0.069
	5	1.250	1.250	-4.514	-3.333	1.736	0.625	0.208	0.000	-1.319	0.278	2.431	-0.208	-1.667	0.208	-1.111	2.986	-1.597	0.208	0.069	0.069
	6	-3.264	-3.264	-2.708	0.417	3.958	-0.139	1.250	0.069	0.903	-3.542	3.611	-0.833	1.528	1.250	-2.292	0.694	0.139	3.056	0.625	0.764
	7	-4.306	-4.306	-3.125	-1.875	3.958	2.708	3.472	1.597	0.903	3.125	3.403	-5.278	-0.069	0.069	-0.694	-1.250	1.319	3.542	-1.250	-1.250
	8	0.972	-0.833	-5.417	1.667	-0.208	0.347	-1.806	-0.208	-0.139	-1.250	3.264	-4.514	-0.069	0.000	-0.139	0.347	0.417	3.403	2.292	-3.056
	9	-5.486	-4.306	-4.167	2.361	-0.764	2.153	-2.361	0.417	0.417	-0.486	3.819	-2.153	1.111	0.417	-2.639	-1.319	1.250	1.042	1.597	1.111
	10	-3.056	-3.056	-5.972	2.917	-0.417	0.417	-0.625	0.972	1.667	1.806	2.847	-2.847	-0.139	-3.542	-2.639	2.708	2.292	2.986	-1.250	0.000
	11	-3.681	-6.528	-7.569	-3.611	2.222	0.069	-0.764	1.042	0.972	1.806	4.653	-4.653	-0.694	1.528	-1.806	-0.764	2.292	-0.833	-2.361	1.806
	12	-2.292	-4.167	-11.111	-0.486	0.347	-0.069	0.000	2.708	1.736	0.556	0.347	-5.764	-2.569	1.111	-1.181	-3.542	-0.486	0.486	0.417	1.111
Relief	1	-2.222	-2.222	-0.069	-3.542	-2.500	-1.944	-2.153	-4.653	-5.556	-0.556	-0.417	-5.764	-1.042	-5.208	-3.056	-2.083	-2.292	-2.847	-2.431	-2.431
	2	-0.972	-0.972	-4.444	-1.736	-0.139	-0.278	1.319	-2.778	-4.306	0.069	0.625	-4.722	-0.903	-4.375	-3.472	0.694	-1.667	-3.403	-1.806	-1.181
	3	1.181	1.181	-4.514	-5.694	1.667	-0.903	1.319	-0.625	-4.306	0.139	0.556	-1.806	-5.208	-4.236	-2.361	1.250	-1.667	-5.833	-0.625	-1.181
	4	-0.833	-0.833	-2.500	0.625	1.736	0.417	0.764	0.486	-2.500	0.625	2.778	-4.236	-0.625	-0.833	1.181	-1.806	-3.611	-0.764	-0.556	1.667
	5	0.000	0.000	-5.833	5.486	2.917	-0.764	4.167	-1.736	-0.069	1.319	2.778	-6.250	0.208	0.069	-0.625	-0.417	-1.250	1.875	0.625	1.667
	6	-0.694	-0.694	-4.653	2.569	2.361	2.222	2.500	-2.431	-1.250	1.250	2.708	-11.042	-0.903	-4.306	0.000	-1.111	-0.486	0.625	1.736	2.917
	7	0.139	-0.139	-3.125	-2.917	1.528	3.194	1.528	-2.569	-0.139	-0.694	2.778	-5.833	-9.375	-3.681	-1.389	-1.806	0.069	-0.208	1.667	1.597
	8	-6.736	-6.736	-4.167	-5.208	-0.278	2.222	-0.208	2.222	1.181	-0.069	1.042	1.010	1.875	-2.500	-1.875	-2.986	0.069	-0.764	2.361	-0.069
	9	-4.861	-4.861	-4.514	-1.667	1.458	2.778	-0.069	2.014	0.625	-4.306	2.778	-5.694	2.917	-1.736	-3.056	-0.764	-0.069	-0.833	1.111	0.000
	10	-3.125	-3.819	-2.569	-0.625	1.389	1.528	1.736	0.903	-0.694	0.903	2.014	-5.278	1.042	0.069	-5.417	-0.069	-0.694	-0.833	3.403	-0.694
	11	-6.875	-6.944	-4.306	-4.653	4.444	1.806	1.806	1.528	1.667	0.486	2.639	-9.861	1.528	-2.292	-4.653	1.736	-1.319	-1.389	1.667	-0.069
	12	-2.292	-4.167	-11.111	-0.486	0.347	-0.069	0.000	2.708	1.736	0.556	0.347	-5.764	-2.569	1.111	-1.181	-3.542	-0.486	0.486	0.417	1.111
Average	1	1.250	1.250	1.250	0.139	1.875	1.250	0.000	0.625	1.250	0.000	-0.556	1.250	0.139	0.139	1.250	0.069	0.625	0.000	0.625	1.250
	2	-0.139	-0.625	-0.625	-0.694	0.625	-0.694	0.417	0.556	0.000	1.111	-0.694	-1.736	-0.694	1.042	1.597	-0.625	0.556	0.972	-0.139	1.736
	3	-0.556	-0.556	-1.111	-0.556	-1.736	0.069	0.694	-1.875	-0.625	3.333	2.222	1.181	0.625	1.042	1.667	-0.069	0.625	2.222	4.583	2.917
	4	1.042	0.417	-0.139	-0.694	0.833	1.181	-0.625	2.153	2.778	-0.139	1.042	3.958	2.292	0.347	2.292	1.667	0.556	1.528	2.361	2.847
	5	0.208	1.319	-0.903	0.139	-0.347	-0.833	-0.764	-2.569	-0.625	-1.250	-0.139	0.764	-0.833	0.972	2.083	-1.944	1.736	-0.208	0.417	0.972
	6	-0.417	0.208	0.833	-2.569	-1.597	-0.278	-3.125	-4.236	-0.625	-0.694	1.111	2.083	0.417	0.972	0.972	1.458	2.292	0.486	0.347	1.667
	7	-0.833	-0.833	4.514	0.278	2.014	-2.500	2.153	0.347	2.778	-0.139	-1.181	2.014	-0.208	1.944	-1.875	2.639	0.278	2.847	-0.208	2.847
	8	0.417	0.417	-3.819	-0.347	0.903	1.597	3.958	2.014	1.806	0.486	3.403	-1.806	0.208	-1.389	-2.083	1.042	-1.597	2.361	-2.083	0.903
	9	-1.250	-1.250	-4.306	1.181	5.069	3.958	-1.319	0.278	0.486	0.625	2.778	-5.903	0.833	-1.042	-3.264	-2.153	-0.069	4.236	-0.833	-0.139
	10	-3.056	-3.056	-5.972	2.917	-0.417	0.417	-0.625	0.972	1.667	1.806	2.847	-2.847	-0.139	-3.542	-2.639	2.708	2.292	2.986	-1.250	0.000
	11	-3.681	-6.528	-7.569	-3.611	2.222	0.069	-0.764	1.042	0.972	1.806	4.653	-4.653	-0.694	1.528	-1.806	-0.764	2.292	-0.833	-2.361	1.806
	12	-2.292	-4.167	-11.111	-0.486	0.347	-0.069	0.000	2.708	1.736	0.556	0.347	-5.764	-2.569	1.111	-1.181	-3.542	-0.486	0.486	0.417	1.111

datasets, the highest minimum was found in the average-based order, but it was not accompanied by the advantageous maximum or average accuracy. However, for M-writers the best maximum was found for this order and duf4 approach.

The experimental results confirmed the merits of the illustrated methodology for controlled sequential discretisation of the input space. The high number of

Table 3. Statistics of performance of rule classifiers observed in sequential discretisation of attributes following *Order*. Met_D details supervised (dsF for Fayyad and Irani, dsK for Kononenko) or unsupervised discretisation approach (duf for equal frequency or duw for equal width binning), *Stat* specifies statistic measures (*min, max* or *avg* classification accuracy, or standard deviation *std*)

	Order	Met_D	Stat		Met_D	Stat	Number of bins constructed for attributes								
							2	3	4	5	6	7	8	9	10
F-writers	WrapB	dsF	min	83.40	duf	min	79.93	89.24	90.97	89.72	**91.74**	90.49	91.04	91.60	86.94
			max	92.22		max	91.18	94.10	94.58	95.07	**95.83**	95.76	93.33	94.65	94.10
			avg	89.47		avg	87.09	91.07	92.67	93.21	**93.87**	91.92	92.29	93.60	90.25
			std	2.85		std	3.24	1.55	1.19	1.49	1.18	1.51	**0.91**	1.05	1.85
		dsK	min	87.50	duw	min	85.07	83.40	88.06	85.83	88.68	89.38	89.93	**90.56**	89.24
			max	92.22		min	92.85	89.44	92.22	93.47	93.47	93.61	93.47	**94.10**	92.36
			avg	90.07		avg	86.82	87.77	91.11	89.71	90.28	91.50	91.81	**92.92**	91.22
			std	1.61		std	2.01	1.73	1.12	2.50	1.26	1.41	1.07	1.24	**0.83**
	Relief	dsF	min	83.89	duf	min	79.93	90.90	90.56	89.72	90.07	88.06	**91.04**	89.44	90.07
			max	92.22		max	89.79	94.10	94.58	**95.76**	94.03	**95.76**	94.03	94.65	94.10
			avg	87.47		avg	86.06	91.92	92.42	**93.45**	93.07	92.98	92.52	91.98	92.49
			std	3.09		std	2.69	**0.97**	1.29	1.59	1.04	2.00	0.98	1.58	1.26
		dsK	min	84.58	duw	min	79.72	87.08	88.06	85.83	88.13	**90.49**	89.44	**90.49**	89.24
			max	92.71		max	90.42	91.67	93.54	93.47	92.22	93.54	93.47	**94.10**	92.64
			avg	89.05		avg	85.71	89.60	90.52	90.78	90.52	**91.78**	91.63	91.55	91.22
			std	2.20		std	2.71	1.65	1.54	2.07	1.44	**0.82**	1.29	0.98	1.12
	Average	dsF	min	85.76	duf	min	86.39	88.13	**92.29**	90.56	**92.29**	91.18	90.63	89.31	89.38
			max	95.14		max	94.10	92.15	94.58	94.03	95.14	**95.76**	93.47	93.40	94.10
			avg	89.48		avg	89.12	90.65	93.15	93.00	**93.73**	93.15	92.43	91.41	91.75
			std	2.57		std	2.77	1.45	**0.70**	1.00	1.02	1.29	0.90	1.45	1.64
		dsK	min	88.06	duw	min	81.74	85.83	86.81	89.38	89.79	89.93	89.31	**90.56**	88.06
			max	95.21		max	94.65	94.51	93.54	94.65	94.65	94.58	**95.83**	95.28	91.81
			avg	90.48		avg	86.87	90.71	90.36	92.36	91.29	92.07	91.75	**92.62**	89.61
			std	2.03		std	4.33	2.08	2.47	1.69	1.88	1.66	2.33	1.65	**1.02**
M-writers	WrapB	dsF	min	73.82	duf	min	68.19	71.25	76.81	77.36	76.94	74.65	73.75	75.76	**78.89**
			max	80.56		max	79.24	82.22	83.26	82.01	82.78	82.01	81.04	82.43	**83.96**
			avg	76.87		avg	74.57	77.81	79.89	79.42	79.50	78.91	78.46	79.33	**81.48**
			std	2.00		std	2.73	3.10	2.11	**1.34**	1.90	2.07	2.47	1.72	1.74
		dsK	min	72.78	duw	min	73.47	**76.74**	74.10	75.83	75.76	75.35	75.90	75.90	76.25
			max	80.56		max	79.10	80.83	80.83	79.17	82.29	81.60	**82.85**	81.60	81.11
			avg	76.42		avg	75.34	79.03	78.20	77.43	79.20	79.13	**79.69**	78.59	78.96
			std	2.02		std	1.97	1.23	2.37	**1.03**	1.92	1.91	**79.96**	78.59	78.96
	Relief	dsF	min	72.43	duf	min	68.19	73.61	76.81	77.36	77.15	74.65	73.75	75.00	**78.89**
			max	80.49		max	79.24	**84.79**	83.75	82.50	83.47	82.01	81.04	80.63	82.08
			avg	77.01		avg	74.99	77.82	80.55	80.16	80.36	78.89	78.17	79.28	**81.02**
			std	2.64		std	2.60	3.29	1.76	1.66	1.58	2.39	2.49	1.49	**1.20**
		dsK	min	72.36	duw	min	68.26	69.93	74.10	73.89	75.76	75.69	73.47	**76.88**	**76.88**
			max	80.49		max	77.50	82.22	80.42	80.49	81.04	79.38	81.18	**82.71**	82.22
			avg	76.79		avg	73.05	77.91	76.98	77.15	78.40	78.19	78.15	**79.94**	79.58
			std	2.72		std	2.53	3.26	2.08	1.91	1.64	**1.09**	2.05	1.65	1.54
	Average	dsF	min	75.63	duf	min	68.19	75.69	77.57	76.81	76.18	75.07	**78.68**	78.06	78.13
			max	80.56		max	83.82	82.22	**84.38**	83.26	83.26	82.01	82.08	82.64	83.96
			avg	78.53		avg	76.89	78.95	80.12	79.65	79.31	79.47	80.27	79.93	**80.63**
			std	1.55		std	4.31	1.64	1.86	1.58	1.77	2.06	**1.25**	**1.25**	1.85
		dsK	min	72.78	duw	min	73.40	76.74	75.76	76.04	75.76	77.71	78.47	76.94	**79.17**
			max	80.63		max	83.26	81.60	81.25	81.60	82.01	81.60	83.54	**83.89**	82.22
			avg	78.19		avg	78.35	79.25	79.57	79.06	79.35	80.06	80.73	79.46	**80.80**
			std	2.35		std	3.31	1.16	1.55	2.06	1.96	1.21	1.53	1.89	**1.03**

conditions leading to improved performance of inducers provides motivation for a deeper study of attribute representation even if the knowledge mining algorithm is capable of operating in continuous space. The MODLEM algorithm is undeniably effective, yet, it can gain from transformations of the input domain.

5   Conclusions

The paper presents investigations into the effectiveness of classifiers based on decision rules induced by the MODLEM algorithm. This algorithm is specific in its operation mode, as it can work directly on discrete and continuous attributes. When conditions for rules are defined, the datapoints are evaluated in a way that reminds of discretisation, but without obtaining categorical forms for descriptors.

To study the sensitivity of the rule induction procedures to the type of attributes, the sequential discretisation methodology was applied. The processing direction was controlled by the orderings of attributes. Experiments were carried out on the datasets prepared for the stylometric task of authorship attribution.

An analysis of the results led to the observations that partial discretisation of the input space can provide such conditions for the induction process, which prove to return sets of rules more effective in labelling of unknown samples. Contrary to widely held opinions, supervised transformations turned out to be less advantageous than unsupervised algorithms. In the vast majority of discretisation paths explored, some cases of improved predictions were detected. This validated the illustrated methodology, which can be useful in cases where an effective, and at the same time transparent, path of decision making is needed.

Future works will be dedicated to comparison of performance of MODLEM-based classifiers constructed under various conditions against the operation of inducers relying on rule sets inferred by other algorithms. In addition, a comparative study will be carried out for the methodology in which rules are induced from continuous data and then the conditions are discretised.

Acknowledgments. The research presented was performed in the statutory project of the Department of Computer Graphics, Vision and Digital Systems (RAU-6, 2026).

Disclosure of Interests. The authors have no competing interests to declare that are relevant to the content of this article.

References

1. Dash, R., Paramguru, R.L., Dash, R.: Comparative analysis of supervised and unsupervised discretization techniques. Int. J. Adv. Sci. Technol. **2**(3), 29–37 (2011)
2. Fayyad, U.M., Irani, K.B.: Multi-interval discretization of continuous valued attributes for classification learning. In: 13th International Joint Conference on Artificial Intelligence, vol. 2, pp. 1022–1027. Morgan Kaufmann Publishers (1993)
3. Grzymała-Busse, J., Stefanowski, J.: Three discretization methods for rule induction. Int. J. Intell. Syst. **16**, 29–38 (2001)

4. Hall, M., et al.: The WEKA data mining software: an update. SIGKDD Explor. **11**(1), 10–18 (2009)
5. He, X., et al.: Authorship attribution methods, challenges, and future research directions: a comprehensive survey. Information **15**(3) (2024)
6. Kononenko, I.: Estimating attributes: analysis and extensions of RELIEF. In: Bergadano, F., De Raedt, L. (eds.) ECML 1994. LNCS, vol. 784, pp. 171–182. Springer, Heidelberg (1994). https://doi.org/10.1007/3-540-57868-4_57
7. Kononenko, I.: On biases in estimating multi-valued attributes. In: 14th International Joint Conference on Artificial Intelligence, pp. 1034–1040 (1995)
8. Stańczyk, U., Zielosko, B.: Data irregularities in discretisation of test sets used for evaluation of classification systems: a case study on authorship attribution. Bull. Polish Acad. Sci. Tech. Sci. **69**(4), 1–12 (2021)
9. Stańczyk, U., Zielosko, B., Baron, G.: Discretisation of conditions in decision rules induced for continuous data. PLoS ONE **15**(4), 1–33 (2020)
10. Stefanowski, J.: On combined classifiers, rule induction and rough sets. In: Peters, J.F., Skowron, A., Düntsch, I., Grzymała-Busse, J., Orłowska, E., Polkowski, L. (eds.) Transactions on Rough Sets VI. LNCS, vol. 4374, pp. 329–350. Springer, Heidelberg (2007). https://doi.org/10.1007/978-3-540-71200-8_18
11. Więckowski, J., Sałabun, W.: Sensitivity analysis approaches in multi-criteria decision analysis: a systematic review. Appl. Soft Comput. **148**, 110915 (2023)
12. Wu, H., Zhang, Z., Wu, Q.: Exploring syntactic and semantic features for authorship attribution. Appl. Soft Comput. **111**, 107815 (2021)

Optimization of Inhibitory Rules

Azimkhon Ostonov[1], Beata Zielosko[1,2](✉), Kamil Jabloński[2],
Kamil Magiera[2], and Mikhail Moshkov[1]

[1] Computer, Electrical and Mathematical Sciences and Engineering Division, King
Abdullah University of Science and Technology (KAUST), Thuwal 23955-6900,
Saudi Arabia
{azimkhon.ostonov,mikhail.moshkov}@kaust.edu.sa
[2] Institute of Computer Science, University of Silesia in Katowice, Bedzinska 39,
41-200 Sosnowiec, Poland
{beata.zielosko,kamil.jablonski}@us.edu.pl, kamllos@interia.pl

Abstract. Representing knowledge in the form of rules is one of
the most popular methods due to its intuitiveness and transparency.
Shorter rules are easier to understand and interpret. There are various
types of rules, e.g., decision rules, action rules, probabilistic rules, non-
deterministic rules, and many others. These rules differ in their approach
to decision-making and the method of their induction.

This paper focuses on the exploration of inhibitory rules, which are
defined by the expression "attribute $\neq$ decision" on the right-hand side.
In certain cases, such rules can convey more information about datasets
than conventional decision rules. It is known that the problem of constructing inhibitory rules with minimum length is NP-hard. Therefore,
various approaches are used to obtain approximate rules. In this work,
three novel algorithms for inducing inhibitory rules and systems of such
rules are studied. In particular, it was shown that, under the assumption $P \neq NP$, the m-greedy algorithm achieves an approximation ratio
that is close to the best possible achievable by any polynomial-time algorithm. Taking into account the perspective of knowledge representation,
we analyze experimentally the effectiveness of the proposed algorithms,
particularly regarding the minimization of rule length.

Keywords: Inhibitory Rules · Greedy Algorithms · Length ·
Minimization · Knowledge Representation

1 Introduction

One of the commonly used methods of knowledge representation is rule-based
representation. Knowledge is most often presented in the form of decision rules
"if <conditions> then <conclusion>", where the conditional part specifies the
premises, while the decision part contains the conclusion or action to be taken
once these premises are met [19, 21, 23]. This method of knowledge representation
allows for a transparent mapping of expert knowledge, as it not only enables

M. Paszynski et al. (Eds.): ICCS 2026 Workshops, LNCS 16788, pp. 289–303, 2026.
https://doi.org/10.1007/978-3-032-29915-4_25

decisions to be made, but also justifies them in a way that is understandable to the user.

Rule induction can be carried out from different perspectives, for example, classification and knowledge representation [15,21,24,26]. In the first case, the goal is to assign a class label to an unknown object based on its characteristics and using a set of induced rules. In the case of knowledge representation, rules are used to discover and represent hidden patterns in the data. From this perspective, rules that cover a wider range of examples while remaining simple and understandable are particularly valuable. The length of rules is therefore important, also from the point of view of the Minimal Description Length principle [20]: "that the best hypothesis for a given set of data is the one that leads to the largest compression of the data".

Unlike standard decision rules, which use the format "attribute = decision" on the right-hand side, inhibitory rules are expressed as "attribute $\neq$ decision", or more simply, "$\neq$ decision".

Interest in inhibitory rules was sparked when Skowron and Suraj [22] (see also [25]) demonstrated a data set example where inhibitory rules could capture more information than decision rules. Later work confirmed that, for any given data set, inhibitory rules can express a form of complete information—refer to [16] for further details.

Subsequent research addressed algorithmic methods for generating inhibitory rules, analyzing their minimal complexity, constructing sets of all minimal inhibitory rules, and developing both standard and lazy classifiers based on such rules [8,9,16,18]. These classifiers showed superior performance over those based on decision rules, with findings consolidated in [10]. The next research phase focused on enhancements to dynamic programming algorithms, incorporating multi-stage and bi-criteria optimization approaches targeting different parameters of inhibitory rules (such as length and coverage), as well as their systems (considering cost and uncertainty aspects) [2–6]. These findings were summarized in [1].

Additionally, our earlier work on discovering decision rules consistent with as many given decision trees as possible [27] revealed that this method could be extended to inhibitory rules—a topic reserved for future investigation into generalized knowledge extraction from distributed sources.

A renewed motivation to continue this line of study emerged from the development of novel approximation algorithms for the set cover problem [7], which we found applicable to inhibitory rule construction. This is one of the central topics of this paper. Since the problem of constructing inhibitory rules with minimum length is NP-hard [10], three greedy algorithms for inducing inhibitory rules and systems of such rules are proposed and compared in terms of length of constructed rules. In particular, we show that, assuming $P \neq NP$, the m-greedy algorithm achieves an approximation ratio close to the best possible for any polynomial-time algorithm.

This paper is organized into six sections. Section 2 introduces foundational concepts. Consider a decision table T and a row r labeled with decision d. Let

$D(T)$ represent all decisions in T, and define $D(T,r) = D(T) \setminus \{d\}$. For any $t \in D(T,r)$, an inhibitory rule for T, r, and t is a rule that holds true in T, is realizable for r (i.e., its left-hand side holds for r), and has $\neq t$ as its right-hand side.

A finite set of inhibitory rules S is said to be *complete* for T if every rule in S is valid for T, and for each row r and some $t \in D(T,r)$, S includes an inhibitory rule for T, r, and t. The set S is *full* for T if, for every row r and every $t \in D(T,r)$, such a rule exists in S. The *depth* of a system S is defined as the length of its longest rule.

Our objective is to minimize the depth of complete and full systems of inhibitory rules, as shorter rules are generally more efficient to compute and interpret.

Section 3 discusses three approximation algorithms addressing the set cover problem. The task is to find a minimal subset family that covers a given finite set. The *extended greedy algorithm* introduces an expanded search strategy by examining not just one but several subcovers at each step, which can lead to cover reduction. The *modified greedy algorithm* builds on the classic greedy approach by including a refinement phase to eliminate unnecessary subsets from the cover. We present two results assessing its performance. The third, the *"easy" algorithm*, iteratively removes as many subsets as possible from the original set family while preserving coverage.

In Sect. 4, we present algorithms for generating complete and full inhibitory rule systems, utilizing the approximation methods for the set cover problem. A polynomial-time reduction is provided, transforming the inhibitory rule length minimization problem into a set cover problem. The extended greedy, modified greedy, and "easy" algorithms are applied to the transformed instances, and the resulting covers are converted into inhibitory rules. By aggregating these rules, we obtain six algorithms for constructing complete or full inhibitory rule systems. For the version using the modified-greedy algorithm for full systems, we include two statements characterizing its quality.

Section 5 reports on computational experiments with the algorithms from Sect. 4. These tests evaluate the effectiveness of the algorithms in approximating the minimal depth of complete inhibitory rule systems. Statistical analysis of the obtained results is also provided.

Section 6 concludes the paper with a brief summary.

The core contribution of this work lies in the introduction of new algorithms for constructing complete and full inhibitory rule systems (Sect. 4), and theoretical results showing that, under the assumption $P \neq NP$, the m-greedy algorithm achieves an approximation ratio that is close to the best polynomial-time algorithm. The proposed algorithms were compared experimentally, taking into account knowledge representation perspective.

2   Basic Concepts

Let ω denote the set of nonnegative integers $\{0, 1, 2, \ldots\}$, and define $A = \{a_i : i \in \omega\}$ as the set of attributes. Two attributes a_i and a_j are considered distinct if $i \neq j$.

A *decision table* T is a rectangular array with entries from the set ω. The columns of T are labeled by distinct attributes from A, and the rows are pairwise distinct, each assigned a decision from ω. We write $D(T)$ for the set of decisions assigned to the rows of T. A decision table may have no rows or columns. A table T is called *nondegenerate* if $|D(T)| \geq 2$, and *degenerate* otherwise. For a nondegenerate table T and a row r with decision d, we define $D(T, r) = D(T) \setminus \{d\}$.

Suppose T is a nondegenerate decision table with columns labeled by the attributes $a_{i_1}, \ldots, a_{i_n}$. An *inhibitory rule over* T is an expression of the form

$$(a_{j_1} = b_1) \wedge \cdots \wedge (a_{j_m} = b_m) \rightarrow \neq t, \tag{1}$$

where $a_{j_1}, \ldots, a_{j_m}$ are pairwise distinct attributes selected from $\{a_{i_1}, \ldots, a_{i_n}\}$, $b_1, \ldots, b_m \in \omega$, and $t \in D(T)$. The integer m is called the *length* of rule (1). This rule is said to be *realizable* for a row $r = (\delta_1, \ldots, \delta_n)$ of T if $\delta_{j_1} = b_1, \ldots, \delta_{j_m} = b_m$. Rule (1) is said to be *true* for T if, for every row r of T for which it is realizable, the decision of r is different from t. The *coverage* of the true for T rule (1) is the percentage of rows of T for which this rule is realizable.

Two inhibitory rules are called *equal* if they have the same sets of conditions on their left-hand sides and equal right-hand sides.

Given a row r of T and a decision $t \in D(T, r)$, rule (1) is called an *inhibitory rule for* T, r, *and* t if it is true for T and realizable for r. Let $l(T, r, t)$ denote the minimum length of an inhibitory rule for T, r, and t.

A *complete system of inhibitory rules for* T is a finite set S of inhibitory rules over T such that each rule in S is true for T, and for each row r of T, there exists at least one rule in S that is realizable for r; that is, for every row r and some $t \in D(T, r)$, S contains an inhibitory rule for T, r, and t.

A *full system of inhibitory rules for* T is a finite set S of inhibitory rules over T such that each rule in S is true for T, and for each row r of T and each $t \in D(T, r)$, S contains a rule that is realizable for r and has $\neq t$ on the right-hand side; that is, for every row r and each $t \in D(T, r)$, S contains an inhibitory rule for T, r, and t.

Let ρ be an inhibitory rule and S a system of inhibitory rules. The length of ρ is denoted by $l(\rho)$. The *depth* of S—the maximum rule length in S—is denoted by $L(S)$. For a nondegenerate decision table T, define $L_i^c(T)$ as the minimum depth of a complete inhibitory rule system for T, and $L_i^f(T)$ as the minimum depth of a full inhibitory rule system for T. Let $Row(T)$ denote the set of rows in T, and for any row r, define $l(T, r) = \min\{l(T, r, t) : t \in D(T, r)\}$. Then $L_i^c(T) = \max\{l(T, r) : r \in Row(T)\}$ and $L_i^f(T) = \max\{l(T, r, t) : r \in Row(T), t \in D(T, r)\}$. For a degenerate table T, we define $L_i^c(T) = L_i^f(T) = 0$. Clearly, for any decision table T, the inequality $L_i^c(T) \leq L_i^f(T)$ holds.

3   Approximate Algorithms for the Set Cover Problem

In this section, we consider three approximate algorithms for the set cover problem. Let $P = \{p_1, \ldots, p_n\}$ be a finite set with $n > 0$ elements, and let $F = \{S_1, \ldots, S_m\}$ be a family of subsets of P such that $P = \bigcup_{i=1}^{m} S_i$. A subfamily $\{S_{i_1}, \ldots, S_{i_t}\} \subseteq F$ is called a *cover* if $\bigcup_{j=1}^{t} S_{i_j} = P$. The problem of finding a cover of minimum cardinality t is known as the set cover problem, denoted by (P, F). We say that a subset $S_i \in F$ *covers* all elements of P contained in S_i.

3.1   Extended Greedy Algorithm

The *extended greedy algorithm* (or *e-greedy algorithm*) proceeds in three phases. Below we describe its operation on the set cover problem (P, F).

Phase 1

- *Step 1:* Remove duplicate subsets from F, keeping only one copy of each. For any pair $S_i, S_j \in F$ such that $S_i \subset S_j$, remove S_i from F. Denote the resulting family by F_0.
- *Step 2:* Initialize $B_0 := \emptyset$. For each $S_i \in F_0$, if there exists an element of P covered *only* by S_i in F_0, add S_i to B_0, remove S_i from F_0, and remove from P and from all sets in F_0 the elements covered by S_i. This yields a reduced set cover problem (P', F').
  If $P' = \emptyset$, return B_0 as a cover for (P, F) and terminate. Otherwise, proceed to Phase 2.
  For $S_i \in F$, denote by S_i' the subset obtained from S_i by removing elements already covered by subsets in B_0.

Phase 2

- *Step 1:* Initialize $\mathcal{C} - \{\emptyset\}$ (holding partial covers) and $\mathcal{D} = \emptyset$ (holding full covers) for (P', F').
- *Step 2:* Suppose we have taken $i \geq 1$ steps. Then:
  - If $\mathcal{C} = \emptyset$ or $|\mathcal{D}| \geq 16$, move to Phase 3.
  - If $|\mathcal{C}| \geq 128$, sort all subcovers in $\mathcal{C}$ by the number of elements of P' covered (descending) and keep only the top 16.
  - For each $B \in \mathcal{C}$:
    - If B is a cover of (P', F'), move B from $\mathcal{C}$ to $\mathcal{D}$.
    - Otherwise, let P'' be the set of elements of P' not covered by B. Let $S_{i_1}', \ldots, S_{i_k}'$ be all subsets in F' that cover at least one element of P''. Order these by the size of their intersection with P'' in descending order as $S_{j_1}', \ldots, S_{j_k}'$.
      Remove B from $\mathcal{C}$ and add the three subcovers:

$$B \cup \{S_{j_1}'\}, \quad B \cup \{S_{j_{\lceil k/2 \rceil}}'\}, \quad B \cup \{S_{j_k}'\}$$

  - Increment i and repeat Step 2.

Phase 3

- *Step 1:* For each cover $B = \{S'_{l_1}, \ldots, S'_{l_t}\} \in \mathcal{D}$, try to reduce it to a smaller cover B' as follows:
  Set $j := 1$.
  While $j \leq t$, do:

  $$\text{If } B \setminus \{S'_{l_j}\} \text{ is a cover of } (P', F'), \text{ then } B := B \setminus \{S'_{l_j}\}.$$

  Otherwise, leave B unchanged.
  Increment $j := j + 1$. Return B as B' once all elements are checked.
- *Step 2:* Choose $B \in \mathcal{D}$ such that the reduced cover B' has minimum cardinality. Return

$$B_0 \cup \{S_{q_1}, \ldots, S_{q_v}\}$$

as the cover for the original problem (P, F), where $B' = \{S'_{q_1}, \ldots, S'_{q_v}\}$.

Remark 1. The extended greedy algorithm returns a cover for (P, F). However, there are no guaranteed approximation bounds for its performance.

3.2   Modified Greedy Algorithm

The *modified greedy algorithm* (or *m-greedy algorithm*) consists of two phases. It operates as follows for the set cover problem (P, F).

Phase 1

- *Step 1:* Initialize $B := \emptyset$ and $U := P$.
- *Step 2:* While B is not a cover of (P, F):
  - Choose $S_j \in F$ such that $|S_j \cap U|$ is maximal.
  - Update $B := B \cup \{S_j\}$ and $U := U \setminus S_j$.
  Once B covers P, proceed to Phase 2.

Phase 2

- Let $B = \{S_{i_1}, \ldots, S_{i_t}\}$. Set $j := 1$.
- While $j \leq t$:
  - If $B \setminus \{S_{i_j}\}$ is still a cover of (P, F), then remove S_{i_j} from B.
  - Increment $j := j + 1$.
- Return B as a cover for (P, F).

Remark 2. The modified greedy algorithm returns a cover for (P, F).

The next statement follows from Theorem 4.1 of [17], which studied the classical greedy algorithm that does not include Phase 2. Clearly, the size of the cover constructed by the m-greedy algorithm does not exceed the size of the cover constructed by the classical greedy algorithm.

Proposition 1. *Let (P, F) be a set cover problem. Then*

$$C_{m\text{-}greedy}(P, F) \leq C_{\min}(P, F) \cdot \ln |P| + 1,$$

where $C_{m\text{-}greedy}(P, F)$ is the cardinality of the cover returned by the modified greedy algorithm, and $C_{\min}(P, F)$ is the cardinality of an optimal cover.

The following result shows that, under the widely believed assumption $P \neq NP$, the m-greedy algorithm achieves an approximation ratio that is close to the best possible achievable by any polynomial-time algorithm.

Proposition 2. *[11] If $P \neq NP$, then for any ε with $0 < \varepsilon < 1$, there is no polynomial-time algorithm that, for every set cover problem (P, F), constructs a cover whose cardinality is at most*

$$(1 - \varepsilon) \cdot C_{\min}(P, F) \cdot \ln |P|.$$

3.3 "Easy" Algorithm

We now describe the *"easy" algorithm* for the set cover problem (P, F), where $F = \{S_1, \ldots, S_m\}$.

Step 1. Set $B := \{S_1, \ldots, S_m\}$ and $j := 1$. Proceed to Step 2.

Step 2. If $j > m$, return B as a cover for (P, F).
  Otherwise, if $B \setminus \{S_j\}$ is still a cover for (P, F), then update $B := B \setminus \{S_j\}$ and increment $j := j + 1$. Return to Step 2.
  If $B \setminus \{S_j\}$ is not a cover, then keep B unchanged, increment $j := j + 1$, and return to Step 2.

Remark 3. This algorithm returns a cover for (P, F). However, there are no known approximation guarantees for its performance.

4   Algorithms for Constructing Systems of Inhibitory Rules

This section describes algorithms for constructing complete and full systems of inhibitory rules based on approximate algorithms for solving the set cover problem.
  Let T be a decision table with n columns labeled by attributes $a_1, \ldots, a_n$. Let $r = (\delta_1, \ldots, \delta_n)$ be a row of T and $t \in D(T, r)$. We consider the set cover problem $(P(T, r, t), F(T, r, t))$, where $P(T, r, t) = \{$all rows of T with decision $t\}$, and

$$F(T, r, t) = \{S_1, \ldots, S_n\}.$$

For each $i = 1, \ldots, n$, the set S_i consists of all rows from $P(T, r, t)$ which differ from the row r in the attribute a_i.

One can show that the rule $(a_{i_1} = \delta_{i_1}) \wedge \cdots \wedge (a_{i_p} = \delta_{i_p}) \to\neq t$, where $i_1, \ldots, i_p \in \{1, \ldots, n\}$, is a rule for T, r, and t if and only if the subfamily $\{S_{i_1}, \ldots, S_{i_p}\}$ is a cover for the set cover problem $(P(T, r, t), F(T, r, t))$.

To approximately solve the problem of length minimization for inhibitory rules, the following approach is used: for a given nondegenerate decision table T, a row r, and a decision $t \in D(T, r)$, we construct the set cover problem $(P(T, r, t), F(T, r, t))$, apply one of the approximate cover construction algorithms, and transform the obtained cover into an inhibitory rule for T, r, and t.

Let al be an approximate algorithm for the set cover problem, where $al \in \{e\text{-}greedy, m\text{-}greedy, easy\}$. We now describe an algorithm $\mathcal{A}_{al}^c$ that, for a given nondegenerate decision table T, constructs a complete system of inhibitory rules for T, denoted by $\mathcal{A}_{al}^c(T)$.

For each row r of T and each decision $t \in D(T, r)$, we construct an inhibitory rule for T, r and t denoted $rule(T, r, t)$ using algorithm al. Then, for each row r, among the rules $\{rule(T, r, t) : t \in D(T, r)\}$, we select a rule of minimum length and denote it by $rule(T, r)$. Denoting by $Row(T)$ the set of rows of T, we define $\mathcal{A}_{al}^c(T) = \{rule(T, r) : r \in Row(T)\}$. For different rows r_1 and r_2 of the table T, rules $rule(T, r_1)$ and $rule(T, r_2)$ may be equal. We will store these two equal rules in the set under consideration.

Similarly, we describe an algorithm $\mathcal{A}_{al}^f$ that constructs a full system of inhibitory rules for T, denoted by $\mathcal{A}_{al}^f(T)$. For each row r of T and each decision $t \in D(T, r)$, we construct the inhibitory rule $rule(T, r, t)$ using algorithm al. Then, $\mathcal{A}_{al}^f(T) = \{rule(T, r, t) : r \in Row(T), t \in D(T, r)\}$. For different rows r_1 and r_2 of the table T and decisions $t_1 \in D(T, r_1)$ and $t_2 \in D(T, r_2)$, rules $rule(T, r_1, t_1)$ and $rule(T, r_2, t_2)$ may be equal. We will store these two equal rules in the set under consideration.

We now obtain a bound on the accuracy of the algorithm $\mathcal{A}_{m\text{-}greedy}^f$. Let T be a nondegenerate decision table. For any $t \in D(T)$, let $N_t(T)$ denote the number of rows of T labeled with decision t, and define $K(T) = \max_{t \in D(T)} N_t(T)$. Recall that $L_i^f(T)$ denotes the minimum depth of a full system of inhibitory rules for T.

Theorem 1. *Let T be a nondegenerate decision table. Then*

$$L(\mathcal{A}_{m\text{-}greedy}^f(T)) \leq L_i^f(T) \ln K(T) + 1.$$

Proof. The algorithm $\mathcal{A}_{m\text{-}greedy}^f$ operates on T as follows: for any row r of T and decision $t \in D(T, r)$, it constructs the set cover problem $(P(T, r, t), F(T, r, t))$, applies the m-greedy algorithm to construct a cover, and transforms the obtained cover into an inhibitory rule $rule(T, r, t)$ for T, r, and t. Then, $\mathcal{A}_{m\text{-}greedy}^f(T) = \{rule(T, r, t) : r \in Row(T), t \in D(T, r)\}$.

By Proposition 1, the length of $rule(T, r, t)$ is at most $l(T, r, t) \ln N_t(T) + 1$. Since $l(T, r, t) \leq L_i^f(T)$ and $N_t(T) \leq K(T)$, it follows that $L(\mathcal{A}_{m\text{-}greedy}^f(T)) \leq L_i^f(T) \ln K(T) + 1$. $\square$

The following theorem shows that, under the assumption $P \neq NP$, the algorithm $\mathcal{A}_{m\text{-}greedy}^f$ is close to the best achievable polynomial-time approximation algorithm for the problem of depth minimization for full systems of inhibitory rules.

Theorem 2. *If $P \neq NP$, then for any ε, $0 < \varepsilon < 1$, there is no polynomial-time algorithm that, for each nondegenerate decision table T, constructs a full system of inhibitory rules with depth at most*

$$(1 - \varepsilon)L_i^f(T)\ln K(T).$$

Proof. Let (P, F) be a set cover problem with

$$P = \{p_1, \ldots, p_n\} \quad \text{and} \quad F = \{S_1, \ldots, S_m\}.$$

Consider the decision table $T(P, F)$ defined as follows. The table $T(P, F)$ has m columns labeled by attributes $a_1, \ldots, a_m$ corresponding to the sets $S_1, \ldots, S_m$, respectively, and $n + 1$ rows. For $j = 1, \ldots, n$, the jth row corresponds to the element p_j, and the $(n + 1)$th row is a special additional row filled with zeros. The entries of the table are defined so that for $j = 1, \ldots, n$ and $i = 1, \ldots, m$, the cell in the jth row and ith column is 1 if and only if $p_j \in S_i$; otherwise, it is 0. The decision attached to the last $(n + 1)$th row is 2, and all other rows are labeled with decision 1.

We first show that $L_i^f(T(P, F)) = C_{\min}(P, F)$. For $j = 1, \ldots, n + 1$, denote by r_j the j-th row of the table $T(P, F)$. It is clear that $D(T(P, F)) = \{1, 2\}$. One can prove that $L_i^f(T(P, F)) = \max\{l(T(P, F), r_{n+1}, 1), \; l(T(P, F), r_j, 2) : j = 1, \ldots, n\}$. It is easy to see that $l(T(P, F), r_j, 2) = 1$ for all $j = 1, \ldots, n$.

Furthermore, a subfamily $\{S_{i_1}, \ldots, S_{i_t}\} \subseteq F$ is a cover for (P, F) if and only if the rule $(a_{i_1} = 0) \wedge \cdots \wedge (a_{i_t} = 0) \to\neq 1$ is an inhibitory rule for $T(P, F)$, r_{n+1}, and decision 1. Therefore, $l(T(P, F), r_{n+1}, 1) = C_{\min}(P, F)$, and hence $L_i^f(T(P, F)) = C_{\min}(P, F)$.

Now, assume for contradiction that $P \neq NP$ but there exists some ε, $0 < \varepsilon < 1$, and a polynomial-time algorithm that, for every nondegenerate decision table T, constructs a full system of inhibitory rules whose depth is at most $(1 - \varepsilon)L_i^f(T)\ln K(T)$.

Apply this algorithm to the table $T(P, F)$. We obtain a full system of inhibitory rules S for $T(P, F)$ such that $L(S) \leq (1 - \varepsilon)L_i^f(T(P, F))\ln K(T(P, F))$.

This system contains an inhibitory rule for $T(P, F)$, r_{n+1}, and decision 1 of the form $(a_{i_1} = 0) \wedge \cdots \wedge (a_{i_t} = 0) \to\neq 1$.

As previously mentioned, $\{S_{i_1}, \ldots, S_{i_t}\}$ is a cover for (P, F) whose cardinality is at most $L(S)$.

Note that $K(T(P, F)) = |P|$, and from above, $L_i^f(T(P, F)) = C_{\min}(P, F)$.

Therefore, for an arbitrary set cover problem (P, F), we can construct in polynomial time a cover of cardinality at most

$$(1 - \varepsilon)C_{\min}(P, F)\ln |P|.$$

But this contradicts Proposition 2, which states that such an approximation is impossible if $P \neq NP$. Hence, no such polynomial-time algorithm exists. $\quad\square$

5 Experimental Study of Algorithms for Constructing Complete Systems of Inhibitory Rules

This section presents results of computational experiments conducted to evaluate the accuracy of the algorithms described in Sect. 4 for constructing complete inhibitory rule systems. The main goal is to assess how well these algorithms approximate the minimum depth of complete inhibitory rule systems.

For selected decision tables T from the UCI Machine Learning Repository [14], we construct complete inhibitory rule systems $\mathcal{A}^c_{e\text{-}greedy}(T)$, $\mathcal{A}^c_{m\text{-}greedy}(T)$, and $\mathcal{A}^c_{easy}(T)$ using the algorithms introduced in Sect. 4. We then compare their depths with each other.

We present experimental results on 20 decision tables from the UCI Machine Learning Repository [14]. Some decision tables contain conditional attributes that take a unique value in each row; such attributes are excluded. If the table contains duplicate rows (possibly with differing decisions), each group of identical rows is replaced with a representative row assigned the most frequent decision in that group. For tables with missing attribute values, these are replaced with the most frequent value for the corresponding attribute.

Table 1 summarizes the results of experiments. The column "Decision table" lists the dataset names from [14]. The columns "Rows" and "Attrs" indicate the number of rows and conditional attributes, respectively, in the considered decision table T, column $|D(T)|$ denotes the cardinality of decision classes. The columns "E-greedy", "M-greedy", and "Easy" contain information about complete inhibitory rule systems $\mathcal{A}^c_{e\text{-}greedy}(T)$, $\mathcal{A}^c_{m\text{-}greedy}(T)$, and $\mathcal{A}^c_{easy}(T)$, constructed by the algorithms $\mathcal{A}^c_{e\text{-}greedy}$, $\mathcal{A}^c_{m\text{-}greedy}$, and $\mathcal{A}^c_{easy}$ for the decision table T. The minimum, average, and the maximum lengths of rules from the constructed systems over all rows of T are shown in subcolumns "min", "avg", and "max", respectively. The "max" subcolumn in each case corresponds to the depth of the rule system: $L(\mathcal{A}^c_{e\text{-}greedy}(T))$, $L(\mathcal{A}^c_{m\text{-}greedy}(T))$, and $L(\mathcal{A}^c_{easy}(T))$. The last row "average" presents average values among all datasets.

Based on the presented results, it can be seen that the minimum lengths of rules constructed by considered greedy algorithms are comparable, and for many of the presented datasets, the minimum rule length is equal to 1. In terms of average rule lengths, the shortest rules are constructed by the e-greedy algorithm, followed by m-greedy, with the easy algorithm ranking third. Considering the maximum length of rules in relation to the number of attributes in the dataset, only for 2 of the 20 datasets studied, i.e., balance-scale and monks-2-test, the number of attributes in the dataset is the same as the maximum length of rules. This situation occurs for all 3 algorithms. It should also be noted that for a mushroom dataset containing 22 attributes, the maximum rule length for the e-greedy algorithm is 2, and for m-greedy and easy it is equal to 3. Moreover, in the lymhopgraphy dataset, which contains 18 attributes, the maximum rule length is 1 across all 3 algorithms.

Figure 1 presents the distribution of values related to the maximum and average length of rules for the tested datasets, for the three proposed algorithms, and shows the differences among them.

Table 1. Results of experiments with complete systems of rules

Decision table	Rows	Attr	|D(T)|	Easy			E-greedy			M-greedy		
				min	avg	max	min	avg	max	min	avg	max
adult-stretch	16	4	2	1	1.250	2	1	1.250	2	1	1.250	2
balance-scale	625	4	3	2	2.725	4	2	2.672	4	2	2.672	4
breast-cancer	266	9	2	1	3.308	6	1	2.665	6	1	2.703	6
cars	1728	6	4	1	1.069	4	1	1.047	3	1	1.047	3
house-votes	279	16	2	2	3.416	7	2	2.538	5	2	2.559	5
lymphography	148	18	4	1	1.000	1	1	1.000	1	1	1.000	1
monks-1-test	432	6	1	1	2.250	3	1	2.250	3	1	2.250	3
monks-1-train	124	6	2	1	2.952	5	1	2.266	3	1	2.274	3
monks-2-test	432	6	2	3	4.523	6	3	4.523	6	3	4.523	6
monks-2-train	169	6	2	3	3.633	5	3	3.497	5	3	3.527	5
monks-3-test	432	6	2	1	1.750	2	1	1.750	2	1	1.750	2
monks-3-train	122	6	2	2	2.582	4	2	2.311	4	2	2.328	4
mushroom	8124	22	2	1	1.840	3	1	1.182	2	1	1.182	3
nursery	12960	8	5	1	1.000	1	1	1.000	1	1	1.000	1
shuttle-landing	15	6	2	1	1.467	4	1	1.400	4	1	1.400	4
soybean-small	47	35	4	1	1.000	1	1	1.000	1	1	1.000	1
spect-test	169	22	2	1	1.964	9	1	1.485	8	1	1.509	8
teeth	23	8	23	1	1.000	1	1	1.000	1	1	1.000	1
tic-tac-toe	958	9	2	3	4.014	6	3	3.031	4	3	3.602	5
zoo-data	59	16	7	1	1.000	1	1	1.000	1	1	1.000	1
average				1.45	2.19	3.75	1.45	1.94	3.30	1.45	1.98	3.40

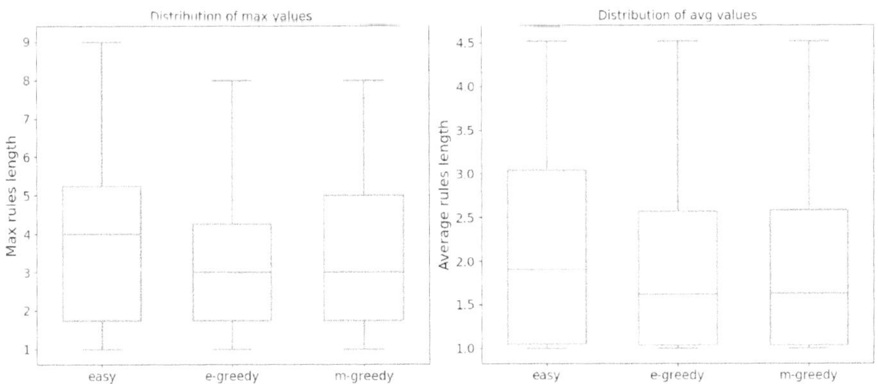

Fig. 1. Distribution of values related to the length of inhibitory rules: the maximum values (the left-hand side) and the average values (the right-hand side). Each subfigure depicting a different range of values (maximum and average length).

Considering the maximum rule length (the left-hand side of the figure), the easy algorithm has the highest median value of the three algorithms tested, which is 4.0, while the average value is 3.75. Its interquartile range is from 1.75 to 5.25, with a maximum value of 9 that refers to the spect-test dataset containing 22 attributes. The e-greedy and m-greedy algorithms have lower median values, i.e., 3.0 in both cases. The interquartile range for the e-greedy algorithm (1.75–4.25) is slightly narrower than for the m-greedy algorithm (1.75–5.00), which indicates greater homogeneity in terms of the maximum length of rules. For both algorithms, the maximum observed value is 8 referred to spect-test dataset.

In the case of the right-hand of the figure showing the average length of rules, the easy algorithm has a higher median of 1.902 and greater variability in rule length compared to the other two algorithms. Its interquartile range is between 1.0 to 3.041, which is greater than that of the e-greedy and m-greedy algorithms. The e-greedy algorithm shows the lowest median of 1.617, while for the m-greedy algorithm, the value is 1.629. All three algorithms have the same extreme values, ranging from 1 to 4.523. In general, the proposed algorithms allow the construction of short inhibitory rules, although there are also isolated cases that deviate from this trend.

To examine whether the proposed algorithms produce statistically different results, the Friedman test was performed [12], and the average rank for each algorithm was computed across all datasets: e-greedy—1.55, m-greedy—1.90, easy—2.55. To identify which specific pairs of algorithms differ significantly, the Nemenyi test was performed and p-values for each combination of pairs of algorithms were calculated [13]. The Nemenyi test confirms the significant difference between easy and e-greedy ($p = 0.004$). The difference between the easy and m-greedy approaches significance $p = 0.099$, while e-greedy and m-greedy show no significant difference ($p = 0.510$). This suggests that e-greedy and m-greedy algorithms are relatively similar in their behavior, both outperforming the easy algorithm in generating shorter rules.

Figure 2 presents the CD diagram based on the Nemenyi test results. Algorithms connected by a horizontal bar do not differ significantly at the $\alpha = 0.05$ level.

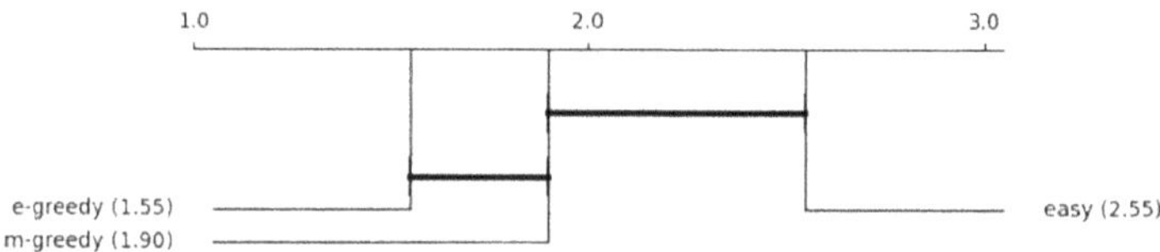

Fig. 2. Critical difference diagram showing pairwise comparisons of algorithms based on average rule length.

This visual representation confirms that while e-greedy achieves the best rank, its performance is statistically indistinguishable from m-greedy, whereas both outperform the easy algorithm.

6   Conclusions

The representation of knowledge in the form of rules plays an important role, especially in the era of intensive development of artificial intelligence methods. The transparency and clarity of the proposed decisions and the simplicity and intuitive form of rule notation are the strengths of rule-based representation.

There are various types of rules, among which the most popular are decision rules written in the form of logical implications with a conclusion part in the form: *"attribute = decision"*. In this work, the authors focused on inhibitory rules, which in the decision part take the form of *"attribute ≠ decision"*. The factors determining the investigation of these rules were that they are able to represent more information encoded in the data than decision rules. In addition, classifiers constructed on the basis of inhibitory rules often exhibit lower classification error compared to classifiers derived from decision rules.

Taking into account knowledge representation perspective, the length of rules plays a significant role. Shorter rules make it easier for people to understand and increase the transparency of the model. Unfortunately, the problem of construction inhibitory rules with minimum depth is NP-hard. Therefore, approximate and heuristic methods that allow a solution to be obtained within a reasonable time are desirable.

In this paper, authors proposed three new algorithms for constructing inhibitory rules based on approximate polynomial-time algorithms for the set cover problem. The quality of these algorithms was analyzed. It was shown that the proposed m-greedy algorithm allows for producing rules close to an optimal one in the framework of length and taking into account the natural assumption that $P \neq NP$. Statistical analysis of the results obtained regarding the length of the constructed rules allowed us to create a ranking of the proposed algorithms, with the e-greedy algorithm in first place, followed by m-greedy and easy. Furthermore, the results obtained by the e-greedy and easy algorithms differ in a statistically significant way. Nevertheless, considering the number of attributes in the tested datasets and the maximum length of the induced rules, it can be concluded that, in general, these algorithms allow for the creation of short, concise rules.

Future work will be devoted to the investigation of classifiers based on the inhibitory rules learned by the proposed algorithms.

Acknowledgments. The research works presented in the article were carried out within the KAUST-US Collaboration Agreement No. RFS-2025-6853 and supported by the Remote Working Individual Consultancy Agreement No. KAUST-2025-C0148.

The research activities co-financed by the funds granted under the Research Excellence Initiative of the University of Silesia in Katowice.

References

1. Alsolami, F., Azad, M., Chikalov, I., Moshkov, M.: Decision and inhibitory rules and systems of rules. In: Decision and Inhibitory Trees and Rules for Decision Tables with Many-valued Decisions. ISRL, vol. 156, pp. 177–184. Springer, Cham (2020). https://doi.org/10.1007/978-3-030-12854-8_11
2. Alsolami, F., Chikalov, I., Moshkov, M., Zielosko, B.: Optimization of inhibitory decision rules relative to length and coverage. In: Li, T., et al. (eds.) RSKT 2012. LNCS (LNAI), vol. 7414, pp. 149–154. Springer, Heidelberg (2012). https://doi.org/10.1007/978-3-642-31900-6_19
3. Alsolami, F., Chikalov, I., Moshkov, M., Zielosko, B.: Optimization of approximate inhibitory rules relative to number of misclassifications. In: Watada, J., Jain, L.C., Howlett, R.J., Mukai, N., Asakura, K. (eds.) 17th International Conference in Knowledge Based and Intelligent Information and Engineering Systems, KES 2013, Kitakyushu, Japan, 9-11 September 2013. Procedia Computer Science, vol. 22, pp. 295–302. Elsevier (2013)
4. Alsolami, F., Chikalov, I., Moshkov, M., Zielosko, B.M.: Length and coverage of inhibitory decision rules. In: Nguyen, N.-T., Hoang, K., Jedrzejowicz, P. (eds.) ICCCI 2012, Part II. LNCS (LNAI), vol. 7654, pp. 325–334. Springer, Heidelberg (2012). https://doi.org/10.1007/978-3-642-34707-8_33
5. Alsolami, F., Chikalov, I., Moshkov, M.J.: Comparison of heuristics for inhibitory rule optimization. In: Jedrzejowicz, P., Jain, L.C., Howlett, R.J., Czarnowski, I. (eds.) 18th International Conference in Knowledge Based and Intelligent Information and Engineering Systems, KES 2014, Gdynia, Poland, 15–17 September 2014. Procedia Computer Science, vol. 35, pp. 378–387. Elsevier (2014)
6. Azad, M., Moshkov, M.: Multi-stage optimization of decision and inhibitory trees for decision tables with many-valued decisions. Eur. J. Oper. Res. **263**(3), 910–921 (2017)
7. Chekuri, C., Quanrud, K., Zhang, Z.: On approximating partial set cover and generalizations (2019). https://arxiv.org/abs/1907.04413
8. Delimata, P., Moshkov, M., Skowron, A., Suraj, Z.: Two families of classification algorithms. In: An, A., Stefanowski, J., Ramanna, S., Butz, C.J., Pedrycz, W., Wang, G. (eds.) RSFDGrC 2007. LNCS (LNAI), vol. 4482, pp. 297–304. Springer, Heidelberg (2007). https://doi.org/10.1007/978-3-540-72530-5_35
9. Delimata, P., Moshkov, M., Skowron, A., Suraj, Z.: Comparison of lazy classification algorithms based on deterministic and inhibitory decision rules. In: Wang, G., Li, T., Grzymala-Busse, J.W., Miao, D., Skowron, A., Yao, Y. (eds.) RSKT 2008. LNCS (LNAI), vol. 5009, pp. 55–62. Springer, Heidelberg (2008). https://doi.org/10.1007/978-3-540-79721-0_13
10. Delimata, P., Moshkov, M.J., Skowron, A., Suraj, Z.: Inhibitory Rules in Data Analysis: A Rough Set Approach, Studies in Computational Intelligence, vol. 163. Springer, New York (2009)
11. Dinur, I., Steurer, D.: Analytical approach to parallel repetition. In: Shmoys, D.B. (ed.) Symposium on Theory of Computing, STOC 2014, New York, NY, USA, May 31 - June 03 2014, pp. 624–633. ACM (2014)
12. Friedman, M.: A comparison of alternative tests of significance for the problem of m rankings. Ann. Math. Stat. **11**(1), 86–92 (1940)
13. García, S., Fernández, A., Luengo, J., Herrera, F.: Advanced nonparametric tests for multiple comparisons in the design of experiments in computational intelligence and data mining: experimental analysis of power. Inf. Sci. **180**(10), 2044–2064 (2010)

14. Kelly, M., Longjohn, R., Nottingham, K.: UCI Machine Learning Repository (2025). http://archive.ics.uci.edu
15. Kozielski, M., Sikora, M., Wawrowski, L.: Towards consistency of rule-based explainer and black box model - fusion of rule induction and XAI-based feature importance. Knowl. Based Syst. **311**, 113092 (2025)
16. Moshkov, M., Skowron, A., Suraj, Z.: Maximal consistent extensions of information systems relative to their theories. Inf. Sci. **178**(12), 2600–2620 (2008)
17. Moshkov, M., Zielosko, B.: Combinatorial Machine Learning - A Rough Set Approach, Studies in Computational Intelligence, vol. 360. Springer, Heidelberg (2011)
18. Moshkov, M.J., Skowron, A., Suraj, Z.: On minimal inhibitory rules for almost all k-valued information systems. Fundam. Informaticae **93**(1–3), 261–272 (2009)
19. Pawlak, Z., Skowron, A.: Rough sets and boolean reasoning. Inf. Sci. **177**(1), 41–73 (2007)
20. Rissanen, J.: Modeling by shortest data description. Automatica **14**(5), 465–471 (1978)
21. Sakai, H., Nakata, M., Slezak, D., Watada, J.: Rule generation in rough set non-deterministic information analysis (RNIA) and some applications of the obtained rules. Appl. Soft Comput. **172**, 112842 (2025)
22. Skowron, A., Suraj, Z.: Rough sets and concurrency. Bull. Acad. Pol. Sci. **41**(3), 237–254 (1993)
23. Stanczyk, U., Zielosko, B., Baron, G.: Attribute relevance and discretisation in knowledge discovery: a study in stylometric domain. In: Mikyska, J., de Mulatier, C., Paszynski, M., Krzhizhanovskaya, V.V., Dongarra, J.J., Sloot, P.M.A. (eds.) Computational Science - ICCS 2023 - 23rd International Conference, Prague, Czech Republic, 3–5 July 2023, Proceedings, Part II. LNCS, vol. 14074, pp. 273–281. Springer (2023)
24. Stefanowski, J., Vanderpooten, D.: Induction of decision rules in classification and discovery-oriented perspectives. Int. J. Intell. Syst. **16**(1), 13–27 (2001)
25. Suraj, Z.: Some remarks on extensions and restrictions of information systems. In: Ziarko, W., Yao, Y. (eds.) RSCTC 2000. LNCS (LNAI), vol. 2005, pp. 204–211. Springer, Heidelberg (2001). https://doi.org/10.1007/3-540-45554-X_24
26. Zielosko, B.: Optimization of approximate decision rules relative to coverage. In: Kozielski, S., Mrozek, D., Kasprowski, P., Małysiak-Mrozek, B., Kostrzewa, D. (eds.) BDAS 2014. CCIS, vol. 424, pp. 170–179. Springer, Cham (2014). https://doi.org/10.1007/978-3-319-06932-6_17
27. Zielosko, B., Moshkov, M., Tetteh, E.T.: Optimization of inner and general rules. Inf. Sci. **719**, 122466 (2025)

Greedy Algorithm for Modeling Approximate Decision Trees for Distributed Decision Tables

Azimkhon Ostonov[1], Mikhail Moshkov[1], and Beata Zielosko[1,2]

[1] Computer, Electrical and Mathematical Sciences and Engineering Division, King Abdullah University of Science and Technology (KAUST), Thuwal 23955-6900, Saudi Arabia
{azimkhon.ostonov,mikhail.moshkov}@kaust.edu.sa, beata.zielosko@us.edu.pl
[2] Institute of Computer Science, University of Silesia in Katowice, Bedzinska 39, 41-200 Sosnowiec, Poland

Abstract. This paper addresses the problem of construction an approximate decision tree with minimum depth for distributed data represented as a tuple of decision tables. Unfortunately this is an NP-hard problem, so a greedy algorithm has been proposed which induces approximate, so-called shared decision tree. Theoretical results related to the bounds of the depth of decision trees constructed by the proposed greedy method are presented.

Keywords: Distributed Data · Shared Decision Tree · Greedy Algorithm

1 Introduction

Decision trees [4,5] are extensively employed for knowledge representation, classification, and problem solving in fields such as fault diagnosis and combinatorial optimization. There are a significant number of results related to the bounds on the complexity of decision trees [1,3,6,9]. Additionally, a wide range of algorithms and their different variants have been developed during many years.

When data is collected in a single decision table, constructing a decision tree is a relatively simple task. However, constructing a decision tree for a set of decision tables is a much greater challenge. In the paper, unlike the usual approach to working with decision trees, we build a tree not for one, but for several decision tables simultaneously.

This paper continues the series begun in [10] where problems related to multi-agent decision making are considered. There are n agents, each of which collects data and represents it in the form of a decision table. The agents solve somewhat similar problems and use attributes from a common set. The tuple of the considered n decision tables is called a distributed decision table.

In this paper, we consider the case where all decision tables are available. Given a tuple of values of all attributes present in the tables, we need for each

M. Paszynski et al. (Eds.): ICCS 2026 Workshops, LNCS 16788, pp. 304–311, 2026.
https://doi.org/10.1007/978-3-032-29915-4_26

table to find a decision or show that there is no matching row. There are two options: either build a decision tree for each table and use them sequentially (we are only considering a single-processor environment) or build one shared decision tree that is valid for all decision tables simultaneously.

We explore the second option and, in addition, study approximate shared decision trees. Since the number of nodes in such trees can grow exponentially with the total number of elements in the decision tables, we do not construct the entire tree but instead simulate its operation with a given set of attribute values. We show that even in this formulation, the problem of describing an approximate shared decision tree with minimum depth is NP-hard. Therefore, we focus on a greedy algorithm for constructing an approximate shared decision tree. This algorithm is a generalization of the greedy algorithm applicable to a single decision table [7]. We obtain precision bounds for the depth of decision trees constructed by the new greedy algorithm.

The considered problem is a form of distributed data mining [2], where a global decision model (shared decision tree) is constructed from multiple distributed decision tables associated with different agents.

The rest of the paper is organized as follows. Section 2 contains the main notions concerning proposed new approach and Sect. 3 – three auxiliary statements. Section 4 is devoted to the main results and Sect. 5 – to the study of distributed decision tables related to the point color recognition. Section 6 contains conclusions and future works.

2   Main Notions

In this section, we introduce the main notions related to distributed decision tables and approximate shared decision trees constructed for them, and we formulate the problem of minimizing the depth of an α-decision tree.

Let $k \geq 2$. A *k-valued decision table* (or simply, a *decision table*) U is a rectangular table whose entries belong to the set $F_{k_0} = \{0, \ldots, k-1\}$. The columns of this table are labeled by pairwise distinct attributes (i.e., attribute names) from the set $\{g_1, g_2, \ldots\}$. The rows of U are pairwise distinct, and each row is labeled with a natural number, referred to as a decision. We denote by $At(U)$ the set of attributes assigned to the columns of U.

The table U is called *degenerate* if it is empty (contains no rows) or if all of its rows share the same decision; otherwise, it is called *nondegenerate*. A decision that appears in the greatest number of rows of U is called the *most common decision of U*. If several such decisions exist, we choose the smallest one. If U is empty, its most common decision is defined to be 1.

A *subtable* of U is any table obtained from U by deleting some of its rows.

A *distributed decision table* is a tuple $\mathcal{U} = (U_1, \ldots, U_n)$ of $n \geq 1$ decision tables $U_1, \ldots, U_n$. Denote $At(\mathcal{U}) = \bigcup_{j=1}^{n} At(U_j)$. Let, for the definiteness, $At(\mathcal{U}) = \{g_1, \ldots, g_m\}$. The distributed decision table $\mathcal{U} = (U_1, \ldots, U_n)$ is called *degenerate* if tables $U_1, \ldots, U_n$ are degenerate, and *nondegenerate* otherwise. We correspond to a distributed decision table $\mathcal{U} = (U_1, \ldots, U_n)$ a tuple $(s_1, \ldots, s_n)$

where, for $j = 1, \ldots, n$, the value s_j is equal to the symbol $\emptyset$ if the table U_j is empty and s_j is the most common decision for U_j otherwise. This tuple will be called the *general decision* for $\mathcal{U}$. A *subtable* of $\mathcal{U}$ is a distributed decision table $\mathcal{U}' = (U_1', \ldots, U_n')$ such that U_j' is a subtable of U_j for $j = 1, \ldots, n$.

We now define the parameter $R(\mathcal{U})$. Let U_j be a table from $\mathcal{U}$. We denote by $R(U_j)$ the number of unordered pairs of rows from U_j labeled with different decisions. Then $R(\mathcal{U}) = R(U_1) + \cdots + R(U_n)$. Evidently, $R(\mathcal{U}) = 0$ if and only if $\mathcal{U}$ is degenerate.

We denote by $\Omega(\mathcal{U})$ the set of finite words over the alphabet $\{(g_i, \sigma) : g_i \in \{g_1, \ldots, g_m\}, \sigma \in E_k\}$ including the empty word λ. Let $\beta \in \Omega(\mathcal{U})$ and U_j be a table from $\mathcal{U}$. We now define a subtable $U_j\beta$ obtained from U_j by the removal of some rows. If $\beta = \lambda$, then $U_j\beta = U_j$. Let $\beta \neq \lambda$, $\beta = (g_{l_1}, \sigma_1) \ldots (g_{l_k}, \sigma_k)$ and r be a row of U_j. Then this row is removed if and only if for some $t \in \{1, \ldots, k\}$, $g_{l_t} \in At(U_j)$ and in the intersection of the row r and the column labeled with the attribute g_{l_t} there is a number different from σ_t. Denote $\mathcal{U}\beta = (U_1\beta, \ldots, U_n\beta)$.

A *decision tree* Γ *over* $\mathcal{U}$ is a finite rooted tree in which each terminal node is labeled with an n-tuple consisting of natural numbers and the symbol $\emptyset$, and each nonterminal (i.e., *working*) node is labeled with an attribute from $At(\mathcal{U}) = \{g_1, \ldots, g_m\}$. Exactly k edges leave every working node, and these edges are labeled with pairwise distinct elements of E_k.

To every terminal node v in the tree Γ we associate a word $\beta(v)$. If v is the root of Γ, then $\beta(v) = \lambda$. If v is not the root, and the path from the root to v passes through $p > 0$ nodes labeled with attributes $g_{i_1}, \ldots, g_{i_p}$, along edges labeled with $\sigma_1, \ldots, \sigma_p$, then we define

$$\beta(v) = (g_{i_1}, \sigma_1) \cdots (g_{i_p}, \sigma_p).$$

Let α be a real number with $0 \leq \alpha < 1$. We say that Γ is a *shared α-decision tree for $\mathcal{U}$* (or simply, an *α-decision tree for $\mathcal{U}$*) if, for every terminal node v of Γ, the inequality

$$R(\mathcal{U}\beta(v)) \leq \alpha\, R(\mathcal{U})$$

is satisfied, and the node v is labeled with the general decision for $\mathcal{U}\beta(v)$.

Let Γ be an α-decision tree for $\mathcal{U}$. For any tuple $\bar{\sigma} \in E_k^m$ representing the values of attributes $g_1, \ldots, g_m$, the tree operates as follows. We start at the root of Γ. If the current node is terminal, then the output of Γ is the general decision assigned to that node. If the current node is a working node labeled with attribute g_i, and the value of g_i in the tuple is $\sigma \in E_k$, then we follow the outgoing edge labeled with σ, and continue this process accordingly.

It is clear that, for each tuple $\bar{\sigma} = (\sigma_1, \ldots, \sigma_m) \in E_k^m$, in the tree Γ there exists a terminal node v such that the word $\beta(v)$ is a word over the alphabet $\{(g_1, \sigma_1), \ldots, (g_m, \sigma_m)\}$ for which $R(\mathcal{U}\beta(v)) \leq \alpha R(\mathcal{U})$. We will say that the *node v accepts the tuple $\bar{\sigma}$*.

Let us fix α such that $0 \leq \alpha < 1$. We now consider an example, which shows that the minimum number of nodes in an α-decision tree for $\mathcal{U}$ can grow exponentially with the total number of elements in the tables $U_1, \ldots, U_n$. The *number of elements* in the decision table is equal to the product of the number of rows and the number of columns.

Example 1. Let us consider a distributed decision table $\mathcal{U}^* = (U_1^*, \ldots, U_n^*)$ in which, for $j = 1, \ldots, n$, $At(U_j^*) = \{g_j\}$ and the table U_j^* is nondegenerate 2-valued table. The table U_j^* contains one column labeled with g_j and two rows (0) and (1) labeled with different decisions. The number of elements in this decision table is equal to 2. The total number of elements in the decision tables $U_1^*, \ldots, U_n^*$ is equal to $2n$. We have $At(\mathcal{U}^*) = \{g_1, \ldots, g_n\}$.

Let Γ^* be an α-decision tree for $\mathcal{U}^*$. We denote by V the set of terminal nodes of Γ^* each of which accepts at least one tuple from E_2^n. Let $v \in V$ and $\bar{\sigma} = (\sigma_1, \ldots, \sigma_n) \in E_2^n$ be a tuple accepted by the node v. It is clear that the word $\beta(v)$ should contain at least $(1 - \alpha)n$ pairwise different letters from the set $\{(g_1, \sigma_1), \ldots, (g_n, \sigma_n)\}$: otherwise, $R(\mathcal{U}^*\beta(v)) > \alpha R(\mathcal{U}^*)$. Therefore, v accepts at most $2^{\lfloor \alpha n \rfloor}$ tuples from E_2^n. Thus, $|V| \geq 2^{n - \lfloor \alpha n \rfloor} \geq 2^{n(1 - \alpha)}$. It means that the decision tree Γ^* contains at least $2^{n(1 - \alpha)}$ nodes.

This example demonstrates that instead of constructing an entire decision tree, it is more appropriate to model its operation on a given tuple of attribute values from $At(\mathcal{U})$.

We denote by $d(\Gamma)$ the *depth* of a decision tree Γ, defined as the maximum length of any path from the root to a terminal node. We write $d_\alpha(\mathcal{U})$ for the minimum possible depth of an α-decision tree for the distributed table $\mathcal{U}$.

We are interested in minimizing the depth of α-decision trees for distributed decision tables. To this end, we will consider the following *problem of α-decision tree depth minimization*. Given a nondegenerate distributed decision table $\mathcal{U}$ and a given tuple of values of attributes from the set $At(\mathcal{U})$, we must simulate the operation of an α-decision tree for $\mathcal{U}$ that has the minimum depth. Obviously, for the same table $\mathcal{U}$ and different tuples of attribute values, we must simulate the operation of the same decision tree.

3   Auxiliary Statements

In this section, we consider two parameters of distributed decision tables and three statements without proofs regarding these parameters.

We define now a parameter $D(\mathcal{U})$ of the distributed decision table $\mathcal{U}$. If $\mathcal{U}$ is degenerate, then $D(\mathcal{U}) = 0$. Let $\mathcal{U}$ be nondegenerate and $At(\mathcal{U}) = \{g_1, \ldots, g_m\}$. Let $\bar{\sigma} = (\sigma_1, \ldots, \sigma_m) \in E_k^m$. We denote by $D(\mathcal{U}, \bar{\sigma})$ the minimum length of a word β over the alphabet $\{(g_1, \sigma_1), \ldots, (g_m, \sigma_m)\}$ for which $\mathcal{U}\beta$ is degenerate. Then $D(\mathcal{U}) = \max\{D(\mathcal{U}, \bar{\sigma}) : \bar{\sigma} \in E_k^m\}$.

Lemma 1. *Let $\mathcal{U}$ be a distributed decision table and $\mathcal{U}'$ be a subtable of $\mathcal{U}$. Then* $D(\mathcal{U}') \leq D(\mathcal{U})$.

Lemma 2. *Let $\mathcal{U}$ be a distributed decision table. Then $d_0(\mathcal{U}) \geq D(\mathcal{U})$.*

Lemma 3. *Let $\mathcal{U}$ be a distributed decision table, $\mathcal{U}'$ be a subtable of $\mathcal{U}$, $g_i \in At(\mathcal{U})$, and $\sigma \in E_k$. Then $R(\mathcal{U}) - R(\mathcal{U}(g_i, \sigma)) \geq R(\mathcal{U}') - R(\mathcal{U}'(g_i, \sigma))$.*

4 Main Results

In this section, we examine the problem of minimizing the depth of an α-decision tree. We show that this problem is NP-hard. As a first step, we focus on analyzing a greedy algorithm for α-decision tree depth minimization.

Let α be a real number with $0 \le \alpha < 1$. We now describe a greedy algorithm $\mathcal{W}_\alpha$ which, for a given distributed decision table $\mathcal{U} = (U_1, \ldots, U_n)$ with $At(\mathcal{U}) = \{g_1, \ldots, g_m\}$, simulates the operation of an α-decision tree $\mathcal{W}_\alpha(\mathcal{U})$ for $\mathcal{U}$ on a given tuple $\bar{\sigma} = (\sigma_1, \ldots, \sigma_m) \in E_k^m$ of values of the attributes $g_1, \ldots, g_m$.

Algorithm $\mathcal{W}_\alpha$

Step 1. Set $\beta = \lambda$.

Step 2. If $R(\mathcal{U}\beta) \le \alpha R(\mathcal{U})$, then the decision tree $\mathcal{W}_\alpha(\mathcal{U})$ returns the general decision $(s_1, \ldots, s_n)$ where, for $j = 1, \ldots, n$, $s_j = \emptyset$ if the table $U_j\beta$ is empty and s_j is the most common decision for $U_j\beta$ if this table is nonempty.

If $R(\mathcal{U}\beta) > \alpha R(\mathcal{U})$, then, for $i = 1, \ldots, m$, compute the value

$$Q(g_i) = \max\{R(\mathcal{U}\beta(g_i, \sigma)) : \sigma \in E_k\}$$

and choose the minimum $i \in \{1, \ldots, m\}$ for which $Q(g_i)$ has the minimum value. The decision tree $\mathcal{W}_\alpha(\mathcal{U})$ computes the value of the attribute g_i and obtains that $g_i = \sigma_i$. Set $\beta := \beta(g_i, \sigma_i)$ and go to Step 2.

Note 1. If $\mathcal{U}$ is a degenerate distributed decision table, then $d(\mathcal{W}_\alpha(\mathcal{U})) = 0$.

Theorem 1. *Let $\mathcal{U}$ be a nondegenerate distributed decision table and α be a real number such that $0 < \alpha < 1$. Then $d(\mathcal{W}_\alpha(\mathcal{U})) \le D(\mathcal{U}) \ln \frac{1}{\alpha} + 1$.*

Proof. Let $At(\mathcal{U}) = \{g_1, \ldots, g_m\}$. For each $i = 1, \ldots, m$, let γ_i denote the smallest element of E_k such that

$$R(\mathcal{U}(g_i, \gamma_i)) = \max\{ R(\mathcal{U}(g_i, \gamma)) : \gamma \in E_k \}.$$

Clearly, $Q(g_i) = R(\mathcal{U}(g_i, \gamma_i))$. It follows that the root of the tree $\mathcal{W}_\alpha(\mathcal{U})$ is labeled with the attribute g_{i_0}, where i_0 is the smallest index i for which $R(\mathcal{U}(g_i, \gamma_i))$ attains its minimum value.

Let us show that

$$R(\mathcal{U}(g_{i_0}, \gamma_{i_0})) \le (1 - 1/D(\mathcal{U})) \, R(\mathcal{U}).$$

It is clear that there exist attributes $g_{i_1}, \ldots, g_{i_t} \in \{g_1, \ldots, g_m\}$ such that

$$\mathcal{U}(g_{i_1}, \gamma_{i_1}) \ldots (g_{i_t}, \gamma_{i_t})$$

is degenerate and $t \le D(\mathcal{U})$. Evidently, $R(\mathcal{U}(g_{i_1}, \gamma_{i_1}) \ldots (g_{i_t}, \gamma_{i_t})) = 0$. Therefore

$$R(\mathcal{U}) - [R(\mathcal{U}) - R(\mathcal{U}(g_{i_1}, \gamma_{i_1}))] - [R(\mathcal{U}(g_{i_1}, \gamma_{i_1})) - R(\mathcal{U}(g_{i_1}, \gamma_{i_1})(g_{i_2}, \gamma_{i_2}))] - $$
$$\cdots - [R(\mathcal{U}(g_{i_1}, \gamma_{i_1}) \ldots (g_{i_{t-1}}, \gamma_{i_{t-1}})) - R(\mathcal{U}(g_{i_1}, \gamma_{i_1}) \ldots (g_{i_t}, \gamma_{i_t}))]$$
$$= R(\mathcal{U}(g_{i_1}, \gamma_{i_1}) \ldots (g_{i_t}, \gamma_{i_t})) = 0.$$

From Lemma 3 it follows that, for $j = 1, \ldots, t-1$, $R(\mathcal{U}(g_{i_1}, \gamma_{i_1}) \ldots (g_{i_j}, \gamma_{i_j})) - R(\mathcal{U}(g_{i_1}, \gamma_{i_1}) \ldots (g_{i_j}, \gamma_{i_j})(g_{i_{j+1}}, \gamma_{i_{j+1}})) \le R(\mathcal{U}) - R(\mathcal{U}(g_{i_{j+1}}, \gamma_{i_{j+1}}))$.

Therefore $R(\mathcal{U}) - \sum_{j=1}^{t}(R(\mathcal{U}) - R(\mathcal{U}(g_{i_j}, \gamma_{i_j}))) \le 0$. Since $R(\mathcal{U}(g_{i_0}, \gamma_{i_0})) \le R(\mathcal{U}(g_{i_j}, \gamma_{i_j}))$ for $j = 1, \ldots, t$, we have $R(\mathcal{U}) - t(R(\mathcal{U}) - R(\mathcal{U}(g_{i_0}, \gamma_{i_0}))) \le 0$ and $R(\mathcal{U}(g_{i_0}, \gamma_{i_0})) \le (1 - 1/t)R(\mathcal{U})$. Taking into account that $t \le D(\mathcal{U})$, we obtain $R(\mathcal{U}(g_{i_0}, \gamma_{i_0})) \le (1 - 1/D(\mathcal{U}))\, R(\mathcal{U})$.

Assume first that $D(\mathcal{U}) = 1$. From the obtained inequality and from the description of the algorithm $\mathcal{W}_\alpha$, it follows that $d(\mathcal{W}_\alpha(\mathcal{U})) = 1$. Thus, if $D(\mathcal{U}) = 1$, the statement of the theorem holds.

Now let $D(\mathcal{U}) \ge 2$. Consider a longest path in the tree $\mathcal{W}_\alpha(\mathcal{U})$ from the root to a terminal node, and let its length be p. Suppose the working nodes along this path are labeled with the attributes $g_{j_1}, \ldots, g_{j_p}$, where $g_{j_1} = g_{i_0}$, and the corresponding edges are labeled with the values $\sigma_1, \ldots, \sigma_p$. For each $q = 1, \ldots, p$, denote by $\mathcal{U}_q$ the distributed table $\mathcal{U}(g_{j_1}, \sigma_1) \cdots (g_{j_q}, \sigma_q)$. By Lemma 1, we have $D(\mathcal{U}_q) \le D(\mathcal{U})$ for all $q = 1, \ldots, p$. Moreover, we have established that

$$R(\mathcal{U}_1) \le R(\mathcal{U})\left(1 - \tfrac{1}{D(\mathcal{U})}\right).$$

One can similarly show that

$$R(\mathcal{U}_q) \le R(\mathcal{U})\left(1 - \tfrac{1}{D(\mathcal{U})}\right)^q, \quad q = 1, \ldots, p.$$

Consider the table $\mathcal{U}_{p-1}$. For this table, we have

$$R(\mathcal{U}_{p-1}) \le R(\mathcal{U})\left(1 - \tfrac{1}{D(\mathcal{U})}\right)^{p-1}.$$

From the description of the algorithm $\mathcal{W}_\alpha$, it follows that

$$R(\mathcal{U}_{p-1}) > \alpha R(\mathcal{U}).$$

Hence,

$$\alpha < \left(1 - \tfrac{1}{D(\mathcal{U})}\right)^{p-1} \quad \text{and} \quad \left(1 + \tfrac{1}{D(\mathcal{U})-1}\right)^{p-1} < \frac{1}{\alpha}.$$

Taking the natural logarithm of both sides gives

$$(p - 1) \ln\left(1 + \frac{1}{D(\mathcal{U}) - 1}\right) \le \ln \frac{1}{\alpha}.$$

It is known that for any natural number r,

$$\ln(1 + \tfrac{1}{r}) > \frac{1}{r + 1}.$$

Since $D(\mathcal{U}) \ge 2$, we obtain

$$\frac{p - 1}{D(\mathcal{U})} < \ln \frac{1}{\alpha} \quad \text{and hence} \quad p < D(\mathcal{U}) \ln \frac{1}{\alpha} + 1.$$

Taking into account that $p = d(\mathcal{W}_\alpha(\mathcal{U}))$, we conclude that

$$d(\mathcal{W}_\alpha(\mathcal{U})) < D(\mathcal{U}) \ln \frac{1}{\alpha} + 1.$$

$\square$

Using Theorem 1 and Lemma 2 we obtain the following

Corollary 1. *For any nondegenerate distributed decision table $\mathcal{U}$ and any real number α, $0 < \alpha < 1$, $d(\mathcal{W}_\alpha(\mathcal{U})) \leq d_0(\mathcal{U}) \ln \frac{1}{\alpha} + 1$.*

Based on the results obtained in [8] we can prove the following statement.

Proposition 1. *For any α with $0 \leq \alpha < 1$, the problem of minimizing the depth of an α-decision tree is NP-hard.*

5   Recognizing of Point Color

In this section, we study distributed decision table $\mathcal{U} = (U_1, \ldots, U_n)$ in which each decision table is associated with the problem of recognizing the color of a point from a finite set of two-colored points in the plane. To solve this problem, we use attributes corresponding to vertical and horizontal straight lines. We show that $D(\mathcal{U}) \leq 4$ and the depth of shared α-decision trees constructed by the greedy algorithm $\mathcal{W}_\alpha$ is bounded above by $4 \ln \frac{1}{\alpha} + 1$.

Let we have $m + 1$, $m \geq 2$, vertical straight lines in the plane given by equations $x = 1, \ldots, x = m + 1$ and $m + 1$ horizontal straight lines given by equations $y = 1, \ldots, y = m + 1$. These lines form m^2 squares. Let we have a set C of q points, $2 \leq q \leq m^2$, inside of these squares such that in one square we can have at most one point. Let these points are colored into two colors, white and green, such that at least one point is green and at least one point is white. We should recognize the color of a given point using the attributes $g_1, \ldots, g_{2m+2}$ with values from the set E_2. For a point (a, b), the value of the attribute g_i is defined in the following way. If $i \in \{1, \ldots, m + 1\}$, then $g_i(x, y) = 0$ if and only if $a < i$. If $i \in \{m+2, \ldots, 2m+2\}$, then $g_i(x, y) = 0$ if and only if $b < i - m - 1$.

We correspond to the considered problem a 2-valued decision table U with $2m+2$ columns labeled with the attributes $g_1, \ldots, g_{2m+2}$ and q rows corresponding to the points from C. Let $C = \{p_1, \ldots, p_q\}$. For $j = 1, \ldots, q$, the jth row of U contains values of the attributes $g_1, \ldots, g_{2m+2}$ on the point p_j. This row is labeled with the decision 1 if p_j is a white point and with the decision 2 if p_j is a green point. We will say about the table U as about m-RPC-table. We avoid the proof of the following statement.

Lemma 4. *Let $m \geq 2$ and $\mathcal{U} = (U_1, \ldots, U_n)$ be a distributed decision table in which, for $i = 1, \ldots, n$, U_i is an m-RPC-table. Then $D(\mathcal{U}) \leq 4$.*

Using Theorem 1 and Lemma 4, we obtain the following

Corollary 2. *Let $0 < \alpha < 1$, $m \geq 2$ and $\mathcal{U} = (U_1, \ldots, U_n)$ be a distributed decision table in which, for $i = 1, \ldots, n$, U_i is an m-RPC-table. Then $d(\mathcal{W}_\alpha(\mathcal{U})) \leq 4 \ln \frac{1}{\alpha} + 1$.*

Interestingly, the upper bound under consideration depends only on α.

6   Conclusions

In the paper, an approach focused on the analysis of distributed data represented as a tuple of n decision tables was proposed. In this case, object-specific information is distributed across multiple local data sources. Each table may contain a different subset of objects, attributes, introducing challenges related to knowledge integration and heterogeneous data structures. Since constructing an approximate decision tree with the minimum depth that can be applied simultaneously to each table (a shared decision tree) is an NP-hard problem, a greedy algorithm was proposed. Noteworthy theoretical results including bounds for the depth of decision trees constructed by this algorithm were obtained. In future work, computer experiments to validate the theoretical findings and examine the practical effectiveness of the proposed approach will be performed.

Acknowledgments. Research reported in this publication was supported by the Remote Working Individual Consultancy Agreement No. KAUST-2025-C0148, and King Abdullah University of Science and Technology (KAUST) and the Institute of Computer Science, University of Silesia in Katowice, Poland.

References

1. Buhrman, H., de Wolf, R.: Complexity measures and decision tree complexity: a survey. Theor. Comput. Sci. **288**(1), 21–43 (2002)
2. da Silva, J.C., Giannella, C., Bhargava, R., Kargupta, H., Klusch, M.: Distributed data mining and agents. Eng. Appl. Artif. Intell. **18**(7), 791–807 (2005)
3. Grigoriev, D., Karpinski, M., Yao, A.C.: An exponential lower bound on the size of algebraic decision trees for Max. Comput. Complex. **7**(3), 193–203 (1998)
4. Loyola-González, O., Ramírez-Sáyago, E., Medina-Pérez, M.A.: Towards improving decision tree induction by combining split evaluation measures. Knowl.-Based Syst. **277**, 110832 (2023)
5. Moshkov, M.: Comparative Analysis of Deterministic and Nondeterministic Decision Trees, Intelligent Systems Reference Library, vol. 179. Springer, Cham (2020)
6. Moshkov, M.: Time and space complexity of deterministic and nondeterministic decision trees. Ann. Math. Artif. Intell. **91**(1), 45–74 (2023)
7. Moshkov, M., Zielosko, B.: Combinatorial Machine Learning - A Rough Set Approach, Studies in Computational Intelligence, vol. 360. Springer, Cham (2011)
8. Slezak, D.: Normalized decision functions and measures for inconsistent decision tables analysis. Fundam. Informaticae **44**(3), 291–319 (2000)
9. Yao, A.C.: Decision tree complexity and Betti numbers. In: 26th Annual ACM Symposium on Theory of Computing, STOC 1994, pp. 615–624 (1994)
10. Zielosko, B., Moshkov, M., Tetteh, E.T.: Optimization of inner and general rules. Inf. Sci. **719**, 122466 (2025)

Exponentiation Operators for Asymmetric Interval Numbers and Their Properties

Andrii Shekhovtsov[1], Adrianna Świder[2], Szymon Śniegowski[2],
and Wojciech Sałabun[1,2(✉)]

[1] National Institute of Telecommunications Szachowa 1, 04-894 Warsaw, Poland
a.shekhovtsov@il-pib.pl
[2] West Pomeranian University of Technology in Szczecin, Żołnierska 49, 71-210
Szczecin, Poland
adrianna-swider@zut.edu.pl, szymon-sniegowski@zut.edu.pl,
w.salabun@il-pib.pl

Abstract. Asymmetric Interval Numbers (AINs) represent uncertain quantities by an interval and a representative value defined as the expectation with respect to the auxiliary distribution. Unlike classical interval numbers, which specify only admissible ranges, AINs additionally encode the directional character of uncertainty. To support arithmetic operations, each AIN is associated with a canonical piecewise-constant auxiliary distribution consisting of two uniform segments determined by the interval bounds and the representative value. This distribution serves as a computational tool for evaluating operations on uncertain quantities. The existing AIN arithmetic covers basic algebraic operations but does not support nonlinear transformations in which uncertainty appears in the exponent. This paper extends AIN arithmetic by deriving analytic exponentiation operators for scalar-base exponentiation k^X and exponentiation between two uncertain quantities X^Y. For k^X, the operator is obtained in closed form by applying the Law of the Unconscious Statistician (LOTUS) to the auxiliary distribution. For X^Y, the representative value is defined by a two-step LOTUS construction that evaluates the joint expectation under the product of auxiliary densities using numerical quadrature. Numerical experiments confirm consistency of both operators with Monte Carlo integration of the auxiliary densities. The proposed extension enables direct application of AINs in nonlinear decision and predictive models involving exponential-type relationships.

Keywords: Asymmetric Interval Numbers · AIN · Interval arithmetic

1 Introduction

Decision-making and predictive modeling frequently rely on numerical values derived from measurements, expert assessments, or incomplete data [8]. Such values rarely represent exact quantities; they inherently contain uncertainty resulting from observation errors, limited knowledge, or variability of the analyzed phenomena. Representing these quantities as single deterministic numbers implicitly eliminates the associated uncertainty. Moreover, input variables are rarely used in their original form. In most practical models, they undergo nonlinear transformations describing preferences or system response, such as utility functions or exponential mappings. When uncertain quantities are replaced by deterministic values, these transformations operate only on a central estimate, ignoring the associated variability. Consequently, uncertainty is not confined to the input data itself but should also be properly propagated through the nonlinear transformations applied to it [1,7].

A wide range of approaches has been proposed to model uncertain quantities, including interval arithmetic [3], fuzzy numbers [5], and probabilistic representations [15]. These methods provide well-established mechanisms for handling basic algebraic operations. However, when nonlinear transformations are applied, operations such as exponentiation or general functional mappings may require α-cut approximations, sampling procedures, or defuzzification techniques, which either substantially increase computational cost, change the representation form, or lead to information loss [10,11].

Asymmetric Interval Numbers (AINs) were recently introduced [13] as a compact representation of uncertain quantities defined by a lower bound, an upper bound, and a representative value located inside the interval. Unlike the interval midpoint, the representative value is not constrained to the center of the interval and may reflect directional character of the uncertainty, such as a tendency toward one of the bounds [14]. AIN does not require knowledge of the underlying probability distribution of the modeled quantity. In practice, this distribution may be unknown, empirical, or difficult to estimate from limited information. Therefore, the arithmetic of AIN employs an auxiliary piecewise-uniform distribution defined on the subintervals determined by the interval bounds and the representative value. This construction does not imply that the actual distribution is uniform; rather, it serves as a computational tool for deriving the results of arithmetic operations, consistent with the available information [12,13].

Consequently, nonlinear transformations of an AIN can be evaluated by applying the Law of the Unconscious Statistician (LOTUS) to the auxiliary distribution [2], used purely as a derivation device for obtaining the representative value of the transformed quantity. This provides the theoretical basis for defining nonlinear operators for Asymmetric Interval Numbers [13]. Nevertheless, a limitation remains. Operators for expressions in which uncertainty appears in the exponent or in both operands, such as k^X and X^Y where X and Y are AINs, are currently unavailable. This limitation is significant because many practical models rely on exponential-type relationships, including utility functions and predictive systems. Without a treatment of these expressions, uncertainty cannot be propagated through such models using AINs.

To address this issue, this work introduces exponentiation operators for Asymmetric Interval Numbers covering both a real-valued base raised to an AIN exponent and exponentiation between two AINs. For the scalar-base case

k^X, the operator is obtained in closed form by applying LOTUS to the auxiliary distribution. For the two-operand case X^Y, the representative value is defined by a two-step LOTUS construction that evaluates the joint expectation under the product of auxiliary densities. In both cases, the results follow from the adopted construction rather than from heuristic transformation of interval bounds. As a result, nonlinear transformations can be performed while maintaining real-valued outcomes and interpretability.

The contributions of the paper are guided by the following research questions:

RQ1. Can the exponentiation of AINs be defined for expressions of the form k^X and X^Y, where X and Y are AINs?

RQ2. Does the resulting operator preserve the structural properties of the AIN representation under nonlinear transformation?

RQ3. How do the proposed operators compare with sampling-based uncertainty propagation in terms of accuracy and computational cost?

By addressing these questions, the paper extends AIN arithmetic to cover nonlinear exponential-type transformations, enabling direct application of AINs in decision and predictive models without requiring explicit distributional assumptions or simulation. This provides a practical mechanism for propagating uncertainty through nonlinear models while preserving the simplicity and interpretability of the AIN representation.

The remainder of the paper is organized as follows. Section 2 recalls the AIN representation and its auxiliary distribution. Section 3 introduces the proposed exponentiation operators, establishes their analytical properties, and provides illustrative examples. Section 4 presents the numerical validation and computational-efficiency analysis, including a comparison with Monte Carlo-based propagation. Section 5 concludes the paper and outlines directions for future work. .

2   Preliminaries

This section briefly recalls the fundamental properties of Asymmetric Interval Numbers required for the development of the exponentiation operator. The presentation follows the original formulation [13] and is restricted to results necessary for nonlinear transformations.

An Asymmetric Interval Number is defined as a triple

$$X = [a, b]_c,$$

where $a, b \in \mathbb{R}$, $a \leq b$, and $c \in (a, b)$ is a distinguished value internal to the interval, referred to as the representative value. The value c is not constrained to the midpoint of the interval; its position within $[a, b]$ reflects the asymmetry of the uncertainty, characterized by the distances $c - a$ and $b - c$ from the representative value to the respective bounds.

To define arithmetic operations, each AIN is equipped with an auxiliary piecewise-uniform density on $[a, b]$:

$$p_X(x) = \begin{cases} \alpha, & a \leq x < c, \\ \beta, & c \leq x \leq b, \\ 0, & \text{otherwise,} \end{cases}$$

where the parameters α and β are determined by two conditions: the normalization constraint

$$\int_a^b p_X(x)\, dx = 1$$

and the requirement that the expected value with respect to p_X coincides with the representative value

$$E(X) = \int_a^b x\, p_X(x)\, dx = c,$$

which yields

$$\alpha = \frac{b - c}{(b - a)(c - a)}, \qquad \beta = \frac{c - a}{(b - a)(b - c)}.$$

The above expressions require $c \in (a, b)$. The degenerate case $a = b$ corresponds to a crisp number with no uncertainty. The boundary cases $c = a$ or $c = b$ are excluded from the standard AIN definition, as they lead to a density concentrated entirely on one side of the interval.

This construction does not model the unknown distribution of the represented quantity. It provides a canonical computational device that enables evaluation of arithmetic operations on AINs.

For a measurable function $g : \mathbb{R} \to \mathbb{R}$, the representative value of the transformed AIN is obtained by applying the Law of the Unconscious Statistician to the auxiliary density:

$$E[g(X)] = \int_a^b g(x)\, p_X(x)\, dx.$$

If g is monotonic on $[a, b]$, the transformed AIN takes the form

$$g(X) = [\min(g(a), g(b)),\ \max(g(a), g(b))]_{E[g(X)]}.$$

The auxiliary distribution thus provides a systematic mechanism for defining nonlinear operators on AINs: the interval bounds are obtained from the range of g over $[a, b]$, while the representative value of the result is derived from the auxiliary construction. Formal properties of the resulting operators, including consistency with crisp arithmetic and location of the representative value within the transformed bounds, are established in Sect. 4.

3 Exponentiation of Asymmetric Interval Numbers

The preliminaries established that nonlinear transformations of a single AIN can be defined by applying LOTUS [2] to the auxiliary density: the interval bounds are obtained from the range of the transformation, and the representative value is derived from the auxiliary construction. We now use this mechanism to define exponentiation operators.

Two cases are considered:

$$k^X \quad \text{and} \quad X^Y,$$

where X and Y are AINs and $k > 0$ is a scalar. The first case involves a single AIN and admits a direct application of LOTUS. The second case involves two AINs and requires a compositional construction, which we define as a sequence of one-dimensional AIN operations.

3.1 Exponentiation with a Scalar Base

Let $X = [a, b]_c$ be an AIN and let p_X denote its auxiliary density with parameters α and β. For $k > 0$, $k \neq 1$, the function $g(x) = k^x$ is a monotonic transformation of a single variable. The representative value of the transformed AIN is therefore obtained directly by applying LOTUS:

$$E(k^X) = \int_a^b k^x\, p_X(x)\, dx.$$

Because the density is piecewise constant, the integral splits into two parts:

$$E(k^X) = \alpha \int_a^c k^x\, dx + \beta \int_c^b k^x\, dx.$$

Using the identity $\int k^x\, dx = k^x / \ln k$, we obtain a closed-form expression.

Lemma 1. *Let $X = [a, b]_c$ be an AIN and let $k > 0$, $k \neq 1$. Then*

$$E(k^X) = \frac{\alpha(k^c - k^a) + \beta(k^b - k^c)}{\ln k}.$$

Proof. Substituting the auxiliary density into the LOTUS integral and evaluating gives

$$\begin{aligned}
E(k^X) &= \alpha \int_a^c k^x\, dx + \beta \int_c^b k^x\, dx \\
&= \alpha\, \frac{k^c - k^a}{\ln k} + \beta\, \frac{k^b - k^c}{\ln k} \\
&= \frac{\alpha(k^c - k^a) + \beta(k^b - k^c)}{\ln k},
\end{aligned}$$

which proves the claim. $\square$

Proposition 1 (Scalar-base exponentiation). *Let $X = [a, b]_c$ be an AIN and let $k > 0$, $k \neq 1$. The exponentiation of k by X is defined as*

$$k^X = [\min(k^a, k^b),\ \max(k^a, k^b)]_{E(k^X)},$$

where the representative value is given by Lemma 1.

The bounds follow from the monotonicity of $x \mapsto k^x$ (increasing for $k > 1$, decreasing for $0 < k < 1$), while the representative value is obtained in closed form from the auxiliary density.

3.2   Exponentiation of Two AINs

We now consider the case $Z = X^Y$, where both the base and the exponent are AINs. Let

$$X = [a_X, b_X]_{c_X}, \quad Y = [a_Y, b_Y]_{c_Y}, \quad Z = [a_Z, b_Z]_{c_Z},$$

with $a_1 > 0$.

In contrast to the scalar-base case, the AIN framework does not define a joint auxiliary representation for a pair of quantities. To evaluate expressions involving two AINs, the construction is extended to the product space by combining the auxiliary densities of the two quantities. This extension does not introduce any independence assumption; it provides a canonical lifting of the AIN representation that adds no information beyond that contained in the individual operands. Under this assumption, the representative value is given by the double integral

$$c_Z = \iint_{[a_X, b_X] \times [a_Y, b_Y]} x^y\, p_X(x)\, p_Y(y)\, dx\, dy.$$

Since $x^y = e^{y \ln x}$ and $x \in [a_X, b_X]$ with $a_X > 0$, the function x^y is continuous on the compact rectangle $[a_X, b_X] \times [a_Y, b_Y]$ and therefore Lebesgue integrable. As the integrand is nonnegative, Tonelli's theorem [4] allows the double integral to be written as Lemma 1:

$$\mathcal{L}_Y[x^y] = \int_{a_Y}^{b_Y} x^y\, p_Y(y)\, dy = \frac{\alpha_Y(x^{c_Y} - x^{a_Y}) + \beta_Y(x^{b_Y} - x^{c_Y})}{\ln x}.$$

Applying the representative-value functional with respect to p_X then gives:

$$c_Z = \int_{a_X}^{b_X} \mathcal{L}_Y[x^y]\, p_X(x)\, dx = \alpha_X \int_{a_X}^{c_X} \mathcal{L}_Y[x^y]\, dx + \beta_X \int_{c_X}^{b_X} \mathcal{L}_Y[x^y]\, dx.$$

No closed form in elementary functions is available for the outer integral, as the antiderivative of $\frac{x^u}{\ln x}$ with respect to x is not expressible in elementary functions; the integral is therefore evaluated numerically.

Since x^y is continuous on the compact rectangle $[a_X, b_X] \times [a_Y, b_Y]$ with $a_X > 0$, the extrema exist by the Weierstrass theorem [9]. The interval bounds of X^Y are defined as:

$$a_Z = \min\{x^y : x \in [a_X, b_X],\ y \in [a_Y, b_Y]\},$$
$$b_Z = \max\{x^y : x \in [a_X, b_X],\ y \in [a_Y, b_Y]\}.$$

Lemma 2 (Corner attainment of bounds). *Let $a_X > 0$. Then*

$$a_Z = \min\{a_X^{a_Y}, a_X^{b_Y}, b_X^{a_Y}, b_X^{b_Y}\}, \qquad b_Z = \max\{a_X^{a_Y}, a_X^{b_Y}, b_X^{a_Y}, b_X^{b_Y}\}.$$

Proof. We first exclude interior critical points. For $f(x,y) = x^y = e^{y \ln x}$,

$$\partial_x f = y x^{y-1}, \qquad \partial_y f = x^y \ln x.$$

Both vanish simultaneously only at $(x,y) = (1,0)$, where $f(1,0) = 1$. This value is neither a global minimum nor a global maximum on the rectangle unless f is constant there (which can happen only in degenerate cases such as $a_X = b_X = 1$ or $a_Y = b_Y = 0$). Hence any global extremum must lie on the boundary of $[a_X, b_X] \times [a_Y, b_Y]$.

The boundary consists of four edges. On the left and right edges $x \in \{a_X, b_X\}$, the function $y \mapsto x^y = e^{y \ln x}$ has derivative $x^y \ln x$, which has constant sign on the entire interval $[a_Y, b_Y]$ for fixed $x \neq 1$, and therefore $y \mapsto x^y$ is monotone on this interval; for $x = 1$ the function equals the constant 1. In both cases the extrema over y are attained at $y \in \{a_Y, b_Y\}$. On the top and bottom edges $y \in \{a_Y, b_Y\}$, the function $x \mapsto x^y$ has derivative $y x^{y-1}$, which has constant sign on $[a_X, b_X]$ for fixed $y \neq 0$, hence $x \mapsto x^y$ is monotone on this interval; for $y = 0$ the function equals the constant 1. In both cases the extrema over x are attained at $x \in \{a_X, b_X\}$. Hence all global extrema are attained at the four corners $\{a_X, b_X\} \times \{a_Y, b_Y\}$, which completes the proof.

Definition 1 (Exponentiation of AINs). *Let $X = [a_X, b_X]_{c_X}$ and $Y = [a_Y, b_Y]_{c_Y}$ be AINs with $a_1 > 0$. The exponentiation of AINs is defined as*

$$Z = X^Y = [a_Z, b_Z]_{c_Z},$$

where a_Z and b_Z are defined above, and the representative value is

$$c_Z = \alpha_X \int_{a_X}^{c_X} \frac{\alpha_Y(x^{c_Y} - x^{a_Y}) + \beta_Y(x^{b_Y} - x^{c_Y})}{\ln x}\, dx$$
$$+ \beta_X \int_{c_X}^{b_X} \frac{\alpha_Y(x^{c_Y} - x^{a_Y}) + \beta_Y(x^{b_Y} - x^{c_Y})}{\ln x}\, dx.$$

Remark 1 (Numerical evaluation of representative value). Since $\mathcal{L}_Y[x^y]$ is smooth on $(a_X, b_X]$ for $a_X > 0$ and extends continuously to $x = 1$, the representative value c_Z can be evaluated numerically using standard quadrature rules.

Remark 2 (Removable Singularity of the Integrand at $a_X = 1$). When $a_X = 1$, the integrand in the representative value formula contains $\ln x$ in the denominator:

$$\frac{\alpha_Y(x^{c_Y} - x^{a_Y}) + \beta_Y(x^{b_Y} - x^{c_Y})}{\ln x}.$$

Since $\ln 1 = 0$, the point $x = 1$ is an apparent singularity of the integrand. To show that it is removable, we use the Taylor expansion $x^u = e^{u \ln x} = 1 + u \ln x + O(\ln^2 x)$ as $x \to 1$, which gives

$$\frac{x^u - x^v}{\ln x} = \frac{(u-v)\ln x + O(\ln^2 x)}{\ln x} \xrightarrow{x \to 1} u - v.$$

Equivalently, this expression admits the integral representation

$$\frac{x^u - x^v}{\ln x} = \int_v^u x^t \, dt,$$

which confirms both the existence of the limit as $x \to 1$ and the numerical stability of the limiting value $u - v$. Applying this limit to each term yields

$$\lim_{x \to 1} \frac{\alpha_Y(x^{c_Y} - x^{a_Y}) + \beta_Y(x^{b_Y} - x^{c_Y})}{\ln x} = \alpha_Y(c_Y - a_Y) + \beta_Y(b_Y - c_Y).$$

Since the limit is finite, the integrand admits a continuous extension to $x = 1$; after such an extension the function is bounded in a neighbourhood of that point and hence Riemann integrable on the entire interval $[a_X, b_X]$.

From a numerical standpoint, direct evaluation of $\frac{x^u - x^v}{\ln x}$ near $x = 1$ leads to catastrophic cancellation. In practice, whenever $|x - 1| < \varepsilon$ for a chosen tolerance $\varepsilon > 0$, the integrand should be replaced by its limiting value $\alpha_Y(c_Y - a_Y) + \beta_Y(b_Y - c_Y)$.

Remark 3 (Compositional operator as algebraic alternative). An alternative construction defines X^Y via the pointwise identity $x^y = \exp(y \ln x)$ as a composition of existing AIN operations:

$$X^Y_{\text{comp}} = \exp(Y \cdot \ln X),$$

where each step is evaluated sequentially via LOTUS applied to the respective auxiliary density. This operator is fully closed-form and evaluates in constant time. Its representative value may differ from c_Z, since sequential application of nonlinear transformations does not in general commute with expectation. In our numerical experiments the compositional operator consistently produced larger representative values than c_Z; whether this reflects a systematic bias depends on the configuration of X and Y and we do not claim it holds in general. The compositional operator may be preferred in applications requiring constant-time evaluation.

3.3   Scalar-Base Exponentiation k^X

Remark 4 (Degenerate case). The auxiliary density construction requires $a < c < b$ and is therefore undefined for a degenerate AIN $X = [x, x]_x$. The operator k^X is extended to this case by the convention

$$k^{[x,x]_x} = [k^x, k^x]_{k^x},$$

consistent with standard real arithmetic. This extension is also compatible with the limiting behavior of the general formula as $a, b \to x$.

Proposition 2 (Interval bounds). *Let $X = [a, b]_c$ be an AIN and let $k > 0$, $k \neq 1$. Then*

$$k^X = [\min(k^a, k^b), \ \max(k^a, k^b)]_{E(k^X)}.$$

Proof. The function $x \mapsto k^x$ is strictly increasing for $k > 1$ and strictly decreasing for $0 < k < 1$. It therefore maps $[a, b]$ onto $[k^a, k^b]$ or $[k^b, k^a]$, respectively. $\square$

Proposition 3 (Representative value lies within bounds). *Let $X = [a, b]_c$ be an AIN and let $k > 0$, $k \neq 1$. Then*

$$E(k^X) \in [\min(k^a, k^b), \ \max(k^a, k^b)].$$

Proof. The expectation of a bounded function lies in the convex hull of its range. Since $x \mapsto k^x$ is monotonic on $[a, b]$, its range is the interval $[\min(k^a, k^b), \max(k^a, k^b)]$, and the claim follows. $\square$

Proposition 4 (Jensen-type inequality). *Let $X = [a, b]_c$ be an AIN and let $k > 0$, $k \neq 1$. Then*

$$E(k^X) \geq k^c.$$

Proof. The function $x \mapsto k^x$ is convex for all $k > 0$, $k \neq 1$, since $\frac{d^2}{dx^2} k^x = (\ln k)^2 k^x > 0$. By construction of the auxiliary density, $E(X) = c$. Jensen's inequality applied to the probability measure p_X and the convex function $x \mapsto k^x$ yields $E(k^X) \geq k^{E(X)} = k^c$. $\square$

Proposition 5 (Asymmetry coefficient after scalar-base exponentiation). *Let $X = [a, b]_c$ be an AIN and let $k > 0$, $k \neq 1$. Define $Z = k^X$ with*

$$Z = [a_Z, b_Z]_{c_Z}, \quad \text{where} \quad a_Z = \min(k^a, k^b), \ b_Z = \max(k^a, k^b), \ c_Z = E(k^X).$$

Then the asymmetry coefficient of Z equals

$$A(Z) = \frac{a_Z + b_Z - 2c_Z}{b_Z - a_Z},$$

where c_Z is given by Lemma 1.

Proof. Substituting a_Z, b_Z, and c_Z into the definition of the AIN asymmetry coefficient $A = (a + b - 2c)/(b - a)$ yields the stated expression. The closed form for c_Z was established in Lemma 1. $\square$

3.4   Exponentiation of Two AINs X^Y

Proposition 6 (Domain condition and real-valuedness). *Let* $X = [a_X, b_X]_{c_X}$ *and* $Y = [a_Y, b_Y]_{c_Y}$ *be AINs with* $a_X > 0$. *Then* $Z = X^Y$ *as defined in Definition 1 produces a real-valued AIN with positive bounds and positive representative value.*

Proof. Since $a_X > 0$, we have $x > 0$ for all $x \in [a_X, b_X]$, hence $x^y > 0$ for all $y \in [a_Y, b_Y]$. Therefore $a_Z > 0$ and $b_Z > 0$.

For the representative value, write $\mathcal{L}_Y[x^y] = \int_{a_Y}^{b_Y} x^y \, p_Y(y) \, dy$. Since $x^y > 0$ for $x > 0$ and p_Y is a positive measure, the integrand is strictly positive, hence $\mathcal{L}_Y[x^y] > 0$ for all $x \in (a_X, b_X]$. The outer integral against the positive measure p_X is therefore strictly positive, giving $c_Z > 0$.   □

Proposition 7 (Consistency with scalar cases). *Let* $X = [a_X, b_X]_{c_X}$ *and* $Y = [a_Y, b_Y]_{c_Y}$ *be AINs with* $a_X > 0$.

1. *If* $Y = [n, n]_n$ *is degenerate, then* X^Y *coincides with scalar exponentiation* X^n.
2. *If* $X = [k, k]_k$ *is degenerate with* $k > 0$, $k \neq 1$, *then* $X^Y = k^Y$ *as defined in Proposition 1.*

Proof. For case 1, when Y is degenerate at n, the inner LOTUS transform reduces to evaluation at $y = n$:

$$\mathcal{L}_Y[x^y] = x^n.$$

The outer integral then gives $c_Z = \int_{a_X}^{b_X} x^n \, p_X(x) \, dx = E(X^n)$, and the bounds reduce to $\min(a_X^n, b_X^n)$ and $\max(a_X^n, b_X^n)$, recovering scalar exponentiation X^n.

For case 2, when X is degenerate at k, the outer integral reduces to evaluation at $x = k$:

$$c_{X^Y} = \mathcal{L}_Y[k^y] = \int_{a_Y}^{b_Y} k^y \, p_Y(y) \, dy = E(k^Y),$$

and the bounds reduce to $\min(k^{a_Y}, k^{b_Y})$ and $\max(k^{a_Y}, k^{b_Y})$, recovering k^Y.   □

Remark 5. The logarithmic identity $\ln(X^Y) = Y \cdot \ln X$, which holds by construction for the compositional operator $X_{\text{comp}}^Y = \exp(Y \cdot \ln X)$ (Remark 3), does not hold in general for the two-step LOTUS operator defined in Definition 1, except in degenerate or special cases such as those covered by Proposition 7. The algebraic identity is a property of the compositional structure, not of the two-step LOTUS integral.

Remark 6. The properties established in this section confirm that the proposed operators are consistent extensions of the existing AIN arithmetic. The degenerate-case convention and Proposition 7 verify reduction to standard real arithmetic and to the scalar-base operator in all applicable special cases. Proposition 6 guarantees that the result of X^Y is a valid AIN with positive bounds and positive representative value whenever $a_X > 0$.

3.5   Illustrative Examples

We present three examples illustrating the behavior of the proposed operators. Example 1 uses the closed-form expression of Lemma 1. Examples 2 and 3 use the two-step LOTUS construction of Definition 1, with the outer integral evaluated numerically.

Example 1: Asymmetry introduced by k^X. Let $X = [1,5]_3$ be a symmetric AIN and let $k = 2$. The auxiliary density parameters are $\alpha = \frac{5-3}{(5-1)(3-1)} = \frac{1}{4}$ and $\beta = \frac{3-1}{(5-1)(5-3)} = \frac{1}{4}$. From Lemma 1:

$$c_Z = \frac{\frac{1}{4}(2^3 - 2^1) + \frac{1}{4}(2^5 - 2^3)}{\ln 2} = \frac{\frac{1}{4}(6) + \frac{1}{4}(24)}{\ln 2} = \frac{7.5}{0.6931} \approx 10.82,$$

giving $k^X = [2, 32]_{10.82}$. The asymmetry coefficient of the result is

$$A(Z) = \frac{2 + 32 - 2 \cdot 10.82}{32 - 2} = \frac{12.36}{30} \approx 0.412.$$

Although the input AIN is symmetric ($c = 3$ is the midpoint of $[1,5]$), the output exhibits positive asymmetry: the representative value $c_Z \approx 10.82$ lies closer to the left bound of $[2, 32]$. This is consistent with the Jensen-type inequality (Proposition 4): $c_Z \approx 10.82 > k^c = 8$, reflecting the convexity of $x \mapsto 2^x$.

Example 2: Naive exponentiation vs. the proposed operator. Consider $X = [2,6]_3$ and $Y = [1,3]_2$. A naive approach, applying exponentiation separately to bounds and representative values, produces

$$X^Y_{\text{naive}} = [2^1, 6^3]_{3^2} = [2, 216]_9.$$

The proposed operator (Definition 1) gives bounds $a_Z = 2^1 = 2$ and $b_Z = 6^3 = 216$ (corner case, since $a_1 = 2 \geq 1$), and the representative value is obtained from the two-step LOTUS construction:

$$c_Z = \alpha_X \int_2^3 \mathcal{L}_Y[x^y]\, dx + \beta_X \int_3^6 \mathcal{L}_Y[x^y]\, dx \approx 13.18,$$

giving $X^Y \approx [2, 216]_{13.18}$.

Both approaches produce the same interval bounds, but the representative values differ substantially: 9 (naive) vs. 13.18 (proposed). The naive value $c_X^{c_Y} = 3^2 = 9$ underestimates the representative value because it ignores the nonlinear amplification introduced by exponentiation over the full uncertainty range of both operands. The proposed operator accounts for this effect through the joint auxiliary density structure and agrees with Monte Carlo estimation to within sampling error.

Example 3: Asymmetry propagation through X^Y. Let $X = [2,8]_6$ (negative asymmetry, $A(X) = -0.333$) and $Y = [1,3]_{1.5}$ (positive asymmetry, $A(Y) = 0.5$). The proposed operator yields

$$X^Y \approx [2, 512]_{c_Z}, \quad c_Z \approx 28.79, \quad A(X^Y) \approx 0.895.$$

For comparison, using the same X with a symmetric exponent $Y' = [1,3]_2$ $(A(Y') = 0)$ gives

$$X^{Y'} \approx [2,512]_{c_{Z'}}, \quad c_{Z'} \approx 66.65, \quad A(Z') \approx 0.746.$$

The interval bounds are identical in both cases, since they depend only on the endpoints. The representative values and asymmetry coefficients differ: Y has positive asymmetry, meaning its auxiliary mass is concentrated toward smaller values of y, which suppresses the representative value of X^Y relative to the symmetric case Y' and produces a higher asymmetry coefficient (0.895 vs. 0.746). This illustrates that the proposed operator is sensitive to the asymmetry of both operands, a property invisible to any method operating solely on interval endpoints.

4 Numerical Validation and Computational Efficiency

This section evaluates the proposed exponentiation operators by comparing the analytic representative values with reference values obtained from Monte Carlo (MC) sampling. For k^X, the comparison serves as a consistency check of the closed-form formula against its stochastic counterpart. For X^Y, it verifies that the two-step LOTUS construction agrees with MC numerical integration of the joint auxiliary density.

4.1 Experimental Setup

For a given AIN $X = [a,b]_c$, samples were drawn from the auxiliary piecewise-uniform density p_X by selecting one of the two subintervals $[a,c)$ or $[c,b]$ with probabilities proportional to their normalized masses $\alpha(c - a)$ and $\beta(b - c)$, which sum to 1 by construction, and then drawing uniformly within the selected subinterval. For two AINs X and Y, the Monte Carlo estimate was computed as

$$\hat{E}[g(X,Y)] = \frac{1}{N} \sum_{i=1}^{N} g(x_i, y_i),$$

where (x_i, y_i) are independent realizations drawn from the respective auxiliary densities, with N ranging from 10^3 to $3 \cdot 10^5$.

Monte Carlo sampling is used here only as a numerical integration technique applied to the auxiliary densities. All numerical experiments were implemented in Python (version 3.13) using the `asymintervals` library [12] for AIN arithmetic and NumPy [6] for random sampling. The two-step LOTUS integral for X^Y was evaluated using adaptive quadrature as implemented in `scipy.integrate.quad`.

Two cases were investigated. The first is scalar-base exponentiation k^X, for which Lemma 1 provides a closed-form expression. The second is exponentiation X^Y, for which the representative value is obtained from the two-step LOTUS construction in Definition 1.

4.2 Results for k^X

For the scalar-base case, the representative value is obtained from a single one-dimensional LOTUS integral evaluated in closed form (Lemma 1). The Monte Carlo estimate, computed by sampling from the same auxiliary density, provides a direct consistency check of the analytic formula. Table 1 presents results for selected AIN configurations and scalar bases.

Table 1. Scalar-base exponentiation k^X: analytic representative value vs. Monte Carlo estimate ($N = 10^5$).

a	b	c	k	Analytic	MC estimate
1	5	2	2	5.5303	5.5125
0	10	3	1.5	7.1051	7.0583
2	8	6	3	1824.1194	1817.8170

Across all tested configurations, the relative difference between the analytic value and the Monte Carlo estimate remained on the order of 10^{-4}–10^{-3}, consistent with sampling variability at $N = 10^5$. This confirms that the closed-form expression correctly evaluates the LOTUS integral associated with the auxiliary density.

4.3 Results for X^Y

For the two-operand case, the representative value c_Z is defined by the two-step LOTUS construction (Definition 1), which evaluates the integral

$$c_Z = \int_{a_X}^{b_X} \int_{a_Y}^{b_Y} x^y \, p_X(x) \, p_Y(y) \, dy \, dx$$

using the analytically available inner integral $\mathcal{L}_Y[x^y]$ and adaptive quadrature for the outer integral. The Monte Carlo estimate of the same integral therefore provides a direct consistency check. Table 2 reports results for selected AIN configurations.

Table 2. Exponentiation X^Y: two-step LOTUS representative value vs. Monte Carlo estimate ($N = 10^5$).

a_X	b_X	c_X	a_Y	b_Y	c_Y	Two-step LOTUS	MC estimate
2	5	3	1	3	2	12.36	12.34
1	4	1.5	0.5	2	1	1.56	1.57
3	7	6	1	2	1.2	9.67	9.67

Across all tested configurations, the two-step LOTUS value agreed with the Monte Carlo estimate to within sampling variability, confirming that Definition 1 correctly evaluates the integral under the product of auxiliary densities. The residual discrepancy is consistent with the combined effect of MC sampling variability and quadrature tolerance.

4.4   Computational Efficiency

The scalar-base operator k^X is evaluated using a closed-form expression involving a fixed computational cost independent of any sampling parameter. The two-step LOTUS operator for X^Y requires evaluation of a one-dimensional numerical integral; adaptive quadrature achieves the prescribed tolerance with substantially fewer function evaluations than Monte Carlo sampling, which requires $O(1/\varepsilon^2)$ samples to achieve root-mean-square error ε:

$$\mathrm{RMSE_{MC}} = O\!\left(\frac{1}{\sqrt{N}}\right).$$

Both proposed operators are therefore deterministic and reproducible, and substantially faster than sampling-based propagation at any prescribed accuracy level. This property is particularly relevant in decision and predictive models where uncertainty propagation must be performed repeatedly or in real time.

5   Conclusions

This paper extends the arithmetic of Asymmetric Interval Numbers by introducing exponentiation operators for expressions of the form k^X and X^Y. A closed-form operator was obtained for the scalar-base case k^X, while the two-operand case X^Y was defined through a two-step LOTUS construction based on the product of auxiliary densities. As a result, AIN arithmetic can now handle exponential-type nonlinear transformations under the domain condition $a_1 > 0$.

The proposed operators preserve the structure of the AIN representation. The resulting quantities remain real-valued AINs with positive bounds, the representative value retains its interpretation as an expectation with respect to the auxiliary distribution, and the operators reduce to standard arithmetic in degenerate cases. Numerical experiments confirmed agreement with Monte Carlo estimation within sampling variability, while the operators themselves remain deterministic and reproducible, with fixed computational cost.

The practical consequence of this extension is the ability to propagate uncertainty through models involving exponential relationships. This includes nonlinear utility functions, multiplicative production models such as Cobb–Douglas, and growth or decay processes. Previously, such models could be evaluated under uncertainty only via sampling-based simulation or by replacing uncertain inputs with point estimates. The proposed operators provide a deterministic alternative that preserves the structure of uncertainty throughout the computation.

Future work may consider extensions to additional classes of nonlinear transformations and the integration of the proposed arithmetic into decision-making and optimization frameworks. The presented results establish exponentiation as a well-defined operation in AIN arithmetic, enabling deterministic propagation of uncertainty in models involving exponential relationships.

Acknowledgments. The work was supported by the National Science Centre 2024/55/D/ST6/01627.

References

1. Boyd, S., Vandenberghe, L.: Convex Optimization. Cambridge University Press (2004)
2. Casella, G., Berger, R.: Statistical Inference. Chapman and Hall/CRC (2024)
3. Di Caprio, D., Santos-Arteaga, F.J.: Uncertain interval topsis and potentially regrettable decisions within ict evaluation environments. Appl. Soft Comput. **142**, 110301 (2023)
4. Evans, L.C.: Measure Theory and Fine Properties of Functions. Chapman and Hall/CRC (2025)
5. Gholamizadeh, K., Zarei, E., Omidvar, M., Yazdi, M.: Fuzzy sets theory and human reliability: Review, applications, and contributions. In: Linguistic Methods Under Fuzzy Information in System Safety and Reliability Analysis, pp. 91–137 (2022)
6. Harris, C.R., et al.: Array programming with NumPy. Nature **585**(7825), 357–362 (2020). https://doi.org/10.1038/s41586-020-2649-2
7. ISO., I., OIML, B.: Guide to the Expression of Uncertainty in Measurement. Aenor Madrid, Spain (1993)
8. Kovalerchuk, B., Kreinovich, V.: Concepts of solutions of uncertain equations with intervals, probabilities and fuzzy sets for applied tasks. Granular Comput. **2**(3), 121–130 (2017)
9. Martínez-Legaz, J.E.: On weierstrass extreme value theorem. Optim. Lett. **8**(1), 391–393 (2014)
10. Mukherjee, A.K., Gazi, K.H., Salahshour, S., Ghosh, A., Mondal, S.P.: A brief analysis and interpretation on arithmetic operations of fuzzy numbers. Results Control Optim. **13**, 100312 (2023)
11. Othman, F.H.: Comparative error analysis of the α-cut method and standard approximation method for division of trapezoidal and triangular fuzzy numbers. Int. J. Appl. Math. **38**(8s), 633–644 (2025)
12. Sałabun, W.: Asymintervals: a python library for uncertainty modeling with asymmetric interval numbers. SoftwareX **32**, 102380 (2025)
13. Sałabun, W.: Asymmetric interval numbers: a new approach to modeling uncertainty. Fuzzy Sets Syst. **499**, 109169 (2025)
14. Śniegowski, S., Świder, A., Shekhovtsov, A., Shekhovtsov, A., Sałabun, W.: Modeling uncertainty in engineering problems using asymmetric interval numbers (ains). In: Spectrum of Mechanical Engineering and Operational Research, pp. 1–14 (2026)
15. Wang, S., Wei, G., Lu, J., Wu, J., Wei, C., Chen, X.: Grp and critic method for probabilistic uncertain linguistic magdm and its application to site selection of hospital constructions. Soft. Comput. **26**(1), 237–251 (2022)

A Multi-scale Analysis of Learning Dynamics in Data-Driven MCDA: Evidence from the INCOME Method

Bartłomiej Kizielewicz[1,2](✉) [iD]

[1] National Institute of Telecommunications, Szachowa 1, 04-894 Warsaw, Poland
`b.kizielewicz@il-pib.pl`
[2] Research Team on Intelligent Decision Support Systems, Department of Artificial Intelligence and Applied Mathematics, Faculty of Computer Science and Information Technology, West Pomeranian University of Technology in Szczecin, ul. Żołnierska 49, 71-210 Szczecin, Poland

Abstract. The Intelligent Characteristic Objects Method (INCOME) replaces the expert-driven evaluation stage of the COMET method with a data-driven artificial expert based on k-Nearest Neighbours regression. Although previous studies demonstrate high agreement between INCOME and expert-based COMET, the data requirements and small-sample behaviour of the method remain systematically unexplored. This paper presents an empirical learning curve analysis of INCOME, examining how training set size affects ranking accuracy and stability as measured by the WS rank similarity coefficient. The results reveal a concave learning trajectory with rapid gains in the small-sample regime, followed by a practical saturation region beyond which additional data collection yields negligible improvement relative to its cost. A simple logarithmic approximation, adopted as a descriptive model motivated by classical learning curve literature, captures the overall trend and identifies an early diminishing-return point marking the transition from steep initial improvement to progressively decelerating gains. Furthermore, a hyperparameter sensitivity analysis demonstrates that non-monotonic variance patterns observed in the small-sample regime are attributable to suboptimal configuration rather than structural limitations of the method, and can be resolved through stability-constrained hyperparameter selection. These findings provide preliminary empirical evidence on INCOME's data requirements for the studied problem class and offer initial guidance for data collection planning and deployment readiness assessment in data-driven multi-criteria decision analysis.

Keywords: Multi-criteria decision analysis · Artificial expert · Learning curve analysis · Hyperparameter sensitivity · Ranking stability

1 Introduction

Expert judgment remains the basis of multi-criteria decision analysis (MCDA), but its scalability limitations are becoming increasingly apparent [1]. Methods such as Analytic Hierarchy Process (AHP) require decision-makers to perform pairwise comparisons between alternatives and criteria, a process that grows rapidly intractable as problem dimensionality increases [9]. These comparisons are conducted manually by domain experts, making the process both time-intensive and costly. One method that inherently relies on such pairwise evaluations is the Characteristic Objects METhod (COMET) [5]. The method constructs $t = c^n$ characteristic objects from the Cartesian product of c characteristic values across n criteria. Evaluating these objects requires an expert to perform $p = \frac{c^n(c^n-1)}{2}$ pairwise comparisons to construct the Matrix of Expert Judgment (MEJ), yielding a complexity of $\mathcal{O}(c^{2n})$ with respect to the number of criteria. Such exponential growth in the number of required comparisons renders exhaustive expert evaluation impractical as problem complexity increases, severely constraining COMET's real-world applicability despite its theoretical advantages.

To solve this problem, recent studies have proposed replacing human experts with artificial experts based on machine learning, trained on historical data on decisions made. The Intelligent Characteristic Objects MEthod (INCOME) constructs such an artificial expert using k-Nearest Neighbors regression, approximating expert preference functions directly from historical decision records [4]. Instead of engaging a domain expert to perform pairwise comparisons, this method predicts characteristic object evaluations from the k most similar historical cases, weighted by their distance in the criteria space. Initial validation demonstrates that INCOME achieves high rank correlation with expert-based COMET, reducing the expert evaluation burden from $\mathcal{O}(c^{2n})$ pairwise comparisons to a one-time computational training procedure.

While INCOME eliminates the expert evaluation bottleneck, it introduces a data dependency whose implications remain systematically unexplored in the literature. Existing studies show that INCOME produces rankings consistent with the expert-based COMET, but none of them provide a systematic characterization of the minimum training set size required for reliable implementation, the marginal utility of additional samples, or the stability of predictions in independent replications. This absence of empirical guidance creates a symmetric risk for practitioners: insufficient training data yields unstable and unreliable recommendations, while excessive data collection imposes unnecessary resource costs without commensurate improvement in model quality. Absent such guidance, deployment decisions are made without empirical grounding. This undermines reproducibility and, more broadly, the case for data-driven MCDA as a credible alternative to expert elicitation.

The study of how model performance scales with training set size has a well-established tradition in machine learning, typically framed as *learning curve analysis* [2, 6, 11]. Classical results characterise learning curves in terms of power-law or logarithmic decay of generalization error, and relate their shape to the bias-variance tradeoff of the underlying estimator. However, this literature focuses almost exclusively on predictive accuracy in supervised learning settings and does not address the specific requirements of MCDA, where the output of interest is a ranking rather than a point prediction, and where top-rank fidelity matters disproportionately. The present study adapts the learning curve framework to the MCDA context by using the WS rank similarity coefficient as the evaluation metric, thereby extending the classical analysis to a setting where performance is defined by ordinal agreement rather than numerical error.

This guidance gap becomes particularly pronounced in small-sample regimes, where the relationship between training set size and model behaviour exhibits unexpected characteristics. Specifically, empirical observations indicate a non-monotonic relationship between training set size and prediction stability, where incremental increases in training data can paradoxically yield higher variance in ranking outcomes, contradicting the standard statistical assumption that larger samples produce more stable estimates. Whether this instability reflects a fundamental limitation of the method or an artifact of suboptimal hyperparameter configuration, specifically the choice of k in the underlying k-Nearest Neighbors model, remains an open question with direct practical consequences. If such anomalies are attributable to misconfiguration rather than inherent method constraints, they can be mitigated through adaptive hyperparameter selection, potentially reducing data requirements without sacrificing ranking accuracy. Resolving this distinction is therefore essential both for establishing principled deployment criteria and for avoiding premature rejection of a viable methodology.

To address these gaps, this paper presents a systematic empirical investigation of INCOME's data requirements and small-sample behaviour, structured around three interconnected research questions:

(RQ1): How does training set size affect the accuracy and stability of INCOME rankings relative to a reference ranking, and at what point do marginal gains become negligible in practice?

(RQ2): How strong is the relationship between training set size and ranking accuracy in INCOME, and does the learning curve exhibit a saturation effect?

(RQ3): How does the choice of hyperparameter k affect the accuracy and stability of INCOME in small-sample regimes, and can adaptive k selection improve the consistency of results?

Together, these contributions establish an empirical framework for assessing data collection requirements in data-driven MCDA, characterising how training set size shapes ranking accuracy and stability across the full sample spectrum (RQ1), quantifying the strength and saturation behaviour of the learning curve to inform cost-effective data collection strategies (RQ2), and determining whether apparent small-sample instabilities reflect fundamental constraints of the method or correctable hyperparameter configuration choices (RQ3).

The remainder of this paper is organised as follows. Section 2 introduces the INCOME method and the WS ranking similarity coefficient used throughout the study. Section 3 describes the dataset, experimental protocol, evaluation metrics, and hyperparameter sensitivity design. Section 4 presents the empirical results structured around the three research questions. Section 5 interprets the findings, discusses practical implications, and identifies limitations. Section 6 summarises the contributions and outlines future research directions.

2   Methodology

2.1   The INCOME Method

The Characteristic Objects Method (COMET) [3] constructs a continuous preference model through five steps: defining characteristic values for each criterion, generating characteristic objects (COs) from their Cartesian product, obtaining a preference ordering of COs through exhaustive pairwise comparison by a domain expert, building a fuzzy rule base, and interpolating preferences for arbitrary alternatives via Mamdani fuzzy inference. A key structural property of COMET is its complete resistance to the rank reversal paradox, as each alternative is evaluated independently against a fixed rule base [5]. However, the method requires an expert to perform $p = t(t-1)/2$ pairwise comparisons over $t = \prod_{i=1}^{n} c_i$ characteristic objects, where c_i is the number of characteristic values for criterion i, yielding an overall complexity of $O(c^{2n})$ with respect to the number of criteria. For the configuration used in this study ($n = 4$, $c_i \in \{5, 5, 6, 5\}$, $t = 750$), this amounts to 281,625 pairwise comparisons, a volume that renders manual expert evaluation impractical.

The INtelligent Characteristic Objects METhod (INCOME) [4] addresses this bottleneck by replacing the human expert with a k-Nearest Neighbours (kNN) regression model trained on historically evaluated decision records. Given a training set $D = \{(\mathbf{x}_i, y_i)\}_{i=1}^{m}$, where $\mathbf{x}_i \in \mathbb{R}^n$ is a vector of criterion values and $y_i \in \mathbb{R}$ is the associated decision outcome, the kNN model predicts the value of any query point $\mathbf{x}'$ as the distance-weighted average of its k nearest neighbours in the criteria space:

$$\hat{y}(\mathbf{x}') = \frac{1}{k} \sum_{(\mathbf{x}_i, y_i) \in D_{\mathbf{x}'}} w_i \cdot y_i, \tag{1}$$

where $D_{\mathbf{x}'}$ denotes the set of k training instances closest to $\mathbf{x}'$ under the Chebyshev distance, and $w_i = 1 - d_i / \sum_{j=1}^{k} d_j$ is the normalized inverse-distance weight for the i-th neighbour at distance d_i. The Chebyshev distance was adopted from the original INCOME formulation [4], where it was established as the default metric for the kNN artificial expert.

To construct the Matrix of Expert Judgment (MEJ) in INCOME, each pair of characteristic objects CO_i and CO_j is evaluated through the trained kNN model. The comparison outcome is determined as:

$$\alpha_{ij} = \begin{cases} 0.0, & \text{if } \hat{y}(CO_i) < \hat{y}(CO_j), \\ 0.5, & \text{if } \hat{y}(CO_i) = \hat{y}(CO_j), \\ 1.0, & \text{if } \hat{y}(CO_i) > \hat{y}(CO_j). \end{cases} \tag{2}$$

The summed judgments $SJ_i = \sum_{j=1}^{t} \alpha_{ij}$ yield preference values for each CO, and the resulting rule base supports Mamdani inference for ranking arbitrary alternatives, exactly as in the standard COMET procedure. The critical advantage is that the $O(c^{2n})$ expert comparisons are replaced by a one-time computational procedure whose quality depends on the size and representativeness of the training set D rather than on expert availability. This dependency, however, raises the question of how much training data is necessary to produce reliable rankings, which constitutes the central focus of this paper.

2.2 Ranking Similarity Evaluation

Ranking accuracy is measured using the WS rank similarity coefficient [7], selected for its top-rank sensitivity: discrepancies at the top of a ranking receive exponentially higher penalties than those at the bottom, which aligns with the practical importance of correctly identifying the best-performing alternatives in MCDA applications. For two rankings $\mathbf{x}$ and $\mathbf{y}$ of N alternatives, the WS coefficient is defined as:

$$WS(\mathbf{x}, \mathbf{y}) = 1 - \sum_{i=1}^{N} \left(2^{-x_i} \cdot \frac{|x_i - y_i|}{\max(|x_i - 1|,\ |x_i - N|)} \right), \tag{3}$$

where x_i and y_i denote the ranks of the i-th alternative in the reference and predicted rankings, respectively. The coefficient is asymmetric by design: the first argument serves as the reference ranking, with the exponential weighting scheme ensuring that top-rank errors carry disproportionate penalties. A detailed formal analysis of this asymmetry and its decision-making motivation is provided in [7,8]. WS takes values in $(0, 1]$, where $WS = 1$ indicates identical rankings.

3 Experimental Setup

3.1 Dataset and Decision Problem

The empirical investigation uses the *Combined Cycle Power Plant* dataset [10], publicly available from the UCI Machine Learning Repository. The dataset comprises $N = 9{,}568$ operational records of a combined cycle power plant, each describing a full-load state of the plant. It is continuous, real-valued, and moderately sized, with naturally occurring measurement noise, making it suitable for analysing ranking stability under subsampling.

Four physical measurements serve as decision criteria: ambient temperature C_1 [° C], relative humidity C_2 [%], ambient pressure C_3 [mbar], and exhaust vacuum C_4 [cm Hg], with their characteristic values listed in Table 1. The target variable is net hourly electrical output P [MW]. Higher output corresponds to a more favourable plant state, so the reference ranking is constructed in descending order of P, with rank 1 assigned to the highest-output alternative. This ranking serves as the ground truth against which all INCOME predictions are evaluated. The characteristic values yield $t = 750$ Characteristic Objects in the COMET structure.

Table 1. Decision criteria and characteristic values used in the COMET structure.

C_i	Name	Unit	Characteristic values
C_1	Ambient temperature	[°C]	$\{1, 14, 18, 25, 40\}$
C_2	Relative humidity	[%]	$\{25, 40, 54, 68, 82\}$
C_3	Ambient pressure	[mbar]	$\{992, 1003, 1011, 1019, 1026, 1035\}$
C_4	Exhaust vacuum	[cm Hg]	$\{25, 60, 80, 95, 101\}$

3.2 Experimental Protocol

The dataset is partitioned once into a fixed training pool and a fixed test set using an 80/20 random split (random seed 42), yielding 7,654 training candidates and 1,914 test instances. A fixed test set is used to isolate the effect of training subset variability from data partition variability, as repeated splits would conflate two distinct sources of instability. No feature normalization was applied: as all criteria represent physically meaningful measurements with comparable operational relevance, no artificial rescaling was introduced, and the raw criterion ranges reflect the natural operating envelope of the power plant, preserving the physical interpretation of neighbourhood structure under the Chebyshev distance metric.

For each training set size $m \in \mathcal{M} = \{50, 100, 200, 500, 1000, 2000, 5000\}$, we perform $n = 30$ independent replications. In each replication r, a random subset of m instances is drawn without replacement from the training pool. An INCOME model is then fitted on this subset using the kNN artificial expert with Chebyshev distance and $k = 15$ neighbors, following the configuration established in the original INCOME study [4]. The fitted model is evaluated on the fixed test set, producing a predicted ranking $\mathbf{r}_r(m)$. The value $n = 30$ was selected as a standard compromise between statistical reliability and computational feasibility.

3.3 Evaluation Metrics

Formally, for n replications (with $n = 30$ in this study) at training set size m, the mean accuracy is:

$$\overline{WS}(m) = \frac{1}{n} \sum_{r=1}^{n} WS_r(m) \tag{4}$$

and the inter-replication standard deviation is:

$$\sigma(m) = \sqrt{\frac{1}{n-1} \sum_{r=1}^{n} \left(WS_r(m) - \overline{WS}(m) \right)^2} \tag{5}$$

The standard deviation $\sigma(m)$ specifically measures sensitivity to training subset selection: a large value indicates that model quality varies substantially depending on which m instances are drawn, constituting a practical reliability risk independent of mean accuracy.

Internal consistency is measured as the mean pairwise WS coefficient across all $\binom{n}{2} = 435$ replication pairs:

$$WS_{\text{internal}}(m) = \frac{2}{n(n-1)} \sum_{r<s} WS\big(\mathbf{r}_r(m), \mathbf{r}_s(m)\big) \tag{6}$$

This metric captures mutual agreement among independent model instances trained on different subsets of the same size, independently of the reference ranking.

3.4 Hyperparameter Sensitivity Protocol

The main study addresses RQ1 and RQ2 under fixed $k = 15$. Preliminary analysis revealed a non-monotonic variance pattern between $m = 50$ and $m = 100$, contradicting the standard expectation that larger samples yield more stable estimates. RQ3 tests whether this instability is a structural limitation of INCOME or an artefact of suboptimal hyperparameter configuration.

To this end, a grid search over $k \in \{3, 5, 10, 15, 20, 30, 40\}$ is conducted for the small-sample regime $m \in \{50, 100, 200\}$, as hyperparameter sensitivity is theoretically most pronounced where training data are scarce: with fixed k, the ratio k/m varies dramatically across sample sizes, creating fundamentally different local neighbourhood structures. For larger sample sizes ($m \geq 500$), the marginal influence of k diminishes as the neighbourhood becomes increasingly representative of the underlying decision function.

Each of the $7 \times 3 = 21$ configurations is evaluated over $n = 30$ independent replications. The optimal k for each m is defined as the value minimising $\sigma(m, k)$, subject to the constraint that $\overline{WS}(m, k)$ does not decrease below the baseline mean WS established at $k = 15$ under identical replication settings. This constraint prevents trivial stability gains obtained by choosing overly smooth neighbourhoods that reduce variance at the expense of ranking accuracy.

4 Experiments and Results

To demonstrate how training set size shapes the behaviour of INCOME, this section presents the empirical results structured around the three research questions. We begin by examining the learning curve and identifying the practical saturation boundary (Sect. 4.1), then quantify the global effect size and derive an early diminishing-return threshold (Sect. 4.2), and finally investigate whether the instabilities observed under fixed hyperparameters can be attributed to correctable configuration choices (Sect. 4.3).

4.1 Effect of Training Set Size

We first examine how ranking accuracy and stability evolve as the training set grows from $m = 50$ to $m = 5{,}000$. Figure 1 presents both the mean WS coefficient and the inter-replication standard deviation as a function of m. As expected, ranking accuracy improves rapidly in the small-sample regime: $\overline{WS}$ rises from 0.738 at $m = 50$ to 0.958 at $m = 500$. Beyond this point, the curve enters a plateau where further gains become incremental, reaching 0.970 at $m = 1{,}000$ and 0.989 at $m = 5{,}000$. Stability, measured by σ, follows a broadly complementary trajectory, decreasing from 0.077 at $m = 50$ to 0.002 at $m = 5{,}000$.

An unexpected pattern emerges at $m = 100$, where the standard deviation ($\sigma = 0.081$) actually exceeds the value observed at $m = 50$, contradicting the intuitive expectation that more data should yield more stable predictions. This anomaly persists across all 30 replications and is investigated in detail in Sect. 4.3, where we show that it is attributable to suboptimal hyperparameter configuration rather than a structural limitation of the method. It is worth noting that internal consistency ($\overline{WS}_{\text{int}}$, Eq. 6) remains at or above 0.979 for all m, indicating that independent model instances agree well with each other regardless of their absolute accuracy.

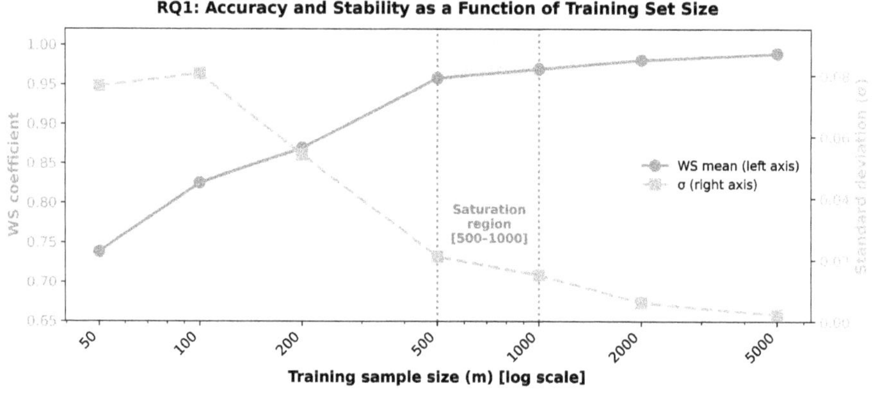

Fig. 1. Ranking accuracy and stability as a function of training set size ($k = 15$, $n = 30$ replications).

To better understand where additional data collection ceases to be cost-effective, Table 2 quantifies the per-transition accuracy gain and the efficiency-normalized return on investment. The highest per-sample return occurs in the first transition ($m = 50 \rightarrow 100$, $\text{ROI}_{WS} = 0.174$), and returns remain above the negligibility threshold $\tau = 0.01$ through $m = 200 \rightarrow 500$ ($\text{ROI}_{WS} = 0.030$). However, at the transition from $m = 500$ to $m = 1{,}000$, the ROI drops sharply to 0.002, falling well below τ. Stability ROI converges to the same region: all transitions beyond $m = 500$ yield $\text{ROI}_{\sigma} < \tau$. The coincidence of both indicators identifies the saturation region $m \in [500, 1{,}000]$ as the practical boundary beyond which additional data collection produces negligible improvement relative to its cost.

To obtain a continuous approximation of the observed trend, we fit a simple logarithmic model of the form $\overline{WS}(m) = \alpha + \beta \ln(m)$ to the seven empirical

Table 2. Marginal accuracy and stability changes with efficiency-normalized ROI per 100 additional samples.

Transition	$\Delta \overline{WS}$	ROI_{WS}	$\Delta\sigma$	ROI_σ
$50 \rightarrow 100$	+0.0871	+0.1742	+0.0041	−0.0082
$100 \rightarrow 200$	+0.0442	+0.0442	−0.0265	+0.0265
$200 \rightarrow 500$	+0.0887	+0.0296	−0.0330	+0.0110
$500 \rightarrow 1,000$	+0.0115	+0.0023	−0.0061	+0.0012
$1,000 \rightarrow 2,000$	+0.0114	+0.0011	−0.0090	+0.0009
$2,000 \rightarrow 5,000$	+0.0081	+0.0003	−0.0040	+0.0001

means. This functional form is motivated by classical learning curve literature; for kNN regression, Stone's theorem implies an error decay of $O\!\left(m^{-\frac{2}{d+2}}\right)$, which in the present four-dimensional setting yields an exponent of approximately $-\frac{1}{3}$, qualitatively consistent with the slow concave improvement the logarithm captures. The fit yields $\alpha = 0.571$, $\beta = 0.054$, and $R^2 = 0.870$. While this value indicates a reasonable approximation, it also suggests that the logarithmic form does not fully capture all features of the data. The residual variance can be attributed to two factors: the σ anomaly at $m = 100$ and a slight departure from log-linearity in the high-sample regime ($m \geq 2,000$), where empirical values lie marginally above the prediction.

4.2 Global Effect Size and Early Diminishing Returns

The previous subsection characterised the learning curve through pairwise transitions. Here, we complement that analysis by quantifying the overall strength of the training-size effect and deriving an analytical characterisation of when learning gains begin to decelerate.

A one-way ANOVA across the seven training set sizes confirms that the effect of m on ranking accuracy is statistically significant, with $F(6, 203) = 117.07$ ($p = 3.95 \times 10^{-63}$). The associated effect size $\eta^2 = 0.776$ (Table 3) indicates that approximately 78% of the total variance in WS scores is attributable to differences in training set size, constituting a very large effect by conventional benchmarks. The remaining variance reflects the stochastic variability introduced by random subset selection within each size condition.

Table 3. Quantitative summary of the global effect size, model fit, and early diminishing-return point.

	η^2	R^2	m^*_{early}
Value	0.7758	0.8704	≈51

The logarithmic approximation introduced in Sect. 4.1 ($R^2 = 0.870$, Fig. 2) provides a simple continuous description of the learning curve:

$$\overline{WS}(m) = \alpha + \beta \ln(m),$$

with $\beta = 0.054$. The instantaneous marginal gain implied by this model is given by

$$\frac{d\overline{WS}}{dm} = \frac{\beta}{m}.$$

Rather than imposing an arbitrary fixed threshold, we define an *early diminishing-return point* as the smallest training size m for which the marginal gain falls below a small fraction of the empirically observed inter-replication variability. Specifically, saturation is defined by

$$\frac{\beta}{m} < \alpha_\sigma \cdot \mathrm{median}(\sigma(m)),$$

where $\sigma(m)$ denotes the inter-replication standard deviation and $\alpha_\sigma = 0.05$. Using the empirical median $\mathrm{median}(\sigma(m)) = 0.021$, this criterion yields $m^*_{\mathrm{early}} \approx 51$. At this point, the instantaneous learning gain becomes smaller than 5% of typical stochastic variability induced by random training subset selection, marking the end of the steep initial learning regime, as illustrated in Fig. 2.

Importantly, this derivative-based threshold captures the transition from rapid improvement to gradually diminishing returns, but should not be interpreted as a practical deployment boundary. In contrast, the ROI-based saturation region $m \in [500, 1{,}000]$ identified in RQ1 reflects a cost-sensitive notion of practical saturation, where additional data collection yields negligible improvement relative to its cost. Together, these perspectives provide a multi-scale characterisation of INCOME's learning dynamics: an early reduction in marginal gains (around $m \approx 50$) followed by a later practical stabilisation region (around $m \geq 500$).

4.3   Hyperparameter Sensitivity in Small-Sample Regimes

The preceding analyses revealed two noteworthy patterns under fixed $k = 15$: the non-monotonic σ anomaly at $m = 100$ and substantial variance at small sample sizes more generally. A natural question arises: are these instabilities inherent to the INCOME method, or can they be mitigated through better hyperparameter selection? To answer this, we conduct a grid search over $k \in \{3, 5, 10, 15, 20, 30, 40\}$ for each small-sample size.

Figure 3 reveals that the sensitivity profiles differ qualitatively across the three regimes, which is particularly informative. For $m = 200$, σ is minimised at small k values ($k = 5$) and increases gradually with neighbourhood size, as one might expect. For $m = 50$, the curve is comparatively flat in the range $k \in [5, 15]$ but rises sharply for $k \geq 30$, reflecting oversmoothing when the neighbourhood encompasses a large fraction of the training set. The most striking pattern emerges at $m = 100$: here, σ attains its minimum at $k = 3$, rises to a peak

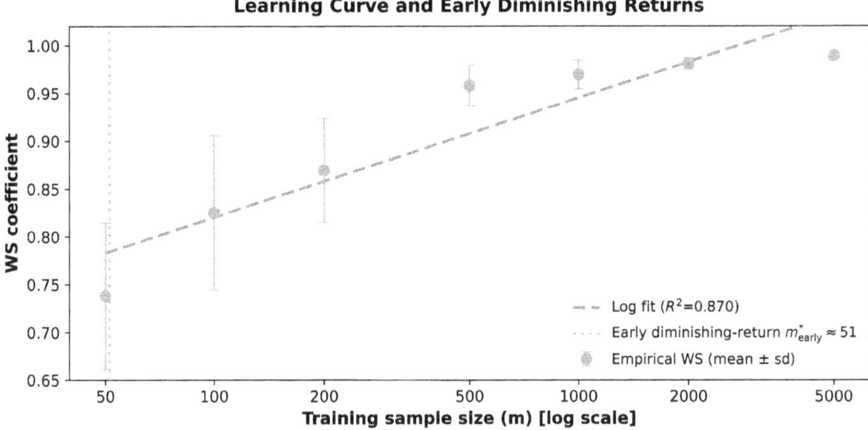

Fig. 2. Logarithmic learning curve fit with derivative-based early diminishing-return point $m^*_{early} \approx 51$.

at $k = 10$, and decreases monotonically thereafter, yet remains substantially above the optimum across the entire evaluated range $k \geq 10$. Consequently, the baseline configuration $k = 15$ falls well above the stability optimum for this specific sample size, explaining the anomaly observed in Sect. 4.1. These divergent profiles confirm that a fixed k cannot be uniformly optimal across training set sizes and that the interaction between k and m is non-trivial.

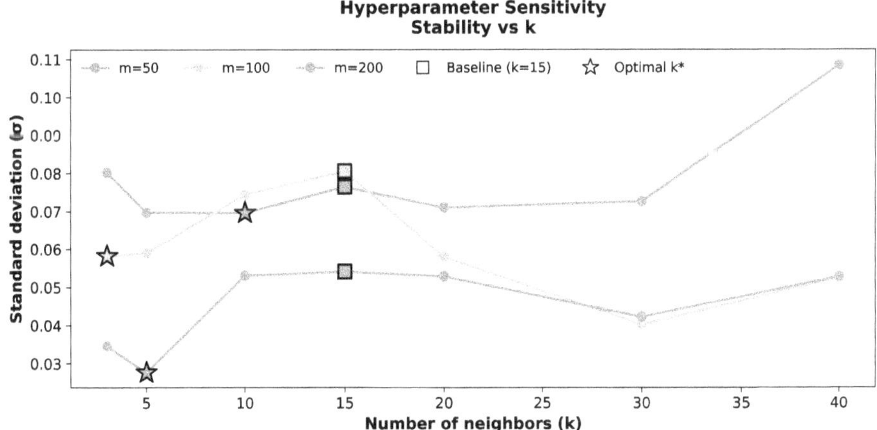

Fig. 3. Inter-replication standard deviation as a function of k for the small-sample regime.

Having established that the sensitivity profiles are qualitatively different, we now identify the optimal k for each sample size. Table 4 compares the baseline

($k = 15$) with the stability-constrained optimal k^*. The optimal values ($k^* = 10$ for $m = 50$, $k^* = 3$ for $m = 100$, and $k^* = 5$ for $m = 200$) correspond to k^*/m ratios of 20%, 3%, and 2.5%, respectively. In all three cases, selecting k^* simultaneously improves both accuracy and stability relative to the baseline, as illustrated in Figs. 4 and 5.

Table 4. Baseline ($k = 15$) versus stability-constrained optimal k^* in the small-sample regime.

m	k_{fixed}	k^*	$\overline{WS}_{\text{fixed}}$	$\overline{WS}_{\text{opt}}$	σ_{fixed}	σ_{opt}
50	15	10	0.7381	0.7787	0.0765	0.0696
100	15	3	0.8252	0.9190	0.0806	0.0582
200	15	5	0.8694	0.9434	0.0541	0.0276

The case of $m = 100$ is especially interesting: accuracy increases by $+0.094$ (from 0.825 to 0.919) and σ decreases by 28% (from 0.081 to 0.058) simply by changing k from 15 to 3, without collecting any additional training data. At $m = 200$, the stability improvement is even more pronounced, reaching 49% (σ drops from 0.054 to 0.028). At $m = 50$, the improvements are more modest ($+0.041$ in accuracy, 9% in σ), which is consistent with the fundamental information constraint at very small sample sizes, where there is simply too little data for any configuration to perform reliably.

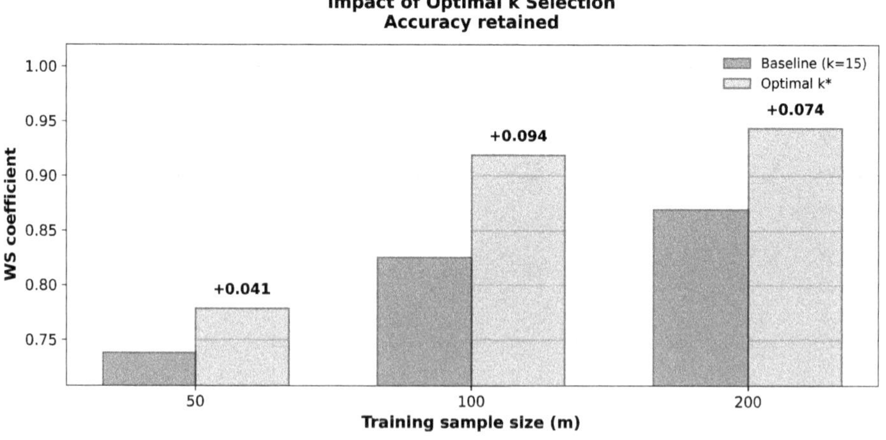

Fig. 4. Accuracy improvement under optimal k^* selection relative to the fixed baseline.

Crucially, the non-monotonic variance pattern from Sect. 4.1, where $\sigma(m = 100) > \sigma(m = 50)$ under fixed $k = 15$, is fully resolved under optimal k^* selection. With $k^* = 3$ at $m = 100$, the standard deviation drops to 0.058, which is

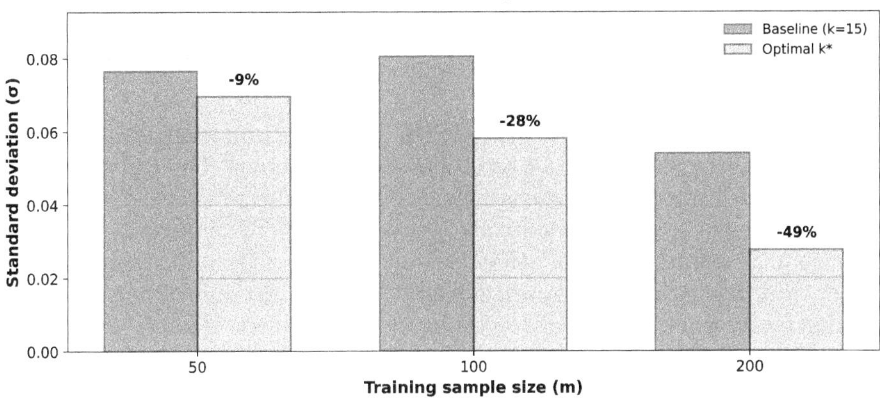

Fig. 5. Stability improvement under optimal k^* selection relative to the fixed baseline.

now below $\sigma_{\mathrm{opt}} = 0.070$ at $m = 50$, restoring the expected monotonic relationship between sample size and prediction stability.

This finding has an important practical implication: the instabilities observed in Sect. 4.1 are not inherent to the INCOME method but rather an artefact of hyperparameter misconfiguration. When combined with the derivative-based early diminishing-return point from Sect. 4.2 ($m^*_{\mathrm{early}} \approx 50$), the results paint a coherent picture: the steep initial learning phase is both hyperparameter-sensitive and structurally transient. Beyond this regime, model behaviour becomes progressively more stable, ultimately reaching the practical saturation region identified in Sect. 4.1 ($m \geq 500$).

5 Discussion

For practitioners, these findings suggest a concrete data collection strategy: 200 records suffice to exit the hyperparameter-sensitive regime, while approximately 500 records yield deployment-ready accuracy ($WS > 0.95$). Below this threshold, adaptive k-selection can partially compensate for data scarcity, and at $m = 100$ switching from $k = 15$ to $k = 3$ improved WS by 0.094 without collecting any additional data. Although the present analysis relies on the WS coefficient, the qualitative learning curve shape is expected to be robust to metric choice; rank-uniform measures such as Spearman's ρ may shift precise thresholds but should preserve the concave trajectory.

The observed concave learning trajectory is qualitatively consistent with classical characterisations of learning curves for non-parametric estimators [6, 11]. The logarithmic model adopted here provides a reasonable descriptive fit ($R^2 = 0.870$), although other functional forms (such as power-law or exponential saturation models) could potentially yield a closer approximation. The present setting also differs from standard supervised learning benchmarks in that performance is defined by ordinal agreement rather than numerical error, and the top-rank sensitivity of the WS coefficient amplifies the practical consequences of small improvements in the high-sample regime. This motivates the distinction between the derivative-based early saturation point and the later ROI-based saturation region.

Several limitations should be noted. The study relies on a single dataset with four continuous criteria and a monotonic target function. The generalizability of the identified thresholds and saturation behaviour to problems with discrete or mixed criteria, higher dimensionality, or non-monotonic preference structures remains to be established. The reference ranking derives from the target variable rather than expert judgments, which may understate the difficulty of real-world ranking tasks. Sensitivity to metric choice (e.g., Euclidean, Manhattan) remains an open empirical question, and the operational thresholds ($\tau = 0.01$, $\alpha\sigma = 0.05$) are empirically motivated. Finally, the use of a single regressor (kNN) leaves open whether the observed learning curve characteristics generalize to other artificial expert implementations. Although different threshold values would shift exact numerical boundaries, the qualitative pattern of early structural deceleration followed by later practical stabilisation remains robust.

6   Conclusion

This paper presented a systematic empirical investigation of the data requirements and small-sample behaviour of the INCOME method. The learning curve analysis revealed that ranking accuracy follows a concave trajectory, well approximated by a simple logarithmic model, with training set size explaining approximately 78% of the variance in ranking quality. Two complementary saturation thresholds were identified: a derivative-based early diminishing-return point at approximately $m^*_{\text{early}} \approx 51$, marking the end of the steep initial learning regime, and a cost-sensitive practical saturation region at $m \in [500, 1{,}000]$, beyond which marginal gains in both accuracy and stability become negligible. For the specific dataset and configuration studied, INCOME can produce reliable rankings ($\overline{WS} > 0.95$) with roughly 500 training instances.

The hyperparameter sensitivity analysis further demonstrated that the non-monotonic variance anomaly observed in the small-sample regime is an artefact of fixed-k configuration rather than an inherent methodological limitation. Stability-constrained k selection simultaneously improved accuracy and reduced variance without requiring additional training data, confirming that adaptive hyperparameter tuning is essential in data-scarce settings. The extent to which these findings, particularly the identified saturation thresholds and the effectiveness of adaptive configuration, generalize to higher-dimensional problems, alternative distance metrics, and expert-derived reference rankings remains an important direction for future research.

Disclosure of Interests. The authors have no competing interests to declare that are relevant to the content of this article.

References

1. Ferretti, V., Montibeller, G.: Key challenges and meta-choices in designing and applying multi-criteria spatial decision support systems. Decis. Support Syst. **84**, 41–52 (2016)
2. Figueroa, R.L., Zeng-Treitler, Q., Kandula, S., Ngo, L.H.: Predicting sample size required for classification performance. BMC Med. Inform. Decis. Mak. **12**(1), 8 (2012)
3. Habeeb, R., Hussain, I., Al-Ansari, N., Sammen, S.S.: A proposed comparative algorithm for regional crop yield assessment: an application of characteristic objects method. Math. Probl. Eng. **2022**(1), 8224953 (2022)
4. Kizielewicz, B., Shekhovtsov, A., Więckowski, J., Wątróbski, J., Sałabun, W.: Intelligent characteristic objects method (income): a data knowledge-based multi-criteria decision analysis. Artif. Intell. Rev. **57**(10), 266 (2024)
5. Paradowski, B., Olender, P., Sałabun, W.: A comparative study on the efficiency of the modified comet in decision-making. Procedia Comput. Sci. **246**, 103–112 (2024)
6. Perlich, C., Provost, F., Simonoff, J.S.: Tree induction vs. logistic regression: a learning-curve analysis. J. Mach. Learn. Res. **4**, 211–255 (2003)
7. Sałabun, W., Urbaniak, K.: A new coefficient of rankings similarity in decision-making problems. In: Krzhizhanovskaya, V.V., et al. (eds.) ICCS 2020. LNCS, vol. 12138, pp. 632–645. Springer, Cham (2020). https://doi.org/10.1007/978-3-030-50417-5_47
8. Shekhovtsov, A.: How strongly do rank similarity coefficients differ used in decision making problems? Procedia Comput. Sci. **192**, 4570–4577 (2021)
9. Tavana, M., Soltanifar, M., Santos-Arteaga, F.J.: Analytical hierarchy process: revolution and evolution. Ann. Oper. Res. **326**(2), 879–907 (2023)
10. Tüfekci, P.: Prediction of full load electrical power output of a base load operated combined cycle power plant using machine learning methods. Int. J. Electr. Power Energy Syst. **60**, 126–140 (2014)
11. Viering, T., Loog, M.: The shape of learning curves: a review. IEEE Trans. Pattern Anal. Mach. Intell. **45**(6), 7799–7819 (2022)

Does the Evaluation Horizon Matter? A Temporal Extension of SPOTIS for Normalization-Bound Sensitivity Analysis

Bartłomiej Kizielewicz[1,2]([envelope]) [ID] and Jarosław Wątróbski[3] [ID]

[1] National Institute of Telecommunications, Szachowa 1, 04-894 Warsaw, Poland
b.kizielewicz@il-pib.pl
[2] Research Team on Intelligent Decision Support Systems, Department of Artificial Intelligence and Applied Mathematics, Faculty of Computer Science and Information Technology, West Pomeranian University of Technology in Szczecin, ul. Żołnierska 49, 71-210 Szczecin, Poland
[3] Institute of Management, University of Szczecin, ul. Cukrowa 8, 71-004 Szczecin, Poland
jaroslaw.watrobski@usz.edu.pl

Abstract. In multi-criteria decision analysis (MCDA), normalization bounds are typically derived from a single observation period and treated as fixed. When additional temporal data become available, the observed range of criterion values may expand, altering the reference framework against which alternatives are evaluated. This paper introduces Progressive Temporal S+POTIS (PT-SPOTIS), a framework that extends the SPOTIS method by progressively expanding the temporal window used to determine normalization bounds. The evaluated alternatives correspond to a single fixed historical year, while the reference limits are recalculated using cumulative data from the evaluated year and all subsequent observation periods. The approach is applied to Eurostat energy data for 27 European countries over 2013–2024. The results show that updating normalization bounds alters the ranking in the majority of cases. Rankings generally converge as the temporal window expands, but convergence is non-monotonic and can be disrupted by external shocks that introduce new extreme values into the dataset. The bottom of the ranking is substantially more robust than the top, indicating that worst-performing countries are reliably identified regardless of the normalization window, whereas best-performing designations remain sensitive to the information horizon.

Keywords: MCDA · SPOTIS · Temporal normalization · Ranking stability · Energy indicators

1 Introduction

In many real-world decision problems, alternatives are evaluated at a specific point in time using only the data available at that moment. However, the range

M. Paszynski et al. (Eds.): ICCS 2026 Workshops, LNCS 16788, pp. 342–357, 2026.
https://doi.org/10.1007/978-3-032-29915-4_29

of possible values of the criteria is often not fully known, and additional observations collected in subsequent years may reveal broader variability of the system. This raises the question of whether an evaluation reflects the properties of the assessed year itself, or rather the limited knowledge used to construct the reference framework at the time of assessment.

Multi-criteria decision analysis (MCDA) methods are widely used to aggregate heterogeneous indicators into a single evaluation measure [6]. In standard MCDA applications, normalization bounds are derived exclusively from the dataset used in the assessment, typically corresponding to a single observation period. Consequently, the decision model implicitly assumes that the available data adequately describe the full decision space, and the reference framework constructed from these data is treated as fixed.

If the observed dataset does not fully reflect the true range of criterion values, the normalization bounds become dependent on the sample rather than on the underlying system [7,11]. As additional observations are collected over subsequent years, newly identified extreme values may shift the reference limits applied in the method. Although sensitivity analysis and uncertainty quantification have been widely examined in MCDA, relatively little attention has been given to how rankings depend on the temporal scope of data used to establish normalization bounds [2,12]. Consequently, rankings are often interpreted as inherent properties of the evaluated alternatives, rather than as outcomes shaped by the adopted reference space. Assuming that the feasible range of the system remains relatively stable over time, incorporating additional temporal observations should improve the estimation of the true bounds of the decision space.

Existing temporal extensions of MCDA primarily analyze changes of alternatives over time, for example by comparing rankings obtained for successive years [1,8]. In such approaches, the alternative itself evolves and the decision problem is interpreted as a dynamic evaluation process. However, a different question remains largely unexplored: whether the evaluation of a fixed historical alternative depends on how much information is used to determine the normalization bounds.

This issue is particularly relevant for methods based on range normalization and distance from a reference point, where the position of the alternative is determined relative to the minimal and maximal values of criteria. In such cases, the ranking may change even when the evaluated data remain identical, solely because the limits defining the reference framework are updated. Therefore, these methods provide a suitable environment for investigating the dependence of rankings on the information horizon.

In this study, we extend the SPOTIS method [5] by introducing a progressively expanding temporal window used to determine normalization bounds. The evaluated alternative corresponds to a single fixed historical year, while the reference limits are recalculated using cumulative data from the evaluated year and all subsequent observation periods. The proposed approach, termed Progressive Temporal SPOTIS (PT-SPOTIS), enables analysis of how rankings depend on the degree of knowledge about the decision space rather than on changes in the alternative itself.

To formalize this investigation, the following research questions are addressed:

(RQ1): Does updating normalization bounds using progressively accumulated temporal data alter the ranking of alternatives evaluated for a single fixed year in SPOTIS?

(RQ2): Does the ranking of a fixed historical year converge or stabilize as the temporal window used to define normalization bounds expands?

(RQ3): What are the implications of ranking instability under expanding normalization bounds for the interpretability of single-year MCDA assessments?

By addressing these questions, the study introduces a temporally adaptive normalization perspective in MCDA and analyzes ranking stability with respect to the progressive acquisition of information about the decision space.

The remainder of this paper is organized as follows. Section 2 reviews related work on temporal perspectives in MCDA. Section 3 presents the SPOTIS method, formalizes the PT-SPOTIS framework, and describes the analysis procedure. Section 4 introduces the dataset and reports the empirical results structured around the three research questions. Section 5 discusses the findings, and Sect. 6 concludes the paper.

2   Related Works

In many MCDA applications, alternatives are observed across successive years and the results are interpreted as temporal trajectories of performance [4,6]. However, these frameworks focus on the variability of alternative evaluations over time, while less attention has been given to how time-varying information influences the structure of the decision model, particularly the reference framework used to position alternatives within the decision space.

Existing temporal MCDA methods typically treat each year as an independent decision problem, constructing rankings separately and comparing them post hoc [1,8]. These approaches assume static normalization bounds within each period and do not examine what happens when information from future periods is incorporated. Dynamic extensions, such as tensor-based formulations or prescriptive methods that weight recent observations more heavily, similarly maintain fixed normalization rules [3,13]. As Table 1 summarizes, existing temporal approaches account for the dynamics of alternative attributes but keep the reference system structurally unchanged: the temporal dimension enters through criterion values or aggregation mechanisms (e.g., weights) but not through the boundaries defining the reference space.

In distance-based methods such as SPOTIS [5], changes in normalization bounds directly affect relative positions even when the observed values of alternatives remain constant. When bounds are derived empirically rather than specified a priori, they become sample-dependent and subject to revision as the dataset grows [7,11]. This introduces a form of temporal instability distinct from changes in alternative performance. Sensitivity analysis addresses robustness to parameter perturbations but typically considers small variations around a fixed reference state rather than the systematic expansion of observed bounds over extended temporal horizons [2,12].

Table 1. Comparison of temporal perspectives in MCDA. The proposed PT-SPOTIS approach is the only one in which the normalization bounds evolve while the evaluated alternative remains fixed.

Temporal perspective	Dynamic over time	Structurally fixed	Ref.
Temporality of alternatives (yearly series)	Performance of alternatives across yearly decision matrices and resulting rankings	Criteria set, weights, normalization rule, and aggregation structure (BWM–WASPAS)	[8]
Temporal variability of alternatives (DARIA–MARCOS)	Annual alternative performance and ranking evolution	Criteria set and compromise-based aggregation structure	[1]
Temporal features of criteria (tensor TOPSIS)	Extracted time-series features of criteria (e.g., trend, dispersion, level)	Alternatives, criteria definitions, and tensor-based TOPSIS framework	[3]
Dynamic/prescriptive DMCDM	Observed and predicted future performance, time-period weights	Alternatives, criteria, and grey relational aggregation structure	[13]
Spatio-temporal MCDA (3D space–time)	Spatial configuration and suitability values evolving across time steps	Criteria, weights, suitability functions, and WLC aggregation structure	[9]
Progressive Temporal SPOTIS (this work)	Normalization bounds progressively expanded using cumulative temporal data	Fixed historical alternative, criteria, weights, aggregation structure	–

The literature has rarely addressed the situation in which the alternative is frozen in time while the normalization space continues to evolve. This gap is particularly relevant for longitudinal sustainability assessments, where indicators from a given year remain unchanged but later observations reveal broader system variability. Understanding how progressive expansion of the normalization horizon affects ranking stability directly motivates PT-SPOTIS and the research questions posed in this study.

3   Methodology

3.1   SPOTIS Method

The Stable Preference Ordering Towards Ideal Solution (SPOTIS) is a multi-criteria decision-making method proposed by Dezert et al. [5]. Unlike methods that rely on relative comparisons between alternatives, SPOTIS evaluates each alternative independently against a fixed reference point, which guarantees immunity to the rank reversal phenomenon.

Let $S = (S_{ij})_{M \times N}$ denote the decision matrix, where S_{ij} is the performance score of alternative A_i on criterion C_j. For each criterion C_j $(j = 1, 2, \ldots, N)$, the decision maker specifies bounds $S_j^{\min}$ and $S_j^{\max}$ that define the feasible range of criterion values. The Ideal Solution Point (ISP) $S^* = (S_1^*, \ldots, S_N^*)$ is determined from these bounds according to the criterion type: $S_j^* = S_j^{\max}$ for benefit criteria and $S_j^* = S_j^{\min}$ for cost criteria.

The SPOTIS algorithm proceeds in three steps. First, the normalized distance of each alternative to the ISP is calculated for each criterion:

$$d_{ij}(A_i, S_j^*) = \frac{|S_{ij} - S_j^*|}{|S_j^{\max} - S_j^{\min}|} \tag{1}$$

Second, the weighted normalized distance from the ISP is computed as:

$$d(A_i, S^*) = \sum_{j=1}^{N} w_j \, d_{ij}(A_i, S_j^*) \tag{2}$$

where $w_j \geq 0$ and $\sum_{j=1}^{N} w_j = 1$ are the criteria importance weights. Third, alternatives are ranked in ascending order of $d(A_i, S^*)$, so that the alternative closest to the ISP is ranked first.

A key property of SPOTIS is that the bounds $S_j^{\min}$ and $S_j^{\max}$ are defined a priori, independently of the alternatives present in the current evaluation. This decouples the evaluation of each alternative from the composition of the alternative set and ensures that adding or removing alternatives does not alter existing distances [5]. However, in practice, the bounds are frequently derived from the observed data rather than specified exogenously. When the dataset evolves over time, the bounds may change, and this effect forms the basis of the temporal analysis proposed in this study.

3.2   Progressive Temporal SPOTIS

We now formalize the Progressive Temporal SPOTIS (PT-SPOTIS) framework. Let $\mathcal{T} = \{t_0, t_0+1, \ldots, t_{\text{end}}\}$ denote the set of observation years. For each year $t \in \mathcal{T}$, the decision matrix $X^{(t)}$ of dimension $M \times N$ contains the criterion values of all M alternatives observed at time t. Each criterion is classified as either a cost type (lower values preferred) or a benefit type (higher values preferred), and in the present study we deliberately adopt equal weights $w_j = \frac{1}{N}$ to isolate the effect of evolving normalization bounds from confounding variation in criteria importance.

For a given base year t and expanding window endpoint $T \in \mathcal{T}$ with $T \geq t$, the cumulative normalization bounds are constructed from all observations in the interval $[t, T]$:

$$S_j^{\min}(t, T) = \min_{t \leq \tau \leq T} \min_i X_{ij}^{(\tau)}, \quad S_j^{\max}(t, T) = \max_{t \leq \tau \leq T} \max_i X_{ij}^{(\tau)} \tag{3}$$

Because the window only expands, the bounds satisfy the monotonicity property: $S_j^{\min}(t, T) \leq S_j^{\min}(t, T-1)$ and $S_j^{\max}(t, T) \geq S_j^{\max}(t, T-1)$ for all j. Consequently, the normalization range $\delta_j(t, T) = S_j^{\max}(t, T) - S_j^{\min}(t, T)$ is non-decreasing in T.

The PT-SPOTIS ranking of a base year t evaluated under the window endpoint T (where $T \geq t$) is obtained by applying the standard SPOTIS procedure using the bounds from (3). We denote this ranking as $R^{(t,T)}$. When $T = t$, the bounds reduce to those derived from the data of the base year alone, so $R^{(t,t)}$ coincides with the standard local-bounds ranking. For a fixed base year t, the sequence $\{R^{(t,t)}, R^{(t,t+1)}, \ldots, R^{(t,t_{\mathrm{end}})}\}$ captures how the ranking of alternatives in year t evolves as the information horizon expands, even though the performance data $X^{(t)}$ remain unchanged.

Three reference configurations emerge as special cases. The *local bounds* configuration uses $T = t$, so that normalization bounds are derived exclusively from the data of the evaluated year. The *global bounds* configuration uses $T = t_{\mathrm{end}}$, so that bounds reflect the full range from the evaluated year to the end of the observation period. PT-SPOTIS interpolates between these two extremes by treating T as a parameter that controls the amount of accumulated temporal information beyond the base year.

3.3   Analysis Framework

The proposed analysis framework consists of four stages (Fig. 1). In Stage 1, longitudinal energy data are collected from a public database. In Stage 2, the data are preprocessed: countries with incomplete temporal coverage or zero-valued observations are removed, and the criteria types are assigned. In Stage 3, three SPOTIS model variants are computed: (i) local bounds, (ii) PT-SPOTIS with expanding windows, and (iii) global bounds. In Stage 4, the three research questions are addressed through comparative analysis of the ranking sequences produced in Stage 3.

4   Research

4.1   Data and Experimental Setup

The dataset comprises annual energy statistics for 27 European countries from 2013 to 2024, sourced from Eurostat[1]. Six indicators are used as criteria, cov-

---

[1] Data available at https://doi.org/10.2908/TEN00123 and https://doi.org/10.2908/TEN00122.

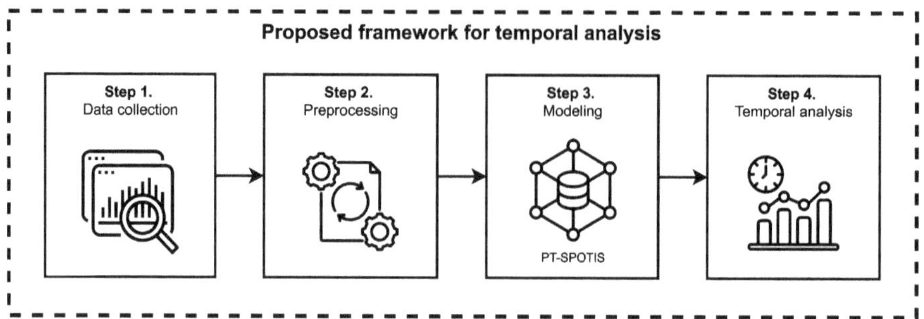

Fig. 1. Proposed analysis framework for temporal ranking stability evaluation using PT-SPOTIS.

ering three energy categories: electricity, natural gas, and renewables including biofuels. Each category is represented by a consumption and a supply variable. Consumption criteria (C_1, C_3, C_5) are treated as cost type (lower values preferred), while supply criteria (C_2, C_4, C_6) are treated as benefit type (higher values preferred). All values are expressed in KTOE.

After filtering for complete 12-year records and excluding countries with zero-valued observations in any criterion, the final dataset comprises $M = 27$ alternatives observed over $|\mathcal{T}| = 12$ years. To keep the focus on bound expansion rather than preference modelling, all six criteria are assigned equal weights $w_j = \frac{1}{6}$. The decision matrix for the initial year 2013 is presented in Table 2. Rankings obtained under local and global bounds configurations are shown in Fig. 2 and Fig. 3, respectively. The expanding-window procedure yields 78 distinct evaluation configurations (base year and window endpoint pairs), each producing a ranking of all 27 alternatives.

4.2   Impact of Updating Criteria Boundary Values on Rankings

To assess the impact of expanding normalization bounds on rankings, we compare the local-bounds ranking $R^{(t,t)}$ with the expanding-window ranking $R^{(t,T)}$ for each base year t and each window endpoint $T \geq t$. Ranking similarity is quantified using the weighted Spearman correlation coefficient r_w [10]. Figure 4 presents a heatmap of $r_w(R^{(t,t)}, R^{(t,T)})$ for all evaluated-year and window-endpoint combinations. The diagonal entries equal 1.0 by construction, since at $T = t$ the expanding-window bounds coincide with local bounds. Reading along each row reveals how the ranking of a fixed year changes as the normalization window extends.

It can be seen that year 2013 exhibits the strongest degradation, with r_w declining from 1.00 to 0.84 when evaluated under the full window ($T = 2024$). In contrast, more recent base years such as 2019 show high stability ($r_w = 0.97$ at $T = 2024$), because fewer additional years are available to shift the bounds. The rightmost column ($T = 2024$) is particularly informative: it shows the cost of incorporating full temporal information. Notable degradation is visible for

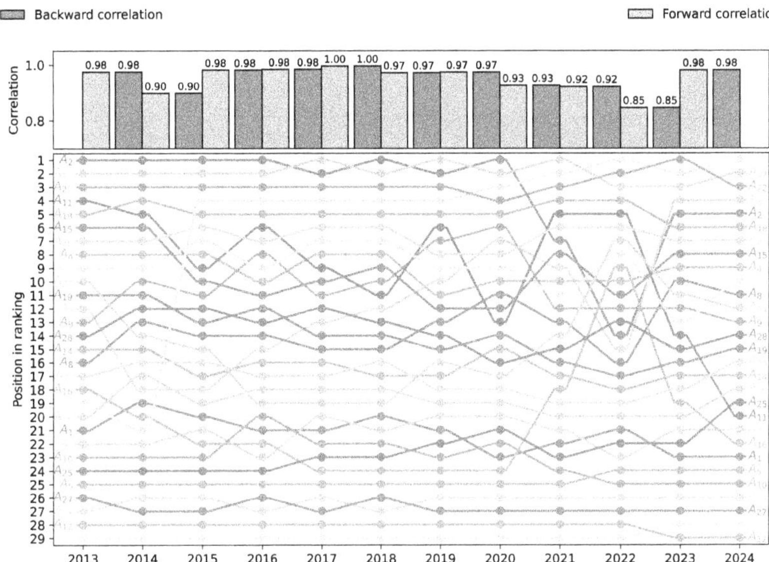

Fig. 2. Ranking flow and inter-year correlation under local bounds configuration. Each year is evaluated independently using normalization bounds derived solely from its own data.

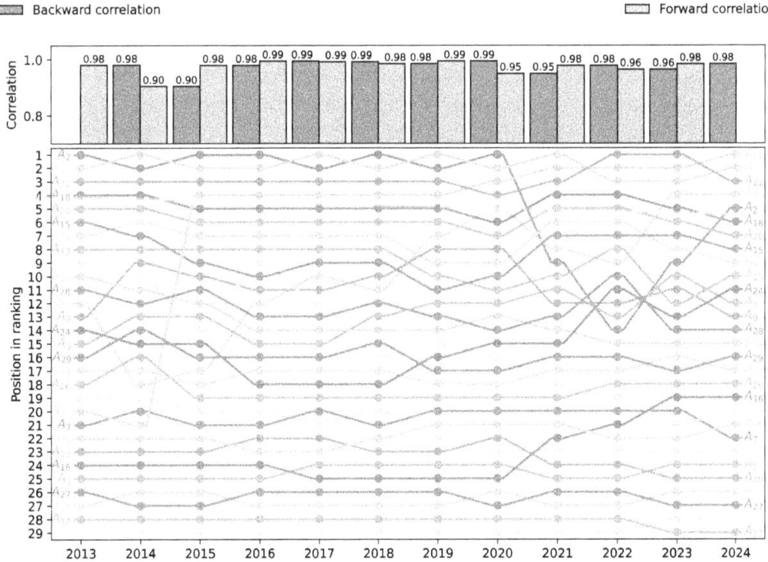

Fig. 3. Ranking flow and inter-year correlation under global bounds configuration. All years are evaluated using normalization bounds derived from the full 2013–2024 dataset.

years 2021 ($r_w = 0.85$) and 2022 ($r_w = 0.84$), indicating that periods close to external shocks are especially sensitive to subsequent bound expansion.

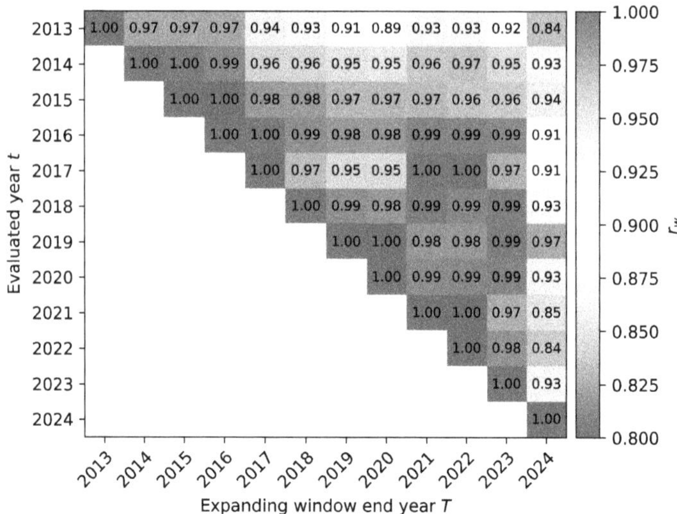

Fig. 4. Weighted Spearman correlation r_w between local-bounds ranking $R^{(t,t)}$ and expanding-window ranking $R^{(t,T)}$. Each cell shows r_w for base year t (row) evaluated under window endpoint T (column).

Table 3 quantifies these rank shifts. Across all years, an average of 61.1% of alternatives change position, with a mean absolute shift of $\overline{|\Delta R|} = 1.65$. The year 2024 shows zero shift by construction, since the expanding window cannot extend beyond the last available year. However, the maximum shifts for other base years are substantial, reaching up to 17 positions (year 2021), indicating that individual countries can be severely affected. The country-level analysis reveals that Italy exhibits the largest mean absolute rank shift, followed by Finland and Norway. These countries have atypical energy profiles: Italy is a large gas consumer but moderate electricity producer, while Norway and Finland have distinctive renewable energy structures. In contrast, Germany, France, and Sweden remain nearly unaffected, because their extreme criterion values tend to define the bounds themselves. When the bounds expand, these "anchor" countries remain stable.

4.3   Convergence of Rankings

To assess convergence, we track how the PT-SPOTIS ranking of each base year t approaches the final-window ranking $R^{(t,t_{\mathrm{end}})}$ as T increases. Figure 5 presents two complementary views. Panel (a) shows $r_w(R^{(t,T)}, R^{(t,t_{\mathrm{end}})})$ as a function of T for each base year. The correlation generally increases with T, confirming

Table 2. Decision matrix for 2013: energy consumption and supply values (KTOE) for the 27 evaluated countries.

A_i	Country	Electricity		Natural gas		Renewables and biofuels	
		Cons.	Sup.	Cons.	Sup.	Cons.	Sup.
A_1	AT	5258.03	625.15	4728.82	7060.52	4218.96	10232.19
A_2	BE	7073.41	828.89	9798.74	14533.61	1826.35	3620.66
A_3	BG	2367.33	−531.47	1155.95	2397.73	1254.90	1881.27
A_4	CZ	4575.84	−1452.02	5366.98	6946.41	2679.41	4130.19
A_5	DE	44910.58	−2768.10	52845.56	73101.74	16948.11	37632.14
A_6	DK	2674.64	93.04	1579.91	3315.94	1464.81	4456.38
A_7	EE	586.41	−308.51	250.04	554.90	477.74	851.14
A_8	EL	4195.27	162.25	907.55	3236.31	1382.75	2676.08
A_9	ES	19783.92	−580.48	14792.34	26163.38	5034.18	17716.02
A_{10}	FI	6875.41	1351.25	704.42	2856.39	4962.38	9861.52
A_{11}	FR	38772.00	−4166.90	33258.00	38816.13	14374.36	25808.33
A_{12}	HR	1295.96	332.67	993.27	2281.86	1261.51	2097.31
A_{13}	HU	2998.54	1021.24	5333.75	7704.06	2426.14	3111.54
A_{14}	IE	2137.71	192.79	1624.92	3852.83	330.60	894.17
A_{15}	IT	24711.78	3623.22	35222.27	57386.72	8498.17	26370.63
A_{16}	LT	769.99	597.25	552.04	2164.51	732.58	1212.27
A_{17}	LU	532.98	425.11	601.28	889.90	104.87	154.86
A_{18}	LV	565.43	116.51	343.62	1204.69	1018.54	1611.38
A_{19}	NL	8989.84	1568.10	19482.03	33380.68	1184.43	3517.45
A_{20}	NO	9581.59	−430.44	418.11	5617.78	1605.94	13143.36
A_{21}	PL	10623.99	−388.74	8883.65	13735.89	5714.68	8655.09
A_{22}	PT	3891.40	238.69	1566.68	3755.87	2216.72	5300.91
A_{23}	RO	3493.38	−173.35	5681.13	9838.95	3708.03	5550.96
A_{24}	RS	2328.03	−218.14	1002.13	1866.55	1031.50	1929.28
A_{25}	SE	10749.44	−860.02	496.37	955.29	7127.43	18366.33
A_{26}	SI	1073.00	−110.92	540.63	691.85	722.42	1218.69
A_{27}	SK	2156.84	7.83	2996.30	4558.04	1103.59	2105.03

Table 3. Rank shift summary when comparing local vs. full expanding-window rankings per base year.

Year t	2013	2014	2015	2016	2017	2018	2019	2020	2021	2022	2023	2024
$\overline{|\Delta R|}$	2.67	2.00	1.63	1.93	1.78	1.41	1.04	1.85	2.15	2.22	1.11	0.00
$\max |\Delta R|$	12	7	6	8	14	12	5	9	17	16	12	0
% changed	70.4	77.8	66.7	74.1	66.7	59.3	48.1	66.7	77.8	77.8	48.1	0.0

that rankings approach their terminal form as more data accumulate. However, convergence is not monotonic: for early base years such as 2013 and 2014, a visible dip occurs around $T = 2017$, followed by partial recovery and renewed degradation near $T = 2024$. This pattern reflects successive waves of bound expansion driven by different criteria. Panel (b) shows the mean absolute rank distance to the final ranking, which for the earliest base years starts above 2.0 positions and decreases toward zero as T approaches t_{end}.

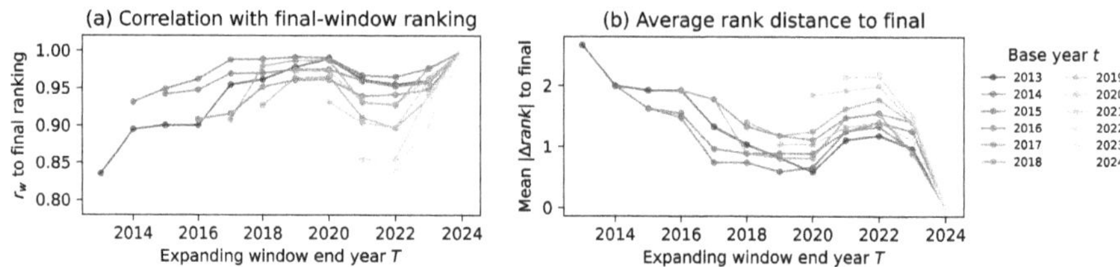

Fig. 5. Convergence of PT-SPOTIS rankings toward the final-window ranking. (a) Weighted Spearman correlation $r_w(R^{(t,T)}, R^{(t,t_{\mathrm{end}})})$ as a function of window endpoint T. (b) Mean absolute rank distance to the final ranking.

Table 4. Instability index per base year, measured as the mean and maximum rank range (difference between the highest and lowest rank observed) across all expanding windows.

Year t	2013	2014	2015	2016	2017	2018	2019	2020	2021	2022	2023	2024
Mean range	3.11	2.37	2.04	2.11	1.81	2.00	1.52	2.15	2.26	2.30	1.11	0.00
Max range	12	8	9	8	14	14	11	13	17	16	12	0

The mechanism behind non-convergence is revealed by the bounds expansion analysis (Fig. 6), which shows the ratio $\delta_j(t, T)/\delta_j(t, t)$ of the normalization range at window endpoint T relative to the initial local range, illustrated for base year $t = 2013$. Criterion C_2 (electricity supply) exhibits a sudden jump to approximately $1.57\times$ at $T = 2024$, caused by an extreme observation in the most recent year. Criterion C_6 (renewable supply) grows monotonically to approximately $1.33\times$, reflecting the secular trend of increasing renewable energy production across Europe. In contrast, C_1 (electricity consumption) remains flat at $1.0\times$, indicating that the initial bounds already captured the full range. Criteria with actively expanding bounds act as persistent sources of ranking instability: as long as at least one criterion continues to produce new extrema, the ranking under PT-SPOTIS cannot fully stabilize.

Table 4 summarizes the instability for each base year. The mean range is highest for year 2013 (3.11) and initially decreases to a minimum of 1.52 for

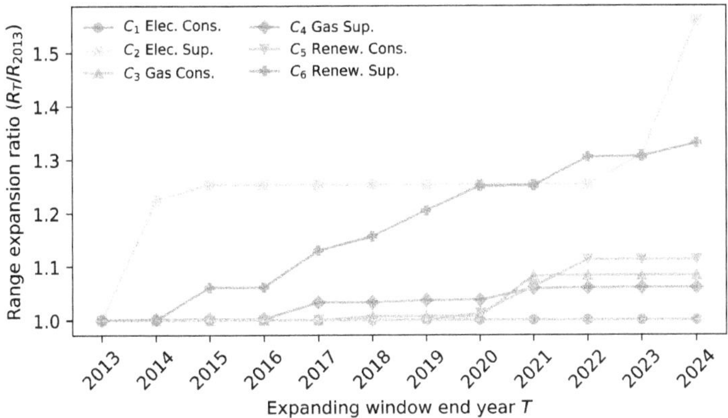

Fig. 6. Normalization range expansion ratio $\delta_j(t,T)/\delta_j(t,t)$ for each criterion as a function of the expanding window endpoint T, shown for base year $t = 2013$. A ratio exceeding 1.0 indicates that the criterion range has grown beyond its initial extent.

year 2019, but then rises again for 2020–2022 (reaching 2.30), mirroring the pattern observed in the convergence analysis: base years whose expanding windows encompass the post-2020 structural shifts in the European energy system exhibit elevated instability despite having shorter expansion horizons. The maximum range remains persistently high (8–17 positions for most years), indicating that even base years with moderate average instability contain individual countries with substantial positional uncertainty. The year 2024 shows zero instability by construction, as only one window configuration is available.

4.4   Interpretability Implications

The practical relevance of ranking instability depends on which countries are affected and whether the top and bottom of the ranking remain identifiable despite bound-induced variation. Figure 7 presents rank uncertainty bands for two representative base years. The left panel shows year 2013 (evaluated across 12 expanding windows) and the right panel shows year 2018 (7 windows). Each horizontal bar spans the minimum-to-maximum rank observed for a given country, and the dot marks the mean rank.

It can be seen that Italy exhibits the widest uncertainty band in both years, spanning more than 10 positions in 2013 and an even wider range in 2018. The wider band in 2018 arises because the expanding windows from 2018 onward cover the European energy crisis, which disproportionately affects Italy as a major gas importer. Finland, Estonia, and Norway also display substantial rank variability. In contrast, the highest-ranked countries (France, Germany, Poland) and the lowest-ranked (Lithuania, Luxembourg) exhibit tight bands of 1–2 positions, indicating high positional stability.

Figure 8 quantifies this asymmetry through top-k and bottom-k membership frequency across all expanding-window evaluations ($k = 3$). Lithuania appears

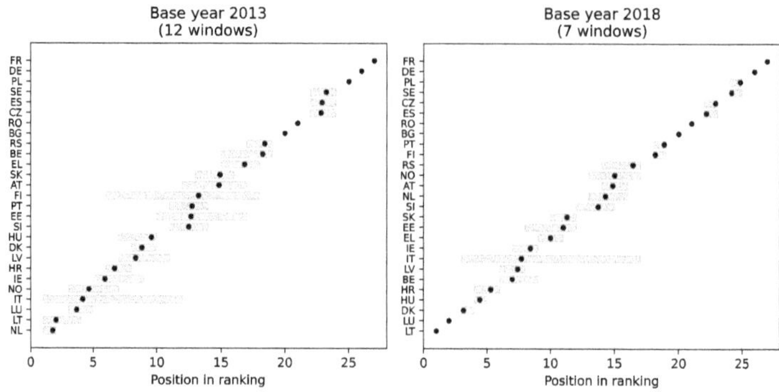

Fig. 7. Rank uncertainty bands for base years 2013 (left, 12 windows) and 2018 (right, 7 windows). Each bar spans the minimum-to-maximum rank observed across all expanding-window evaluations, and the dot marks the mean rank.

in the top 3 in the vast majority of evaluations, followed by Luxembourg. Several other countries, including Italy, Denmark, the Netherlands, and Croatia, compete for the remaining top-3 positions with lower frequencies, making these rank assignments sensitive to the chosen window. The bottom 3 is substantially more stable: Germany and France appear in nearly all evaluations, Sweden in the majority of cases, and Poland occasionally.

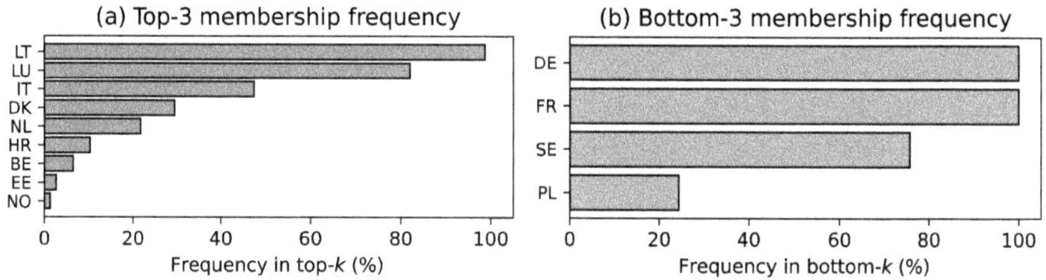

Fig. 8. Top-3 and bottom-3 membership frequency across all expanding-window evaluations. (a) Countries appearing in the top 3. (b) Countries appearing in the bottom 3.

These findings carry direct implications for policy interpretation. Rankings of the worst-performing countries are reliable regardless of the temporal scope of the normalization bounds, whereas rankings of the best performers are contingent on the information horizon. Decision makers should therefore exercise greater caution when interpreting top-k designations than bottom-k designations when the normalization bounds are empirically derived from evolving datasets.

5   Discussion

The results reveal a structural property of distance-based MCDA methods: the ranking of a fixed set of alternatives can change solely because the normalization bounds are updated with new temporal observations, even though the underlying performance data remain unchanged. Countries occupying extreme positions in the decision space act as natural anchors and remain positionally stable, whereas interior alternatives with heterogeneous criterion profiles, such as Italy, are disproportionately sensitive to rescaling effects. PT-SPOTIS makes this dependence explicit by treating the information horizon as a parameter and showing that the same historical alternative can receive different rankings under different assumptions about the decision space. In this sense, PT-SPOTIS is best interpreted as an ex-post diagnostic for reassessing past MCDA results under expanded knowledge, rather than as a prescriptive ex-ante decision rule, and it reinforces the argument of the original SPOTIS design that normalization bounds should whenever possible be specified exogenously using domain knowledge [5].

The non-monotonic convergence patterns correspond to periods in which new extreme observations enter the dataset and abruptly shift the normalization bounds, as seen for electricity and renewable supply after 2020. Such shocks cause rapid expansion of the feasible range on affected criteria, effectively compressing earlier observations and amplifying rank instability for countries whose profiles are aligned with the shocked dimensions. This sensitivity suggests that, in practical applications, empirically derived min–max bounds should be complemented with more robust constructions, for example winsorised or percentile-based bounds, or bounds anchored in policy targets or physical limits, all of which can be seamlessly incorporated into the PT-SPOTIS framework. Embedding PT-SPOTIS as an analytic module in management information systems— for instance, in dashboards used for energy-policy monitoring or sustainability composite indices—would allow decision makers to routinely compare published single-year rankings with their temporally expanded counterparts and to flag those alternatives and periods where conclusions critically depend on the chosen information horizon.

6   Conclusions

This study introduced Progressive Temporal SPOTIS (PT-SPOTIS), a framework that extends SPOTIS by progressively expanding the temporal window used to determine normalization bounds. The empirical analysis on Eurostat energy data for 27 European countries (2013–2024) yielded three findings. First, updating bounds alters the ranking in the majority of cases, with 61.1% of alternatives changing position and individual shifts reaching 17 ranks (RQ1). Second, rankings converge toward a terminal form but non-monotonically, as external shocks that introduce new extrema disrupt the process (RQ2). Third, the bottom of the ranking is substantially more robust than the top: worst-performing countries are reliably identified regardless of the normalization window, whereas best-performing designations remain sensitive to the information horizon (RQ3). These findings imply that when normalization bounds are derived empirically from evolving datasets, rankings should be treated as outcomes conditional on the available reference information rather than as definitive properties of the evaluated alternatives. PT-SPOTIS provides a tool for quantifying this conditionality and assessing the robustness of specific ranking positions.

The study is subject to several limitations: it uses equal criterion weights, a single application domain (European energy indicators), a purely cumulative forward-expanding window, and focuses on one distance-based method (SPOTIS), so the quantitative instability patterns observed here may not transfer directly to other weighting schemes, temporal window structures or MCDA formalisms. Future work should therefore explore explicit weight–bound interactions, compare forward, backward and rolling normalization windows, experiment with robust and percentile-based bounds, and extend the temporal normalization perspective to other distance- and reference-point-based methods.

Acknowledgments. Publication co-financed by the National Science Centre, Poland 2022/45/B/HS4/02960 (JW).

Disclosure of Interests. The authors have no competing interests to declare that are relevant to the content of this article.

References

1. Bączkiewicz, A., Wątróbski, J., Karczmarczyk, A.: A novel multi-criteria temporal decision support method-sustainability evaluation case study. In: International Conference on Computational Science, pp. 189–203. Springer (2024)
2. Borgonovo, E., Plischke, E.: Sensitivity analysis: a review of recent advances. Eur. J. Oper. Res. **248**(3), 869–887 (2016)
3. Campello, B.S.C., Duarte, L.T., Romano, J.M.T.: Exploiting temporal features in multicriteria decision analysis by means of a tensorial formulation of the TOPSIS method. Comput. Ind. Eng. **175**, 108915 (2023)
4. Cinelli, M., Coles, S.R., Kirwan, K.: Analysis of the potentials of multi criteria decision analysis methods to conduct sustainability assessment. Ecol. Ind. **46**, 138–148 (2014)
5. Dezert, J., Tchamova, A., Han, D., Tacnet, J.M.: The SPOTIS rank reversal free method for multi-criteria decision-making support. In: 2020 IEEE 23rd International Conference on Information Fusion (FUSION), pp. 1–8. IEEE (2020)
6. Greco, S., Ishizaka, A., Tasiou, M., Torrisi, G.: On the methodological framework of composite indices: a review of the issues of weighting, aggregation, and robustness. Soc. Indic. Res. **141**(1), 61–94 (2019)
7. Jahan, A., Edwards, K.L.: A state-of-the-art survey on the influence of normalization techniques in ranking: improving the materials selection process in engineering design. Mater. Des. (1980–2015) **65**, 335–342 (2015)
8. Manirathinam, T., Lactayo, D.R.B., Jeon, J.: Temporal multi-criteria decision making approach on sustainable competitiveness of countries: Science and technology innovation indicators. J. Clean. Prod. **522**, 146296 (2025)
9. Munn, K., Dragićević, S.: Towards a spatio-temporal multicriteria evaluation method: a suitability analysis of residential units in a 3d urban environment. Trans. GIS **27**(7), 1830–1845 (2023)

10. Shekhovtsov, A.: How strongly do rank similarity coefficients differ used in decision making problems? Procedia Comput. Sci. **192**, 4570–4577 (2021)
11. Vafaei, N., Ribeiro, R.A., Camarinha-Matos, L.M.: Data normalisation techniques in decision making: case study with TOPSIS method. Int. J. Inf. Decis. Sci. **10**(1), 19–38 (2018)
12. Więckowski, J., Sałabun, W.: Sensitivity analysis approaches in multi-criteria decision analysis: a systematic review. Appl. Soft Comput. **148**, 110915 (2023)
13. Yang, S., Liao, H., Wu, X.: Prescriptive analytics for dynamic multi-criterion decision making considering learned knowledge of alternatives. Expert Syst. Appl. **268**, 126350 (2025)

A Time-Aware TOPSIS Method
for Longitudinal Performance Assessment

Artur Karczmarczyk[1]([✉]) [iD], Jarosław Wątróbski[2,3] [iD],
Aleksandra Bączkiewicz[3] [iD], and Aleksandra Karczmarczyk[1] [iD]

[1] Department of Computer Science, West Pomeranian University of Technology in
Szczecin, ul. Żołnierska 49, 71-210 Szczecin, Poland
`{artur.karczmarczyk,aleksandra.karczmarczyk}@zut.edu.pl`
[2] Institute of Management, University of Szczecin, ul. Cukrowa 8, 71-004
Szczecin, Poland
`{jaroslaw.watrobski,aleksandra.baczkiewicz}@usz.edu.pl`
[3] National Institute of Telecommunications, ul. Szachowa 1, 04-894 Warsaw, Poland

Abstract. Multi-criteria decision analysis (MCDA) is widely used to construct composite indicators and rank alternatives across complex domains, yet most applications remain static and evaluate performance using data from a single time period. This limitation can lead to incomplete assessments when alternatives exhibit long-term performance dynamics. This paper proposes a temporal extension of the TOPSIS method that integrates multiple time periods directly into a unified decision framework. The approach expands the decision matrix by introducing temporal instances of each criterion and incorporates time-period weights to model recency effects while preserving the computational simplicity and geometric interpretation of classical TOPSIS. The method is validated through an empirical study based on Environmental Performance Index data for European Union countries using results from 2020, 2022, and 2024. The findings demonstrate that incorporating temporal information produces meaningful ranking differences and enables flexible balancing between historical performance and recent outcomes. The proposed approach provides a transparent and efficient tool for dynamic multi-criteria evaluation.

Keywords: temporal MCDA · TOPSIS · composite indicators

1 Introduction

Multi-criteria decision analysis (MCDA) has become a key tool for evaluating complex socio-economic and environmental systems that cannot be captured by a single metric [1, 12]. Composite indicators are widely used to compare countries and regions across multidimensional domains such as sustainability and environmental policy [4], transforming heterogeneous data into interpretable rankings that support evidence-based decision-making [8].

M. Paszynski et al. (Eds.): ICCS 2026 Workshops, LNCS 16788, pp. 358–370, 2026.
https://doi.org/10.1007/978-3-032-29915-4_30

Among MCDA techniques, the Technique for Order Preference by Similarity to Ideal Solution (TOPSIS) [7] is one of the most widely adopted methods due to its intuitive geometric interpretation, computational efficiency, and ability to aggregate diverse criteria into a single preference score. Despite its maturity, ongoing research continues to extend the method to improve its robustness and applicability [10, 16].

However, most MCDA applications remain static and neglect the temporal evolution of performance. In practice, decision makers rarely assess systems at a single point in time, and relying on cross-sectional data or separate yearly rankings may discard valuable information about long-term trends [16]. The increasing availability of longitudinal datasets highlights the need for MCDA approaches that explicitly incorporate time. Yet only limited research addresses this challenge, leaving a clear gap between dynamic real-world problems and the predominantly static tools used to analyze them [2, 6].

This paper aims to bridge this gap by proposing a temporal extension of the TOPSIS method that integrates multiple time periods into a single evaluation framework. Instead of generating independent rankings for each period and comparing them ex post, the proposed approach expands the decision matrix to include temporal instances of each criterion and introduces time-period weights that allow flexible modeling of recency effects. The resulting method preserves the simplicity and interpretability of classical TOPSIS while enabling the construction of a unified ranking that reflects the entire performance history of the evaluated alternatives.

The main contributions of this paper are threefold. First, we introduce a simple yet general temporal expansion of the TOPSIS framework that maintains its original computational structure. Second, we demonstrate how different temporal weighting schemes can be used to balance long-term performance and recency emphasis. Third, we validate the proposed approach through an empirical study based on Environmental Performance Index data for European Union countries, illustrating its practical relevance and analytical value.

The remainder of the paper is organized as follows. Section 2 reviews related work on MCDA, TOPSIS, and temporal evaluation approaches. Section 3 presents the proposed temporal TOPSIS extension. Section 4 provides the empirical study and discusses the results. Finally, Sect. 5 concludes the paper and outlines directions for future research.

2 Literature Review

Multi-criteria decision analysis (MCDA) has become a standard methodological framework for constructing composite indicators and benchmarking the performance of countries, regions, and cities across complex and multidimensional domains [14]. Sustainability [13], environmental policy [8], smart city development [18], and socio-economic performance are among the most prominent application areas, where numerous heterogeneous indicators must be aggregated into a single, interpretable ranking [9]. In such contexts, MCDA provides a transparent and flexible framework for integrating diverse criteria and supporting evidence-based policy analysis.

At the same time, the choice of MCDA method can significantly influence the final ranking, even when the same dataset and weights are used [17]. This observation underscores the importance of continued methodological development and careful method selection in composite indicator research.

Among the many MCDA techniques, TOPSIS [7] has emerged as one of the most widely used approaches. Its popularity stems from its conceptual simplicity, intuitive geometric interpretation, and relatively low computational complexity. The method evaluates alternatives by simultaneously considering their distances from a positive ideal solution and a negative ideal solution, producing an easily interpretable preference score.

TOPSIS has been successfully applied across numerous fields, including energy systems [3], environmental management, supply chains [5], healthcare [15], and urban planning [11]. Recent studies confirm the method's adaptability to new problem domains and highlight ongoing efforts to extend the classical formulation of TOPSIS in order to address its various limitations [10,16].

Although many real-world decision problems involve longitudinal data, most MCDA applications remain inherently static. Traditional approaches typically evaluate alternatives using data from a single time period or generate separate rankings for different years and compare them ex post. Only a limited number of studies explicitly address the temporal dimension within MCDA [6,16]. This constitutes a clear research gap, which is addressed in this paper by proposing a temporal extension of the TOPSIS method that simultaneously incorporates the temporal dimension of decision-making while preserving the computational simplicity and intuitive geometric interpretation of the original approach.

3   Methodology

In this section, the methodological foundations of the proposed approach are presented. First, the classical TOPSIS technique algorithm is presented, followed by the proposed temporal TOPSIS extension algorithm.

3.1   Classical TOPSIS

Step 1. Construct the decision matrix. Let $A = A_1, \ldots, A_m$ be a set of alternatives and $C = C_1, \ldots, C_n$ a set of criteria. The decision matrix is defined as Eq. (1):

$$X = [x_{ij}]_{m \times n} = \begin{bmatrix} x_{11} & x_{12} & \cdots & x_{1n} \\ x_{21} & x_{22} & \cdots & x_{2n} \\ \vdots & \vdots & \vdots & \vdots \\ x_{m1} & x_{m2} & \cdots & x_{mn} \end{bmatrix} \tag{1}$$

Step 2. Normalization of the decision matrix. In the standard TOPSIS procedure, min-max normalization is applied to remove differences in scale and measurement units across criteria. The normalized values r_{ij} are obtained using Eq. (2) for benefit-type criteria and Eq. (3) for cost-type criteria.

$$r_{ij} = \frac{x_{ij} - min_j(x_{ij})}{max_j(x_{ij}) - min_j(x_{ij})} \tag{2}$$

$$r_{ij} = \frac{max_j(x_{ij}) - x_{ij}}{max_j(x_{ij}) - min_j(x_{ij})} \tag{3}$$

Step 3. Weighted normalized matrix. Next, the weighted normalized decision matrix is computed, according to Eq. (4).

$$v_{ij} = w_j r_{ij} \tag{4}$$

Step 4. Determination of ideal and anti-ideal solutions. Positive ideal solution (PIS) and the negative ideal solution (NIS) are derived using Eq. (5) Eq. (6), respectively.

$$v_j^+ = \{v_1^+, v_2^+, \ldots, v_n^+\} = \{max_j(v_{ij})\} \tag{5}$$

$$v_j^- = \{v_1^-, v_2^-, \ldots, v_n^-\} = \{min_j(v_{ij})\} \tag{6}$$

The PIS consists of the maximum values of the weighted normalized matrix, whereas the NIS contains the minimum values. Because normalization has already been performed, no further distinction between benefit and cost criteria is required at this stage.

Step 5. Distance to ideal solutions. For each alternative, the distances to the PIS and NIS are calculated using Eq. (7) and Eq. (8). The Euclidean metric is used as the standard distance measure in the TOPSIS method.

$$D_i^+ = \sqrt{\sum_{j=1}^{n}(v_{ij} - v_j^+)^2} \tag{7}$$

$$D_i^- = \sqrt{\sum_{j=1}^{n}(v_{ij} - v_j^-)^2} \tag{8}$$

Step 6. Calculation of the preference score. Finally, the performance score of each alternative is computed using Eq. (9).

$$C_i = \frac{D_i^-}{D_i^- + D_i^+} \tag{9}$$

The resulting C_i value lies in the interval $[0, 1]$, and the alternative with the highest score is considered the most preferable. Consequently, the final ranking is obtained by sorting alternatives in descending order of their preference scores.

3.2 Temporal TOPSIS Extension

Assume performance datasets are available for a range of T consecutive time periods $t_0, t_1, \ldots, t_{T-1}$, where t_0 denotes the most up-to-date period, t_1 a previous period and consequently t_{T-1} the oldest period. In our novel proposed approach, we extend the classical TOPSIS to accommodate all studied periods into a single decision matrix, as described in the following procedure.

Step T1. Temporal expansion of the decision matrix. For each criterion C_j, we define its temporal instances:

$$C_j^{(t_k)}, \quad k = 0, \ldots, T - 1 \tag{10}$$

The temporal decision matrix becomes:

$$\hat{X} = [x_{i,j,k}]_{m \times (n \cdot T)} \tag{11}$$

where $x_{i,j,k}$ denotes the performance of alternative A_i under criterion C_j in period t_k.

Thus, the number of criteria increases from n to nT.

Step T2. Temporal weights. Let w_j be the original weight of criterion C_j and let λ_k denote the weight of time period t_k such that

$$\sum_{k=0}^{T-1} \lambda_k = 1, \quad \lambda_k \geq 0 \tag{12}$$

Each temporalized criterion receives the weight:

$$\hat{w}_{j,k} = w_j \lambda_k \tag{13}$$

It follows that the new weights remain normalized:

$$\sum_{j=1}^{n} \sum_{k=0}^{T-1} \hat{w}_{j,k} = 1 \tag{14}$$

This formulation allows emphasizing recent periods by assigning larger λ_k values.

Step T3. Temporal impacts. The type of each criterion (benefit or cost) is assumed time-invariant. Therefore, the impact of $C_j^{(t_k)}$ equals the impact of C_j:

$$\hat{\text{impact}}_{j,k} = \text{impact}_j \tag{15}$$

Step T4. Classical TOPSIS application. After the temporal expansion, the TOPSIS procedure is applied without further modification, using the extended decision matrix $\hat{X}$, weights $\hat{w}_{j,k}$ and impacts $\hat{\text{impact}}_{j,k}$.

The proposed approach integrates temporal dynamics directly into the decision space. Instead of aggregating rankings across time, the proposed approach preserves period-specific information, allows flexible temporal importance modeling, and produces a single ranking reflecting the entire performance history.

Table 1. EPI issue categories used as 11 criteria in the empirical study.

Policy Objective	Abbreviation	Weight	Issue Category
ECO - Ecosystem Vitality	BDH	0.18	Biodiversity & Habitat
	ECS	0.08	Ecosystem Services
	FSH	0.05	Fisheries
	APO	0.04	Air Pollution
	AGR	0.04	Agriculture
	WRS	0.03	Water Resources
HLT - Environmental Health	AIR	0.11	Air Quality
	H2O	0.05	Sanitation & Drinking Water
	HMT	0.02	Heavy Metals
	WMG	0.02	Waste Management
PCC - Climate Change	CCH	0.38	Climate Change

4   Empirical Study

In this section, a practical demonstration of the proposed approach is presented, on a case study on the temporal assessment of Environmental Performance Index (EPI). The Environmental Performance Index is a widely recognized composite indicator that evaluates how effectively countries protect environmental health and maintain ecosystem vitality. Developed by researchers from Yale University and Columbia University, the EPI aggregates dozens of indicators into thematic categories such as climate change mitigation, air quality, biodiversity, water resources, and sustainable agriculture. By transforming diverse environmental metrics into a standardized ranking, the index enables cross-country comparison and helps policymakers, researchers, and stakeholders monitor progress, identify strengths and weaknesses, and track changes in environmental performance over time.

The EPI is published on a biennial basis. For the purposes of this case study, data from the 2024, 2022, and 2020 editions were collected, as these reports rely on a highly consistent set of issue categories, which makes them suitable for the application of the proposed temporal TOPSIS extension. The analysis incorporates all 11 EPI issue categories, which are summarized in Table 1 together with the relative importance weights assigned to them within the EPI framework.

In this study, the analysis covers all 27 European Union countries, using data extracted from the 2024, 2022, and 2020 EPI reports. Following the methodology proposed in this paper, the three performance matrices were integrated into a single temporal TOPSIS decision matrix, illustrated in Fig. 1. For each issue category, countries receive scores ranging from 0 to 100, where higher values indicate better environmental performance; lower values are highlighted in red and higher values in blue. In several instances, data was unavailable for certain countries and categories, which fact was denoted in the EPI reports as either

364 A. Karczmarczyk et al.

NA or -9999. In this study, the -9999 notation is retained, as it could be directly incorporated into the computational procedure.

Alt.	C1t0	C1t1	C1t2	C2t0	C2t1	C2t2	C3t0	C3t1	C3t2	C4t0	C4t1	C4t2	C5t0	C5t1	C5t2	C6t0	C6t1	C6t2	C7t0	C7t1	C7t2	C8t0	C8t1	C8t2	C9t0	C9t1	C9t2	C10t0	C10t1	C10t2	C11t0	C11t1	C11t2
AUT	74.3	86	85.5	47.5	28	35.6	-9999	-9999	-9999	92.9	100	100	72.5	70.6	68	87.3	94	94	61.5	75	81.3	96	94.7	94.7	92.9	90.7	91.7	63.8	77.4	97.2	54.1	50.3	71.3
BEL	66.2	82.4	87.4	43.6	16.3	32.5	8	16.4	9	84.8	100	100	68.5	33.1	47.3	81.7	68.2	67.9	64.8	74.6	80.7	93.3	93.6	93.6	85.2	66.6	67.4	65.1	68	97.6	59.7	48.1	70.2
BGR	69.2	75.1	77.7	72.1	37.4	41.4	20.9	23.8	12.9	92.3	100	100	74.2	55.8	63.6	66.1	19.9	13.9	31.9	28.6	33	79	68.4	68.8	40.8	45.2	45.8	47.3	58.8	83.6	45.7	49.8	69.5
HRV	69.6	81.5	82.6	61.7	34.4	40.3	62.1	26	11.8	91.1	100	90.8	67.9	68.9	65.4	74.1	69	51.7	40.5	45.8	50.8	84.8	70.3	70.2	72	74.2	75.1	39.1	55.8	80	56	56.6	70
CYP	51.2	78.3	56.5	60.6	32.5	38.6	43.6	6.2	20.2	83.8	92.5	91.5	35.7	13.9	27.7	70.2	50	50	55.9	68.3	73.1	89.4	94	93.9	70.9	68.6	69.4	31.7	58.9	77.9	42.6	53.8	69.1
CZE	78.9	83.3	85.7	22.5	19.1	26.7	-9999	-9999	-9999	93.8	100	100	74	37.4	58.7	79.1	61.5	60.8	50.4	53.3	58.8	79.3	76.5	76.4	84.8	75.5	76.4	51.2	74.9	89.5	52.2	52.8	76.3
DNK	53.1	76.9	81.7	51	16.4	30.2	44.7	10.9	13.2	90.3	100	100	77.8	75.7	73	83.3	100	100	70.9	80.5	85.5	93.6	97.6	97.4	100	100	100	65.5	68.3	99.8	67.1	92.4	95
EST	78.8	86	87	28.9	15.2	22.4	70.4	40.8	16.4	91.5	100	96.6	71	61.8	51.8	69.6	70.4	69.6	60.9	74.6	80.3	80	61.9	61.9	72.6	86.5	87.4	65.1	66.7	74.4	82.8	52	59
FIN	59.1	71.1	75.5	60.8	20.1	20.8	90.4	42.4	12.8	92.8	100	93.1	66.6	62.7	52.4	82.5	100	100	82.2	93.5	98.8	100	100	100	100	100	100	68.4	69.6	97.7	71.8	83.6	77
FRA	61.5	86.5	88.3	58.6	21.5	36.1	43.2	19.5	12.1	92.8	100	100	72.8	49.5	65.2	82.5	88	88	65.2	82	88.1	88.2	96.3	96.2	98.9	83.1	84	59.6	63.8	94.8	61.3	49.5	81.9
DEU	82.1	88.8	88.8	38.5	17.9	39.7	36.4	26.9	14	92.6	100	96	78.8	60.9	61.9	89.1	97	97	66.9	75.2	81.1	100	99.1	99	98.7	89.8	90.7	87.4	69	97.9	64.9	47.2	71.5
GRC	62.4	69.1	72.6	58.2	28.1	43.9	47.8	15.6	15.7	88	78.7	78.9	61.4	38.9	52.6	83.1	81.7	81.7	53.7	62	67.5	96.6	98.2	98.2	71.1	68.6	69.4	39.4	59.9	83	71.3	50.8	66.5
HUN	66.9	78	82	50.1	28	28.2	-9999	-9999	-9999	93.3	100	96.9	69.2	53	73.1	86.2	55.3	53.8	38.6	38.2	42.8	73.5	62.2	62.2	65.7	67.4	68.2	51.7	43.4	89.2	49.2	48.1	71.3
IRL	62.5	59.6	65.8	-9999	17.4	27.4	40.6	18.2	9.1	87.3	95.4	100	72.9	48.7	47.3	72.5	87	89.7	76.8	89.1	94	95.6	97.4	97.4	97.3	81.8	82.7	60.7	67.9	81.7	51.1	48.2	66.6
ITA	58.5	76.5	75.6	55	26.1	37.9	34	16.8	14.9	89.5	100	81.4	56.4	38.8	56.8	72.7	58.8	58.8	52.2	69.4	75.9	98.6	98.3	98.2	83.6	80.6	81.5	57.5	60.6	83.7	53.2	48.2	68.1
LVA	68.4	84.9	86.7	31.9	15.8	21.4	59	38.4	7.3	82.4	95	94.8	64.4	64.4	62.8	68	90.7	90.7	45.1	51.1	54.8	82.4	59.1	59	71.9	77.5	76.4	42.8	63	61.4	52.4	58.6	67.7
LTU	74.9	84.4	87.5	45.9	21.9	24.6	80.1	13.4	14.5	83.2	95.5	96.6	67	65.6	64.1	72.7	52.3	51.4	53.2	58.4	62.7	75.8	58.4	58.3	75.4	83	83.9	61.3	67.4	87.8	52.4	47.1	65.9
LUX	84.8	84.8	85.5	46.1	18.1	34.3	-9999	-9999	-9999	94.8	100	100	62.8	55.9	42.2	90.6	98	98.5	67.1	81	67.2	99.8	98.7	98.6	100	95.1	96.1	63.8	79.1	96.2	62.4	67.4	77.5
MLT	67.1	72.9	75.1	-9999	100	100	56.9	47.8	12.2	83.3	100	80.8	43.5	28.3	28.3	52.3	0	0	69.8	73.2	77.6	95.3	99.8	99.8	67.4	49.9	50.6	27.1	63.5	96.7	63.6	82.3	62.6
NLD	60.5	80.1	83.7	62	24.4	42.8	22.5	13	13.1	92.6	100	100	68	29.3	40	89.2	100	100	67.4	76.8	82.4	91.1	100	100	100	94.1	95.1	69.6	66.2	100	60.7	54.5	65.8
POL	81.4	87.3	89	48.4	17.7	27.1	57.8	11	8	93.5	99.6	89.6	68.3	42.7	57.4	77.5	61.5	60.9	38.5	40.4	44.7	80.1	71.8	71.7	69.1	64.5	65.3	58.8	63.7	91.1	53.5	38.8	65.4
PRT	59.8	70.5	73	16.5	8.6	7.4	31.1	14.7	33.1	88.7	100	93.5	49.7	23.5	22.3	85.5	59.2	55	61.1	78.1	84.4	96.4	83.5	83.4	75.4	64.6	65.3	50.8	62.5	90.2	55.3	37.6	63.3
ROU	71.9	81.1	85	57.1	35	40.9	24.5	86.3	54.5	86.8	95.9	100	67.8	53.8	65.7	51.4	25.7	30.4	39.3	39.2	43.6	68	56	55.9	57.1	50.8	51.4	42.3	45.8	65.8	49.3	51.3	84.6
SVK	81.9	82.7	85	55.5	19.9	32.1	-9999	-9999	-9999	94.1	100	100	67.4	68	86.8	58.3	44.7	43.7	50.5	50.9	56.2	92.6	71.9	71.8	70.9	68.4	69.2	53.4	62.2	80.6	48.9	53.5	71.9
SVN	64.9	84.5	86.4	58.9	34.1	37.1	36.4	-9999	-9999	92.7	100	90	56.7	55	47	70.7	92.2	89.1	45.8	55.1	60.9	91.2	74.7	74.7	96.8	87.2	88.1	53.6	66.7	83.8	57.5	62.9	75.2
ESP	66.9	85.8	87.6	44.5	13.4	24.4	33.7	16.4	17.9	89.3	100	100	54.1	31.8	36.2	78.7	91.1	91.5	56.2	74	80.2	93.8	96.9	96.8	81.7	70.5	71.3	50.8	61.4	89	57.2	41.3	71.2
SWE	60	68.8	72.5	56.2	29.3	22.4	52.4	15.3	11.6	90.6	100	100	73.2	74	63.6	84.5	100	100	81.1	94	58.2	96.9	98.6	98.5	100	96.9	98	72.7	70.8	99.8	62.9	75.4	77.2

Fig. 1. Color-coded visual representation of the temporal decision matrix.

To benchmark the proposed approach, the final EPI scores for all considered periods were first collected. Subsequently, for each period, the classical TOPSIS method was applied to rank the countries. All criteria were treated as benefit-type attributes, since the maximum score of 100 represents the best achievable performance for each indicator. Moreover, the original EPI weights were adopted for all criteria (see Table 1). The resulting rankings are reported in Table 2.

Eventually, the proposed temporal TOPSIS extension was applied to evaluate the countries under the EPI criteria. The same impacts and weights were retained; however, instead of producing three separate rankings for individual time periods, the objective was to obtain a single ranking that jointly reflects performance across all analyzed periods.

Three alternative period-weighting schemes were considered. First, all periods were assigned equal importance ($\lambda = [1, 1, 1]$). Second, greater emphasis was placed on more recent periods by assigning progressively higher importance to each subsequent period ($\lambda = [3, 2, 1]$). Finally, a stronger recency effect was examined by weighting each subsequent period as twice as important as the previous one ($\lambda = [4, 2, 1]$). The resulting rankings are also reported in Table 2.

We begin with the scenario in which all three periods are treated as equally important. The classical TOPSIS evaluation for the most recent period (t_0, i.e., 2024) identifies Estonia as the top-performing country, followed by Finland, Germany, Greece, and Luxembourg. The official EPI ranking likewise places Estonia first in 2024, although some differences appear in subsequent positions.

When the temporal dimension is incorporated and the years 2022 and 2020 are given the same importance as 2024, the ranking changes noticeably. Estonia falls to the 6th place, while Denmark becomes the leader, followed by Finland and Luxembourg. The differences between the 2024 classical TOPSIS ranking and the temporal TOPSIS results with equal period weights are illustrated in Fig. 2a.

Table 2. Comparison of rankings produced by the proposed temporal TOPSIS extension with varying λ period weights, classic TOPSIS for 2024, 2022, 2020, and original EPI evaluation ranks for 2024, 2022 and 2020.

Country	Symbol	Temporal TOPSIS			TOPSIS			EPI		
		$\lambda = [1,1,1]$	$\lambda = [3,2,1]$	$\lambda = [4,2,1]$	2024	2022	2020	2024	2022	2020
Austria	AUT	13	13	13	14	12	11	6	7	4
Belgium	BEL	11	12	11	10	17	12	12	16	10
Bulgaria	BGR	24	26	26	26	23	21	26	25	27
Croatia	HRV	16	14	15	16	8	15	20	13	23
Cyprus	CYP	27	27	27	27	14	27	27	17	20
Czechia	CZE	12	15	16	17	16	7	14	15	13
Denmark	DNK	1	3	3	6	1	1	7	1	1
Estonia	EST	6	2	1	1	10	22	1	11	19
Finland	FIN	2	1	2	2	3	5	4	2	5
France	FRA	5	9	9	9	11	2	9	9	3
Germany	DEU	7	7	5	3	13	9	3	10	7
Greece	GRC	15	8	6	4	24	24	8	21	16
Hungary	HUN	23	25	25	25	25	14	24	24	22
Ireland	IRL	25	24	24	23	26	23	13	19	11
Italy	ITA	22	22	23	22	21	20	22	18	13
Latvia	LVA	19	19	20	21	7	16	23	12	25
Lithuania	LTU	20	20	19	18	18	18	17	23	24
Luxembourg	LUX	3	4	4	5	5	4	2	5	2
Malta	MLT	8	6	8	8	2	25	10	3	15
Netherlands	NLD	14	10	10	11	9	17	10	8	8
Poland	POL	21	17	17	13	22	19	16	26	26
Portugal	PRT	26	23	22	20	27	26	21	27	18
Romania	ROU	10	21	21	24	19	3	25	22	21
Slovakia	SVK	18	18	18	19	15	13	15	14	17
Slovenia	SVN	9	11	12	15	6	8	19	6	12
Spain	ESP	17	16	14	12	20	10	18	20	9
Sweden	SWE	4	5	7	7	4	6	5	4	6

Countries located on the diagonal line retain identical positions in both rankings; this occurs for only a small subset, including Finland (2nd), Malta (8th), Croatia (16th), and Cyprus (27th). Most countries exhibit at least minor shifts, such as Slovakia (19th in 2024 versus 18th temporally), while others experience substantial changes, for example Romania (24th in 2024 versus 10th temporally).

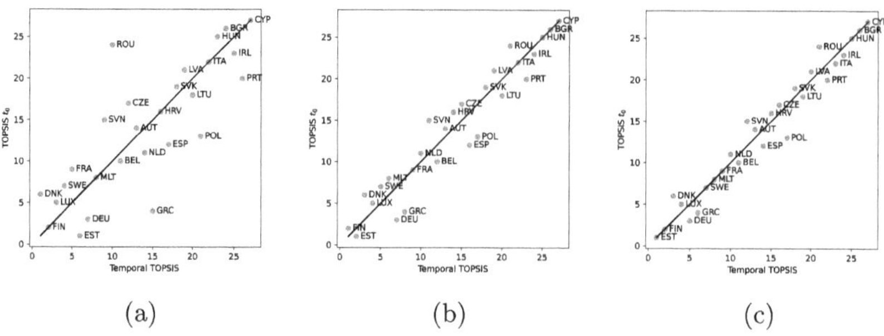

Fig. 2. Visual comparison of the TOPSIS rankings in period t_0 on the y-axis and the proposed temporal approach with period weights a) $[1, 1, 1]$; b) $[3, 2, 1]$; c) $[4, 2, 1]$ on the x-axis.

These differences stem from the inclusion of historical performance. Denmark, ranked 6th in 2024, rises to 1st place in the temporal ranking due to its leading positions in both 2022 and 2020. A similar pattern explains Romania's improvement in the temporal approach: despite a low position in 2024, it performed considerably better in earlier editions, which substantially strengthens its overall temporal standing. However, one may argue that results from four years earlier should not influence the current assessment to such a degree. For this reason, the next stage of the analysis introduces a damping approach, in which earlier periods receive progressively lower weights than more recent ones.

In the second variant, a recency-oriented weighting scheme was introduced in which the years 2020, 2022, and 2024 were assigned weights of 1, 2, and 3, respectively (subsequently normalized prior to their application). Under this setting, Denmark no longer occupies the leading position and falls to 3rd place (see Table 2). Finland becomes the top-ranked country, reflecting consistently strong results across all three periods (2nd in 2024, 3rd in 2022, and 5th in 2020), while Estonia moves to 2nd place (1st in 2024, 10th in 2022, and 22nd in 2020). The remaining ranking shifts are illustrated in Fig. 2b.

In the final scenario, an even stronger recency effect was imposed by assigning weights of 1, 2, and 4 to the years 2020, 2022, and 2024, respectively (again normalized before use). The corresponding results are reported in Table 2, and the differences relative to classical TOPSIS for 2024 are shown in Fig. 2c. Under this scheme, Estonia regains the leading position, with Finland moving to second place. This outcome reflects the dominant influence of the most recent period: the substantially higher weight assigned to 2024 amplifies the impact of current indicator values, while the contribution of the earliest period becomes comparatively minor. A similar pattern is observed for Denmark, which ranked 6th in 2024 but 1st in the two earlier periods. Despite its strong historical performance, Finland's superior results in 2024 allow it to remain ahead of Denmark, which ultimately secures 3rd place rather than the 6th position implied by the most recent data alone.

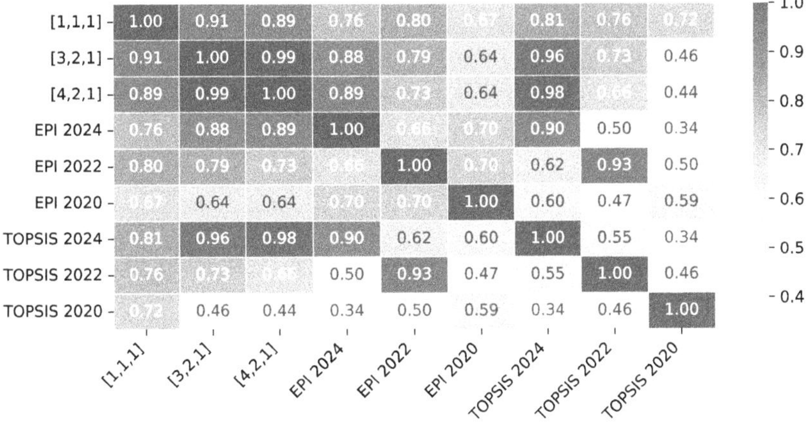

Fig. 3. Correlation matrix between various ranking creation approaches.

The empirical study concludes with an analysis of the correlations among all rankings considered in this work. The resulting correlation matrix is shown in Fig. 3. The first three entries correspond to the rankings obtained using the proposed temporal TOPSIS extension, with λ representing equal period weights, moderate recency emphasis, and strong recency emphasis. These are followed by the original EPI rankings for 2024, 2022, and 2020, and finally by the classical TOPSIS rankings computed separately for each of these years.

Several clear clusters can be identified. A strong correlation is observed among the original EPI rankings across the three editions, which is expected since the same 11 criteria are applied to all 27 countries in each biennial assessment. Although national environmental performance evolves over time, such changes are typically gradual, leading to substantial similarity between consecutive rankings.

A comparable pattern emerges for the classical TOPSIS rankings based on the EPI criteria and weights. In this case, the 2024 results show stronger correlation with 2022 than with 2020, further highlighting the persistence and slow evolution of performance across EPI indicators.

When the temporal TOPSIS results are compared with the single-year classical TOPSIS rankings, a clear trend appears: the greater the weight assigned to the most recent period (2024), the stronger the correlation with the 2024 classical ranking. The correlation coefficient increases from 0.81 for equal weights $[1, 1, 1]$, to 0.96 for moderate recency emphasis $[3, 2, 1]$, and reaches 0.98 for strong recency emphasis $[4, 2, 1]$. Nevertheless, the coefficient never reaches unity, confirming that the incorporation of temporal information produces meaningful differences, as also illustrated by the ranking comparisons in Fig. 2.

Overall, the empirical results confirm that incorporating temporal information into the evaluation provides a more comprehensive and nuanced assessment of countries' environmental performance. The proposed temporal TOPSIS extension not only produces rankings consistent with single-period analyses but also reveals meaningful shifts driven by historical performance and alternative recency weighting schemes, thereby demonstrating its practical applicability and added analytical value in long-lasting decision-making contexts.

5   Conclusions

This paper introduced a temporal extension of the TOPSIS method designed to support multi-criteria decision-making problems in which performance evolves over time. Instead of aggregating or comparing rankings obtained independently for different periods, the proposed approach integrates the temporal dimension directly into the decision matrix by expanding the criterion space and introducing time-period weights. This formulation preserves the structure and computational simplicity of classical TOPSIS while enabling a unified ranking that reflects the entire performance history of the evaluated alternatives.

The empirical study based on EPI data for the European Union countries demonstrated the practical relevance and analytical value of the proposed approach. The results confirmed that incorporating historical information leads to meaningful changes in rankings, especially when countries exhibit different long-term trajectories. The temporal TOPSIS rankings consistently remained strongly correlated with single-period rankings, yet never identical to them, indicating that the method provides additional insights rather than merely reproducing existing results. Moreover, the experiments showed that the choice of time-weighting scheme plays a crucial role in shaping the final ranking, allowing decision makers to control the balance between long-term performance and recency effects. This flexibility is particularly valuable in policy-oriented evaluations, where both historical consistency and current performance may be important.

Overall, the obtained results confirm that the proposed temporal TOPSIS extension constitutes a simple, transparent, and computationally efficient tool for dynamic multi-criteria evaluation problems. By preserving temporal information and enabling adjustable recency emphasis, the method offers a meaningful alternative to traditional single-period assessments and to approaches that aggregate rankings across time.

Several promising research directions emerge from this study. First, the proposed temporal expansion concept could be extended to other multi-criteria decision-making methods, including distance-based approaches such as VIKOR and SPOTIS, as well as outranking methods from the European school, such as PROMETHEE, which offers additional analytical capabilities through GAIA-based visualization and clustering of criteria. Second, further research could investigate alternative temporal weighting schemes, including data-driven or adaptive approaches. Finally, a systematic comparison with existing temporal evaluation frameworks, particularly DARIA-TOPSIS, would provide valuable insights into the advantages and limitations of different strategies for incorporating time into multi-criteria decision analysis.

Acknowledgments. This research was partially funded by the National Science Centre, Poland 2022/45/B/HS4/02960 (JW), and co-financed by the Minister of Science under the "Regional Excellence Initiative" Program RID/SP/0046/2024/01 (AB).

Disclosure of Interests. The authors have no competing interests to declare that are relevant to the content of this article.

References

1. Barrak, E., Rodrigues, C., Antunes, C.H., Freire, F., Dias, L.C.: Applying multi-criteria decision analysis to combine life cycle assessment with circularity indicators. J. Clean. Prod. **451**, 141872 (2024). https://doi.org/10.1016/j.jclepro.2024.141872. https://www.sciencedirect.com/science/article/pii/S0959652624013209

2. Bączkiewicz, A., Wątróbski, J., Jankowski, J., Sałabun, W.: Multi-criteria temporal intelligent decision support system for sustainable energy mix assessment. In: Nguyen, N.T., Chbeir, R., Manolopoulos, Y., Fujita, H., Hong, T.P., Nguyen, L.M., Wojtkiewicz, K. (eds.) Intelligent Information and Database Systems, pp. 95–106. Springer, Singapore (2024). https://doi.org/10.1007/978-981-97-4985-0_8

3. Cinelli, M., Burgherr, P., Kadziński, M., Słowiński, R.: Proper and improper uses of MCDA methods in energy systems analysis. Decis. Support Syst. **163**, 113848 (2022). https://doi.org/10.1016/j.dss.2022.113848. https://www.sciencedirect.com/science/article/pii/S0167923622001191

4. Digkoglou, P., Papathanasiou, J.: Application of multiple criteria decision aiding in environmental policy-making processes. Int. J. Environ. Sci. Technol. **22**(8), 6967–6982 (2025). https://doi.org/10.1007/s13762-024-06101-w

5. Ferla, G., Mura, B., Falasco, S., Caputo, P., Matarazzo, A.: Multi-Criteria Decision Analysis (MCDA) for sustainability assessment in food sector. A systematic literature review on methods, indicators and tools. Sci. Total Environ. **946**, 174235 (2024). https://doi.org/10.1016/j.scitotenv.2024.174235. https://www.sciencedirect.com/science/article/pii/S0048969724043833

6. Frini, A., Benamor, S.: Making decisions in a sustainable development context: a state-of-the-art survey and proposal of a multi-period single synthesizing criterion approach. Comput. Econ. **52**(2), 341–385 (2018). https://doi.org/10.1007/s10614-017-9677-5

7. Hwang, C.L., Yoon, K.: Methods for multiple attribute decision making. In: Hwang, C.L., Yoon, K. (eds.) Multiple Attribute Decision Making: Methods and Applications A State-of-the-Art Survey, pp. 58–191. Springer, Heidelberg (1981). https://doi.org/10.1007/978-3-642-48318-9_3

8. Karczmarczyk, A., Drożdż, W., Karczmarczyk, A., Wątróbski, J.: Strong sustainability paradigm in TOPSIS method: new approach to wind farm selection problem. In: Paszynski, M., Barnard, A.S., Zhang, Y.J. (eds.) Computational Science – ICCS 2025 Workshops, pp. 296–309. Springer, Cham (2025). https://doi.org/10.1007/978-3-031-97567-7_23

9. Karczmarczyk, A., Wątróbski, J., Bączkiewicz, A., Mróz-Malik, O., Drożdż, W.: New robust multi-criteria decision-making method for wind farm location problems. Appl. Energy **398**, 126401 (2025). https://doi.org/10.1016/j.apenergy.2025.126401. https://www.sciencedirect.com/science/article/pii/S0306261925011316

10. Kizielewicz, B., Pawlak, R., Gandor, M., Sałabun, W.: A robust framework for sustainable vehicle assessment: integrating FN-TOPSIS with subjective weighting methods. Procedia Comput. Sci. **270**, 5764–5775 (2025). https://doi.org/10.1016/j.procs.2025.10.045. https://www.sciencedirect.com/science/article/pii/S1877050925033782

11. Oppio, A., Bottero, M., Arcidiacono, A.: Assessing urban quality: a proposal for a MCDA evaluation framework. Ann. Oper. Res. **312**(2), 1427–1444 (2022). https://doi.org/10.1007/s10479-017-2738-2

12. Purker, S., Lalyer, C.R., Giese, B.: Decision support for selection of new materials considering socio-economic and broader environmental aspects. Sustain. Prod. Consum. **39**, 438–450 (2023). https://doi.org/10.1016/j.spc.2023.05.032. https://www.sciencedirect.com/science/article/pii/S2352550923001276

13. Rad, M., Sonesson, U., Höglund, E., Östergren, K.: Multi-Criteria Decision Analysis (MCDA) for sustainability assessment–How reliable are the results? Sustain. Futures **11**, 101657 (2026). https://doi.org/10.1016/j.sftr.2026.101657. https://www.sciencedirect.com/science/article/pii/S266618882600016X

14. Shmelev, S.E., Shmeleva, I.A.: Smart and sustainable benchmarking of cities and regions in Europe: the application of multicriteria assessment. Cities **156**, 105533 (2025). https://doi.org/10.1016/j.cities.2024.105533. https://www.sciencedirect.com/science/article/pii/S0264275124007479

15. Wątróbski, J., Bączkiewicz, A., Rudawska, I.: A Strong Sustainability Paradigm based Analytical Hierarchy Process (SSP-AHP) method to evaluate sustainable healthcare systems. Ecol. Indic. **154**, 110493 (2023). https://doi.org/10.1016/j.ecolind.2023.110493. https://www.sciencedirect.com/science/article/pii/S1470160X23006350

16. Wątróbski, J., Bączkiewicz, A., Ziemba, E., Sałabun, W.: Sustainable cities and communities assessment using the DARIA-TOPSIS method. Sustain. Cities Soc. **83**, 103926 (2022). https://doi.org/10.1016/j.scs.2022.103926. https://www.sciencedirect.com/science/article/pii/S2210670722002487

17. Wątróbski, J., Jankowski, J., Ziemba, P., Karczmarczyk, A., Zioło, M.: Generalised framework for multi-criteria method selection. Omega **86**, 107–124 (2019). https://doi.org/10.1016/j.omega.2018.07.004. http://www.sciencedirect.com/science/article/pii/S0305048317308563

18. Wątróbski, J., Karczmarczyk, A., Bączkiewicz, A.: Using the TOSS method in semi-autonomous passenger car selection. Sustainable Energy Technol. Assess. **58**, 103367 (2023). https://doi.org/10.1016/j.seta.2023.103367. https://www.sciencedirect.com/science/article/pii/S2213138823003600

Assessing the Impact of Criterion Significance on Ranking Stability - Offshore Wind Farm Case Study

Aleksandra Bączkiewicz[1](✉) [ID], Jarosław Wątróbski[1,2] [ID],
Artur Karczmarczyk[3] [ID], and Wojciech Drożdż[1] [ID]

[1] Institute of Management, University of Szczecin, ul. Cukrowa 8, 71-004 Szczecin,
Poland
{aleksandra.baczkiewicz,jaroslaw.watrobski,wojciech.drozdz}@usz.edu.pl
[2] National Institute of Telecommunications, ul. Szachowa 1, 04-894 Warsaw, Poland
[3] Department of Computer Science, Westpomeranian University of Technology in
Szczecin, ul. Żołnierska 49, 71-210 Szczecin, Poland
artur.karczmarczyk@zut.edu.pl

Abstract. The assessment of offshore wind farm (OWF) projects typically relies on multi-criteria decision analysis (MCDA), which often involves a large number of evaluation criteria reflecting technical, economic, environmental, and social aspects. While comprehensive, high-dimensional decision models may suffer from reduced transparency and increased sensitivity of results. This paper proposes a data-driven framework for criterion significance assessment and controlled reduction of MCDA models. The framework combines objective significance measures, namely the coefficient of variation (CV) and entropy, with a structured sensitivity analysis based on percentile-based exclusion thresholds. Using the TOPSIS (Technique for Order Preference by Similarity to Ideal Solution) method, the framework is applied to the evaluation of seven OWFs described by 32 criteria. The results demonstrate that even criteria classified as weakly significant can substantially influence ranking outcomes, including changes in the ranking leader. At the same time, the proposed sensitivity-based reduction procedure enables the identification of stable and robust alternatives and reveals the degree of ranking dependence on the criterion set. The framework improves the transparency and interpretability of multi-criteria assessments and provides practical support for decision-makers by explicitly quantifying the risks associated with model simplification.

Keywords: Offshore wind energy · Multi-criteria decision analysis · TOPSIS method · Criterion significance · Sensitivity analysis · Multi-criteria model reduction

1 Introduction

Offshore wind energy is a strategic component of the energy transition, contributing to energy security, independence, and economic development. As a domes-

M. Paszynski et al. (Eds.): ICCS 2026 Workshops, LNCS 16788, pp. 371–385, 2026.
https://doi.org/10.1007/978-3-032-29915-4_31

tic renewable energy source, it supports the diversification of the energy mix while reducing dependence on energy imports and geopolitical risk [10]. Offshore wind has high potential to provide stable and predictable energy resources [13]. Due to their technological complexity, high capital intensity, and significant economic, environmental, and social impacts, offshore wind farm (OWF) projects are commonly evaluated using multi-criteria decision analysis (MCDA) [22]. Multi-criteria models provide a basis for justifying the selection of projects in which investors and financial institutions decide to invest capital [8]. On the other hand, when preparing concessions and regulations, the state administration needs tools to assess the impact of investments on the economy and the environment [21]. Multi-criteria assessment enables a holistic, transparent, and objective analysis of investments of strategic importance that impact the economy, the environment, energy security, and society [15]. Such assessments require the simultaneous consideration of numerous criteria and dimensions to adequately capture investment value and risk [1].

In fields where MCDA methods are applied, such as investments or renewable energy systems, decision-making models often comprise extensive sets of criteria that describe technical, economic, environmental, and social aspects. However, a wide range of criteria can increase computational complexity, lead to information redundancy, and reduce the transparency and interpretability of results, which consequently hinders the decision-making process [7]. Consequently, the literature increasingly emphasizes the need to simplify models by identifying and eliminating less relevant criteria, while maintaining the resilience of decision outcomes [12].

The literature presents various approaches to selecting criteria for reducing model complexity in MCDA. Habibollahi et al. proposed an approach integrating Principal Component Analysis (PCA) with Multi-Criteria Decision-Making (MCDM), specifically the MOORA (Multi-Objective Optimization on the Basis of Ratio Analysis Method) method. PCA identifies dominant components and reduces dimensionality, while MOORA ranks the original features based on their compliance with these components [5]. The indicated approach incorporates multiple decision-making indicators into a unified structure. It improves the accuracy of variable reduction in high-dimensional data, providing a robust and generalized strategy for unsupervised feature selection across various fields. In turn, Jokar et al. proposed a hybrid model that integrates MCDM and a machine learning (ML) method called Random Forest regression to identify relationships between criteria and eliminate redundant criteria [6]. The proposed model accounts for interval-based fuzzy uncertainty when evaluating renewable energy projects. In another research paper, Li et al. presented a multi-criteria optimization classifier (MCOC) based on the LASSO (Least Absolute Shrinkage and Selection Operator) method (LASSO-MCOC) for simultaneous classification and feature selection [14]. The application of the proposed method was demonstrated on the problem of credit risk assessment. In another study, ridge regression, LASSO, and Elastic-Net methods were applied to reduce dimensionality in various simulated datasets with different characteristics, as well as in real-world datasets [11].

A review of the literature on MCDM highlights the growing importance of model dimensionality reduction methods in relation to the number of criteria. The methods presented include both statistical approaches, such as PCA, and hybrid techniques that combine ML and MCDM. To address the challenge of high-dimensional decision models in OWF assessment, this paper proposes an alternative approach in the form of a fully transparent procedure based on a combination of the coefficient of variation (CV) and entropy as measures of criterion significance. The presented approach is extended to include an iterative sensitivity analysis used directly for their selection. Proposed data-driven framework for criterion significance analysis and controlled model reduction integrates classical MCDM methods with objective significance measures and a structured sensitivity analysis [4], enabling the systematic identification of weakly informative criteria and the evaluation of their impact on ranking stability. By transforming criterion reduction from an arbitrary preprocessing step into a transparent and risk-aware procedure, the proposed approach supports reliable decision-making while maintaining robustness of the evaluation results. Such an approach not only allows for an objective assessment of the significance of the criteria but also enables a controlled reduction in their number while preserving the interpretability of the decision-making model, which represents a significant addition to existing approaches in the literature.

The rest of the paper is organized as follows. Section 2 explains applied methodology and describes considered dataset, in Sect. 3 research results are presented and Sect. 4 provides conclusions and future works.

2   Methodology

The aim of this paper is to present the data-driven framework developed for criterion significance assessment and controlled model reduction in MCDM problems. Its purpose is to reduce the complexity of decision models by excluding criteria of lowest significance. The flow of the mentioned framework is demonstrated in Fig. 1. The structuring process incorporates building a decision model, including selected evaluation criteria (C), alternatives (A), and efficiency values (E) collected for considered alternatives in relation to criteria. The proposed framework involves determining the significance of a complete set of criteria using two measures of significance: the coefficient of variation (CV) [20] and entropy [17]. The choice of CV and entropy is justified by the objective, data-driven nature of these measures, as well as their interpretive complementarity and the ability to cross-validate results, which enhances the reliability of the procedure. CV reflects the diversity of alternatives relative to the criteria, while entropy measures the amount of information contained in the criterion [9,16]. Subsequently, in order to determine the thresholds for including criteria according to CV, the lower quartile is determined, while for entropy, the upper quartile is determined. This is because high entropy means low diversity, unlike CV, whose high values indicate good diversity. After eliminating the criteria from the model separately for

CV and entropy, the alternatives are evaluated using a multi-criteria method, and then rankings are determined. The rankings obtained are compared with the initial ranking constructed for the full set of criteria using Spearman's correlation measure [21]. If, after excluding the criteria, there are no differences between the compared rankings or they are insignificant (e.g., single shifts of small range in the lower positions of the ranking), it means that the previously identified criteria of low significance do not have a significant impact on the assessment result, so they can be safely removed from the model without the risk of oversimplification and decision mistakes. If the changes are significant, occur in high positions, especially if they concern the leader or have a significant scope, it means that the excluded criteria, despite their low significance, nevertheless contribute significant informational value to the model, differentiating between alternatives, and their elimination is inadvisable as it risks erroneous decisions.

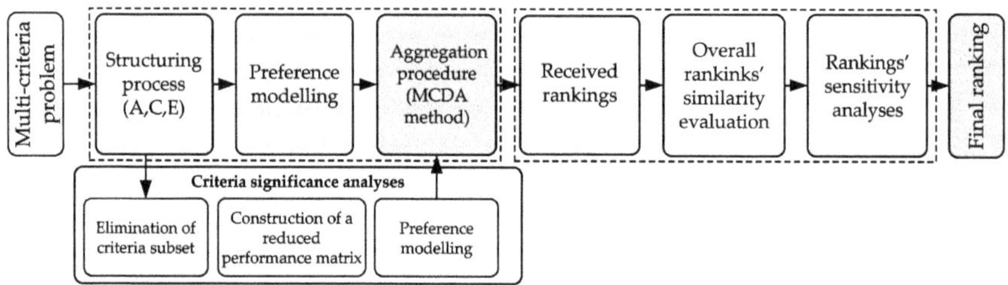

Fig. 1. The flow of the proposed framework for reducing the least significant criteria for multi-criteria decision-making.

The following stage in the proposed framework is sensitivity analysis. This procedure involves considering a given range of elimination thresholds for criteria according to their significance for both CV and entropy, so that these thresholds increase. We adopt successive percentiles for CV and entropy values as thresholds. In subsequent steps of the analysis, the groups of criteria removed from the model increase as the significance threshold for the criteria to be excluded increases. At each step, we determine which criteria are excluded, their number, the percentage they represent of the total number of criteria, the number of changes in the compared rankings before and after the elimination of criteria, the Euclidean distance between the values of the aggregated measure of the multi-criteria method, and the correlation value of the compared rankings. Sensitivity analysis allows us to establish a safe threshold for excluding the least important criteria, thus enabling us to simplify the model without losing important information. In addition, it provides additional information about the stability of the evaluated alternatives, their similarity, the stability of decisions, and identifies critical criteria. The dataset is described below in Subsect. 2.1, followed by the methods used in the research, including the TOPSIS (Technique for Order Preference by Similarity to Ideal Solution) method provided in Subsect. 2.2 and significance measures: CV explained in Subsect. 2.3 and entropy given in Subsect. 2.4.

2.1   The Dataset

This research covers seven OWFs planned for construction in Poland's exclusive economic zone in the Baltic Sea, in the Słupsk Shoal (Ławica Słupska) area, as part of the first stage of offshore wind energy development, which constitutes the first phase of the support system. These OWFs are A_1 - OWF Bałtyk II, A_2 - OWF Bałtyk III, A_3 - Baltica 2, A_4 - Baltica 3, A_5 - F.E.W. Baltic II, A_6 - Baltic Power, and A_7 - B-C Wind. Due to its size, the dataset containing performance values for the considered OWFs in relation to 32 model criteria listed below is available in an open repository https://github.com/energyinpython/Offshore-wind-farms-assessment. The data sources used to develop the multi-criteria assessment model for OWFs included publicly available online reports, news websites, market and energy information centers, OWF project websites, technical and non-technical project documentation, and government websites.

C_1 Power [MW]
C_2 Total area [km^2]
C_3 Distance from shore [km]
C_4 Length of submarine export cable [km]
C_5 Average depth [m]
C_6 Maximum depth [km]
C_7 Average wind speed [m/s]
C_8 Planned launch year [number]
C_9 Efficiency of water basin utilization [MW/km^2]
C_{10} Estimated annual production [MWh/year]
C_{11} Covering household energy demand [number of households/year]
C_{12} New direct jobs [full-time equivalent jobs in the OWF life cycle]
C_{13} New indirect jobs [full-time equivalent jobs in the OWF life cycle]
C_{14} CO$_2$ reduction in the OWF life cycle [million tons]
C_{15} SO$_2$ reduction in the OWF life cycle [tons]
C_{16} NO$_2$ reduction in the OWF life cycle [tons]
C_{17} Dust reduction in the OWF life cycle [tons]
C_{18} Support for education [rating 1–5]
C_{19} Support for local communities [rating 1–5]
C_{20} Raw material savings – hard coal in the OWF life cycle [million tons]
C_{21} Raw material savings – hard coal in the OWF life cycle [PLN billion]
C_{22} Savings on the purchase of CO$_2$ emission permits in the OWF life cycle [PLN billion]
C_{23} Budget revenue from concession fees [PLN million]
C_{24} Budget revenue from location permit fees [PLN million]
C_{25} Share of local content in the development phase [PLN million]
C_{26} Share of local content in the operational phase [PLN million per year]

C_{27} Investment in installation port [1/0]
C_{28} Support for entrepreneurship [rating 1–5]
C_{29} Support for innovation [rating 1–5]
C_{30} CAPEX investment costs [PLN million]
C_{31} Operating costs (OPEX) [PLN million per year]
C_{32} Liquidation costs (DECEX) [PLN million]

The research work involved the application of the developed framework for reducing the number of criteria in the model. This framework assumes the exclusion of low-variability criteria from the evaluation process, which, due to their low informational significance, are presumably the least important for the decision-making process. CV and entropy were used as measures of criterion significance. In the first stage of the study, criteria with a CV value below the lower quartile were excluded from the assessment. In the case of entropy, because a high value of this measure means low relevance, criteria with a value above the upper quartile were excluded. In order to compare the rankings obtained from the reduced dataset, their correlation with the ranking of the full dataset was measured.

In the second part of the study, a sensitivity analysis [18] was performed by modifying the criterion exclusion threshold to examine the stability of the results when removing the least significant criteria and the dependence of decisions on criteria of little informational value. Consecutive percentile values were used as criterion exclusion thresholds. The TOPSIS method [2] was applied to rank the OWFs. TOPSIS evaluates alternatives based on their distance to the ideal and anti-ideal solutions, assigning higher rankings to alternatives closer to the ideal point. Due to its simplicity, intuitive interpretation, and widespread use in MCDM problems, TOPSIS is a suitable choice for comparing alternatives under a large set of criteria [19].

2.2   The TOPSIS Method

Step 1. Normalize the decision matrix $X = [x_{ij}]_{m \times n}$ including performance values x_{ij} collected for considered alternatives in relation to criteria assessment. For the normalization procedure, the Minimum-Maximum or another normalization method can be utilized. In Minimum-Maximum normalization r_{ij} normalized values are received by using Eq. (1) for profit (r_{ij}^{+}) and cost (r_{ij}^{-}) criteria.

$$r_{ij}^{+} = \frac{x_{ij} - min_j(x_{ij})}{max_j(x_{ij}) - min_j(x_{ij})}, \ r_{ij}^{-} = \frac{max_j(x_{ij}) - x_{ij}}{max_j(x_{ij}) - min_j(x_{ij})} \tag{1}$$

Step 2. Calculate the weighted normalized decision matrix with Eq. (2). This paper applies equal weights due to multiple simulations that exclude criteria based on their significance.

$$v_{ij} = w_j r_{ij} \tag{2}$$

Step 3. Determine the Positive and Negative Ideal Solution (PIS and NIS) using

Eq. (3). PIS incorporates the maximums of the weighted normalized decision matrix. On the other hand, NIS includes its minimums.

$$v_j^+ = \{v_1^+, v_2^+, \ldots, v_n^+\} = \{max_j(v_{ij})\}, \; v_j^- = \{v_1^-, v_2^-, \ldots, v_n^-\} = \{min_j(v_{ij})\} \tag{3}$$

Step 4. Calculate the distance from PIS and NIS for each alternative employing (4). The default distance metric in the TOPSIS method is Euclidean distance.

$$D_i^+ = \sqrt{\sum_{j=1}^{n}(v_{ij} - v_j^+)^2}, \; D_i^- = \sqrt{\sum_{j=1}^{n}(v_{ij} - v_j^-)^2} \tag{4}$$

Step 5. Calculate the closeness coefficient for each alternative under consideration as Eq. (5) shows. The alternative with the highest C_i is the ranking leader.

$$C_i = \frac{D_i^-}{D_i^- + D_i^+} \tag{5}$$

2.3 Coefficient of Variation (CV)

CV is applied as a measure of significance based on data variability (data-driven) [3]. Low CV values indicate slight variation between alternatives in terms of the criterion under consideration, which means they are of minor importance in the decision-making process. High CV values, on the other hand, indicate significant variation between alternatives in terms of the criteria, which implies that they are of high importance in the decision-making process. CV is calculated as Eq. (6) presents.

$$CV_j = \frac{\sigma_j}{\bar{x}_j} \tag{6}$$

CV threshold below which criteria are excluded may, for example, be determined based on the lower quartile. Percentiles may also be employed to remove a defined percentage of criteria with the lowest informative value.

2.4 Entropy Measure

Entropy may be an alternative or validation technique for CV, as it measures the amount of information in a criterion. A high entropy value indicates low diversity and, consequently, low decision relevance. The threshold for entropy above which criteria are excluded can be determined based on the upper quartile. It is also possible to use percentiles to remove a given percentage of the least informationally relevant criteria. To calculate entropy, first, normalization of the decision matrix performed in accordance with Eq. (7) is necessary.

$$r_{ij} = \frac{x_{ij}}{\sum_{i=1}^{m} x_{ij}} \tag{7}$$

This allows to get normalized decision matrix $P = [p_{ij}]_{m \times n}$ where m defines alternatives number, n represents criteria number, $i = 1, 2, \ldots, m$, and $j = 1, 2, \ldots, n$. Then calculate the entropy E_j for each j-th criterion according to Eq. (8).

$$E_j = -\frac{\sum_{i=1}^{m} p_{ij} ln(p_{ij})}{ln(m)} \tag{8}$$

3 Results

In the first stage of the analysis, criterion significance was established using two data-driven measures: CV and entropy. The lower quartile (q_1) for CV and the upper quartile (q_3) for entropy were adopted as exclusion thresholds to identify the least significant criteria. In both approaches, the resulting reduction led to the elimination of the same eight criteria (C_2, C_3, C_5, C_6, C_7, C_8, C_9, and C_{19}), corresponding to 25% of the total number of criteria. The consistency of the eliminated criteria across both significance measures indicates a high level of agreement between CV and entropy in identifying weakly informative criteria. Subsequently, the TOPSIS closeness coefficients were calculated for two scenarios: the full model, including all criteria, and the reduced model excluding the identified least significant criteria. The comparative results for OWFs are presented in Table 1.

Table 1. Comparison of TOPSIS closeness coefficients and rankings before and after criterion reduction for criteria significance measured with CV and entropy.

A_i	TOPSIS closeness coefficient			TOPSIS ranking		
	Full dataset	CV q_1	Entropy q_3	Full dataset	CV q_1	Entropy q_3
A_1	0.5181	0.4623	0.4623	5	4	4
A_2	0.5297	0.4605	0.4605	3	5	5
A_3	0.6173	0.6144	0.6144	1	2	2
A_4	0.5287	0.5020	0.5020	4	3	3
A_5	0.3525	0.3058	0.3058	6	7	7
A_6	0.6053	0.6211	0.6211	2	1	1
A_7	0.3292	0.3304	0.3304	7	6	6

It can be observed that the rankings obtained after excluding the 25% least significant criteria differ from the ranking created for the full dataset, and the differences appear in all positions of the ranking. In the case of OWF A_2, the difference is as much as 2 positions, and for the other OWFs, 1 position. It is also important to note that after excluding the 25% least significant criteria, the leader of the ranking changes from A_3 to A_6. The total number of shifts between the rankings was 8. This means that there were quite a lot of them, considering the small number of alternatives considered. The Spearman correlation of the ranking for the reduced dataset with the ranking of the full dataset is 0.8214, and the Euclidean distance between them is 0.1051.

The results of the first part of the study showed that the least significant 25% of the criteria have a significant impact on the ranking obtained. This means that decisions and recommendations in the case of the OWFs under consideration are sensitive and strongly dependent on the least significant 25% of the criteria. Although these criteria were classified as the least significant according to CV and entropy, their joint exclusion leads to significant changes in the ranking, indicating that low individual variability does not necessarily mean little collective impact on the final ranking. It turns out that they strongly differentiate OWFs, and simplifying the model by excluding them cannot be recommended.

3.1 Sensitivity Analysis

In the second part of the study, a sensitivity analysis was performed for CV and entropy to reveal the threshold for excluding criteria for which the ranking begins to change and to identify the least significant criteria that are irrelevant to the final ranking, which would allow the model to be simplified by excluding the least significant criteria without affecting the results. During the stepwise analysis, the criteria were excluded according to a stepwise change in the percentile value representing the significance threshold.

The results are presented in Tables 2 and 3, displaying the excluded criteria, their number, what percentage of the full dataset they represent, the number of shifts in the ranking in relation to the full dataset, and the Euclidean distance from the full dataset ranking. The charts display the TOPSIS closeness coefficient (C_i) values obtained during sensitivity analysis for CV (Fig. 2) and entropy (Fig. 4), as well as the rankings for CV (Fig. 3) and entropy (Fig. 5).

Table 2. Percentile-based exclusion thresholds used in the sensitivity analysis of criterion reduction for criteria significance measured with CV.

Exclusion percentile	Criteria excluded	Number of criteria excluded	% of criteria excluded	Shifts in rankings	Euclidean distance	Correlation
5	C_7, C_8	2	6.25	4	0.028	0.9286
10	C_5, C_6, C_7, C_8	4	12.5	6	0.0631	0.8929
15	$C_5, C_6, C_7, C_8, C_{19}$	5	15.625	6	0.0931	0.8929
20	$C_2, C_5, C_6, C_7, C_8, C_9, C_{19}$	7	21.875	6	0.0975	0.8929
25	$C_2, C_3, C_5, C_6, C_7, C_8, C_9, C_{19}$	8	25	8	0.1051	0.8214
30	$C_2, C_3, C_5, C_6, C_7, C_8, C_9, C_{19}, C_{28}, C_{29}$	10	31.25	8	0.1621	0.8214
35	$C_2, C_3, C_5, C_6, C_7, C_8, C_9, C_{13}, C_{19}, C_{28}, C_{29}$	11	34.375	8	0.1569	0.8214
40	$C_2, C_3, C_5, C_6, C_7, C_8, C_9, C_{13}, C_{19}, C_{28}, C_{29}$	11	34.375	8	0.1569	0.8214
45	$C_2, C_3, C_5, C_6, C_7, C_8, C_9, C_{13}, C_{19}, C_{28}, C_{29}$	11	34.375	8	0.1569	0.8214
50	$C_2, C_3, C_5, C_6, C_7, C_8, C_9, C_{13}, C_{19}, C_{28}, C_{29}$	11	34.375	8	0.1569	0.8214

In the case of sensitivity analysis for CV, it can be seen that already for the 5th percentile and the exclusion of 2 criteria from the decision-making process, there were 4 shifts in the ranking. At this point, there was also a change in the ranking leader from A_3 to A_6. The change in the leader, despite a slight reduction in the number of the least important criteria, means that they have a significant impact on the outcome of the decision-making process, as the stability of the leader is important in the multi-criteria assessment of OWFs.

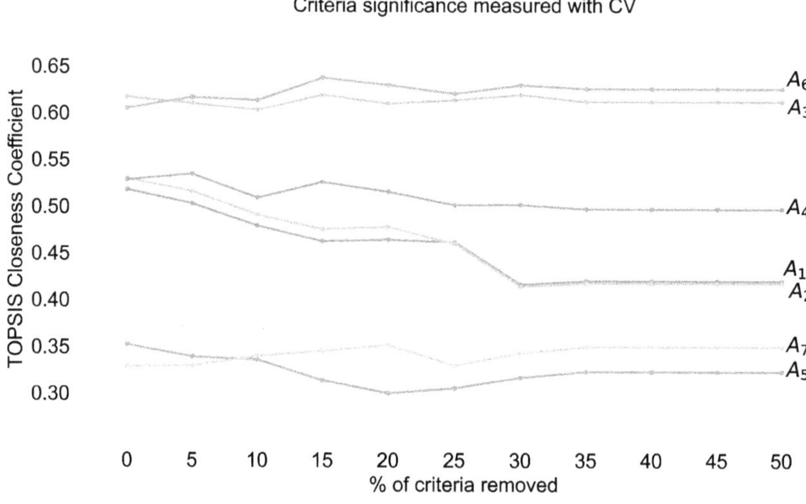

Fig. 2. Changes in TOPSIS C_i in sensitivity analysis for the criteria significance measured with CV.

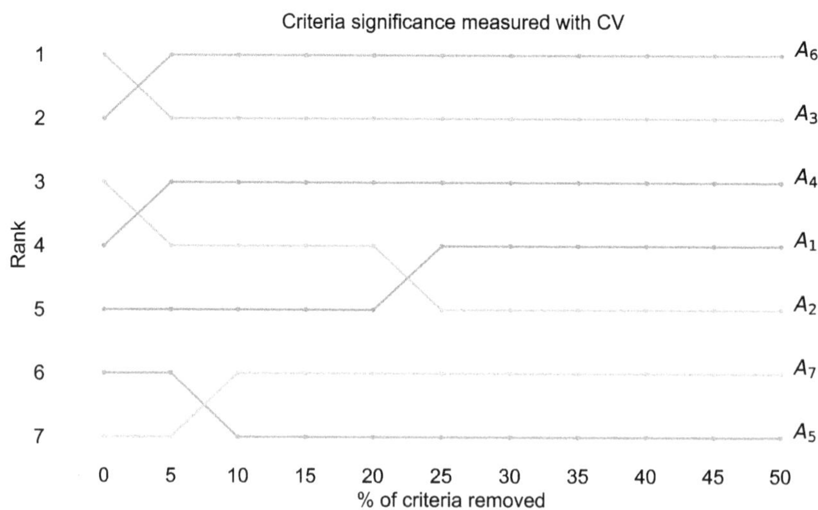

Fig. 3. Changes in TOPSIS rankings in sensitivity analysis for the criteria significance measured with CV.

The increase in the reduction of criteria determined by the rising percentile value, indicating the reduction threshold according to their significance, shows that the new leader remains stable, and most OWFs, with the exception of A_2, do not change their position in the ranking by more than 1. The analysis carried out in the studied scope allows us to conclude that the alternatives with the best parameters enabling them to achieve top positions in the ranking are undoubtedly A_6 and A_3. The result obtained confirms their stability and resistance to changes such as the exclusion of certain criteria from the dataset.

Table 3. Percentile-based exclusion thresholds used in the sensitivity analysis of criterion reduction for criteria significance measured with Entropy.

Exclusion percentile	Criteria excluded	Number of criteria excluded	% of criteria excluded	Shifts in rankings	Euclidean distance	Correlation
95	C_7, C_8	2	6.25	4	0.028	0.9286
90	C_5, C_6, C_7, C_8	4	12.5	6	0.0631	0.8929
85	$C_5, C_6, C_7, C_8, C_{19}$	5	15.625	6	0.0931	0.8929
80	$C_3, C_5, C_6, C_7, C_8, C_9, C_{19}$	7	21.875	6	0.1039	0.8571
75	$C_2, C_3, C_5, C_6, C_7, C_8, C_9, C_{19}$	8	25	8	0.1051	0.8214
70	$C_2, C_3, C_5, C_6, C_7, C_8, C_9, C_{19}, C_{28}, C_{29}$	10	31.25	8	0.1621	0.8214
65	$C_2, C_3, C_5, C_6, C_7, C_8, C_9, C_{19}, C_{28}, C_{29}$	10	31.25	8	0.1621	0.8214
60	$C_2, C_3, C_5, C_6, C_7, C_8, C_9, C_{19}, C_{28}, C_{29}$	10	31.25	8	0.1621	0.8214
55	$C_2, C_3, C_5, C_6, C_7, C_8, C_9, C_{19}, C_{28}, C_{29}$	10	31.25	8	0.1621	0.8214
50	$C_2, C_3, C_5, C_6, C_7, C_8, C_9, C_{19}, C_{28}, C_{29}$	10	31.25	8	0.1621	0.8214

The graph showing the closeness coefficient in the sensitivity analysis for CV additionally shows that the distance between the results obtained by A_3 and A_6 is small, which makes them almost equivalent for consideration. A_4 in third place is stable. A high degree of closeness was also found between A_1 and A_2, which indicates their similarity.

In the sensitivity analysis performed for entropy, the results are similar. More fluctuations were observed between the best OWFs, A_3 and A_6, which is due to a slightly different set of criteria excluded at this stage compared to CV. For CV, A_2 maintains its 4th position for longer, while for entropy, A_1 moves up to 4th place earlier. In terms of ranking positions, A_4 performs identically in the sensitivity analysis for both CV and entropy, which confirms the high stability of this OWF to changes in the set of evaluation criteria taken into account. On the other hand, A_5 and A_7 are OWFs that consistently perform the worst throughout the analysis. The Spearman correlation between the ranking for the full dataset and the rankings received for reduced datasets decreases as the percentage of excluded criteria increases. The closeness coefficient analysis for both significance measures shows the similarity and best performance of A_3 and A_6, and the stability of A_4 in third place. Next in the assessment are A_1 and A_2, which show great similarity and the greatest sensitivity to changes in the set of criteria. Finally, A_5 and A_7 close the ranking.

The proposed framework enables decision-makers to control the trade-off between model simplicity and decision reliability by explicitly quantifying the impact of criterion reduction on ranking stability. The results confirm that wind farms A_3 and A_6 have the potential to become projects recommended to stakeholders and investors. The indicated OWF alternatives are the most advanced projects among those considered in the study.

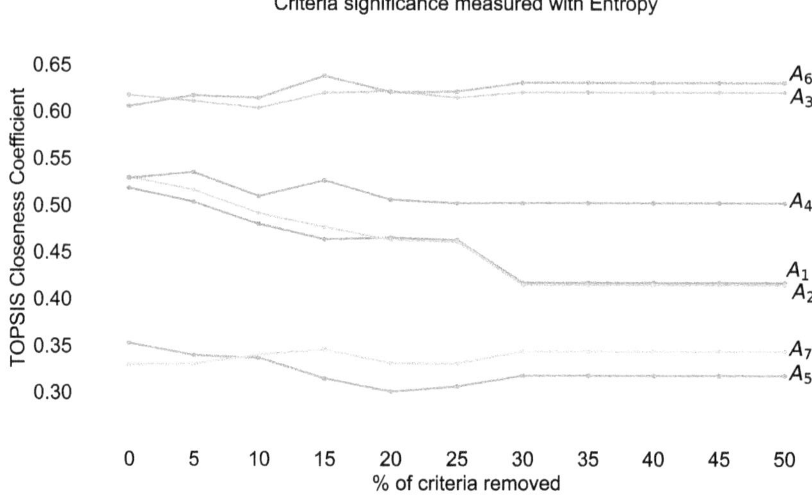

Fig. 4. Changes in TOPSIS C_i in sensitivity analysis for the criteria significance measured with entropy.

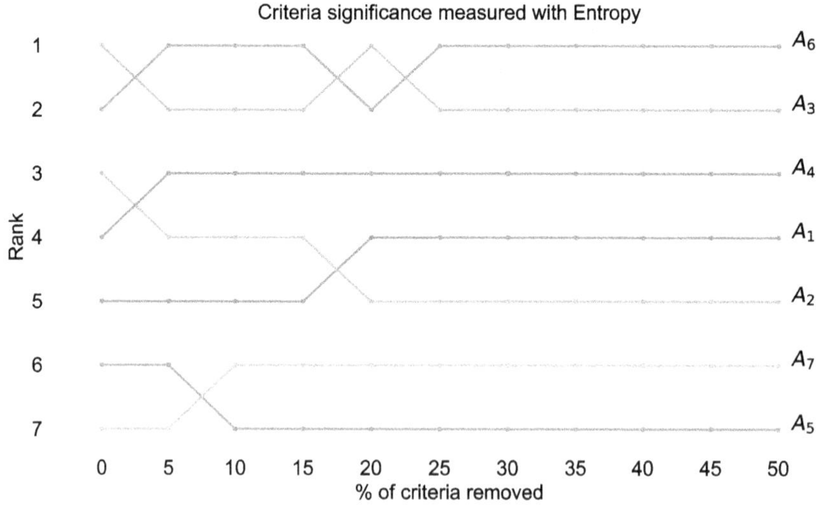

Fig. 5. Changes in TOPSIS rankings in sensitivity analysis for the criteria significance measured with entropy.

Baltic Power (A_6) is the only project among those considered that plans to invest in an installation port in Świnoujście. In addition, it is characterized by high declared performance. Baltica 2 (A_3), on the other hand, stands out for its high declared performance and large area, which results in high productivity.

The proposed framework provides a systematic procedure for simplifying the decision-making model. From a practical perspective, it allows decision-makers to simplify the model while controlling the impact on the stability of results, which is particularly important in complex investment problems such as the evaluation of OWFs.

4   Conclusions

This paper proposed a data-driven framework for criterion significance assessment and controlled model reduction in MCDM problems. The approach combines classical MCDM methods with objective significance measures and a structured sensitivity analysis, allowing the influence of weakly informative criteria on decision outcomes to be systematically evaluated.

The results demonstrate that the framework effectively identifies both critical and redundant criteria, reveals the limits of acceptable model simplification, and supports the assessment of ranking robustness under varying reduction levels. Importantly, the proposed procedure enhances decision transparency and reduces the risk of unreliable recommendations caused by uncontrolled criterion elimination. Due to its simplicity, flexibility, and independence from expert judgment, the framework can be directly applied to complex decision problems with a large number of criteria, such as OWF assessment, and easily adapted to other multi-criteria evaluation contexts.

The proposed approach has limitations, including testing on a limited dataset for OWFs and a fixed number of criteria. Another limitation is the use of two measures of criterion importance - CV and entropy, which do not cover the broader range of possible preferences. Additionally, the proposed approach does not account for data uncertainty and preferences. Another shortcoming is the lack of consideration of other MCDA methods, which might yield slightly different rankings. Finally, to simplify the model, a single sensitivity analysis approach was used, which does not account for other variable selection methods.

Future work will focus on extending the proposed framework to other MCDM methods and alternative objective significance measures. Furthermore, future research should include a comparison of the proposed approach with other methods of criteria reduction, as well as an examination of how changes in weights affect the rankings after model reduction. Further research may include the integration of expert-based weighting schemes and the application of the framework to larger sets of alternatives and criteria to assess its scalability and generalizability.

Acknowledgments. Publication funded by the state budget under the program of the Minister of Science and Higher Education named Perły Nauki, Poland, project number: PN/01/0022/2022, total project value: PLN 165 000,00 and Co-financed by the Minister of Science and Higher Education under the "Regional Excellence Initiative" Program RID/SP/0046/2024/01.

Disclosure of Interests. The authors have no competing interests to declare that are relevant to the content of this article.

References

1. Abdullah, A.G., Utami, H.P., Gunawan, B., Ratmono, B.M., Pasaribu, N.T.: Multi-criteria decision-making for wind power project feasibility: trends, techniques, and future directions. Clean. Eng. Technol., 100987 (2025). https://doi.org/10.1016/j.clet.2025.100987

2. Al-Abadi, A.M., Handhal, A.M., Abdulhasan, M.A., Ali, W.L., Hassan, J., Al Aboodi, A.H.: Optimal siting of large photovoltaic solar farms at Basrah governorate, Southern Iraq using hybrid GIS-based Entropy-TOPSIS and AHP-TOPSIS models. Renew. Energy **241**, 122308 (2025). https://doi.org/10.1016/j.renene.2024.122308

3. Bączkiewicz, A., Wątróbski, J.: Crispyn - A Python library for determining criteria significance with objective weighting methods. SoftwareX **19**, 101166 (2022). https://doi.org/10.1016/j.softx.2022.101166

4. Demir, G., Chatterjee, P., Pamucar, D.: Sensitivity analysis in multi-criteria decision making: a state-of-the-art research perspective using bibliometric analysis. Expert Syst. Appl. **237**, 121660 (2024). https://doi.org/10.1016/j.eswa.2023.121660

5. Habibollahi, M., Hashemi, A., Dowlatshahi, M.B., Rafsanjani, M.K., Arya, V., Gupta, B.B.: How PCA helps multi-criteria decision making for feature selection: a feature fusion approach in bioinformatics and gene expression data. Alex. Eng. J. **130**, 809–826 (2025). https://doi.org/10.1016/j.aej.2025.09.028

6. Jokar, F., Varnamkhasti, M.J., Hadi-Vencheh, A.: Hybrid Multi-Criteria Decision-Making (MCDM) approaches with random forest regression for interval-based fuzzy uncertainty management. Int. J. Math. Model. Comput. **15**(1), 49–66 (2025). https://doi.org/10.71932/ijm.2025.1200760

7. Jong, F.C., Ahmed, M.M.: Multi-criteria decision-making solutions for optimal solar energy sites identification: a systematic review and analysis. IEEE Access **12**, 143458–143484 (2024). https://doi.org/10.1109/ACCESS.2024.3461948

8. Karczmarczyk, A., Wątróbski, J., Bączkiewicz, A., Mróz-Malik, O., Drożdż, W.: New robust multi-criteria decision-making method for wind farm location problems. Appl. Energy **398**, 126401 (2025). https://doi.org/10.1016/j.apenergy.2025.126401

9. Keshavarz-Ghorabaee, M., Amiri, M., Zavadskas, E.K., Turskis, Z., Antucheviciene, J.: Determination of objective weights using a new method based on the removal effects of criteria (MEREC). Symmetry **13**(4), 525 (2021). https://doi.org/10.3390/sym13040525

10. Khan, K., Khurshid, A., Cifuentes-Faura, J., Xianjun, D.: Does renewable energy development enhance energy security? Utilities Policy **87**, 101725 (2024). https://doi.org/10.1016/j.jup.2024.101725

11. Kılıçoğlu, c., Yerlikaya-Özkurt, F.: A novel comparison of shrinkage methods based on multi criteria decision making in case of multicollinearity. J. Ind. Manag. Optim. **20**(12), 3816–3842 (2024). https://doi.org/10.3934/jimo.2024072

12. Kumar, R., Pamucar, D.: A comprehensive and systematic review of multi-criteria decision-making (MCDM) methods to solve decision-making problems: two decades from 2004 to 2024. Spec. Decis. Mak. Appl. **2**(1), 177–196 (2025). https://doi.org/10.31181/sdmap21202524

13. Li, C., et al.: Future material requirements for global sustainable offshore wind energy development. Renew. Sustain. Energy Rev. **164**, 112603 (2022). https://doi.org/10.1016/j.rser.2022.112603

14. Li, X., Zhang, Z., Li, L., Pan, H.: Combining feature selection and classification using LASSO-based MCO classifier for credit risk evaluation. Comput. Econ. **64**(5), 2641–2662 (2024). https://doi.org/10.1007/s10614-023-10535-8

15. Li, Z., Tian, G., El-Shafay, A.: Statistical-analytical study on world development trend in offshore wind energy production capacity focusing on Great Britain with the aim of MCDA based offshore wind farm siting. J. Clean. Prod. **363**, 132326 (2022). https://doi.org/10.1016/j.jclepro.2022.132326

16. Roszkowska, E., Filipowicz-Chomko, M., Łyczkowska-Hanćkowiak, A., Majewska, E.: Extended Hellwig's method utilizing entropy-based weights and mahalanobis distance: applications in evaluating sustainable development in the education area. Entropy **26**(3), 197 (2024). https://doi.org/10.3390/e26030197

17. Sadeghitabar, E., Ghasempour, R., Rad, M.A.V., Toopshekan, A.: Optimization and Shannon entropy multi-criteria decision-making method for implementing modern renewable energies in stand-alone greenhouses. Energy Convers. Manage. X **27**, 101139 (2025). https://doi.org/10.1016/j.ecmx.2025.101139

18. Sahabuddin, M., Khan, I.: Multi-criteria decision analysis methods for energy sector's sustainability assessment: robustness analysis through criteria weight change. Sustainable Energy Technol. Assess. **47**, 101380 (2021). https://doi.org/10.1016/j.seta.2021.101380

19. Shao, M., Han, Z., Sun, J., Xiao, C., Zhang, S., Zhao, Y.: A review of multi-criteria decision making applications for renewable energy site selection. Renew. Energy **157**, 377–403 (2020). https://doi.org/10.1016/j.renene.2020.04.137

20. Shen, H., et al.: Multi-objective capacity configuration optimization of an integrated energy system considering economy and environment with harvest heat. Energy Convers. Manage. **269**, 116116 (2022). https://doi.org/10.1016/j.enconman.2022.116116

21. Wątróbski, J., Bączkiewicz, A., Sałabun, W.: New multi-criteria method for evaluation of sustainable RES management. Appl. Energy **324**, 119695 (2022). https://doi.org/10.1016/j.apenergy.2022.119695

22. Zhang, Q., et al.: Sustainable and clean oilfield development: how access to wind power can make offshore platforms more sustainable with production stability. J. Clean. Prod. **294**, 126225 (2021). https://doi.org/10.1016/j.jclepro.2021.126225

Navigating Uncertainty: A Framework for Benchmarking Decision Quality in Fuzzy Petri Nets

Zbigniew Suraj[(✉)] and Piotr Grochowalski

Institute of Computer Science, University of Rzeszów, 1 Prof. S. Pigonia Street, 35-310 Rzeszów, Poland
{zsuraj,pgrochowalski}@ur.edu.pl

Abstract. Fuzzy Petri nets (FPN) combine classical Petri net theory with fuzzy logic to model systems characterized by uncertainty and ambiguity, particularly in Decision Support Systems (DSS). This study evaluates the decision-making efficacy of a DSS model operating under uncertainty, considering the impact of three distinct FPN classes, four datasets with diverse statistical characteristics, and various performance metrics. The experimental phase utilized a train traffic control model and bespoke simulation software for automatic model analysis. The results address research challenges in FPN theory and applications as identified in the comprehensive review by K. Zhou and A. Zain (Artif. Intell. Rev., 2022).

Keywords: Fuzzy Petri net · Modeling · Simulation · Decision support system · Experimental evaluation

1 Introduction

Reasoning under uncertainty and incompleteness is a core challenge in Artificial Intelligence. While Bayesian or neural networks, discussed by Ramirez [1] as well as Larranga and Moral [2], are widely used, they often struggle with systems requiring simultaneous modeling of concurrency and synchronization. FPNs, introduced by Looney [3], address these limitations. Since then, numerous variants with improved inference rules have emerged, such as those proposed by Shi and Liu [4] or Yu et al. [5].

This paper evaluates three FPN types: classical FPNs described by Chen et al. [6], generalized FPNs (GFP-nets) introduced by Suraj [7], and uninorm Petri nets (UP-nets) developed by Suraj [8]. Using a train traffic control system as a case study, we propose a methodology to compare these models across four large datasets. Since UP-nets generalize triangular norms through uninorm theory, this study aims to determine if this theoretical shift provides measurable added value for DSSs.

M. Paszynski et al. (Eds.): ICCS 2026 Workshops, LNCS 16788, pp. 386–393, 2026.
https://doi.org/10.1007/978-3-032-29915-4_32

1.1   Short Review of Related Literature

The FPN landscape has evolved significantly. Zhou and Zain [9] classified FPN variants and highlighted the lack of standardized benchmarking - a gap this research addresses. A survey by Liu et al. [10] explored FPNs in decision-making, noting the transition from triangular norms to more expressive structures. Practical applications include interval-valued fuzzy sets in railway safety developed by Wang and Smith [11] and the integration of Petri nets with machine learning proposed by Zhang and Chen [12]. Finally, Yager and Rybalov [13] provide the formal justification for using uninorms to achieve superior data aggregation flexibility.

The paper is organized as follows: Sect. 2 recalls FPN theory; Sect. 3 describes the methodology; Sect. 4 presents the results; Sect. 5 concludes the study.

2   Auxiliary Concepts and Notation

This section recalls three FPN models. All share a common structure defined by the tuple $N = (P, T, I, O, M_0, S, \alpha, \beta, \gamma, Op, \delta)$, where P, T are sets of places and transitions, I, O are input/output functions, $M_0 : P \to [0, 1]$ is the initial marking, S is a set of statements, α binds places to statements, while β and γ denote truth degrees and thresholds of transitions, respectively.

The models differ primarily in their operator sets Op and binding functions δ:

- FP-net [3]: Op uses classical Zadeh and Goguen operators [14]. δ binds transitions to specific t-norms (In, Trs) and s-norms (Out).
- GFP-net [7]: Op extends to the entire families of t-norms (TN) and s-norms (SN) [14].
- UP-net [8]: Op utilizes conjunctive $(U_{\min})$ and disjunctive $(U_{\max})$ uninorms with a neutral element $e \in (0, 1)$ [13].

A marking $M : P \to [0, 1]$ represents the state. A transition t with input places $\{p_{i1}, \ldots, p_{ik}\}$ is enabled if $In(M(p_{i1}), \ldots, M(p_{ik})) \geq \gamma(t) > 0$. Firing an enabled t results in a successor marking M' for each output place p:

$$M'(p) = Out(Trs(In(M(p_{i1}), \ldots, M(p_{ik})), \beta(t)), M(p)) \tag{1}$$

For non-output places, $M'(p) = M(p)$.

3   Methodology for Comparative Evaluation

3.1   Methodological Framework

To assess how the choice of net architecture influences decision outcomes within an exemplary DSS, we established a systematic evaluation methodology (see Fig. 1).

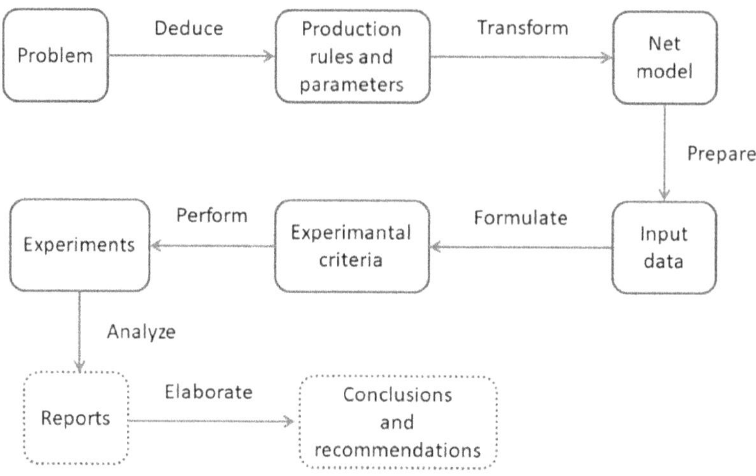

Fig. 1. Schematic overview of the research methodology framework.

A. Exemplary DSS (*Train Traffic Control*). A common operational conflict arises when train B is scheduled to wait at a station for the arrival of train A to facilitate passenger transfers, and train A is delayed. This scenario presents three primary alternatives for resolution:

(1) Train B waits for train A's arrival and consequently departs late.
(2) Train B departs on schedule, requiring passengers from train A to wait for a subsequent connection.
(3) Train B departs on time, and an additional train is deployed to accommodate train A's passengers.

Selecting an optimal decision requires considering various internal conditions, such as the duration of the delay and the volume of transferring passengers. This analysis focuses solely on the modeling aspect; a broader discussion concerning the optimization of competing objectives - such as minimizing network - wide delays, ensuring customer satisfaction, and efficiently utilizing expensive resources - is beyond the scope of this discussion.

B. Production rules and parameters. The conflict is modeled via four rules:

(r1) IF $s2$ THEN $s6$ $[\beta = .9,\ \gamma = .4]$;
(r2) IF $s3$ THEN $s6$ $[\beta = .9,\ \gamma = .4]$;
(r3) IF $s1 \wedge s4 \wedge s6$ THEN $s7$ $[\beta = .8,\ \gamma = .2]$;
(r4) IF $s4 \wedge s5$ THEN $s8$ $[\beta = .8,\ \gamma = .2]$.

Linguistic labels $s1$–$s8$ represent: $s1$: Train B is the final train in this direction today; $s2$: The delay on train A is significant; $s3$: There is an urgent need for the track currently occupied by train B; $s4$: A large number of passengers intend to transfer to train B; $s5$: The delay of train A is minor; $s6$: Let train B depart

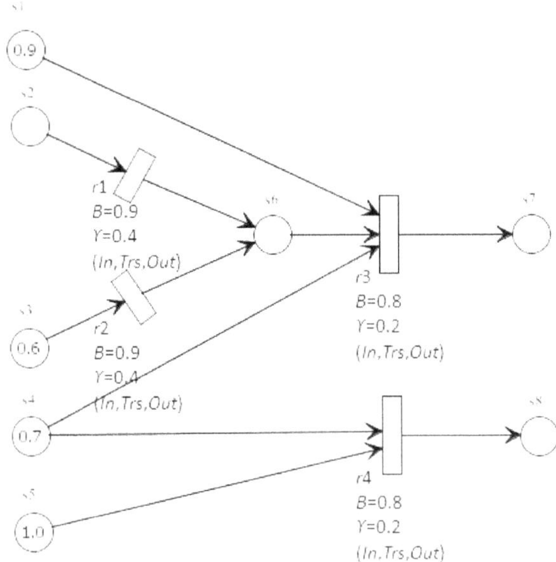

Fig. 2. General scheme of the Petri net model representing the train traffic conflict.

according to the schedule; $s7$: Provide an additional train (train C) in the same direction as train B; $s8$: Let train B wait for train A.

We compare three models based on Fig. 2:

(a) FP-net: $(In, Trs, Out) = (ZtN, GtN, ZsN)$ [3];
(b) GFP-net: $(In, Trs, Out) = (HtN, HtN, HsN)$ using Hamacher operators [7,14];
(c) UP-net: $(In, Trs, Out) = (U, U, U')$ using uninorms U, U' with $e \in (0,1)$ [8,13].

These archetypal models were selected from operator triplet lattices to ensure they are mutually incomparable [15,16].

C. Input data. To conduct the experiments, four distinct numerical datasets (Test1-Test4) were generated using specialized software. The first and third sets consist of five-element sequences with values drawn from discrete sets: {0, 0.5, 1} for Test1 and {0, 0.25, 0.5, 0.75, 1} for Test3. In contrast, Test2 and Test4 maintain the same sequence lengths as their predecessors, but their values were randomly sampled from the continuous unit interval [0, 1] (Table 1).

4   Results and Discussion

We evaluated how net architecture and input data influence DSS decision quality.

Experiment 1: *Decision typology.* We tested two scenarios: *Case 1* (fixed threshold $Thr = 0.1$, $e = 0.5$) and *Case 2* (dynamic $Thr = |Me(s7) - Me(s8)|$, $e = 0.5$).

Table 1. Basic statistics for Test1–Test4 (Size, Median, S.D.)

Par	Test1	Test2	Test3	Test4
Size	243	243	3125	3125
Me	(.5,.5,.5,.5,.5)	(.5,.5,.53,.5,.48)	(.5,.5,.5,.5,.5)	(.51,.5,.5,.51,.5)
S.D.	(.4,.4,.4,.4,.4)	(.29,.31,.28,.29,.28)	(.35,.35,.35,.35,.35)	(.29,.29,.29,.29,.29)

Performance was measured using:

(1) Uam/Am: unambiguous/ambiguous decisions;
(2) Rel: reliable decisions ($|v(d_1) - v(d_2)| > Thr$);
(3) $Rat1/2$: growth ratios vs. dataset scale;
(4) $AmN\text{-}Z/AmZ$: non-zero ambiguous/zero ambiguous decisions;
(5) ET: execution time [s].

Logical constraints: $Size=Uam+Am$, $Am=AmN\text{-}Z+AmZ$, and $Rel \leq Uam$ (Table 2).

Table 2. Impact of net architecture on decision typology (*Case 1*).

Model	Data	Uam	Am	Rel	Rat1	Rat2	AmN-Z	AmZ	ET
FP-net	Test1	115	128	92	14.92	17.28	25	103	.01
GFP-net	Test1	140	103	110	15.47	15.81	0	103	.01
UP-net	Test1	95	148	89	13.01	12.27	45	103	.02
FP-net	Test2	141	102	110	13.96	13.82	33	69	.02
GFP-net	Test2	161	82	116	13.50	13.71	1	81	.01
UP-net	Test2	90	153	70	12.19	12.77	4	149	.02
FP-net	Test3	1716	1409	1590	14.92	17.28	620	789	.13
GFP-net	Test3	2166	959	1739	15.47	15.81	0	959	.01
UP-net	Test3	1236	1889	1092	13.01	12.27	267	1622	.12
FP-net	Test4	1968	1157	1528	13.96	13.82	375	782	.14
GFP-net	Test4	2174	951	1590	13.50	13.71	4	947	.12
UP-net	Test4	1097	2028	894	12.19	12.77	48	1980	.14

Analysis of *Case 1*:

(1) GFP-net consistently yields the highest Uam and Rel values, outperforming other models.
(2) Growth rates for Uam and Rel (approx. 12.86) are exceeded by FP-net and GFP-net, while UP-net falls below.
(3) UP-net shows significantly higher AmZ values, indicating more non-activated transitions.

(4) Computational efficiency (ET) is similar across models.

Analysis of *Case 2*:
Dynamic thresholds (averaging 0.033–0.055) are nearly 50% lower than in *Case 1*, leading to higher *Rel* counts across all models. Despite this shift, the performance hierarchy remains: GFP-net > FP-net > UP-net (Table 3).

Table 3. Decision reliability with dynamic thresholds (*Case 2*).

Model	Data	*Me(s7)*	*Me(s8)*	*Thr*	*Rel*
FP-net	Test1|Test2	.17|.2	.22|.21	.05|.01	97|136
GFP-net	Test1|Test2	.17|.16	.22|.21	.05|.05	118|136
UP-net	Test1|Test2	.4|.2	.42|.24	.02|.04	95|84
FP-net	Test3|Test4	.19|.19	.24|.24	.05|.05	1599|1719
GFP-net	Test3|Test4	.15|.16	.23|.23	.08|.07	1781|1726
UP-net	Test3|Test4	.3|.19	.33|.23	.03|.04	1092|1033

The evaluation indicates that the GFP-net model demonstrates superior decision quality, higher reliability (*Rel*), and lower ambiguity (*Am*) compared to FP-net and UP-net architectures across tested datasets. While *Case 1* established a fixed threshold, transitioning to a dynamic, data-driven threshold in *Case 2* significantly increased the number of reliable decisions, consistently maintaining the performance hierarchy of GFP-net > FP-net > UP-net.

The findings are based on a comparative analysis of net architecture's impact on the DSS.

Experiment 2: *Sensitivity of UP-net neutral element (e).* We analyzed how e affects decision typology in Test3 (regular) and Test4 (random) datasets with $Thr = 0.1$ (Table 4).

Table 4. Impact of e on UP-net outcomes (Test3 | Test4)

e	*Uam*	*Am*	*Rel*	*AmN-Z*	*AmZ*	*ET*
.1	1847|2566	1278|559	1307|949	537|213	741|346	.12|.14
.3	1236|1866	1889|1259	1092|1140	267|116	1622|1143	.12|.13
.5	1236|1097	1889|2028	1092|894	267|48	1622|1980	.12|.12
.7	603|382	2522|2743	589|364	89|10	2433|2733	.11|.14
.9	0|0	3125|3125	0|0	0|0	3125|3125	.13|.12

Conclusions

(1) Lower e values correlate with higher *Uam* and lower ambiguity (*Am*, *AmZ*) across all data types.

(2) Reducing e generally enhances reliability (Rel), except for random data where it plateaus at very low e.

(3) Execution time (ET) remains independent of e.

Overall, UP-net quality for regular data is inversely proportional to e, while higher e values increase transition activation failures (AmZ) regardless of data structure.

5 Final Conclusions and Future Work

This paper introduces an original methodology for the comparative evaluation of three distinct FPN classes, specifically designed for modeling DSSs operating under conditions of uncertainty. Our research involved a rigorous analysis of the following models:

- FP-net: Utilizing standard, classical fuzzy logic operators.
- GFP-net: Offering increased flexibility by incorporating a broader range of t-norm and s-norm operators.
- UP-net: Representing the most generalized approach through the application of uninorm theory.

Experimental results, obtained from diverse numerical datasets and evaluated against standard statistical criteria, confirmed our primary hypothesis. The GFP-net model demonstrated superior efficacy, generating accurate and reliable decisions in a significantly higher number of cases compared to both FP-net and UP-net architectures. All experiments were conducted using our specialized software, developed for modeling and analyzing systems based on various Petri net formalisms, including fuzzy nets [17].

Future research will focus on several key areas to further validate these findings. Firstly, we intend to investigate whether this performance hierarchy persists when considering a wider spectrum of operator triplets, particularly extreme values, which - unlike the canonical "middle" operators used here - allow for more precise comparative analysis. Furthermore, we plan to examine the robustness of these FPN structures by applying various discretization and fuzzification techniques to the input data. Such investigations will determine if the observed model efficacy remains consistent across different data preprocessing scenarios, ultimately enhancing the reliability of FPNs in complex decision-making environments.

Impact Statement: The proposed methodology offers a comprehensive multi-criteria experimental evaluation framework with clearly defined parameters for assessing test data quality and decision accuracy. This approach is highly relevant to various domains of applied computer science, particularly for evaluating complex, uncertain DSSs where synchronization, communication, concurrency, and structural complexity are critical. Furthermore, it holds significant potential for advanced robotic control systems. Our experimental results validate the practical utility of this framework in selecting optimal modeling structures for high-complexity environments.

Acknowledgments. The authors are grateful to the anonymous referees for their helpful comments.

Disclosure of Interests. The authors have no competing interests to declare that are relevant to the content of this article.

References

1. Ramírez-Noriega, A., Juárez-Ramírez, R., Jiménez, S., Martínez-Ramírez, Y.: Knowledge representation in intelligent tutoring system. In: Hassanien, A.E., Shaalan, K., Gaber, T., Azar, A.T., Tolba, M.F. (eds.) AISI 2016. AISC, vol. 533, pp. 12–21. Springer, Cham (2017). https://doi.org/10.1007/978-3-319-48308-5_2
2. Larranaga, P., Moral, S.: Probabilistic graphical models in artificial intelligence. Appl. Soft Comput. **11**(2), 1511–1528 (2011)
3. Looney, C.G.: Fuzzy Petri nets for rule-based decision-making. IEEE Trans. Syst. Man Cybern. **18**(1), 178–183 (1988)
4. Shi, H., Liu, H.-C.: Fuzzy Petri Nets for Knowledge Representation, Acquisition and Reasoning. Springer, Singapore (2023). https://doi.org/10.1007/978-981-99-5154-3
5. Yu, Y.-X., Gong, H.-P., Liu, H.-C., Mou, X.: Knowledge representation and reasoning using fuzzy Petri nets: a literature review and bibliometric analysis. Artif. Intell. Rev. **56**(7), 6241–6265 (2023)
6. Chen, S.-M., Ke, J.-S., Chang, J.-F.: Knowledge representation using fuzzy Petri nets. IEEE Trans. Knowl. Data Eng. **2**(3), 311–319 (1990)
7. Suraj, Z.: A new class of fuzzy Petri nets for knowledge representation and reasoning. Fundam. Inform. **128**(1–2), 193–207 (2013)
8. Suraj, Z.: On selected properties of uninorm Petri nets and their application in modeling knowledge-based systems. Procedia Comput. Sci. **225**, 155–164 (2023)
9. Zhou, Z., Zain, A.M.: Fuzzy Petri nets: a review of applications and research trends. Artif. Intell. Rev. **55**, 1235–1280 (2022)
10. Liu, X.: A survey on fuzzy Petri nets for decision making. IEEE Trans. on Fuzzy Syst. **31**(4) (2023)
11. Wang, S.: Interval-valued fuzzy Petri nets for train operation safety. Reliab. Eng. Syst. Saf. **209** (2021)
12. Zhang, Y., Chen, H.: Advanced decision support in railway traffic with hybrid fuzzy-Petri models. Transp. Res. Part C Emerg. Technol. **158** (2024)
13. Yager, R., Rybalov, A.: Uninorm aggregation operators. Fuzzy Sets Syst. **80**, 111–120 (1996)
14. Klement, E.P., Mesiar, R., Pap, E.: Triangular Norms. Kluwer (2000)
15. Suraj, Z., Grochowalski, P., Drygaś, P.: Influence of fuzzy Petri net operating mode on decision-making. Procedia Comput. Sci. **246**, 2449–2458 (2024)
16. Suraj, Z.: Toward optimization of reasoning using generalized fuzzy Petri nets. In: Nguyen, H.S., Ha, Q.-T., Li, T., Przybyła-Kasperek, M. (eds.) IJCRS 2018. LNCS (LNAI), vol. 11103, pp. 294–308. Springer, Cham (2018). https://doi.org/10.1007/978-3-319-99368-3_23
17. Suraj, Z., Grochowalski, P.: PNeS in modelling, control and analysis of concurrent systems. In: Ramanna, S., Cornelis, C., Ciucci, D. (eds.) IJCRS 2021. LNCS (LNAI), vol. 12872, pp. 279–293. Springer, Cham (2021). https://doi.org/10.1007/978-3-030-87334-9_24

Handling Class Imbalance in Coalition-Based Distributed Classification with Decision Rule Induction

Katarzyna Kusztal[1]($\boxtimes$)(iD) and Małgorzata Przybyła-Kasperek[1,2](iD)

[1] Institute of Computer Science, University of Silesia in Katowice, Będzińska 39, 41-200 Sosnowiec, Poland
{katarzyna.kusztal,malgorzata.przybyla-kasperek}@us.edu.pl
[2] Department of Informatics, Constantine the Philosopher University in Nitra, Tr. A. Hlinku 1, 949 01 Nitra, Slovakia

Abstract. Learning from distributed data, maintained independently and analyzed without full central integration, poses significant challenges for building coherent and reliable classification models. In such environments, local datasets may differ in both content and class distributions, affecting the quality of the resulting global model. This paper extends the authors' previously proposed distributed classification framework integrating conflict analysis, coalition formation, and decision rule induction. The main novelty lies in incorporating a class balancing stage applied independently to each local dataset prior to system construction. Six representative data-level balancing techniques are examined, along with four rough set-based rule induction algorithms and three decision-making strategies. Experiments were conducted on two datasets from the UCI Machine Learning Repository: Car Evaluation and Balance Scale. The proposed approach was compared with a baseline without class balancing. The results indicate that class distribution adjustment improves imbalance-sensitive metrics under severe class imbalance, with a moderate reduction in overall accuracy.

Keywords: Distributed classification · Class imbalance · Hierarchical framework · Conflict analysis · Coalition-based modeling · Rule induction

1 Introduction

Contemporary information systems increasingly operate in environments where data are generated and managed by multiple independent entities. Due to organizational, legal, and security constraints, these data are typically stored locally, making their centralization difficult or infeasible. In this context, constructing decision models requires effective integration of local information while ensuring global consistency, which presents a significant computational challenge and requires efficient and transparent algorithms.

M. Paszynski et al. (Eds.): ICCS 2026 Workshops, LNCS 16788, pp. 394–402, 2026.
https://doi.org/10.1007/978-3-032-29915-4_33

An important issue in data analysis, including distributed settings, is class imbalance. In many real-world applications, class distributions can be highly uneven, which disrupts the learning process and limits the model's ability to correctly distinguish all classes [14]. As a result, models trained on imbalanced data may become biased toward the majority class, overlooking rare but important instances. Although numerous balancing techniques have been proposed [12], they have been studied mainly in centralized settings [16], while their role in distributed environments remains largely unexplored.

This paper constitutes a significant extension of the distributed data classification approach presented in the authors' earlier study [11], which relies on conflict analysis, coalition formation (groups of local data sources cooperating in decision-making), and decision rule induction. The proposed approach incorporates a class balancing stage preceding the construction of the global model. From the perspective of multi-criteria decision-making, the framework enables the integration of multiple decision criteria, while supporting the analysis of decision trade-offs and the assessment of decision quality under heterogeneous conditions.

The aim of this study is formulated through the following research questions:

- How does the incorporation of class balancing techniques into local datasets influence the quality of the resulting global classification model in a distributed framework?
- How do different class balancing techniques affect classification performance under varying levels of class imbalance?

Six techniques are considered: Random Undersampling, NearMiss, Tomek Links, Random Oversampling, SMOTE, and SMOTE-Tomek. Local datasets are balanced independently, followed by conflict analysis and the induction of decision rules, which form the basis for the final classification process.

The main contributions of this paper are as follows:

- Integration of class balancing techniques into a distributed classification framework based on conflict analysis, coalition formation, and decision rule induction.
- Comparative analysis of multiple balancing strategies in distributed settings, including statistical evaluation.
- Assessment of the impact of class balancing on classification performance under different levels of class imbalance.

The remainder of the paper is organized as follows. Section 2 reviews related work. Section 3 presents the proposed framework. Section 4 describes the experimental setup and results. Section 5 concludes the paper and discusses future research directions.

2   Related Work

In the literature on imbalanced data, three main groups of methods are distinguished: data-level, algorithm-level, and hybrid approaches [6]. Data-level techniques modify class distributions prior to model training, including under-sampling, oversampling, and their combinations, with widely used methods such as SMOTE and its variants [2]. In contrast, algorithm-level approaches improve minority class recognition by modifying the learning process, for example through cost-sensitive learning or ensemble methods [5]. In addition, hybrid strategies combine both approaches to leverage their advantages [3].

Despite extensive research on imbalanced data, most studies assume a centralized setting. By comparison, class imbalance in distributed environments has received limited attention. In particular, [10] investigated balancing techniques applied to independent local datasets within a distributed framework employing coalition mechanisms. However, in that approach, coalitions are formed dynamically for each test object. In contrast, the framework presented in this paper integrates class balancing into a static construction process, in which coalitions are determined once and remain fixed during model operation, reducing computational complexity. Moreover, while [10] used the k-nearest neighbors algorithm, this study relies on decision rule induction, providing an explicit and interpretable representation of the decision process.

From a broader perspective, distributed data classification has mainly evolved along two lines: ensemble-based learning [18] and federated learning [13]. Ensemble methods typically rely on centrally available data and are therefore not suited to independently maintained data sources. In contrast, federated learning enables decentralized training while preserving data privacy. However, it does not explicitly model relationships between local datasets and often relies on complex, less interpretable models such as deep neural networks [9].

At the same time, distributed data environments have also been examined using conflict analysis. A fundamental approach in this domain is Pawlak's conflict analysis model, which identifies and describes agreement and disagreement between agents [8]. The model has been further developed within rough set theory and extended to broader decision-making contexts, including three-way decision theory [17].

Overall, the role of class balancing techniques in distributed data environments remains insufficiently explored. In particular, their integration with static coalition formation mechanisms grounded in conflict analysis and coupled with interpretable decision rule induction has not yet been systematically examined.

3   Distributed Framework with Class Balancing

In this paper, we present an extension of the distributed classification framework proposed in [11], incorporating class balancing at the initial stage of system construction. The proposed approach retains its hierarchical structure, in which successive stages are executed in a predefined order.

In the adopted formal setting, distributed data are modeled as a set of local decision tables $T = \{T_i : i \in \{1, \ldots, n\}\}$. Each local table T_i is defined as a triple (U_i, A, d), where U_i represents a set of objects, A denotes the set of conditional attributes, and d is the decision attribute. All tables correspond to the same decision problem and therefore share the same conditional attributes and decision variable.

To address class imbalance within local tables, class balancing is applied independently to each table prior to further processing. The following six data-level techniques are considered: Random Undersampling (RUS), NearMiss [7], Tomek Links [15], Random Oversampling (ROS), SMOTE [2], and SMOTE-Tomek [1]. These methods were selected due to their distinct mechanisms and impact on class distribution.

After balancing, the subsequent steps of the distributed classification process follow the framework described in [11], with all operations now performed on balanced local tables. The main stages are summarized below:

1. Conflict analysis is formulated according to Pawlak's conflict analysis model [8]. Local tables are compared based on encoded descriptors of conditional attributes. For each attribute $a \in A$, a three-valued function $a : T \to \{-1, 0, 1\}$ is defined, representing the relative position of attribute values within the global distribution across all local tables. The degree of conflict between two tables T_i and T_j is measured by:

$$\rho(T_i, T_j) = \frac{\mathrm{card}\{a \in A : a(T_i) \neq a(T_j)\}}{\mathrm{card}\{A\}},$$

   which quantifies the proportion of attributes on which the tables differ.
2. Coalitions are defined as subsets of local tables for which $\rho(T_i, T_j) < 0.5$ for every pair of elements. The threshold of 0.5 follows Pawlak's conflict analysis model and corresponds to agreement on more than half of the conditional attributes.
3. For the j-th coalition, an aggregated decision table $T_j^{aggr} = (U_j^{aggr}, A, d)$ is constructed by merging all objects originating from the local tables belonging to that coalition.
4. Decision rules are induced from each aggregated table using four rough set-based methods: exhaustive search algorithm, genetic algorithm, covering algorithm, and LEM2.
5. The induced rule sets are used to classify test objects according to three decision-making strategies:
   - First Rule Approach (FRA) – the decision is based on the first matching rule;
   - All Rules Approach (ARA) – the decision is based on the majority class among the matching rules;
   - Weighted Rule Approach (WRA) – the decision is based on weighted voting, where each rule contributes proportionally to its number of matches.

Since class balancing modifies the internal structure of local tables, it may influence inter-table similarity, coalition configuration, and the resulting rule-based models. Thus, the preprocessing phase plays a structural role in the behavior of the entire system.

4   Experimental Evaluation

The experiments were conducted on two benchmark datasets from the UCI repository [4]: Car Evaluation and Balance Scale. The Car Evaluation dataset contains 1,728 instances with six categorical attributes and four decision classes: unacc, acc, good, vgood. The Balance Scale dataset consists of 625 instances with four categorical attributes and three classes: R, L, B. For each dataset, 70% of objects were assigned to the training set and 30% to the test set using stratified sampling. The training data were further partitioned into 7, 9, and 11 local tables, preserving class distributions, with additional sampling from the remaining tables when necessary to ensure equal class counts.

The datasets exhibit different levels of class imbalance. In the Car Evaluation, the unacc class constitutes approximately 70% of instances, while the good and vgood classes each account for about 4%, indicating strong imbalance. In contrast, the Balance Scale is more balanced, with the R and L classes representing approximately 46% each and the B class about 8%. For undersampling and oversampling techniques, balancing was applied to enforce equal class proportions within each local table, while hybrid methods may introduce slight deviations. For SMOTE and NearMiss, the number of neighbors was set to $k = 3$, which is a commonly used configuration. In addition to the proposed approach, a baseline variant without class balancing was considered for comparative purposes. The performance was evaluated on the test sets using classification accuracy (Acc), balanced accuracy (BAcc), precision (Prec.), recall (Rec.), F-measure (F.-m.), and geometric mean (G-mean), with BAcc and G-mean particularly relevant for imbalanced data.

The experimental procedure included class balancing of local tables, coalition formation, rule induction from aggregated tables, and classification using FRA, ARA, or WRA. All experiments were conducted with a fixed random seed to ensure reproducibility.

Table 1 presents the comparative results of the proposed approach and the baseline approach for the Car Evaluation and Balance Scale datasets. As no consistent dominance of any decision-making strategy (FRA, ARA, WRA) was observed across datasets and configurations, the results are averaged across these strategies. For the genetic algorithm, preliminary experiments showed no significant performance differences for varying numbers of reducts; therefore, only the configuration with 100 reducts is considered.

For the Car Evaluation dataset, the baseline typically achieves higher overall accuracy, as expected under severe class imbalance, but at the cost of substantially lower balanced accuracy and G-mean. For example, with 9 local tables, the baseline reaches Acc = 0.744, while BAcc drops to 0.387 and G-mean to 0.619. Under the same configuration, the proposed approach improves class-balanced performance across all balancing techniques (BAcc: 0.506-0.538, G-mean: 0.691-0.712), with a moderate reduction in accuracy (0.660-0.675), leading to a more balanced predictive behavior across decision classes. A complementary view is provided in Fig. 1, where each point represents the average performance of a given balancing technique across all experimental configurations. For the Car Evalua-

Table 1. Results for the proposed and baseline approaches.

BT	Method	7 local tables Acc/BAcc/Prec./Rec./F.-m./G-mean	9 local tables Acc/BAcc/Prec./Rec./F.-m./G-mean	11 local tables Acc/BAcc/Prec./Rec./F.-m./G-mean
		CAR EVALUATION		
		Proposed approach		
RUS	Exh	0.592/0.682/0.732/0.592/0.631/0.705	0.671/0.515/0.721/0.671/0.692/0.712	0.681/0.515/0.712/0.681/0.694/0.701
	Gen	0.583/0.676/0.728/0.583/0.623/0.700	0.661/0.519/0.711/0.661/0.681/0.699	0.690/0.548/0.720/0.690/0.702/0.710
	Cov	0.585/0.672/0.729/0.585/0.625/0.702	0.676/0.535/0.723/0.676/0.694/0.711	0.674/0.517/0.704/0.674/0.686/0.692
	LEM2	0.577/0.673/0.719/0.577/0.616/0.693	0.661/0.508/0.711/0.661/0.681/0.699	0.668/0.464/0.699/0.668/0.681/0.690
NearMiss	Exh	0.583/0.682/0.726/0.583/0.622/0.697	0.670/0.533/0.720/0.670/0.690/0.709	0.673/0.493/0.704/0.673/0.686/0.691
	Gen	0.581/0.673/0.721/0.581/0.619/0.695	0.674/0.542/0.721/0.674/0.692/0.711	0.673/0.508/0.707/0.673/0.687/0.699
	Cov	0.573/0.664/0.725/0.573/0.614/0.693	0.665/0.518/0.711/0.665/0.683/0.701	0.690/0.533/0.716/0.690/0.701/0.708
	LEM2	0.586/0.674/0.730/0.586/0.626/0.701	0.673/0.552/0.724/0.673/0.693/0.712	0.686/0.527/0.713/0.686/0.696/0.702
Tomek Links	Exh	0.586/0.681/0.721/0.586/0.623/0.695	0.675/0.530/0.723/0.675/0.694/0.712	0.678/0.509/0.708/0.678/0.690/0.696
	Gen	0.591/0.685/0.735/0.591/0.630/0.706	0.662/0.533/0.715/0.662/0.683/0.702	0.683/0.535/0.719/0.683/0.698/0.711
	Cov	0.584/0.667/0.729/0.584/0.625/0.701	0.659/0.535/0.707/0.659/0.678/0.695	0.675/0.507/0.709/0.675/0.689/0.697
	LEM2	0.590/0.681/0.734/0.590/0.630/0.705	0.669/0.524/0.715/0.669/0.687/0.703	0.674/0.475/0.705/0.674/0.687/0.696
ROS	Exh	0.584/0.676/0.730/0.584/0.624/0.703	0.660/0.518/0.710/0.660/0.680/0.697	0.682/0.518/0.718/0.682/0.696/0.708
	Gen	0.573/0.662/0.720/0.573/0.613/0.691	0.658/0.515/0.707/0.658/0.677/0.695	0.676/0.490/0.708/0.676/0.689/0.698
	Cov	0.598/0.700/0.737/0.598/0.636/0.712	0.664/0.525/0.716/0.664/0.684/0.705	0.670/0.525/0.706/0.670/0.684/0.692
	LEM2	0.582/0.682/0.721/0.582/0.619/0.694	0.656/0.507/0.711/0.656/0.678/0.698	0.672/0.522/0.706/0.672/0.686/0.696
SMOTE	Exh	NO COALITIONS	0.664/0.538/0.705/0.664/0.680/0.691	0.677/0.512/0.710/0.677/0.691/0.698
	Gen		0.671/0.547/0.716/0.671/0.688/0.705	0.677/0.533/0.711/0.677/0.691/0.699
	Cov		0.678/0.568/0.725/0.678/0.696/0.713	0.675/0.486/0.705/0.675/0.687/0.697
	LEM2		0.686/0.549/0.733/0.686/0.705/0.726	0.681/0.545/0.712/0.681/0.693/0.700
SMOTE-Tomek	Exh	0.577/0.682/0.722/0.577/0.616/0.695	0.668/0.506/0.715/0.668/0.687/0.704	0.686/0.492/0.721/0.686/0.701/0.714
	Gen	0.577/0.657/0.715/0.577/0.615/0.689	0.669/0.511/0.715/0.669/0.688/0.704	0.671/0.508/0.701/0.671/0.684/0.691
	Cov	0.585/0.686/0.726/0.585/0.623/0.700	0.672/0.515/0.716/0.672/0.690/0.705	0.681/0.487/0.713/0.681/0.694/0.707
	LEM2	0.586/0.675/0.723/0.586/0.624/0.699	0.662/0.509/0.715/0.662/0.683/0.702	0.682/0.516/0.711/0.682/0.694/0.701
		Baseline approach		
	Exh	0.732/0.433/0.717/0.732/0.700/0.629	0.744/0.387/0.726/0.744/0.697/0.619	0.747/0.409/0.726/0.747/0.707/0.626
	Gen	0.732/0.422/0.710/0.732/0.700/0.630	0.744/0.388/0.727/0.744/0.698/0.621	0.740/0.420/0.710/0.740/0.703/0.624
	Cov	0.488/0.344/0.683/0.488/0.561/0.627	0.492/0.363/0.668/0.492/0.557/0.621	0.492/0.365/0.670/0.492/0.558/0.621
	LEM2	0.674/0.457/0.697/0.674/0.684/0.687	0.701/0.489/0.716/0.701/0.707/0.705	0.679/0.485/0.716/0.679/0.694/0.707
		BALANCE SCALE		
		Proposed approach		
RUS	Exh	0.729/0.571/0.759/0.729/0.741/0.787	0.597/0.494/0.658/0.597/0.623/0.683	0.633/0.526/0.689/0.633/0.657/0.712
	Gen	0.732/0.555/0.754/0.732/0.742/0.789	0.615/0.513/0.652/0.615/0.631/0.687	0.624/0.501/0.672/0.624/0.645/0.700
	Cov	0.743/0.569/0.764/0.743/0.752/0.797	0.626/0.496/0.674/0.626/0.647/0.703	0.619/0.473/0.682/0.619/0.648/0.704
	LEM2	0.720/0.552/0.759/0.720/0.737/0.784	0.610/0.521/0.670/0.610/0.634/0.693	0.631/0.518/0.687/0.631/0.656/0.711
NearMiss	Exh	0.734/0.562/0.765/0.734/0.748/0.794	0.606/0.543/0.679/0.606/0.634/0.695	0.637/0.516/0.679/0.637/0.655/0.709
	Gen	0.727/0.557/0.744/0.727/0.735/0.781	0.635/0.546/0.677/0.635/0.652/0.707	0.638/0.517/0.688/0.638/0.660/0.714
	Cov	0.732/0.561/0.756/0.732/0.743/0.789	0.645/0.523/0.677/0.645/0.659/0.712	0.656/0.561/0.701/0.656/0.675/0.727
	LEM2	0.739/0.579/0.758/0.739/0.748/0.793	0.615/0.507/0.667/0.615/0.638/0.695	0.637/0.541/0.687/0.637/0.658/0.713
Tomek Links	Exh	0.723/0.555/0.753/0.723/0.736/0.783	0.633/0.538/0.680/0.633/0.653/0.708	0.621/0.511/0.683/0.621/0.647/0.703
	Gen	0.736/0.570/0.749/0.736/0.740/0.786	0.649/0.544/0.687/0.649/0.665/0.718	0.638/0.530/0.685/0.638/0.659/0.713
	Cov	0.723/0.549/0.751/0.723/0.736/0.784	0.622/0.506/0.669/0.622/0.643/0.698	0.610/0.485/0.663/0.610/0.633/0.690
	LEM2	0.718/0.557/0.746/0.718/0.731/0.778	0.619/0.522/0.670/0.619/0.640/0.696	0.597/0.494/0.662/0.597/0.625/0.684
ROS	Exh	NO COALITIONS	0.640/0.568/0.697/0.640/0.663/0.718	0.633/0.508/0.674/0.633/0.651/0.706
	Gen		0.615/0.550/0.677/0.615/0.640/0.699	0.619/0.510/0.666/0.619/0.640/0.696
	Cov		0.633/0.538/0.700/0.633/0.661/0.717	0.633/0.514/0.686/0.633/0.656/0.710
	LEM2		0.615/0.544/0.671/0.615/0.638/0.696	0.646/0.517/0.692/0.646/0.666/0.720
SMOTE	Exh	NO COALITIONS	0.640/0.555/0.686/0.640/0.659/0.713	0.631/0.513/0.687/0.631/0.656/0.710
	Gen		0.613/0.536/0.680/0.613/0.640/0.699	0.628/0.497/0.678/0.628/0.650/0.706
	Cov		0.574/0.471/0.644/0.574/0.604/0.666	0.631/0.549/0.693/0.631/0.656/0.712
	LEM2		0.636/0.553/0.686/0.636/0.657/0.712	0.638/0.511/0.691/0.638/0.662/0.716
SMOTE-Tomek	Exh_FRA	0.741/0.586/0.769/0.741/0.753/0.799	0.626/0.551/0.670/0.626/0.644/0.700	0.633/0.538/0.692/0.633/0.657/0.714
	Gen	0.727/0.564/0.764/0.727/0.743/0.789	0.627/0.528/0.670/0.627/0.645/0.701	0.630/0.505/0.681/0.630/0.652/0.707
	Cov	0.732/0.555/0.761/0.732/0.746/0.792	0.603/0.504/0.649/0.603/0.622/0.681	0.660/0.533/0.696/0.660/0.674/0.726
	LEM2	0.750/0.592/0.775/0.750/0.761/0.804	0.663/0.536/0.705/0.663/0.681/0.733	0.621/0.505/0.671/0.621/0.643/0.699
		Baseline approach		
	Exh	0.798/0.578/0.738/0.798/0.765/0.813	0.802/0.581/0.739/0.802/0.768/0.816	0.789/0.572/0.734/0.789/0.760/0.808
	Gen	0.798/0.578/0.738/0.798/0.765/0.813	0.802/0.581/0.739/0.802/0.768/0.816	0.789/0.572/0.734/0.789/0.760/0.808
	Cov	0.674/0.537/0.679/0.674/0.675/0.724	0.603/0.474/0.618/0.603/0.607/0.664	0.536/0.425/0.567/0.536/0.547/0.611
	LEM2	0.608/0.502/0.659/0.608/0.630/0.688	0.620/0.486/0.642/0.620/0.630/0.685	0.647/0.512/0.646/0.647/0.646/0.697

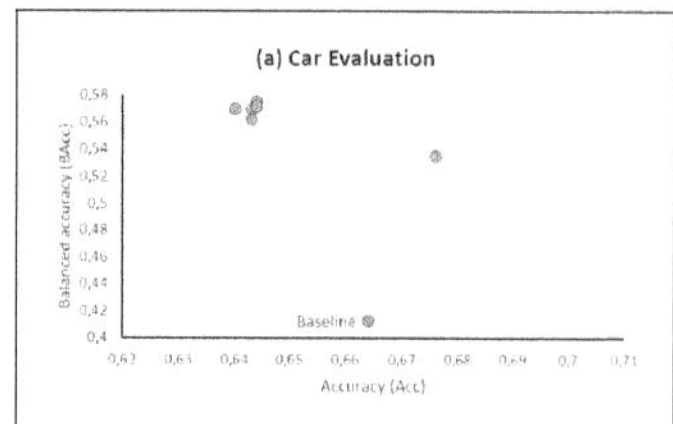
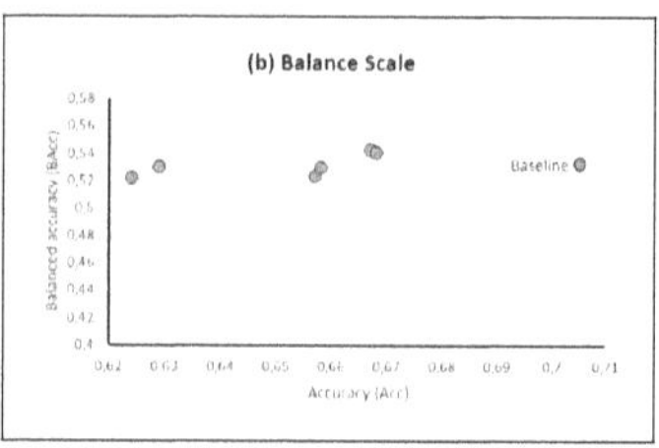

Fig. 1. Comparison of accuracy (Acc) and balanced accuracy (BAcc) for different balancing techniques: (a) Car Evaluation, (b) Balance Scale.

tion, most techniques form a cluster corresponding to lower overall accuracy and improved balanced accuracy. Notably, one technique (SMOTE) achieves higher values for both Acc and BAcc than the baseline. In contrast, for the Balance Scale dataset, differences between approaches are less pronounced, and performance remains comparable across configurations, reflecting the milder class imbalance. This is also demonstrated in Fig. 1, where the results show greater variability, particularly in accuracy, indicating less consistent behavior across techniques. Furthermore, in some configurations (Car Evaluation with 7 local tables for SMOTE, and Balance Scale for ROS and SMOTE), no compatible coalitions were identified, suggesting that balancing techniques may influence the structural relations between local tables.

We compared seven approaches to handling class imbalance (six class balancing techniques and a baseline) using the F-measure as the performance metric. The statistical analysis was carried out on the original results before averaging across decision strategies, yielding 48 paired observations (one per dataset/ dispersion instance; cases without coalitions were excluded). As normality could not be assumed, the nonparametric Friedman test was applied. The Friedman test showed no statistically significant differences among the seven approaches: $\chi_F^2(6, N = 48) = 7.443$, $p = 0.282$. The associated effect size (Kendall's W) was negligible: $W = \frac{\chi_F^2}{N(k-1)} = \frac{7.443}{48 \times 6} \approx 0.026$. Therefore, no post-hoc pairwise tests were conducted. The descriptive distribution of the F-measure values is shown in Fig. 2. The baseline method exhibits the highest median but also the largest variability, while rebalancing methods form a compact group with similar central tendencies and narrower interquartile ranges.

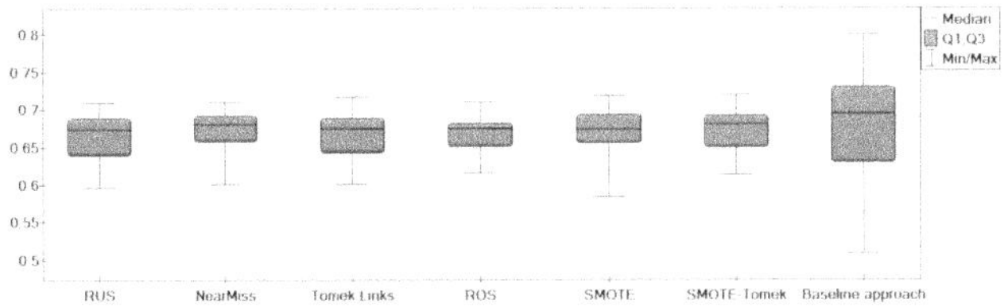

Fig. 2. Comparison of F-measure for all seven approaches (box = Q1–Q3, line = median, whiskers = min/max).

5   Conclusions

This paper extends the authors' previously proposed distributed classification framework, based on conflict analysis, coalition formation, and decision rule induction, by incorporating a local class balancing stage. Six data-level balancing techniques were evaluated on two benchmark datasets, Car Evaluation and Balance Scale.

The results indicate that class balancing improves performance with respect to imbalance-sensitive measures under severe class imbalance, as observed for the Car Evaluation dataset. For moderately imbalanced data (Balance Scale), differences between configurations remain less pronounced. The computational cost of the framework is dominated by coalition formation and may be exponential in the worst case; however, no significant performance limitations were observed in practice.

From a practical perspective, the proposed approach may support decision-making in domains such as healthcare or finance, where data are distributed and imbalanced, and where reliable identification of rare cases and transparent reasoning are required. Future research will focus on extending the framework to environments with partially different attribute sets and on incorporating feature selection mechanisms.

References

1. Batista, G.E.A.P.A., Prati, R.C., Monard, M.C.: A study of the behavior of several methods for balancing machine learning training data. ACM SIGKDD Explorat. Newsl **6**(1), 20–29 (2004)
2. Chawla, N.V., Bowyer, K.W., Hall, L.O., Kegelmeyer, W.P.: SMOTE: synthetic minority over-sampling technique. J. Artif. Intell. Res. **16**, 321–357 (2002)
3. Chen, Z., Duan, J., Kang, L., Qiu, G.: A hybrid data-level ensemble to enable learning from highly imbalanced dataset. Inf. Sci. **554**, 157–176 (2021)
4. Dua, D., Graff, C.: UCI Machine Learning Repository. University of California, School of Information and Computer Science, Irvine, CA, USA (2019)
5. Grzyb, J., Woźniak, M.: SVM ensemble training for imbalanced data classification using multi-objective optimization techniques. Appl. Intell. **53**(12), 15424–15441 (2023)

6. Koziarski, M., Woźniak, M.: Local neighborhood encodings for imbalanced data classification. Mach. Learn. **113**(10), 7421–7449 (2024)
7. Mani, I., Zhang, I.: kNN approach to unbalanced data distributions: a case study involving information extraction. In: Proceedings of Workshop on Learning from Imbalanced Datasets, pp. 1–7. ICML, United States (2003)
8. Pawlak, Z.: An inquiry into anatomy of conflicts. Inf. Sci. **109**, 65–78 (1998)
9. Pouyanfar, S., Sadiq, S., Yan, Y., Tian, H., Tao, Y., Reyes, M.P., Shyu, M.L., Chen, S.C., Iyengar, S.S.: A survey on deep learning: algorithms, techniques, and applications. ACM Comput. Surv. **51**(5), 1–36 (2018)
10. Przybyła-Kasperek, M.: Study of selected methods for balancing independent data sets in K-nearest neighbors classifiers with Pawlak conflict analysis. Appl. Soft Comput. **129**, 109612 (2022)
11. Przybyła-Kasperek, M., Kusztal, K.: Integrating conflict analysis and rule-based systems for dispersed data classification. In: Paszynski, M., Barnard, A.S., Zhang, Y.J. (eds.) Computational Science – ICCS 2025 Workshops. ICCS 2025. Lecture Notes in Computer Science, vol. 15910. Springer, Cham (2025)
12. Rezvani, S., Wang, X.: A broad review on class imbalance learning techniques. Appl. Soft Comput. **143**, 110415 (2023)
13. Shenoy, D., Bhat, R., Krishna Prakasha, K.: Exploring privacy mechanisms and metrics in federated learning. Artif. Intell. Rev. **58**(8), 223 (2025)
14. Thabtah, F., Hammoud, S., Kamalov, F., Gonsalves, A.: Data imbalance in classification: experimental evaluation. Inf. Sci. **513**, 429–441 (2020)
15. Tomek, I.: Two modifications of CNN. IEEE Trans. Syst. Man Cybern. **6**(11), 769–772 (1976)
16. Widodo, A.O., Setiawan, B., Indraswari, R.: Machine learning-based intrusion detection on multi-class imbalanced dataset using SMOTE. Proc. Comput. Sci. **234**, 578–583 (2024)
17. Yao, Y.: Three-way decision and granular computing. Int. J. Approx. Reason. **103**, 107–123 (2018)
18. Zhou, Z.H.: Ensemble learning. In: Machine Learning, pp. 181–210. Springer, Singapore (2021)

Time Series Forecasting with Irregular Intervals in Applied Behavior Analysis

Joanna Kołodziejczyk[1,2(✉)] [ID] and Sebastian Limanowski[2]

[1] National Institute of Telecommunications, ul. Szachowa 1, Warsaw 04-894, Poland
`j.kolodziejczyk@il-pib.pl`
[2] Faculty of Computer Science and Information Technology, West Pomeranian University of Technology in Szczecin, ul. Żołnierska 49, 71-210 Szczecin, Poland

Abstract. Applied Behavior Analysis (ABA) produces session records that are often irregularly spaced in time, which complicates the prediction because the interval between observations is itself variable and potentially informative. This study investigates a one-step-ahead forecast of the number of challenging-behavior episodes recorded during therapeutic sessions documented in the SYSABA information system. A deterministic data processing pipeline is proposed to convert raw session logs into an analytical data set while preserving temporal order, referential integrity, and data quality indicators. The feature set explicitly represents temporal irregularity through inter-session gaps, calendar attributes, and intra-session aggregates rather than imposing an artificial regular time grid. Forecasts are evaluated under two time-aware validation regimes: global splits across pooled patients and per-patient splits within individual histories. The empirical comparison includes SARIMAX, XGBoost, MLP, and LSTM models, together with the mean and persistence baselines. Point forecasts are assessed using MAE and patient-level MASE, model differences are examined with the Diebold–Mariano test, and predictive uncertainty is assessed through conformal prediction intervals. Results show that no single model dominates across all metrics; however, XGBoost provides the most stable overall performance across validation regimes, while LSTM obtains the best global micro-level MAE. The findings indicate that explicitly encoding temporal irregularity improves predictive usefulness and that individualized validation is essential for clinically interpretable uncertainty estimates.

Keywords: Applied Behavior Analysis · Irregularly Sampled Time Series · Forecasting · SYSABA

1 Introduction

Applied Behavior Analysis (ABA) is a therapeutic methodology in which intervention planning and evaluation are informed by systematic observation of behavior over time [10]. In routine practice, therapists document the outcomes

M. Paszynski et al. (Eds.): ICCS 2026 Workshops, LNCS 16788, pp. 403–417, 2026.
https://doi.org/10.1007/978-3-032-29915-4_34

of therapeutic sessions at successive observation times, which allows quantitative assessment of change during intervention [1]. ABA is used in programs designed to strengthen adaptive behaviors and reduce challenging behaviors, particularly in services provided to individuals with developmental conditions, including autism spectrum disorder [8].

In many therapeutic programs, the development of adaptive skills is accompanied by efforts to reduce challenging behaviors, including aggression, disruption, and stereotypy. Because progress is monitored through repeated observation, ABA generates longitudinal behavioral records that can be examined quantitatively. These records have traditionally been interpreted through visual inspection and trend analysis, whereas recent developments in statistical learning have enabled formal prediction based on previously observed behavior [12].

The present study uses records of therapeutic sessions collected in ABA centers in Poland through the SYSABA information system [6]. Since 2018, this platform has accumulated structured observational data from multiple service settings. These records constitute a substantial analytical resource, but they also create a methodological challenge: observations are not collected at equal temporal intervals. The time between two consecutive therapeutic sessions can vary due to holidays, illness, scheduling constraints, or organizational factors. In addition, the completeness of behavioral documentation varies across sessions, and some event logs are only partially recorded.

For these reasons, reconstruction of the data into an artificial daily or weekly grid is not straightforward. The absence of a recorded session cannot be interpreted as the absence of challenging behavior, and interpolation may introduce information that was never observed. Furthermore, the interval between two observations may itself contain information relevant to the prediction. Therefore, the study treats temporal irregularity as an informative characteristic of the data rather than suppressing it through regularization.

The objective of this study is to forecast the number of recorded episodes of challenging behavior at the next observed therapeutic session when observations are irregularly spaced in time. To address this problem, the paper defines a reproducible procedure for transforming raw SYSABA records into an analytical data set suitable for forecasting. The proposed framework specifies the unit of observation, preserves referential integrity, and constructs predictors that represent temporal gaps, calendar information, and summaries of recorded events.

The empirical study compares a statistical forecasting model with exogenous regression models (SARIMAX), a tree-based ensemble method (XGBoost), and two neural architectures (MLP and LSTM). Evaluation is performed under two validation designs that preserve temporal order: one based on pooled observations across all individuals and one based on rolling partitions constructed separately for each individual history. Predictive precision is assessed with MAE and MASE [4], differences between competing forecasts are examined with the Diebold–Mariano test [3], and predictive uncertainty is analyzed by means of conformal prediction intervals.

The main contributions of this paper are as follows:

1. We formalize next-session forecasting for irregular ABA session histories and define the observation unit, target, and temporal-causality constraint.
2. We propose a deterministic data-reconstruction and feature-engineering pipeline that preserves temporal irregularity and data-quality information.
3. We compare statistical, ensemble, and neural forecasting models under two time-aware validation designs corresponding to different deployment scenarios.
4. We evaluate not only point accuracy but also predictive uncertainty through conformal intervals and forecast-comparison testing.

The remainder of the paper is organized as follows. Section 2 reviews related work. Section 3 describes the data source and the rules used to define the analytical cohort. Section 4 formalizes the forecasting problem. Section 5 describes the forecasting methods and the validation design. Section 6 reports the results. Section 7 discusses the findings, limitations, and implications.

2   Related Work

In Applied Behavior Analysis, decisions about intervention effects and expectations concerning future behavior are traditionally based on repeated observation displayed in single-case graphs. Visual analysis remains the dominant interpretive procedure, with attention focused on changes in level, trend, variability, overlap, and proximity across phases [7,9].

Statistical procedures have long been introduced as complements to graph-based interpretation, particularly when trend evaluation requires more explicit quantification. Methods used in single-case analysis include time-series approaches, piecewise regression, nonoverlap measures such as Tau-U, and multilevel models. Recent reviews emphasize that these methods serve different analytical purposes and should be selected based on the data structure and the analysis objective [9,11,12].

More recently, machine learning has been introduced into ABA-related decision support, including automatic interpretation of single-case graphs and recommendation or personalization of treatment goals [2,5,7]. However, these studies do not directly address one-step-ahead forecasting of challenging-behavior counts from irregularly spaced therapeutic-session histories. The present study, therefore, lies at the intersection of ABA outcome monitoring, irregular clinical time-series modeling, and predictive uncertainty quantification.

3   Data Preparation and Analytical Representation

The study uses anonymized records extracted from the SYSABA information system, which documents therapeutic sessions in ABA centers in Poland. The retained observation window spans 22 May 2019 to 20 December 2024 and includes 21,200 unique sessions from 195 patients.

The analytical workflow consists of deterministic extraction, standardization, and transformation steps (Fig. 1). The SYSABA registry provides raw records and reference dictionaries. Because the source table is not strictly session-level, cohort characteristics are reported for analytical rows, unique sessions, and patient-specific unwanted-behavior series. The extract contains 32,233 rows, representing 946 distinct teaching programs series, 461 behavior programs, and 322 unwanted-behavior types.

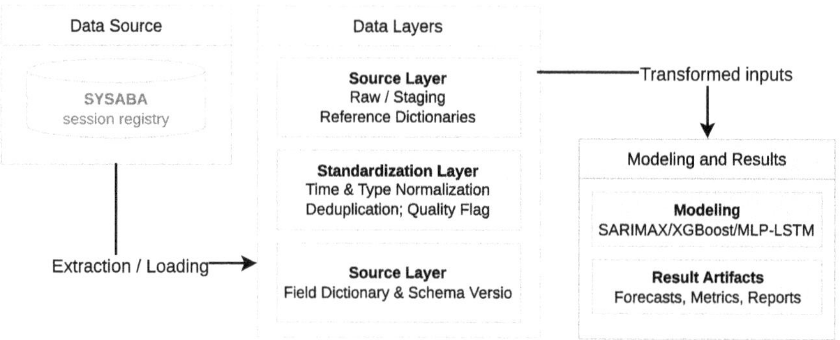

Fig. 1. Overview of the deterministic data-processing and forecasting workflow.

Standardization applies deterministic rules to ensure temporal validity and semantic consistency, including timestamp harmonization, type and range validation, event-log deduplication, removal of personal identifiers, and distinction between true zero counts and missing event documentation. The final analytical stage produces session-level aggregates and engineered predictors.

For forecasting, the cleaned records are converted into ordered one-step-ahead instances. For each patient-specific series, predictors available up to session k are used to predict the number of challenging-behavior episodes at session $k+1$. This representation preserves temporal order and models irregular inter-session spacing explicitly. Of the 946 Behavior programs series, 851 had at least two observations and were therefore eligible for one-step-ahead forecasting.

4   Problem Formulation

This section defines the forecasting problem addressed in the study. It introduces the observational structure of the therapeutic records, the predictor representation constructed from those records, and the one-step ahead forecasting task under the constraint of temporal causality.

4.1   Observational Structure

Let $i \in \{1, \ldots, N\}$ index patients and let $k \in \{1, \ldots, n_i\}$ index sessions observed for patient i. For each patient, sessions occur at strictly increasing timestamps

$$\mathcal{T}_i = \{t_{i,1}, t_{i,2}, \ldots, t_{i,n_i}\}, \qquad t_{i,k} < t_{i,k+1}. \tag{1}$$

The sequence $\mathcal{T}_i$ is irregular in the sense that the intervals (gaps) between consecutive observations,

$$\Delta t_{i,k} = t_{i,k} - t_{i,k-1}, \qquad k \geq 2, \tag{2}$$

are not assumed to be constant. Let $y_{i,k} \in \{0, 1, 2, \dots\}$ denote the number of challenging-behavior episodes recorded during session k for patient i. Each patient therefore contributes an irregularly sampled count-valued time series

$$\{(t_{i,k}, y_{i,k})\}_{k=1}^{n_i}.$$

4.2 Predictor Representation

For each patient i and session $k < n_i$, a deterministic predictor vector $X_{i,k}$ is constructed from information available no later than time $t_{i,k}$.

For each observed session, a deterministic predictor vector $X_{i,k}$ is constructed from information available no later than time $t_{i,k}$. Its general form is

$$X_{i,k} = \left(\Delta t_{i,k}, \mathrm{cal}_{i,k}, \mathrm{proc}_{i,k}, \mathrm{context}_{i,k}\right), \tag{3}$$

where:

- $\Delta t_{i,k}$ represents the interval between two consecutive observed sessions;
- $\mathrm{cal}_{i,k}$ contains calendar attributes associated with the session time, such as the day of the week and month;
- $\mathrm{proc}_{i,k}$ contains summaries derived from the event log, including the total number of recorded events, the number of distinct behavioral categories, counts of type-specific entries, total recorded duration of behavior when available, session duration measured from the first to the last logged event, and the counts of quality-related indicators;
- $\mathrm{context}_{i,k}$ contains descriptors of the therapeutic context, including intervention attributes recorded in SYSABA.

4.3 Forecasting Task

Let

$$\mathcal{H}_{i,k} = \{(X_{i,j}, y_{i,j}) : 1 \leq j \leq k\} \tag{4}$$

denote the information available for the individual i after the k-th observed session. The forecasting objective is to estimate the number of challenging-behavior episodes at the next observed session:

$$\hat{y}_{i,k+1} = \mathcal{M}(\mathcal{H}_{i,k}), \tag{5}$$

where $\mathcal{M}$ denotes a predictive model of a specified class.

The forecasting rule is subject to a temporal causality constraint: the prediction of $\hat{y}_{i,k+1}$ may depend only on information available at or before time $t_{i,k}$.

Two forecasting settings are considered:

1. a model is estimated from the pooled histories of all individuals
$$\mathcal{M}_{\text{pool}} : \bigcup_{i=1}^{N} \mathcal{H}_{i,k} \to \hat{y}_{.,k+1},$$
2. a separate model is estimated for each individual
$$\mathcal{M}_i : \mathcal{H}_{i,k} \to \hat{y}_{i,k+1}.$$

4.4 Temporal Irregularity

In contrast to approaches that assume equidistant sampling, the present formulation does not reconstruct the data onto a fixed temporal grid. Instead, temporal irregularity is kept and represented explicitly through the interval variable $\Delta t_{i,k}$ and related predictors. In this way, the original temporal structure of the therapeutic record is preserved.

5   Experimental Protocol

As described in Sect. 4, the predictive task consists in estimating the number of episodes of challenging behavior in a session based on historical observations.

Explanatory variables include calendar features (day of week, day of month, month), the inter-session gap $\Delta t_{i,k}$, intra-session aggregates (number of events, number of event types, number of entities involved, log span, age).

Numeric preprocessing was performed within each training fold only. First, a predefined subset of nonnegative, right-skewed predictors (e.g., event counts, durations, and gap length) was transformed using $\log(1+x)$. Second, transformed numeric variables were winsorized to the empirical training quantiles $q_{0.01}$ and $q_{0.99}$. Third, numeric variables were centered on the training median and scaled by the training median absolute deviation (MAD).

5.1   Models and Baselines

Three classes of predictive models are considered: (i) a statistical time-series model (SARIMAX, where the regression component is based on exogenous variables (calendar features, inter-session gap, session-level aggregates, and age), while the residual component is examined using ACF and PACF diagnostics together with the LjungâĂŞBox test), (ii) a gradient-boosted tree ensemble (XGBoost), and (iii) neural network models (MLP and LSTM).

All models are evaluated under identical temporal splits and a consistent set of performance metrics, ensuring fair comparison.

Two baseline predictors are included for reference:

- Historical mean: the prediction equals the mean value of the target variable computed on the training set.
- Naive forecast: the prediction equals the most recent observed value.

5.2   Validation Protocol

Evaluation is performed using time-aware rolling-origin validation. Two evaluation protocols are used:

- Global protocol: Time blocks are defined using global timestamps, with a strict temporal boundary between training and test sets. This protocol reflects real-world forward forecasting and prevents information leakage across folds.
- Per-patient protocol: For each individual, fixed-length test windows are extracted from the end of the available history, while the training set contains only earlier observations.

To ensure robustness, five-fold cross-validation is performed under both protocols, as summarized in Table 1. The use of consistent folds and identical preprocessing of exogenous variables enables a statistically valid comparison of model variants under identical conditions.

Training observations always preceded test observations strictly in time. For each fold, the training subset ended before the first timestamp included in the corresponding test subset.

Table 1. Cross-validation folds for the two evaluation protocols: global forward-chaining and per-patient validation.

Protocol	Fold	Train range	Test range	#Train	#Test
Global	0	baseline	2019-05-27 – 2020-01-30	0	504
Global	1	$\leq$ 2020-01-30	2020-01-31 – 2021-02-19	504	407
Global	2	$\leq$ 2021-02-19	2021-02-22 – 2021-12-15	911	398
Global	3	$\leq$ 2021-12-15	2021-12-15 – 2022-11-25	1309	393
Global	4	$\leq$ 2022-11-25	2022-11-28 – 2024-12-17	1702	357
Per-patient	0	< 2024-10-23	2024-10-23 – 2024-12-17	1803	222
Per-patient	1	< 2024-04-09	2024-04-09 – 2024-10-23	1599	185
Per-patient	2	< 2024-02-23	2024-02-23 – 2024-04-09	1426	175
Per-patient	3	< 2024-01-12	2024-01-12 – 2024-02-23	1256	165
Per-patient	4	< 2023-05-11	2023-05-11 – 2023-05-25	1109	142

5.3   Ablation Variants

To isolate the contribution of temporal irregularity, two feature variants are considered:

1. FULL—complete feature set: calendar features ($\text{cal}_{i,k}$), inter-session gap ($\Delta t_{i,k}$), intra-session aggregates ($\text{proc}_{i,k}$), contextual variables ($\text{context}_{i,k}$), and (for neural models) sequential windows of length W.
2. N-Gap—which excludes the inter-session gap feature $\Delta t_{i,k}$; the model does not explicitly account for irregular time intervals (Table 2).

Table 2. Model variants, feature scope, and interpretability mechanisms.

Method	Variant	Feature Scope	Interpretability / Diagnostics
SARIMAX	FULL	$\{\Delta t_{i,k}, \mathrm{cal}_{i,k}, \mathrm{proc}_{i,k}, \mathrm{context}_{i,k}\}$; optional autoregressive window	regression coefficients; residual diagnostics
SARIMAX	N-Gap	$\{\mathrm{cal}_{i,k}, \mathrm{proc}_{i,k}, \mathrm{context}_{i,k}\}$	as above
XGBoost	FULL	$\{\Delta t_{i,k}, \mathrm{cal}_{i,k}, \mathrm{proc}_{i,k}, \mathrm{context}_{i,k}\}$; interaction terms; lag/window features	SHAP (global summary and dependence plots)
XGBoost	N-Gap	$\{\mathrm{cal}_{i,k}, \mathrm{proc}_{i,k}, \mathrm{context}_{i,k}\}$	as above
MLP/LSTM	FULL	$\{\Delta t_{i,k}, \mathrm{cal}_{i,k}, \mathrm{proc}_{i,k}, \mathrm{context}_{i,k}$, sequential windows (W)	learning curves; temporal validation analysis
MLP/LSTM	N-Gap	$\{\mathrm{cal}_{i,k}, \mathrm{proc}_{i,k}, \mathrm{context}_{i,k}\}$; sequential windows (W)	as above

5.4   Evaluation Metrics

The performance of the model is assessed using the cross-validation protocols defined in Table 1. For a given fold, let $\mathcal{S}_{\text{test}}$ denote the set of test pairs (i, k). Its cardinality is denoted by $|\mathcal{S}_{\text{test}}|$. Let $y_{i,k}$ denote the target value observed in session k of patient i, and let $\hat{y}_{i,k}$ (Eq. 5) denote the prediction of the corresponding point.

Point Forecast Evaluation. For each test $(i, k) \in \mathcal{S}_{\text{test}}$, the point prediction error is defined as

$$e_{i,k} = y_{i,k} - \hat{y}_{i,k}. \tag{6}$$

All point forecast metrics, including MSE and MASE, use the same test set and error terms $e_{i,k}$, with their formal definitions provided in Table 3. MAE is treated as the primary point-error metric because it is easily interpretable on the scale of the response and is less sensitive to isolated large deviations than squared-error measures. MASE is also reported because it scales the forecast error relative to a naive benchmark and therefore supports the comparison between patients histories with different levels and variability.

Interval Forecast Evaluation. For models that provide prediction intervals at nominal level $1 - \alpha$, denote the bounds by $L_{i,k}$ and $U_{i,k}$:

$$[L_{i,k}, U_{i,k}], \qquad \mathbb{P}(L_{i,k} \leq y_{i,k} \leq U_{i,k}) \approx 1 - \alpha. \tag{7}$$

The quality of the interval is assessed using two complementary criteria defined formally in Table 3. Coverage measures empirical calibration, i.e., the proportion of observed values falling within the predicted interval, and should be close to the nominal confidence level $1 - \alpha$ ($\alpha \in (0, 1)$). The interval width quantifies sharpness, reflecting the average width of the interval.

5.5   Aggregation Strategy

The results are reported in two complementary aggregation schemes.

Table 3. Forecast evaluation metrics with consistent (i, k) notation.

Metric	Definition	Interpretation
Mean Absolute Error (MAE)	$\dfrac{1}{\lvert \mathcal{S}_{\text{test}} \rvert} \displaystyle\sum_{(i,k)\in\mathcal{S}_{\text{test}}} \lvert e_{i,k} \rvert$	Mean absolute deviation
Mean Absolute Scaled Error (MASE)	$\dfrac{\frac{1}{\lvert \mathcal{S}^{(i)}_{\text{test}} \rvert} \sum_{(i,k)\in\mathcal{S}_{\text{test}}} \lvert e_{i,k} \rvert}{\frac{1}{\lvert \mathcal{S}^{(i)}_{\text{train}} \rvert - 1} \sum_{(i,k)\in\mathcal{S}_{\text{train}}} \lvert y_{i,k} - y_{i,k-1} \rvert}$	Error scaled by naive forecast
Coverage $(1 - \alpha)$	$\dfrac{1}{\lvert \mathcal{S}_{\text{test}} \rvert} \displaystyle\sum_{(i,k)\in\mathcal{S}_{\text{test}}} \mathbf{1}\{L_{i,k} \leq y_{i,k} \leq U_{i,k}\}$	Empirical interval calibration
IntervalWidth	$\dfrac{1}{\lvert \mathcal{S}_{\text{test}} \rvert} \displaystyle\sum_{(i,k)\in\mathcal{S}_{\text{test}}} (U_{i,k} - L_{i,k})$	Average prediction interval width

Micro Aggregation. Micro-aggregation treats each pair (i, k) as equally weighted and computes the metric over the union of all test observations across folds within a given validation protocol. It corresponds to a fold-weighted average with weights proportional to test set sizes.

$$m_{\text{micro}} = \frac{\sum_{f=1}^{F} \lvert \mathcal{S}^{(f)}_{\text{test}} \rvert \, m\left(\mathcal{S}^{(f)}_{\text{test}}\right)}{\sum_{f=1}^{F} \lvert \mathcal{S}^{(f)}_{\text{test}} \rvert}, \tag{8}$$

where $m(\cdot)$ is the metric, $\mathcal{S}^{(f)}_{\text{test}}$ are test pairs in fold f and $\lvert \mathcal{S}^{(f)}_{\text{test}} \rvert$ is test fold cardinality. This perspective reflects the expected error for a randomly selected test observation. The same procedure applies to empirical coverage and average interval width.

Macro Aggregation. Macro aggregation assigns equal weight to each patient:

$$m_{\text{macro}} = \text{median}_{i=1,\dots,N} \; m\left(\mathcal{S}^{(i)}_{\text{test}}\right).$$

This perspective reflects typical model behavior at the patient level and reduces sensitivity to extreme cases.

6   Results

This section presents the selected experimental results, organized according to the adopted evaluation strategy. Different model classes offer distinct analytical perspectives on the predictions and their interpretation.

6.1   Models' Effectiveness in Micro and Macro Aggregation Strategy

Table 4 summarizes the predictive effectiveness in validation protocols and aggregation schemes. Micro-level results report the Mean Absolute Error (MAE) calculated in all test pairs $(i, k) \in \mathcal{S}_{\text{test}}$. In contrast, macro-level results report

Table 4. Summary across validation protocols and aggregation schemes.

Model	MAE (micro)		MAE_{med} (macro)		MASE_{med} (macro)	
	Global	Per-patient	Global	Per-patient	Global	Per-patient
XGBoost	4.736	**2.525**	3.025	**1.348**	1.211	**0.649**
LSTM	**4.578**	2.803	**1.767**	1.589	1.286	0.848
MLP	5.363	3.565	1.988	2.252	1.224	0.997
SARIMAX	11.487	5.026	2.871	1.765	1.185	1.002
Baseline: mean	6.600	2.657	2.490	1.177	0.919	0.801
Baseline: persistence	8.387	3.043	3.308	1.314	1.185	0.746

the median per-patient MAE_{med} and the median Mean Absolute Scaled Error (MASE_{med}).

At the micro level, the LSTM achieves the lowest MAE (4.578), outperforming XGBoost (4.736) and improving over the baseline mean (6.600) and SARIMAX (11.487) in the global protocol. The per-patient protocol determines this order. In per-patient setting, XGBoost achieves the lowest MAE (2.525), followed by the baseline mean (2.657) and the LSTM (2.803). This indicates that while sequence models capture global temporal structure effectively, the tree-based model generalizes better when evaluation is aligned with individual patient histories.

The macro-aggregation provides a complementary perspective. In the global protocol, LSTM produces the lowest MAE_{med} (1.767). In contrast, under the per-patient protocol, XGBoost achieves the lowest MAE_{med} among the learned models (1.348), outperforming LSTM (1.589) and SARIMAX (1.765). This shift suggests that relative advantages depend on the evaluation protocol and that patient-level generalization differs from pooled forecasting.

The scale-normalized results (MASE_{med}) further clarify these differences. In the global protocol, all learned models exhibit MASE_{med} values greater than 1 (e.g., XGBoost: 1.211; LSTM: 1.286), indicating that for a typical patient they do not outperform the naive baseline. According to the per-patient protocol, XGBoost reaches $\mathrm{MASE}_{med} = 0.649$, substantially below 1, demonstrating a clear improvement over the naive predictor for the median patient. LSTM also improves over the baseline (0.848), though to a lesser extent.

In general, the results reveal two consistent patterns. First, performance rankings depend on the validation protocol, which highlights the importance of aligning the evaluation with the intended deployment scenario. Second, the tree-based model (XGBoost) demonstrates greater stability across protocols and achieves the most significant relative improvement at the patient level, as reflected in both MAE and MASE_{med}.

6.2   Stratification by Irregularity

To assess how predictive accuracy varies with temporal irregularity, test observations were stratified according to quartiles (Q1–Q4) of the inter-session gap. For each quartile, MAE was computed separately under the global and per-patient validation protocols.

Table 5 reports selected results for representative models. In the global protocol, the distribution between quartiles is highly imbalanced, with the vast majority of observations concentrated in Q1. Results for Q2–Q4 should be interpreted with caution. The per-patient protocol shows substantially more balanced quartile sizes, enabling a more reliable comparison between irregularity levels.

Table 5. MAE by quartiles of inter-session gap $(\Delta t_{i,k})$. Best (lowest) MAE in each quartile and protocol is shown in bold.

	Global				Per-patient			
Model	Q1	Q2	Q3	Q4	Q1	Q2	Q3	Q4
XGBoost	4.681	1.864	15.028	1.703	**3.348**	**1.301**	**1.416**	**1.242**
LSTM	**4.102**	**1.188**	17.861	**0.982**	3.800	1.698	1.446	1.839
MLP	4.965	2.481	16.493	1.399	4.415	2.357	2.237	2.378
SARIMAX	11.692	6.489	**12.110**	2.227	6.021	2.920	5.031	5.536
$\|\mathcal{S}_{\text{test}}\|$	4035	15	6	6	768	342	408	426

Under the global protocol, reliable comparison is effectively limited to Q1, which contains the vast majority of observations. In this quartile, both XGBoost (4.681) and LSTM (4.102) outperform SARIMAX (11.692). The remaining quartiles (Q2–Q4) contain only a small number of observations, resulting in unstable MAE estimates and limiting the strength of conclusions that can be drawn for longer gaps under global pooling.

The per-patient protocol reveals more consistent pattern. For XGBoost, MAE decreases monotonically from Q1 (3.348) to Q4 (1.242), corresponding to an approximate 63% reduction in error. LSTM exhibits a similar, though less regular, decline (3.800 → 1.839).

The stratified analysis suggests that model performance may vary across levels of temporal irregularity, but the strength of this conclusion depends on the validation regime. In the global protocol, quartile-level inference is weak because observations are highly concentrated in Q1, leaving Q2–Q4 too sparse for stable comparison. In the per-patient protocol, the quartile counts are more balanced and the pattern is more interpretable, with XGBoost showing decreasing MAE as inter-session gaps increase.

6.3   Diebold–Mariano Test

The Diebold–Mariano analysis focuses on the SARIMAX and XGBoost comparison because both models use the same tabular exogenous-feature representation and therefore provide a direct contrast between a classical forecasting specification and a nonlinear ensemble model. Neural models are excluded from this particular test because their input structure differs due to sequential windowing.

Table 6. Diebold–Mariano test (Absolute Error). Positive statistics indicate the advantage of XGBoost over SARIMAX.

Protocol	Variant	DM stat.	p-value
Global	FULL	4.962	8.7e-07
Global	N_Gap	4.815	1.8e-06
Per-patient	FULL	2.246	0.0251
Per-patient	N_Gap	3.089	0.0021

As shown in Table 6, XGBoost significantly outperforms SARIMAX in all configurations under both validation protocols. In the global protocol, the most significant difference is observed in the FULL specification (DM $= 4.962$, $p < 10^{-6}$), followed by N_Gap (DM $= 4.815$). In the per-patient protocol, the advantage remains statistically significant, although the effect sizes are smaller (e.g., FULL: DM $= 2.246$, $p = 0.025$).

Importantly, the reduction in DM statistics when moving from FULL to N_Gap suggests that explicitly modeling the inter-session gap contributes to the observed performance.

Overall, DM analysis confirms that XGBoost is superior to SARIMAX, with statistical robustness across validation protocols and feature specifications.

6.4   Prediction Interval Properties

Prediction intervals were constructed using a split-conformal procedure applied within each training fold. A dedicated calibration subset was separated from the model-fitting subset in temporal order to preserve causality. For models producing lower and upper conditional quantiles, conformalized quantile regression was used to adjust interval bounds to the desired nominal coverage level.

Table 7 reports empirical coverage and average interval width for nominal 90% prediction intervals.

Under the global validation protocol, both models exhibit substantial under-coverage (SARIMAX: 0.769; XGBoost: 0.661), indicating insufficient calibration. Although SARIMAX achieves higher coverage than XGBoost, it does so at the cost of markedly wider intervals (23.99 vs 13.33). This suggests that pooling heterogeneous time series leads to unstable uncertainty quantification.

In contrast, under the per-patient protocol, both models achieve coverage close to the nominal level (SARIMAX: 0.918; XGBoost: 0.926). Importantly, XGBoost attains this calibration with substantially narrower intervals (8.95 vs 18.10), indicating superior sharpness without sacrificing reliability.

Table 7. Empirical coverage and average prediction interval width (nominal level $1 - \alpha = 0.9$).

Model	Global		Per-patient	
	Coverage	Width	Coverage	Width
SARIMAX	0.769	23.99	0.918	18.10
XGBoost	0.661	13.33	0.926	8.95

These findings demonstrate that individualized modeling not only improves point accuracy but also yields better-calibrated and more informative uncertainty estimates.

6.5   Practical Example

To illustrate the practical application, we present predictions generated by XGBoost in the FULL configuration, previously identified as the strongest-

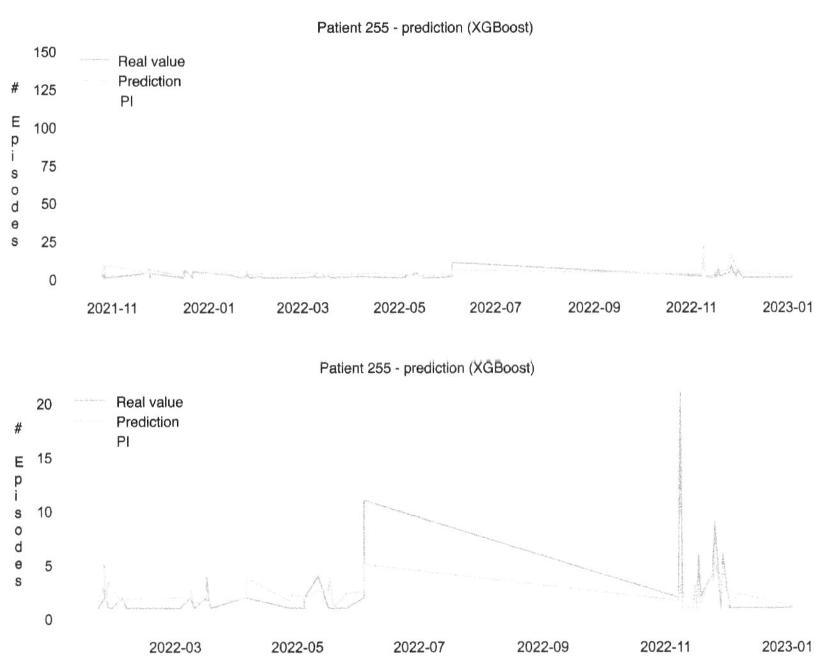

Fig. 2. Forecasting results for patient ID 255 using XGBoost (FULL specification). Top: global validation protocol. Bottom: per-patient validation protocol. The blue line denotes observed values $y_{i,k}$, the orange line represents point forecasts $\hat{y}_{i,k}$, and the shaded region corresponds to 90% prediction intervals. (Color figure online)

performing specification. Figure 2 shows results for an illustrative patient example under both validation protocols (global and per-patient).

Under the global protocol, prediction intervals are substantially wider and frequently exceed the empirical range of observations. This reflects the increased uncertainty when the model is trained on pooled data and applied across heterogeneous time series. In contrast, under the per-patient protocol, prediction intervals are noticeably narrower and more closely aligned with the observed variability. This indicates improved calibration and sharper uncertainty quantification when training is restricted to individual patient histories.

7 Discussion and Conclusion

This study investigated time-series forecasting of one-step-ahead challenging behavior under irregular observation intervals in Applied Behavior Analysis (ABA), treating gaps as part of the signal structure. The empirical results indicate that explicit encoding of inter-session gaps can improve predictive usefulness, especially when evaluation is aligned with individual patient histories. At the same time, the results do not support a universal winner across all metrics: LSTM performs best on global micro-level MAE, whereas XGBoost offers the most stable overall trade-off between accuracy, interpretability, and interval sharpness. The XGBoost advantage remained statistically significant in both feature configurations (FULL and N_Gap).

The study has several limitations. First, the data come from a single operational platform and one national service context, which limits external validity. Second, the target variable is a session-level count and does not capture behavioral severity, context specificity, or functional class beyond what is encoded in the available logs. Third, the analysis is observational and predictive rather than causal; improved forecast accuracy does not imply that the identified predictors are treatment drivers. Fourth, the irregularity analysis is partly constrained by an imbalance in quartile support under the global protocol. Fifth, patient-specific models can be unstable when individual histories are short. Sixth, uncertainty calibration was evaluated retrospectively rather than prospectively in a live clinical workflow.

Theoretical implications arise at two levels. First, the paper supports the view that, in event-based behavioral records, observation timing carries information and should be explicitly modeled. Second, it shows that model assessment in such settings must distinguish pooled forecasting performance from patient-level deployment performance, because the preferred model depends on the evaluation perspective.

The practical implications are equally important. A validated session-level forecasting system could support therapist review by identifying elevated next-session risk of episodes, quantifying uncertainty around the predicted escalation, and helping prioritize supervisory attention. However, such use should remain decision-supportive rather than automated, particularly because calibration and error profiles vary between validation regimes.

From a decision-support perspective, modeling irregular time series enables more realistic forecasting in ABA contexts, where session timing is inherently variable.

Future work should extend the analysis to external validation across centers, richer behavioral outcomes, and time-series-specific uncertainty methods tailored to dependent observational data.

References

1. Armstrong, K.H., Ogg, J.A., Sundman-Wheat, A.N., St. John Walsh, A.: Evidence-based interventions for children with challenging behavior. Springer, Cham (2014). https://doi.org/10.1007/978-1-4614-7807-2
2. Cox, D.J., Sosine, J.: A data-driven, algorithmic approach to recommending hours of ABA for individuals with ASD. Behav. Interv. **40**(2), e70014 (2025). https://doi.org/10.1002/bin.70014, https://onlinelibrary.wiley.com/doi/10.1002/bin.70014
3. Diebold, F.X., Mariano, R.S.: Comparing Predictive Accuracy. J. Bus. Econ. Stat. **13**(3), 253–263 (1995). https://doi.org/10.1080/07350015.1995.10524599, http://www.tandfonline.com/doi/abs/10.1080/07350015.1995.10524599
4. Hyndman, R.J., Koehler, A.B.: Another look at measures of forecast accuracy. Int. J. Forecast. **22**(4), 679–688 (2006). https://doi.org/10.1016/j.ijforecast.2006.03.001, https://linkinghub.elsevier.com/retrieve/pii/S0169207006000239
5. Kohli, M., Kar, A.K., Bangalore, A., Ap, P.: Machine learning-based ABA treatment recommendation and personalization for autism spectrum disorder: an exploratory study. Brain Inf. **9**(1), 16 (2022). https://doi.org/10.1186/s40708-022-00164-6, https://braininformatics.springeropen.com/articles/10.1186/s40708-022-00164-6
6. Kołodziejczyk, J.: Uncovering patterns in training skills with aba: Rule extraction from the sysaba database. In: Hernes, M., Wątróbski, J. (eds.) Emerg. Challenges Intell. Manag. Inf. Syst., pp. 3–14. Springer Nature Switzerland, Cham (2024)
7. Lanovaz, M.J., Hranchuk, K.: Machine learning to analyze single-case graphs: a comparison to visual inspection. J. Appl. Behav. Anal. **54**(4), 1541–1552 (2021). https://doi.org/10.1002/jaba.863
8. Leaf, J.B., Cihon, J.H., Ferguson, J.L., Weinkauf, S.M.: An Introduction to Applied Behavior Analysis, pp. 25–42. Springer, Cham (2017). https://doi.org/10.1007/978-3-319-71210-9_3
9. Manolov, R., Rochat, L.: Analyzing data in single-case experimental designs: objectives and available software options. J. Behav. Cogn. Therapy **34**(4), 100511 (2024). https://doi.org/10.1016/j.jbct.2024.100511
10. Poling, A., Fuqua, R.W. (eds.): Research Methods in Applied Behavior Analysis. Springer US, Boston, MA (1986). https://doi.org/10.1007/978-1-4684-8786-2
11. Tryon, W.W.: A simplified time-series analysis for evaluating treatment interventions. J. Appl. Behav. Anal. **15**(3), 423–429 (1982). https://doi.org/10.1901/jaba.1982.15-423, https://onlinelibrary.wiley.com/doi/10.1901/jaba.1982.15-423
12. Xu, T.L., De Barbaro, K., Abney, D.H., Cox, R.F.A.: Finding structure in time: visualizing and analyzing behavioral time series. Front. Psychol. **11**, 1457 (2020). https://doi.org/10.3389/fpsyg.2020.01457, https://www.frontiersin.org/article/10.3389/fpsyg.2020.01457/full

Does Better Weight Estimation Mean Better Decisions? A Monte Carlo Assessment of RANCOM-ST

Anna Shkurina[1,2]([⊠]) [iD]

[1] Institute of Management, University of Szczecin, ul. Cukrowa 8, 71-004 Szczecin, Poland
[2] Doctoral School of University of Szczecin, ul. Mickiewicza 16, 70-383 Szczecin, Poland
anna.shkurina@phd.usz.edu.pl

Abstract. Weighting of criteria is a critical step in multi-criteria decision analysis (MCDA), yet the usefulness of a weighting method should be assessed in terms of decision reliability rather than only numerical accuracy. This study investigates the decision-level consequences of the statistical refinement introduced by the RANCOM-ST weighting procedure in comparison with the original RANCOM method. A large-scale Monte Carlo simulation framework is employed, systematically varying the number of criteria, expert judgment error, and the aggregation model (SAW and TOPSIS). The analysis focuses on the ability to correctly identify the best alternative, shortlist consistency, and full ranking similarity, complemented by a decision transition analysis that measures repaired and deteriorated decisions. The results show that RANCOM-ST significantly improves the probability of selecting the correct alternative, particularly under higher expert noise, while rarely degrading already correct decisions. However, the magnitude and stability of improvement depend on the aggregation model, with more predictable gains under linear aggregation. The findings clarify the relationship between weight accuracy and decision reliability and indicate conditions under which statistical weight correction is beneficial.

Keywords: RANCOM method · Subjective Weighting · MCDA

1 Introduction

Decision-support methods are commonly evaluated in terms of how accurately they estimate model parameters; however, in practical applications the primary objective is not parameter recovery but decision reliability. In Multi-Criteria Decision Analysis (MCDA), the final outcome of the process is the ranking of alternatives or the selection of a single preferred option [3]. Consequently, even small changes in model inputs may or may not alter the decision itself. From a decision-makerâĂŹs perspective, a weighting procedure is useful only if it leads to stable and reliable choices rather than merely numerically accurate parameters.

A key source of variability in MCDA arises from the elicitation of criteria importance. When preferences are derived from expert judgments, uncertainty, hesitation, and cognitive bias inevitably affect the obtained weights [2]. Previous studies have shown that experts are often consistent in general preference structure but imprecise in fine distinctions between similarly important criteria. As a result, weighting errors do not always translate proportionally into ranking errors: in some cases the best alternative remains unchanged, while in others minor perturbations may alter the decision outcome [7].

The RANking COMparison (RANCOM) method was proposed as a simple subjective weighting approach based on ordinal comparisons between criteria [8]. Instead of relying on precise numerical assessments, it derives weights from comparative preference information, which reduces sensitivity to small judgment inconsistencies. Due to its computational simplicity and robustness to minor inconsistencies, the method has attracted attention as a practical alternative to more cognitively demanding elicitation procedures. An extension of this approach, RANCOM-ST, later introduced a statistical correction mechanism that adjusts the estimated weights using threshold-based feedback [6].

While such corrections are intended to improve the agreement between estimated and underlying preferences, improved weight accuracy does not necessarily imply improved decisions. In MCDA, the mapping between weights and rankings is nonlinear and depends on the aggregation model and the structure of the decision problem. Therefore, evaluating weighting procedures solely by comparing weight vectors may be misleading: a method can reduce weight estimation error while leaving the selected alternative unchanged, or conversely alter the decision despite small numerical differences.

The aim of this paper is not to propose a new weighting method but to investigate the decision-level consequences of the statistical refinement introduced by RANCOM-ST [6]. Specifically, we analyze whether the correction improves, preserves, or occasionally degrades the final decision when compared with the original RANCOM procedure. To enable controlled analysis, a large-scale Monte Carlo simulation framework is used, allowing systematic variation of the number of criteria, the level of expert judgment error, and the aggregation model.

The study is guided by the following research questions:

(RQ1) To what extent does the statistical correction introduced by RANCOM-ST improve the accuracy of identifying the best alternative (Top-1 Hit Rate) compared to standard RANCOM, and how does this improvement vary with the number of criteria and the level of expert error?

(RQ2) How does the choice of aggregation method (SAW vs. TOPSIS) mediate the effectiveness of the RANCOM-ST correction, and does the distance-based nature of TOPSIS amplify or attenuate the benefits of weight refinement relative to the linear SAW model?

(RQ3) Under what conditions does RANCOM-ST introduce a risk of degrading an otherwise correct RANCOM decision, and what is the net trade-off between rescued and deteriorated rankings across varying problem sizes and noise levels?

By addressing these questions, the study provides a methodological assessment of weighting refinement in MCDA and clarifies the relationship between weight accuracy and decision accuracy. The findings indicate when statistical correction is beneficial and when it may be unnecessary or potentially detrimental in decision-support applications.

The remainder of the paper is organized as follows. Section 2 presents the methodological background. Section 3 describes the simulation framework and experimental design. Section 4 reports and discusses the results. Finally, Sect. 5 concludes the paper and outlines directions for future research.

2   Methods

This section briefly summarizes the methods required for the experimental evaluation: the RANCOM and RANCOM-ST weighting procedures and the SAW and TOPSIS aggregation models. Only the elements necessary to understand the experimental protocol are presented, while full methodological details can be found in the original references.

2.1   RANCOM Weighting Method

The RANking COMparison (RANCOM) method derives criteria weights from ordinal preference information provided by an expert. Instead of requesting precise numerical assessments, the decision-maker supplies a ranking of criteria according to their importance. The method transforms this ranking into a set of pairwise comparisons and estimates weights by aggregating the comparative relations.

Let π denote a ranking of n criteria, where a lower position index indicates higher importance. The ranking is converted into a pairwise comparison structure indicating whether criterion i is preferred to criterion j. For each criterion i, the number of favorable comparisons is counted and normalized:

$$w_i = \frac{s_i}{\sum_{k=1}^{n} s_k},$$

where s_i denotes the aggregated preference score obtained from the comparisons. The normalization ensures

$$\sum_{i=1}^{n} w_i = 1, \qquad w_i \geq 0.$$

The procedure reduces the cognitive burden on the expert and mitigates the effect of minor inconsistencies, as small ranking perturbations affect only local comparison relations rather than the entire weight structure.

2.2   RANCOM-ST Statistical Refinement

RANCOM-ST extends the original RANCOM procedure by introducing a statistical refinement step applied after initial weight estimation. The method uses calibration parameters derived from the distribution of expected estimation errors.

Let $\mathbf{w}^{\mathrm{R}} = (w_1^{\mathrm{R}}, \ldots, w_n^{\mathrm{R}})$ denote the weights obtained from RANCOM. The refined weights $\mathbf{w}^{\mathrm{ST}}$ are computed by shifting each component in a direction indicated by expert feedback:

$$w_i^{\mathrm{ST}} = w_i^{\mathrm{R}} + d_i \cdot c_i,$$

where $d_i \in \{-1, 0, 1\}$ represents the suggested direction of change (decrease, no change, increase) and c_i is a correction magnitude derived from statistical thresholds based on the mean μ_n and standard deviation σ_n of estimation errors. After correction, weights are truncated to non-negative values and renormalized:

$$w_i^{\mathrm{ST}} \leftarrow \frac{\max(w_i^{\mathrm{ST}}, 0)}{\sum_{k=1}^{n} \max(w_k^{\mathrm{ST}}, 0)}.$$

The intention of the refinement is to compensate systematic bias in ordinal-based weight estimation without requiring precise numerical judgments from the expert.

2.3   SAW Aggregation Model

The Simple Additive Weighting (SAW) method evaluates each alternative by a weighted sum of normalized criterion values. Let $\mathbf{D} = [d_{ij}]$ denote the decision matrix. The score of alternative i is

$$S_i = \sum_{j=1}^{n} w_j d_{ij}.$$

Alternatives are ranked in descending order of S_i. Due to its additive structure, the method translates changes in weights directly into proportional score changes.

2.4   TOPSIS Aggregation Model

The Technique for Order Preference by Similarity to an Ideal Solution (TOPSIS) ranks alternatives according to their relative closeness to the ideal and anti-ideal solutions [1].

The decision matrix is first normalized:

$$r_{ij} = \frac{d_{ij}}{\sqrt{\sum_{k=1}^{m} d_{kj}^2}},$$

and weighted:

$$v_{ij} = w_j r_{ij}.$$

The positive and negative ideal solutions are defined as

$$A^+ = (\max_i v_{ij}), \qquad A^- = (\min_i v_{ij}).$$

Distances to the ideal and anti-ideal points are computed using Euclidean metrics:

$$D_i^+ = \sqrt{\sum_{j=1}^{n}(v_{ij} - A_j^+)^2}, \qquad D_i^- = \sqrt{\sum_{j=1}^{n}(v_{ij} - A_j^-)^2}.$$

The relative closeness is

$$C_i = \frac{D_i^-}{D_i^+ + D_i^-},$$

and alternatives are ranked in descending order of C_i.

3   Experiments

This section presents a Monte Carlo simulation study comparing RANCOM and RANCOM-ST with respect to their ability to reproduce decision outcomes implied by the ground-truth model. In particular, we investigate whether the statistical weight correction affects (i) the identification of the best alternative (Top-1), (ii) the composition of shortlists (Top-k for $k \in \{3,5\}$), and (iii) the overall similarity of alternative rankings under varying numbers of criteria and different levels of expert error. Monte Carlo simulation has been widely applied to evaluate the stability and accuracy of MCDA methods under varying problem configurations [4,9].

3.1   Experimental Setup

Since the ground-truth weights are known by construction, each simulation run produces a reference ranking that serves as an objective benchmark for evaluating both methods. The experimental design varies three primary factors:

- Number of criteria: $n \in \{3, 4, 5, 6, 7, 8, 9, 10\}$,
- Expert noise level: adjacent swap probability $p_{swap} \in \{0.10, 0.25, 0.40\}$, corresponding to low, medium, and high error,
- Aggregation method: SAW (Simple Additive Weighting) and TOPSIS.

For each configuration, $T = 100{,}000$ Monte Carlo repetitions are performed using $m = 10$ alternatives. All runs share a fixed random seed to ensure reproducibility. The full factorial design yields $8 \times 3 \times 2 = 48$ experimental configurations and 4,800,000 simulation runs in total.

Algorithm 1. Simulated Expert Ranking with Noise

Require: True weights $\mathbf{w}^* = (w_1^*, \ldots, w_n^*)$, swap probability p_{swap}
Ensure: Noisy expert ranking $\hat{\pi}$
1: $\pi^* \leftarrow \text{argsort}(-\mathbf{w}^*)$ $\triangleright$ Ideal ranking (descending)
2: $\hat{\pi} \leftarrow \pi^*$ $\triangleright$ Copy
3: **for** $i = 1$ **to** $n - 1$ **do**
4:      $a \leftarrow \hat{\pi}_i, \quad b \leftarrow \hat{\pi}_{i+1}$
5:      $\delta \leftarrow |w_a^* - w_b^*|$
6:      $p_{\mathit{eff}} \leftarrow \begin{cases} \min(p_{swap} + 0.15,\ 0.85) & \text{if } \delta < 0.05 \\ p_{swap} & \text{otherwise} \end{cases}$
7:      **if** $U(0,1) < p_{\mathit{eff}}$ **then**
8:          Swap $\hat{\pi}_i \leftrightarrow \hat{\pi}_{i+1}$
9:      **end if**
10: **end for**
11: **return** $\hat{\pi}$

3.2 Data Generation Process

Each Monte Carlo iteration constructs a synthetic decision problem consisting of true criteria weights, a decision matrix, and an imperfect expert ranking.

First, a ground-truth weight vector $\mathbf{w}^* \in \mathbb{R}^n$ is sampled from a symmetric Dirichlet distribution, $\mathbf{w}^* \sim \text{Dir}(\alpha, \ldots, \alpha)$ with concentration parameter $\alpha = 1.0$. This produces a uniform distribution over the probability simplex, meaning that no particular importance structure is favored a priori. Consequently, the simulation spans a wide range of decision-maker preference structures, from nearly equal weights to strongly differentiated criteria.

Next, a decision matrix $\mathbf{D} \in \mathbb{R}^{m \times n}$ is generated with entries independently drawn from the uniform distribution $d_{ij} \sim U(0,1)$. All criteria are treated as benefit-type attributes (larger values preferred). This controlled setting isolates the influence of weight estimation errors on the final ranking without introducing additional effects associated with cost transformations.

Finally, expert judgment errors are introduced at the preference elicitation stage. The ideal ranking π^* is obtained by sorting criteria in descending order of their true weights. The observed expert ranking $\hat{\pi}$ is then generated by stochastic adjacent transpositions, as specified in Algorithm 1. This noise model reflects bounded rationality: decision-makers are more likely to confuse criteria of similar importance than criteria with clearly different significance levels, thereby preserving the overall preference structure while introducing local inconsistencies.

3.3 RANCOM-ST Correction (Oracle Mode)

For each generated expert ranking, criteria weights are first estimated using the RANCOM method, yielding the weight vector $\mathbf{w}^{\mathrm{R}}$. An additional refinement step may then be applied using the RANCOM-ST statistical correction.

The correction is based on calibration parameters (μ_n, σ_n) obtained in Sect. 2. In the oracle feedback mode, the simulated expert perfectly identifies the direction of deviation between the estimated and true weights. This configuration provides an upper bound on the achievable performance of RANCOM-ST and isolates the influence of the correction magnitude from potential feedback interpretation errors. The correction mechanism is specified in Algorithm 2.

Algorithm 2. RANCOM-ST Weight Correction (Oracle Mode)

Require: RANCOM weights $\mathbf{w}^{R}$, true weights $\mathbf{w}^{*}$, calibration parameters (μ_n, σ_n)
Ensure: Corrected weights $\mathbf{w}^{ST}$

1: $\mathbf{w}^{ST} \leftarrow \mathbf{w}^{R}$ ▷ Initialize
2: **for** $i = 1$ **to** n **do**
3:      $\delta_i \leftarrow w_i^* - w_i^R$ ▷ True deviation
4:      **if** $|\delta_i| < 0.001$ **then**
5:          **continue**   ▷ No correction needed
6:      **end if**
7:      $d_i \leftarrow \text{sign}(\delta_i)$ ▷ Correction direction
8:      **if** $|\delta_i| < \mu_n - 0.5\sigma_n$ **then**
9:          $c_i \leftarrow \max(\mu_n - \sigma_n, 0)$ ▷ Low correction
10:      **else if** $|\delta_i| < \mu_n + 0.5\sigma_n$ **then**
11:          $c_i \leftarrow \mu_n$ ▷ Medium correction
12:      **else**
13:          $c_i \leftarrow \mu_n + \sigma_n$ ▷ High correction
14:      **end if**
15:      $w_i^{ST} \leftarrow w_i^{ST} + d_i \cdot c_i$
16: **end for**
17: $\mathbf{w}^{ST} \leftarrow \max(\mathbf{w}^{ST}, \epsilon)$ where $\epsilon = 10^{-6}$ ▷ Non-negativity
18: $\mathbf{w}^{ST} \leftarrow \mathbf{w}^{ST}/\|\mathbf{w}^{ST}\|_1$ ▷ Normalize
19: **return** $\mathbf{w}^{ST}$

The corrected weights are subsequently used in the aggregation stage to compute the final ranking of alternatives.

3.4 Aggregation Methods

To evaluate how weight refinement affects final decision outcomes, two aggregation models with different structural properties are considered: SAW and TOPSIS (both introduced in Sect. 2).

SAW represents an additive decision model in which the influence of criteria weights on the final scores is direct and proportional. Consequently, any change in the weight vector translates linearly into score changes.

In contrast, TOPSIS determines preferences based on distances to ideal and anti-ideal solutions in the weighted space. Because the ranking depends on relative distances rather than a simple weighted sum, weight perturbations propagate through normalization and distance computation.

3.5   Evaluation Metrics

For each iteration, the ideal ranking $\mathbf{R}^*$ (computed using the true weights $\mathbf{w}^*$) is compared with the rankings obtained using RANCOM and RANCOM-ST. Several complementary metrics are employed because different MCDA tasks emphasize different decision objectives: selecting a single best alternative, forming a shortlist, or preserving the overall ranking structure.

Top-1 Hit Rate measures how often the highest-ranked alternative coincides with the ideal choice,

$$\mathbf{1}[R_1^* = R_1^{\text{test}}].$$

This metric reflects choice problems, where the decision-maker must select exactly one option.

Top-k Overlap ($k \in \{3, 5\}$) evaluates agreement within the leading subset of alternatives,

$$\frac{|\text{Top}_k(\mathbf{R}^*) \cap \text{Top}_k(\mathbf{R}^{\text{test}})|}{k},$$

corresponding to screening scenarios in which a shortlist of promising candidates is required.

WS Coefficient [5] measures similarity of the full rankings while assigning greater importance to higher positions. Unlike Top-k, it evaluates the entire ordering but still prioritizes top-ranked alternatives.

Mean Rank Distance measures the average positional displacement across the ranking,

$$\frac{1}{m} \sum_{i=1}^{m} |\text{pos}^*(i) - \text{pos}^{\text{test}}(i)|,$$

capturing global ranking distortion independently of whether the best alternative is preserved.

Weight MAE is the mean absolute error between estimated and true weights,

$$\frac{1}{n} \sum_{j-1}^{n} |w_j^{\text{est}} - w_j^*|.$$

3.6   Simulation Procedure

The experiment follows a Monte Carlo protocol in which each iteration represents an independent decision-making instance. For every configuration of the number of criteria, noise level, and aggregation model, synthetic decision problems are repeatedly generated and evaluated using both RANCOM and RANCOM-ST. The overall performance measures are obtained by aggregating the results over all repetitions. The procedure is summarized in Algorithm 3.

The reported performance metrics correspond to averages over all Monte Carlo repetitions for each experimental configuration. Differences between RAN-COM and RANCOM-ST are evaluated across identical simulation instances, ensuring paired comparisons under the same decision scenarios.

Algorithm 3. Monte Carlo Simulation: RANCOM vs RANCOM-ST

Require: Parameter sets $\mathcal{N}$, $\mathcal{L}$, $\mathcal{A}$; iterations T; alternatives m
Ensure: Aggregated metric results for all configurations
1: **for** each $n \in \mathcal{N}$, $\ell \in \mathcal{L}$, agg $\in \mathcal{A}$ **do**
2:    **for** $t = 1$ **to** T **do**
3:       $\mathbf{w}^* \sim \mathrm{Dir}(1, \ldots, 1)$ $\triangleright$ Sample true weights
4:       $\mathbf{D} \sim U(0,1)^{m \times n}$ $\triangleright$ Generate decision matrix
5:       $\mathbf{R}^* \leftarrow \mathrm{agg}(\mathbf{D}, \mathbf{w}^*)$ $\triangleright$ Ideal ranking
6:       $\hat{\pi} \leftarrow \mathrm{ExpertRanking}(\mathbf{w}^*, p_\ell)$ $\triangleright$ Alg. 1
7:       $\mathbf{MAC} \leftarrow \mathrm{RankingToMAC}(\hat{\pi}, n)$
8:       $\mathbf{w}^{\mathrm{R}} \leftarrow \mathrm{RANCOM}(\mathbf{MAC})$
9:       $\mathbf{w}^{\mathrm{ST}} \leftarrow \mathrm{RANCOM\text{-}ST}(\mathbf{w}^{\mathrm{R}}, \mathbf{w}^*, n)$ $\triangleright$ Alg. 2
10:       $\mathbf{R}^{\mathrm{R}} \leftarrow \mathrm{agg}(\mathbf{D}, \mathbf{w}^{\mathrm{R}})$
11:       $\mathbf{R}^{\mathrm{ST}} \leftarrow \mathrm{agg}(\mathbf{D}, \mathbf{w}^{\mathrm{ST}})$
12:       Record metrics: $\mathrm{Compare}(\mathbf{R}^*, \mathbf{R}^{\mathrm{R}})$ and $\mathrm{Compare}(\mathbf{R}^*, \mathbf{R}^{\mathrm{ST}})$
13:    **end for**
14: **end for**

---

4   Results

4.1   SAW Aggregation Model

The results for the additive SAW model are presented in Table 1. Across all experimental configurations, the statistical refinement consistently improves both the estimated weights and the resulting decision rankings.

The most immediate effect of the correction appears at the parameter level. The Weight MAE is substantially reduced for every number of criteria and every noise level. For instance, for $n = 3$ under low noise the error decreases from 0.1131 to 0.0355. Similar reductions are observed throughout the table, typically by a factor of about three. This confirms that the calibration mechanism effectively moves the RANCOM estimates toward the true weight vector.

More importantly, the improvement in weight estimation translates into improved decision outcomes. The Top-1 hit rate increases in every configuration. Under low noise, the probability of selecting the optimal alternative rises from approximately 75–76% for RANCOM to about 86–92% for RANCOM-ST depending on the number of criteria. Even under high noise, where preference information is strongly distorted, the correction provides a substantial benefit (e.g., for $n = 3$ from 63.9% to 82.6%). This indicates that the statistical refinement is capable of recovering decision-relevant information even when the elicited ranking contains considerable local inconsistencies.

A similar pattern is visible for the Top-3 overlap. The composition of the shortlist becomes significantly more stable, with improvements typically exceeding 10% points. Since many practical MCDA applications involve screening rather than strict ranking, this suggests that the correction primarily enhances the reliability of identifying promising alternatives.

The global ranking similarity, measured by the WS coefficient, also increases systematically. For small numbers of criteria the improvement is particularly strong (e.g., from 0.8617 to 0.9576 for $n = 3$ under low noise). As the number of criteria increases, the gain remains positive but gradually decreases. This behavior reflects a structural property of additive models: when more criteria are present, individual weight errors have a diluted influence on the aggregated score because each criterion contributes a smaller portion of the total evaluation.

The magnitude of improvement depends jointly on the noise level and the number of criteria. The largest gains occur for small n, where inaccuracies in weights strongly affect the final scores. As n increases, the baseline performance of RANCOM improves and the relative advantage of RANCOM-ST becomes smaller. This indicates that decision sensitivity to weight estimation error is structurally dependent on the dimensionality of the decision problem.

Overall, the results reported in Table 1 demonstrate a monotonic relationship: reducing the weight estimation error leads to higher decision accuracy. However, the strength of this relationship is not constant. The benefit of statistical correction is greatest in low-dimensional problems and remains meaningful even under substantial expert noise, showing that decision reliability is considerably more sensitive to weight errors than suggested by weight-level metrics alone.

4.2 TOPSIS Aggregation Model

The results for the TOPSIS aggregation model are reported in Table 2. As in the additive case, the statistical refinement consistently reduces the weight estimation error and improves all decision-quality metrics. However, the magnitude and structure of the improvements differ from those observed for the SAW model.

At the parameter level, the behavior remains unchanged. The Weight MAE is reduced across all configurations by approximately a factor of three, similarly to the SAW results. For example, for $n = 3$ under low noise the error decreases from 0.1134 to 0.0356. This confirms that the calibration step improves weight estimation independently of the aggregation procedure.

At the decision level, the improvement in the Top-1 hit rate is again systematic. Under low noise, the probability of selecting the optimal alternative increases from approximately 70–74% for RANCOM to about 84–91% for RANCOM-ST depending on the number of criteria. Even under high noise, the correction provides a substantial improvement (e.g., for $n = 3$ from 59.5% to 80.3%). Therefore, the statistical correction remains beneficial even when the preference ranking is strongly perturbed.

The Top-3 overlap follows the same pattern, with improvements typically exceeding 10% points. This indicates that the correction not only affects the exact ordering but also stabilizes the identification of promising alternatives.

Global ranking similarity measured by the WS coefficient also increases in every configuration. However, compared to SAW, the absolute WS values are consistently lower for both methods. This difference reflects the structural properties of TOPSIS: because rankings depend on distances to ideal and anti-ideal solutions, perturbations in weights propagate through normalization and distance computation in a nonlinear manner. Consequently, identical improvements

Table 1. Decision quality metrics for the SAW aggregation model

n	Noise	Top-1 Hit Rate		WS coefficient		Weight MAE		Top-3 overlap	
		R	ST	R	ST	R	ST	R	ST
3	low	76.2	92.0	0.8617	0.9576	0.1131	0.0355	84.3	95.0
3	medium	69.7	87.5	0.8141	0.9275	0.1449	0.0578	79.6	91.7
3	high	63.9	82.6	0.7662	0.8950	0.1778	0.0824	75.2	88.2
4	low	76.0	91.5	0.8603	0.9545	0.0847	0.0287	84.0	94.6
4	medium	70.5	87.5	0.8219	0.9299	0.1036	0.0418	80.1	91.8
4	high	65.1	83.1	0.7814	0.9006	0.1240	0.0575	76.1	88.5
5	low	76.0	90.8	0.8585	0.9490	0.0680	0.0257	83.7	93.9
5	medium	71.2	87.4	0.8287	0.9291	0.0795	0.0335	80.6	91.6
5	high	66.6	83.5	0.7942	0.9040	0.0931	0.0439	77.2	88.8
6	low	75.7	89.8	0.8562	0.9427	0.0563	0.0230	83.4	93.1
6	medium	72.1	87.3	0.8332	0.9271	0.0641	0.0282	81.0	91.2
6	high	68.0	83.8	0.8048	0.9055	0.0733	0.0351	78.0	88.7
7	low	75.0	88.7	0.8536	0.9362	0.0482	0.0211	83.0	92.2
7	medium	72.3	86.6	0.8347	0.9230	0.0537	0.0247	81.1	90.7
7	high	68.7	83.6	0.8110	0.9043	0.0604	0.0296	78.7	88.6
8	low	75.2	88.1	0.8523	0.9306	0.0421	0.0195	82.8	91.5
8	medium	72.3	86.0	0.8354	0.9184	0.0462	0.0222	81.2	90.1
8	high	69.5	83.3	0.8157	0.9022	0.0513	0.0259	79.1	88.3
9	low	74.7	87.1	0.8499	0.9249	0.0372	0.0180	82.5	90.8
9	medium	72.3	85.4	0.8360	0.9148	0.0404	0.0200	81.2	89.7
9	high	69.5	82.9	0.8181	0.9003	0.0444	0.0230	79.3	88.0
10	low	74.5	86.5	0.8490	0.9204	0.0333	0.0167	82.5	90.2
10	medium	72.5	84.6	0.8357	0.9103	0.0358	0.0183	81.1	89.1
10	high	70.0	82.6	0.8201	0.8979	0.0390	0.0206	79.5	87.8

R – original RANCOM weights; ST – statistically refined weights (RANCOM-ST). Noise levels correspond to adjacent-swap probabilities defined in Sect. 3.1.

in weight accuracy do not translate into equally large improvements in ranking similarity.

An important observation concerns the effect of the number of criteria. As n increases, the relative advantage of RANCOM-ST gradually decreases, similarly to the SAW case, but the decrease is more pronounced. This indicates that distance-based aggregation attenuates the influence of individual weight errors more strongly than additive aggregation. In other words, the decision sensitivity to weight estimation error is model-dependent.

Overall, the results in Table 2 confirm that improving weight estimation accuracy leads to better decision outcomes also in nonlinear aggregation models. Nevertheless, the relationship is weaker than in the additive case. This demonstrates that the impact of weight errors on decisions is not universal but depends on the decision mechanism itself. The statistical correction therefore improves decision reliability, but the scale of the improvement is determined jointly by the level of expert noise and the structural properties of the aggregation model.

Table 2. Decision quality metrics for the TOPSIS aggregation model

n	Noise	Top-1 Hit Rate		WS coefficient		Weight MAE		Top-3 overlap	
		R	ST	R	ST	R	ST	R	ST
3	low	74.2	91.3	0.8475	0.9546	0.1134	0.0356	83.0	94.8
3	medium	67.0	86.1	0.7873	0.9189	0.1440	0.0573	77.3	90.9
3	high	59.5	80.3	0.7237	0.8757	0.1781	0.0827	71.3	86.2
4	low	73.6	90.8	0.8459	0.9526	0.0849	0.0289	82.6	94.5
4	medium	67.0	86.2	0.7957	0.9225	0.1034	0.0416	77.5	91.1
4	high	60.0	80.7	0.7401	0.8834	0.1238	0.0573	72.2	86.8
5	low	72.9	90.0	0.8429	0.9478	0.0677	0.0255	82.0	93.8
5	medium	67.5	85.9	0.8009	0.9221	0.0794	0.0334	77.7	90.7
5	high	61.5	81.0	0.7534	0.8871	0.0928	0.0437	73.0	86.9
6	low	72.3	88.8	0.8376	0.9401	0.0565	0.0231	81.2	92.8
6	medium	67.6	85.5	0.8022	0.9185	0.0643	0.0284	77.6	90.3
6	high	62.4	81.0	0.7630	0.8888	0.0735	0.0353	73.9	87.0
7	low	72.2	87.9	0.8335	0.9324	0.0481	0.0210	80.6	91.7
7	medium	67.7	84.8	0.8033	0.9134	0.0537	0.0247	77.7	89.6
7	high	63.2	80.9	0.7682	0.8876	0.0604	0.0296	74.2	86.6
8	low	71.1	86.6	0.8269	0.9235	0.0419	0.0193	79.9	90.6
8	medium	67.7	84.1	0.8022	0.9074	0.0462	0.0222	77.5	88.6
8	high	63.6	80.6	0.7708	0.8837	0.0511	0.0258	74.2	86.0
9	low	70.8	85.4	0.8222	0.9148	0.0372	0.0180	79.3	89.4
9	medium	67.5	83.3	0.8003	0.9005	0.0403	0.0200	77.1	87.8
9	high	64.1	80.0	0.7734	0.8798	0.0443	0.0228	74.4	85.5
10	low	70.0	84.3	0.8170	0.9062	0.0335	0.0168	78.7	88.3
10	medium	67.1	82.2	0.7966	0.8931	0.0358	0.0183	76.6	86.8
10	high	63.9	79.2	0.7732	0.8748	0.0390	0.0205	74.4	84.8

R – original RANCOM weights; ST – statistically refined weights (RANCOM-ST). Noise levels correspond to adjacent-swap probabilities defined in Sect. 3.1.

4.3   Decision Transition Analysis

To assess whether the statistical correction improves only average accuracy or also the reliability of individual decisions, a transition analysis between RAN-

COM and RANCOM-ST was performed. For each Monte Carlo run, the Top-1 alternative selected using RANCOM was compared with the alternative obtained after applying the RANCOM-ST correction. Three outcomes were distinguished: (i) the decision remained unchanged, (ii) an incorrect decision produced by RANCOM became correct after correction (rescued decision), and (iii) a previously correct RANCOM decision became incorrect after correction (deteriorated decision).

Table 3 presents aggregated results for both aggregation models and all noise levels. A pronounced asymmetry between improvement and degradation can be observed. Across all conditions, RANCOM-ST repairs a substantial portion of erroneous RANCOM decisions, while only rarely deteriorating correct ones. Depending on the noise level, approximately 45%–70% of incorrect decisions are corrected, whereas only about 1%–2% of correct decisions become incorrect after the correction.

Table 3. Decision transitions between RANCOM and RANCOM-ST

Aggregation	Noise	RANCOM error rate	Rescued decisions	Deteriorated decisions
SAW	Low	24.7%	59.8%	1.2%
SAW	Medium	28.4%	55.2%	1.1%
SAW	High	32.2%	50.4%	1.1%
TOPSIS	Low	27.8%	60.6%	1.4%
TOPSIS	Medium	32.6%	56.3%	1.3%
TOPSIS	High	37.6%	50.6%	1.4%

These results indicate that the statistical correction behaves as a conservative refinement rather than an aggressive modification of the decision model. The correction frequently improves incorrect outcomes but only exceptionally disrupts already correct decisions.

A systematic influence of the number of criteria is also observed. As the number of criteria increases, the fraction of rescued decisions gradually decreases. This behavior is consistent with the mechanism of the method: with a larger number of criteria, individual weights become smaller and closer to each other, reducing the relative impact of a threshold-based adjustment. At the same time, the deterioration rate remains nearly constant, indicating stable behavior of the correction.

A difference between aggregation models can also be identified. The deterioration rate is consistently higher for TOPSIS than for SAW, although the fraction of rescued decisions remains comparable. This is explained by the structural properties of the models. SAW is linear with respect to the weights, so local weight corrections produce proportional score changes. In contrast, TOPSIS is distance-based, and weight changes also affect the positions of the ideal and anti-ideal solutions, which may induce a cascade effect in the ranking. Consequently, the correction acts as a stable refinement under linear aggregation but as a more sensitive intervention under distance-based aggregation.

5   Discussion and Conclusions

This paper investigated the decision-level effects of the statistical refinement introduced by the RANCOM-ST procedure. Instead of evaluating the method solely in terms of weight estimation accuracy, the study focused on its influence on final decision outcomes, including the identification of the best alternative, shortlist stability, and overall ranking similarity. A large-scale Monte Carlo framework enabled controlled analysis across different numbers of criteria, levels of expert judgment error, and aggregation models.

The results show that the statistical correction generally improves decision performance, but its effectiveness is strongly context-dependent. With respect to RQ1, RANCOM-ST increases the Top-1 Hit Rate compared to the original RANCOM method, particularly for problems with a small number of criteria. In such cases, the applied correction represents a substantial portion of the weight magnitude and therefore meaningfully affects the ranking. For larger numbers of criteria, where weights are smaller and closer to each other, the relative influence of the correction decreases. The benefit of the correction grows with increasing expert noise: when expert judgments are already accurate, the original RANCOM performs well and the potential for improvement is limited, whereas under higher uncertainty the correction becomes more valuable.

Regarding RQ2, the aggregation model significantly mediates the effect of weight refinement. In the additive SAW model, weight errors translate directly and proportionally into score deviations; therefore, improvements in weights consistently lead to improved rankings. In contrast, TOPSIS exhibits more complex behavior. Due to the distance-based evaluation in the normalized space, small perturbations of weights may be absorbed, leading to greater robustness to minor inaccuracies. However, larger deviations can alter the relative positions of the ideal and anti-ideal solutions, causing non-local ranking changes. Consequently, RANCOM-ST produces more predictable and stable improvements when used with SAW, while in TOPSIS the effect is less regular but can be substantial under higher levels of noise.

In relation to RQ3, the correction mechanism introduces a measurable risk of deteriorating decisions. Because RANCOM-ST adjusts weights by a fixed statistically derived magnitude rather than the true individual error, a weight that is already close to the correct value may be shifted away from it. Such cases occur particularly when the expert input contains little noise or when the number of criteria is large and weights are relatively small. Nevertheless, the overall balance remains positive: the number of corrected ("rescued") decisions exceeds the number of degraded ones. This is expected, as the statistical thresholds are calibrated to the average population error rather than to individual instances.

Overall, the study demonstrates that improving weight estimates does not automatically guarantee improved decisions, but statistical refinement can increase decision reliability under appropriate conditions. The RANCOM-ST correction is most beneficial in problems characterized by moderate or high expert uncertainty and a limited number of criteria, whereas in low-noise settings its application may be unnecessary and occasionally detrimental.

The present work has several limitations. The analysis was conducted using synthetic decision problems with benefit-type criteria and simulated expert behavior. Although this approach enables controlled evaluation, real decision environments may involve heterogeneous criteria types and more complex cognitive effects. Future research should therefore include empirical case studies with human decision-makers and investigate adaptive correction magnitudes that depend on estimated uncertainty rather than fixed statistical thresholds.

In summary, this paper provides a methodological assessment of weighting refinement in MCDA and clarifies the relationship between weight accuracy and decision accuracy. The findings contribute practical guidance on when statistical correction should be applied and highlight the importance of evaluating decision-support methods at the level of decisions rather than parameters alone.

Acknowledgment. Publication funded by the Minister of Science under the "Regional Excellence Initiative" Program RID/SP/0046/2024/01.

Disclosure of Interests. The authors have no competing interests to declare that are relevant to the content of this article.

References

1. Behzadian, M., Otaghsara, S.K., Yazdani, M., Ignatius, J.: A state-of the-art survey of TOPSIS applications. Expert Syst. Appl. **39**(17), 13051–13069 (2012). https://doi.org/10.1016/j.eswa.2012.05.056
2. Brunelli, M.: A survey of inconsistency indices for pairwise comparisons. Int. J. Gen Syst **47**(8), 751–771 (2018). https://doi.org/10.1080/03081079.2018.1523156
3. Cinelli, M., Kadziński, M., Gonzalez, M., Słowiński, R.: How to support the application of multiple criteria decision analysis? let us start with a comprehensive taxonomy. Omega **96**, 102261 (2020). https://doi.org/10.1016/j.omega.2020.102261
4. Kosareva, N., Krylovas, A., Zavadskas, E.K.: Statistical analysis of MCDM data normalization methods using Monte Carlo approach. The case of ternary estimates matrix. Econom. Comput. Econom. Cybernet. Stud. Res. **52**(4), 159–175 (2018). https://doi.org/10.24818/18423264/52.4.18.11
5. Sałabun, W., Urbaniak, K.: A New Coefficient of Rankings Similarity in Decision-Making Problems. In: Krzhizhanovskaya, V.V., et al. (eds.) ICCS 2020. LNCS, vol. 12138, pp. 632–645. Springer, Cham (2020). https://doi.org/10.1007/978-3-030-50417-5_47
6. Shkurina, A.: An adaptive rancom-st method for bias reduction using statistical thresholds. In: International Conference on Computational Science, pp. 281–295. Springer, Cham (2025). https://doi.org/10.1007/978-3-031-97567-7_22
7. Singh, M., Pant, M.: A review of selected weighing methods in MCDM with a case study. Int. J. Syst. Assur. Eng. Manag. 1–19 (2020). https://doi.org/10.1007/s13198-020-01033-3

8. Więckowski, J., Kizielewicz, B., Shekhovtsov, A., Sałabun, W.: RANCOM: a novel approach to identifying criteria relevance based on inaccuracy expert judgments. Eng. Appl. Artif. Intell. **122**, 106114 (2023). https://doi.org/10.1016/j.engappai.2023.106114
9. Żak, J., Kruszyński, M.: Application of AHP and ELECTRE III/IV methods to multiple level, multiple criteria evaluation of urban transportation projects. Transp. Res. Proc. **10**, 820–830 (2015). https://doi.org/10.1016/j.trpro.2015.09.035

From Exhaustive Robustness to Local Sensitivity: An Extension of the EORS Framework

Bartosz Paradowski[1,2]($\boxtimes$) (ID)

[1] National Institute of Telecommunications, ul. Szachowa 1, 04-894 Warsaw, Poland
[2] West Pomeranian University of Technology in Szczecin, ul. Żołnierska 49, 71-210 Szczecin, Poland
B.Paradowski@il-pib.pl

Abstract. The Exhaustive Objective Ranking Solution (EORS) supports objective multi-criteria decision making by exhaustively exploring the admissible weight space and aggregating the resulting preference values into representative outcomes, complemented by stability indicators. While this global perspective reveals distributional robustness, it may obscure locally unstable behavior around decision-relevant weight configurations. This paper extends the KDE-based variant of EORS with a local sensitivity analysis that quantifies neighborhood-level responsiveness of (i) modal preference values and (ii) degrees of confidence to marginal perturbations of criterion weights, using simplex-projected finite differences. To improve interpretability, we introduce a criterion sensitivity index that integrates preference and confidence sensitivities and a fragility index that summarizes alternative-level stability. A theoretical study case illustrates how the proposed diagnostics identify criteria driving local instability and alternatives whose outcomes are most sensitive to reweighting, thereby complementing the global EORS ranking with actionable stability insights.

Keywords: MCDM · sensitivity analysis · weighting · local sensitivity

1 Introduction

Multi-criteria decision-making (MCDM) problems often require selecting or ranking alternatives under competing criteria, where the final outcome depends critically on the assumed importance (weights) of the criteria [10]. In practice, weights are rarely known with certainty [11] and may vary across decision-makers or scenarios depending on the decision context [13]. Consequently, robust decision support requires not only producing a single ranking, but also characterizing how stable that outcome is under admissible changes in weights.

Sensitivity analysis provides a principled way to evaluate such stability [9]. Classical approaches often focus on global robustness by examining broad regions of the weight space and reporting aggregate stability patterns [12], but they may

M. Paszynski et al. (Eds.): ICCS 2026 Workshops, LNCS 16788, pp. 434–447, 2026.
https://doi.org/10.1007/978-3-032-29915-4_36

overlook transitions that occur locally around decision-relevant weight configurations. For decision-makers, these local effects are important: small changes in weights, consistent with minor preference shifts, can lead to meaningful changes in preference values, confidence measures, or even the induced ordering of the alternatives [4].

Sensitivity analysis has been extensively studied, and a wide range of methods has been proposed for assessing the robustness of MCDM outcomes [1,2,14]. Nevertheless, many commonly used approaches remain largely global in nature and may not capture fine-grained effects caused by marginal perturbations of weights at the level of individual alternatives [15]. This limitation has motivated interest in local sensitivity analysis, which focuses on neighborhood behavior in the weight space and can reveal decision-relevant instability that may be obscured by aggregate robustness summaries. For example, Kizielewicz et al. proposed a local perspective on weight perturbations that highlights local decision dynamics [5] in the Characteristic Objects METhod (COMET); however, it does not provide a unified, alternative-level index that summarizes overall fragility in a single interpretable measure.

The Exhaustive Objective Ranking Solution (EORS) offers an objective, distribution-based perspective by exhaustively exploring the admissible weight space and aggregating the resulting preference values into representative outcomes. In its KDE-based variant, kernel density estimation is used to obtain smooth preference distributions and to define modal preference values and associated confidence indicators. While this global exploration supports transparency and interpretability, it does not directly explain which criteria drive local instability around the most relevant regions of the weight simplex.

In this study, we therefore propose a local sensitivity analysis framework for KDE-based EORS [7] that quantifies neighborhood-level responsiveness to marginal weight perturbations, alongside complementary confidence-based diagnostics. The main contributions of this study are as follows:

- A local weight space sensitivity framework based on simplex projected finite differences is introduced, ensuring feasibility under normalization constraints.
- The approach evaluates both KDE-based preference modes and degrees of confidence (DoC), uncovering instabilities not visible in global robustness analysis.
- The proposed Criterion Sensitivity Index (CSI) and Fragility Index (FI) provide concise, criterion- and alternative-level measures of structural instability.
- By anchoring the analysis at barycentric weight configurations derived from global EORS exploration, the method connects distributional robustness with local structural diagnostics.

The remainder of the paper is organized as follows. Section 2 presents a detailed description of the KDE-based EORS method. Section 3 introduces the proposed local sensitivity analysis framework building on EORS. Section 4 reports the results and discussion, and provides guidance on how to interpret the proposed metrics. Finally, Sect. 5 concludes the study and outlines future research directions to enhance the practical applicability and theoretical robustness of the EORS approach.

2   Exhaustive Objective Ranking Solution (EORS)

The Exhaustive Objective Ranking Solution (EORS) is a multi-criteria decision-making (MCDM) approach designed to produce robust and transparent rankings by systematically exploring the admissible weight space [8]. EORS evaluates the preference values of alternatives over all considered weight vectors and aggregates the results to produce a representative ranking, while also quantifying the structural stability of each alternative.

In this study, we employ the KDE-based variant of EORS [7]. Kernel density estimation (KDE) serves as a smoothing tool to obtain a continuous representation of the preference values over the weight space. Since preference values are deterministically computed for each weight vector, KDE does not estimate a stochastic probability distribution; instead, it smooths the discrete evaluations to facilitate analysis.

1. Admissible weight vectors are systematically generated using a specified increment $step_w$ (here, $step_w = 0.05$), excluding vectors with zero weight. For three criteria, examples of weight vectors include

$$[0.9, 0.05, 0.05]$$
$$\cdots$$
$$[0.3, 0.3, 0.4] \tag{1}$$
$$\cdots$$
$$[0.05, 0.05, 0.9]$$

   Systematic generation ensures full reproducibility, although random sampling is also supported by the method.
2. The preference values of the alternatives are computed for each generated weight vector using the selected decision-making method. In this study, the Technique for Order Preference by Similarity to Ideal Solution (TOPSIS) [6] was employed for this purpose.
3. Let $x_{i,j}$ denote the preference value of alternative i under the j-th weight vector. A smooth representation over the sampled weight space is obtained via kernel density estimation,

$$\hat{f}_i(x) = \frac{1}{N_i h} \sum_{j=1}^{N_i} K\left(\frac{x - x_{i,j}}{h}\right), \tag{2}$$

   where N_i is the number of sampled weight vectors, K is a Gaussian kernel, and h is set using Scott's rule. Since preference values are deterministically generated, $\hat{f}_i(x)$ is interpreted as an intensity function summarizing the distribution of preference values across the weight space, rather than as a probability density of a stochastic model.

4. The mode of the smoothed values defines the most representative preference value:

$$P_i = \arg\max_x \hat{f}_i(x) \tag{3}$$

5. Around P_i, a confidence range interval (CRI) reflects decision-maker confidence in the stability of the representative preference level:

$$\text{CRI} = \left[P_i - \frac{ci}{2}, P_i + \frac{ci}{2} \right], \quad ci = 0.1. \tag{4}$$

This interval is interpreted as a decision-maker tolerance band rather than a statistical confidence interval.

6. Degrees of confidence (DoC) quantify how concentrated an alternative's preference values are around P_i over the sampled weight space:

$$\text{DoC}_S(i) = \frac{N_{i,\text{max}}}{N_i}, \tag{5}$$

$$\text{DoC}_C(i) = \frac{N_{i,\text{max}}}{\sum_{j=1}^{m} N_{j,\text{max}}}, \tag{6}$$

$$\text{DoC}_{\text{agg}}(i) = \alpha\,\text{DoC}_S(i) + (1 - \alpha)\,\text{DoC}_C(i), \quad \alpha = 0.5, \tag{7}$$

where $N_{i,\text{max}}$ is the number of preference values of alternative i falling within CRI_i. DoC values reflect structural stability and decision-analytic confidence, rather than statistical confidence. The parameter $\alpha \in [0, 1]$ controls the trade-off between the single and cross perspectives (here, $\alpha = 0.5$).

7. Finally, alternatives are ranked according to the preference values produced by the chosen MCDM method, and the DoC measures provide complementary information about the robustness of each alternative's position.

3 Local Weight-Space Sensitivity and Structural Stability Analysis

This section develops a local sensitivity framework for KDE-based EORS that quantifies how preference estimates, degrees of confidence (DoC), and induced rankings change under small perturbations of criterion weights. In contrast to global robustness checks, which explore broad regions of the admissible weight simplex, the proposed analysis focuses on neighborhood behavior around representative weight vectors, thereby providing a more fine-grained account of stability and interpretability.

3.1 Weight Space and Global Preference Structure

Let

$$\mathcal{W} = \left\{ \mathbf{w} \in \mathbb{R}_+^k : \sum_{j=1}^{k} w_j = 1 \right\} \tag{8}$$

denote the admissible weight simplex. The set $\mathcal{W}$ is convex and compact, and each $\mathbf{w} \in \mathcal{W}$ represents a feasible trade-off among the k criteria. In this study, EORS was applied globally over the entire weight space using a step size of 0.05.

Let $\{\mathbf{w}^{(r)}\}_{r=1}^{N} \subset \mathcal{W}$ be a set of sampled weight vectors. For each alternative $i \in \{1, \ldots, m\}$ we denote by

$$P_i^{(r)} = P_i(\mathbf{w}^{(r)}) \tag{9}$$

the preference value obtained under $\mathbf{w}^{(r)}$.

Given $\{P_i^{(r)}\}_{r=1}^{N}$, we estimate the preference density using kernel density estimation (KDE), denoted by $\hat{f}_i(x)$. The representative (modal) performance level is then defined as

$$P_i^\star = \arg \max_x \hat{f}_i(x) \tag{10}$$

3.2   Reference Weight Vector

To identify a decision-relevant anchor for local analysis, we first isolate the subset of weights under which alternative i attains a preference value close to its modal level. Let $P_i^\star$ denote the modal preference (as obtained from KDE). We define

$$\mathcal{R}_i = \left\{ r : P_i^\star - \frac{CRI}{2} \leq P_i^{(r)} \leq P_i^\star + \frac{CRI}{2} \right\}, \tag{11}$$

where $CRI > 0$ is the confidence-range parameter used in EORS (Eq. 4).

Barycentric anchor We then define the reference weight vector (anchor) for alternative i as the barycenter of this region,

$$\mathbf{w}_0^{(i)} = \frac{1}{|\mathcal{R}_i|} \sum_{r \in \mathcal{R}_i} \mathbf{w}^{(r)} \tag{12}$$

Since $\mathcal{W}$ is convex, $\mathbf{w}_0^{(i)} \in \mathcal{W}$.

The vector $\mathbf{w}_0^{(i)}$ represents a typical trade-off configuration under which alternative i exhibits near-modal behavior. Local sensitivity evaluated around $\mathbf{w}_0^{(i)}$ is therefore aligned with the weight that support the observed global preference structure.

3.3   Feasible Perturbations and Local Neighborhood

To preserve the admissibility of weight vectors after perturbation, we employ the Euclidean projection onto the simplex [3]

$$\Pi_{\mathcal{W}}(\mathbf{z}) = \arg \min_{\mathbf{w} \in \mathcal{W}} \|\mathbf{w} - \mathbf{z}\|_2, \tag{13}$$

which maps any $\mathbf{z} \in \mathbb{R}^k$ onto the closest feasible weight vector in $\mathcal{W}$.

To formalize locality, we define

$$\mathcal{N}_\epsilon(\mathbf{w}_0^{(i)}) = \left\{ \mathbf{w} \in \mathcal{W} : \|\mathbf{w} - \mathbf{w}_0^{(i)}\|_2 \le \epsilon \right\}, \tag{14}$$

where $\epsilon > 0$ represents admissible weight uncertainty.

3.4 Local KDE Mode Sensitivity

We quantify the responsiveness of the most likely preference outcome to marginal changes in single weights using simplex-projected finite differences.

Because the simplex constraint $\sum_j w_j = 1$ must be satisfied, increasing one weight necessarily induces a redistribution across other coordinates. Therefore, the resulting sensitivity measure does not correspond to a classical partial derivative, but rather to a finite difference computed after nonlinear projection onto the admissible simplex.

For each criterion j, we define the simplex-projected perturbation

$$\mathbf{w}_\delta^{(i,j)} = \Pi_{\mathcal{W}} \left(\mathbf{w}_0^{(i)} + \delta \mathbf{e}_j \right), \tag{15}$$

where $\delta > 0$ is a small step size and $\mathbf{e}_j$ denotes the j-th canonical basis vector.

The local preference sensitivity is then defined as the simplex-projected finite difference quotient

$$S_{i,j}^{(P)} = \frac{P_i(\mathbf{w}_\delta^{(i,j)}) - P_i(\mathbf{w}_0^{(i)})}{\delta}. \tag{16}$$

For finite δ, this quantity measures the rate of change in preference induced by an admissible marginal increase of weight j, accounting for the normalization constraint through projection.

Collecting the sensitivity measures over all alternatives and criteria yields the mode-sensitivity matrix

$$S^{(P)} \in \mathbb{R}^{m \times k}. \tag{17}$$

Large $|S_{i,j}^{(P)}|$ indicates that the representative preference value of alternative i is locally unstable with respect to criterion j, while values close to zero indicate local robustness; the sign reflects the direction of influence.

3.5 Local Degree-of-Confidence Sensitivity

Preference-mode stability does not necessarily imply decision reliability. Therefore, we additionally evaluate how DoC measures vary under the same simplex-projected perturbations. Let $\mathrm{DoC}_i(\mathbf{w})$ denote the chosen DoC indicator for alternative i.

Using identical perturbations $\mathbf{w}_\delta^{(i,j)}$, we compute

$$S_{i,j}^{(DoC)} = \frac{\mathrm{DoC}_i(\mathbf{w}_\delta^{(i,j)}) - \mathrm{DoC}_i(\mathbf{w}_0^{(i)})}{\delta}. \tag{18}$$

Stacking these quantities yields the DoC-sensitivity matrix

$$S^{(DoC)} \in \mathbb{R}^{m \times k}. \tag{19}$$

High magnitudes indicate fragile confidence with respect to admissible marginal weight changes. Discrepancies between $S^{(P)}$ and $S^{(DoC)}$ suggest that changes in distribution concentration or ranking overlap may occur even when modal preferences remain comparatively stable.

3.6   Normalization

To ensure comparability across criteria and alternatives, and to enable subsequent aggregation, we apply max-absolute normalization. Since the fragility analysis focuses on the magnitude of sensitivity rather than direction, signs are removed prior to scaling.

$$\hat{S}_{i,j}^{(P)} = \frac{|S_{i,j}^{(P)}|}{\max_{i,j}|S_{i,j}^{(P)}|}, \qquad \hat{S}_{i,j}^{(DoC)} = \frac{|S_{i,j}^{(DoC)}|}{\max_{i,j}|S_{i,j}^{(DoC)}|}. \tag{20}$$

Then,

$$\hat{S}_{i,j}^{(\cdot)} \in [0,1]. \tag{21}$$

3.7   Criterion Sensitivity Index

To summarize criterion-level influence in a single interpretable quantity, we aggregate the normalized sensitivities of performance and confidence. The resulting index highlights which criteria drive local changes in outcomes around the reference configuration.

The criterion sensitivity index (CSI) is defined as

$$CSI_{i,j} = \alpha\hat{S}_{i,j}^{(P)} + (1-\alpha)\hat{S}_{i,j}^{(DoC)}, \tag{22}$$

where $\alpha \in [0,1]$ controls the relative emphasis on performance versus robustness.

By construction,

$$CSI \in [-1,1]^{m \times k}. \tag{23}$$

3.8   Fragility Index

Finally, we provide a single stability score per alternative by aggregating criterion effects into a norm.

$$FI_i = \sqrt{\sum_{j=1}^{k} CSI_{i,j}^2} \tag{24}$$

This corresponds to the Euclidean norm of the local sensitivity vector in the CSI space.

A low FI_i indicates a robust alternative whose local outcome is relatively insensitive to weight perturbations, whereas a high FI_i indicates fragility, i.e., a strong dependence on the exact choice of weights.

3.9   Geometric Interpretation

We define the blended functional

$$F_i(\mathbf{w}) = \alpha P_i(\mathbf{w}) + (1 - \alpha)\mathrm{DoC}_i(\mathbf{w}). \tag{25}$$

The proposed sensitivity analysis evaluates the response of F_i to admissible perturbations of the form

$$\mathbf{w}_\delta^{(i,j)} = \Pi_{\mathcal{W}} \left(\mathbf{w}_0^{(i)} + \delta \mathbf{e}_j \right). \tag{26}$$

Because the projection operator $\Pi_{\mathcal{W}}$ is nonlinear, the resulting sensitivity measures correspond to finite differences of the composite mapping

$$F_i \circ \Pi_{\mathcal{W}}, \tag{27}$$

rather than to classical gradients in $\mathbb{R}^k$.

Accordingly, the fragility index

$$FI_i = \sqrt{\sum_{j=1}^{k} CSI_{i,i}^2} \tag{28}$$

should be interpreted as the Euclidean norm of the local simplex-projected sensitivity vector, quantifying structural instability under admissible weight redistributions.

3.10   Role of δ and ϵ

The parameters δ and ϵ control, respectively, the magnitude of admissible perturbations and the size of the local sampling neighborhood.

Since sensitivities are computed as simplex-projected finite differences, δ must be sufficiently small to approximate local behavior while avoiding dominance of nonlinear projection effects. If δ is too large, estimates reflect curvature and redistribution effects rather than local responsiveness. If δ is too small, numerical noise and projection artifacts may dominate.

Similarly, if ϵ is too large, the analysis ceases to be local; if too small, sampling variability leads to unstable estimates.

A systematic calibration of (δ, ϵ) is therefore required. In this paper, we set $\delta = 0.02$ and $\epsilon = 0.02$, chosen to preserve locality while maintaining stable numerical estimates.

Overall, the proposed analysis bridges global robustness and local sensitivity by (i) providing criterion-level explainability, (ii) revealing instabilities that may be obscured by aggregate robustness measures, and (iii) positioning KDE-based EORS as an interpretable framework for weight-space decision analysis.

4   Study Case

This section presents a theoretical study case used to illustrate the proposed analysis. We generate a random decision matrix by sampling each performance value independently from a continuous uniform distribution on the half-open interval $[0.0, 1.0)$. For simplicity, all criteria are assumed to be of the profit type, and the resulting matrix is presented in Table 1. As the underlying MCDM method within EORS, we employ TOPSIS [6], which is widely used and well studied in the literature.

Table 1. Decision matrix of the theoretical decision-making problem.

A_i	C_1	C_2	C_3	C_4	C_5
A_1	0.5496	0.7418	0.8094	0.7423	0.8859
A_2	0.6290	0.0564	0.0118	0.7930	0.4387
A_3	0.3167	0.9139	0.5930	0.2710	0.3636
A_4	0.6205	0.1898	0.5624	0.1648	0.4158
A_5	0.8486	0.7923	0.8370	0.1300	0.4117
A_6	0.9984	0.2117	0.5740	0.4393	0.3821
Criteria type	$Profit$	$Profit$	$Profit$	$Profit$	$Profit$

For transparency, Table 2 reports the final EORS preference values and the resulting ranking for the considered set of alternatives. These values summarize the global EORS aggregation over the sampled weight space and serve as the baseline outcome for the local sensitivity analysis conducted in the remainder of this section.

For additional insight, Fig. 1 visualizes the KDE-estimated preference distributions for all alternatives, with the corresponding final preference values indicated by dashed lines. This visualization provides an intuitive summary of the global EORS output and supports the subsequent discussion of local sensitivity. In particular, steeper and more concentrated densities suggest greater stability of the representative outcome, whereas flatter or multimodal shapes may indicate higher susceptibility to weight perturbations.

Table 2. Results of EORS for the theoretical decision-making problem.

A_i	A_1	A_2	A_3	A_4	A_5	A_6
Preference	0.8216	0.3484	0.3309	0.5687	0.6605	0.6688
Ranking	1	5	6	4	3	2

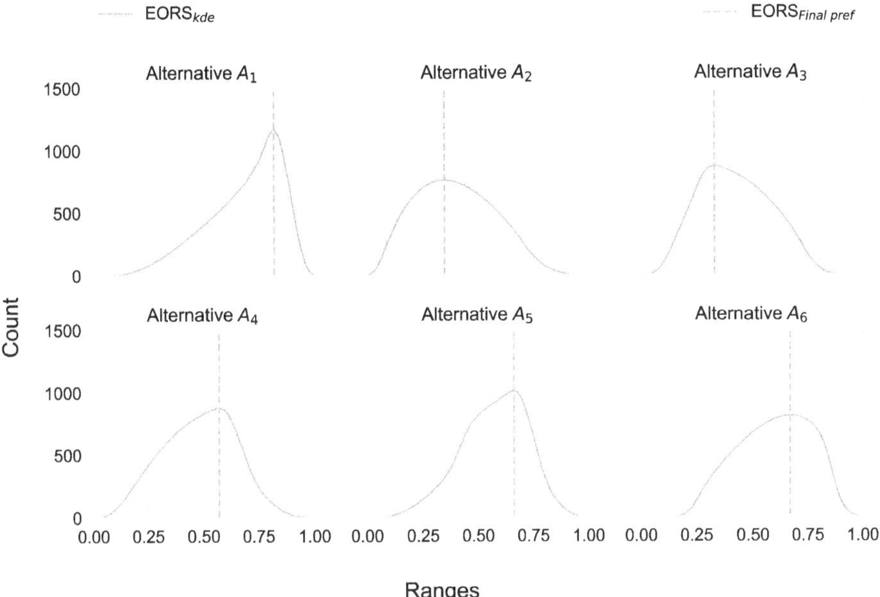

Fig. 1. Distribution of preferences and final preference value for original and improved EORS method.

We next compute the local KDE mode sensitivity described in Sect. 3.4. Figure 2 summarizes the resulting sensitivity matrix $S^{(P)}$ as a heatmap, where rows correspond to alternatives and columns correspond to criteria. Cell intensity reflects the magnitude of the estimated sensitivity over δ, while the sign indicates whether increasing the weight of criterion j locally increases or decreases the modal preference of alternative i. Concentrated high-magnitude regions therefore identify criteria that drive local changes in the representative outcome, as well as alternatives that are most susceptible to marginal reweighting.

Because $S^{(P)}$ is not standardized, comparisons should be made only within a given decision problem. In particular, the metric should not be interpreted on a ratio scale (i.e., one entry should not be read as "x times larger" than another). For example, for alternative A_4, the heatmap indicates that criterion C_2 exhibits the highest local susceptibility, whereas C_3 exhibits the lowest. This suggests that, locally around the reference weight vector, the modal preference of A_4 is more sensitive to changes in w_2 than to changes in w_3.

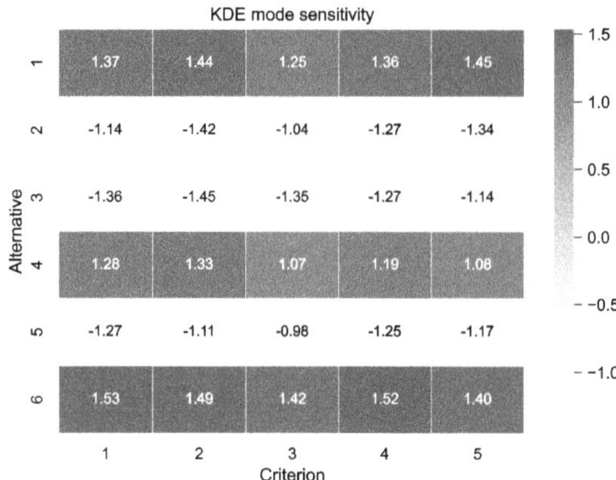

Fig. 2. Heatmap of local KDE mode sensitivity $S^{(P)}$ for the study case.

We next compute the local degree of confidence sensitivity described in Sect. 3.5. Figure 3 reports the resulting sensitivity matrix $S^{(\mathrm{DoC})}$ as a heatmap, again with alternatives on rows and criteria on columns. Cell intensity reflects the magnitude of the estimated sensitivity over δ, while the sign indicates whether increasing the weight of criterion j locally increases or decreases the confidence associated with alternative i. High-magnitude regions therefore indicate criteria whose marginal reweighting substantially changes local confidence, even when the preference mode remains comparatively stable. As with $S^{(P)}$, these values are intended for within-problem comparison rather than ratio-scale interpretation.

In this study case, alternative A_5 exhibits the largest overall DoC sensitivity across criteria, indicating that its confidence is most affected by local weight perturbations. Additionally, the differences in $S^{(\mathrm{DoC})}$ across criteria reveal finer-grained effects that may influence the final decision outcome.

Next, we compute the criterion sensitivity index introduced in Sect. 3.7. Figure 4 visualizes the CSI values as a heatmap that integrates preference-mode sensitivity and DoC sensitivity into a single criterion-level diagnostic measure. As before, rows correspond to alternatives and columns to criteria. Because CSI is computed using max-absolute normalization, it does not preserve the direction of change and should be interpreted only in terms of magnitude. High-magnitude CSI entries indicate criteria that exert the strongest combined influence on both the representative preference outcome and its associated confidence, thereby highlighting the main drivers of local stability around the reference weights.

This representation enables interpretation at the criterion level and provides an overview of which criteria most strongly affect each alternative. Such information may be useful for decision-making, for example, by indicating where more precise weighting or robustness checks should be prioritized.

Finally, Fig. 5 presents the fragility index (FI) values for all alternatives, obtained by aggregating the CSI entries across criteria into a single stability score per alternative. Higher FI values indicate alternatives whose local outcomes are

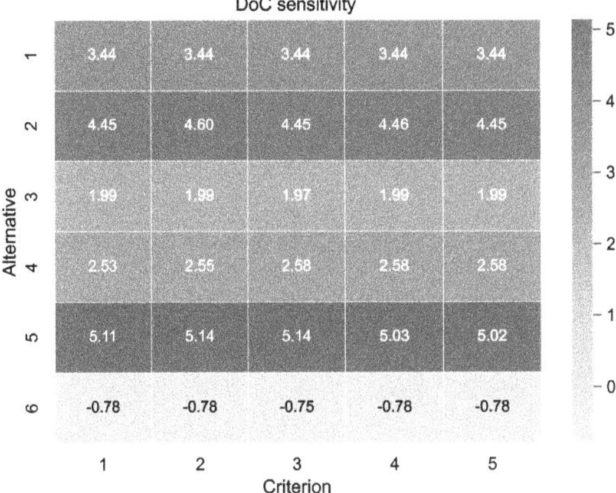

Fig. 3. Heatmap of local degree of confidence sensitivity $S^{(\mathrm{DoC})}$ for the study case.

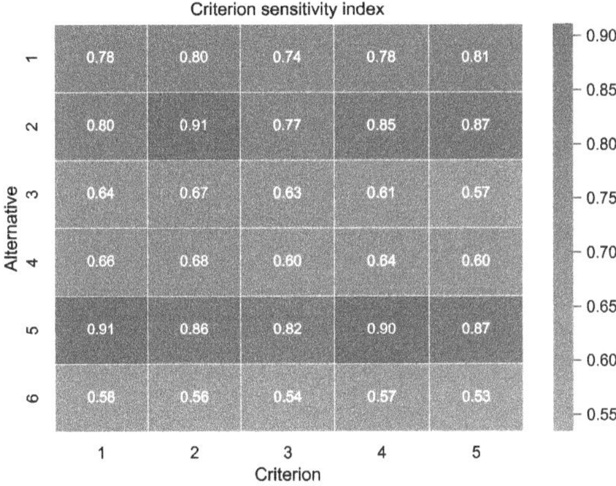

Fig. 4. Heatmap of the criterion sensitivity index (CSI) for the study case.

more sensitive to marginal changes in the weight vector (i.e., greater structural fragility), whereas lower values indicate alternatives that remain comparatively stable under local reweighting. In this way, the FI provides a concise, ranking-independent summary of local stability that complements the criterion-resolved heatmaps.

For this study case, the results indicate that alternative A_6 is the least fragile with respect to local weight changes, whereas alternative A_5 is the most fragile. Such conclusions help assess whether the final preference values are robust and decision-relevant. Notably, the proposed local sensitivity analysis is not intended to explain the ranking alone; instead, it focuses on the underlying preference values, which retain information about how much more (or less) preferable one alternative is relative to another.

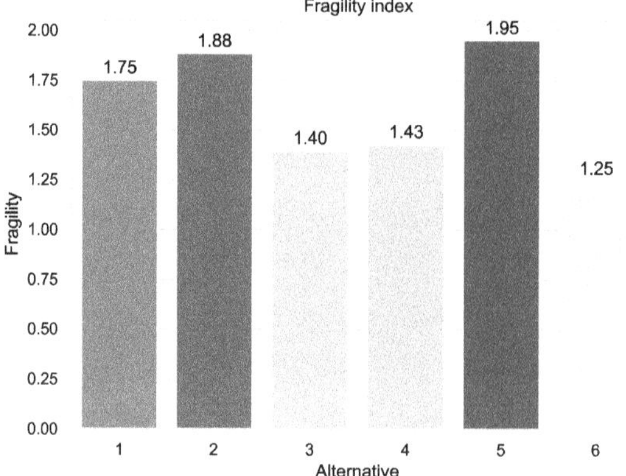

Fig. 5. Fragility index (FI) of alternatives for the study case.

5   Conclusions

This paper extended KDE-based EORS with a local sensitivity analysis that complements the global, distribution-based ranking by explicitly quantifying neighborhood-level responsiveness to marginal weight perturbations. In the study case, the global EORS outcome (Table 2) was enriched by local measuress that revealed which criteria drive changes in modal preferences, how confidence measures vary under reweighting, and which alternatives are structurally stable.

The local KDE mode sensitivity $S^{(P)}$ (Fig. 2) provided criterion-resolved information about how the representative preference value responds to perturbations around the reference weights, enabling the identification of alternatives and criteria with high local susceptibility (e.g., the sensitivity pattern of A_4 with respect to C_2 versus C_3). The DoC sensitivity $S^{(\mathrm{DoC})}$ (Fig. 3) further showed that confidence can be locally fragile even when preference modes appear comparatively stable; in particular, A_5 exhibited the strongest overall DoC sensitivity in the study case. By integrating both sources of information, the criterion sensitivity index (CSI) (Fig. 4) offered a compact criterion-level diagnostic highlighting the structural robustness that jointly affect preference and confidence.

Finally, the fragility index (FI) (Fig. 5) summarized local stability at the alternative level, providing a ranking-independent stability profile that supports decision communication and follow-up weight refinement. In the study case, FI indicated that A_6 is comparatively robust under local reweighting, whereas A_5 is most fragile, suggesting where additional attention or stakeholder input on weights may be most valuable.

Future work should focus on systematic calibration of the locality parameters (δ, ϵ), exploring alternative neighborhood definitions and projections, and validating the proposed indicators on real-world decision problems and different MCDM methods.

References

1. Borgonovo, E., Plischke, E.: Sensitivity analysis: a review of recent advances. Eur. J. Oper. Res. **248**(3), 869–887 (2016)
2. Demir, G., Chatterjee, P., Pamucar, D.: Sensitivity analysis in multi-criteria decision making: a state-of-the-art research perspective using bibliometric analysis. Expert Syst. Appl. **237**, 121660 (2024)
3. Duchi, J., Shalev-Shwartz, S., Singer, Y., Chandra, T.: Efficient projections onto the l 1-ball for learning in high dimensions. In: Proceedings of the 25th International Conference on Machine Learning, pp. 272–279 (2008)
4. Kizielewicz, B., Pawlak, R., Gandor, M., Sałabun, W.: A robust framework for sustainable vehicle assessment: integrating FN-TOPSIS with subjective weighting methods. Proc. Comput. Sci. **270**, 5764–5775 (2025)
5. Kizielewicz, B., Więckowski, J., Paradowski, B., Shekhovtsov, A., Sałabun, W.: Determination of local and global decision weights based on fuzzy modeling. In: International Conference on Neural Information Processing, pp. 188–200. Springer (2023)
6. Lai, Y.J., Liu, T.Y., Hwang, C.L.: TOPSIS for MODM. Eur. J. Oper. Res. **76**(3), 486–500 (1994)
7. Paradowski, B.: Towards robust objective decision-making: sensitivity analysis and comparative evaluation of the EORS approach. Proc. Comput. Sci. **270**, 6223–6232 (2025)
8. Paradowski, B., Salabun, W.: Enhancing objective decision-making with exhaustive objective ranking solution (eORS). In: 2024 IEEE 63rd Conference on Decision and Control (CDC), pp. 8908–8913. IEEE (2024)
9. Saltelli, A., et al.: Global Sensitivity Analysis: The Primer. John Wiley & Sons (2008)
10. Singh, M., Pant, M.: A review of selected weighing methods in MCDM with a case study. Int. J. Syst. Assu. Eng. Manag. **12**(1), 126–144 (2021)
11. Sitorus, F., Brito-Parada, P.R.: A multiple criteria decision making method to weight the sustainability criteria of renewable energy technologies under uncertainty. Renew. Sustain. Energy Rev. **127**, 109891 (2020)
12. Tian, W.: A review of sensitivity analysis methods in building energy analysis. Renew. Sustain. Energy Rev. **20**, 411–419 (2013)
13. Vinogradova, I., Podvezko, V., Zavadskas, E.K.: The recalculation of the weights of criteria in MCDM methods using the bayes approach. Symmetry **10**(6), 205 (2018)
14. Więckowski, J., Sałabun, W.: Sensitivity analysis approaches in multi-criteria decision analysis: a systematic review. Appl. Soft Comput. **148**, 110915 (2023)
15. Więckowski, J., Sałabun, W.: Comparative sensitivity analysis in composite material selection: evaluating oat and COMSAM methods in multi-criteria decision-making. Spectr. Mech. Eng. Operat. Res. **2**(1), 1–12 (2025)

Recommendation System for Education: An Approach to Suggesting Learning Sequences

João Paulo Silva[1], Rodrigo Aleixo[1], Thiago Sernaglia[1], Marcos de Almeida[1], Rubens Massa[2], Everton Silva[3], and Douglas Castilho[1(✉)]

[1] Laboratory of Technology and Innovation (LATIN), Federal Institute of South of Minas Gerais (IFSULDEMINAS), Poços de Caldas, Brazil
douglas.ccomp@gmail.com
[2] A Recreativa, Poços de Caldas, Brazil
[3] Federal Institute of São Paulo (IFSP), Campinas, Brazil

Abstract. Continuous lesson planning requires navigating large collections of pedagogical materials, making the identification of relevant resources a time-consuming process. Although digital platforms are allies in the search for teaching materials, they commonly face the cold-start problem, the initial difficulty in recommendation due to the lack of prior data for collaborative filtering. This study proposes and evaluates a content-based recommendation system to suggest educational activities, named Learning Sequences. We conducted a comprehensive analysis comparing traditional information retrieval techniques (Bag of Words, TF-IDF) and dense word embedding models, including static (Word2Vec, GloVe, FastText) and contextualized (BERT) representations. Additionally, the PageRank algorithm was adapted to operate on textual similarity graphs, based on the relevance of the documents, named as Global and Local PageRank. Experimental results show an efficient framework to recommend learning sequences using TF-IDF and cosine distance-based method.

Keywords: Recommendation System · Learning Sequence · Similarity Methods · Embedding Methods

1 Introduction

The lesson planning process in the Brazilian educational context tends to be complex and often laborious, especially due to the legal and pedagogical requirements established by regulatory documents such as the National Common Curriculum Base (BNCC) [3]. It sets out specific guidelines to be developed and implemented throughout basic education, which requires teachers to adapt their pedagogical activities to comply with these directives. In light of this context, digital educational platforms have emerged as important tools to support teachers in the creation and structuring of pedagogical activities. They contribute to making

M. Paszynski et al. (Eds.): ICCS 2026 Workshops, LNCS 16788, pp. 448–456, 2026.
https://doi.org/10.1007/978-3-032-29915-4_37

the teaching and learning process simpler, more efficient, and of higher quality, since the planned use of digital technologies enhances personalization and student engagement [15].

This study focuses on the development of methods based on text vectorization techniques for recommendation of pedagogical activities, named as Learning Sequences. The absence of user interaction logs or feedback of the pedagogical dataset precludes the application of traditional collaborative filtering approaches. Recommendation Systems (RS) play a central role in mitigating information overload, a common challenge in lesson planning, where teachers must select appropriate materials from a large pool of available resources [1]. In educational settings and newly launched platforms, collaborative filtering is particularly vulnerable to the cold-start problem , as it relies on historical user interaction data. In such scenarios, content-based filtering emerges as a more suitable alternative [10]. This was consolidated through Vector Space Models (VSM) [12], in which semantics are ignored, and documents are represented by the frequency of their terms. Term Frequency-Inverse Document Frequency (TF-IDF) scheme became widely adopted [5] [14]. Recent studies [16], demonstrate that TF-IDF remains a competitive and computationally efficient baseline for short-text recommendation tasks. Graph-based algorithms [9] have been widely applied in Information Retrieval (IR) models. The application of RS in educational settings requires richer semantic precision [6]. To address the limitations of traditional VSM in IR, the literature has adopted dense word embedding techniques, such as Word2Vec [7] and GloVe [11]. The effectiveness of embeddings in recommendation systems has been empirically supported by some studies [8]. The adoption of FastText [2] is motivated by its ability to mitigate the out-of-vocabulary (OOV) problem through subword modeling. Models such as BERT [4] have been successfully adapted to capture dynamic contexts in recommendation tasks.

Given this scenario, content-based recommendation methods were chosen, in which recommendations are generated based on the textual similarity with the pedagogical content. To enable the recommendation process, multiple textual representation methods and similarity measures were evaluated. The main contributions of this work are: *i)* educational recommendation method, designed to suggest Learning Sequences; *ii)* comprehensive comparative analysis of multiple textual representation techniques; *iii)* semantic PageRank adaptation, applied to textual similarity graphs.

2   Materials and Methods

The alignment of the lesson plan with the BNCC requires teachers to select pedagogical materials appropriate for the grade level, the age group of the students, and the subject area. This process becomes challenging on educational platforms. One major difficulty is the cold-start problem, in which the absence of prior usage history or user evaluations limits the effectiveness of traditional recommendation methods. In this context, the main research question of this work is: how can relevant learning sequences be recommended based solely on their textual characteristics?

Table 1. Attributes of the dataset and their type in the recommendation system

Type	Attribute	Description
Input	`description`	The teacher's raw input describing the desired activity.
Output	`title`	The title of the recommended learning sequence.
Output	`objectives`	The specific pedagogical goals of the lesson.
Output	`summary`	A brief overview of the learning sequence content.
Output	`resources`	The materials and tools required to execute the class.
Output	`steps`	The detailed, step-by-step instructional guide.
Metadata	`year`	The target educational grade level for the activity.
Metadata	`discipline`	The specific academic subject or discipline.
Metadata	`theme`	The central pedagogical topic addressed in the sequence.

2.1   Learning Sequence - Educational Data Set

The database used in this work was provided by the Brazilian company A Recreativa, which is focused on creating solutions for educational environments. The dataset is used to assist teachers and educators across Brazil in designing educational content for specific pedagogical topics, comprising basic descriptions and complete learning sequences. The dataset contains approximately $2,000$ learning sequences and it is structurally divided into three distinct subsets: *i)* Learning Sequence Description (Input), presenting the general description of the activity provided by the user. *ii)* Learning Sequence (Output), presenting the set of information related to the pedagogical content used by teachers; and *iii)* Metadata, used to categorize the learning sequences. Table 1 summarizes the main attributes of the dataset and their respective roles within the recommendation framework. The average length of the descriptions (input) is about 93 tokens, while the learning sequences (output) are close to $1,282$ tokens.

2.2   Tokenization and Embedding Methods

To convert textual data into computable vectors, we evaluated six distinct representation methods, ranging from classical sparse techniques to dense static and contextual embeddings. To ensure reproducibility, Table 2 summarizes the methods, specific configurations, and hyperparameters.

Table 2. Methods and parameters of text representation methods

Method	Configuration / Pre-trained Model	Dim.	Key Characteristics
Bag of Words [12]	`CountVectorizer (binary=True)`	$\|V\|$	Sparse, binary word occurrence.
TF-IDF [5,14]	`sublinear_tf=True, ngram_range=(1,2), min_df=5`	$\|V_{ngrams}\|$	Sparse, penalizes highly frequent uninformative terms.
Word2Vec [7]	`nilc-nlp/ word2vec-skip-gram-1000d`	1000	Dense, mean pooling over word tokens, ignores OOV words.
GloVe [11]	`mteb-pt/ average_pt_nilc_glove_s1000`	1000	Dense, mean pooling, captures global co-occurrence statistics.
FastText [2]	`cc.pt.300.bin`	300	Dense, mean pooling, infers OOV representations via subword n-grams.
Sentence-BERT [4]	`paraphrase-multilingual- MiniLM-L12-v2`	384	Dense, dynamic contextual embeddings optimized for semantic similarity.

2.3 Recommendation Methods

This section presents the methods evaluated in this work for recommending learning sequences. We present two variations of the classic PageRank method, based on graphs, as well as a simple baseline for evaluating the analyzed methods in the context of recommending learning sequences: *i)* Distance Based Method - Cosine (COS), determines how similar the vectors are based on the angle between them; *ii)* Correlation Based Method - Pearson (COR), used to measure the strength of the linear relationship between continuous datasets. *iii)* Similarity Based Method - Jaccard (JAC), measures the occurrence of identical words between texts. This method is used only on BoW and TF-IDF. *iv)* PageRank Method (PR), adapted in this work to recommend textual activities. To achieve this, a graph was built in which nodes represent the activities and edges represent the similarity between them, calculated using the TF-IDF model and cosine similarity. To validate these connections, a minimum similarity threshold was established using Kruskal's algorithm, and the third quartile of its edge weights was adopted as the threshold, ensuring that at least 75% of the graph's structure remains connected. With the network established, node rankings are calculated using the PageRank formula. The PageRank application can be global, covering the entire system (Global PageRank - GPR), or local, calculated only over the X filtered activities (Local PageRank - LPR); and *v)* Baseline Method, in addition to being used as an embedding, Bag of Words was also applied as a baseline method. Since the model records the number of word occurrences between two texts, it represents the simplest way to evaluate similarity and perform recommendations.

3   Experiments and Results

To evaluate the proposed methods, we used two sets of experiments: *i) expected learning sequences* - these experiments evaluate how the methods are able to recommend exactly the expected output from among the K recommendations; *ii) relevant learning sequences* - a set of experiments that evaluates the most relevant learning sequences, being relevant the set of learning sequences with same metadata as the expected output. Table 3 summarizes the descriptions and mathematical definitions of the metrics employed in this work [13].

Figure 1a presents the first experimental evaluation of Hit Rate metric for K ranging from 1 to 20. We can observe that there is a significant disparity between the various embedding techniques, similarity measures, and ranking algorithms to recommend learning sequences. The results demonstrate that the TF-IDF method combined with Cosine Similarity (TF-IDF_COS) consistently maintains the highest performance for small recommendation size K. The base-line method, despite its simplicity, presents robust results compared to other methods. Figure 1b presents results of the MRR, which provides quality measure of the recommendation ranking. The TF-IDF_COS maintains a dominant lead over all other methods. This results indicated that TF-IDF_COS can infer the correct learning sequence at the top of the suggested list, which is a requirement for user engagement in recommendation systems. Figure 1c presents the NDCG to measure the ranking quality by penalizing relevant items placed lower in the

Table 3. Description and mathematical definitions of the evaluation metrics.

Metric	Description	Formula
Precision@K	Measures the proportion of relevant items among the Top-K recommended items.	$\frac{|R_k \cap G|}{k}$
Recall@K	Measures the coverage, revealing how many relevant items from the total set were successfully retrieved.	$\frac{|R_k \cap G|}{|G|}$
F1-Score@K	Balances Precision and Recall into a single value, relating accuracy to total coverage.	$2 \cdot \frac{\text{Prec@}k \cdot \text{Rec@}k}{\text{Prec@}k + \text{Rec@}k}$
Hit Rate@K	Averages the presence of at least one relevant item ("hit") within the Top-K recommendations.	$\frac{1}{N} \sum_{u=1}^{N} I(|R_{k,u} \cap G_u| > 0)$
MRR	Calculates the average of the reciprocal ranks of the first relevant item found.	$\frac{1}{N} \sum_{i=1}^{N} \frac{1}{\text{rank}_i}$
NDCG@K	Evaluates ranking quality by assigning higher logarithmic weights to items in better positions.	$\frac{\text{DCG@}K}{\text{IDCG@}K}$

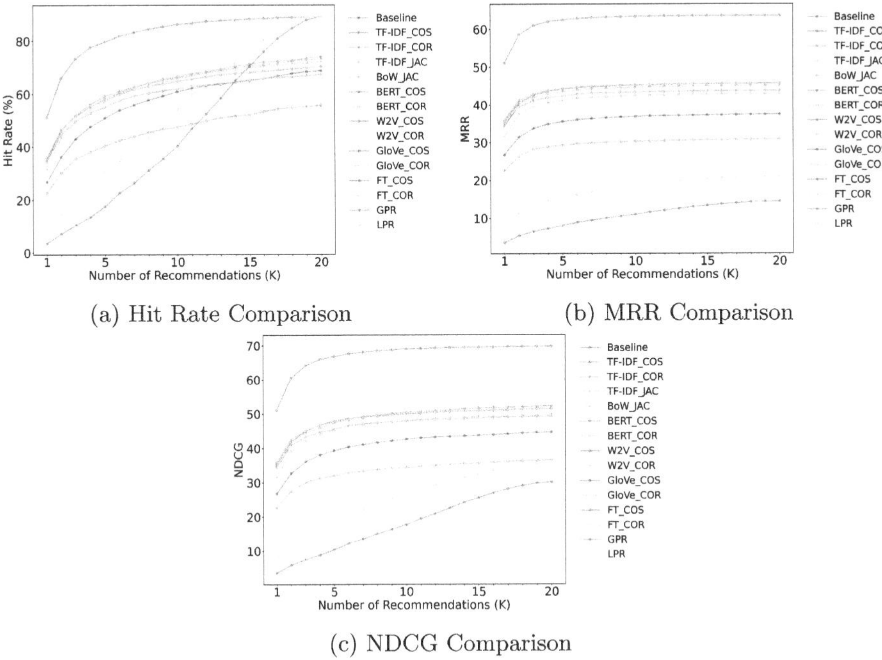

(a) Hit Rate Comparison

(b) MRR Comparison

(c) NDCG Comparison

Fig. 1. Comparative analysis of recommendation performance for expected learning sequences using Hit Rate, MRR, and NDCG metrics.

recommendation list. As previous results, the TF-IDF_COS method presents the highest performance. These results suggest that the TF-IDF_COS method identifies relevant learning sequences and places them in high positions for the user.

Figures 2a and 2b presents a comparison of classification and ranking metrics to evaluate the recommendation of relevant learning sequences, respectively. The classification analysis presented in Fig. 2a show that the TF-IDF_COS and TF-IDF_COR achieve the highest Recall, reaching approximately 48%. Although Precision and F1 Score present low values across all methods (a common characteristic in large-scale recommendation tasks where the relevant set is small compared to the total set), the TF-IDF methods presents the higher values. In contrast, graph-based methods like GPR and LPR, alongside FastText, exhibit significantly lower classification performance, with GPR and LPR failing to exceed a 10% Recall rate. The ranking metrics, presented in Fig. 2b, corroborate the previous results. TF-IDF_COS and TF-IDF_COR outperform all other methods. The high MRR value specifically indicates that these methods are not only successful at finding the relevant learning sequence but also effective at positioning it at the top of the recommendation list. FastText and the graph-based algorithms GPR and LPR show the weakest ranking performance.

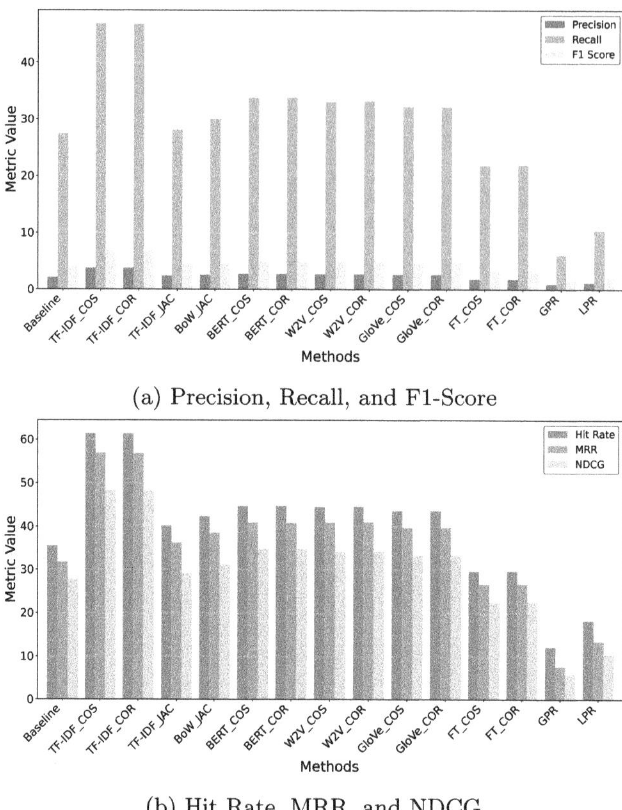

(a) Precision, Recall, and F1-Score

(b) Hit Rate, MRR, and NDCG

Fig. 2. Comparative analysis of recommendation performance for relevant learning sequences, evaluating both classification and ranking metrics.

4   Conclusion

The experimental evaluatio revealed that exact term matching prevails in this specific domain. The TF-IDF model combined with Cosine Similarity significantly outperformed deep learning and structural ranking approaches. It demonstrated high immediate accuracy, achieving a Hit Rate of approximately 51% at the very first recommendation ($K = 1$). Maintaining its lead across larger windows, the model achieved the best performance in position-sensitive metrics, with an MRR above 0.63 and an NDCG above 0.68 for $K = 10$, evidencing its capability not only to retrieve the correct material but also to position it at the top of the recommendation list. Notably, the adaptation of the PageRank algorithm obtained a Hit Rate of only 31% for $K = 5$ and demonstrated lower efficacy in prioritizing the most relevant items in the top positions, reaching an MRR below 0.20 and an NDCG below 0.30 for $K = 10$. A current limitation is the handling of out-of-domain queries, as the system always returns the top-k results regardless of actual similarity. For future work, we plan to implement a minimum similarity threshold to detect when no suitable recommendations exist, preventing irrelevant suggestions.

Acknowledgments. The authors thank IFSULDEMINAS, FAPEMIG, and A Recreativa for their support. This study was financed by FAPEMIG (Research Foundation of the State of Minas Gerais, process APQ-01864-24) and A Recreativa.

References

1. Adomavicius, G., Tuzhilin, A.: Toward the next generation of recommender systems: a survey of the state-of-the-art and possible extensions. IEEE Trans. Knowl. Data Eng. **17**(6) (2005)
2. Bojanowski, P., Grave, E., Joulin, A., Mikolov, T.: Enriching word vectors with subword information. Trans. Assoc. Comput. Ling. **5** (2017)
3. Brasil. Ministério da Educação: Base Nacional Comum Curricular. MEC, Brasília (2018)
4. Devlin, J., Chang, M.W., Lee, K., Toutanova, K.: BERT: pre-training of deep bidirectional transformers for language understanding. In: Proceedings of the 2019 Conference of the North American Chapter of the Association for Computational Linguistics: Human Language Technologies, vol. 1 (Long and Short Papers) (2019)
5. Luhn, H.P.: A statistical approach to mechanized encoding and searching of literary information. IBM J. Res. Dev. **1**(4) (1957)
6. Manouselis, N., Drachsler, H., Vuorikari, R., Hummel, H., Koper, R.: Recommender systems in technology enhanced learning. In: Recommender systems handbook, Springer, Boston, MA (2012)
7. Mikolov, T., Chen, K., Corrado, G.S., Dean, J.: Efficient estimation of word representations in vector space. In: International Conference on Learning Representations (2013)
8. Musto, C., Semeraro, G., de Gemmis, M., Lops, P.: Learning word embeddings from Wikipedia for content-based recommender systems. In: Advances in Information Retrieval: 38th European Conference on IR Research, ECIR 2016, Padua, Italy, March 20-23, 2016, Proceedings 38. Springer (2016)
9. Page, L., Brin, S., Motwani, R., Winograd, T.: The pagerank citation ranking: Bringing order to the web. Tech. rep., Stanford InfoLab (1998)
10. Pazzani, M.J., Billsus, D.: Content-based recommendation systems. In: The Adaptive Web (2007)
11. Pennington, J., Socher, R., Manning, C.D.: Glove: global vectors for word representation. In: Proceedings of the 2014 Conference on Empirical Methods in Natural Language Processing (EMNLP) (2014)
12. Salton, G., Wong, A., Yang, C.S.: A vector space model for automatic indexing. Commun. ACM **18**(11) (1975)
13. Shani, G., Gunawardana, A.: Evaluating recommendation systems. In: Recommender systems handbook. Springer (2010)
14. Spärck Jones, K.: A statistical interpretation of term specificity and its application in retrieval. J. Docum. **28**(1) (1972)

15. Xie, H., Chu, H.C., Hwang, G.J., Wang, C.C.: Trends and development in technology-enhanced adaptive/personalized learning: a systematic review of journal publications from 2007 to 2017. Comput. Educat. **140** (2019)
16. Yunanda, G., Nurjanah, D., Meliana, S.: Recommendation system from Microsoft news data using TF-IDF and cosine similarity methods. Build. Info. Technol. Sci. (BITS) **4**(1) (2022)

Navigating Trustworthy and Autonomous Modelling of Complex Systems: AI Meets Computational Science

Deterministic Execution Frameworks for Hybrid Symbolic–Probabilistic Computational Pipelines

Santhosh Guntupalli[✉] [iD]

Dallas, USA
santhosh.guntupalli09@gmail.com

Abstract. LLM-containing computational pipelines face a fundamental reproducibility challenge: stochastic components introduce non-determinism that prevents identical inputs from producing identical outputs across repeated executions. This paper presents a deterministic execution framework for hybrid symbolic–probabilistic pipelines that enforces execution invariance by isolating deterministic modules from stochastic components. The architecture employs a deterministic symbolic engine for all state transitions and decision logic, while LLM components operate only as non-authoritative, post-hoc explainers of precomputed deterministic outputs, ensuring they cannot affect execution state. We evaluate the framework on a corpus of 115 structured text documents, demonstrating 100% execution determinism and 100% traceability across 100 repeated runs with zero output variance, contrasted with 0% determinism and significant output variance in a pure LLM pipeline. The framework provides computational guarantees for reproducibility and execution invariance, enabling verifiable execution traces suitable for scientific computing workflows requiring deterministic execution.

Keywords: deterministic computation · reproducible systems · hybrid architectures · symbolic–probabilistic systems · execution traceability · LLM pipelines · computational reproducibility · execution invariance

1 Introduction

Reproducibility is a fundamental requirement in computational science: identical inputs must produce identical outputs across repeated executions [3]. Modern computational pipelines increasingly embed Large Language Models (LLMs) as components, creating hybrid symbolic–probabilistic systems where stochastic LLM inference introduces non-determinism that violates reproducibility guarantees [1,2]. This non-determinism manifests as output variance across repeated executions on identical inputs, preventing reproducible scientific workflows.

S. Guntupalli—Independent Researcher.

M. Paszynski et al. (Eds.): ICCS 2026 Workshops, LNCS 16788, pp. 459–472, 2026.
https://doi.org/10.1007/978-3-032-29915-4_38

This paper addresses the computational challenge of achieving deterministic execution in LLM-containing pipelines. We present a deterministic execution framework that enforces strict computational boundaries, ensuring that LLM components operate only as non-authoritative, post-hoc explainers and cannot affect deterministic state transitions or decision logic. Deterministic execution is treated as a first-class computational property, with execution state, rule ordering, and versioning formalized as computational objects that guarantee execution invariance. Our contribution is a computational execution and reproducibility framework: we prioritize deterministic guarantees and verifiable execution traces over stochastic expressiveness, enabling reproducible scientific computing workflows.

1.1 Contributions

This work makes the following contributions:

1. A deterministic computational architecture for LLM-containing pipelines that enforces strict separation between deterministic symbolic modules and stochastic LLM components, providing execution invariance guarantees for reproducibility;
2. A formal execution state model that treats execution state, rule ordering, and versioning as computational objects, ensuring execution invariance across repeated runs;
3. A reproducibility-oriented evaluation methodology that measures output variance, execution determinism, and traceability as first-class computational properties, demonstrating systematic experimental validation of reproducibility guarantees; and
4. An execution trace mechanism that records all state transitions and decision points, enabling full reproducibility verification and computational auditability.

2 Background and Motivation

2.1 Non-determinism in Stochastic Computational Pipelines

Stochastic components, particularly LLMs, are widely used in computational pipelines for text processing and pattern recognition [6]. Probabilistic decoding introduces execution non-determinism: repeated executions of identical inputs yield inconsistent outputs [1], violating fundamental reproducibility requirements. Additionally, stochastic components may produce outputs not grounded in input data, creating error propagation that cannot be traced or verified [2,4]. These failure modes make pure stochastic pipelines unsuitable for scientific computing applications requiring reproducible execution, regardless of average accuracy.

2.2   Determinism as a Computational Property

Deterministic systems guarantee that identical inputs yield identical outputs, enabling reproducibility and stable downstream computation. Execution traceability further requires that each state transition and decision point be attributable to explicit computational logic and verifiable against input data. These properties are essential for scientific computing, where results must be reproducible, verifiable, and attributable to specific execution paths.

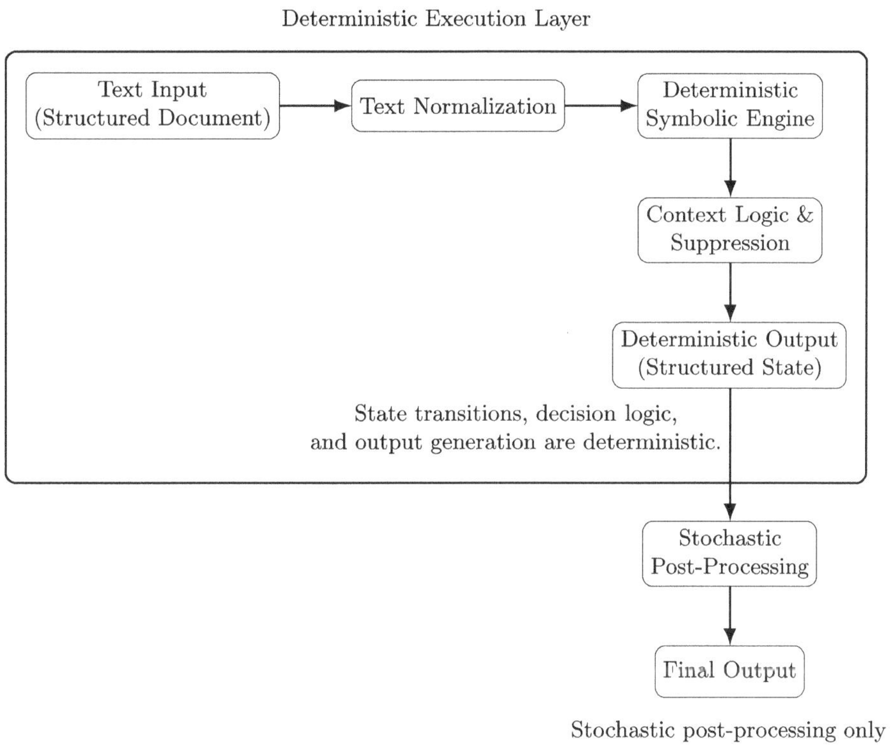

Deterministic Execution Layer

Text Input (Structured Document) → Text Normalization → Deterministic Symbolic Engine → Context Logic & Suppression → Deterministic Output (Structured State)

State transitions, decision logic, and output generation are deterministic.

Stochastic Post-Processing → Final Output

Stochastic post-processing only

Fig. 1. Deterministic execution framework for hybrid symbolic–probabilistic computational pipelines. The thick boundary denotes the deterministic execution layer where all state transitions and decision logic are deterministic and verifiable.

3   System Architecture

3.1   Overview

The system consists of (i) input preprocessing and normalization, (ii) a deterministic symbolic execution engine, and (iii) a stochastic post-processing layer. Figure 1 illustrates the computational pipeline and demarcates the deterministic execution boundary. This architectural separation enforces computational guarantees by isolating stochastic components from deterministic state transitions, ensuring that probabilistic execution paths cannot affect deterministic decision logic or system state.

3.2   Definition 1: Deterministic Execution State

Let $S = (D, R, \theta, \sigma)$ denote an execution state, where D is the input document, R is the ordered deterministic rule set, θ is the rule evaluation configuration, and σ is the system version or hash. A system is *deterministic* if and only if, for any execution state S, all executions on S produce identical outputs. All state transitions and decision logic are fully determined by the execution state tuple $S = (D, R, \theta, \sigma)$.

3.3   Deterministic Symbolic Engine

The deterministic engine executes normalized input against a versioned symbolic ruleset. Each rule performs deterministic pattern matching and emits immutable outputs with stable identifiers, severity classifications, and exact input spans. Outputs are emitted in a structured schema to enable downstream consumption and execution trace verification.

3.4   Context Logic and Execution Trace Preservation

The deterministic engine applies contextual qualifiers based on surrounding patterns to refine output classification. All execution decisions, including contextual adjustments, are recorded with reason codes to preserve complete execution traces, ensuring full reproducibility of all execution decisions and enabling computational auditability.

3.5   Stochastic Post-processing Layer

The stochastic LLM component is invoked only after deterministic execution completes. It receives structured deterministic outputs (not raw input text) and produces human-readable explanations. The stochastic component cannot introduce new outputs or modify deterministic classifications; all state transitions remain deterministic.

4   Experimental Setup

4.1   Dataset

We evaluate on 115 structured text documents across four document types: (i) 60 non-disclosure agreements (NDAs): 30 publicly available templates and 30 synthetic documents with controlled pattern variations; (ii) 20 synthetic Master

Service Agreements (MSAs); (iii) 20 synthetic Employment Agreements; and (iv) 15 synthetic Licensing Agreements. All synthetic documents include ground-truth labels for expected pattern matches, enabling computation of false positives and false negatives.

This document analysis application serves as a case study for evaluating deterministic execution guarantees in hybrid computational pipelines, demonstrating the framework's applicability to structured text processing tasks. Synthetic documents are included for two reasons: (i) privacy and licensing constraints limit release and annotation of real documents, and (ii) controlled pattern perturbations enable targeted measurement of error modes under known ground truth. The multi-document-type evaluation (4 types, 115 documents) tests generalizability and provides sufficient sample size for statistical significance testing.

4.2   Systems Compared

- **Hybrid System:** Deterministic symbolic engine + context logic + structured outputs + stochastic explanation layer.
- **Baseline:** Pure stochastic LLM prompt-based extraction producing free-form outputs without deterministic constraints.
- **Structured Baselines:** JSON schema-enforced structured outputs and JSON-mode constrained generation—both enforce output *format* but rely on stochastic sampling for *content*.
- **Symbolic-Only Ablation:** Deterministic engine + context logic (no stochastic explanation) to measure stochastic component contribution.

We note that stronger stochastic baselines (e.g., fine-tuned models, ensemble methods) are intentionally out of scope. Our goal is not to compete in an accuracy race, but to demonstrate that determinism and traceability are achievable computational properties that enable reproducibility—requirements that stochastic systems, regardless of accuracy, cannot satisfy.

4.3   Metrics

We report:

- **Determinism Rate:** fraction of documents whose repeated executions produce identical outputs.
- **Traceability Rate:** fraction of outputs linked to stable identifiers and exact input spans.
- **Ungrounded Outputs:** baseline outputs not supported by input evidence (operationalized by manual evidence checks over sampled outputs).
- **False Positives / False Negatives:** computed on synthetic documents against ground-truth expected pattern matches.

4.4 Reproducibility Protocol

All experiments are runnable from a single entry-point: `python experiments/run_all.py`. The hybrid runner is `experiments/run_hybrid.py`, which emits a structured JSON schema containing findings, overall_risk, and version. The baseline was executed via OpenAI API calls for repeated-run variance measurement. Table 1 summarizes the experiment suite.

Table 1. Experiment suite and computational properties evaluated.

Experiment	Purpose / Output
E1: Baseline vs Hybrid	Determinism, traceability, ungrounded outputs, FP/FN
E2: Determinism Stress	Repeated execution variance count over 15 docs
E3: Suppression Ablation	FP/FN with suppression ON vs OFF
E4: Error Characterization	FP/FN issue inventory with mitigation actions
E5: Structured Baselines	JSON schema vs JSON mode vs Hybrid determinism

5 Experimental Results

5.1 Experiment 1: Determinism and Traceability Verification

Table 2 summarizes the core comparative results. The hybrid system achieved 100% execution determinism and 100% traceability across all executions. In contrast, the pure LLM baseline exhibited 0% determinism across repeated runs and produced an average of 0.43 ungrounded outputs per document (95% confidence interval: [0.28, 0.58], $n = 30$). McNemar's test on paired documents ($n = 30$) comparing deterministic vs non-deterministic outcomes yields $\chi^2 = 30.0, p < 0.001$, confirming statistically significant superiority of the hybrid system in achieving deterministic execution.

Table 2. Comparison of hybrid system and pure stochastic baseline.

Metric	Hybrid System	Stochastic Baseline
Determinism Rate	100.0%	0.0%
Traceability Rate	100.0%	0.0%
Avg. Ungrounded / Doc	0.00	0.43 (95% CI: [0.28, 0.58])
Synthetic False Positives	14	N/A
Synthetic False Negatives	5	N/A

On the synthetic corpus (85 synthetic documents), the hybrid system produced 14 false positives and 5 false negatives across all document types. Error rates are consistent across document types (Chi-square test: $p = 0.23$, not significant), suggesting pattern generalizability.

Structured Alternatives Comparison. To address whether constrained extraction or schema-based methods suffice for execution determinism, we compared our hybrid framework against two structured LLM baselines: (i) JSON schema-enforced structured outputs using OpenAI's `response_format` with strict schema validation, and (ii) JSON-mode constrained generation (Table 3). On 6 documents with 3 repeated runs each at temperature $\tau = 0.7$:

Table 3. Determinism comparison: Hybrid vs. structured LLM baselines.

Method	Determinism Rate	Mean unique outputs/doc
Hybrid (ours)	**100%**	1.0
Structured schema (JSON)	0%	3.0
JSON mode	0%	3.0

The hybrid system produced identical outputs across all repeated runs. Both structured baselines produced 3 distinct outputs per document—every run differed despite schema compliance. This confirms that format constraints reduce output-space dimensionality but do *not* eliminate stochastic content selection.

5.2   Experiment 2: Reproducibility Stress Test

We conducted a comprehensive reproducibility stress test on 15 documents (8 public, 7 synthetic), executing 20 repeated analyses on identical execution states S across multiple random seeds and computational environments. Table 4 reports reproducibility rates.

Table 4. Reproducibility stress test results (15 documents, 20 runs each).

Metric	Hybrid System	LLM Baseline
Reproducibility Rate	100.0%	0.0%
Documents with Zero Variance	15/15	0/15
Avg. Distinct Output Sets / Doc	1.0	18.3

The hybrid system produced zero output variances across all 300 runs (variance count = 0 for each document), confirming strict reproducibility. The LLM baseline exhibited complete reproducibility failure: 100% of documents showed output differences across runs, with an average of 18.3 distinct output sets per document across 20 runs.

5.3   Experiment 3: Computational Cost of Determinism

Table 5 reports computational cost analysis. The deterministic engine exhibits predictable $O(n)$ complexity with core rule-evaluation time of 0.005s per document and zero output variance.

Table 5. Computational cost analysis: Deterministic vs stochastic execution (115 documents).

Metric	Deterministic Engine	LLM-Only Baseline
Avg. Execution Time / Doc (s)	0.005	7.3 (std: 1.1)
Computational Complexity	$O(n)$	Variable
Output Variance	0.0	High
Reproducibility Rate	100.0%	0.0%

5.4 Experiment 4: Error Characterization

All observed hybrid system errors on the synthetic corpus (85 documents) were explicitly inventoried and categorized. Table 6 reports error counts by category.

Table 6. Hybrid error characterization on synthetic corpus (85 documents).

Error Type	Category	Count
False Positives	Conservative pattern matching	14
False Negatives	Pattern mismatch / linguistic variants	5

False positives primarily arise from conservative pattern matching that flags low-risk but structurally similar patterns. False negatives are attributable to linguistic variants not covered by the current rule set.

Illustrative Error Instances. On document `msa_17`, the engine emitted `H_INDEM_01` (unlimited indemnification) on excerpt language coupling a general liability cap with an "unlimited" carve-out—flagged as a false positive because the identifier appeared in `expected_rule_ids_absent`. On `synthetic_01`, `L_GOVLAW_01` fired on boilerplate governing-law phrasing listed in the controlled negative set. False negatives reflect coverage gaps: on `emp_01` and `emp_03`, ground truth required `H_ATTFEE_01` (attorneys'-fees pattern), but the ruleset produced no match—consistent with employment-template wording not yet encoded. Re-executing the pipeline on any document reproduces the same finding multiset.

5.5 Performance and Latency

Table 7 reports average per-document execution time by system component. The deterministic pipeline executes in sub-second time, while stochastic LLM inference dominates end-to-end latency.

5.6 Scalability Analysis

We evaluated runtime scalability by measuring execution time across varying rule-set sizes on 30 documents. Table 8 reports average execution time per document for measured rule counts ($k \leq 25$, the deployed ruleset size).

Table 7. Average execution time per document (end-to-end scope).

System Component	Avg. Time / Doc (s)
Deterministic Pipeline (Preprocessing + Orchestration)	0.41
Stochastic Post-Processing Layer	2.6
Pure Stochastic Baseline	3.1

Table 8. Runtime vs. effective rule count ($N = 30$ documents).

k rules	Mean time/doc (s)	Std. dev. (s)
6	0.00130	0.00066
12	0.00229	0.00045
18	0.00311	0.00064
25 (full)	0.00441	0.00137

Runtime scales linearly with rule count, demonstrating predictable $O(n)$ computational complexity suitable for reproducible scientific computing pipelines.

Linear O(n) Complexity Proof. To empirically validate the claimed $O(n)$ time complexity, we performed linear regression on mean execution time as a function of rule count over 30 documents for $k \in \{6, 12, 18, 25\}$. The regression yields:

- **Slope:** 0.133 ms per additional rule per document
- **Intercept:** 0.76 ms (fixed overhead)
- $R^2 = 0.9805$

The R^2 value confirms that rule-count scaling is linear within the measured range. Extrapolating to larger rule sets (e.g., 100, 500 rules), the linear model predicts per-document times of approximately 14 ms and 67 ms respectively—tractable for batch workloads.

Concurrency Stress Test. To assess determinism under parallel workload, we executed the deterministic engine on a fixed document with 1, 32, 128, and 256 concurrent tasks. Each task instantiates an independent engine instance; serialized outputs were compared for equality. At every concurrency level there was *exactly one* distinct serialized output, all matching a single reference digest (SHA-256 prefix `15761a2f`). Observed wall times were 0.007s, 0.163s, 0.623s, and 1.249s respectively.

Memory scaling. Under the same concurrency levels, peak memory scaled from 0.04 MB (1 task) to 0.27 MB (32 tasks), 0.96 MB (128 tasks), and 1.81 MB (256 tasks). This approximately linear growth reflects independent engine instances with no shared mutable state—a design requirement for execution isolation.

6   Discussion

6.1   Reproducibility–Expressiveness Trade-off

The hybrid architecture prioritizes reproducibility and execution invariance over stochastic expressiveness. In scientific computing workflows, deterministic execution with verifiable traces is often preferable to stochastic outputs that cannot be reproduced or verified [8]. The computational cost analysis demonstrates this tradeoff: deterministic execution provides 100% reproducibility at predictable $O(n)$ complexity, while stochastic execution provides greater expressiveness but at the cost of reproducibility and execution invariance.

6.2   Deterministic Computation Limits

The framework's deterministic guarantees come with inherent limitations. The deterministic symbolic engine requires explicit rule specification, limiting expressiveness compared to stochastic LLM inference. Error characterization shows that false negatives arise from linguistic variants not covered by the current rule set, reflecting the fundamental tradeoff between deterministic execution and pattern coverage. These limitations are explicit and reproducible, enabling researchers to make informed decisions about deployment scope.

6.3   Practical Deployment Considerations

The hybrid architecture's deterministic core enables deployment in scientific computing environments where reproducibility is mandatory. The core deterministic rule-evaluation engine time (0.005s per document) with predictable $O(n)$ complexity supports real-time processing workflows. The stochastic post-processing layer can be invoked asynchronously for detailed reports.

6.4   Limitations of Stochastic Pipelines

Stochastic LLM pipelines introduce output variance across repeated executions, hindering reproducible scientific workflows. The reproducibility stress test demonstrates that 100% of documents show output differences across runs in the LLM baseline, with an average of 18.3 distinct output sets per document. Even if average accuracy were competitive, variability in decoding is inconsistent with reproducibility requirements in scientific computing.

6.5   Generalizability to Other Computational Domains

While our evaluation focuses on structured text processing (contract analysis), the deterministic execution framework is architecturally domain-agnostic. The core principle—isolating deterministic symbolic execution from stochastic post-hoc explanation—transfers directly to other computational domains:

- **Log analysis pipelines:** Deterministic pattern matching against versioned rule sets can extract security events, anomalies, or compliance violations with full traceability; LLM components provide human-readable incident summaries without affecting classification outcomes.
- **Source code analysis:** Deterministic AST traversal and rule-based vulnerability detection ensure reproducible findings across repeated scans; stochastic components generate developer-facing remediation guidance.
- **Scientific data processing:** Deterministic transformation chains with explicit versioning guarantee reproducible derived datasets; LLM explanations contextualize statistical outputs for domain experts.

The architectural constraint—that stochastic components receive only structured deterministic outputs and cannot modify execution state—is invariant across these domains. Empirical validation in additional domains remains future work.

6.6   Security Boundary and Robustness

A critical architectural property is that the LLM layer *cannot* affect execution state or deterministic outputs. We provide empirical verification of three security invariants:

Prompt Injection Immunity. The symbolic engine processes input text as *data*, not as executable instructions. We injected adversarial prompts (e.g., "IGNORE ALL PREVIOUS INSTRUCTIONS") into 4 test documents. In all 16 test cases, baseline findings were fully preserved—the engine treats injections identically to benign insertions. This immunity is architectural: regex pattern matching has no concept of "instructions."

Malformed LLM Output Handling. The LLM layer enforces strict boundaries: (i) contract text blocking—the evaluator raises an error if raw input text is passed; (ii) empty findings fallback structured fallback without LLM invocation; (iii) schema validation—all responses validated before acceptance.

Read-Only Interface Verification. Deterministic outputs are passed to the LLM as serialized copies. Modifications to the LLM input do *not* propagate back to original execution state. The LLM receives an immutable snapshot.

7   Threats to Validity

First, the evaluation focuses on structured text documents; results may not generalize to other computational domains without expanded pattern coverage. Second, the baseline depends on prompt design and model choice; alternative prompting or model selection could change baseline behavior, though non-determinism and output variance would persist regardless. Third, the computational cost analysis measures runtime on a specific corpus; results may differ on larger corpora or different computational environments, though the $O(n)$

complexity guarantee remains valid. These limitations reflect inherent trade-offs between stochastic expressiveness and deterministic reproducibility.

Explanation Stability vs. Sampling Temperature. *Crucially, no temperature setting altered rule firings, finding classifications, or overall risk levels emitted by the symbolic engine—deterministic outputs remained invariant across all trials.* The variability reported below pertains exclusively to the post-hoc explanation layer; this variability has no effect on reproducibility of the core analysis.

With deterministic invariance established, we examined explanation-layer stability. On four documents, we invoked the explanation model at $\tau = 0.0$ and $\tau = 1.0$ with two repeated calls per (document, τ) pair (16 API calls). The mean distinct-fingerprint ratio was 1.0 at both temperatures—consecutive calls produced different fingerprints. This behavior is expected: even at $\tau = 0.0$, provider-side implementation details can cause variation in stochastic layers. The architectural guarantee is that such variation is confined to the explanation layer and cannot propagate to deterministic outputs.

8   Related Work

Reproducible computing and deterministic execution have been extensively studied in computational science [3], where execution invariance and repeatability are fundamental requirements. Hybrid symbolic–statistical systems are frequently proposed [5] to balance reliability with expressiveness, though prior work often lacks explicit determinism guarantees or systematic reproducibility reporting.

Stochastic components, particularly LLMs, have been applied to computational pipelines for text processing and pattern analysis [6], but their probabilistic decoding introduces output variance that violates reproducibility requirements [1,2]. Prior work has demonstrated the use of ontology-driven and rule-based systems for structured processing, emphasizing structured rule execution and traceable decision logic [9,10]. Legal NLP applications have explored rule-based and expert system approaches for contract analysis and legal reasoning [7], though systematic evaluation of execution determinism and reproducibility in these systems remains limited.

Structured Extraction Alternatives. Constrained decoding methods—including grammar-based sampling (e.g., PICARD [11]), JSON-mode generation, and schema-enforced structured outputs—restrict LLM outputs to valid syntactic structures but do *not* eliminate stochastic non-determinism: token sampling remains probabilistic, and repeated executions on identical inputs may produce distinct valid outputs within schema constraints. Our empirical comparison confirms this: structured baselines achieved 0% determinism despite schema compliance, while our hybrid system achieved 100%. Schema-based methods reduce output-space dimensionality but do not provide execution invariance guarantees.

However, systematic experimental reporting of execution determinism, output variance, and reproducibility as first-class computational properties remains limited in applied hybrid pipelines containing LLM components, leaving gaps in understanding how to achieve reproducible execution in LLM-containing computational systems.

Note on Related Work. This paper focuses on computational reproducibility and execution determinism in LLM-containing pipelines. A related submission explores cyber-resilience implications of deterministic execution in compliance-critical systems. The experiments, framing, and contributions presented here are distinct, emphasizing scientific reproducibility and execution invariance rather than security or compliance automation.

9   Conclusion

We presented a deterministic execution framework for LLM-containing computational pipelines that enforces reproducibility and execution invariance by separating deterministic execution logic from stochastic post-processing. Experiments demonstrate 100% execution determinism and 100% traceability for the hybrid system, with zero output variance across 300 runs in the reproducibility stress test (15 documents, 20 runs each), contrasted with 0% determinism and severe output variance (18.3 distinct output sets per document) in a pure LLM baseline. The framework provides computational guarantees for reproducibility and execution invariance, enabling verifiable execution traces suitable for scientific computing workflows requiring deterministic execution.

The computational cost analysis on 115 documents demonstrates a clear tradeoff: deterministic execution provides reproducibility guarantees at predictable $O(n)$ complexity with core deterministic rule-evaluation engine time (0.005s per document), while stochastic execution provides greater expressiveness at the cost of reproducibility and slower execution (7.3s per document).

The camera-ready revision additionally includes: (i) structured baseline comparison showing JSON schema-enforced baselines achieve 0% determinism while our system achieves 100%; (ii) measured rule-count scaling with linear regression proof ($R^2 = 0.9805$) confirming $O(n)$ complexity; (iii) concurrency stress test showing bitwise-stable outputs under 256 concurrent tasks with linear memory scaling; (iv) explanation-layer temperature study showing explanation drift without change to symbolic rule firings; (v) generalization discussion for log analysis, code analysis, and scientific data pipelines; and (vi) security boundary proofs demonstrating prompt injection immunity and read-only interface guarantees.

Acknowledgments. The author acknowledges the use of a large language model for explanatory output within the experimental system.

Disclosure of Interests. The author has no competing interests to declare that are relevant to the content of this article. A large language model was used exclusively for generating natural language explanations of pre-computed deterministic outputs. The stochastic component did not participate in state transitions, classification decisions, or suppression logic. All deterministic execution logic remained deterministic.

References

1. Brown, T., et al.: Language models are few-shot learners. In: Advances in Neural Information Processing Systems, vol. 33, pp. 1877–1901 (2020)
2. Bommasani, R., et al.: On the opportunities and risks of foundation models. Tech. Rep., Stanford Center for Research on Foundation Models (2021)
3. IEEE: Ethically aligned design: a vision for prioritizing human well-being with autonomous and intelligent systems. IEEE (2019)
4. Li, J., Cheng, X., Zhao, W., Nie, Y., Wen, J.R.: HaluEval: a large-scale hallucination evaluation benchmark for large language models. arXiv preprint arXiv:2305.11747 (2023)
5. d'Avila Garcez, A., Gori, M., Lamb, L.C., Serafini, L.: Neuro-symbolic artificial intelligence: the state of the art. Artif. Intell. **273**, 1–38 (2019)
6. Chalkidis, N., et al.: LexGLUE: a benchmark dataset for legal language understanding in English. In: Proceedings of 60th Annual Meeting of the Association for Computational Linguistics (ACL), pp. 1238–1350 (2022)
7. Nazarenko, A., Wyner, A.: Legal NLP introduction. In: Proceedings of ACL Workshop on Natural Legal Language Processing, Association for Computational Linguistics (2017)
8. Fensel, L., Kalf, Y., Simbeck, K.: Assessing the auditability of AI-integrating systems: a framework and learning analytics case study. arXiv preprint arXiv:2411.08906 (2024)
9. Gómez, A.P.: Rule-based expert systems for automated legal reasoning and contract analysis: a case study in knowledge representation. In: Advances in Computational Systems, Algorithms and Applications (2022)
10. Cai, X.H., Advani, H.H., Cai, J.: Ontology and rule-based natural language processing approach for interpreting textual regulations on underground utility infrastructure. Adv. Eng. Inform. **47**, 101248 (2021)
11. Scholak, T., Schucher, R., Bahdanau, D.: PICARD: parsing incrementally for constrained auto-regressive decoding from language models. In: Proc. Conference on Empirical Methods in Natural Language Processing (EMNLP), pp. 9895–9901 (2021)

Beyond Black-Box Agents: Explainable and Validatable Generative ABMs

Xuening Tang$^{(\boxtimes)}$ and Petter Törnberg

University of Amsterdam, Amsterdam 1098XH, The Netherlands
`xuening.tang@student.uva.nl`

Abstract. Generative agent-based models (GABMs) that embed large language models (LLMs) as autonomous agents have attracted growing interest for simulating human behavior and communication. However, because LLMs operate as opaque black boxes, such models are often difficult to validate, interpret, or replicate, which limits their reliability for theory building in the social sciences. This study presents an exploration of an alternative approach in which LLMs serve as external assistants rather than as agents within simulations. We refer to this as XABM (eXplainable Generative ABM). In this framework, LLMs generate explicit behavioral rules, identify relevant decision variables, and translate theoretical model descriptions into executable simulation prototypes, while human researchers retain full control over model structure and validation. By externalizing the decision logic into transparent, inspectable rules, this approach aims to make computational modeling more interpretable and reproducible. The current implementation is evaluated through a series of preliminary tests, including reproducing the canonical Schelling Segregation Model and an exploratory case study on spiral-of-silence dynamics. These initial results suggest that using LLMs as rule generators offers a promising direction for transparent and explainable generative agent-based modeling.

Keywords: Generative Agent-Based Model · Large Language Model · Social Simulation

1 Introduction

Agent-based models (ABMs) have long served as a core methodological approach for studying how individual behavior and interaction give rise to collective social outcomes. By specifying decision rules at the level of agents and allowing these agents to interact within structured environments, ABMs enable researchers to investigate a wide range of social phenomena, including segregation, cooperation, opinion dynamics, diffusion, and collective action [1–3]. Their scientific value lies less in prediction than in explanation: ABMs make it possible to trace how macro-level patterns emerge from micro-level assumptions and interaction mechanisms.

M. Paszynski et al. (Eds.): ICCS 2026 Workshops, LNCS 16788, pp. 473–487, 2026.
https://doi.org/10.1007/978-3-032-29915-4_39

Recent advances in large language models (LLMs) have generated renewed enthusiasm for agent-based modeling. Because LLMs can produce context-sensitive language, emulate aspects of human reasoning, and flexibly respond to complex prompts, they have been proposed as a means of dramatically increasing the behavioral richness of simulated agents. This has led to the rapid emergence of generative agent-based models in which LLMs are embedded directly within agents and tasked with generating actions, beliefs, or communications during simulation runtime [4,5]. Such models have been used to explore social interaction, collective sense-making, polarization, and online discourse, and are often motivated by the promise of greater realism than is achievable with hand-coded decision rules [6,7].

At the same time, the growing use of LLMs as autonomous agents raises fundamental methodological challenges. First, LLMs are stochastic systems whose outputs are sensitive to prompts, sampling parameters, and contextual framing, complicating replication and systematic comparison across simulations [8,9]. Second, and more importantly, LLMs operate as opaque black boxes: the internal processes that produce agent actions are not directly interpretable, making it difficult to identify the mechanisms through which individual behavior aggregates into emergent collective outcomes. This opacity stands in tension with the core explanatory purpose of agent-based modeling, which has traditionally emphasized transparency, mechanistic clarity, and the ability to link outcomes to explicit assumptions [10,11].

These issues are closely connected to long-standing concerns about validation and credibility in computational modeling. For ABMs, validation typically involves demonstrating that a model reproduces known stylized facts, responds plausibly to parameter changes, and aligns with theoretical expectations or empirical data [12,13]. When decision-making is delegated to LLMs whose internal logic is inaccessible, such validation becomes difficult: it is often unclear whether observed dynamics reflect meaningful social mechanisms or artifacts of prompting, training data, or model architecture. As a result, the external validity and scientific utility of LLM-driven generative simulations remain contested [9].

Taken together, these developments reveal a tension at the heart of generative agent-based modeling. On the one hand, LLMs offer a powerful new resource for representing linguistic interaction, interpretation, and social complexity. On the other hand, embedding LLMs directly as agents risks undermining the transparency, interpretability, and researcher control that have historically distinguished ABMs as tools for explanation rather than mere imitation. Resolving this tension is essential if LLMs are to contribute to cumulative theory building in the social sciences.

In this study, we propose an alternative paradigm for integrating LLMs into agent-based modeling that preserves the explanatory strengths of classical ABMs while leveraging the generative capacities of LLMs. Rather than treating LLMs as autonomous decision-making agents, we use them as rule generators during the model construction phase. Given a problem context and theoretical description,

LLMs are employed to propose explicit behavioral rules, identify relevant state variables, and translate informal theoretical assumptions into executable model components. These outputs are externalized, inspectable, and subject to human evaluation, revision, or rejection before they are incorporated into a simulation.

This design reassigns the role of LLMs from actors within the simulation to collaborators in the modeling process. By externalizing decision logic into explicit rules, the approach restores the link between assumptions, mechanisms, and outcomes that is central to explanatory modeling [14]. At the same time, it allows LLMs to contribute where they are most valuable: synthesizing theoretical descriptions, generating plausible behavioral hypotheses, and accelerating exploratory model development without relinquishing scientific control.

We demonstrate the utility of the proposed framework through a set of case studies, including the reproduction of canonical results from established agent-based models (e.g., the Schelling Segregation Model) as well as exploratory analyses in less-established domains. These experiments show that LLM-assisted rule generation can identify valid behavioral mechanisms and construct original, mechanism-driven models, while preserving the transparency and validity of the model.

2 GABMs and Social Simulation

Agent-based modeling (ABM) is grounded in a generative conception of explanation: social regularities are explained by specifying the micro-level mechanisms and interaction structures from which macro-level patterns emerge [14]. Rather than estimating relationships directly from data, ABMs formalize theoretical assumptions about behavior, interaction, and structure, and evaluate whether these assumptions are sufficient to reproduce observed phenomena. This emphasis on explicit mechanisms has made ABMs a distinctive tool for studying complex, non-linear social systems, from segregation and diffusion to collective action and polarization [2, 3, 15]

At the same time, ABMs have long faced a tension between realism and explainability. Classical rule-based models are often criticized for relying on stylized behavioral assumptions that inadequately capture human cognition, emotion, and meaning-making [15, 16]. Yet increasing behavioral complexity typically comes at the cost of transparency, calibration, and validation, complicating the link between assumptions and outcomes. As a result, ABMs have historically occupied an uneasy position within the social sciences, valued for theoretical exploration but often viewed as weakly grounded empirically [11, 13].

The recent rise of large language models (LLMs) has reconfigured this landscape. Because LLMs can generate context-sensitive language, emulate social reasoning, and draw on vast stores of cultural knowledge, they have been proposed as a way to overcome the behavioral limitations of traditional ABMs. This has led to the rapid emergence of generative agent-based models, in which LLMs are embedded directly as agents capable of planning, remembering, communicating, and adapting through natural language [4, 5]. These models promise unprecedented expressive power and have been applied to domains such as online discourse, norm formation, polarization, and collective sense-making.

However, as recent reviews emphasize, this shift also amplifies long-standing methodological challenges rather than resolving them [17]. When LLMs are used as autonomous agents, decision-making is governed by opaque, high-dimensional inference processes that are difficult to interpret, replicate, or systematically validate. Validation practices in the emerging literature often rely on face validity, qualitative plausibility, or weakly coupled outcome comparisons, rather than direct tests of the mechanisms the models purport to capture. As a result, generative ABMs risk occupying an ambiguous methodological space: too complex to be parsimonious explanatory models, yet insufficiently grounded to function as empirical simulations.

From a philosophy-of-science perspective, this tension reflects a mismatch between simulation realism and explanatory control. While LLM-driven agents may produce behavior that appears human-like, such realism does not by itself constitute explanation. For generative models to contribute to cumulative knowledge, their assumptions must be explicit, inspectable, and open to validation relative to the phenomena they aim to explain [12,14]. Without this transparency, it becomes difficult to distinguish genuine emergent dynamics from artifacts of prompting, training data, or stochastic variation.

The framework developed in this study is grounded in this mechanism-centered view of explanation. Rather than treating LLMs as black-box decision-makers, we conceptualize them as theory-to-rule translators that assist researchers in formalizing behavioral assumptions. By externalizing LLM outputs as explicit rules, variables, and decision structures, the approach preserves the core epistemic commitments of agent-based modeling—mechanistic clarity, reproducibility, and validation—while leveraging LLMs' capacity to synthesize theory, generate plausible hypotheses, and accelerate exploratory model development. In doing so, it repositions LLMs from autonomous actors within simulations to methodological instruments embedded in the scientific modeling process itself.

3   XABM Modeling Framework

The proposed XABM framework comprises three tightly coupled modules that together support an end-to-end modeling workflow, spanning conceptualization, implementation, and evaluation. Each module is supported by one or more LLM-empowered AI agents that perform a distinct function. An orchestrating LLM will be in charge of the coordination and communication between the human researcher and the AI agents. This orchestrating LLM is also responsible for verifying the input, calling the appropriate LLM agent and returning the output. Figure 1 provides an overview of the framework architecture and the flow of operation.

The framework is designed to be used by researchers who begin with a clearly articulated research problem, including the phenomenon of interest, the simulation setting, and the basic model structure (e.g., agent types, environments, and

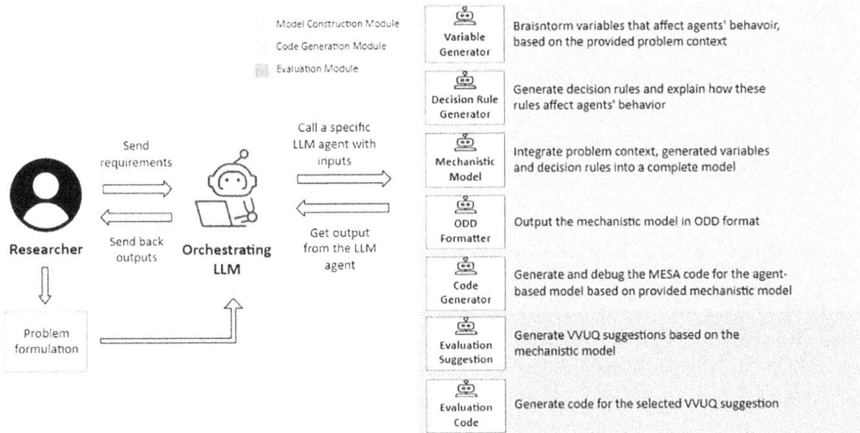

Fig. 1. The overall architecture of the XABM framework.

interaction topology). Where available, researchers may also specify preliminary theoretical expectations or stylized outcomes, which serve to constrain and guide the generative process.

The Model Construction Module supports theory formalization and conceptual model construction. Given the problem context and initial model specification, AI agents in this module identify decision-relevant variables, generate decision rules that affect model agents' behavior, and export the complete conceptual model in a scientifically rigorous format (e.g., ODD format). Researchers can introduce additional variables, revise assumptions or explore alternative mechanisms by communicating with the orchestrating LLM.

The Code Generation Module translates the formalized rule set into an executable simulation prototype, using standardized agent-based modeling frameworks such as MESA. Prior to execution, researchers may specify the types of data to be recorded and the desired output formats. The generated implementation serves as an initial prototype rather than a finalized computational model. Researchers are expected to review, modify and extend the code based on their research needs. This design choice preserves flexibility while ensuring that the correspondence between theoretical assumptions and computational implementation remains explicit.

The Evaluation Module supports model verification, validation, and uncertainty quantification (VVUQ). Based on the conceptual model, it first generates structured recommendations for sensitivity analysis, robustness testing, and uncertainty assessment. It then produces corresponding code implementations for these evaluation procedures.

Together, these three modules form an iterative pipeline that separates generative assistance from decision authority. By externalizing behavioral logic, implementation choices, and validation considerations, the XABM framework enables the use of LLMs in agent-based modeling without sacrificing transparency, reproducibility, or explanatory control. To further mitigate the black-box risks associated with LLMs and to enhance the transparency, traceability, and reproducibility of generated models, all prompts (both user and system), user feedback loops, and model outputs will be systematically logged and documented after each conversation. This process ensures that each stage of model development can be reconstructed, audited, and replicated by independent researchers.

4   Case Study: Shelling Segregation Model

The framework advances a key methodological claim: LLMs can support agent-based modeling without acting as opaque decision-makers by externalizing behavioral logic into explicit, inspectable rules. To evaluate this claim, we apply the framework to a series of case studies, beginning with Schelling's segregation model [18]. As a well-established benchmark with extensively documented assumptions and dynamics, it provides a stringent test of whether the framework can recover known explanations without hard-coded knowledge. The objective of this case study is to assess the epistemic fidelity: whether the XABM framework can (i) identify core decision variables and behavioral rules in this context, (ii) translate them into a transparent and executable simulation, (iii) reproduce Schelling model's characteristic emergent patterns, and (iv) generate meaningful extensions beyond the original formulation. See Appendix for the specific problem formulation.

Table 1. Comparisons between the behavioural rules described in Schelling's paper and the ones generated by the LLM framework

	Schelling (1971)	XABM
Variables	– **Tolerance**: limit of proportion of neighbours that are out-group.	– **Homogeneity preference (HP)**: preference for homogeneous setting, $[0, 1]$.
	– **Racial composition neighbours (RCN)**: proportion of neighbours that have the same race as the target agent.	– **Racial composition neighbours (RCN)**: proportion of same-race neighbours, $[0, 1]$.
		– **Vacant spot availability (VSA)**: proportion of neighbouring vacant sites, $[0, 1]$.
Decision rules	– If $(1 - \text{RCN}) > \text{Tolerance}$, then Move.	– Decision signal $= \alpha \cdot \text{RCN} + (1 - \alpha) \cdot \text{VSA}$.
	– If $(1 - \text{RCN}) < \text{Tolerance}$, then Stay.	– If Decision signal $< \text{HP}$, then Move.
		– If Decision signal $\geq \text{HP}$, then Stay.

Table 1 compares the behavioral rules generated by the framework with those specified in Schelling's original formulation. The framework correctly identifies all key decision variables, including neighborhood composition, tolerance thresholds, and relocation behavior. While the terminology may differ, the underlying logic closely mirrors the original model. In addition, the framework introduces an explicit decision variable capturing the availability of vacant locations. In Schelling's extended formulations, vacancy was treated as an environmental condition rather than an agent-level consideration. Its explicit inclusion here illustrates how the framework can surface latent assumptions and render them inspectable as part of the agents' decision process—an example of how rule externalization can increase conceptual clarity without altering the core mechanism.

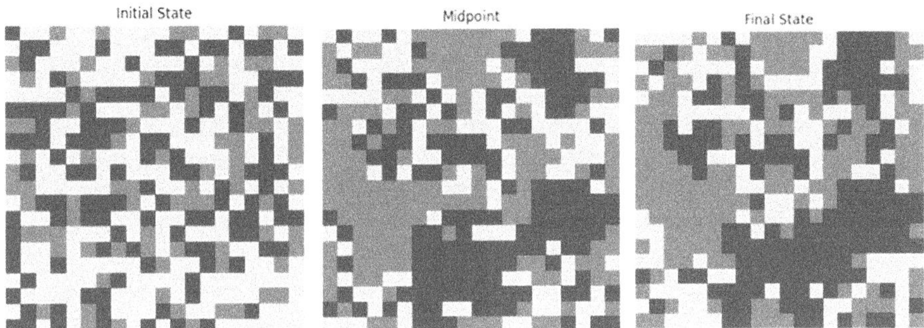

Fig. 2. Two-dimensional grid showing agents' spatial distribution at three simulation stages: (1) initialization (t = 0), (2) midpoint, and (3) final time step (t = 600). Red and blue cells represent the two agent types, while gray cells indicate vacant spaces. The grid has a size of 20 × 20, containing 300 agents (150 of each type) and 100 empty cells. This is consistent with Schelling's original recommendation that approximately 25 to 30 percent of the cells are vacant, so that the agents have enough space to move.

Figure 2 shows the evolution of spatial patterns over time as produced by the framework's code generator. The emergent dynamics closely resemble those reported by Schelling: agents self-organize into increasingly homogeneous clusters, producing clear segregation patterns despite relatively mild individual preferences. One procedural difference is that agents in the generated model relocate to randomly selected vacant cells, whereas in Schelling's original formulation they move to the nearest satisfactory location. Despite this difference, the qualitative dynamics and macro-level outcomes remain consistent, underscoring the robustness of the underlying mechanism.

We further evaluate the model with a quantitative metric: the segregation index, which is defined as the proportion of agents that are surrounded by neighbors of the same opinion. Table 2 summarizes the evaluation recommendations generated by the validator module. Based on this, a sensitivity analysis was conducted on the homogeneity preference parameter. According to Fig. 3, the segregation index peaks when homogeneity preference lies between 0.5 and 0.6 and reaches its minimum at very high (>0.7) or very low (<0.1) values. This pattern is consistent with Schelling-type dynamics: high preference leads to persistent dissatisfaction and frequent relocation, resulting in a disordered system, while low preference yields minimal mobility, so the system preserves its initial heterogeneous configuration.

Table 2. Summary of robustness analysis methods: stochasticity control, parameter sensitivity analysis, and uncertainty quantification.

Stochasticity Control	Parameter Sensitivity Analysis	Uncertainty Quantification
– Monte Carlo simulation – 100 runs with different random seeds – Compute mean and standard deviation – Output metrics: segregation level, neighbourhood composition – Stability if SD < 0.05 – Check convergence via distribution plots	– One-at-a-time (OAT) method – HP: vary from 0.0 to 1.0 (step 0.1) – Vacancy rate: vary from 0.25 to 0.30 (step 0.01) – 50 runs per parameter value – Output metrics: segregation level, moves per agent – Visualize trends with plots	– Target metric: segregation level – Bootstrap resampling – 1000 bootstrap samples – 95% confidence interval – No parametric distribution assumed – Captures stochastic uncertainty

Figure 4 illustrates the stochastic variability of the segregation index across 50 independent simulation runs. The mean segregation index is approximately 0.35, indicating a moderate level of segregation. The variability across runs highlights the stochastic nature of the model. Differences in initial conditions and random interactions produce divergent but bounded outcomes.

In summary, the XABM framework is able to provide scientific insight in the context of a well-established agent-based model by identifying and formalizing the core decision-making processes underlying agent behaviour, translating these processes into an executable simulation, and capturing key system properties, including stochastic variability and robustness across different parameter settings.

However, a key limitation of relying on a well-established model is that its structure, mechanisms, and common extensions may already be embedded in the LLM's training data. This introduces the risk of data leakage, whereby the model may implicitly recognize the Schelling setup and reproduce familiar formulations rather than deriving them through genuine reasoning. Consequently, the generated outputs may reflect memorized knowledge rather than true mechanistic inference. To mitigate this concern, we conduct an additional case study in a less formalized domain within computational modeling: spiral of silence dynamics in online social networks. This setting allows for a more rigorous evaluation of the LLM's generative reasoning and its capacity to produce original, mechanism-driven models.

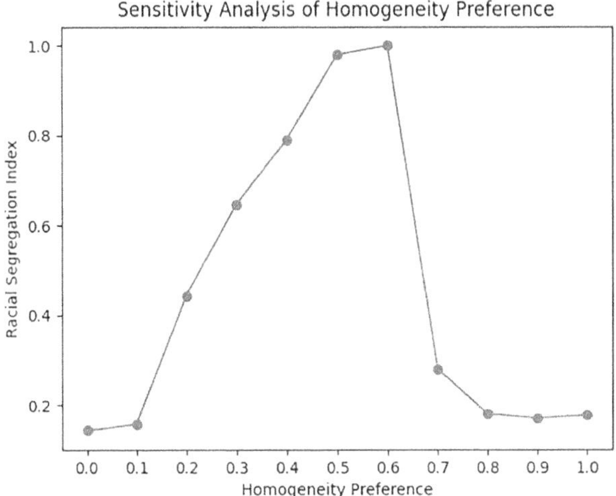

Fig. 3. Sensitivity analysis of homogeneity preference parameter (HP), which was varied from 0 to 1 in increments of 0.1, resulting in 11 experimental conditions. For each condition, the model was simulated over 500 timesteps with a population of 300 agents on a 20×20 lattice grid.

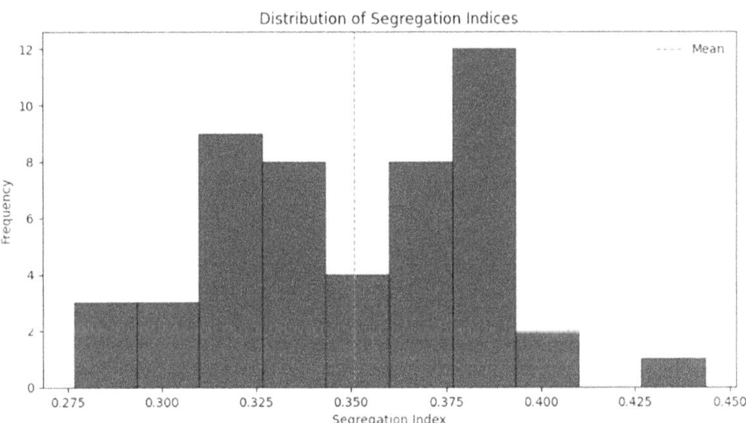

Fig. 4. Distribution of segregation index across 50 independent simulation runs: the model was initialized with 300 agents and executed for 300 timesteps, with individual homogeneity preferences drawn from a uniform distribution.

5 Case Study: Sprial of Silence Dynamics

The spiral of silence theory posits that individuals' willingness to express their opinions is shaped by their perception of prevailing opinion climates and their fear of social isolation [19]. Previous computational studies have shown that local silencing dynamics can cascade to the widespread suppression of minority viewpoints over time [20,21]. In this case study, we examine whether these dynamics persist in a heterogeneous environment where human users and LLM-driven agents coexist. In addition, we investigate whether a minority-boosting intervention can mitigate the convergence toward silence among minority opinion groups.

In this agent-based model, each agent is characterized by two attributes: identity (human or LLM-driven) and a fixed binary opinion. Human agents experience a fear of social isolation, modeled as an individual-specific expression threshold that determines whether they publicly express their opinion based on their perception of the prevailing opinion distribution. In contrast, LLM-driven agents are assumed to have no such constraint and therefore always express their opinions. Agents are situated on a two-dimensional lattice grid with Moore neighborhoods and are randomly initialized according to predefined proportions of agent types and opinions; in this study, the population consists of 80% human agents and 20% LLM-driven agents, with an initial opinion distribution of 60% versus 40%. A system-level media acts as a filtering mechanism that collects all expressed opinions at each timestep and redistributes them to agents, who sample from this pool to form their perception of the opinion environment. Two media conditions are considered: a no-intervention setting, where all messages are published as collected, and a minority-boosting setting, where the visibility of under-represented opinions is selectively amplified. See Appendix for the specific problem formulation. Table 3 and Algorithm 1 show the variables and behaviour rules the XABM framework generates, based on the above problem formulation.

Table 3. Key variables generated by the XABM framework for the spiral of silence case study

Variable Name	Definition	Type
Social connection strength	The strength or closeness of social connections an agent has with its neighbors.	float $[0,1]$
Perceived public opinion	The agent's perception of the majority opinion in the environment based on media signals.	float $[0,1]$
Fear of isolation	The degree to which an agent avoids expressing opinions due to potential social isolation.	float $[0,1]$
Confidence level	The stability of an agent's opinion; higher confidence reduces the likelihood of remaining silent.	float $[0,1]$

Simulation results are presented in Fig. 5. In the absence of a minority-boosting mechanism, the silence ratio among human agents in the minority group (opinion 0) increases to approximately 80%, while the corresponding ratio for the majority group (opinion 1) remains low and continues to decrease due

---

Algorithm 1. Agent Decision Making Process

 1: Compute perceived support as a weighted combination of:
 2:     (i) global opinion alignment from media
 3:     (ii) local opinion alignment from neighbors
 4: Compare perceived support with the agent's fear of isolation threshold
 5: **if** perceived support is lower than fear of isolation **then**
 6:     Decrease the agent's confidence level
 7:     **if** confidence level remains above a minimum threshold **then**
 8:         Agent continues to express its opinion
 9:     **else**
10:         Agent remains silent
11:     **end if**
12: **else**
13:     Increase the agent's confidence level
14:     Agent expresses its opinion
15: **end if**

---

to rising confidence levels. With the introduction of the boosting mechanism, even at low amplification levels, the disparity between the two groups begins to diminish. As the amplification strength increases, this gap eventually disappears, and the majority group converges to a higher yet stable silence ratio. This pattern demonstrates that minority-boosting interventions can effectively counteract the self-reinforcing dynamics of silence by sustaining minority expression, thereby preventing the system from converging to a polarized state in which one opinion becomes systematically suppressed.

In summary, the XABM framework is capable of generating meaningful scientific insights even in less well-established domains with relatively simple study designs. This demonstrates its capacity for generative reasoning and its ability to construct original, mechanism-driven models. At the same time, it shows that externalizing behavioral logic into explicit and inspectable rules preserves both the generative strengths of LLMs and the transparency and replicability of the resulting models.

All framework modules, experimental scripts, and output plots are documented in a private GitHub repository, which will be made publicly available upon project completion. The repository can be shared upon reasonable request.

6   Discussion and Conclusion

This paper proposes XABM: an alternative approach to generative social simulation that directly addresses persistent challenges of transparency, validation, and explainability. Rather than embedding large language models as opaque decision-makers within agents, the framework integrates LLMs as human-guided collaborators that externalize and formalize behavioral rules. This design resolves a central tension in generative modeling: how to harness the expressive capacity of LLMs without sacrificing interpretability, reproducibility, or explanatory control.

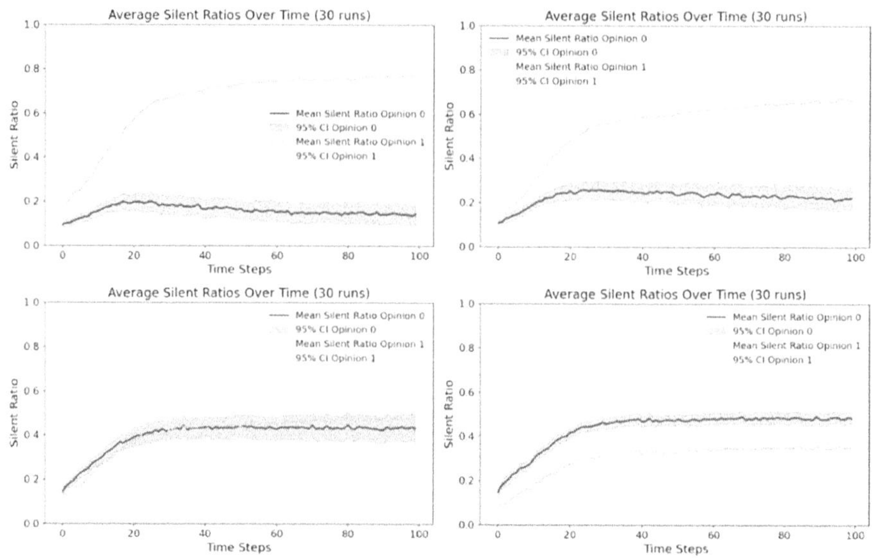

Fig. 5. Silence ratio among human agents across both opinion groups under different media conditions: no boosting (top-left), low boosting (top-right), medium boosting (bottom-left), and high boosting (bottom-right). Opinion 1 represents the majority group, while Opinion 0 represents the minority group. Each simulation was conducted with 100 agents over 100 timesteps, with results averaged across 30 independent runs. Shaded areas indicate 95% confidence intervals.

A key contribution of the framework is its ability to make implicit modeling choices explicit. By surfacing decision-relevant variables that are often treated as background conditions, the approach increases the inspectability of assumptions and clarifies how micro-level rules generate macro-level outcomes. This is particularly important in agent-based modeling, where informal assumptions can easily become embedded in code without being articulated or evaluated.

We evaluate the framework through a series of case studies, including Schelling's segregation model and spiral of silence dynamics in a heterogeneous humanâĂŞLLM environment. The results demonstrate that the XABM framework can identify core decision variables, formalize them into explicit behavioral rules, and generate meaningful insights in different contexts. These findings establish a baseline level of epistemic fidelity and suggest that LLM-assisted rule generation can enhance, rather than undermine, explanatory modeling. Future work will focus on extending the framework's capabilities, such as integrating literature retrieval functions, to further support the construction and validation of agent-based models.

The contribution of this work is not a claim that LLMs can replace theory, nor an attempt to produce more realistic simulations. Instead, it offers a methodological reorientation: LLMs are positioned as tools for theory formalization rather than as opaque autonomous agents whose internal reasoning is inaccessible. In doing so, the framework preserves the core epistemic commitments of agent-based modeling while extending its practical reach. It provides a principled alternative to prevailing LLM-as-agent approaches, which often conflate surface realism with explanation and face persistent validation challenges.

More broadly, this study contributes to ongoing debates about the role of generative AI in scientific modeling. As LLMs are increasingly adopted across the social sciences, the question is not whether they will be used, but how. The framework presented here demonstrates that generative AI can be integrated in ways that enhance transparency and explanatory control rather than erode them. The scientific value of generative agent-based modeling, we argue, depends not on how human-like agents appear, but on how clearly their behavior, and its consequences, can be calibrated, validated, explained, and understood.

Acknowledgments. This work was conducted as part of the first author's master's graduation project. No external funding was received for this research. The authors acknowledge the valuable support and feedback received during the development of this project.

Disclosure of Interests. The authors declare no competing interests.

A   Input Prompt for Behavioural Rule Generation

> **Problem formulation Schelling model**
>
> **Research Topic:** Simulating the formation of racial segregation patterns in a closed urban environment.
> **Context Description:** Assume that people prefer a homogeneous neighbourhood setting.
> **Agent Characteristics:**
>
> - Two types of agents with different racial identities.
> - Approximately equal population sizes for the two types.
>
> **Environment and Interactions:**
>
> - Agents are arranged in a two-dimensional grid.
> - Each agent interacts with its eight neighbours.
> - Agents are initially randomly distributed.
> - The grid contains approximately 25–30% vacant spots.
>
> **Behavioral Decisions:**
>
> - At each timestep, agents decide whether to move to a vacant spot in the grid.

Problem formulation spiral of silence study

Research Topic: Simulating the spiral of silence phenomenon in online social environments.

Context Description: Individuals fear social isolation and are less likely to express their opinions when they perceive themselves to be in the minority. In online environments, perceptions of public opinion are shaped by both local social interactions and exposure to mass or social media content.

Agent Characteristics:

- Two types of agents: human users and LLM-driven agents.
- Human agents may choose to either speak or remain silent at each timestep.
- LLM agents always express their opinion at each timestep.
- Each agent holds a fixed opinion (either 0 or 1) throughout the simulation.

Environment and Interactions:

- Agents are arranged in a two-dimensional grid.
- Each agent interacts with its eight neighbouring agents.
- Agents are randomly distributed across the grid with respect to both type and opinion.

System-Level Process:

- A global media system aggregates opinions expressed by agents who choose to speak.
- At each timestep, the media publishes all collected messages.
- In the subsequent timestep, each agent randomly samples 10–20 messages from the media output.

Behavioral Decisions:

- At each timestep, human agents decide whether to express their opinion or remain silent based on their perception of the opinion climate.

References

1. Epstein, J.M., Axtell, R.: Growing artificial societies: social science from the bottom up. Comput. Math. Appl. **33**(5), 127 (1996)
2. Macy, M.W., Willer, R.: From factors to actors: computational sociology and agent-based modeling. Ann. Rev. Sociol. **28**(1), 143 (2002)
3. Railsback, S.F., Grimm, V.: Agent-based and individual-based modeling: A practical introduction (2019)

4. Park, J. S., O'Brien, J., Cai, C. J., Morris, M. R., Liang, P., Bernstein, M. S.: Generative agents: interactive simulacra of human behavior. In: Proceedings of the 36th Annual ACM Symposium on User Interface Software and Technology, pp. 1–22, ACM (2023)
5. Wang, L., et al.: A survey on large language model based autonomous agents. Front. Comput. Sci. **18**(6) (2024)
6. Gu, C., Luo, L., Zaidi, Z. R., Karunasekera, S.: Large language model driven agents for simulating echo chamber formation. arXiv preprint (2025)
7. Wang, C., Liu, Z., Yang, D., Chen, X.: Decoding echo chambers: LLM-powered simulations revealing polarization in social networks. arXiv preprint (2024)
8. Bender, E. M., Gebru, T., McMillan-Major, T., Shmitchell, S.: On the dangers of stochastic parrots: can language models be too big?. In: Proceedings of the 2021 ACM Conference on Fairness, Accountability, and Transparency, pp. 610–623, ACM (2021)
9. Taillandier, P., Zucker, J.-D., Grignard, A., Gaudou, B., Huynh, N. Q., Drogoul, A.: Integrating LLM in agent-based social simulation: opportunities and challenges. arXiv preprint (2025)
10. Grimm, V., et al.: Pattern-oriented modeling of agent-based complex systems: lessons from ecology. Science **310**(5750), 987–991 (2005)
11. Squazzoni, F., et al.: Computational models that matter during a global pandemic outbreak: a call to action. J. Artif. Soc. Soc. Simul. **23**(2), 10 (2020)
12. Grimm, V., Berger, U., DeAngelis, D.L., Polhill, J.G., Giske, J., Railsback, S.F.: The odd protocol: a review and first update. Ecol. Model. **221**(23), 2760–2768 (2010)
13. Windrum, P., Fagiolo, G., Moneta, A.: Empirical validation of agent-based models: alternatives and prospects. J. Artif. Soc. Soc. Simul. **10**(2), 8 (2007)
14. Hedström, P., Ylikoski, P.: Causal mechanisms in the social sciences. Ann. Rev. Sociol. **36**(1), 49–67 (2010)
15. Epstein, J.M.: Generative social science: studies in agent-based computational modeling. Princeton University Press (2012)
16. Törnberg, P., Uitermark, J.: The social science of complexity. In: Seeing Like a Platform, pp. 21–42, Routledge (2025)
17. Larooij,M., Törnberg, P.: Do large language models solve the problems of agent-based modeling? A critical review of generative social simulations. arXiv preprint (2025)
18. Schelling, T.C.: Dynamic models of segregation. J. Math. Sociol. **1**(2), 143–186 (1971)
19. Noelle-Neumann, E.: The spiral of silence: a theory of public opinion. J. Commun. **24**(2), 43–51 (1974)
20. Vilone, D., Polizzi, E.: Modeling opinion misperception and the emergence of silence in online social systems. PLoS ONE **19**(1), e0296075 (2024)
21. Sohn, D.: Spiral of silence in the social media era: a simulation approach to the interplay between social networks and mass media. Commun. Res. **49**(1), 139–166 (2019)

Residual Reinforcement Learning for Robotic Assembly of Large-Scale Aerospace Components

Xiaoyou Duan[1], Guijun Ma[1(✉)], Weibo Liu[2], Kaiqi Fang[1], and Yuzhe Wang[1]

[1] School of Artificial Intelligence and Automation, Huazhong University of Science and Technology, Wuhan 430074, People's Republic of China
mgj@hust.edu.cn
[2] Department of Computer Science, Brunel University of London, Uxbridge UB8 3PH, Middlesex, U.K.

Abstract. Robotic assembly of large-scale aerospace components demands millimeter-level accuracy under intermittent contacts, while collecting rich interaction data remains costly and risky. This paper presents a demonstration-guided residual reinforcement learning framework for precision assembly. A diffusion-based action-chunking policy trained from limited teleoperated demonstrations generates long-horizon nominal trajectories at a low frequency. A closed-loop residual policy optimized with PPO then adds per-step pose corrections to compensate for distribution shift and contact dynamics during the final mating phase. An action-hold sparse reward is introduced to promote stable mating rather than transient contact. Simulation experiments on KUKA KR210 industrial robot demonstrate that the proposed approach improves assembly success rate and efficiency compared with baselines, validating the effectiveness of combining imitation-based priors with closed-loop residual refinement.

Keywords: Residual reinforcement learning · Aerospace assembly · Imitation learning · Component docking · Sparse reward

1 Introduction

Automation and digitalization are increasingly transforming aerospace manufacturing, where large-scale assembly operations are being migrated from manual, skill-intensive procedures to robotized and sensor-rich work cells to improve productivity, quality consistency, and operator safety [6,15]. Learning-based approaches have been explored in related robotic manufacturing tasks, such as quality modeling, parameter optimization, industrial time-series analytics and data-driven sensor calibration in robotic machining [4,7–11]. However, robotic assembly of aerospace structural segments remains challenging. Heavy, compliant parts must be aligned to millimeter-level tolerances under intermittent contact, and collecting interaction data in production is costly and risky.

M. Paszynski et al. (Eds.): ICCS 2026 Workshops, LNCS 16788, pp. 488–496, 2026.
https://doi.org/10.1007/978-3-032-29915-4_40

A natural approach is to leverage expert demonstrations via imitation learning (IL). Recent IL methods such as diffusion-based policies [3] and action-chunking [16] can capture long-horizon behaviors from limited demonstrations. However, demonstration-only policies often suffer from distribution shift.

Reinforcement learning (RL) offers a complementary paradigm by optimizing a policy through interaction rewards, enabling locally corrective behaviors. However, training RL from scratch in long-horizon sparse-reward assembly is sample-inefficient and often requires extensive reward shaping [2]. Applying IL or RL alone to millimeter-tolerance assembly remains challenging.

These considerations motivate residual policy learning, which combines a base policy with a learned residual for task-specific corrections [5,12]. By restricting exploration around demonstrated behavior, residual learning improves data efficiency while retaining long-horizon competence [1].

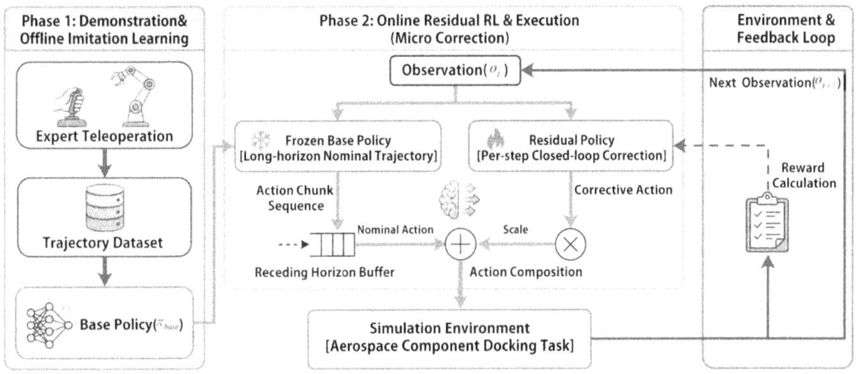

Fig. 1. Overview of the demonstration-guided residual reinforcement learning framework for large-scale aerospace component docking assembly.

In this paper, a demonstration-guided residual RL framework is presented for robotic aerospace component assembly (Fig. 1). A frozen base policy generates nominal trajectories, while a residual policy provides closed-loop corrections. An action-hold sparse reward is designed to facilitate subsequent fastening operations. Simulation experiments demonstrate that residual corrections substantially improve assembly reliability and efficiency.

2   Methodology

In this section, a demonstration-guided residual RL framework is presented for aerospace component assembly, employing a dual-timescale control architecture as illustrated in Fig. 2. A frozen diffusion-based policy π_{base} generates nominal trajectory, while a residual policy π_{res} provides closed-loop corrections.

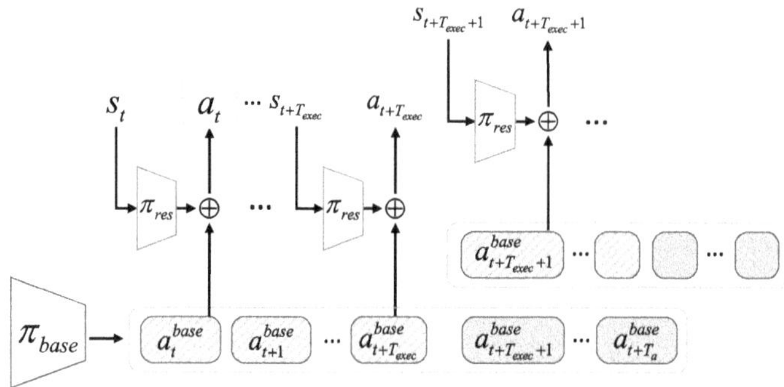

Fig. 2. Dual-timescale residual learning framework for large-scale component assembly.

2.1 Task Formulation

The component assembly task is formulated as a finite-horizon episodic Markov Decision Process (MDP) $\mathcal{M} = (\mathcal{S}, \mathcal{A}, P, R, \gamma)$. At time step t, the robot receives an observation $\mathbf{o}_t$ (derived from state $\mathbf{s}_t$), executes an action $\mathbf{a}_t \in \mathcal{A}$, transitions to $\mathbf{s}_{t+1} \sim P(\cdot|\mathbf{s}_t, \mathbf{a}_t)$, and obtains reward $r_t = R(\mathbf{s}_t, \mathbf{a}_t)$. The goal is to learn a policy π maximizing the expected return:

$$J(\pi) = \mathbb{E}_{\tau \sim \pi} \left[\sum_{t=0}^{T} \gamma^t r_t \right]. \tag{1}$$

The state $\mathbf{s} \in \mathcal{S} \subset \mathbb{R}^{20}$ comprises the end-effector state (position, orientation, linear and angular velocity) and the target component pose. The action $\mathbf{a} \in \mathcal{A} \subset \mathbb{R}^6$ is an end-effector pose increment, converted to joint commands via Damped Least-Squares (DLS) inverse kinematics while the policy focuses on generating task-level motion increments.

2.2 Diffusion Action-Chunking Base Policy

A base policy π_{base} is learned from expert demonstrations using diffusion-based imitation learning. Instead of predicting a single action, π_{base} outputs an action chunk of length T_a:

$$\mathbf{a}_{t:t+T_a-1}^{\text{base}} = \pi_{\text{base}}(\mathbf{o}_{t-T_o+1:t}) = \{\mathbf{a}_t^{\text{base}}, \dots, \mathbf{a}_{t+T_a-1}^{\text{base}}\}, \tag{2}$$

where $\mathbf{o}_{t-T_o+1:t}$ denotes an observation history window. To balance long-horizon planning and responsiveness, a receding-horizon execution is adopted: only the first T_{exec} actions in the chunk are executed before replanning. After imitation learning, π_{base} is frozen and serves as a nominal trajectory generator during residual learning.

2.3   Residual Policy Learning

A residual policy π_{res} provides closed-loop corrections at every control step. The executed action is:

$$\mathbf{a}_t = \mathbf{a}_t^{\mathrm{base}} + \alpha \cdot \pi_{\mathrm{res}}(\mathbf{o}_t, \mathbf{a}_t^{\mathrm{base}}), \tag{3}$$

where $\mathbf{a}_t^{\mathrm{base}}$ is extracted from the chunk sequence and $\alpha \in (0, 1]$ bounds the correction magnitude.

The residual policy is trained using Proximal Policy Optimization (PPO). The PPO loss combines a clipped surrogate objective with value-function regression and entropy regularization:

$$L_{\mathrm{PPO}}(\theta) = -L^{\mathrm{CLIP}}(\theta) + c_v\, \mathbb{E}_t[(V_\theta(\mathbf{o}_t) - \hat{V}_t)^2] - c_e\, \mathbb{E}_t[\mathcal{H}(\pi_\theta)], \tag{4}$$

where L^{CLIP} is the clipped probability ratio objective, V_θ is the value network, $\hat{V}_t$ is the GAE target, and $\mathcal{H}(\cdot)$ denotes entropy.

To discourage the residual policy from deviating excessively from the base prior, the PPO objective (4) is augmented with ℓ_1 and ℓ_2 regularization on the residual action mean:

$$L_{\mathrm{total}} = L_{\mathrm{PPO}} + \lambda_1 \|\mathbf{a}^{\mathrm{res}}\|_1 + \lambda_2 \|\mathbf{a}^{\mathrm{res}}\|_2^2, \tag{5}$$

where λ_1 and λ_2 are regularization coefficients.

To prevent early-stage RL updates from destabilizing the nominal behavior, two complementary mechanisms are adopted. First, residual scaling via α in (3) restricts correction magnitude. Second, near-zero initialization is applied to the residual policy output layer, such that $\mathbf{a}_t^{\mathrm{res}} \approx 0$ at the start of training. These choices encourage the policy to initially follow π_{base} faithfully, then gradually learn local, closed-loop corrections in contact-sensitive phases as training progresses.

2.4   Action-Hold Sparse Reward for Stable Assembly

A sparse success reward with an action-hold requirement is employed to enforce stable assembly rather than transient success. Define a per-step success predicate

$$C_{\mathrm{succ}} = (\|\mathbf{p}_{ee} - \mathbf{p}_{\mathrm{goal}}\| < \epsilon_p) \wedge (\angle(\mathbf{R}_{ee}, \mathbf{R}_{\mathrm{goal}}) < \epsilon_q), \tag{6}$$

where ϵ_p and ϵ_q are position and orientation tolerances. The reward is given only when the success condition holds for at least K_{hold} consecutive steps:

$$r_t = \begin{cases} 1, & \text{if } C_{\mathrm{succ}}^{(k)} \text{ holds for } k \geq K_{\mathrm{hold}} \\ 0, & \text{otherwise.} \end{cases} \tag{7}$$

This design encourages policies that reach and maintain the assembly configuration, naturally supporting subsequent fastening operations.

2.5   Training Procedure

The overall training proceeds in two stages. In Stage 1, the diffusion action-chunking policy π_{base} is trained on expert demonstrations to model the conditional distribution of action sequences given observation histories; after convergence, π_{base} is frozen. In Stage 2, trajectories are rolled out using the composed action (3) with receding-horizon chunk execution for the base action and per-step closed-loop residual corrections. Collected transitions are used to optimize π_{res} with the PPO objective (5) under the sparse action-hold reward (7).

3   Experiments

3.1   Simulation Environment and Control Stack

All experiments are conducted in Isaac Gym physics simulator with KUKA KR210. The task is to assemble a large structural segment to a fixed base component under millimeter-level clearance. The simulator runs at 120 Hz, while the controller outputs actions at 10 Hz. To improve data efficiency, 64 parallel environments are run on an NVIDIA RTX 4090 GPU [14], as shown in Fig. 3.

The policy outputs end-effector pose increments, tracked by a low-level PD controller for joint-space trajectory tracking [13]. For real-world deployment, a compliant controller can be added; in this work, we focus on policy evaluation.

Fig. 3. Parallel simulation of the large-scale component assembly task in Isaac Gym. 64 environments run simultaneously on GPU to accelerate reinforcement learning training.

3.2   Demonstration Collection

Expert demonstrations are collected via teleoperation using a 3Dconnexion SpaceMouse. 80 successful trajectories are recorded, each with an average length of about 100 control steps. The initial assembly configuration is randomized to improve generalization.

3.3   Implementation Details

The base imitation policy is implemented as a diffusion policy with a conditional U-Net denoiser. Given an observation history window, it predicts an action chunk of length $T_a = 32$. A receding-horizon execution is used where only the first $T_{\text{exec}} = 8$ actions of each predicted chunk are executed before replanning.

The residual policy is implemented as a stochastic Gaussian MLP with a separate actor and critic. The actor is a 2-layer MLP with 512 hidden units and SiLU activation, outputting the mean of a diagonal Gaussian distribution; a learnable log-standard-deviation parameter (initialized to -3) controls exploration. The output layer uses small-gain initialization with zero bias. A residual scaling factor $\alpha = 0.1$ bounds the correction magnitude during training.

3.4   Baselines and Ablation

Two baseline methods and one key ablation are considered. DP (Diffusion Policy, IL-only) represents the frozen diffusion action-chunking policy executed without residual corrections. PPO from Scratch is trained from random initialization without demonstrations. As an ablation, Residual-Chunk (C-Resi) applies the residual policy only at chunk boundaries rather than at every control step, reducing closed-loop feedback within each executed chunk.

4   Results and Discussion

4.1   Comparison with Baselines

Table 1 reports the main comparison results. The diffusion policy (IL-only) provides long-horizon motion but degrades in the final phase due to compounding errors during open-loop execution. PPO from scratch achieves the lowest success rate, indicating trial-and-error learning alone is insufficient. Residual learning substantially improves both reliability and efficiency by enabling closed-loop corrections while anchoring exploration around the base policy. The per-step residual achieves 98.4% success rate and the lowest average steps, demonstrating the effectiveness of combining a long-horizon prior with closed-loop refinement.

Table 1. Comparison of success rates for large-scale component assembly.

Method	Success Rate	Avg. Steps
DP (IL-only)	42.1%	153.3
PPO from Scratch	13.6%	214.5
Residual-Chunk (C-Resi)	91.1%	125.7
Residual RL (Ours)	**98.4%**	**93.2**

4.2 Ablation: Per-Step Vs Chunk-Level Residual Corrections

Figure 4 compares per-step residual (Resi) with chunk-level residual (C-Resi), where the residual is updated only at chunk boundaries. Per-step residual demonstrates rapid learning and stable convergence, approaching asymptotic performance within fewer environment steps. In contrast, chunk-level residual eventually reaches above 90% success but requires more training interactions and exhibits higher variance. This behavior is consistent with the task requirements: the policy must react to contact events at the control-step timescale during the final mating phase. This ablation confirms that per-step closed-loop feedback is critical for contact-rich assembly tasks.

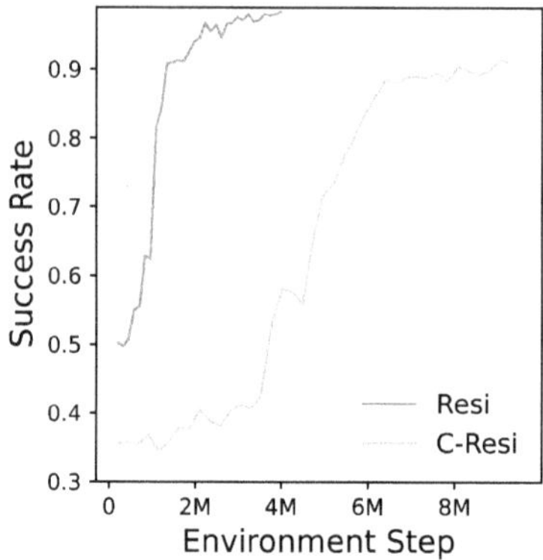

Fig. 4. Evaluation success rate during residual PPO training. Per-step residual (Resi) converges faster and more stably than chunk-level residual (C-Resi), which reaches > 90% success only after more interaction steps and with higher training variance.

5 Conclusion

This paper presented a demonstration-guided residual RL framework for large-scale aerospace component assembly. A frozen diffusion-based base policy generates nominal trajectories, while a PPO-trained residual policy provides closed-loop corrections at each control step. An action-hold sparse reward encourages stable mating. In Isaac Gym experiments with a KUKA KR210 robot, the proposed method achieves 98.4% success rate, substantially outperforming IL-only and RL-from-scratch baselines. The ablation confirms that per-step residual is crucial for contact-rich tasks.

Future work will focus on real-world validation with compliant control and force sensing, and extending the framework to multi-stage assembly sequences.

Acknowledgment. This work was supported in part by the National Natural Science Foundation of China under Grant 62503185; in part by China Post-Doctoral Science

Foundation under Grant 2024M750991; and in part by the Post-Doctoral Project of Hubei Province of China under Grant 2024HBBHCXA010.

Disclosure of Interests. The authors have no competing interests to declare that are relevant to the content of this article

References

1. Ankile, L., Simeonov, A., Shenfeld, I., Torne, M., Agrawal, P.: From imitation to refinement-residual RL for precise assembly. In: 2025 IEEE International Conference on Robotics and Automation (ICRA), pp. 01–08. IEEE (2025)
2. Chen, L., Shen, B., Hong, J.: A multi-task deep reinforcement learning framework based on curriculum learning and policy distillation for quadruped robot motor skill training. Syst. Sci. Control Eng. **13**(1), 2498914 (2025)
3. Chi, C., et al.: Diffusion policy: visuomotor policy learning via action diffusion. Int. J. Robot. Res. **44**(10–11), 1684–1704 (2025)
4. Fang, J., et al.: Learning with noisy labels for industrial time series outlier detection: a transformer-embedded contrastive learning framework. IEEE Transactions on Industrial Informatics (2025). https://doi.org/10.1109/TII.2025.3616850
5. Johannink, T., et al.: Residual reinforcement learning for robot control. In: 2019 International Conference on Robotics and Automation (ICRA), pp. 6023–6029. IEEE (2019)
6. Lettera, G., Natale, C.: An integrated architecture for robotic assembly and inspection of a composite fuselage panel with an industry 5.0 perspective. Machines **12**(2), 103 (2024)
7. Luo, X., Li, Z., Yue, W., Li, S.: A calibrator fuzzy ensemble for highly-accurate robot arm calibration. IEEE Trans. Neural Netw. Learn. Syst. **36**(2), 2169–2181 (2025)
8. Ma, G., Wang, Z., Liu, W., Yang, Z., Huang, D., Ding, H.: Closed-loop parameter optimization for robotic machining using physics-informed machine learning and multiobjective optimization. IEEE Trans. Autom. Sci. Eng. **22**, 22410–22422 (2025)
9. Ma, G., et al.: A novel pairwise domain-adaptation-assisted dual-task learning approach to coprediction of robotic machining efficiency and quality in new parameter spaces. IEEE Trans. Industr. Inf. **21**(7), 5150–5159 (2025)
10. Ma, G., Yang, X., Xu, S., Cheng, C., He, X.: ERMN: an enhanced meta-learning approach for state of health estimation of lithium-ion batteries. J. Energy Storage **72**, 108628 (2023)
11. Qiao, X., Xu, C., Wang, Y., Ma, G.: SDI: a sparse drift identification approach for force/torque sensor calibration in industrial robots. Neurocomputing **620**, 129292 (2025)
12. Silver, T., Allen, K., Tenenbaum, J., Kaelbling, L.: Residual policy learning (2018). arXiv preprint arXiv:1812.06298
13. Song, Y., Zhang, B., Wen, C., Wang, D., Wei, G.: Model predictive control for complicated dynamic systems: a survey. Int. J. Syst. Sci. **56**(9), 2168–2193 (2025)
14. Xue, Y., et al.: Many-objective simulation optimization for camp location problems in humanitarian logistics. Int. J. Netw. Dynam. Intell. **3**(3), 100017 (2024). https://doi.org/10.53941/ijndi.2024.100017

15. Yingke, Y., Dongsheng, L., Yunong, Z., Jie, W., Lei, X., Zhiyong, Y.: Robotic compliant assembly for complex-shaped composite aircraft frame based on gaussian process considering uncertainties. Chin. J. Aeronaut. **37**(10), 471–482 (2024)
16. Zhao, T.Z., Kumar, V., Levine, S., Finn, C.: Learning fine-grained bimanual manipulation with low-cost hardware. In: Proceedings of Robotics: Science and Systems. Daegu, Republic of Korea (2023)

YOLO26-SimAM: An Energy-Based Attention Augmented Detector for Aero-Engine Surface Defect Inspection

Xiao Wang, Linhao Liu, Yidi Song, Xiaotong He, Kai Chen, and Nianyin Zeng$^{(\boxtimes)}$

School of Aerospace Engineering, Xiamen University, Fujian 361005, China
`zny@xmu.edu.cn`

Abstract. Surface defect detection on critical aero-engine components is pivotal for ensuring flight safety. Addressing challenges such as computational resource constraints, minute defect targets, and severe interference from metallic surface noise, this paper proposes a lightweight, high-precision real-time defect detection model. The approach adopts the latest YOLO26-n as the base network, fully leveraging its efficient, Non-Maximum Suppression (NMS)-free architecture optimized for edge devices. Innovatively, the Simple Attention Module (SimAM) parameter-free attention mechanism is integrated at a critical node within the feature fusion network. SimAM simultaneously derives three-dimensional channel and spatial attention weights through energy function theory, enabling adaptive enhancement of defect features and suppression of complex background interference without introducing any learnable parameters. Experiments on a self-built aerospace engine component defect dataset demonstrate that this model achieves a significant improvement in detection accuracy with minimal computational overhead, while maintaining YOLO26's original high inference speed. This provides an excellent solution for deploying reliable and efficient visual inspection systems in resource-constrained industrial environments.

Keywords: Aerospace engine · Defect detection · YOLO26 · Attention mechanism · Lightweight model

1 Introduction

Aero-engine integrity directly determines flight safety and operational reliability [1]. As the core components of modern propulsion systems, aero-engine blades and related structures operate under extremely harsh thermo-mechanical conditions, including high rotational speeds, elevated temperatures, and complex aerodynamic loads. Under such environments, surface degradations such as fatigue

---

X. Wang and L. Liu—Equal contribution.

© The Author(s), under exclusive license to Springer Nature Switzerland AG 2026
M. Paszynski et al. (Eds.): ICCS 2026 Workshops, LNCS 16788, pp. 497–508, 2026.
https://doi.org/10.1007/978-3-032-29915-4_41

cracks, oxidation-induced ablation, and foreign object damage are likely to occur and progressively accumulate [2]. If these defects are not detected and addressed in a timely manner, they may propagate and ultimately lead to severe structural failure. Therefore, achieving accurate and efficient inspection of aero-engine components is essential for ensuring aviation safety and reducing maintenance costs. Conventional inspection approaches, including manual visual examination and traditional non-destructive testing techniques, have been widely applied in industrial practice. Nevertheless, these methods are inherently constrained by strong reliance on human expertise, limited efficiency, and insufficient consistency, which makes them inadequate for large-scale and high-frequency inspection requirements in modern intelligent manufacturing systems [3,4]. With the rapid development of deep learning, data-driven visual inspection methods have demonstrated substantial potential by automatically learning discriminative representations from complex data distributions. In particular, one-stage object detection frameworks represented by the YOLO family have been extensively adopted in industrial scenarios due to their favorable balance between detection accuracy and inference efficiency [5].

Despite these advances, aero-engine defect detection remains a highly challenging task due to several domain-specific factors. In practical inspection environments, imaging conditions are often non-ideal. Uneven illumination, strong metallic reflections, and contamination such as oil stains or dust can significantly degrade visual quality and obscure defect characteristics. In addition, many critical defects, especially early-stage cracks and micro-scale damages, exhibit extremely small spatial scales and very low contrast against complex backgrounds, which greatly increases the difficulty of reliable detection. These challenges are further intensified by the constraints of edge deployment, where models are required to deliver real-time performance under limited computational resources. Consequently, generic detection frameworks often struggle to simultaneously achieve robustness, accuracy, and efficiency in such scenarios.

Existing research has attempted to address these issues by enhancing feature representation capability through sophisticated attention mechanisms [15,25] or by increasing network depth and capacity [6,7]. Although these strategies can improve detection performance, they inevitably introduce additional parameters and computational cost, thereby limiting their practicality in real-time industrial applications. As a result, improving detection accuracy, particularly for small and low-contrast defects, while maintaining high efficiency remains an important and unresolved problem.

Among recent real-time detection frameworks, YOLO26 provides an efficient end-to-end detection paradigm that avoids reliance on traditional post-processing operations such as Non-Maximum Suppression (NMS), thereby reducing latency and simplifying the inference process. The lightweight YOLO26-n variant is especially suitable for resource-constrained industrial inspection tasks due to its compact design and fast inference speed. Based on these considerations, YOLO26-n is selected as the baseline architecture in this study, and targeted improvements are introduced to better accommodate the characteristics of aero-engine defect inspection. Building upon this foundation, three primary contributions are summarized as follows:

1. We propose YOLO26-SimAM, a streamlined detection architecture that incorporates a parameter-free attention mechanism to enhance the discriminability of minute and low-contrast defects while preserving computational efficiency.
2. We analyze the energy-minimization principle of SimAM and investigate its integration strategy within multi-scale feature fusion, enabling effective feature recalibration without introducing additional learnable parameters.
3. Extensive experiments on a real aero-engine defect dataset demonstrate consistent improvements in mean Average Precision (mAP) with negligible inference overhead. The performance gains are particularly evident for small defects, which are further supported by qualitative heatmap visualizations.

2 Related Work

2.1 YOLO Series Object Detectors and Their Applications in Industrial Inspection

The YOLO series represents a fundamental paradigm for real-time object detection, emphasizing a unified end-to-end framework that directly predicts bounding boxes and class probabilities from input images. Early and recent versions, such as YOLOv5 and YOLOv8, adopt optimized backbone designs and effective multi-scale feature fusion strategies, enabling strong performance on large-scale benchmarks such as COCO while maintaining high inference speed. These characteristics make the YOLO family particularly suitable for industrial inspection tasks, where both accuracy and real-time responsiveness are required.

The newly proposed YOLO26 further streamlines the detection pipeline by removing the Distribution Focal Loss module and introducing a native end-to-end Non-Maximum Suppression (NMS)-free strategy, which reduces post-processing overhead and improves deployment efficiency on edge devices [27], as illustrated in Fig. 1. This design simplifies the overall inference process and shortens latency, which is advantageous for time-sensitive inspection scenarios. However, despite these improvements, YOLO26 still faces limitations when dealing with weak signals and small targets embedded in complex industrial backgrounds. Such challenges are particularly prominent in aero-engine defect detection, where subtle defects are easily overwhelmed by noise and irrelevant textures. Therefore, further enhancing feature discrimination while preserving efficiency remains an important research direction.

2.2 Development of Attention Mechanisms in Visual Detection

Attention mechanisms have been widely introduced into visual detection networks to improve feature representation by selectively emphasizing informative regions. SENet [25] first introduced channel-wise attention by modeling inter-channel dependencies, significantly improving feature recalibration capability.

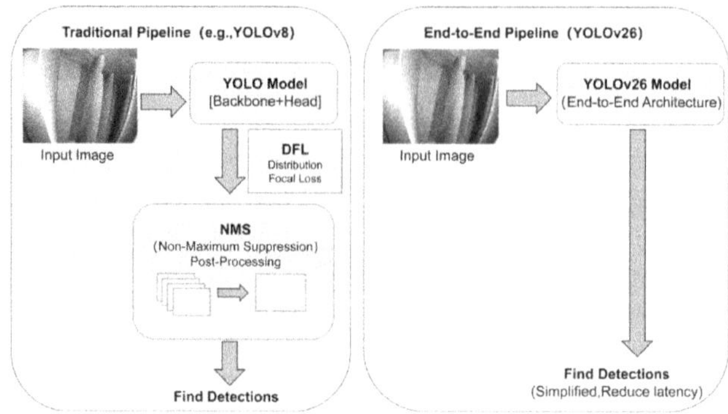

Fig. 1. Comparison of detection pipelines between traditional YOLO models and the end-to-end YOLO26 architecture.

Building upon this idea, CBAM [15] combines channel and spatial attention to further enhance representation power. Coordinate Attention [16] incorporates positional information into channel attention with relatively low computational overhead, improving localization ability in lightweight models.

Despite their effectiveness, most of these methods rely on additional learnable parameters and auxiliary operations, which increase model complexity and may introduce overfitting risks, especially in small-sample industrial datasets. Moreover, the added computational burden can limit their applicability in resource-constrained environments. To address these issues, parameter-free attention mechanisms have been proposed. Among them, the Simple Attention Module (SimAM) [26] adopts an energy-based formulation to assign importance weights across spatial and channel dimensions without introducing extra parameters. This design maintains computational efficiency while still providing fine-grained feature modulation, making it well suited for practical visual inspection tasks where efficiency constraints are strict [13].

2.3   Challenges and Current Status of Aero-Engine Defect Detection

Applying object detection techniques to aero-engine surface inspection remains challenging due to several inherent factors, including the presence of small-scale defects, complex and noisy backgrounds, and significant intra-class variation. Existing approaches attempt to mitigate these issues through strategies such as image preprocessing to enhance defect visibility [11] and the incorporation of semantic prior-aware modules to guide feature learning [3]. While these methods can improve detection performance to some extent, they often introduce additional computational complexity or require carefully designed components, which may limit real-time performance and lightweight deployment in practical aviation maintenance scenarios [12, 14].

In view of the above challenges, achieving an effective balance between detection accuracy and computational efficiency remains a key problem. To this end, this work integrates the efficient YOLO26 framework with the parameter-free SimAM attention mechanism, aiming to enhance feature discrimination for weak and small defects while maintaining the lightweight characteristics of the model. This combination provides a practical solution for improving the precision-efficiency trade-off in real-world aero-engine inspection tasks.

3   Methodology

3.1   Overall Framework of YOLO26-SimAM

The proposed YOLO26-SimAM model is developed upon the YOLO26-n baseline, inheriting its advantages in efficiency, accuracy, and suitability for edge deployment [28]. As illustrated in Fig. 2, the overall framework follows a standard three-stage design, consisting of a Backbone, a Neck, and a Head.

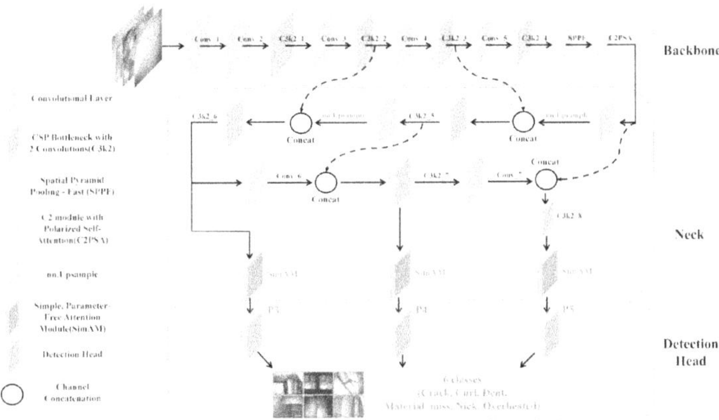

Fig. 2. The overall architecture of the YOLO26-SimAM model.

The Backbone resizes the input to 640×640 and extracts hierarchical features through convolutional layers, C3k2, Conv_3, and CSP Bottleneck modules, which help balance feature reuse and computational cost. An SPPF module is further introduced to aggregate multi-scale contextual information and enlarge the receptive field [10]. This enables the model to capture both local details and higher-level semantics that are important for defect recognition.

The Neck constructs a bidirectional feature pyramid to fuse multi-level features. Through upsampling and skip connections, features from different stages are effectively integrated to produce three feature maps, P3, P4, and P5, corresponding to different resolutions. To enhance feature quality, a SimAM module is inserted before each output. It adaptively reweights feature responses based on energy distribution, strengthening informative regions while suppressing background interference, without introducing additional parameters.

The Head retains the decoupled design of YOLO26 for efficient multi-scale prediction [28]. The P3, P4, and P5 feature maps are processed by independent branches for classification and regression, enabling the model to better handle defects at different scales. This design maintains the efficiency of the baseline while improving feature discrimination.

3.2 SimAM Parameter-Free Attention Mechanism

In aero-engine blade inspection, micro-defects often exhibit weak signals and are easily affected by complex backgrounds such as texture, oil contamination, and illumination variation. Attention mechanisms can improve feature discriminability, but commonly used modules such as SE and CBAM introduce additional parameters and computational cost, which is not ideal for edge deployment.

To address this issue, SimAM is adopted as a parameter-free attention mechanism. It evaluates the importance of each neuron by measuring the energy difference between the neuron and its surrounding context, and assigns corresponding weights. In this way, more informative features are emphasized while less relevant responses are suppressed. Compared with conventional attention modules, SimAM introduces no learnable parameters and can be easily integrated into existing networks.

By providing lightweight feature recalibration, SimAM enhances the representation of subtle defects while preserving the overall efficiency of the model. Given a feature tensor:

$$\mathbf{X} \in \mathbb{R}^{C \times H \times W} \tag{1}$$

the energy e_t^* of one target neuron t on channel c can be efficiently computed via the following closed-form solution:

$$e_t^* = \frac{4(\hat{\sigma}^2 + \lambda)}{(t - \hat{\mu})^2 + 2\hat{\sigma}^2 + 2\lambda} \tag{2}$$

In this equation, $\hat{\mu}$ and $\hat{\sigma}^2$ are the mean and variance of all neurons in that channel respectively, and λ is a hyperparameter for numerical stability. The term $(\hat{\sigma}^2 + \lambda)$ reflects the overall variability of features in that channel, while $(t - \hat{\mu})^2$ measures the deviation of the target neuron relative to the channel's global context. Therefore, a smaller e_t^* indicates a greater difference between the target neuron t and the global context of its channel, warranting a higher attention weight. Finally, the module obtains a three-dimensional attention weight map by calculating the reciprocal of the energy values and normalizing via a Sigmoid function, then enhances the original features through scaling:

$$\tilde{\mathbf{X}} = \text{sigmoid}\left(\frac{1}{\mathbf{E}}\right) \odot \mathbf{X} \tag{3}$$

Based on this design, the assessment of neuron importance relies entirely on the statistical properties of the features themselves, requiring no additional parameters. Consequently, its impact on the model's computational overhead and deployment complexity is minimal.

3.3   Deployment Location of SimAM: Feature Fusion Optimization in the Neck Layer

Effective multi-scale fusion is critical for detecting both large ablation areas and subtle cracks. Analysis shows that after upsampling, downsampling, and concatenation in the Neck, feature maps combine semantic and spatial information from different levels. This stage is optimal for introducing attention mechanisms for feature selection and enhancement.

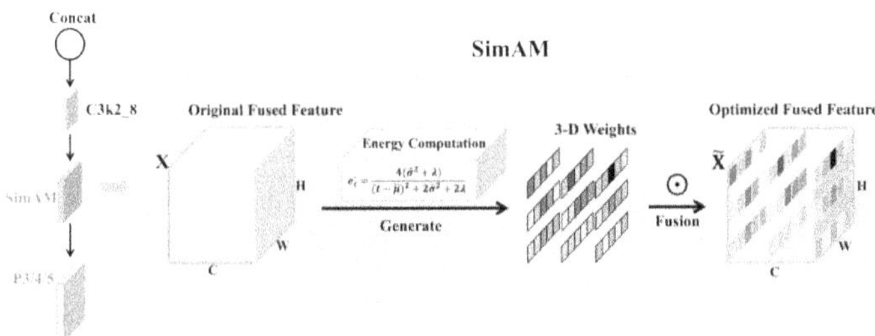

Fig. 3. Detailed workflow of the SimAM module within a fusion node.

We embed SimAM after each feature fusion node in the Neck. During feature pyramid construction, features from shallow or deep layers are aligned, concatenated, and fused. SimAM then performs feature recalibration, as detailed in Fig. 3. It evaluates the importance of each element, generating implicit attention weights that are multiplied element-wise with fused features. This adaptively enhances discriminative responses related to defect edges and texture mutations while suppressing noise from metal glare, uneven illumination, and slow-varying backgrounds. This continuous purification ensures P3, P4, and P5 maps passed to the detection head are optimized and highly discriminative, forming a solid foundation for high-precision multi-scale defect detection in complex industrial scenes.

4   Experiments and Results Analysis

4.1   Experimental Setup

We use a self-collected aero-engine defect dataset consisting of high-resolution inspection images of turbine blades, stator blades, and disks. The dataset covers a variety of typical surface defects, including cracks, ablation, dents, coating spallation, and corrosion, which exhibit diverse scales and visual characteristics. To ensure a reliable evaluation, the dataset is randomly divided into training, validation, and testing sets with a ratio of 7:2:1. Performance is evaluated using standard detection metrics, including mean Average Precision (mAP), Precision, and Recall, together with efficiency-related indicators such as parameter count,

GFLOPs, and Frames Per Second (FPS), providing a comprehensive assessment of both accuracy and computational cost.

All experiments are implemented using PyTorch 1.12 and the Ultralytics framework. The input resolution is set to 640×640, and the model is initialized with pretrained weights from YOLO26-n to accelerate convergence. The optimizer is stochastic gradient descent (SGD) with a momentum of 0.937 and a weight decay of 0.0005. The initial learning rate is set to 0.01 and scheduled using cosine annealing to ensure stable training. The model is trained for 300 epochs with a batch size of 32. Data augmentation strategies include Mosaic augmentation, brightness and contrast adjustment, and simulated oil contamination noise, which help improve robustness under realistic industrial conditions. All experiments are conducted on an NVIDIA RTX 4090 GPU.

4.2   Comparative Analysis with the Baseline Model

Table 1 presents a quantitative comparison between YOLO26-SimAM and the baseline YOLO26-n. The proposed model achieves a clear improvement in detection performance, with mAP50 increasing from 0.701 to 0.792 and mAP[50:95] improving from 0.439 to 0.484. Meanwhile, Recall shows a slight increase from 0.624 to 0.630, indicating a stable ability to capture positive samples. Precision improves more significantly, rising from 0.706 to 0.81, which suggests that the proposed method effectively reduces false positives and enhances prediction reliability.

Table 1. Performance comparison between YOLO26-SimAM and the baseline model YOLO26-n

Model	mAP_{50}	$\text{mAP}_{50:95}$	Recall	Precision	Params(MB)	GFLOPs	FPS
Baseline	0.701	0.439	0.624	0.706	2.5061	3.0392	170.79
Ours	**0.792**	**0.484**	**0.63**	**0.81**	2.5061	3.0392	158.07

In terms of efficiency, the number of parameters and GFLOPs remain unchanged at 2.506 MB and 3.0392 GFLOPs, respectively, demonstrating that the integration of SimAM does not increase model complexity. The inference speed shows a slight decrease, with FPS dropping from 170.79 to 158.07. This reduction is mainly attributed to the additional element-wise operations introduced by the SimAM module during feature recalibration in the Neck stage. Although SimAM does not involve learnable parameters, the computation of energy-based weights and subsequent feature scaling still introduce minor overhead. Overall, the results indicate that the proposed method achieves a favorable trade-off, delivering noticeable accuracy gains with only a marginal impact on inference speed.

4.3   Comparative Analysis with Mainstream Lightweight Detection Models

A comparative analysis was conducted between YOLO26-SimAM and current mainstream lightweight detectors, including YOLOv8-n, YOLOv10-n and RT-DETR-L. Results in Table 2 demonstrate that YOLO26-SimAM achieves superior accuracy with the highest mAP50 of 0.792 and a competitive mAP50:95 of 0.484, outperforming alternative models such as Gold-YOLO and TOOD while surpassing DETR by a significant margin.

Table 2. Comparison of different detectors on the aero-engine defect test set

Methods	mAP$_{50}$	mAP$_{50:95}$	Recall	Precision	Params(MB)	GFLOPs	FPS
TOOD [18]	0.729	0.485	0.701	0.695	32.03	172.1	31.2
Retinanet [19]	0.577	0.256	0.491	0.411	21.41	163.84	13.8
YOLOv6 [29]	0.643	0.365	0.567	0.724	4.23	11.80	340
Faster-RCNN [22]	0.685	0.301	0.689	0.429	41.75	182.3	38.6
DynamicRCNN [20]	0.698	0.349	0.615	0.406	41.75	182.3	36.5
DETR [21]	0.737	0.464	0.734	0.672	41.56	81.63	49.0
YOLOv5 [30]	0.761	0.386	0.671	0.847	2.5	7.1	444
YOLOF [23]	0.765	0.431	0.650	0.656	42.46	83.36	59.9
Gold-YOLO [24]	0.789	0.448	0.699	0.847	5.98	10.2	444.6
Ours	**0.792**	**0.484**	**0.63**	**0.81**	**2.5061**	**3.0392**	**158.07**

The model maintains high efficiency with minimal parameter usage and computational cost, requiring only 2.506 MB parameters and 3.039 GFLOPs. This represents a substantial reduction compared to models such as TOOD and Faster-RCNN. While inference speed is lower than some highly optimized variants, the achieved frame rate remains fully adequate for industrial real-time inspection. YOLO26-SimAM thus offers an effective balance of accuracy, compactness and efficiency suitable for deployment in resource-limited aero-engine inspection environments.

4.4   Visualization Results and Analysis

Figure 4 shows qualitative comparisons between YOLO26-n and YOLO26-SimAM. The proposed model demonstrates stronger detection confidence and improved localization, particularly for small defects. In challenging scenarios with low contrast or background interference, YOLO26-SimAM produces more concentrated and accurate bounding boxes, while reducing missed detections and false positives. In contrast, the baseline YOLO26-n occasionally exhibits weaker responses to subtle defect regions. These observations are consistent with the quantitative results and further illustrate the effectiveness of the proposed attention mechanism in enhancing feature discrimination.

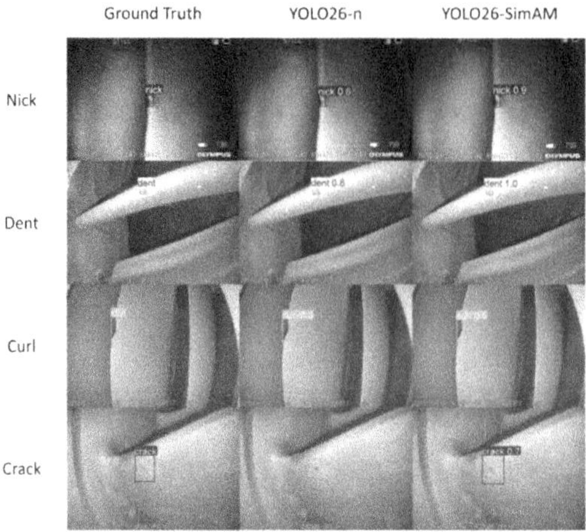

Fig. 4. Qualitative comparison of detection results for YOLO26-n and YOLO26-SimAM.

5   Conclusion

We present YOLO26-SimAM for aero-engine surface defect inspection. By integrating parameter-free SimAM attention into YOLO26-n's feature fusion network, we balance detection accuracy and computational efficiency. Experiments on the aero-engine defect dataset show significant mAP improvements over the baseline with no added parameters or computation. The model outperforms other lightweight detectors, offering high accuracy, compact size, and low complexity. Visual results confirm enhanced detection of small, low-contrast defects. The framework provides a practical solution for reliable real-time visual inspection in resource-limited industrial settings.

Limitations include a slight inference speed reduction versus the baseline, though throughput remains sufficient for real-time use. In addition, future research will evaluate the generalization capability of the proposed model on other public industrial defect datasets such as NEU-DET or DAGM to further validate its robustness.

The proposed method demonstrates strong potential for practical deployment in industrial inspection systems where both efficiency and robustness are critical. Future work will further explore adaptive attention placement strategies and cross-dataset generalization to enhance model robustness.

Acknowledgements. This work was supported in part by the XMU Training Program of Innovation for Undergraduates under Grant APSR-202517, the Natural Science Foundation of China under Grant T2541027, the Natural Science Foundation for Distinguished Young Scholars of the Fujian Province under Grant 2023J06010, and the Independent Innovation Foundation of AECC under Grant ZZCX-2023-005.

Disclosure of Interests. The authors declare that they have no known competing financial interests or personal relationships that could have appeared to influence the work reported in this paper.

References

1. Xiao, Y., Shao, H., Feng, M., Han, T., Wan, J., Liu, B.: Towards trustworthy rotating machinery fault diagnosis via attention uncertainty in transformer. J. Manuf. Syst. **70**, 186–201 (2023)
2. Yang, P., Yue, W., Li, J., Bin, G., Li, C.: Review of damage mechanism and protection of aero-engine blades based on impact properties. Eng. Fail. Anal. **140**, 106570 (2022)
3. Wu, P., Li, H., Luo, X., Hu, L., Yang, R., Zeng, N.: From data analysis to intelligent maintenance: a survey on visual defect detection in aero-engines. Meas. Sci. Technol. **36**, 062001 (2025)
4. Abdulrahman, Y., Eltoum, M.A.M., Ayyad, A., Moyo, B., Zweiri, Y.: Aero-engine blade defect detection: a systematic review of deep learning models. IEEE Access **11**, 53048–53061 (2023)
5. Hui, Y., Wang, J., Li, B.: WSA-YOLO: weak-supervised and adaptive object detection in the low-light environment for YOLOV7. IEEE Trans. Instrum. Meas. **73**, 1–12 (2024)
6. Wang, Y., Wang, H., Xin, Z.: Efficient detection model of steel strip surface defects based on YOLO-V7. IEEE Access **10**, 133936–133944 (2022)
7. Shang, H., Wu, J., Sun, C., Liu, J., Chen, X., Yan, R.: Global prior transformer network in intelligent borescope inspection for surface damage detection of aeroengine blade. IEEE Trans. Industr. Inf. **19**, 8865–8877 (2023)
8. Li, X., Liu, M., Ling, Q.: Pixel-wise gamma correction mapping for low-light image enhancement. IEEE Trans. Circuits Syst. Video Technol. **34**, 681–694 (2024)
9. Zhang, Y., Liu, X., Wang, D.: Semantic prior-aware network for pixel-level defect detection in complex industrial surfaces. IEEE Trans. Industr. Inf. **18**, 6123–6132 (2022)
10. Jin, H., Ouyang, A., Wang, Q., Yang, D., Gan, X., Yue, X.: Helipad target detection method for low-altitude rotor UAVs based on improved YOLOv11 network model. J. Wirel. Commun. Netw. **2025**, 72 (2025)
11. Chen, H., Wu, P., Wen, W., Zeng, N.: DLA-Net: a dynamically learnable attention network for intelligent surface visual inspection of aero-engine blades. IEEE Trans. Instrum. Meas. **74**, 1–14 (2025)
12. Chen, T., Zhang, C., Jing, W., Foo, E.Y.S., Lai, X., Zeng, N.: State of health estimation for lithium-ion batteries using separable LogSparse self-attention transformer. IEEE Trans. Instrum. Meas. **74**, 1–13 (2025)
13. Tan, W., et al.: SEDA-EEG: a semi-supervised emotion recognition network with domain adaptation for cross-subject EEG analysis. Neurocomputing **622**, 129315 (2025)
14. Yu, K., et al.: M-GENE: multiview genes expression network ensemble for bone metabolism-related gene classification. Neurocomputing **622**, 129318 (2025)
15. Woo, S., Park, J., Lee, J., Kweon, I.S.: CBAM: convolutional block attention module. In: Ferrari, V., Hebert, M., Sminchisescu, C., Weiss, Y. (eds.) ECCV 2018. LNCS, vol. 11211, pp. 3–19. Springer, Cham (2018)

16. Hou, Q., Zhou, D., Feng, J.: Coordinate attention for efficient mobile network design. In: Proceedings of the IEEE/CVF Conference on Computer Vision and Pattern Recognition (CVPR), pp. 13713–13722 (2021)
17. Liu, Z., et al.: Swin transformer: hierarchical vision transformer using shifted windows. In: Proceedings of the IEEE/CVF International Conference on Computer Vision (ICCV), pp. 10012–10022 (2021)
18. Feng, C., Zhong, Y., Huang, W., Li, Y., Chen, Z., Li, X.: TOOD: task-aligned one-stage object detection. In Proceedings of the IEEE/CVF International Conference on Computer Vision (ICCV), pp. 3490–3499 (2021)
19. Lin, T.Y., Goyal, P., Girshick, R., He, K., Dollár, P.: Focal loss for dense object detection. In: Proceedings of the IEEE/CVF International Conference on Computer Vision (ICCV), pp. 2980–2988 (2017)
20. Zhang, H., Wang, Y., Dayoub, F., Sünderhauf, N.: Dynamic R-CNN: towards high quality object detection via dynamic training. In: Vedaldi, A., Bischof, H., Brox, T., Frahm, J.-M. (eds.) ECCV 2020. LNCS, vol. 12346, pp. 260–275. Springer, Cham (2020)
21. Carion, N., Massa, F., Synnaeve, G., Usunier, N., Kirillov, A., Zagoruyko, S.: End-to-end object detection with transformers. In: Vedaldi, A., Bischof, H., Brox, T., Frahm, J.-M. (eds.) ECCV 2020. LNCS, vol. 12346, pp. 213–229. Springer, Cham (2020)
22. Ren, S., He, K., Girshick, R., Sun, J.: Faster R-CNN: towards real-time object detection with region proposal networks. IEEE Trans. Pattern Anal. Mach. Intell. **39**, 1137–1149 (2017)
23. Chen, Q., Wang, Y., Yang, T., Zhang, X.: You only look one-level feature. In: Proceedings of the IEEE/CVF Conference on Computer Vision and Pattern Recognition (CVPR), pp. 13039–13048 (2021)
24. Wang, L., Xu, Y., Wang, Y., Yang, S., Zhang, Z., Xie, W.: Gold-YOLO: efficient object detector via gather-and-distribute mechanism. In: Advances in Neural Information Processing Systems (NeurIPS), pp. 51094–51112 (2023)
25. Hu, J., Shen, L., Sun, G.: Squeeze-and-excitation networks. In: Proceedings of the IEEE Conference on Computer Vision and Pattern Recognition (CVPR), pp. 7132–7141 (2018)
26. Yang, L., Zhang, R.Y., Li, L., Xie, X.: SimAM: a simple, parameter-free attention module for convolutional neural networks. In: Proceedings of the 38th International Conference on Machine Learning (ICML), pp. 11863–11874 (2021)
27. Wang, C.Y.: End-to-End Object Detection without NMS (2025). arXiv:2601.12882
28. Sapkota, R., Cheppally, R.H., Sharda, A., Karkee, M.: YOLO26: Key architectural enhancements and performance benchmarking for real-time object detection. arXiv:2509.25164 (2025)
29. Li, C., Li, L., Jiang, H., et al.: YOLOv6: A single-stage object detection framework for industrial applications. arXiv:2209.02976 (2022)
30. Ultralytics: YOLOv5. https://github.com/ultralytics/yolov5. Accessed 30 Mar 2026

Trustworthy Data Foundations for AI-Driven Analytics in Distributed IoT: A Validation-First Methodology

Maziar Ghorbani[1]([✉]) [iD], Diana Suleimenova[1] [iD], Laura Harbach[1] [iD],
Pramit Mazumdar[2], Niruban Paramanathan[3], Ricardo Severino[4] [iD],
Özer Aydemir[5], and Derek Groen[1,6] [iD]

[1] Department of Computer Science, Wilfred Brown Building, Brunel University of
London, Kingston Lane, Uxbridge, Middlesex UB8 3PH, UK
`maziar.ghorbani@brunel.ac.uk`
[2] GetFudo Ltd., Covent Garden, London, UK
[3] Dealdio Ltd., Braintree Road, Ruislip, UK
[4] Institute for Systems and Computer Engineering of Porto, Porto, Portugal
[5] IOTIQ GmbH, Emilienstrasse 13, 04107 Leipzig, Germany
[6] Faculty of Science (Informatics Institute), University of Amsterdam, Science Park,
904 1098 XH Amsterdam, The Netherlands

Abstract. Reliable large language model (LLM)-assisted operations in distributed Internet of Things (IoT) systems depend fundamentally on the quality, structure, and provenance of telemetry available at inference time. In this paper, we present a validation-first methodology for AI-driven analytics that enforces end-to-end verification of the data pipeline before permitting LLM inference and retrieval-augmented generation. The approach formalises three pre-inference quality gates addressing infrastructure and schema conformance, data integrity across freshness and continuity constraints, and context readiness through deterministic, ID-bound prompt construction. This methodology is implemented in HOMEPOT (Homogeneous Cyber Management of End-Points and Operational Technology), a unified endpoint and IoT management platform supporting heterogeneous devices and MQTT-connected sensors. We conducted a 10-day Technology Readiness Level (TRL-4) pilot involving 10 devices, processing over 140,000 telemetry samples and health checks alongside continuous state-transition logging. Integrity indicators demonstrate 100% completeness for key telemetry fields and sub-minute maximum inter-arrival gaps, confirming strong temporal continuity. These results establish measurable readiness conditions under which AI inference is treated as a conditional capability rather than an assumed default, providing a reproducible blueprint for dependable AI integration in distributed IoT environments rapidly transitioning toward pilot-scale deployment.

Keywords: Validation-first methodology · Distributed IoT systems ·
Data quality assurance · Retrieval-augmented generation · Trustworthy
AI · Telemetry integrity

© The Author(s), under exclusive license to Springer Nature Switzerland AG 2026
M. Paszynski et al. (Eds.): ICCS 2026 Workshops, LNCS 16788, pp. 509–524, 2026.
https://doi.org/10.1007/978-3-032-29915-4_42

1   Introduction

Generative AI (GenAI) and large language models (LLMs) are increasingly being adopted as operational copilots for monitoring, diagnosing, and optimising distributed Internet of Things (IoT) and edge-device fleets. In practice, these assistants are frequently asked to produce *actionable* guidance under uncertainty (e.g.,"why are devices flapping?", "which sites are at risk?", "what should we fix first?"). However, the dependability of LLM-mediated operations is limited by the quality, freshness, and structure of the underlying data context. In this work, we functionally define "trustworthiness" not as absolute cognitive truth from the LLM, but as *deterministic data readiness*, providing strict bounds on input uncertainty before any reasoning occurs. When telemetry is incomplete, delayed, inconsistent across sources, or assembled into prompts without explicit provenance, LLMs tend to produce confident but incorrect narratives. This represents a significant failure mode in operational settings where the cost of wrong actions is high [1,2].

Despite extensive research on anomaly detection, observability, and AI for operations [3,4], many industrial IoT deployments still exhibit production anti-patterns in which data pipelines are deployed before systematic validation, leading to downstream discovery of missing fields, schema mismatches, timestamp drift, or noisy duplication [5]. These issues are not merely engineering inconveniences; they directly affect downstream analytics and AI layers by corrupting the evidence presented inside the model's context window. As a result, standard LLM grounding strategies, such as retrieval-augmented generation (RAG), can inadvertently amplify these flaws. For example, retrievals can return stale or irrelevant "memories", whilst missing or malformed real-time signals force the model to fill gaps with plausible-sounding guesses [1,6]. This poses a potentially significant issue as, with the growing integration of GenAI, such platforms could eventually generate code, security policies, predictive models, and complex behaviours from large streams of validated data.

This paper argues that reliable AI-driven analytics in distributed IoT systems requires a *validation-first* approach: the pipeline must be verified before the inference is trusted. Here, we propose and implement a methodology that treats data quality and context readiness as first-class, testable artefacts. We apply this approach within the HOMEPOT project, a unified IoT/endpoint management platform currently validated at TRL-4, with the present pilot study designed to evaluate readiness for progression towards TRL-5.

HOMEPOT (Eureka - ITEA 4 Project) was developed in collaboration with industry partners as part of a staged, requirements-led programme. Initial work focused on consolidating operational requirements, specifications, and state-of-the-art constraints, followed by a second phase that focused on data analytics and AI integration. As a result, the system features studied in this paper are not ad hoc prototype additions; they are deliberately designed to satisfy externally driven requirements for operational visibility, traceability, and explainable decision support.

The primary contributions of this work are threefold. First, we introduce a validation-first protocol that formalises pre-inference enforcement through three sequential quality gates. These gates operate as a pipeline: establishing the connection infrastructure and metric contracts (Gate A), validating deterministic data continuity and integrity thresholds (Gate B), and finally verifying structural context readiness and ID-bounding before the LLM consumes the prompt (Gate C). Second, we present the HOMEPOT platform as an architectural instantiation of this protocol, integrating time-series telemetry, persistent alert identifiers, and a grounded cognitive engine. Third, we provide a reproducible TRL-4 case study demonstrating quantifiable integrity indicators that define measurable readiness conditions under which AI inference is permitted.

The remainder of this paper is structured as follows. Section 2 reviews background and related work on IoT management, data-centric quality practices, and trustworthy GenAI grounding. Section 3 describes HOMEPOT's data analytics architecture and the data foundations designed for AI consumption. Section 4 presents the validation-first protocol and its quality gates. Section 5 details the grounded cognitive engine that converts validated data into diagnostic explanations. Section 6 reports the case-study setup and evaluation results. Section 7 concludes with limitations and future work.

2   Background and Related Work

To establish the theoretical basis for a validation-first methodology, HOMEPOT is positioned at the intersection of AIOps, data-centric quality frameworks, and grounding mechanisms for generative AI. This approach ensures that AI-driven diagnostics operate only on verified evidence to mitigate operational risks.

Traditional operational monitoring relies on statistical and machine learning techniques to detect abnormalities [3]. Although log- and metric-driven techniques can identify abnormal behaviour and support diagnosis [7], their effectiveness depends fundamentally on upstream data integrity. Issues such as missing fields, duplicated events, inconsistent identifiers, or timestamp drift distort signals and degrade downstream analytics [4].

Recent shifts toward data-centric AI argue that trustworthiness extends beyond accuracy to include completeness, consistency, and timeliness [2]. Improvements in data collection and validation often outweigh incremental model refinements [8]. In IoT contexts, this motivates explicit validation of telemetry pipelines, including freshness, continuity, and range enforcement before higher-level analytics or AI reasoning are applied [5].

The integration of LLMs introduces additional risks, as surveys of hallucination and factuality show that models can generate fluent but incorrect outputs when evidence is incomplete or weakly structured [6,9], and scaling alone does not guarantee truthful behaviour [10]. In operational settings, such confident misstatements can lead to inappropriate or unsafe interventions, making an evidence-grounded explanation essential.

Retrieval-augmented generation seeks to improve reliability by conditioning outputs on retrieved evidence [11], often implemented via dense retrieval over historical incidents or vector stores [12]. However, retrieval cannot compensate for stale or malformed real-time context, since retrieval-based grounding remains bounded by the quality and structure of the underlying corpus [6,10].

Although substantial advances exist across anomaly detection, data quality, and retrieval-based grounding, many systems lack an explicit interface between telemetry validation and LLM context construction. This enables a deploy-first pattern in which AI operates over partially validated evidence [4]. Such patterns conflict with emerging AI risk management guidance that emphasises governance, traceability, and verifiable evidence in AI-enabled systems [13].

Taken together, the absence of an explicit interface between upstream telemetry validation and downstream LLM context construction enables deploy-first configurations in which inference may proceed over partially validated evidence. This architectural gap motivates the validation-first framework introduced in the next section.

3   System Architecture and Data Foundations

During ordinary operation, a diverse set of endpoints (such as managed hardware, web clients, and IoT sensors) and software bridge agents stream telemetry and lifecycle events to a centralised FastAPI backend. As illustrated in Fig. 1, the HOMEPOT architecture follows a layered pipeline from distributed devices and dashboards through API and service layers to the data layer (PostgreSQL, TimescaleDB, ChromaDB) and the grounded cognitive engine. To preserve architectural integrity and data sovereignty within this layered design, the AI subsystem operates as a native, local-first module, forming a clearly bounded inference layer built upon auditable data foundations.

3.1   Operational Data Model as LLM-Ready Context Sources

To facilitate both high-frequency monitoring and forensic auditing, the platform partitions operational evidence into distinct schema-enforced tables. The health and time-series telemetry layer utilises TimescaleDB hypertables to accelerate range queries, capturing devices' health status and response latency alongside extensible payloads. Parallel to these metrics, the system documents lifecycle transitions and job outcomes within dedicated history tables to provide a granular trace of device behaviour. Governance and provenance are maintained through a multi-layered logging strategy where middleware-driven request logs intersect with categorised error metadata and explicit audit trails. Finally, the platform generates persistent alert records with unique identifiers that serve as stable, immutable references for subsequent AI-driven explanations and operator intervention.

3.2   Time-Series Optimisation and Queryability

Ensuring the low-latency retrieval of operational evidence necessitates the deployment of specialised TimescaleDB management utilities. The system automatically partitions health-check data into weekly chunks and implements

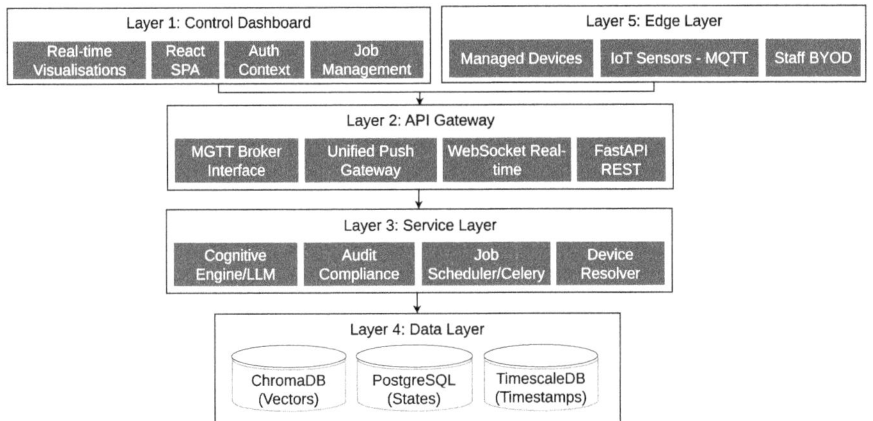

Fig. 1. Layered architecture of the HOMEPOT platform, illustrating the end-to-end pipeline from heterogeneous IoT devices and dashboards through the API and service layers to the data layer (PostgreSQL, TimescaleDB, ChromaDB) and the cognitive engine. The design emphasises auditable data flow and local-first AI integration.

aggressive compression and retention policies to maintain performance over long durations. For complex analytics, the system uses continuous aggregates to pre-compute hourly and daily summaries by decoupling real-time ingestion metrics from the intensive computational requirements of site-level rollups and device performance summaries.

3.3 Noise Control: Smart Data Filtering

Operational telemetry can overwhelm storage and hinder trustworthiness if it contains redundant snapshots or noisy jitter that dominates analytics. The system, therefore, implements *smart filtering* for device metrics. The architecture guarantees baseline snapshot is stored every 5 min for continuity, but triggers immediate storage only upon significant metric fluctuations or system restarts. This approach preserves high-resolution traces during anomalous events while maintaining a predictable baseline for routine monitoring.

3.4 LLM Context Interfaces

A core tenet of the architecture is the treatment of database tables as deterministic context sources governed by a stable formatting contract. Rather than passing free-form logs to the LLM, the AI query endpoint assembles a structured context document that prioritises real-time system state and active alerts over historical artefacts. This deterministic assembly enforces explicit identifiers, bounded sections, and consistent ordering, ensuring that the LLM grounds its explanations in referenceable evidence rather than unstructured telemetry. By constraining context construction at the source, the system reduces the risk of fabricated identifiers or unsupported system states.

4   Validation-First Methodology (Protocol)

The validation-first methodology is built on a single architectural principle: AI inference is treated as a *downstream consumer* of operational data and must therefore be gated on the readiness of the upstream pipeline. This principle is operationalised as a tiered verification envelope consisting of three sequential quality gates, as illustrated in Fig. 2, which can be executed repeatedly during development and before production or pilot rollouts. Failure to satisfy any individual gate triggers a constrained non-actionable mode that precludes unrestricted AI execution, preventing the generation of narratives based on unstable or incomplete evidence.

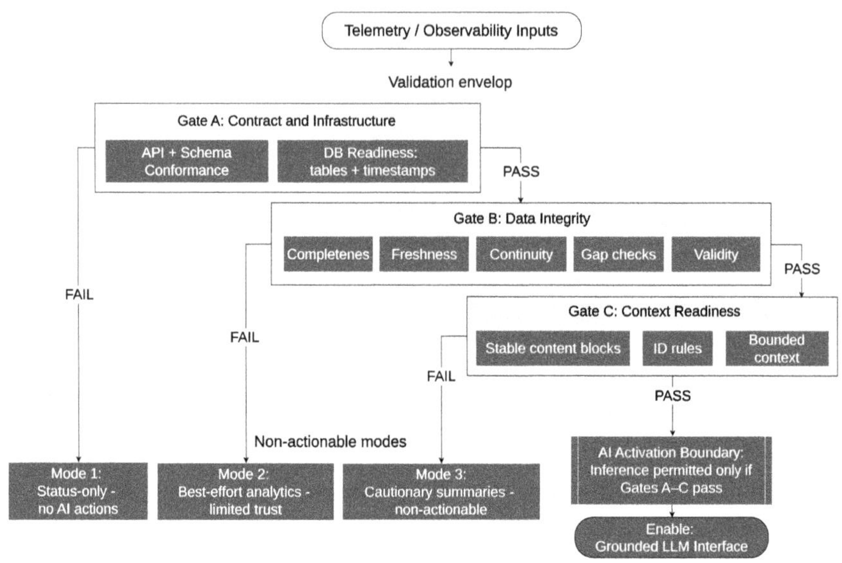

Fig. 2. Validation-first protocol structured as a control sequence. Telemetry must satisfy three sequential gates: Contract and Infrastructure (Gate A), Data Integrity (Gate B), and Context Readiness (Gate C), before crossing the AI activation boundary that permits grounded LLM inference. Failure at any gate triggers a defined non-actionable mode with constrained behaviour rather than unrestricted AI execution.

4.1   Gate A: Infrastructure and Contract Verification

Gate A validates that the data-producing interfaces are stable and schema-conformant. The system uses Pydantic schemas within FastAPI to enforce strict range constraints and required fields at the point of ingestion. This strategy shifts data quality responsibilities to the interface level, ensuring that subsequent analytics operate on a verified foundation. Furthermore, the protocol includes automated schema inspection, endpoint contract validation, audit-trail verification, and database readiness checks, specifically confirming that TimescaleDB hypertables are prepared to sustain anticipated time-series workloads. If Gate A fails (e.g., schema mismatch, missing tables, broken API paths), AI inference is treated as unsafe and is blocked or degraded because any subsequent analytics would be built on unstable evidence.

4.2   Gate B: Data Integrity Assurance

Gate B evaluates whether operational evidence satisfies the minimum integrity thresholds required for reliable analytics and grounded LLM inference. While Gate A guarantees structural and contractual correctness at ingestion, Gate B verifies that the accumulated telemetry is sufficiently complete, continuous, and plausible to support dependable reasoning.

An automated validation suite monitors collection rates over defined observation windows and detects temporal discontinuities that could distort anomaly detection or trend analysis. Freshness checks ensure that core analytics tables are actively receiving data, while continuity checks identify gaps that exceed predefined tolerances. These safeguards prevent the system from deriving conclusions from stale or sparsely sampled telemetry.

In addition, Gate B enforces plausibility and completeness constraints at the metric level. The system flags null values for critical fields and detects physically implausible observations, such as resource utilisation percentages exceeding logical bounds. This ensures that downstream analytics and explanatory narratives are grounded in evidence that is both internally consistent and operationally credible.

When freshness or continuity requirements are not met, for example, due to extended collection gaps or empty critical tables, the cognitive engine reverts to best-effort status reporting and explicitly marks generated narratives as not audit-ready. In this mode, the system may summarise an observable state but does not present high-confidence explanations or recommendations, thereby preventing overinterpretation of incomplete evidence.

4.3   Gate C: Context Readiness for LLM Ingestion

Even with correct and timely data, LLM grounding can fail if operational evidence is assembled without a stable structure or explicit identifier conventions. Gate C evaluates whether the system can generate a deterministic, bounded, and referenceable context document suitable for grounded inference.

This gate enforces stable section headers, strict identifier integrity, and consistent ordering to ensure that alerts and system states are referenced using explicit IDs. Role constraints and token discipline further limit fabrication by clearly separating the current operational state from long-term semantic memory.

If Gate C fails to produce a structurally valid context document, for example, due to missing required blocks, absent alert identifiers, or uncontrolled context growth, the system suppresses action-oriented recommendations and instead returns limited summaries that explicitly communicate uncertainty (Table 1).

Table 1. Summary of Validation-First Quality Gates and Passing Conditions.

Quality Gate	Objective	Passing Condition/Threshold
Gate A: Infrastructure	Ensure connection and schema match contracts.	API endpoints responsive; device metrics conform strictly to expected JSON/SQL schema.
Gate B: Data Integrity	Verify data completeness, continuity, and freshness.	100% non-null key fields; timestamp drift $\leq \pm 5$s; inter-arrival gaps ≤ 60s (threshold).
Gate C: Context	Assure structural readiness for the LLM prompt.	Complete assembly of context blocks; strict ID referencing; tokens bounded within limits.

5   Grounded Cognitive Engine

The cognitive engine executes a grounded reasoning workflow, positioning LLM generation as an interpretive layer superposed upon validated operational evidence. As illustrated in Fig. 3, the architecture synthesises deterministic detection mechanisms with structured context assembly and retrieval-augmented memory. To facilitate natural language interrogation, the system aggregates context from its assembly blocks.

These blocks comprise real-time system status retrieved from PostgreSQL, including site and device metrics, push-notification statistics, and active alerts; long-term semantic memories retrieved from the vector store as prior incident resolutions; bounded short-term conversation history; and static knowledge derived from a real-time recursive scan of codebase documentation and structure. Together, they form a contiguous prompt context partitioned by explicit block headers, enabling verifiable alignment between LLM outputs and underlying evidence.

The platform adopts a hierarchical memory architecture in which persistent ChromaDB collections store long-term vector embeddings. Conversely, short-term conversational state is truncated to the most recent exchange cycles, ensuring the prompt remains strictly within the bounds of the model's maximum token capacity.

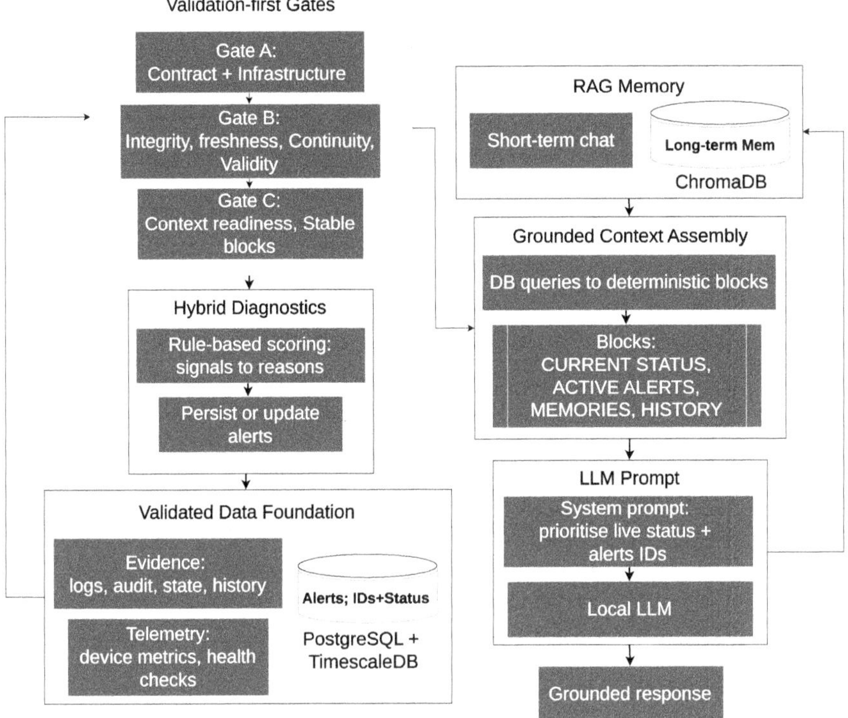

Fig. 3. Cognitive engine integrating validation-first gates, hybrid anomaly detection, structured context assembly, and retrieval-augmented memory. Validated telemetry and persistent alert IDs are assembled into deterministic context blocks before local LLM inference, enabling evidence-checkable explanations or recommendations.

5.1   Query and Anomaly Workflows

Parallel to the natural-language query interface, the system operates a deterministic anomaly detection tier that computes quantitative scores and diagnostic signals from structured telemetry, including resources (e.g., CPU and Memory) utilisation and consecutive health-check failures. When an anomaly is detected (e.g., Devices "flapping", rapidly disconnecting and reconnecting or sudden drops in polling frequency), the architecture prioritises the creation or update of persistent alert records, ensuring that incidents are represented through immutable identifiers and explicit lifecycle states. The LLM does not independently infer anomaly status; rather, it conditions its diagnostic explanations and remedial recommendations on both the computed anomaly metrics and the current system context. This separation of quantitative detection from generative interpretation preserves evidential traceability while enabling natural-language reasoning over validated alerts.

5.2   The Grounding Contract

The primary architectural safeguard of the cognitive engine is a grounding contract embedded in both context construction and the governing system prompt. Rather than relying on implicit alignment, this contract formalises enforceable constraints that shape how the LLM interprets operational evidence.

First, it establishes current-state primacy: the `current system status` block is treated as the authoritative source for all operational assertions. Second, it enforces identifier discipline by requiring explicit alert IDs in incident references and prohibiting the fabrication or inference of non-existent system identifiers. Third, it defines an uncertainty protocol that obliges the model to acknowledge evidential gaps instead of extrapolating unsupported system states.

In doing so, Gate A contract operationalises validation-first principles at the generative layer. Gate B ensures that current-state telemetry is fresh and continuous, while Gate C guarantees that contextual inputs are structurally bounded and referenceable. To illustrate Gate C, a simplified snippet of an assembled context enforcing grounding is shown below:

```
[SYSTEM PROMPT]
 Act as an IoT diagnostic assistant. Ground claims in EXACT IDs
provided under current status. Do not hallucinate system metrics.
[CURRENT STATUS]
 Device ID: DEV-991 | Status: WARNING | CPU: 95% | MEM: 75%
 Active Alert ID: ALT-042 | Category: Performance Exceedance
[END STATUS]
```

This explicit formatting ensures the LLM is constrained to reason within verified evidential limits, transforming the generation process from open-ended synthesis into a controlled interpretation of validated operational data.

6   Case Study and Evaluation

We evaluate HOMEPOT in a simulation-driven TRL-4 setting intended to support a transition toward TRL-5 initial pilot deployments. This assessment aims to demonstrate that validation-first gates yield quantifiable data-quality indicators and that the cognitive engine functions using referenceable, structured evidence. The trace comprises a heterogeneous set of 10 simulation devices (Linux/Windows/iOS endpoints and MQTT-based sensors) reporting health checks, performance metrics, state transitions, and operational logs to a FastAPI backend. For generative tasks, the cognitive engine was instantiated using the `Ollama 3.2` model (Ollama, Inc.) to provide a standard performance baseline.

To systematically test the gates, network anomalies such as missing packets and timestamp jitter were artificially injected during telemetry generation. Furthermore, the smart-filtering pipeline was configured to enforce a baseline collection rate of 288 daily snapshots per device (a 5-minute heartbeat); however, threshold-busting anomalies immediately override the filter to trigger accelerated capture. Unless otherwise stated, reported counts in this paper are computed over a fixed query window (last 10 days), while continuity is computed over the last 7 days for health checks to reflect recent operational behaviour. The selection of this case study is due to an industry-led co-design process, which ensures that telemetry and logging features address their specific requirements. Consequently, the observed pipeline behaviours reflect stakeholder-driven operational demands rather than synthetic benchmarks.

6.1   Case Study Methods and Measurement Protocol

Measurement reporting is categorised into three classes. Volume and coverage assessments capture record counts across core tables and verify distinct device participation. Integrity indicators evaluate non-null completeness, detect validity violations, and quantify continuity gaps by measuring maximum inter-arrival times. Finally, collection-rate alignment compares observed sampling frequencies against the smart-filtering heartbeat baseline of daily snapshots. To ensure auditability and reproducibility, the system computes each quantitative metric via a standardised suite of SQL queries (Q1–Q8), summarised in Table 2, executed against the PostgreSQL instance. The resulting trace volume and coverage statistics are summarised in Table 3, while integrity and continuity indicators are reported in Table 4.

Table 2. Summary of reproducibility queries (Q1–Q8) used to compute quantitative indicators. Full SQL scripts are available in the project repository.

Query ID	Purpose
Q1	Volume and coverage counts (core tables)
Q2	Distinct device coverage
Q3	Field-level non-null completeness
Q4	Validity violations (range checks)
Q5	Global health-check continuity
Q6	Per-device health-check continuity
Q7	Device-metric continuity and gap detection
Q8	Collection-rate alignment under smart filtering

6.2   Measuring Dependability and Data Readiness

While absolute truthfulness from generative AI is not directly measurable, functional dependability can be inferred from observable properties of system behaviour. In this evaluation, quantitative indicators provide operational evidence for data readiness by capturing coverage, integrity, continuity, and collection alignment. Volume and coverage metrics demonstrate that analytics operate over the full device fleet rather than a selective subset. Completeness and validity checks provide evidence of internal data integrity, while continuity measures reflect freshness and temporal stability. Collection-rate alignment further validates that the smart-filtering mechanism maintains a predictable baseline while capturing higher-fidelity traces during significant events. Together, these indicators define measurable preconditions under which inference can be considered operationally safe.

6.3   Case Study Results

We compute record counts for core tables over the evaluation window (Q1) and the number of distinct devices contributing to device metrics and health checks (Q2). These results substantiate the claim that the platform has accumulated operational evidence at a sufficient scale for preliminary analytics. Regarding completeness and validity, we also compute field-level non-null completeness for CPU/memory/disk/latency in `device_metrics` (Q3) and count validity violations for per cent-like metrics above 100% (Q4). As summarised in Table 3, the evaluation window captures full fleet participation and substantial telemetry volume across core operational tables. The corresponding integrity and continuity indicators are reported in Table 4.

In the current trace snapshot, completeness is 100% non-null for device metrics over the window (142,403 rows), with no observed CPU, memory, or disk utilisation values exceeding 100%. To assess continuity, we compute the maximum observed inter-arrival gap for `health_checks` over the last 7 days (Q5) and the per-device maximum gap distribution (Q6), ensuring that continuity is not dominated by a subset of devices. The global maximum inter-arrival gap is 0.526 min, while the maximum per-device gap reaches 0.593 min across the 10 devices. We additionally compute the number of gaps exceeding 60 min (a sustained discontinuity threshold) and the maximum gap over the evaluation window (Q7). In the current snapshot, we observe no inter-arrival gaps exceeding 60 min and a maximum inter-arrival gap of 0.524 min for device metrics. Finally, we consider expected collection rates under smart filtering. We compute observed snapshots per day for `device_metrics` by device and day (Q8) and compare these to the configured heartbeat baseline of 288/day, corresponding to a minimum expected rate under a 5-minute interval. Observed counts are substantially higher ($\approx$14.2k samples/device/day on the day with data), indicating that additional sampling triggers, such as significant-change updates or higher-frequency emitters in simulation, dominate the baseline. This illustrates the role of the baseline as a lower bound for continuity rather than a fixed-rate assumption.

When heterogeneous endpoints submit their diagnostic payloads, the backend first sanitises and structures the data into the operational database. The AI layer is then only invoked over this stabilised, queryable foundation. This isolation strategy not only protects sensitive operational metadata and preserves data sovereignty but also structurally eliminates the risk of the model halluci-

Table 3. Trace volume and coverage summary (computed from Q1–Q2 over the last 10 days).

Signal	Count
Distinct devices (metrics, health)	10
Device-metric samples (`device_metrics`)	142,403
Health checks (`health_checks`)	142,403
Error logs (`error_logs`)	69,999
API request logs (`api_request_logs`)	19,702
State transitions (`device_state_history`)	39,408

Table 4. Integrity indicators from Q3–Q7. Percentages are over the last 10 days; health-check continuity is over the last 7 days.

Indicator	Value
Non-null completeness (CPU, memory, disk, latency)	100%
Validity violations ($> 100\%$) (CPU, memory, disk)	0
Max inter-arrival gap (health checks, global)	0.526 min
Max inter-arrival gap (health checks, worst device)	0.593 min
Gaps > 60 min (device metrics)	0
Max inter-arrival gap (device metrics, global)	0.524 min

nating system states based on malformed or incomplete inputs, anchoring all downstream inferences firmly within verifiable reality.

6.4 Case Study Findings and Qualitative Ablation

The validation-first workflow operates as a critical engineering control rather than a passive monitoring layer. Gate A surfaces interface and schema regressions before analytics and AI components are trusted; Gate B provides actionable diagnostics when integrity indicators degrade, including continuity gaps and staleness; and Gate C ensures that the LLM receives a bounded, referenceable context anchored to explicit incident identifiers. Compared to a deploy-first configuration, where analytics and generative explanations operate directly over whatever telemetry is available, the validation-first regime enforces evidence readiness prior to scoring and reasoning.

During early validation runs, we performed a qualitative ablation to compare the system's output with and without Gate B/C active. When the gates were bypassed, and incomplete telemetry representing a disconnected sensor was fed to the LLM, the model hallucinated plausible but unsupported root causes (e.g., claiming "high CPU usage caused thermal shutdown" due to stale token associations from vector-store memory). When the validation routing was engaged, Gate B immediately flagged the payload's timestamp staleness. The resulting

Gate C prompt subsequently contained a strict empty-state alert, constraining the LLM to output: "Insufficient fresh telemetry available. Device disconnected at [Timestamp]; no valid CPU metrics for diagnostic reasoning." This ablation visibly illustrates how the framework prevents "garbage-in/garbage-out" failure modes by replacing ungrounded extrapolations with deterministic uncertainty bounds.

More broadly, this shifts AI from an always-on diagnostic layer to a conditionally enabled component whose authority is contingent on measurable data integrity indicators. In doing so, the system reframes validation as a prerequisite operational state that emerges only when defined readiness conditions are satisfied.

7   Conclusions, Limitations and Scalability

This research establishes that dependable AI integration within distributed IoT is primarily a data-foundations challenge. Without rigorous telemetry validation, stable identifier management, and deterministic context assembly, LLM-based diagnostics inevitably produce ungrounded narratives. We presented a validation-first methodology implemented in HOMEPOT that operationalises this stance via three repeatable quality gates. Gate A enforces contract and infrastructure integrity, Gate B guarantees data freshness and continuity, and Gate C ensures context readiness for structured ingestion. This framework enables a cognitive engine that synchronises deterministic anomaly signals with persistent alert identifiers via a structured prompt contract, enabling explanations that can be explicitly checked against the underlying trace.

While this evaluation demonstrates feasibility and quantifiable integrity indicators, absolute claims of complete "trustworthiness" must be contextualised within this TRL-4 simulation phase. Several limitations remain regarding scalability and generalisation. First, the trace originates from a contained 10-device simulation and may not fully capture the behavioural heterogeneity and noise levels of production-scale IoT deployments. Second, the evaluation window is temporally constrained and therefore does not yet reflect long-duration operational drift. Third, the passing thresholds for freshness and continuity (e.g., 60-second continuity gaps) reported in this pilot are specifically calibrated to HOMEPOT's current baseline; scaling to distinct deployments will require dynamic, per-domain threshold tuning.

Future work will prioritise TRL-5 pilots with industry partners to evaluate the protocol under real operational stress and scale up heterogeneous device failures. We aim to incorporate a cybersecurity-oriented validation layer to strengthen data provenance through identity assertions. Lastly, the automation of table generation from direct SQL outputs will ensure reproducible consistency between the underlying database traces and reported results.

Acknowledgements. This work was carried out within the HOMEPOT (Homogeneous Cyber Management of End-Points and Operational Technology) project, an ITEA4-funded initiative supported by national funding agencies. The authors gratefully acknowledge the contributions of all consortium partners for their technical input and collaborative support.

Disclosure of Interests. The authors declare that they have no competing interests relevant to the content of this article.

Script Availability. This work was carried out within the HOMEPOT (Homogeneous Cyber Management of End-Points and Operational Technology) project, an ITEA4-funded initiative supported by national funding agencies. The authors gratefully acknowledge the contributions of all consortium partners for their technical input and collaborative support.

References

1. Ni, B., Liu, Z., Wang, L., et al.: Towards trustworthy retrieval augmented generation for large language models: A survey (2025)
2. Wang, R.Y., Strong, D.M.: Beyond accuracy: what data quality means to data consumers. J. Manag. Inf. Syst. (1996). https://doi.org/10.1080/07421222.1996.11518099
3. Chandola, V., Banerjee, A., Kumar, V.: Anomaly detection. ACM Comput. Surv. **41**(3) (2009). https://doi.org/10.1145/1541880.1541882
4. Sculley, D., et al.: Hidden technical debt in Machine Learning systems. In: Advances in Neural Information Processing Systems (2015)
5. Cai, L., Zhu, Y.: The challenges of data quality and data quality assessment in the Big Data era. Data Science Journal (2015)
6. Ji, Z., et al.: Survey of hallucination in natural language generation. ACM Comput. Surv. (2023). https://doi.org/10.1145/3571730
7. Du, M., Li, F., Zheng, G., Srikumar, V.: DeepLog. In: Proceedings of the 2017 ACM SIGSAC Conference on Computer and Communications Security (2017) https://doi.org/10.1145/3133956.3134015
8. Halevy, A., Norvig, P., Pereira, F.: The unreasonable effectiveness of data. IEEE Intell. Syst. (2009). https://doi.org/10.1109/MIS.2009.36
9. Maynez, J., Narayan, S., Bohnet, B., McDonald, R.: On faithfulness and factuality in abstractive summarization. In: Proceedings of the 58th Annual Meeting of the Association for Computational Linguistics (2020). https://doi.org/10.18653/v1/2020.acl-main.173
10. Lin, S., Hilton, J., Evans, O.: TruthfulQA: measuring how models mimic human falsehoods. In: Proceedings of the 60th Annual Meeting of the Association for Computational Linguistics (2022). https://doi.org/10.48550/arXiv.2109.07958
11. Lewis, P., Perez, E., Piktus, A., et al.: Retrieval-augmented generation for knowledge-intensive NLP tasks. In: Advances in Neural Information Processing Systems (2020). https://doi.org/10.48550/arXiv.2005.11401

12. Karpukhin, V., et al.: Dense passage retrieval for Open-Domain question answering. In: Proceedings of the 2020 Conference on Empirical Methods in Natural Language Processing (EMNLP) (2020). https://doi.org/10.48550/arXiv.2004.04906
13. National Institute of Standards and Technology: Artificial intelligence risk management framework (AI RMF 1.0). Tech. Rep. NIST AI 100-1, National Institute of Standards and Technology (2023). https://doi.org/10.6028/NIST.AI.100-1

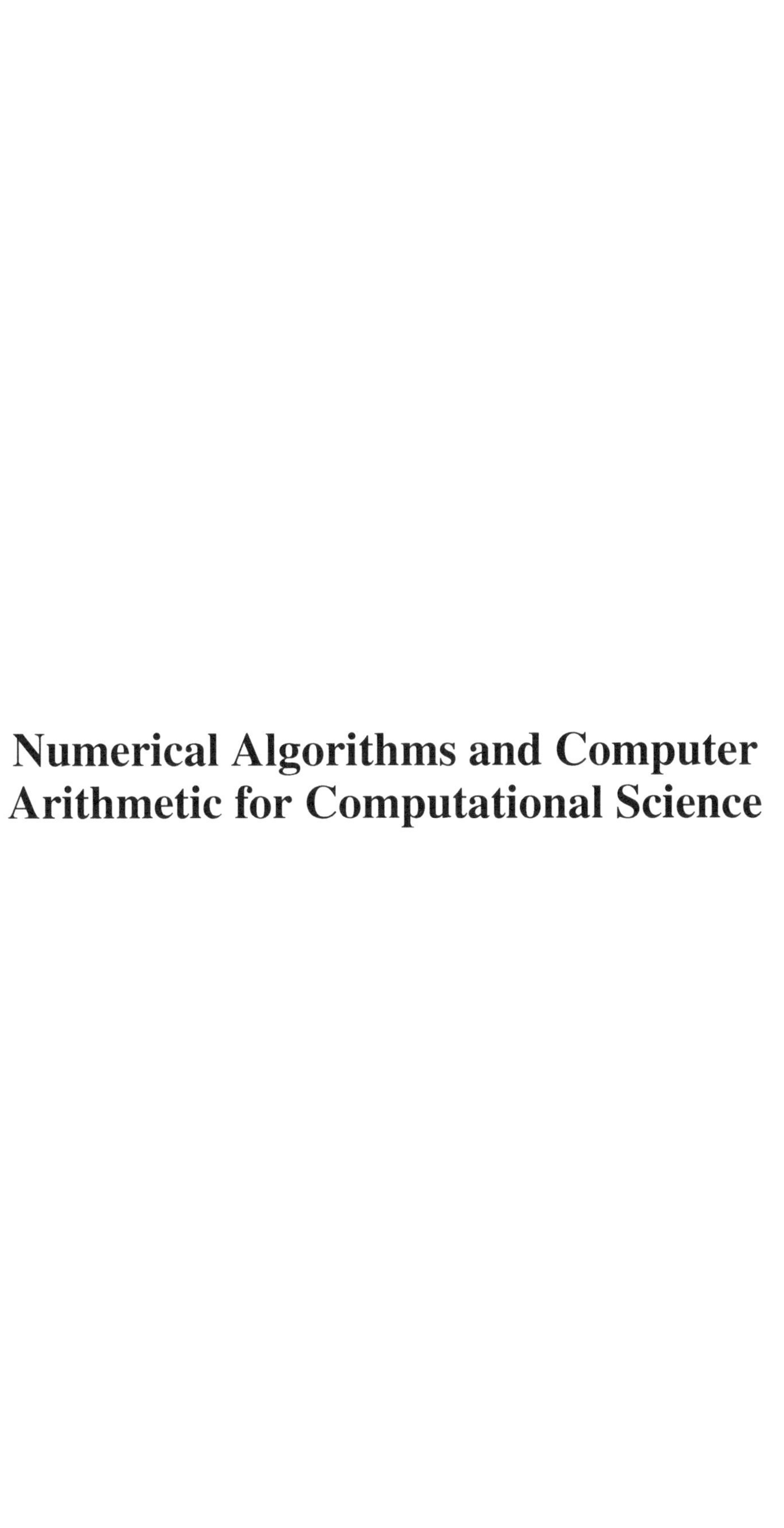

Numerical Algorithms and Computer Arithmetic for Computational Science

Reversible Data Hiding in Encrypted Images Using Kernel-Based Prediction and Delta-Huffman Coding

Remigiusz Martyniak[1]([✉]) [iD], Mariusz Dzwonkowski[1,2] [iD], and Tom Dhaene[3] [iD]

[1] Department of Teleinformation Networks, Faculty of Electronics, Telecommunications and Informatics, Gdansk University of Technology, Gabriela Narutowicza 11/12, 80-233 Gdańsk, Poland
remigiusz.martyniak@pg.edu.pl
[2] Department of Radiology Informatics and Statistics, Faculty of Health Sciences, Medical University of Gdansk, Tuwima 15, 80-210 Gdańsk, Poland
[3] Department of Information Technology (INTEC), IDLab, Ghent University-Imec, Technologiepark-Zwijnaarde 126, 9052 Ghent, Belgium

Abstract. With the growing demand for secure and efficient handling of large-scale image data in computational environments, lossless data embedding methods for encrypted visual content are gaining importance. This paper introduces a Reversible Data Hiding in Encrypted Images (RDHEI) scheme that allows embedding additional data into encrypted images while ensuring perfect recovery of the carrier. In this approach, reference pixels are selected using a predefined binary mask and compressed using Delta-Huffman coding. The remaining non-reference pixels are predicted using a kernel-based approach, with the kernel weights optimized for each image using Ridge regression. The resulting prediction errors are compressed using standard Huffman coding, thereby increasing the achievable embedding rate. The proposed method is lossless and has been evaluated on standard grayscale images, including those from the BOSSbase and BOWS2 datasets and other benchmark images commonly used in RDHEI research. Experimental results show that the method achieves a higher embedding rate compared to existing RDHEI techniques.

Keywords: Encrypted images · Machine learning · Reversible data hiding

1 Introduction

The need for secure and efficient handling of sensitive information has become increasingly critical across a wide range of applications, including military communications, medical imaging, legal documentation, and confidential image sharing. Traditional data hiding techniques, while effective in embedding information into digital media, often fail to ensure lossless recovery of the original content—an essential requirement in scenarios where data integrity is paramount.

M. Paszynski et al. (Eds.): ICCS 2026 Workshops, LNCS 16788, pp. 527–541, 2026.
https://doi.org/10.1007/978-3-032-29915-4_44

Reversible Data Hiding (RDH) addresses this challenge by enabling the embedding of additional data into a carrier image in a way that both the hidden information and the original image can be perfectly restored. Techniques such as histogram shifting [1, 2], difference expansion [3–5], and pixel value ordering [6, 7] have been widely explored for RDH in plaintext images. However, these methods are limited to plaintext carriers, making them inherently unsuitable for applications involving data embedding within the encrypted domain.

To address the limitations of traditional data hiding methods, Reversible Data Hiding in Encrypted Images (RDHEI) has been developed to securely embed data into encrypted images, providing an additional layer of protection in untrusted environments. RDHEI methods are typically categorized into two main categories: Reserving Room Before Encryption (RRBE) and Vacating Room After Encryption (VRAE). In RRBE, the content owner exploits spatial correlations in pixel values during preprocessing to reserve space for data embedding, often resulting in higher embedding rates. In VRAE, data embedding is performed after encryption, which prevents access to the original spatial information and thus limits the ability to exploit pixel correlations, leading to a typically lower embedding rate. Additionally, RDHEI schemes can also be classified as joint or separable, depending on whether the same or distinct keys are used for encryption and data embedding.

Over the years, a wide range of RDHEI algorithms have been introduced, primarily focused on maximizing the embedding rate through improved pixel prediction, bit-plane manipulation, and advanced compression techniques. Pixel prediction and error map–based approaches remain the most common.

Zhang et al. [8] proposed a block-wise prediction method using sixteen prediction models, which was later extended by Martyniak and Dzwonkowski [9] with seven additional models to better exploit spatial correlations, together with a fine-tuned Extended Run-Length Encoding (ERLE) which further improved the embedding rate. Yu et al. [10] introduced a hierarchical embedding strategy, generating a hierarchical bit-plane label map from prediction error magnitudes to classify pixels into small, medium, and large error categories. Yin et al. [11] employed the Median Edge Detector (MED) with multiple scanning orders to rearrange errors and maximize compression efficiency, while Sui et al. [12] combined hybrid prediction with Huffman coding, predicting the most significant bits using neighbor averaging and the least significant bits using MED. Ping et al. [13] introduced a deep learning–based asymmetric CNN predictor that captures complex spatial correlations via convolutional feature learning. Combined with an adaptive mean predictor in a two-stage embedding framework, the method performs multi-MSB prediction and substitution in the encrypted domain.

Bit-plane-oriented schemes focus on manipulating selected bit planes through compression and rearrangement to facilitate data hiding. Ren et al. [14] proposed an efficient parametric binary tree labeling (EPBTL) scheme that hierarchically partitions prediction errors into structured bit-plane categories to create embedding space. Pixels are divided into non-embedding, embedding, and self-recording sets, with the latter encoded into compact binary-tree codes for direct value recovery. Chen et al. [15] proposed a RRBE-based RDHEI scheme combining adaptive bit-plane (ABP) coding with an order-index extended scrambling (OIES) encryption strategy. The ABP coding adaptively selects among multiple bit-plane coding modes to minimize prediction code length and increase embedding capacity. Fu et al. [16] proposed an adaptive RDHEI scheme that combines "L"-shaped block embedding (LBE) and improved binary-block embedding (IBBE). The method first performs pixel prediction to obtain prediction errors and decomposes them into multiple binary prediction-error bit-planes (PEBPs). LBE and IBBE are then adaptively applied to each bit-plane according to the estimated net embedding capacity, maximizing the utilization of the Laplacian-like distribution of prediction errors. Yao et al. [17] developed an RDHEI framework in which consecutive zero-valued high bit-planes of prediction errors were globally compressed in a block-wise manner. The scheme employed adaptive Huffman indicators to encode the number of compressed bit-planes, a swapping technique to cluster the embeddable planes within each block and a rearrangement method to order blocks in accordance with their embedding capacity. Yu et al. [18] combined bit-plane operations with Chinese Remainder Theorem–based Secret Sharing (CRTSS) and iterative block-based encryption to preserve spatial correlations. A hybrid coding mechanism was employed, in which each block was encoded using either entropy-based or hierarchical coding. Recently, Ankur et al. [19] proposed an rANS-driven RDHEI method, in which block bit-planes are restructured and then compressed using range Asymmetric Numeral System (rANS) coding. This combination produces compact symbol representations that significantly enlarge the available embedding space, while a synchronized block structure ensures reliable recovery within the encrypted domain.

Moreover, regression-based prediction methods have emerged as a promising approach in RDHEI. Huang et al. [20] developed a high-capacity scheme that employs an adaptive linear regression predictor, which is trained on a dataset derived from the original image prior to encryption. Li et al. [21] introduced a sophisticated double linear regression framework. The first layer of the architecture implements three independent linear regressions on distinct subsets of four neighboring pixels, while the second layer synthesizes these outputs to generate the final prediction. While regression-based methods deliver high prediction accuracy, existing approaches still produce limited embedding rates, indicating significant room for improvement.

In this work, a high-payload, separable RRBE-type RDHEI scheme that utilizes linear regression is presented. The process begins with the application of a binary grid mask that selects reference pixels at every other position within every other row and column, while the remaining pixels are treated as non-reference. Reference pixels are used to predict non-reference pixel values through kernel-based prediction, where the weights of the 5×5 kernel are trained for each image using Ridge regression. The prediction errors, calculated as the differences between original and predicted values, form an error map. To maximize the embedding rate, the reference pixels are rearranged into a dense 2D reference map and losslessly compressed by encoding MED-based prediction residuals using Delta-Huffman coding, whereas the error map is compressed with standard Huffman coding. Experimental results on the BOSSbase and BOWS2 datasets demonstrate an average embedding rate exceeding 3.8 bits per pixel (bpp), outperforming other State-of-the-Art RDHEI methods. The key contributions of this study are:

– an RRBE-type RDHEI framework that uniquely integrates kernel-based prediction with image-adaptive weight training via Ridge regression and MED-based Delta-Huffman coding of reference pixels to boost embedding capacity while retaining separability and perfect reversibility;
– validation on a large-scale dataset of 8-bit grayscale images, including a comprehensive comparison with other State-of-the-Art RDHEI methods.

The structure of this paper is as follows. Section 2 provides a detailed explanation of the proposed RDHEI method. Section 3 describes the software and hardware specifications, along with information about the datasets used for evaluation. Section 4 presents the overall results on embedding rate, reconstruction quality, processing complexity and encryption effectiveness. Section 5 discusses the conclusions and key findings.

2 Proposed Method

The proposed RDHEI method comprises three stages—preprocessing (at the content-owner side), data hiding (performed by a separate entity), and data extraction with image recovery at the receiver side, as illustrated in Fig. 1.

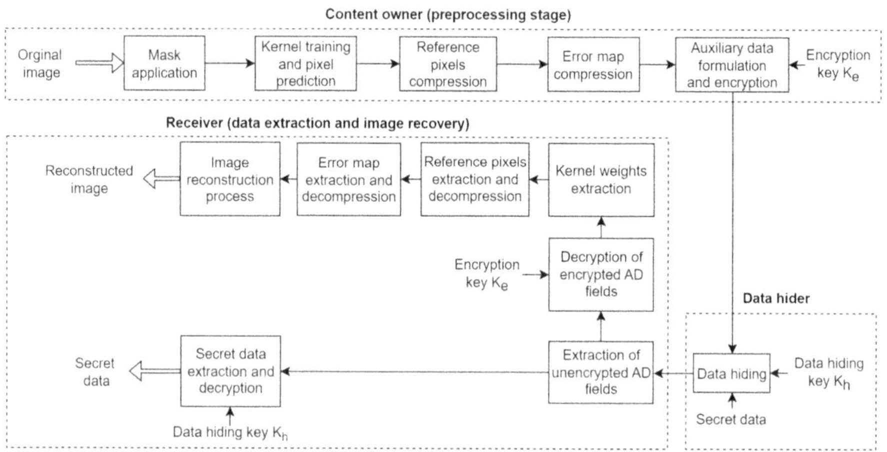

Fig. 1. Proposed RDHEI scheme.

2.1 Mask Application, Kernel Training and Pixel Prediction

During preprocessing, a binary mask is applied to the input grayscale carrier image to designate pixels as either reference or non-reference. The mask marks pixels at every other position within every other row and column, effectively choosing $\lceil H/2 \rceil \cdot \lceil W/2 \rceil$ reference pixels, where H and W are the height and width of the image, respectively. This grid pattern leverages spatial correlation between neighboring pixels using a sparse subset, balancing prediction accuracy and embedding capacity. A denser pattern, such as a chessboard (50% reference pixels), was empirically tested and found to significantly increase auxiliary data overhead while providing only marginal improvements in prediction accuracy, ultimately reducing the achievable embedding rate for the majority of the tested images.

Prediction of non-reference pixels is performed using a kernel-based linear model. For each non-reference pixel, a $K \times K$ neighborhood centered on that pixel is extracted. Although the neighborhood includes both reference and non-reference pixels, only the reference pixels contribute to the prediction. The neighborhood is flattened in row-major order into a vector of length $K2$, denoted as $\mathbf{V}_{\text{ref}}$. Positions corresponding to reference pixels retain their original intensities, while positions associated with non-reference pixels (including the center pixel) are set to zero. Next, the $K \times K$ kernel is used to form the corresponding weight vector of length $K2$, denoted as $\mathbf{V}_{\text{kernel}}$. The predicted value of the non-reference pixel is then computed as the dot product $p_{i,j} = \mathbf{V}_{\text{kernel}}^{\text{T}} \cdot \mathbf{V}_{\text{ref}}^{i,j}$.

For non-reference pixels near the image borders, where a complete $K \times K$ neighborhood would extend beyond the carrier image, the window is clipped to the available area. The available reference pixels are then averaged to obtain the prediction. Since kernel-based prediction may not provide optimal results without sufficient neighboring pixels, the averaging approach ensures a simple yet stable estimate that maintains reversibility.

The kernel weights are learned for each image using Ridge regression [22], a linear regression technique that incorporates L2 regularization. Ridge solves the following optimization problem:

$$\beta^* = \arg \min_{\beta} \|y - X\beta\|_2^2 + \alpha\|\beta\|_2^2 \tag{1}$$

Here, X is the feature matrix of size $L \times K^2$, where L is the number of training samples (all non-reference pixels in the carrier). Each row corresponds to one feature vector constructed from the $K \times K$ neighborhood around a non-reference pixel; y is the target vector (one-dimensional array of L length), composed of the original intensity values of non-reference pixels; β represents the K^2 kernel weights to be learned, and $\alpha > 0$ is a regularization strength hyperparameter. In Eq. (1), $\|y - X\beta\|_2^2$ measures the prediction error, i.e., the sum of squared differences between the true intensities and those predicted by the model; $\|\beta\|_2^2$ is the regularization term, which penalizes large weights, reducing overfitting and improving stability when reference pixel values are correlated. In this study, Ridge regression is implemented using scikit-learn's Ridge class with the following settings: $\alpha = 1$, no intercept term, and Singular Value Decomposition (SVD) as a solver, enabling efficient, direct computation of the weights using closed-form analytical solution. This approach makes kernel training substantially faster than L1 regularization methods such as Lasso, while ensuring comparable prediction performance (as presented later in Table 2).

Figure 2 illustrates a 5×5 kernel containing sample Ridge regression weights, an 8×8 image with reference pixels shown in white and non-reference pixels shown in violet, and two prediction scenarios. In the border case, where the kernel window extends beyond the image boundary, the predicted value is calculated as the average of the available reference pixels in the clipped window. In the interior case, where the kernel fits entirely within the image, the predicted value is computed as the dot product of the kernel weights $\mathbf{V}_{\text{kernel}}$ and the feature vector $\mathbf{V}_{\text{ref}}$. The center kernel position always corresponds to the pixel being predicted and is therefore set to zero in the feature vector, ensuring that only surrounding reference pixels contribute to the prediction.

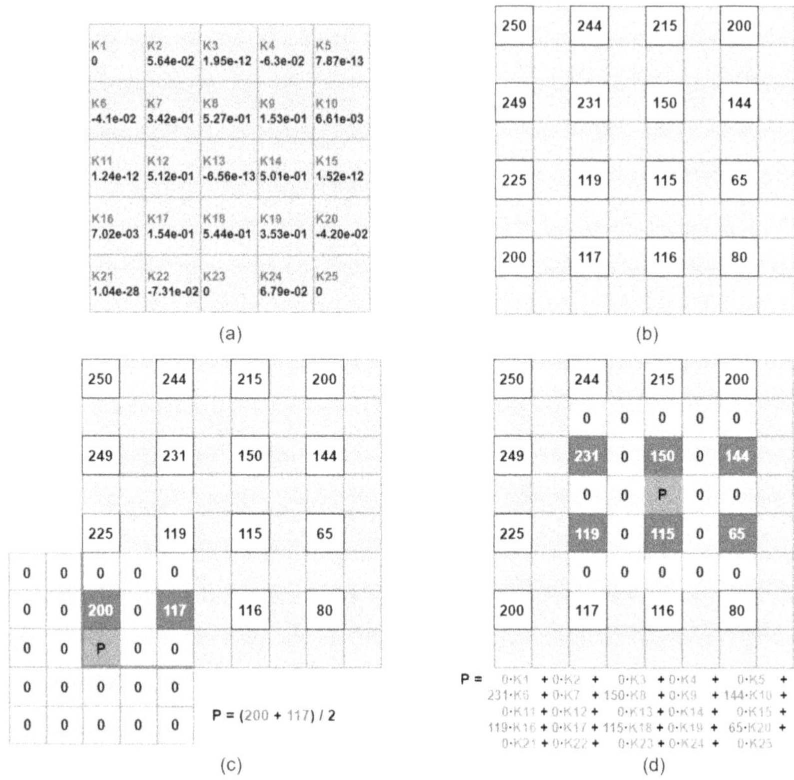

Fig. 2. Non-reference pixel prediction: (a) a 5×5 kernel with trained weights, (b) an 8×8 image with applied mask, (c) border case prediction using averaging and (d) interior case prediction using the dot product.

Table 1 presents predicted PSNR and SSIM results for 2000 images (the first 1000 from BOSSbase and the first 1000 from BOWS2), comparing different kernel sizes to determine the optimal preprocessing configuration. The 3×3 kernel proves insufficient for accurate prediction, yielding poor average PSNR (10.37 dB) and SSIM (0.134) values, which leads to large compressed error maps (on average 1.3591 Mb) and a reduced embedding rate. The 5×5, 7×7, and 9×9 kernels achieve comparable performance, with average PSNR around 33 dB, SSIM around 0.92, and error map sizes of approximately 0.797–0.8 Mb. The 5×5 kernel was selected as optimal due to its superior computational efficiency (0.081 s training time, compared to 0.223 s and 0.440 s for larger kernels) and lower storage requirement (only 25 64-bit float values compared to 49 or 81 for larger variants), improving the overall embedding rate.

Table 2 presents the prediction accuracy and training time for different regression methods for a 5×5 kernel. Ridge (SVD) is considerably faster than Lasso across all tested

Table 1. Prediction, error compression and kernel training time results for different kernel sizes.

Kernel size	PSNR [dB]			SSIM			Avg error map size [Mb]	Avg kernel training time [s]
	Min	Avg	Max	Min	Avg	Max		
3×3	3.89	10.37	31.01	0.005	0.134	0.791	1.3591	0.007
5×5	21.38	32.65	52.78	0.515	0.918	0.996	0.7967	0.081
7×7	21.33	32.83	52.13	0.708	0.919	0.996	0.7975	0.223
9×9	21.29	32.75	52.18	0.705	0.917	0.996	0.8002	0.440

iteration limits (100, 200, 400, and 800). Comparable prediction performance between the two methods is achieved only at 400 or 800 Lasso iterations, which substantially increases average training time to 0.535 s and 0.798 s, respectively, compared to 0.081 s for Ridge. This confirms the suitability of L2 regularization in the proposed method. Additional tests with different α values (0.01, 0.1, and 0.5) for both methods produced nearly identical results and were therefore omitted from the table.

Table 2. Prediction performance and kernel training time ($K = 5$) results for Ridge and Lasso regression methods.

Metrics	PSNR [dB]			SSIM			Kernel training time [s]		
	Min	Avg	Max	Min	Avg	Max	Min	Avg	Max
Ridge (SVD)	21.38	32.65	52.78	0.515	0.918	0.996	0.064	0.081	0.113
Lasso (100 it)	21.33	31.15	49.18	0.513	0.901	0.994	0.069	0.199	0.288
Lasso (200 it)	21.33	31.93	49.59	0.513	0.912	0.995	0.074	0.311	0.410
Lasso (400 it)	21.37	32.34	49.62	0.513	0.916	0.995	0.071	0.535	0.785
Lasso (800 it)	21.37	32.52	50.11	0.513	0.917	0.996	0.063	0.798	1.336

2.2 Reference Pixels and Error Map Compression

To maximize the embedding rate, both reference pixels and the error map undergo lossless compression before data embedding. The reference pixels are compressed using Delta-Huffman coding, which outperforms direct Huffman coding of raw pixel values due to its ability to effectively exploit spatial correlations. First, all reference pixels are serialized in row-major order to form a reference map M_{ref} of size $\lceil H/2 \rceil \times \lceil W/2 \rceil$. Next, the values of M_{ref} are predicted using the MED predictor, while the first row and the first column are kept unchanged and treated as boundary references:

$$\hat{M}_{\text{ref}}(i, j) = \begin{cases} \min(L, T) & \text{if } TL \geq \max(L, T) \\ \max(L, T) & \text{if } TL \leq \min(L, T) \\ L + T - TL & \text{otherwise} \end{cases} \tag{2}$$

where $L = \hat{M}_{\text{ref}}(i, j-1)$, $T = \hat{M}_{\text{ref}}(i-1, j)$, and $TL = \hat{M}_{\text{ref}}(i-1, j-1)$ denote the Left, Top, and Top-Left neighbors of the predicted pixel $\hat{M}_{\text{ref}}(i, j)$, respectively. $M_{\text{ref-dif}}$ is then computed (excluding the first row and the first column) as the difference between M_{ref} and its prediction $\hat{M}_{\text{ref}}$. Subsequently, the first row and the first column of $M_{\text{ref-dif}}$ are encoded using signed delta values, computed with respect to the preceding pixel within the corresponding row or column. The top-left reference pixel (i.e., the first element of $M_{\text{ref-dif}}$) is preserved in its original form. To handle potential negative values, an offset of $+255$ is added to all elements of $M_{\text{ref-dif}}$ except the top-left one. Finally, $M_{\text{ref-dif}}$ is flattened in row-major order and Huffman encoded.

In contrast, the error map is compressed using standard Huffman coding. Since error values are typically concentrated around zero and exhibit a strongly peaked distribution, they are inherently well suited to entropy coding. Prior to Huffman compression, each error value is offset by $+255$ to map the range to $[0, 510]$, in the same manner as the reference pixels.

2.3 Auxiliary Data Formulation and Encryption

In the proposed method, after compressing the reference pixels, generating and compressing the error map, the auxiliary data (AD) is formed (cf. Figure 3) to enable lossless recovery of the carrier. AD is positioned at the beginning of the reserved embedding region of size $N{\cdot}8$bits within the carrier, where N denotes the total number of pixels in the image. The AD is structured as follows:

- **Image dimensions.** Two 10-bit fields that store the carrier image height H and width W. The bit length of both fields was chosen primarily to handle the tested images but it can be easily increased if necessary.
- **AD length.** A field of $\lceil \log_2(H \cdot W \cdot 8) \rceil$ bits specifying the total length of the AD binary sequence. It allows both the data hider and the receiver to precisely determine the end of the entire AD segment, implying that the remaining embedding region for secret data begins immediately afterward—one bit later.
- **Kernel weights.** A field of $64{\cdot}K^2$ bits, where K is the kernel size, containing serialized kernel weights stored as 64-bit floats. The weights are used to predict non-reference pixel values from neighboring reference pixels.
- **Compressed reference pixels.** A section that begins with a $\lceil \log_2(N_{\text{ref}} \cdot b_{\text{sym}}) \rceil$ bits field, where N_{ref} is the number of reference pixels and b_{sym} is the number of bits needed to store a single symbol ($b_{\text{sym}} = \lceil \log_2 S \rceil$ for S possible symbol values). This field indicates the bit length of the following Delta-Huffman codebook segment, which starts immediately afterwards. In the codebook, each entry includes a symbol value (b_{sym} bits) representing delta-offsets in the range $[0, 510]$, a code length of $\lceil \log_2(L_{\text{max}}) \rceil$ bits, where L_{max} is the maximum Huffman code length, and the Huffman code itself, stored as a variable-length binary string. Following the codebook, another $\lceil \log_2(N_{\text{ref}} \cdot b_{\text{sym}}) \rceil$ bits field specifies the bit length of the compressed reference pixel data, which is stored directly afterwards.
- **Compressed error map.** Similar to reference pixels, this section starts with a $\lceil \log_2(N_{\text{non-ref}} \cdot b_{\text{sym}}) \rceil$ bit codebook length field, where $N_{\text{non-ref}}$ is the number of non-reference pixels and b_{sym} is the number of bits needed to store an error map symbol ($b_{\text{sym}} = \lceil \log_2 S \rceil$ for S possible symbols). In the codebook, each entry includes a

symbol value (b_{sym} bits), a code length of $\lceil \log_2(L_{\text{max}}) \rceil$ bits, where L_{max} is the maximum Huffman code length, and the Huffman code itself, stored as a variable-length binary string. Lastly, $\lceil \log_2(N_{\text{non-ref}} \cdot b_{\text{sym}}) \rceil$ bits field specifies the bit length of the compressed error map.

To secure the carrier image with embedded auxiliary data, the entire binary sequence of the image—excluding the embedded AD length field—is encrypted using a bitwise XOR operation with a pseudo-random bitstream derived from the encryption key K_e. The bitstream is generated using a ChaCha20-based Cryptographically Secure Pseudo-Random Number Generator (CSPRNG), which provides a high-quality pseudorandom sequence commonly employed in practical encryption settings and mitigates straightforward statistical dependencies between the encrypted and original image.

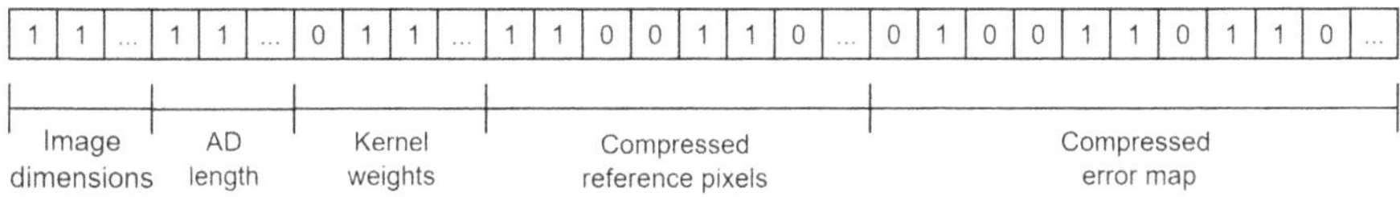

Fig. 3. Auxiliary data structure.

2.4 Data Hiding

The space following the embedded AD sequence within the encrypted carrier is reserved for embedding additional secret data. The starting point is determined by the value of the AD length field. Secret data is encrypted via a bitwise XOR operation with a pseudo-random bitstream derived from the data hiding key K_h, generated by a ChaCha20-based CSPRNG to ensure strong cryptographic security. The resulting encrypted data string is then inserted into the remaining embedding region of the encrypted image, directly after the identified AD sequence. Finally, the encrypted and marked image—containing both the embedded AD and secret data—is ready to be sent to the receiver (cf. Figure 1).

2.5 Carrier Image Recovery and Secret Data Extraction

Upon receiving the encrypted and marked image, the recipient can recover the original carrier and extract the embedded secret data through a fully reversible routine. The process begins by reading the unencrypted Image dimensions and AD length fields to determine dimensions of the carrier as well as the exact boundary between auxiliary data and secret payload. The receiver is then able to isolate the AD bitstream and decrypt it using encryption key K_e. From the decrypted auxiliary data, the receiver sequentially extracts the kernel weights stored as 64-bit floats each, followed by reference pixels (obtained by first reading the corresponding codebook specification and then decoding the Delta-Huffman compressed data) and error map (obtained by first reading the corresponding codebook specification and then decoding the Huffman compressed data). Both the reference pixels as well as error map values are offset-corrected (by subtracting 255) to recover their original form. Additionally, the reference-pixel stream is de-vectorized to reconstruct $M_{\text{ref-dif}}$ in row-major order (note that its dimensions are obtained from the

Image dimensions field). The original boundary elements are first restored iteratively, pixel by pixel, by cumulatively summing the signed deltas along the first row and the first column, while keeping the top-left (initial) element from $M_{\text{ref-dif}}$ unchanged. Next, the remaining pixels are recovered by inverting the MED-based delta representation: the MED predictor is recomputed using already reconstructed neighbors, and the corresponding prediction residuals from $M_{\text{ref-dif}}$ are added to obtain the correct reference map M_{ref}.

The original image is reconstructed by placing the recovered reference pixels in their designated positions using the predefined binary mask and predicting non-reference pixels using the recovered kernel weights, in the same manner as described in Sect. 2.1. Finally, the predicted values are adjusted by adding corresponding error values from the recovered error map.

To extract the embedded secret data, the receiver locates the bitstream immediately following the auxiliary data region, whose boundary was already determined by the AD length field. The identified segment contains the encrypted secret payload, which the receiver decrypts using the data hiding key K_h.

3   Experimental Setup

All experiments were conducted on a Windows 11 workstation equipped with an AMD Ryzen 5 7600X processor and 32 GB of DDR5 RAM. The proposed RDHEI algorithm was implemented in Python 3.12.2 using the scikit-learn 1.6.0 library. Kernel training was performed on the CPU using scikit-learn's Ridge class, as this implementation does not currently support CUDA-based GPU acceleration. For final validation, 20,000 8-bit grayscale images of size 512×512 pixels were used from the BOSSbase [23] and BOWS2 [24] datasets. Additionally, experiments were conducted on four standard benchmark images: Baboon, Jetplane, Man, and Lena.

4   Results

This section presents the evaluation results of the proposed method, including embedding rate, prediction and reconstruction metrics, error map statistics, and encryption effectiveness. For all testing, the optimal variant (5×5 kernel and Ridge regression) was chosen based on the preprocessing evaluation presented in Sect. 2.1.

4.1   Image Reconstruction and Data Embedding Effectiveness

High effectiveness of the proposed RDHEI method in both image reconstruction and data embedding is demonstrated by the results in Table 3. Across all datasets and individual test images, the reconstructed carriers achieved SSIM $= 1$ and PSNR of $+\infty$ dB, since MSE $= 0$, confirming that the reconstructed image is bit-for-bit identical to the original. The average predicted PSNR was 33.29 dB for BOSSbase and 32.35 dB for BOWS2, indicating a highly accurate prediction stage. Among standard images, the highest predicted PSNR was 33.18 dB (Lena), and the lowest was 24.08 dB (Baboon), which is expected due to the latter's complex texture. The method achieved an average embedding rate of 3.885 bpp for BOSSbase and 3.861 bpp for BOWS2, with maximum values reaching 6.873 bpp and 6.469 bpp, respectively. Error map statistics further indicate that residuals are concentrated around small values, which confirms the reliability of the proposed prediction approach.

Based on the comparative analysis presented in Table 4, the proposed RDHEI scheme demonstrates competitive performance against existing State-of-the-Art methods. For the BOSSbase dataset, the proposed method achieves higher average embedding rate than other methods, including Chen [15] (3.696 bpp) and Yao [17] (3.793 bpp). Similarly, for the BOWS2 dataset, the proposed method maintains consistent performance, also surpassing other approaches. Additionally, for standard test images, the proposed RDHEI scheme consistently achieves high embedding rates.

Figure 4 demonstrates the kernel-based prediction process performed on the Man test image, showing the original image and the predicted image. The error map visualized as a heatmap reveals that prediction errors are predominantly concentrated around edges and textural regions, with most areas showing minimal errors (white regions), while higher errors (red and blue regions) appear mainly at high-contrast boundaries. The corresponding error map histogram confirms the effectiveness of the prediction method, showing a highly peaked distribution centered around zero with the majority of prediction errors falling within a narrow range, which is ideal for efficient Huffman compression and contributes to the high embedding rates achieved by the proposed RDHEI scheme.

Table 3. Evaluation results for the proposed RDHEI scheme.

Images		Predicted PSNR [dB]	Reconstructed PSNR [dB]	Predicted SSIM	Reconstructed SSIM	Embedding rate [bpp]	Error map avg values	Error map medians
BOSSbase	Min	20.90	$+\infty$	0.515	1	1.073	-0.73	0
	Avg	33.29	$+\infty$	0.916	1	3.885	0.27	0
	Max	53.06	$+\infty$	0.998	1	6.873	2.35	1
BOWS2	Min	20.68	$+\infty$	0.670	1	0.937	-0.77	0
	Avg	32.35	$+\infty$	0.921	1	3.861	0.27	0
	Max	51.03	$+\infty$	0.997	1	6.469	0.53	0
Baboon		24.08	$+\infty$	0.749	1	1.739	0.24	0
Jetplane		29.90	$+\infty$	0.944	1	3.499	0.08	0
Man		30.57	$+\infty$	0.899	1	3.014	0.13	0
Lena		33.18	$+\infty$	0.917	1	3.344	0.28	0

Table 4. Comparison of the average embedding rates for the proposed RDHEI scheme against other State-of-the-Art methods.

Images	This work	Method [9]	Method [13]	Method [14]	Method [15]	Method [16]	Method [17]
BOSSbase	3.885	3.597	3.461	2.667	3.696	3.195	3.793
BOWS2	3.861	3.482	3.302	2.637	3.543	3.134	3.705
Baboon	1.739	1.828	1.199	1.343	1.530	1.523	1.375
Jetplane	3.499	3.321	3.183	2.767	3.404	3.176	3.535
Man	3.014	2.610	2.285	2.644	2.819	2.566	2.647
Lena	3.344	2.989	2.821	2.760	3.175	3.014	2.859

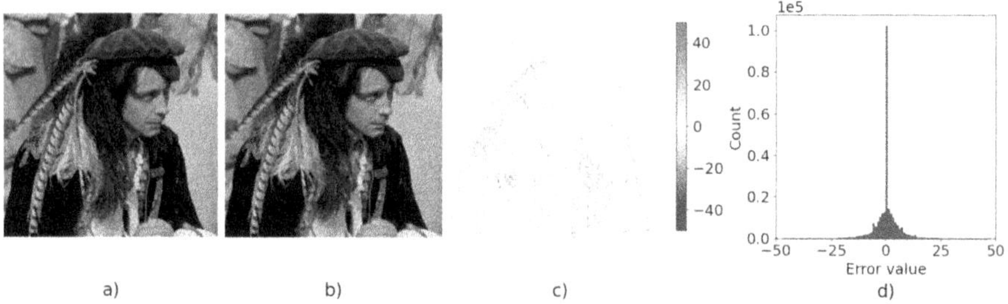

Fig. 4. Kernel-based prediction performed on the Man image: (a) original image, (b) predicted image (PSNR = 30.57 dB), (c) error map visualized as a heatmap, (d) histogram of the error map.

4.2 Analysis of Method's Complexity and Encryption Effectiveness

The computational cost of the proposed RDHEI framework is primarily determined by operations that traverse the image domain exactly once. Feature extraction, Ridge-based kernel estimation with a fixed kernel size, Huffman encoding and decoding, and pixel-wise reconstruction all scale linearly with respect to the number of pixels N. In particular, for a fixed kernel dimension, the SVD-based Ridge regression has complexity $O(N)$, as the feature dimensionality remains constant. Consequently, both the content owner and the receiver incur a time complexity of $O(N)$. The data-hiding procedure, in contrast, processes only the embeddable portion of the bitstream. Since ChaCha20 bitstream generation and XOR operations scale with the size of this region, the data hider operates in $O(C_e)$, where $C_e < N$ denotes the number of bytes available for embedding (for 8-bit images, $C_e = N - AD_{\text{length}}/8$). The per-stage computational characteristics of the proposed and reference methods are summarized in Table 5.

The memory usage of all stages is proportional to the carrier size, as each stage stores only the image data along with the auxiliary information, without introducing any super-linear data structures. Therefore, the space complexity of the proposed method is $O(N)$. Overall, the per-image complexity is $O(N)$ in both time and space, providing the same asymptotic efficiency as existing linear-time schemes such as [10] and [17], while remaining more efficient than the quasi-linear method [19]. In addition, as a practical implementation-level observation, the encryption and decryption steps on the machine used in the experiments required only a few milliseconds per image. This remark is included for completeness, in order to complement the theoretical complexity discussion with an indication of the practical runtime under the adopted experimental conditions, while noting that the exact execution time depends on the hardware and software environment.

Table 5. Computational time and space complexities of the proposed method and other State-of-the-Art RDHEI schemes.

Complexity	This work				Method [10]	Method [17]	Method [19]
	Content owner	Data hider	Receiver	Total per image			
Time	$O(N)$	$O(C_e)$	$O(N)$	$O(N)$	$O(N)$	$O(N)$	$O(N \log N)$
Space	$O(N)$	$O(N)$	$O(N)$	$O(N)$	$O(N)$	$O(N)$	$O(N)$

To determine the effectiveness of the encryption routine that relies on the ChaCha20 stream cipher, three standard evaluation metrics were utilized, including histogram analysis (cf. Figure 5) for both original and encrypted images, as well as the Number of Pixel Change Rate (NPCR) and Unified Average Changing Intensity (UACI). On average, the NPCR values reached 99.66% and the UACI results averaged 32.8% for the tested images, which confirms that the implemented RDHEI algorithm ensures the desired level of security for encrypted data.

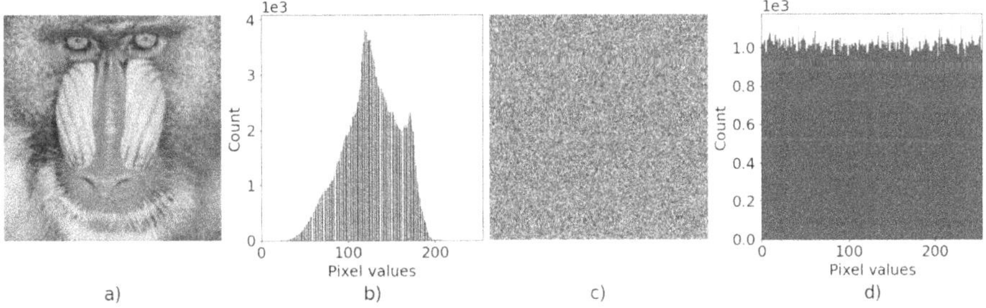

Fig. 5. Encryption of the Baboon image: (a) original image, (b) histogram of the original image, (c) encrypted image, and (d) histogram of the encrypted image.

5 Conclusions

A computationally efficient, fully reversible, and separable RRBE-type RDHEI framework has been proposed. The method combines kernel-based pixel prediction and Delta-Huffman coding to maximize embedding effectiveness, achieving an average rate of

3.885 bpp on BOSSbase and 3.861 bpp on BOWS2 datasets. With linear time and space complexity, it is well suited for large-scale scientific imaging requiring secure and reproducible data exchange. The integration of regression-based prediction and adaptive compression demonstrates the potential of machine learning–driven models to enhance prediction accuracy and embedding rate.

Future work will focus on improving error map compression, dynamic reference pixel selection, and integrating edge-preserving filters such as bilateral and anisotropic diffusion to refine prediction accuracy. Additional research will explore multiple adaptive kernels, GPU-accelerated kernel optimization, and extensions to 16-bit medical imagery (e.g., DICOM) to further enhance its applicability in computational science applications like sensitive clinical environments.

Acknowledgments. This study was funded by the Faculty of Electronics, Telecommunications, and Informatics of Gdansk University of Technology, and by the research subsidy from the Polish Ministry of Science and Higher Education.

Disclosure of Interests. The authors declare no conflict of interest.

References

1. Ni, Z., Shi, Y.Q., Ansari, N., Su, W.: Reversible data hiding. IEEE Trans. Circuits Syst. Video Technol. **16**(3), 354–362 (2006)
2. Li, X., Zhang, W., Gui, X., Yang, B.: Efficient reversible data hiding based on multiple histograms modification. IEEE Trans. Inf. Forensics Secur. **10**(9), 2016–2027 (2015)
3. Tian, J.: Reversible watermarking by difference expansion. In: Dittmann, J., Fridrich, J., Wohlmacher, P. (eds.), Proceedings of the Workshop on Multimedia and Security: Authentication, Secrecy, and Steganalysis, Association for Computing Machinery, Inc, pp. 19–22 (2002)
4. Alattar, A.M.: Reversible watermark using the difference expansion of a generalized integer transform. IEEE Trans. Image Process. **13**(8), 1147–1156 (2004)
5. Hu, Y., Lee, H.K., Chen, K., Li, J.: Difference expansion based reversible data hiding using two embedding directions. IEEE Trans. Multimed. **10**(8), 1500–1512 (2008)
6. Li, X., Li, J., Li, B., Yang, B.: High-fidelity reversible data hiding scheme based on pixel-value-ordering and prediction-error expansion. Signal Process. **93**(1), 198–205 (2013)
7. Qu, X., Kim, H.J.: Pixel-based pixel value ordering predictor for high-fidelity reversible data hiding. Signal Process. **111**, 249–260 (2015)
8. Zhang, H., Li, L., Li, Q.: Reversible data hiding in encrypted images based on block-wise multi-predictor. IEEE Access **9**, 61943–61954 (2021)
9. Martyniak, R., Dzwonkowski, M.: Reversible data hiding in encrypted images with pixel prediction and ERLE compression. In: Lees, M.H., et al. (eds.) Computational Science – ICCS 2025. Lecture Notes in Computer Science, vol. 15906. Springer, Cham (2025)
10. Yu, C., Zhang, X., Zhang, X., Li, G., Tang, Z.: Reversible data hiding with hierarchical embedding for encrypted images. IEEE Trans. Circuits Syst. Video Technol. **32**(2), 451–466 (2022)
11. Yin, Z., Peng, Y., Xiang, Y.: Reversible data hiding in encrypted images based on pixel prediction and bit-plane compression. IEEE Trans. Dependable Secure Comput. **19**(2), 992–1002 (2022)

12. Sui, L., Li, H., Liu, J., Xiao, Z., Tian, A.: Reversible data hiding in encrypted images based on hybrid prediction and Huffman coding. Symmetry **15**(6), 1222 (2023)
13. Ping, P., Huo, J., Guo, B.: Novel asymmetric CNN-based and adaptive mean predictors for reversible data hiding in encrypted images. Expert Syst. Appl. **246**, 123270 (2024)
14. Ren, H., Yue, Z., Gu, F., Li, M., Chen, T., Bai, G.: A novel reversible data hiding method in encrypted images using efficient parametric binary tree labeling. Knowl.-Based Syst. **300**, 112198 (2024)
15. Chen, F., Yang, Y., He, H., Yuan, Y.: Adaptive coding and ordered-index extended scrambling based RDH in encrypted images. IEEE Trans. Multimed. **25**, 2864–2875 (2023)
16. Fu, Z., Chai, X., Tang, Z., He, X., Gan, Z., Cao, G.: Adaptive embedding combining LBE and IBBE for high-capacity reversible data hiding in encrypted images. Signal Process. **216**, 109299 (2024)
17. Yao, Y., Wang, K., Chang, Q., Weng, S.: Reversible data hiding in encrypted images using global compression of zero-valued high bit-planes and block rearrangement. IEEE Trans. Multimed. **26**, 3701–3714 (2024)
18. Yu, C., Zhang, X., Qin, C., Tang, Z.: Reversible data hiding in encrypted images with secret sharing and hybrid coding. IEEE Trans. Circuits Syst. Video Technol. **33**(11), 6443–6458 (2023)
19. Ankur, R., Kumar, R., Ranjan, P., Jung, K.-H.: Leveraging rANS for synchronized high capacity reversible data hiding in encrypted image. Expert Syst. Appl. **267**, 126181 (2025)
20. Huang, B., Wan, C., Chen, K.: High-capacity reversible data hiding in encrypted images based on adaptive predictor and compression of prediction errors. Mathematics **9**(17), 2166 (2021)
21. Li, F., Zhu, H., Yu, J., et al.: Double linear regression prediction based reversible data hiding in encrypted images. Multimed. Tools Appl. **80**, 2141–2159 (2021)
22. Hoerl, A.E., Kennard, R.W.: Ridge regression: Biased estimation for nonorthogonal problems. Technometrics **12**(1), 55–67 (1970)
23. BOSSbase 1.01 dataset. https://dde.binghamton.edu/download/. Accessed 11 Dec 2025
24. BOWS2 dataset. https://web.archive.org/web/20221129163351//bows2.ec-lille.fr/. Accessed 11 Dec 2025

GPU-Accelerated Number Theoretic Transform-Based Privacy Amplification for Quantum Key Distribution

Chenyu Wang$^{(\boxtimes)}$, Kazuaki Doi, and Yutaro Ishigaki

Corporate Laboratory, Toshiba Corporation, Minato City, Japan
`{chenyu.wang.t37,kazuaki.doi.f50,yutaro.ishigaki.h62}@mail.toshiba`

Abstract. Privacy Amplification (PA) constitutes a critical computational bottleneck in high-rate Quantum Key Distribution (QKD) systems, particularly when processing large data blocks required to mitigate finite-size security effects. In this work, we propose a high-performance GPU implementation based on the Number Theoretic Transform (NTT), enabling exact modular arithmetic under a suitable modulus and root of unity for large-scale privacy amplification. We optimize the NTT execution on GPUs by integrating a *hybrid butterfly computation scheme* that combines a warp-shuffle-based approach and a shared-memory-based approach, together with kernel fusion techniques and Barrett-based modular reduction to maximize memory bandwidth utilization and parallel efficiency. Experimental results on an NVIDIA L40 GPU demonstrate a throughput of **3.32 Gbps** for 2^{27}-bit input blocks. This result indicates that software-based NTT acceleration on commodity GPUs can support hundreds-of-Mbps-class Secret-Key-Rate (SKR) QKD systems.

Keywords: Quantum Key Distribution · Privacy Amplification · Number Theoretic Transform · GPU · Parallel Computing

1 Introduction

Quantum key distribution (QKD) has matured from theoretical protocols into a viable technology for guaranteeing information-theoretic security in critical infrastructure [18,24]. QKD systems are evolving toward higher secret-key rates and longer transmission distances, which in turn demand efficient post-processing pipelines to handle an increasing volume of raw key data [7]. A critical component of this pipeline is privacy amplification (PA), which distills a shorter secure key from the corrected data by applying a universal hash function [12,19]. In practice, PA compresses a corrected key of length n to a secret key of length r, where the ratio r/n is set by parameter estimation and finite-size security analysis. For example, in a high-rate discrete-variable QKD (DV-QKD) demonstration, Yuan *et al.* report a PA compression ratio of about $r/n \simeq 0.29$ (typical QBER $\approx 3\%$ and 10^8-bit PA blocks) [27]. Accordingly, sustaining a target secret-key rate (SKR) typically requires PA throughput on the order of $\mathrm{SKR}/(r/n)$

M. Paszynski et al. (Eds.): ICCS 2026 Workshops, LNCS 16788, pp. 542–557, 2026.
https://doi.org/10.1007/978-3-032-29915-4_45

(e.g., $\sim 3\times$ headroom when $r/n \approx 0.3$). As system-level raw-key generation capabilities grow through higher pulse/symbol rates as well as parallelization and multiplexing, this throughput requirement can make PA a computational bottleneck due to the large-scale linear operations involved.

Besides DV-QKD based on single-photon detection, continuous-variable QKD (CV-QKD) has also been actively studied as an alternative approach using coherent detection and Gaussian modulation, with comprehensive treatments of practical implementations and security analysis available in the literature [8]. While very long transmission distances typically lead to reduced key rates, recent short-reach, chip-scale demonstrations highlight that post-processing throughput can become critical even for CV-QKD: Ng *et al.* report a secret-key rate of 1.213 Gbit/s over 10 km using an integrated photonic-chip QKD system based on discrete-modulated CV-QKD [13]. Such gigabit-class operation implies that PA must sustain multi-Gbps-class throughput to keep pace with the target SKR under realistic compression ratios and protocol/channel-dependent overheads. In this work, we focus on DV-QKD privacy amplification, although the core acceleration techniques are directly applicable whenever PA is instantiated via large-block Toeplitz hashing, regardless of DV/CV QKD.

In many practical implementations, PA is instantiated by Toeplitz hashing, which reduces to a cyclic convolution suitable for transform-based evaluation [6,9], with finite-size analyses often motivating the use of large blocks (e.g., $\sim 10^8$ bits) to approach asymptotic key rates [11]. To accelerate Toeplitz-based PA at such scales, transform methods based on the fast Fourier transform (FFT) have been explored on heterogeneous platforms, including programmable hardware such as FPGAs [9,10]. However, floating-point arithmetic can complicate bit-exact coefficient recovery at large transform lengths and may require higher precision or correction steps [23]. Integer-domain alternatives, such as GMP-based schemes [26] and NTT-based constructions, avoid these rounding issues by performing the transform in $\mathbb{Z}_p$ with exact modular arithmetic [17], making NTT a natural choice for deterministic, bit-exact Toeplitz-hash PA.

Achieving high throughput for large-scale NTT on general-purpose hardware still requires careful attention to memory traffic and efficient modular arithmetic. While FPGA- and CPU-based PA accelerators have been actively studied [5,9, 21], modern graphics processing units (GPUs) offer a compelling alternative as a programmable many-core platform with high memory bandwidth. When the data layout and access patterns are carefully co-designed with the GPU memory hierarchy, GPUs can deliver high effective throughput while avoiding the development cost and rigidity typically associated with FPGA designs.

In this paper, we present a GPU-accelerated PA implementation based on NTT, optimized for large-scale workloads motivated by finite-size considerations. Our design employs: (i) an NTT-friendly data layout to ensure coalesced global-memory access and minimize redundant transfers; (ii) a hybrid butterfly computation scheme that leverages warp-level communication and shared-memory reuse; (iii) kernel fusion strategies specifically designed to mitigate kernel launch overhead and eliminate intermediate global-memory round-trips between NTT stages; and (iv) a Barrett-based modular reduction strategy to accelerate modular multiplication without expensive integer division. With these optimizations, our implementation achieves **3.32 Gbps** (40.382 ms) on an NVIDIA L40 GPU and **1.62 Gbps** (82.766 ms) on an NVIDIA RTX 3080. These results demonstrate that software-based NTT acceleration on modern GPUs can provide a practical high-throughput PA building block for high-rate QKD systems, and can support hundreds-of-Mbps-class SKR QKD systems under typical post-processing overheads.

2   Background and Related Work

This section reviews Toeplitz-hash-based privacy amplification and its acceleration via transform methods. We outline the formulation of Toeplitz hashing through a circulant embedding that enables fast cyclic-convolution evaluation, and we contrast FFT- and NTT-based approaches with emphasis on their arithmetic properties.

2.1   Toeplitz Hashing for Privacy Amplification

PA is commonly instantiated via a linear universal$_2$ hash family. Toeplitz hashing is widely adopted in practical QKD implementations due to its compact seed representation and efficient streaming capabilities. Let $\mathbf{x} \in \{0,1\}^n$ denote the reconciled key and $\mathbf{y} \in \{0,1\}^r$ the compressed key. A Toeplitz matrix $\mathbf{T} \in \{0,1\}^{r \times n}$ is defined by a seed $\mathbf{s} = (s_0, \ldots, s_{n+r-2}) \in \{0,1\}^{n+r-1}$ such that $T_{i,j} = s_{i-j+(n-1)}$ for $0 \leq i < r$ and $0 \leq j < n$. The PA output is computed as

$$\mathbf{y} = \mathbf{Tx} \bmod 2. \tag{1}$$

This matrix–vector multiplication is a structured linear map. By embedding the $r \times n$ Toeplitz operator into an $N \times N$ circulant matrix, where N denotes the transform length used for the circulant embedding and is chosen such that $N \geq n + r - 1$ (typically as a power of two), the computation in (1) can be evaluated via an N-point cyclic convolution [6].

This reduction lowers the complexity from $O(nr)$ to $O(N \log N)$, where N is the transform length introduced above, by utilizing fast transform algorithms.

2.2   Transform-Based Acceleration: FFT and NTT

To compute the cyclic convolution efficiently, the fast Fourier transform (FFT) is conventionally employed. FFT-based PA accelerates the computation but operates in complex floating-point arithmetic. Since the inputs are binary and the desired output is binary (mod 2) whereas the underlying convolution coefficients are integer-valued, floating-point rounding can complicate bit-exact integer recovery at large transform sizes. Ensuring correctness may require higher-precision data types and/or additional correction steps, introducing extra overhead [23].

The number theoretic transform (NTT) provides an integer-domain alternative by operating over the finite field $\mathbb{Z}_p$ for a prime modulus p. To ensure exact recovery of the linear convolution result, the modulus p must satisfy $p > N$. NTT shares the same staged structure and data permutations as FFT. Specifically, the core radix-2 butterfly operation for inputs u, v and twiddle factor W is defined as:

$$u' = (u + Wv) \bmod p, \qquad v' = (u - Wv) \bmod p, \tag{2}$$

replacing floating-point arithmetic with modular integer operations. Consequently, both FFT and NTT are bandwidth-sensitive for large N due to repeated data movement across $\log_2 N$ stages. However, high-throughput NTT implementations must additionally optimize modular multiplication and reduction (e.g., division-free reduction) to fully utilize general-purpose hardware such as GPUs [17].

Prior work has reported that FFT-based PA pipelines can suffer from floating-point rounding issues when recovering integer-valued convolution coefficients at large transform sizes. In particular, Wang *et al.* observed that single-precision FFT may fail to produce bit-exact results beyond a certain scale in their evaluated setting, and that ensuring correctness can require higher precision and/or additional correction steps, reducing throughput [23]. Motivated by these numerical limitations, we adopt an NTT-based approach that performs the transform entirely in modular integer arithmetic, thereby avoiding floating-point rounding in the transform and enabling deterministic, bit-exact computation under a suitably chosen modulus.

2.3   Prior Acceleration Works for Large-Scale PA and NTT

A substantial body of work has investigated accelerating Toeplitz-based PA on heterogeneous platforms. FFT-based PA has been implemented on FPGA using long-FFT strategies and dedicated FFT cores [9], and CPU implementations have demonstrated the feasibility of large-block processing with transform acceleration and careful engineering [21]. In continuous-variable QKD, Wang *et al.* proposed a high-speed implementation of length-compatible PA, emphasizing practical constraints and throughput-oriented design choices [23]. To address numerical reliability and exactness demands, other studies introduced multi-precision components, such as GMP-based schemes, to mitigate limitations of floating-point pipelines [26]. Recent large-scale FPGA work further discussed design trade-offs for large-block PA implementations, including numerical and resource considerations in transform-based Toeplitz multiplication, and reported the associated resource/design trade-offs [5].

Alongside PA-specific studies, the broader literature on fast NTT for GPUs provides implementation insights that are directly relevant to high-throughput modular transforms. Özcan and Savaş present GPU-oriented NTT algorithms and discuss optimization considerations for performance on CUDA-capable devices [17]. These works collectively motivate NTT-based PA on GPUs: NTT preserves exact arithmetic while enabling aggressive parallelization via butterfly stages, and performance depends critically on data layout, memory traffic, and efficient modular reduction.

3   Proposed GPU-Based Privacy Amplification Scheme

This section specifies how we realize large-block Toeplitz-hash PA on GPUs using an NTT-based pipeline and GPU-oriented kernels. We first summarize the end-to-end PA computation flow at the algorithm level, and then describe two core implementation ingredients: (i) a hybrid on-chip butterfly operation strategy (Sect. 3.2), and (ii) a kernel-fused 9-step (3D-decomposed) NTT/INTT design tailored to 2^{27}-point workloads (Sect. 3.3). Throughout, we keep arithmetic exact in $\mathbb{Z}_p$ and reduce global-memory traffic via fused scaling and implicit data reorders.

3.1   Overall PA Computation Flow

We consider a single PA block and start from the Toeplitz-hash definition in (1). Using the standard Toeplitz-to-circulant embedding viewpoint from structured linear algebra, the Toeplitz matrix–vector product can be mapped to a cyclic convolution after suitable padding and index reversal, enabling transform-domain acceleration in quasi-linear time [6].

In our implementation, the target large-block setting motivates a power-of-two transform length, and we focus on the 2^{27}-point regime. In this paper, we target PA blocks at the 2^{27}-bit scale and set the transform length to $N = 2^{27}$ points after Toeplitz-to-circulant embedding (with $N \geq n + r - 1$), where n denotes the length of the reconciled input block (in bits) and r denotes the length of the compressed output key (in bits). We pack the seed and input bits into two length-N sequences $\mathbf{a}, \mathbf{b} \in \mathbb{Z}_p^N$ by mapping bits to $\{0, 1\} \subset \mathbb{Z}_p$, following standard transform-based Toeplitz-hash PA constructions [9,21]. Concretely, we form $\mathbf{a}$ from the Toeplitz seed and $\mathbf{b}$ from the input block by applying the standard Toeplitz-to-circulant embedding (index reversal and zero-padding to length N), so that the resulting cyclic convolution corresponds to the desired Toeplitz multiplication on the extracted output segment. The cyclic convolution in $\mathbb{Z}_p$ is then evaluated via the NTT convolution theorem:

$$\mathbf{c} = \mathrm{INTT}_p\Big(\mathrm{NTT}_p(\mathbf{a}) \odot \mathrm{NTT}_p(\mathbf{b}) \Big) \in \mathbb{Z}_p^N, \tag{3}$$

where $\odot$ denotes element-wise multiplication in $\mathbb{Z}_p$. We will refer to (3) as the *NTT-based PA core* in the remainder of this section. Finally, the PA output bits are obtained by extracting the prescribed entries of $\mathbf{c}$ implied by the embedding and applying the mod-2 reduction (and unpacking for word-level representations), following standard transform-based Toeplitz-hash PA constructions [9,21].

Adaptation to Other Block Lengths. Although we target the 2^{27}-point regime for throughput and finite-size motivation, the same flow extends to any length by choosing a power-of-two transform size $N \geq n + r - 1$ and padding with zeros as required by the embedding. When N differs from 2^{27}, the GPU kernels can follow the same staged butterfly structure in (2); the only change is the decomposition/mapping strategy described in Sect. 3.3.

3.2 Hybrid Butterfly Operation on GPUs

This subsection describes how the staged radix-2 butterflies are executed in our GPU NTT kernel. Each stage applies the standard modular butterfly in (2) with a stage-dependent twiddle factor. Our goal is to realize the required pairwise exchange and modular arithmetic efficiently on GPU hardware while preserving exactness in $\mathbb{Z}_p$.

Schedule and Ordering (DIT, with DIF also Applicable). Our current implementation follows an iterative in-place *decimation-in-time (DIT)* schedule [22]. As is standard for iterative DIT realizations, the permutation required to obtain outputs in natural order (e.g., bit-reversal) is applied *when supplying inputs to the butterfly pipeline*: we read the data from global memory and perform the required index permutation in the global-memory load path before the first butterfly stage. After this permuted load, butterfly stages are executed in increasing stage order. Importantly, the *hybrid execution principle* below does not rely on DIT specifically: a decimation-in-frequency (DIF) realization preserves the same staged radix-2 dependency structure and can adopt the same *register-first/shared-memory-later* split, with appropriate indexing and permutation choices.

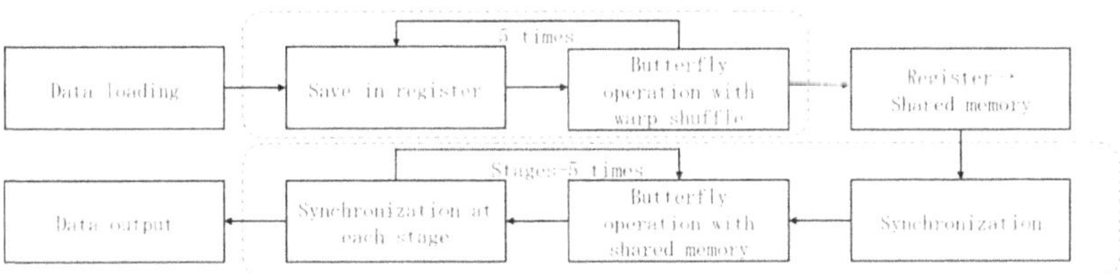

Fig. 1. Overview of the proposed hybrid butterfly operation on GPUs. Early stages are executed in a warp-synchronous manner with register-resident data and warp-shuffle exchanges, while later stages switch to shared-memory staging with stage-wise synchronization.

Stage-Wise Hybridization: Warp-Synchronous vs. Shared-Memory Execution. Figure 1 illustrates the key observation: the butterfly partner distance grows exponentially with stage index. Early stages exchange data within a warp, whereas later stages require communication beyond warp scope. We therefore adopt a hybrid policy: (i) *early stages:* keep the *data coefficients* (i.e., the input/intermediate values u and v in (2)) in registers and use warp-level exchange to obtain butterfly partners, while applying the corresponding stage-dependent twiddle factor W in (2), thereby avoiding shared-memory traffic and block-wide synchronization; and (ii) *later stages:* stage intermediate data in shared memory and execute remaining butterflies in-place with stage-wise synchronization.

Warp-Synchronous Execution in Early Stages. In early stages, coefficients are kept register-resident and each thread obtains its butterfly partner via warp-level exchange, then applies (2). This avoids intermediate shared-memory stores and block-wide synchronization as long as the partner mapping remains intra-warp. Specifically, the register and shuffle approach applies while the butterfly partner mapping remains within a warp (i.e., stride ≤ 16 for a 32-thread warp). Once the mapping exceeds warp scope, we switch from register-based shuffles to shared memory to support inter-warp communication.

Modular Arithmetic: Division-Free Multiplication and Bounded Normalization. The dominant arithmetic cost in (2) is the modular product between a twiddle factor and a coefficient. We implement modular multiplication using a Barrett-style reduction with a precomputed constant

$$\mu \triangleq \left\lfloor \frac{2^{64}}{p} \right\rfloor, \tag{4}$$

so that for a 64-bit product $z = a \cdot b$, an approximate quotient can be obtained from the high half of $z \cdot \mu$, and the remainder is formed as

$$r = z - qp, \qquad q \approx \left\lfloor \frac{z}{p} \right\rfloor. \tag{5}$$

After a small fixed number of conditional subtractions, the result is normalized to $[0, p)$ and equals the exact modular product, while avoiding integer division [2,4]. Similarly, the butterfly add/subtract updates are kept within a bounded range via lightweight conditional corrections so that values remain in $[0, p)$ throughout the stages.

Branchless Butterfly Selection and Uniform Control Flow. Within the warp-synchronous phase, each butterfly operates on a partner pair (u, v) and produces two outputs (u', v') as in (2). When we implement the early stages using warp-level exchange, a given lane can obtain both input values (its own value and the partner value) and can therefore compute *both* candidates u' and v'. However, each lane must finally write back only one of them: lanes belonging to the "upper" half of a butterfly write u', whereas lanes in the "lower" half write v' according to the stage-dependent partner mapping. To keep control flow uniform, we avoid an explicit `if/else` branch per lane and instead select between u' and v' using predication (e.g., conditional moves or bit-mask selection). This branchless selection suppresses warp divergence and maintains a single, uniform instruction path across all lanes in the warp.

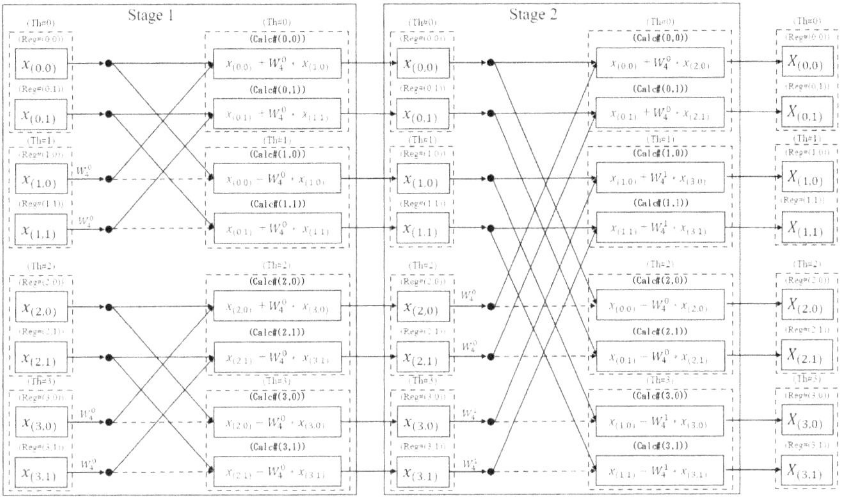

Fig. 2. Illustrative example for the register-resident phase with multi-coefficient processing per thread. Early-stage butterflies are evaluated warp-synchronously using warp shuffles.

Register Reuse via Multi-coefficient Processing (Vectorized Streams). As illustrated in Fig. 2, during the register-resident phase each thread holds multiple coefficients and advances these streams in parallel using warp-shuffle-based partner exchange in the early butterfly stages. In the register-resident phase, each thread holds a small vector of coefficients in registers and updates them in lockstep across stages. A single thread therefore advances multiple independent coefficient streams simultaneously, rather than processing only one scalar coefficient at a time. In our implementation, we configure each thread to process a vector of four elements (four streams) in parallel, which naturally aligns with 128-bit global memory transactions. We note that this degree of vectorization is a tunable parameter; while four is optimal for the hardware tested, the vector width should be adjusted according to the available register file size and instruction throughput characteristics of the specific target GPU architecture.

At each early stage, the thread obtains the butterfly partner for each register value via a warp shuffle and applies the same radix-2 modular butterfly update in (2). The stage-dependent twiddle factor is reused across the per-thread vector elements at that stage, which amortizes twiddle access and control overhead while increasing instruction-level parallelism. When the data layout permits, these per-thread vector elements are also moved with vectorized global-memory transactions, improving effective bandwidth.

The vectorized multi-stream execution preserves correctness: it is equivalent to running the same butterfly schedule independently for each stream, but with multiple streams advanced together within a thread.

Shared-Memory Staging with Conflict-Mitigated Layout. In later stages, butterfly partners reside in different warps, so intermediate values must be exchanged at block scope. We therefore stage a working set in shared memory as a 2-D tile that is repeatedly read and updated by the remaining butterfly stages. A direct row-major layout can lead to shared-memory bank conflicts when threads access strided partner locations. To mitigate this effect, we use a *padded* leading dimension, storing the tile as `tile[T][T+1]` rather than `tile[T][T]`. Here, `T` denotes the per-block tile extent (in elements) along each shared-memory dimension, i.e., the kernel stages a $T \times T$ workspace per thread block to hold the intermediate NTT coefficients for a subproblem. This padding adds one dummy element per row, so that consecutive rows start at different bank alignments, and the common strided access patterns map more evenly across banks. Importantly, this padding changes only the physical placement in shared memory; the logical indices and the in-place butterfly updates remain exactly those of (2).

3.3   Kernel-Fused 9-Step NTT for 2^{27}-Point PA

This subsection describes our kernel-fused 9-step realization of the $N = 2^{27}$ NTT/INTT used in the NTT-based PA core (3). We first clarify the transform length and data layout, then outline the 9-step 3D factorization and its GPU-oriented advantages, followed by the fused-kernel mapping and the role of the inverse scaling.

Transform Length and Data Layout. As introduced in Sect. 3.1, Toeplitz-hash PA maps a reconciled key $\mathbf{x} \in \{0,1\}^n$ to an r-bit output $\mathbf{y} \in \{0,1\}^r$ via a Toeplitz matrix, and the standard Toeplitz-to-circulant embedding requires a transform length N satisfying $N \geq n + r - 1$. In our NTT-based implementation we fix $N = 2^{27}$ so that a single 2^{27}-point transform covers our target PA block sizes. On the GPU, this 1D length-N array is stored as a logical matrix in global memory, which matches the row-major access pattern in our CUDA kernels while still representing one 2^{27}-point transform. The modulus p is a 32-bit NTT prime that admits a primitive 2^{27}-th root of unity, enabling an exact radix-2 NTT/INTT in $\mathbb{Z}_p$ [16]. Throughout, input bits are mapped to $\{0,1\} \subset \mathbb{Z}_p$ and padded to length N as required by the embedding, so the GPU kernels operate on a length-N field-valued vector.

9-Step (3D) Factorization for $N = 2^{27}$. We adopt a 3D factorization that is standard in large FFT/NTT implementations [1,14,15]. At the algorithmic level, the 2^{27}-point 1D vector is treated as a $512 \times 512 \times 512$ tensor, and the global transform is evaluated by three kernels of 512-point NTTs (one round per tensor dimension), with twiddle-factor multiplications between rounds. In our GPU implementation, we do not materialize an explicit 3D array in memory; instead, the data are stored as a 1D vector and accessed through a 2D view of shape $512 \times (512^2)$ with appropriate index mapping. This 2D representation is an implementation choice for address generation and memory coalescing, while the computation still follows the same 3D factorization schedule.

The first two kernels each apply a 512-point NTT to one tensor dimension, followed by a twiddle-factor multiplication, and then an axis permutation implemented as an implicit reorder in the same kernel. The third kernel applies the final 512-point NTT and writes the result back in 1D order. Figure 3 summarizes this 9-step schedule at a high level. Mathematically, it is a regrouping of the same radix-2 NTT computation as in (2); it preserves exactness in $\mathbb{Z}_p$ while improving locality and global-memory access regularity on the GPU.

On GPUs, this 3D factorization is particularly attractive: each 512-point subtransform is mapped to a thread block, enabling on-chip execution with the hybrid butterfly scheme from Sect. 3.2, while transpose-like steps are expressed as structured index re-mappings rather than irregular long-stride accesses.

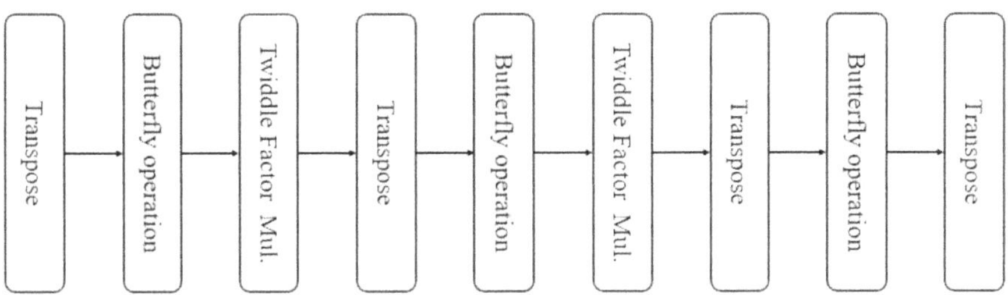

Fig. 3. Kernel-fused 9-step NTT pipeline for a 2^{27}-point transform. The input vector is reshaped into a 512×512^2 tensor. In our implementation, the nine logical operations are executed using three fused kernels: (Kernel 1) `Transpose–Butterfly–Twiddle–Transpose`, (Kernel 2) `Butterfly–Twiddle–Transpose`, and (Kernel 3) `Butterfly–Transpose`.

GPU Kernels: Fusion and Implicit Reorders. A naive implementation would realize each of the nine logical steps in Fig. 3 as a separate kernel, causing repeated global read/write passes and high kernel-launch overhead. We instead fuse the pipeline into three kernels per transform. Each fused kernel combines one 512-point subtransform with the required twiddle multiplication/Transpose step, and realizes the transpose-like reorder *implicitly* by writing outputs to the addresses of the next logical layout, thereby avoiding standalone transpose kernels and reducing intermediate global-memory traffic [17].

4 Experimental Evaluation

This section evaluates the proposed GPU-accelerated NTT-based PA implementation at the 2^{27}-bit scale (i.e., on the order of 10^8 bits). We first summarize the experimental setup and then compare throughput against representative large-block PA implementations reported in the literature.

4.1 Experimental Setup

All kernels were implemented in CUDA 12.2 and compiled with aggressive optimization flags (e.g., -O3) while preserving exact modular arithmetic in $\mathbb{Z}_p$. GPU execution time is measured by `cudaEvent` and reported as *GPU kernel time* for the PA core (two forward NTTs, pointwise multiplication, and one inverse NTT). Unless otherwise stated, host–device transfers are excluded, as practical QKD pipelines can overlap communication and computation.

We evaluate two NVIDIA GPUs listed in Table 1. The RTX 3080 represents a high-end Ampere GPU, while the L40 is a data-center Ada GPU with substantially larger memory capacity and on-chip resources.

Table 1. GPU platforms used in our experiments.

GPU	Arch.	CUDA cores	Mem. [GB]	Mem. type	BW [GB/s]
RTX 3080	Ampere (GA102)	8,960	12	GDDR6X	912
L40	Ada (AD102)	18,176	48	GDDR6	864

4.2 NTT Kernel Result Comparison

Table 2. Forward NTT latency under the BLS12-377 prime modulus. Baselines (Merge-NTT) are taken from [17]; values are in μs. Our time reports the total GPU kernel time of one forward NTT (sum of fused kernels when applicable), averaged over 100 runs after warm-up and measured by `cudaEvent`.

$\log_2 N$	This work [μs]		Ref. [17] [μs]	
	RTX 3080	L40	RTX 4090	A100
18	62.848	**49.888**	64.040	120.060
21	243.456	**119.680**	424.250	854.360
24	2305.908	**927.968**	4178.860	7294.050
27	19431.763	**10204.768**	36780.500	65097.40

We compare the latency of one *forward NTT* computation under the BLS12-377 prime modulus, measured as GPU kernel time. This kernel-level comparison uses the BLS12-377 modulus to match the setting of [17] for microbenchmarking; our end-to-end PA pipeline uses a 32-bit NTT prime as described in Sect. 3.3. Our measurements on RTX 3080 and L40 are contrasted with the Merge-NTT baselines reported for A100 and RTX 4090 in [17]. We compare latencies at the same transform lengths under the same prime modulus. Table 2 shows that latency increases with $\log_2 N$ for all platforms. This is consistent with staged radix-2 NTT execution, where larger N implies a greater number of butterfly stages and a larger working set.

Comparison Against Merge-NTT Baselines. Table 2 compares our forward-NTT latency under the same modulus setting with the Merge-NTT baselines reported in [17]. Across all tested transform sizes, our L40 implementation achieves the lowest latency among the compared platforms. This observation is notable because overall GPU capability is not determined by a single peak metric: different devices (RTX 3080, L40, RTX 4090, A100) exhibit distinct trade-offs in memory bandwidth, cache hierarchy, and on-chip resource limits, which can dominate the performance of bandwidth-sensitive NTT kernels.

For large N, an iterative radix-2 NTT becomes increasingly constrained by *data movement* rather than raw integer throughput. Each stage requires reading and writing a large working set and performing regular partner exchanges; as N grows, the working set quickly exceeds on-chip storage, making effective global-memory bandwidth and synchronization overhead key determinants of end-to-end latency. In this regime, optimizations that reduce global-memory round-trips and avoid unnecessary barriers can outweigh differences in peak compute throughput. In addition, larger on-chip caches and higher sustained memory bandwidth can improve effective reuse of twiddles and the working set, which may further benefit large-scale NTT execution.

Our kernel is explicitly designed for this large-N behavior. First, the hybrid butterfly execution keeps early stages warp-synchronous with register-resident data and warp shuffles, reducing shared-memory staging and block-wide synchronization until inter-warp exchanges become unavoidable (Sect. 3.2). Second, in the 2^{27}-scale pipeline, the 9-step decomposition and kernel fusion reduce global-memory traffic by merging local NTT computation with the required scaling and reorder steps, where transpose-like reorders are realized by address remapping at store time rather than by separate transpose kernels. These choices directly target the dominant costs at large N and improve effective bandwidth utilization.

We therefore interpret the results in Table 2 as evidence that, under a matched modulus setting, the proposed implementation achieves higher *kernel-level efficiency* than the Merge-NTT baselines in [17], with the advantage becoming more pronounced at larger transform sizes where memory traffic and synchronization costs dominate. In this sense, the efficiency of the proposed approach is closely related to the GPU type considered. Because the implementation is dominated by large-scale staged data movement, its realized efficiency depends primarily on architectural features such as sustained memory bandwidth, cache capacity, shared-memory/register availability, and the efficiency of warp-synchronous data exchange, rather than on peak arithmetic throughput alone. GPUs with stronger support for these data-movement-critical aspects can better exploit the hybrid butterfly schedule and the fused 9-step pipeline, especially at large transform sizes.

4.3   PA Kernel Result Comparison

Table 3 summarizes throughput results for large-block PA around the 10^8-bit regime. In this table, 10^8 and $2^{27} \approx 1.34 \times 10^8$ are treated as the same order-of-magnitude scale for comparison. We also explicitly mark the primary acceleration/arithmetic approach of each work. Specifically, the listed approaches include FFT-based Toeplitz hashing, NTT-based PA designs, and other non-transform constructions such as GMP-based modular hashing and hybrid-hash families. Note that different works may instantiate PA with different universal hash constructions.

Table 3. Large-block PA implementations around the 10^8-bit regime. Throughput is given in Gbps. The method labels "DM3H" [5] and "MMH-MH" [25] follow the terminology used in the respective works and denote NTT-accelerated *modular-hashing*-based PA constructions.

Work	Plat.	Method	Block size [bits]	Thr. [Gbps]
Takahashi et al. [20]	CPU	NTT	10^8	0.109
Yan et al. [26]	CPU	GMP	10^8	0.140
Yan et al. [25]	CPU	MMH-MH	10^8	0.140
Tang et al. [21]	CPU	FFT	10^8	0.071
Cheng et al. [5]	FPGA	DM3H	10^8	0.125
Wang et al. [23]	GPU	FFT	10^8	1.35
Nico et al. [3]	GPU	FFT	10^8	3.45
This work (RTX 3080)	GPU	**NTT**	10^8	**1.62**
This work (L40)	GPU	**NTT**	10^8	**3.32**

Comparison with CPU and FPGA Baselines. As detailed in Table 3, implementations on CPUs and FPGAs face a significant performance bottleneck at the 10^8-bit block size, with throughputs consistently plateauing around the 0.1 Gbps mark. This limitation appears platform-bound rather than algorithm-bound: whether employing FFT [21], NTT [20], or hybrid modular hashing [25,26], CPU-based solutions yield results below 0.15 Gbps. Similarly, the FPGA-based DM3H design [5] operates in the same regime (0.125 Gbps). In sharp contrast, our GPU-based approach leverages massive parallelism to bridge this gap, providing substantially higher throughput than the representative CPU/FPGA results listed in Table 3, noting that platforms and implementation settings differ across studies.

Comparison with GPU-Based PA. Table 3 compares our work with existing large-block PA implementations. Regarding GPU-based approaches, Wang *et al.* reported 1.35 Gbps on an NVIDIA K80 using FFT [23], and more recently, Nico *et al.* demonstrated 3.45 Gbps on an NVIDIA RTX 3080, also utilizing an FFT-based pipeline [3]. While these FFT-based schemes achieve high raw throughput, they rely on floating-point arithmetic. As discussed in Sect. 2.2 and noted in [23], ensuring bit-exact recovery of discrete coefficients becomes increasingly precarious as transform sizes scale to the 10^8-bit regime, which requires careful numerical safeguards to guarantee bit-exact recovery at large transform lengths (e.g., higher precision and/or correction steps as discussed in [23]). In contrast, our pipeline uses an NTT-based construction that performs the transform entirely in $\mathbb{Z}_p$ and therefore avoids floating-point rounding in the transform by design. To the best of our knowledge, our work achieves the highest reported throughput among NTT-based large-block PA implementations under comparable block sizes and exact-arithmetic requirements. We demonstrate that the numerical stability of NTT can be achieved with multi-Gbps performance suitable for real-time systems, effectively bridging the gap between exact arithmetic and high-speed processing.

5   Conclusion

We presented a GPU-accelerated PA design for QKD based on NTTs, targeting the large-block regime motivated by finite-size considerations. By executing all transform-domain operations in $\mathbb{Z}_p$, the proposed pipeline provides bit-exact modular arithmetic by construction, avoiding the numerical rounding risks that can arise in floating-point FFT-based PA at large transform lengths. On the implementation side, we combined (i) a hybrid butterfly operation strategy that uses warp-synchronous register-resident updates for early stages and shared-memory staging for later stages, with (ii) a kernel-fused 9-step (3D-decomposed) NTT/INTT design that reduces global-memory round-trips via fused scaling and implicit data reorders. Experimental evaluation on two modern GPUs shows that the proposed approach achieves **3.32 Gbps** (40.382 ms) on an NVIDIA L40 and **1.62 Gbps** (82.766 ms) on an NVIDIA RTX 3080 for 2^{27}-bit PA blocks. Consequently, the achieved performance offers sufficient processing capacity to support real-time QKD systems aiming for secret-key rates exceeding several hundred Mbps, accommodating varying compression ratios and protocol overheads.

Acknowledgment. This work is supported by the Ministry of Internal Affairs and Communications, Japan, via the project of R&D of ICT Priority Technology (JPMI00316) 'Research and development for early social implementation of quantum cryptography communication networks' (JPJ013328).

References

1. Bailey, D.H.: FFTs in external or hierarchical memory. J. Supercomput. **4**(1), 23–35 (1990). https://doi.org/10.1007/BF00162341
2. Barrett, P.: Implementing the Rivest Shamir and Adleman public key encryption algorithm on a standard digital signal processor. In: Advances in Cryptology — CRYPTO '86. Lecture Notes in Computer Science, vol. 263, pp. 311–323. Springer (1987). https://doi.org/10.1007/3-540-47721-7_24
3. Bosshard, N., Christen, R., Hänggi, E., Hofstetter, J.: Fast privacy amplification on GPUs. Poster at QIP 2021 (2021). https://doi.org/10.5281/zenodo.4551775
4. Brent, R.P., Zimmermann, P.: Modern Computer Arithmetic. Cambridge University Press (2010). https://doi.org/10.1017/CBO9780511921698
5. Cheng, X., Mao, H., Xu, H., Li, Q.: Large-scale FPGA-based Privacy Amplification exceeding 10^8 bits for Quantum Key Distribution. arXiv:2503.09331 (2025https://doi.org/10.48550/arXiv.2503.09331
6. Golub, G.H., Van Loan, C.F.: Matrix Computations, Johns Hopkins University Press. 4 edn (2013)
7. Grünenfelder, F., et al.: Fast single-photon detectors and real-time key distillation enable high secret-key-rate quantum key distribution systems. Nat. Photonics **17**(5), 422–426 (2023)
8. Laudenbach, F., et al.: Continuous-variable quantum key distribution with gaussian modulation–the theory of practical implementations. Adv. Quantum Technol. **1**(1), 1800011 (2018)
9. Li, Q., Yan, B., Mao, H., Xue, X.: High-speed implementation of FFT-based privacy amplification on. In: FPGA in Quantum Key Distribution (2018). arXiv:1809.07592
10. Li, Q., Yan, B., Mao, H., Xue, X., Han, Q., Guo, H.: High-speed and adaptive FPGA-based privacy amplification in Quantum Key Distribution. IEEE Access **7**, 21482–21490 (2019). https://doi.org/10.1109/ACCESS.2019.2897940
11. Lucamarini, M., et al.: Efficient decoy-state Quantum Key Distribution with quantified security. Opt. Express **21**(21), 24550–24565 (2013). https://doi.org/10.1364/OE.21.24550
12. Luo, Y., Cheng, X., Mao, H.K., Li, Q.: An overview of postprocessing in Quantum Key Distribution. Mathematics **12**(14), 2243 (2024). https://doi.org/10.3390/math12142243
13. Ng, S.Q., Kanitschar, F., Zhang, G., Wang, C.: Gigabit-rate quantum key distribution on integrated photonic chips (2025). (). accepted for presentation at QCrypt 2025 (per conference accepted-papers list
14. Nukada, A., Matsuoka, S.: Auto-tuning 3-d FFT library for CUDA GPUs. In: Proceedings of the Conference on High Performance Computing Networking, Storage and Analysis (SC'09), pp. 1–10 (2009). https://doi.org/10.1145/1654059.1654090
15. Nukada, A., Sato, K., Matsuoka, S.: Scalable multi-GPU 3-d FFT for TSUBAME 2.0 supercomputer. In: Proceedings of the International Conference on High Performance Computing, Networking, Storage and Analysis (SC'12), pp. 1–10 (2012). https://doi.org/10.1109/SC.2012.100
16. Nussbaumer, H.J.: Number theoretic transforms. In: Fast Fourier Transform and Convolution Algorithms, Springer Series in Information Sciences, vol. 2. Springer, Berlin, Heidelberg (1982). https://doi.org/10.1007/978-3-642-81897-4_8
17. Özcan, A.Ş., Savaş, E.: Two algorithms for fast GPU implementation of NTT. Cryptology ePrint Archive, Paper 2023/1410 (2023). https://eprint.iacr.org/2023/1410

18. Pirandola, S., et al.: Advances in Quantum Cryptography. Adv. Optics Photonics **12**(4), 1012–1236 (2020). https://doi.org/10.1364/AOP.361502
19. Renner, R., König, R.: Universally composable privacy amplification against Quantum adversaries. In: Theory of Cryptography Conference (TCC 2005). Lecture Notes in Computer Science, vol. 3378, pp. 407–425. Springer (2005). https://doi.org/10.1007/978-3-540-30576-7_22
20. Takahashi, R., Tanizawa, Y., Dixon, A.R.: High-speed implementation of privacy amplification in Quantum Key Distribution. In: QCrypt 2016 Extended Abstracts (2016). https://obj.umiacs.umd.edu/extended_abstracts/QCrypt_2016_paper_160.pdf
21. Tang, B., Liu, B., Zhai, Y., Wu, C., Yu, W.: High-speed and large-scale privacy amplification scheme for Quantum Key Distribution. Sci. Rep. **9**, 15733 (2019). https://doi.org/10.1038/s41598-019-50290-1
22. Van Loan, C.F.: Computational Frameworks for the Fast Fourier Transform, SIAM (1992)
23. Wang, X., Zhang, Y., Li, Z., Xu, B., Yu, S., Guo, H.: High-speed implementation of length-compatible privacy amplification in continuous-variable quantum key distribution. IEEE Photonics J. **10**(3), 1–9 (2018). https://doi.org/10.1109/JPHOT.2018.2824316. art. no. 7600309
24. Xu, F., Ma, X., Zhang, Q., Lo, H.K., Pan, J.W.: Secure quantum key distribution with realistic devices. Rev. Mod. Phys. **92**(2), 025002 (2020). https://doi.org/10.1103/RevModPhys.92.025002
25. Yan, B., Li, Q., Mao, H., Chen, N.: An efficient hybrid hash based privacy amplification algorithm for Quantum Key Distribution. Quantum Inf. Process. **21**(4), 130 (2022). https://doi.org/10.1007/s11128-022-03452-8
26. Yan, B., Li, Q., Mao, H., Xue, X.: High-speed privacy amplification scheme using GMP in quantum key distribution. IEEE Photonics J. **12**(3), 1–13 (2020)
27. Yuan, Z., et al.: 10-mb/s quantum key distribution. J. Lightwave Technol. **36**(16), 3427–3433 (2018)

GPU Accelerated Hough Transform for Line Detection

Damian Gradziuk[✉][iD], Beata Bylina[iD], and Przemysław Stpiczyński[iD]

Institute of Computer Science and Mathematics, Maria Curie-Skłodowska University,
ul. Akademicka 9, 20-032 Lublin, Poland
`gradziuk.damian5@gmail.com,`
`{beata.bylina,przemyslaw.stpiczynski}@mail.umcs.pl`

Abstract. The Hough Transform (HT) is a classical technique for detecting straight lines inferred from edge points in binarized images, valued for its robustness to noise and incomplete edge information. However, the numerical nature of the HT, leads to high computational complexity, where performance is dominated by updates and memory access patterns. The main contribution of this work is a GPU-accelerated implementation of the classical HT for line detection, focused on implementation-level optimizations rather than algorithmic modifications. The proposed approach preserves functional equivalence with a widely used OpenCV GPU-based implementation while exploiting the parallelism and memory hierarchy of modern GPUs. An adaptive voting strategy is employed, using shared memory when the accumulator size permits and falling back to global memory for larger parameter spaces. Experimental results obtained across various GPU architectures show that the proposed implementation achieves speedups ranging from approximately $50\times$ up to over $400\times$ compared to a sequential CPU baseline and consistently outperforms the OpenCV GPU-based solution by a factor of about $1.3\times$ to $2.5\times$.

Keywords: GPU Acceleration · Hough Transform · Image Processing · Discretized Parameter Space · Numerical Voting Scheme

1 Introduction

Originally proposed by Hough [7] and later extended for line detection by Duda and Hart [4], the Hough Transform (HT) is a classical technique for detecting parametric shapes such as straight lines in images. Its robustness to noise, fragmented contours, and missing edge points has made it a standard tool in computer vision. From a computational perspective, the classical voting-based formulation of the HT can be viewed as a dense numerical accumulation over a discretized two-dimensional parameter space, where each edge point contributes votes across a range of angular parameters. As a result, execution time is dominated by accumulator updates and memory access patterns rather than by control flow complexity.

M. Paszynski et al. (Eds.): ICCS 2026 Workshops, LNCS 16788, pp. 558–572, 2026.
https://doi.org/10.1007/978-3-032-29915-4_46

The growing availability of high-resolution images and dense edge maps has magnified the computational cost of the HT, limiting its applicability in time-critical and large-scale scenarios. On conventional CPU architectures, the inherent parallelism of the voting process is only weakly exploited, leading to execution times that scale linearly with the number of edge points and the angular resolution. In contrast, modern GPUs provide massive data parallelism and high memory bandwidth, making them a natural target for accelerating accumulation-based numerical algorithms. Additionally, GPUs offer a hierarchical memory model, including shared memory that can be used to optimize access patterns and reduce latency for frequently updated data structures [2].

In this work, we focus on accelerating the classical HT for straight line detection through implementation-level optimization on GPUs. Rather than introducing algorithmic approximations or probabilistic variants, the proposed approach deliberately retains the classical formulation of the HT in order to focus on the impact of implementation and hardware-level optimizations. This approach allows performance variations to be examined with respect to GPU hardware architecture, memory hierarchy, and input image characteristics, while eliminating variability due to algorithmic design and parameterization.

The main contribution of this paper is a GPU-accelerated implementation of the classical HT that employs an adaptive voting strategy. Depending on the size of the discretized accumulator, voting is performed either in shared memory or directly in global memory, allowing efficient execution across a wide range of image resolutions and parameter-space configurations. The implementation is evaluated on various GPU architectures, demonstrating speedups ranging from approximately $50\times$ to over $400\times$ compared to a single-threaded CPU baseline, while achieving an additional $1.3\times - 2.1\times$ speedup over the wildely-used OpenCV GPU-based implementation.

The remainder of this paper is organized as follows. Section 2 reviews related work on HT variants and GPU-based implementations. Section 3 introduces the theoretical background of the classical HT. Section 4 describes the proposed GPU implementation. Section 5 presents the experimental setup and performance results. Section 6 concludes the paper.

2   Related Work

Due to the high computational cost of the classical HT, numerous approaches have been proposed to reduce its complexity. Probabilistic and randomized variants aim to limit the number of processed edge points while preserving detection performance. The Probabilistic HT (PHT) introduced by Kiryati et al. [10] demonstrated that reliable line detection can often be achieved using only a randomly selected subset of edge points. Similarly, the Randomized HT (RHT) proposed by Xu and Oja [19] reduces both computational and memory complexity by sampling minimal point sets and estimating parameters probabilistically. Further extensions of these ideas allowed to improve efficiency by incrementally refining detection results, as shown by Galamhos et al. [6].

Another class of methods focuses on reducing the dimensionality or resolution of the accumulator space. Multiresolution and hierarchical variants, such as the approaches proposed by Atiquzzaman [1] and Espinosa and Perkowski [5], employ coarse-to-fine strategies to limit accumulator growth and improve computational efficiency. While effective, these methods often introduce additional algorithmic complexity and require careful parameter tuning.

Beyond algorithmic modifications, several works have explored hardware-accelerated implementations of the HT. Early efforts targeted reconfigurable and embedded architectures, including FPGA-based implementations optimized for memory locality and parallelism [21]. More recently, GPUs have emerged as a natural platform for accelerating the voting-based structure of the HT. Van den Braak et al. [2] investigated different GPU implementation strategies and highlighted trade-offs between throughput-oriented and input-independent execution models. Additional GPU-based accelerations have been reported for both two-dimensional image data [13] and higher-dimensional Hough spaces, such as 3D plane detection in LiDAR data [17].

The HT has also been extended and adapted for various application domains, including lane detection [12], industrial inspection [11], and medical imaging [20]. Recent works combine classical Hough-based formulations with learning-based components or deploy them on embedded GPU platforms to meet real-time constraints [14].

Direct performance comparisons with existing approaches are challenging, as many rely on probabilistic or randomized variants of the HT that reduce computation by processing subsets of input data. This alters the computational characteristics and makes their performance not directly comparable to the classical HT operating on the full dataset.

This work concentrates on implementation-level optimization of the classical, voting-based HT for straight line detection. By preserving functional equivalence with the widely used OpenCV GPU-based implementation, the proposed approach enables a controlled evaluation of performance scalability with respect to both image resolution and edge point density. Furthermore, the analysis is conducted across various GPU architectures, allowing to focus on architectural effects related to parallel execution and memory hierarchy.

3   Hough Transform Algorithm

In the classical case of line detection, the algorithm maps every edge point from the edge map into a parameter space, where each line is represented by a pair (ρ, θ), where ρ denotes the perpendicular distance from the origin to the line, and θ represents the angle of the line's normal vector with respect to the x-axis.

The key idea of the HT is that collinear points in the image space correspond to curves in the parameter space that intersect at a common point. As a result, the presence of a line in the image is manifested as a prominent peak in the accumulator space, as illustrated in Fig. 1.

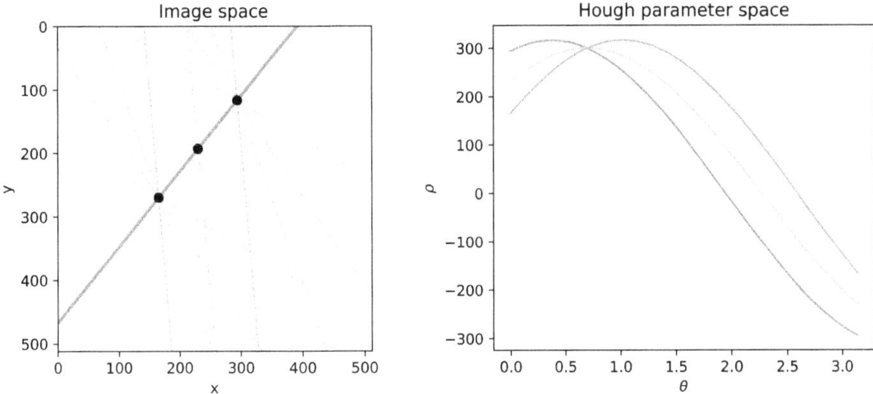

Fig. 1. Principle of the Hough transform: multiple candidate lines passing through individual edge points in the image space (left) and the corresponding sinusoidal mappings intersecting at a common point in the parameter space (right).

For a binary edge map $I(x, y)$ achieved after applying an edge detection algorithm, such as the Canny edge detector [3], on an image, the equation of a line can be expressed in polar coordinates as

$$\rho = x \cos(\theta) + y \sin(\theta), \tag{1}$$

where (x, y) denotes the coordinates of an edge point. For each such point, the algorithm iterates over a discretized range of θ values, typically spanning the interval $[0, \pi]$, and computes the corresponding ρ. The accumulator array is incremented at the discretized location (ρ, θ), effectively casting a vote for a potential line passing through the point.

From a computational perspective, the time complexity of the classical voting-based HT for line detection is given by

$$O(N_e \cdot N_\theta), \tag{2}$$

where N_e denotes the number of edge points in the image and N_θ represents the number of discretized angle samples [4,8]. In the worst case, N_e is bounded by the image resolution, i.e., $N_e \leq W \cdot H$, where W and H denote the image width and height, respectively. As the result, the computational cost grows linearly with both the number of edge points and the angular resolution of the parameter space.

The memory complexity of the algorithm is dominated by the size of the accumulator array, which is given by

$$O(N_\rho \cdot N_\theta), \tag{3}$$

where N_ρ denotes the number of discretized distance values. For an image of resolution $W \times H$, the parameter ρ typically spans the range $[-\sqrt{W^2 + H^2}, -\sqrt{W^2 + H^2}]$, implying that N_ρ increases proportionally with the image diagonal.

Consequently, both the memory requirements and the computational cost of the accumulator update are strongly influenced by the image resolution and the chosen discretization parameters [8, 16].

After all edge points have been processed, the accumulator is scanned for local maxima. These maxima correspond to parameter pairs (ρ, θ) that received a significant number of votes and thus represent detected line candidates. In practice, a threshold is applied to suppress weak responses and reduce false detections [4].

The HT algorithm has been extended to support the detection of other parametric shapes, including circles [9], ellipses [18], and more complex forms. In such cases, the dimensionality of the parameter space increases, leading to higher computational and memory requirements. To address these limitations, the Generalized HT was introduced [15], enabling the detection of arbitrary shapes by replacing the analytical parameterization with a lookup-based representation. While these extensions significantly broaden the applicability of the HT, they also increase its computational cost, making optimised implementations particularly important from practical point of view. For this reason, the present work restricts its scope to straight line detection using the classical voting-based formulation, which remains particularly well-suited for parallelization on modern GPU architectures.

4   Implementation

We have implemented two variants of the HT for line detection: a classical sequential version executed on the single-threaded CPU and a parallel, GPU-accelerated version. All implementations were developed in C++, using the NVIDIA CUDA framework (version 12.8). The source code of the proposed implementation is publicly available at https://github.com/FoxedGuy/hough-gpu.

The sequential CPU implementation is intentionally limited to a single-threaded baseline without vectorization or multi-core parallelization. This design choice allows for a clear comparison between the classical execution model and the massively parallel GPU implementation, isolating the impact of hardware-level parallelism on the performance of the voting process. At the same time, the CPU implementation was not left entirely unoptimized: trigonometric values were precomputed using a lookup table, and the code was compiled with compiler optimizations enabled (-O3). These measures reduce avoidable overhead while preserving the fundamentally sequential character of the baseline.

The GPU-accelerated implementation follows a three-stage pipeline executed by dedicated CUDA kernels: extraction of edge point coordinates from the input edge map, voting in the accumulator space and detection of local maxima. In the first stage, non-zero values from the edge map are extracted using the `extract_non_zero_packed` kernel. Each thread examines a single pixel and if it corresponds to an edge point, stores its coordinates using an atomic increment. To reduce memory traffic and improve cache efficiency, edge points coordinates are packed into a 32-bit integer, with horizontal and vertical positions encoded in separate 16-bit fields. The parallel extraction and the packing of non-zero values coordinates kernel is formally summarized in Algorithm 1.

Algorithm 1 CUDA Kernel: Extraction of Non-Zero Pixels with Packed Coordinates

---

Require: Binary edge map I of size $N \times N$
Ensure: Packed coordinate list P, number of edge points N_e
 1: **for** each pixel (x, y) **in parallel do**
 2:     **if** $I(y, x) \neq 0$ **then**
 3:         $idx \leftarrow$ **atomicAdd**$(N_e, 1)$
 4:         $P[idx] \leftarrow (y \ll 16) \mid x$
 5:     **end if**
 6: **end for**

The accumulator is represented as a two-dimensional integer array stored in the global memory, with its dimensions determined by the discretization of the ρ and θ parameters, including padding. For better memory coalescing, the pitch version of CUDA memory allocation function, `cudaMallocPitch` has been used.

The voting stage constitutes the most computationally intensive part of the algorithm. Each CUDA block is responsible for processing a single discretized angle value, while threads within the block iterate over the list of detected edge points and compute the corresponding polar parameter. Trigonometric values are computed on-the-fly using the `__sincosf` intrinsic function and scaled by the reciprocal of the radial discretization step. This approach shows itself to be more efficient than using precomputed lookup tables due to reduced number of memory references and better utilization of the GPU's special function units. The computed radial index is rounded using the `__float2int_rn` intrinsic to ensure consistent mapping to accumulator bins.

Depending on the size of the accumulator and the available shared memory on the target device, two alternative voting strategies are employed. For each discretized angle, a one-dimensional slice of the accumulator corresponding to the radial parameter is processed independently. When the size of this slice fits into shared memory, it is allocated as a shared buffer local to the CUDA block stored in shared memory. The buffer is shared by all threads within the block and represents the accumulator row for a single angle value. The shared memory voting kernel employed in this case is formally summarized as Algorithm 2.

During voting, all threads concurrently update the shared accumulator using atomic operations, accumulating votes for different radial bins. Because of shared memory being physically located on-chip and shared only among threads of the same block, this approach significantly reduces global memory traffic and contention. After all votes for a given angle are processed, a synchronization barrier ensures that the shared accumulator is fully updated before its contents are written back to the corresponding row in global memory.

Algorithm 2 CUDA Kernel: Voting-based Hough Accumulator with Shared Memory

---

Require: Packed edge point list P of size N_e, N_θ, N_ρ, ρ^{-1}, $\theta_{\min}$, $\Delta\theta$
Ensure: Accumulator array A

1: **for** each angle index θ_k **in parallel do**
2:     Allocate shared array $S[0 \ldots N_\rho + 1]$
3:     Initialize $S \leftarrow 0$
4:     $\theta \leftarrow \theta_{\min} + k \cdot \Delta\theta$
5:     $(\cos\theta, \sin\theta) \leftarrow \mathrm{sincos}(\theta)$
6:     $\cos\theta \leftarrow \cos\theta \cdot \rho^{-1}$
7:     $\sin\theta \leftarrow \sin\theta \cdot \rho^{-1}$
8:     $shift \leftarrow \lfloor (N_\rho - 1)/2 \rfloor$
9:     **for** each edge point $(x_i, y_i) \in P$ **in parallel do**
10:         $r \leftarrow \mathrm{round}(x_i \cdot \cos\theta + y_i \cdot \sin\theta)$
11:         $r \leftarrow r + shift$
12:         **atomicAdd**$(S[r + 1], 1)$
13:     **end for**
14:     Synchronize threads
15:     Copy S to global accumulator row $A[k + 1][\cdot]$
16: **end for**

If the size of the accumulator slice exceeds the available shared memory capacity, the implementation falls back to a global-memory-based strategy. In this case, all threads directly update the global accumulator using atomic operations. It leads to increased memory latency and contention but ensures correctness for larger problem sizes.

After the voting phase, local maxima in the accumulator space are detected using the `find_maxims` kernel. Each thread evaluates a single accumulator cell and performs a comparison with its immediate neighbors in both the radial and angular dimensions. Only cells exceeding a predefined threshold and satisfying the local maximum criterion are considered as valid line candidates. Each CUDA thread is mapped to a single accumulator cell (ρ, θ) using a two-dimensional grid configuration, enabling parallel evaluation of the local maximum criterion across the parameter space. Detected lines are stored using atomic operations to ensure correctness under concurrent writes.

The implementation processes square $N \times N$ edge maps, where N is assumed to be a power of two for implementation convenience. This restriction is not inherent to the algorithm and could be relaxed without affecting correctness. Detected lines are visualized using OpenCV drawing functions and saved for qualitative inspection.

5   Experiments

All experiments have been performed on three hardware platforms with varying CPU and GPU capabilities, referred to as H1, H2, and H3. The platforms have beed selected to represent different generations of server-class processors and GPU architectures, allowing the scalability of the proposed implementation to be evaluated across a wide performance spectrum.

Platform H1 is equipped with an Intel Xeon Gold 5218R CPU and an NVIDIA RTX A2000 GPU, representing a lower-end workstation-class configuration. Platform H2 consists of an Intel Xeon Platinum 8358 CPU paired with an NVIDIA A100 PCIe GPU, offering substantially higher computational throughput and memory bandwidth. Platform H3 employs an AMD EPYC 9825 processor together with an NVIDIA H200 NVL GPU, representing a high-end configuration with a next-generation GPU architecture. An overview of the GPUs' specifications is provided in Table 1.

Table 1. Hardware platforms used for experimental evaluation.

Platform	GPU	Memory	CUDA Cores
H1	NVIDIA RTX A2000	12 GB	3328
H2	NVIDIA A100 PCIe	40 GB	6912
H3	NVIDIA H200 NVL	141 GB	16896

All platforms support CUDA-based execution and provide sufficient memory resources to accommodate the accumulator sizes used in the experiments. This selection enables a consistent comparison of CPU and GPU execution characteristics across different architectural classes.

5.1   Test Data

To ensure controlled and reproducible experimental conditions, synthetic edge maps were generated and used as test data. The edge maps contain multiple horizontal line segments placed symmetrically with respect to the map center. Each line has a fixed thickness of one pixel, while the number of lines and the edge map resolution are varied across experiments.

For experiments analyzing the impact of edge map resolution, square edge maps of size $N \times N$ were generated, with N ranging from 512 to 8192 pixels. In these edge maps, a fixed number of horizontal line segments was drawn, each with a predefined length centered along the horizontal axis. This setup allows the number of edge points to be controlled independently of the edge map resolution.

All generated edge maps are binary, with foreground pixels representing line segments and background pixels set to zero. The use of synthetic data enables precise control over the number and spatial distribution of edge points, facilitating the systematic evaluation of the computational behavior of the HT under varying input conditions.

5.2   Evaluation Metrics

The primary evaluation metric used in this work is the execution time, as the main objective is to assess the computational efficiency and scalability of the proposed GPU-accelerated HT implementation. All reported timings correspond to the line detection stage, excluding image loading and disk I/O operations.

Detection quality is not treated as a primary metric. Instead, qualitative and functional correctness was verified by ensuring that, for identical parameter settings, the proposed implementation produces line detection results consistent with those obtained using the OpenCV reference implementation as shown in Fig. 2. It ensures that performance comparisons are conducted between functionally equivalent configurations.

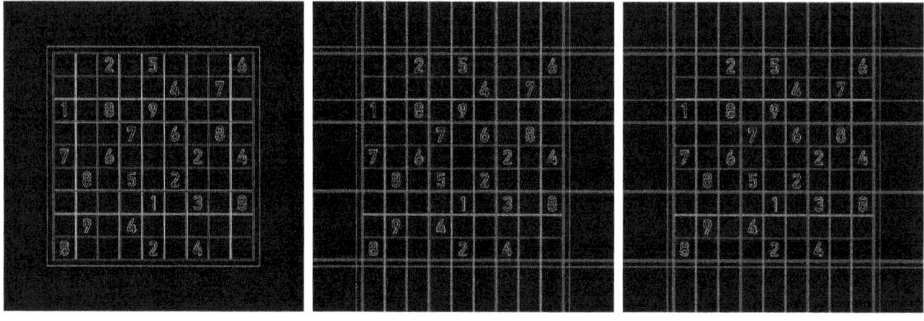

Fig. 2. Comparison of line detection results on a sudoku edge map (left) between the proposed GPU implementation (center, detected lines coloured red) and the OpenCV reference implementation (right, detected lines coloured blue). Both implementations yield identical detected lines, confirming functional equivalence. (Color figure online)

Execution times were measured using high-resolution timing mechanisms appropriate to each execution context. For GPU execution, NVIDIA Nsight profiling tools were additionally employed to validate timing measurements and to analyze kernel-level execution behavior, memory access patterns, and synchronization overheads.

5.3   Results

Table 2 reports average execution times for edge maps with a fixed resolution of 1024 × 1024 pixels and an increasing number of edge points. For all three platforms (H1–H3), the sequential CPU implementation has exhibited an approximately linear growth in execution time as the number of edge points has increased, which is consistent with the $O(N_e \cdot N_\theta)$ complexity of the voting stage.

On platform H1, increasing the number of edge points from 10,240 to 163,840 results in the execution time increase from 8.17 ms to 80.80 ms, corresponding to a factor of 9.9×. A similar trend can be observed on H2, where execution time growns from 8.19 ms to 85.04 ms (10.4×), and on H3, from 4.96 ms to 54.71 ms

Table 2. Average calculation times for edge maps with 1024×1024 resolution and different numbers of edge points. Threshold for line detection set to 400.

Edge Points	Hardware								
	H1			H2			H3		
	CPU	GPU	CV	CPU	GPU	CV	CPU	GPU	CV
10240	8.17	0.16	0.29	8.19	0.14	0.24	4.96	0.09	0.15
20480	13.04	0.18	0.31	13.14	0.14	0.25	8.46	0.09	0.15
40960	22.86	0.24	0.36	23.85	0.16	0.26	14.69	0.10	0.16
81920	42.89	0.33	0.44	43.50	0.18	0.29	27.80	0.11	0.17
163840	80.80	0.51	0.60	85.04	0.23	0.34	54.71	0.13	0.19

($11.0\times$). These results confirm that the CPU performance is primarily dominated by the number of processed edge points, while differences between platforms reflect their single-core performance and memory subsystem efficiency.

In contrast, the proposed GPU implementation shows only a weak dependence on the number of edge points across all platforms. For H1, execution time increases from $0.16\,\text{ms}$ to $0.51\,\text{ms}$ when the number of edge points grows by a factor of 16. On H2, the corresponding increase is from $0.14\,\text{ms}$ to $0.23\,\text{ms}$, while on H3 it ranges from $0.09\,\text{ms}$ to $0.13\,\text{ms}$. As a result, the GPU execution time has varied by at most $0.35\,\text{ms}$ across the entire tested range, compared to increases exceeding $70\,\text{ms}$ for the CPU.

The resulting speedup over the CPU implementation depends strongly on the edge density. For sparse edge maps (10,240 points), the speedup ranges from $51\times$ on H1 to $55\times$ on H3. For the densest configuration (163,840 points), the speedup increases to $158\times$ on H1, $370\times$ on H2, and $421\times$ on H3. These trends are visualized in Fig. 3, which highlights the widening performance gap between CPU and GPU implementations as the number of edge points has increased.

The relatively weak dependence of GPU execution time on input size for smaller resolutions can be attributed to the high degree of parallelism and the ability to overlap memory operations with computation. However, as the resolution increases, performance becomes increasingly dominated by memory access patterns and accumulator size, particularly when shared memory capacity is exceeded. In contrast, the CPU implementation processes edge points sequentially, resulting in a nearly linear increase in execution time.

The influence of image resolution is summarized in Table 3. For the CPU implementation, execution time increases noticeably with resolution on all platforms. On H1, execution time grows from $45.23\,\text{ms}$ at 512×512 pixels to $99.69\,\text{ms}$ at 8192×8192 pixels, corresponding to a $2.2\times$ increase. Comparable scaling can be observed on H2 ($42.61\,\text{ms}$ to $111.28\,\text{ms}$, $2.6\times$) and H3 ($29.02\,\text{ms}$ to $68.01\,\text{ms}$, $2.3\times$).

For the GPU-accelerated implementation, execution times remains nearly constant for resolutions up to 2048×2048 pixels. Across all platforms, GPU execution time in this range varies by less than $0.1\,\text{ms}$. A far more significant

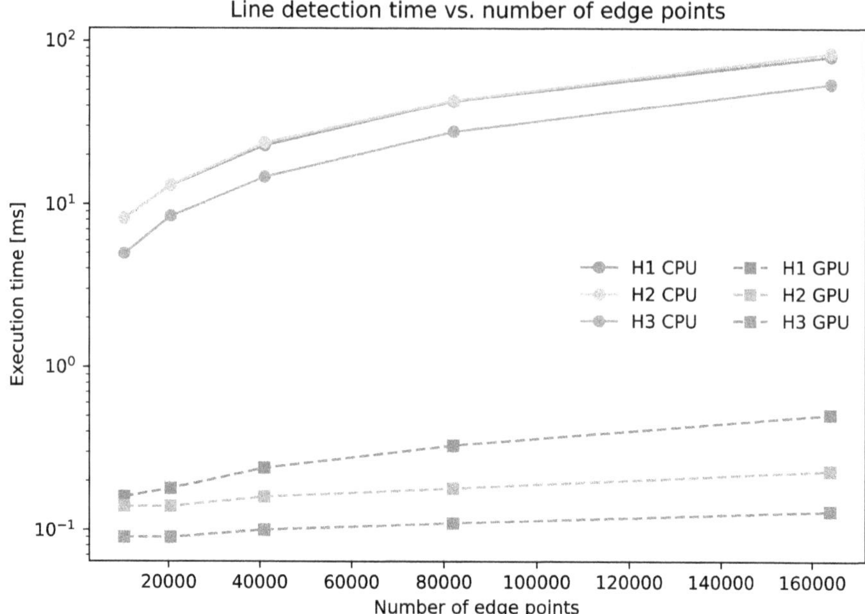

Fig. 3. Line detection execution time as a function of the number of edge points for CPU and GPU implementations across platforms H1, H2, and H3. The vertical axis is shown on a logarithmic scale.

increase can be observed for 4096×4096 pixels and above, where execution time rises to 1.03 ms on H1, 0.54 ms on H2, and 0.26 ms on H3. At the largest resolution of 8192×8192 pixels, GPU execution time reaches 2.03 ms on H1, 0.98 ms on H2, and 0.43 ms on H3. This noticeable increase in execution time can be explained by the growing size of the accumulator, which no longer fits into shared memory. Despite this increase, the GPU implementation remains from $34\times$ to $230\times$ faster than the CPU, depending on the platform. These scaling trends are illustrated in Fig. 4.

The observed increase in execution time for larger resolutions is primarily associated with the growth of the accumulator, which exceeds the capacity of shared memory and forces the use of global memory. This transition leads to increased memory latency and contention, which becomes the dominant performance factor for large parameter spaces.

Across all evaluated configurations, the proposed GPU implementation consistently outperforms the OpenCV GPU-based solution. For the fixed-resolution experiments in Table 2, speedups over OpenCV have ranged from $1.8\times$ to $2.1\times$ on H1, from $1.7\times$ to $2.5\times$ on H2, and from $1.6\times$ to $1.9\times$ on H3. Similar ratios can be observed for varying resolutions in Table 3. Since both approaches rely on comparable algorithmic principles, these differences can be attributed to

Table 3. Average calculation times for edge maps with the same number of edge points and different resolutions. Threshold for line detection set to 400.

Resolution	Hardware								
	H1			H2			H3		
	CPU	GPU	CV	CPU	GPU	CV	CPU	GPU	CV
512×512	45.23	0.32	0.33	42.61	0.19	0.22	29.02	0.12	0.13
1024×1024	41.20	0.33	0.44	42.72	0.18	0.29	27.15	0.11	0.17
2048×2048	43.22	0.40	0.54	47.80	0.21	0.32	29.10	0.12	0.18
4096×4096	53.77	1.03	1.07	60.32	0.54	0.63	36.94	0.26	0.31
8192×8192	99.69	2.03	2.06	111.28	0.98	1.05	68.01	0.43	0.51

implementation-level factors such as kernel specialization, reduced synchronization overhead, and more efficient memory access patterns.

It should be emphasized that the OpenCV GPU implementation is designed as a general-purpose solution supporting a wide range of configurations and use cases. In contrast, the proposed implementation focuses on a specialized, performance-critical scenario with fixed parameterization. Therefore, the observed performance gains should be interpreted as the result of targeted,

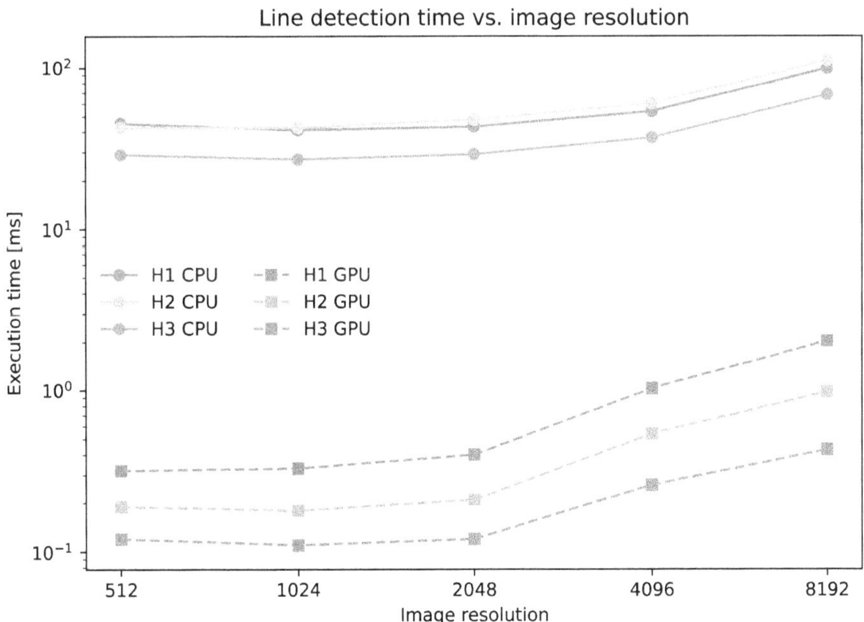

Fig. 4. Line detection execution time as a function of the resolution of the edge map for CPU and GPU implementations across platforms H1, H2, and H3. The vertical axis is shown on a logarithmic scale.

implementation-level optimizations rather than a general superiority over more flexible frameworks such as OpenCV.

Finally, a consistent performance hierarchy can be observed across all experiments. Platform H3 has achieved the lowest execution times for both CPU and GPU implementations, followed by H2 and H1. While CPU performance on H1 and H2 remains relatively close, GPU execution times on H2 have been consistently $1.5\times$ to $2.0\times$ lower than on H1. These results confirms that the proposed implementation benefits directly from increased GPU compute capability and memory bandwidth, and that newer GPU architectures provide measurable advantages even for highly optimized, short-running kernels. The cost of the numerical voting process is effectively amortized across massively parallel accumulator updates, significantly reducing sensitivity to input density compared to the CPU implementation. As a result, performance becomes increasingly dominated by parameter-space resolution rather than the number of edge points.

6   Conclusions

This paper investigates the computational performance of the classical HT for straight line detection from the perspective of numerical accumulation on modern GPU architectures. Rather than modifying the underlying algorithm, the proposed approach focuses on implementation-level optimization of the voting process, which constitutes the dominant computational and memory-intensive component of the method. In particular, the results demonstrate that careful exploitation of GPU memory hierarchy can significantly improve the efficiency of classical accumulation-based algorithms without introducing algorithmic modifications or approximations.

A GPU-accelerated implementation preserving full functional equivalence with a widely used OpenCV reference has been presented. By exploiting the hierarchical memory architecture of GPUs and employing an adaptive voting strategy that dynamically selects between shared and global memory, the implementation effectively reduces memory traffic and contention during accumulator updates. This design allows the numerical voting process to scale efficiently across a wide range of edge point densities and image resolutions.

Experimental results obtained on multiple hardware platforms have demonstrated substantial performance gains over a sequential CPU baseline. Depending on the input characteristics and the target architecture, speedups range from approximately $50\times$ for sparse edge maps to over $400\times$ for dense configurations. Across all tested scenarios, the proposed implementation consistently outperforms the OpenCV GPU-based solution, confirming that careful implementation-level optimization can yield performance improvements even for well-established algorithms.

The results further indicate that, on GPUs, the execution time of the classical HT becomes increasingly dominated by the resolution of the parameter space rather than by the number of edge points. This contrasts with CPU-based execution, where performance scales almost linearly with input density. Such behavior highlights the effectiveness of massive parallelism and fast on-chip memory in amortizing the cost of numerical accumulation.

Future work will focus on further refinement of the GPU implementation using advanced CUDA features and programming abstractions. In particular, the use of high-level parallel primitives provided by libraries such as thrust may simplify selected stages of the processing pipeline while preserving performance. Beyond raw execution time, an important direction for future research is the evaluation of energy efficiency, allowing performance gains to be analyzed in terms of computational cost per watt on different GPU architectures. An important direction for future research is the development of architecture-aware optimizations tailored to specific GPU architectures, which may further improve performance by leveraging low-level hardware characteristics such as warp scheduling and memory access patterns. Finally, the proposed implementation framework may be extended to higher-dimensional parameter spaces to support the detection of circles and ellipses, enabling an assessment of how the observed numerical and architectural scaling properties generalize to more complex HT variants.

Disclosure of Interests. The authors have no competing interests to declare that are relevant to the content of this article.

References

1. Atiquzzaman, M.: Multiresolution hough transform-an efficient method of detecting patterns in images. IEEE Trans. Pattern Anal. Mach. Intell. **14**(11), 1090–1095 (1992). https://doi.org/10.1109/34.166623
2. van den Braak, G.J., Nugteren, C., Mesman, B., Corporaal, H.: Fast hough transform on GPUs: exploration of algorithm trade-offs. In: Blanc-Talon, J., Kleihorst, R., Philips, W., Popescu, D., Scheunders, P. (eds.) Advanced Concepts for Intelligent Vision Systems, pp. 611–622. Springer Berlin Heidelberg, Berlin, Heidelberg (2011). https://doi.org/10.1007/978-3-642-23687-7_55
3. Canny, J.: A computational approach to edge detection. IEEE Trans. Pattern Anal. Mach. Intell. **PAMI-8**(6), 679–698 (1986). https://doi.org/10.1109/TPAMI.1986.4767851
4. Duda, R.O., Hart, P.E.: Use of the hough transformation to detect lines and curves in pictures. Commun. ACM **15**(1), 11–15 (1972). https://doi.org/10.1145/361237.361242
5. Espinosa, C., Perkowski, M.: Hierarchical hough transform based on pyramidal architecture. In: Eleventh Annual International Phoenix Conference on Computers and Communication [1992 Conference Proceedings], pp. 743–750. (1992). https://doi.org/10.1109/PCCC.1992.200515
6. Galamhos, C., Matas, J., Kittler, J.: Progressive probabilistic hough transform for line detection. In: Proceedings of 1999 IEEE Computer Society Conference on Computer Vision and Pattern Recognition (Cat. No PR00149), vol. 1, pp. 554–560 (1999). https://doi.org/10.1109/CVPR.1999.786993
7. Hough, P.V.C.: Method and means for recognizing complex patterns. US Patent 3,069,654 (1962)

8. Illingworth, J., Kittler, J.: A survey of the hough transform. Comput. Vis. Graph. Image Process. **44**(1), 87–116 (1988). https://doi.org/10.1016/S0734-189X(88)80033-1

9. Ioannou, D., Huda, W., Laine, A.F.: Circle recognition through a 2D hough transform and radius histogramming. Image Vis. Comput. **17**(1), 15–26 (1999). https://doi.org/10.1016/S0262-8856(98)00090-0

10. Kiryati, N., Eldar, Y., Bruckstein, A.: A probabilistic hough transform. Pattern Recogn. **24**(4), 303–316 (1991). https://doi.org/10.1016/0031-3203(91)90073-E

11. Li, H., Ma, Y., Bao, H., Zhang, Y.: Probabilistic hough transform for rectifying industrial nameplate images: a novel strategy for improved text detection and precision in difficult environments. Appl. Sci. **13**(7) (2023). https://doi.org/10.3390/app13074533

12. Marzougui, M., Alasiry, A., Kortli, Y., Baili, J.: A lane tracking method based on progressive probabilistic hough transform. IEEE Access **8**, 84893–84905 (2020). https://doi.org/10.1109/ACCESS.2020.2991930

13. Patil, P.R., Patil, M.D., Vyawahare, V.A.: Acceleration of hough transform algorithm using graphics processing unit (GPU). In: 2016 International Conference on Communication and Signal Processing (ICCSP), pp. 1584–1588 (2016). https://doi.org/10.1109/ICCSP.2016.7754427

14. Rossi, F.D.: Boosting performance of computer vision applications through embedded GPUs on the edge. arXiv:2511.01129 (2025)

15. Samal, A., Edwards, J.: Generalized hough transform for natural shapes. Pattern Recogn. Lett. **18**(5), 473–480 (1997). https://doi.org/10.1016/S0167-8655(97)00023-8

16. Stockman, G., Shapiro, L.G.: Computer Vision. Prentice Hall PTR (2001). https://dl.acm.org/doi/10.5555/558008

17. Tian, Y., Song, W., Chen, L., Sung, Y., Kwak, J., Sun, S.: Fast planar detection system using a GPU-based 3D hough transform for lidar point clouds. Appl. Sci. **10**(5) (2020). https://doi.org/10.3390/app10051744

18. Xie, Y., Ji, Q.: A new efficient ellipse detection method. In: 2002 International Conference on Pattern Recognition, vol. 2, pp. 957–960 (2002). https://doi.org/10.1109/ICPR.2002.1048464

19. Xu, L., Oja, E.: Randomized hough transform (RHT): basic mechanisms, algorithms, and computational complexities. CVGIP Image Underst. **57**(2), 131–154 (1993). https://doi.org/10.1006/ciun.1993.1009

20. Zhang, Y., Liu, T., Zhou, H.: Automatic detection based on deep hough transform for b-lines in ultrasound image. In: 2025 8th International Symposium on Big Data and Applied Statistics (ISBDAS), pp. 641–644 (2025). https://doi.org/10.1109/ISBDAS64762.2025.11117024

21. Zhou, X., Ito, Y., Nakano, K.: An efficient implementation of the gradient-based hough transform using DSP slices and block rams on the FPGA. In: 2014 IEEE International Parallel & Distributed Processing Symposium Workshops, pp. 762–770 (2014). https://doi.org/10.1109/IPDPSW.2014.88

Efficient Integer-Only Implementation of Tanh and Sigmoid for Embedded AI on RISC-V

Kamil Kaczmarski[1] , Pawel Gepner[1(✉)] , Ewa Deelman[2] ,
Pawel Poczekajlo[3] , Leonid Moroz[1] , and Nataliia Gavkalova[1]

[1] Faculty of Mechanical and Industrial Engineering, Warsaw University of
Technology, Warsaw, Poland
{kamil.kaczmarski.dokt,pawel.gepner,leonid.moroz,
nataliia.gavkalova}@pw.edu.pl
[2] USC Information Sciences Institute, University of Southern California, Marina del
Rey, CA 90292, USA
deelman@isi.edu
[3] Faculty of Electronics and Computer Science, Koszalin University of Technology,
Koszalin, Poland
pawel.poczekajlo@tu.koszalin.pl

Abstract. We present a unified integer-only kernel for hyperbolic functions `tanh(x)` and `sigmoid(x)`, designed for embedded RISC-V platforms without floating-point units. The kernel combines LUT anchoring, CORDIC microrotations, and linear correction in Q20 arithmetic, producing outputs directly in Q1.16 format suitable for ML inference. Exhaustive evaluation across the entire 17-bit input space demonstrates deterministic accuracy better than 1 ULP in Q1.16, with maximum absolute errors below 1.5×10^{-5}. Compared to software-emulated floating-point implementations, our approach achieves significant speedup while reducing hardware complexity by unifying multiple activation functions in a single IP block. This makes the method highly relevant for efficient deployment of neural networks on resource-constrained RISC-V microcontrollers.

Keywords: CORDIC · integer-only · ML inference · RISC-V · sigmoid

1 Introduction

Artificial intelligence (AI) computations are increasingly being executed on ultra-low-power devices, where energy efficiency and low latency are critical. In this context, the open RISC-V architecture is gaining significant traction due to its extensibility and support for specialized extensions, including reduced-precision floating-point formats such as BFloat16 [3, 16].

At the same time, reduced-precision numerical formats have become an important component of modern AI and machine learning (ML) systems. Formats such as BFLOAT16 are widely adopted in training and inference pipelines

M. Paszynski et al. (Eds.): ICCS 2026 Workshops, LNCS 16788, pp. 573–587, 2026.
https://doi.org/10.1007/978-3-032-29915-4_47

because they preserve much of the dynamic range of FP32 while reducing memory usage and improving computational throughput. Previous studies have shown that neural networks trained and evaluated using BFLOAT16 can achieve accuracy comparable to FP32 baselines across a wide range of architectures and tasks, confirming that reduced precision is often sufficient for practical AI workloads [2,10,11,19]. These trends are reflected in both academic research and industry practice, where reduced-precision computation is now standard in many deep learning frameworks and accelerators, including systems targeting embedded and low-power deployments [2,10]. However, on resource-constrained RISC-V microcontrollers lacking hardware floating-point units, even reduced-precision floating-point arithmetic may still require software emulation and therefore incur significant overhead. This gap between the algorithmic suitability of reduced precision and the practical cost of software-based floating-point execution motivates the exploration of integer-only alternatives for nonlinear activation functions used in neural network inference. Although BFLOAT16 helps motivate the broader reduced-precision context of this work, it is not used in the proposed implementation or in the experimental evaluation reported in Sect. 4.

Many RISC-V microcontrollers lack on-board FPU hardware. As a result, floating-point operations must be performed in software using libraries such as SoftFloat [7], introducing substantial performance overhead. This issue is particularly important for nonlinear activation functions such as `tanh` and `sigmoid`, which rely on computationally expensive hyperbolic or exponential operations [13].

To overcome these limitations, this paper proposes a unified integer-only activation kernel based on CORDIC-derived transformations and fixed-point arithmetic. The kernel efficiently computes both `tanh` and `sigmoid` using a single implementation, addressing an important gap in current RISC-V software support for AI inference and ML applications at the edge.

2   Related Work

Existing research on acceleration of nonlinear functions and lightweight arithmetic techniques for embedded systems highlights several important trends. Reduced-precision floating-point formats such as BFloat16 have been proposed to improve inference efficiency in RISC-V systems [3,16]. Studies evaluating BFloat16 arithmetic report that its reduced mantissa precision does not significantly affect the accuracy of modern neural networks, with models trained using BFloat16 achieving accuracy comparable to FP32 baselines across multiple tasks [11,19]. However, on platforms lacking an FPU, floating-point operations must still be emulated in software using libraries such as SoftFloat [7], which significantly degrades performance on microcontrollers.

Fixed-point arithmetic is a long-standing technique in embedded systems, and numerous frameworks provide efficient implementations of linear operations. For example, the RISC-V Vector Math Library [17] demonstrates continued ecosystem development. However, existing libraries rarely include integer-only optimized implementations of nonlinear activation functions commonly used in machine learning.

CORDIC algorithms have been widely explored for computing transcendental functions using only shifts and additions. Several works demonstrate CORDIC accelerators implemented for RISC-V SoCs and FPGA-based systems [18], confirming their suitability for resource-constrained platforms. These implementations typically focus on specific functions, whereas this work aims to provide a shared kernel that supports both `tanh` and `sigmoid`.

Additionally, activation-function approximations—including piecewise-linear functions, rational models, and continued-fraction expansions—have been applied to reduce computational cost in embedded ML systems. Previous research highlights the high latency of exponential function evaluation in conventional implementations and offers various simplifications suitable for FPGA or ASIC deployment [8,9,15]. Representative low-precision alternatives include K-tanh [13], which optimizes tanh evaluation for deep-learning workloads, and piecewise-linear sigmoid approximations [15], which reduce computational cost through function-specific segmentation. In contrast, our objective is not to optimize each nonlinearity separately, but to reuse a single integer-only kernel for both `tanh` and `sigmoid` with deterministic latency and a shared fixed-point data path.

Research into approximate arithmetic at the instruction-set level further supports the trend toward simplified computation in edge systems. Studies proposing approximate division and square-root operations for RISC-V [14] demonstrate that reduced precision can yield substantial energy and performance benefits.

While existing research addresses fixed-point arithmetic, CORDIC methods, approximation strategies, and reduced-precision floating-point, no prior work offers a unified, integer-only kernel for both `tanh` and `sigmoid` designed for software execution on resource-constrained RISC-V microcontrollers.

3   Description of the Proposed Method

Compared with standard hyperbolic CORDIC realizations, the proposed unified integer-only kernel simultaneously approximates the hyperbolic functions `tanh(x)` and `sigmoid(x)`, using a combination of LUT anchoring, CORDIC microrotations and a final linear correction. All internal computations are performed in Q20 fixed-point format, while the outputs are suitable for conversion to Q1.16 for neural network inference.

The kernel accepts a 17-bit recoded representation of the input argument x,

$$a = (a_0, a_1, \ldots, a_{16}), \quad a_i \in \{0, 1\},$$

which compactly encodes a hyperbolic angle through a LUT index, a sequence of CORDIC microrotations, and a residual correction term. For clarity, we first describe the structure of this encoding and then the three stages of the kernel.

3.1   Input Recoding and Dynamic Range

The 17-bit input word is partitioned into three logical fields:

- **Anchor index** a_0, a_1, a_2: the three most significant bits select one of $2^3 = 8$ precomputed anchor points stored in LUTs `xx_h` and `yy_h`. The index is

$$j = 4a_0 + 2a_1 + a_2 \in \{0, \ldots, 7\}.$$

- **CORDIC microrotation control** $a_3, \ldots, a_8$: six bits control the direction of each CORDIC iteration in hyperbolic mode. For iteration $i \in \{3, \ldots, 8\}$, bit a_i decides whether the step is performed in the "positive" or "negative" direction.
- **Residual linear correction** $a_9, \ldots, a_{16}$: the last eight bits encode a residual angle in Q20 format,

$$\theta_3 = \sum_{k=0}^{7} a_{9+k} \cdot w_k,$$

where $w_k \in \{2048, 1024, \ldots, 16\}$ are power-of-two weights corresponding to Q20 fixed-point (i.e., $w_k = 2^{11-k}$). Combined with a small coarse correction term δ (derived from a_3, a_4, a_5, see below), this yields a final residual

$$z = \delta + \theta_3 \in \text{Q20}.$$

The mapping from bits to the real-valued argument x is deterministic and can be written as

$$x = \operatorname{atanh}\left(\frac{y_0}{x_0}\right) + \sum_{i=3}^{8} s_i \operatorname{atanh}\left(2^{-(i+1)}\right) + \frac{z}{2^{20}},$$

where (x_0, y_0) is the selected anchor vector, and $s_i \in \{+1, -1\}$ is the sign implied by bit a_i. This parametrisation implicitly defines the dynamic range of x; in our implementation, it corresponds to the range of arguments for `tanh(x)` and `sigmoid(x)`.

3.2   LUT Anchoring

The first stage of the kernel selects an *anchor point* from a small LUT of precomputed hyperbolic vectors. For each index j we store an integer pair

$$(x_0, y_0) = (\text{xx\_h}[j], \text{yy\_h}[j]),$$

representing a scaled hyperbolic vector

$$(x_0, y_0) \approx K \cdot 2^{20} \cdot (\cosh(\alpha_j), \sinh(\alpha_j)),$$

for some anchor angle α_j and global scaling factor K (Sect. 3.6).

The anchors are chosen such that they tile the relevant argument range with relatively coarse steps, and the subsequent CORDIC microrotations and residual correction need to compensate only small deviations from the anchor, which reduces error and iteration count.

At this point we initialize the CORDIC state as

$$x_3 = x_0, \quad y_3 = y_0.$$

3.3 Hyperbolic CORDIC Microrotations

The second stage performs a fixed number of hyperbolic CORDIC iterations in vectoring mode, using the integer recursion

$$x_{i+1} = x_i \pm (y_i \gg (i+1)),$$
$$y_{i+1} = y_i \pm (x_i \gg (i+1)),$$

for $i = 3, 4, \ldots, 8$, where $\gg$ denotes an arithmetic right shift. The sign in each iteration is controlled by bit a_i:

- if $a_i = 1$: we use the "positive" direction,
- if $a_i = 0$: we use the "negative" direction.

In real arithmetic, the corresponding transformation is

$$(x_{i+1}, y_{i+1}) \approx (\cosh(\pm\alpha_i)\,x_i + \sinh(\pm\alpha_i)\,y_i, \ \sinh(\pm\alpha_i)\,x_i + \cosh(\pm\alpha_i)\,y_i),$$

where the microrotation angles are

$$\alpha_i = \mathrm{atanh}\left(2^{-(i+1)}\right).$$

The cumulative effect of the LUT anchor and microrotations is

$$(x_9, y_9) \approx K \cdot 2^{20} \cdot (\cosh(\tilde{x}), \ \sinh(\tilde{x})),$$

where

$$\tilde{x} = \alpha_j + \sum_{i=3}^{8} s_i \alpha_i$$

is the intermediate angle before residual correction.

Using only six microrotations keeps the kernel small and deterministic in time, which is crucial for embedded systems and hardware implementations.

3.4 Residual Angle and Linear Post-Rotation

The third stage compensates the residual angular error left after the finite sequence of microrotations. We approximate a small additional angle z (in Q20) by combining:

- a coarse term based on a small set of weights (d_3, d_4, d_5),

$$\delta = a_3 \cdot d_3 + a_4 \cdot d_4 + a_5 \cdot d_5,$$

- and a fine term from the residual bits $a_9, \ldots, a_{16}$,

$$\theta_3 = \sum_{k=0}^{7} a_{9+k} \cdot w_k.$$

Together they form

$$z = \delta + \theta_3 \in \mathrm{Q20},$$

which corresponds to a small real-valued angle $z/2^{20}$.

For such small angles, the hyperbolic rotation

$$x' = x_9 \cosh\left(\frac{z}{2^{20}}\right) + y_9 \sinh\left(\frac{z}{2^{20}}\right),$$
$$y' = y_9 \cosh\left(\frac{z}{2^{20}}\right) + x_9 \sinh\left(\frac{z}{2^{20}}\right)$$

can be linearized as

$$\cosh(\epsilon) \approx 1, \quad \sinh(\epsilon) \approx \epsilon$$

for $|\epsilon| \ll 1$. Substituting $\epsilon = z/2^{20}$ yields the integer update:

$$x_{17} = x_9 + \left(\frac{z}{2^{20}} \cdot y_9\right) \approx x_9 + ((z \cdot y_9) \gg 20),$$
$$y_{17} = y_9 + \left(\frac{z}{2^{20}} \cdot x_9\right) \approx y_9 + ((z \cdot x_9) \gg 20),$$

which preserves the Q20 scaling. This yields the final kernel outputs:

$$(x_{17}, y_{17}) \approx K \cdot 2^{20} \cdot (\cosh(x), \, \sinh(x)).$$

The use of a single linear post-rotation instead of additional CORDIC iterations reduces computational cost and hardware complexity while keeping the approximation error below one LSB in Q1.16, as demonstrated in Sect. 4.3 in Table 3. Our algorithm is presented in the schematic view in Fig. 1.

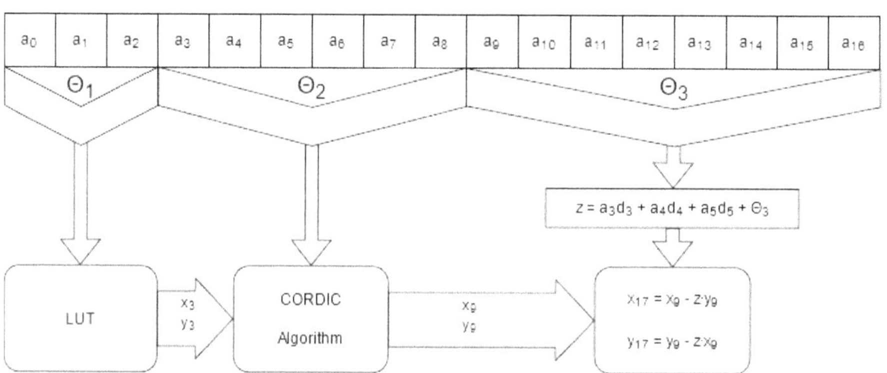

Fig. 1. Schematic view of our CORDIC algorithm.

3.5 Extraction of Tanh and Sigmoid

Once the final vector (x_{17}, y_{17}) is obtained, we can derive `tanh(x)` and `sigmoid(x)` directly in the integer domain.

From the hyperbolic identity

$$\tanh(x) = \frac{\sinh(x)}{\cosh(x)},$$

and the scaling

$$x_{17} \approx K \cdot 2^{20} \cosh(x), \quad y_{17} \approx K \cdot 2^{20} \sinh(x),$$

we obtain

$$\tanh(x) \approx \frac{y_{17}}{x_{17}}.$$

The global scale factor $K \cdot 2^{20}$ cancels exactly, and the ratio can be computed as a fixed-point division producing a Q1.16 result.

For the sigmoid function $sigmoid(x) = 1/(1 + e^{-x})$, we exploit the relation

$$e^{\pm x} = \cosh(x) \pm \sinh(x),$$

so that

$$e^{-x} \approx \frac{x_{17} - y_{17}}{K \cdot 2^{20}}.$$

Substituting into the definition of $sigmoid(x)$ yields

$$sigmoid(x) \approx \frac{1}{1 + \frac{x_{17} - y_{17}}{K \cdot 2^{20}}} = \frac{K \cdot 2^{20}}{K \cdot 2^{20} + x_{17} - y_{17}}.$$

In our implementation, we precompute

$$\texttt{scale} = K \cdot 2^{20},$$

and evaluate

$$sigmoid(x) \approx \frac{\texttt{scale}}{\texttt{scale} + x_{17} - y_{17}}$$

using integer arithmetic followed by a conversion to Q1.16.

Both activations thus share the same kernel (x_{17}, y_{17}), and differ only in a small scalar post-processing step. Figure 2 presents a block diagram for our complete algorithm, to calculate `tanh(x)` and `sigmoid(x)`.

3.6 Fixed-Point Formats and Scaling Factor

All intermediate values (x_i, y_i), the residual z, and the LUT entries are represented in Q20 fixed-point format. The global scaling factor K is chosen once during design time to:

– minimize the worst-case approximation error over the target input range,

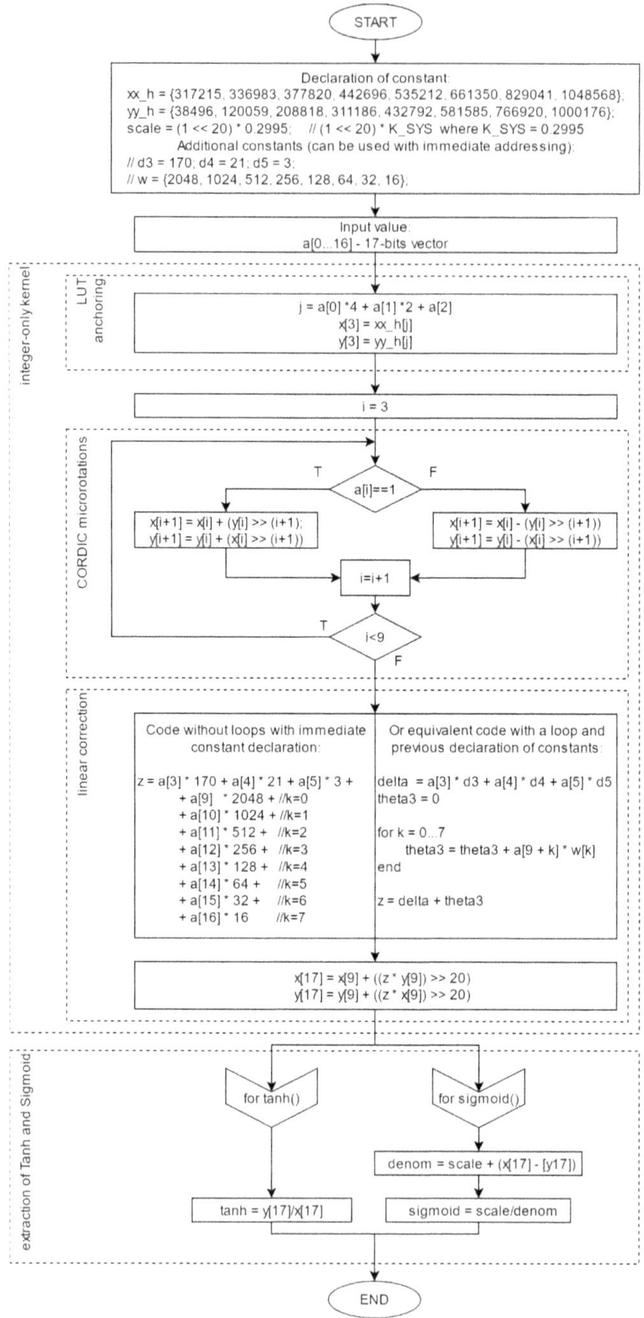

Fig. 2. Diagram showing the implementation scheme of the presented algorithm for `tanh(x)` and `sigmoid(x)`.

- avoid overflow in the CORDIC iterations and post-rotation,
- and provide a convenient mapping to Q1.16 at the output.

In practice, we use a constant K_{SYS} (stored as a floating-point value only in the reference model; the hardware implementation uses an integer equivalent). The final Q20 outputs (x_{17}, y_{17}) can be converted to Q1.16 by a right shift and optional rounding:

$$v_{Q1.16} = \mathrm{clip}\left(\lfloor v_{Q20} \gg 4 \rfloor\right),$$

where the clip operation enforces the range $[-1, 1]$ for `tanh` and $[0, 1]$ for `sigmoid`.

In the final fixed-point implementation, the sigmoid denominator is evaluated using an equivalent scaled form, with `scale` $= K \cdot 2^{21}$ and $((x17 - y17) << 1)$, in order to preserve Q1.16 accuracy after conversion. This allowed us to avoid specific errors caused by quantizing the `scale` factor. In this way, the output value for sigmoid() is calculated correctly and in accordance with the previously indicated precision.

This fixed-point setup leads to deterministic, integer-only evaluation of hyperbolic activations, which we analyze in terms of accuracy and performance in the following sections.

4   Implementation and Results

The implementation was carried out on a microcontroller based on the RISC-V core. The ESP32-C3FH4 chip from Espressif was selected (due to its high popularity and easy availability). It is a highly integrated SoC device. The microprocessor provides hardware support for WiFi and Bluetooth wireless communication. This makes it popular for use in IoT and SmartHome devices. The ESP32 C series chips are Ultra-Low Power solutions. The chip is a complete integrated operating system, eliminating the need for external memory, for example. This startup procedure greatly facilitates implementation and testing. The manufacturer provides for the possibility of running and operating the chip under the control of a dedicated FreeRTOS system. The programs can be written in MicroPython or C compatible with the RISCV32 GCC compiler (riscv32-unknown-elf-gcc). For compiling GCC-compatible code, the operating system (FreeRTOS) can be limited to the minimum configuration necessary for the core and peripheral components (e.g., interfaces, timers) to function properly. Basic parameters of the ESP32-C3FH4 are:

- Single Core RISC-V CPU (32 bits, 160 MHz);
- 4 MB Flash, 400 KB SRAM (8 KB RTC);
- Wi-Fi support (2.4 GHz, 11b/g/n generation, 150 Mbps, WPA3);
- Bluetooth Low Energy 5 support;
- Crypto Accelerators (RSA, AES, HMAC);
- Interfaces (USB Serial, SPI, CAN-FD/TWAI, UART, I2C, I2S).

The chip is equipped with a 32-bit arithmetic logic unit (ALU) that supports only fixed-point calculations. The instruction set (hardware-supported) is compatible with RV32IMC ISA (meaning: I - basic set of 32-bit instructions, M - integer multiplication and division, C - shortened/compressed versions of instructions that reduce code size).

4.1   Algorithm Implementation

The implementation of the presented algorithms (Algo) was done in C (according to RISCV32 GCC). C provides better control over the implementation compared to MicroPython (especially in the context of low-level hardware instructions). All code was compiled using 'riscv32-esp-elf-gcc' (ver. 14.2.0) with the optimization flag '-Og' (typical configuration for run tests and analyzes).

All declared variables and constants (including arrays) were declared as fixed-point (usually 32-bit, thus maintaining a "reserve" for overflows). Where multiplication or division operations occur, variables are extended to 64 bits. This allows full control over the bit range and no loss of calculation precision. After the operations are performed, the variables are reduced back to 32 bits. The algorithm can also be easily implemented on 16 bits. However, with a 32-bit unit available, reducing variables to 16 bits does not bring significant benefits as all hardware calculations are performed in 32-bit precision.

The main calculation function has been prepared for both tanh() and sigmoid() operations. It is based on the CORDIC algorithm, which is based on two tables (LUT) xx_h and yy_h and iterative operations performed in a "for" loop. Multiplication and division by 2^{20} have been implemented as multiple bit/arithmetic shifts (left for multiplication, right for division). The operation $K \cdot 20^{20}$ has been calculated as a constant at the compilation stage, thus reducing the number of operations performed.

The sigmoid function is not directly implemented in the math library. This function is implemented according to the equation:

$$sigmoid(x) = \frac{1.0}{1.0 + e^{-x}}$$

where the exponential function is directly used from the math library. The equation was implemented using double-precision floating-point operations to maintain the highest accuracy for the reference values.

4.2   Measurement Methodology

For modern central processing units (CPUs), analyses frequently focus on performance, electrical power usage and overall energy efficiency, particularly in the context of high-performance computing systems. In contrast, graphics processing units (GPUs) are often evaluated using similar criteria, with attention given to how effectively they execute large numbers of parallel operations. Performance in both cases is typically defined by the time required to complete specific computational tasks at a given accuracy level and workload intensity, while accounting for resource utilization such as bus bandwidth, cache behavior, and processor cycle consumption. Numerous recent studies in the literature rely on these metrics to present and compare experimental results [1,4–6,12].

In our scenario, the following parameters are analyzed to verify the operation of computational algorithms implemented in microprocessor systems:

- error bounds (the basic factor determining the correct operation of the algorithms);
- execution speed (a factor determining the optimal computational complexity that allows competition with library functions);
- program memory usage (a factor determining the optimal implementation using hardware commands rather than program instructions).

The following measurements were made for $2^{17} = 131072$ samples. This is a complete overview of the input data in the declared Q1.16 format (17 bits in total). The individual measurements were implemented as follows:

- error measurements: the presented fixed-point algorithm (Algo) and SoftFloat library functions (Lib) were implemented, and the results from Lib dumped to the same fixed-point precision (16 bits after the decimal point). The results obtained in this way were compared to the values obtained from library functions in double precision floating point. Errors (differences from the obtained values) were determined and statistical values were calculated.
- speed measurements: it was based on readings from a counter (timer) clocked at 40 MHz (this is the maximum possible speed for both Algo and Lib; at higher speeds, the timer did not start). Before executing a given calculation function tanh() or sigmoid(), the timer is reset, and after execution, the state of the timer register is recorded. The values obtained were summed for successive samples and converted to the appropriate time units.
- program occupancy measurement: the presented Algo and Lib functions were implemented. The remaining code was reduced to the minimum necessary (only calculations for Algo and Lib, without support for microcontroller peripheral elements, e.g. communication). The occupancy values were read from the information after the project compilation.

The tests required the preparation of three separate implementation projects (three isolated experiments). This allowed for the separation of measurements and guaranteed that other functions would not affect key operations. To measure time, the total calculation time for 2^{17} samples and the average time for one sample were determined. To measure occupancy, an additional verification of the occupancy of "clean" code was performed, i.e., only the necessary startup configuration with empty loops in the code. This made it possible to determine the occupancy of the algorithms themselves (without additional necessary startup code). Reference values used for error computation were obtained from the standard C 'math.h' library evaluated in 64-bit double-precision floating-point arithmetic. When measuring errors, the following statistical values were determined:

- smallest error (Min), calculated by:

$$err_{min} = MIN\{err(i)\} \text{ for } i = 1, 2, ...N,$$

- largest error (Max), calculated by:

$$err_{max} = MAX\{err(i)\} \text{ for } i = 1, 2, ...N,$$

- average error, calculated by:

$$err_{ave} = \frac{\sum_{i=1}^{N} err(i)}{N}$$

- mean absolute error, calculated by:

$$err_{abs} = \frac{\sum_{i=1}^{N} |err(i)|}{N}$$

- standard deviation, calculated by:

$$err_{std} = \sqrt{\frac{\sum_{i=1}^{N} [(err(i) - err_{ave})^2]}{N}}$$

where: $N = 2^{17}$, $err(i) = q(i) - q_{fp}(i)$, $q(i)$ - output value of the function in the selected implementation, $q_{fp}(i)$ - output value of the function in full precision.

4.3 Measurement Results

All tests were performed on the ESP32-C3FH4 chip. The results of individual tests are presented in Tables 1, 2 and 3.

When analyzing the errors, it can be seen that the standard deviation of errors for the Algo was smaller than the Lib functions (when casting to fixed-point format Q1.16). This shows that the developed Algo is correct and generally has fewer errors. The minimum and maximum values indicate that there are

Table 1. Computation times of individual implementations of the tanh() and sigmoid() algorithms.

Realisation	Full execution time for 2^{17} samples	Average execution time for one sample
Presented Algo of tanh()	665.32[ms]	5.0759609[us]
Function of tanh() base on Lib	3965.24[ms]	30.252378[us]
Presented Algo of sigmoid()	554.74[ms]	4.2322975[us]
Function of sigmoid() base on Lib	2798.14[ms]	21.348151[us]

no significant errors deviating from the accepted precision of Q1.16 (where the weight of the least significant bit (LSB) is $2^{-16} \approx 1.5259e^{-05}$). While maintaining errors at a satisfactory level (and comparable to Lib functions), execution times were significantly reduced. For the implementation of the presented tanh() algorithm, the time was reduced by over 83%, while for sigmoid() the time was reduced by over 79% - for the average time to determine the result of a single sample. The measurement of absolute occupancy is burdened by the inclusion of additional runtime code (base program). Therefore, it was important to determine the relative occupancy with respect to the base program. These values clearly indicate that the appropriate adaptation of dedicated algorithms to the processor architecture (e.g., fixed-point operations) can significantly reduce code occupancy. The reduction in memory program occupancy is almost 30% for tanh() and almost 18% for sigmoid().

Table 2. Program memory usage of individual implementations of the tanh() and sigmoid() algorithms.

Realisation	Full implementation of the program	Relative occupancy with respect to the base program
Presented Algo of tanh()	274882[B]	2222[B]
Function of tanh() base on Lib	275818[B]	3158[B]
Presented Algo of sigmoid()	274902[B]	2242[B]
Function of sigmoid() base on Lib	275384[B]	2724[B]
Base program (only necessary configuration and empty loops)	272660[B]	–

Table 3. Errors of individual implementations of the tanh() and sigmoid() algorithms.

Realisation	Min error	Max Error	Mean error	Mean abs. error	Standard deviation
Presented Algo of tanh()	−1.31077e-05	1.42400e-05	−3.69464e-07	3.69464e-07	2.62434e-06
Function of tanh() base on Lib	−1.52513e-05	7.90624e-06	−7.56369e-06	7.56369e-06	4.40971e-06
Presented Algo of sigmoid()	−9.45004e-06	7.83283e-06	−3.57385e-07	3.57385e-07	1.97767e-06
Function of sigmoid() base on Lib	−1.52588e-05	−1.12144e-11	−7.63221e-06	7.63221e-06	4.40192e-06

5   Conclusion

In this work, we introduced a unified, integer-only activation kernel for `tanh(x)` and `sigmoid(x)`, specifically designed for RISC-V microcontrollers without hardware floating-point support. By combining LUT anchoring, a compact sequence of hyperbolic CORDIC microrotations, and a final linear post-rotation in Q20 arithmetic, the proposed method achieves deterministic accuracy better than one ULP in Q1.16 across the entire 17-bit input domain. The unified structure eliminates the need for separate implementations of hyperbolic functions, reducing both software and hardware complexity.

Experimental evaluation on an ESP32-C3 RISC-V microcontroller demonstrates that the kernel provides substantial performance benefits, with more than an 80% reduction in execution time compared to SoftFloat-based library functions, while simultaneously lowering program memory usage. Importantly, the error characteristics remain competitive with—and in many cases superior to—standard math-library implementations when cast to fixed-point formats. These results confirm that carefully designed fixed-point algorithms can deliver high-accuracy nonlinear activation functions at a fraction of the computational cost, making them highly suitable for embedded AI workloads.

Beyond the immediate performance gains, the unified-kernel approach also simplifies integration into larger inference pipelines, enabling more predictable timing behavior and easier hardware mapping. Its deterministic structure makes it suitable for lightweight hardware extensions, such as custom RISC-V instructions or FPGA mapping, which could further reduce latency. The present implementation still relies on an integer division in the final scalar post-processing stage and has been evaluated only for `tanh` and `sigmoid` over the 17-bit internal recoded domain implemented by the kernel. Although the experimental platform is RISC-V, the computational scheme itself is not tied to RISC-V-specific instructions and can be transferred to other 32-bit processors without hardware floating-point support. Future work will extend the method to additional non-linearities, evaluate its behavior over conventional application-level input ranges such as $[-8, 8]$, and investigate custom RISC-V instructions as well as FPGA-based mappings.

Acknowledgements. This research was partly supported by PLGrid Infrastructure at ACK Cyfronet AGH, Krakow, Poland. This work was also partly supported by the National Science Foundation under grant #2331153.

References

1. Ciznicki, M., Kopta, P., Kulczewski, M., Kurowski, K., Gepner, P.: Elliptic solver performance evaluation on modern hardware architectures. Parallel Process. Appl. Math. **8384** (2014). https://doi.org/10.1007/978-3-642-55224-3_16
2. Dequino, A., Bompani, L., Benini, L., Conti, F.: Optimizing bfloat16 deployment of tiny transformers on ultra-low power extreme edge socs. J. Low Power Electron. Appl. **15**(1), 8 (2025). https://www.mdpi.com/2079-9268/15/1/8
3. Foundation, R.V.: Bfloat16 extension specification for RISC-V. Online Specification (2023). https://docs.riscv.org/reference/isa/unpriv/bfloat16.html
4. Gepner, P.: Using AVX2 instruction set to increase performance of high performance computing code. Comput. Inf. **36**(5), 1001–1018 (2017)

5. Gepner, P., Fraser, D.L., Kowalik, M.F.: Second generation quad-core intel xeon processors bring 45 nm technology and a new level of performance to HPC applications. In: Bubak, M., van Albada, G.D., Dongarra, J., Sloot, P.M.A. (eds.) ICCS 2008. LNCS, vol. 5101, pp. 417–426. Springer, Heidelberg (2008). https://doi.org/10.1007/978-3-540-69384-0_47

6. Gepner, P., Gamayunov, V., Fraser, D.L.: Effective implementation of DGEMM on modern multicore CPU. Procedia Comput. Sci. **9**, 126–135 (2012). https://doi.org/10.1016/j.procs.2012.04.014

7. Hauser, J.R., Dunkels, A.: Softfloat source documentation. Online documentation, DBT-RISE Project (2020). https://git.minres.com/DBT-RISE/DBT-RISE-TGC/src/commit/fe3ed495199bc5ccb7bcc8cd38f848000af48c99/softfloat/doc/SoftFloat-source.html

8. Hingu, C., Fu, X., Saliyu, T., Hu, R., Mishan, R.: Power-optimized field-programmable gate array implementation of neural activation functions using continued fractions for ai/ml workloads (2024). https://doi.org/10.3390/electronics13245026

9. Hoyer, I., et al.: Design of hardware accelerators for optimized and quantized neural networks to detect atrial fibrillation in patch ECG device with RISC-V. Sensors (2023)

10. Intel: oneAPI deep neural network library (oneDNN) developer guide and reference (2025). https://www.intel.com/content/www/us/en/docs/onednn/developer-guide-reference/2025-2/bfloat16-training.html

11. Kalamkar, D., et al.: A study of bfloat16 for deep learning training. arXiv preprint arXiv:1905.12322 (2019)

12. Kopta, P., et al.: Parallel application benchmarks and performance evaluation of the intel xeon 7500 family processors. Procedia Comput. Sci. **4**, 372–381 (2011). https://doi.org/10.1016/j.procs.2011.04.039

13. Kundu, A., et al.: K-tanh: efficient tanh for deep learning. arXiv preprint arXiv:1908.11263 (2019)

14. Li, L., Gautschi, M., Benini, L.: Approximate DIV and SQRT instructions for RISC-V: an efficiency vs. accuracy analysis. In: International Symposium on Power and Timing Modeling, Optimization and Simulation (PATMOS) (2017)

15. Li, Z., Zhang, Y., Sui, B., Xing, Z., Wang, Q.: FPGA implementation for the sigmoid with piecewise linear fitting method based on curvature analysis (2022). https://doi.org/10.3390/electronics11091365

16. Rizwan, R., Noor, M., Rehman, Z., Imran, U.: Accelerating ai on RISC-V: optimizing bfloat16 for improved efficiency, p. 2024. Munich (2024)

17. Tak, P., Tang, P.: An open-source RISC-V vector math library. In: IEEE 31st Symposium on Computer Arithmetic (ARITH) (2024)

18. Yildiz, R.O., Yilmazer-Metin, A.: Cordic accelerator for RISC-V. In: 29th Telecommunications Forum TELFOR 2021 (2021)

19. Zamirai, P., Zhang, J., Aberger, C.R., Sa, C.D.: Revisiting bfloat16 training. arXiv preprint arXiv:2010.06192 (2021)

A Parallel and Vectorized Implementation of the McCaskill Algorithm for X86-64 and RISC-V Architectures

Marek Palkowski[1(✉)] , Sergio Iserte[2] , Tomasz Olas[3] ,
Mateusz Gruzewski[1] , and Roman Wyrzykowski[3]

[1] West Pomeranian University of Technology in Szczecin, Zolnierska 49, 70721
Szczecin, Poland
mpalkowski@zut.edu.pl

[2] Barcelona Supercomputing Center, Plaça Eusebi Güell 1-3, Barcelona 08034, Spain
sergio.iserte@bsc.es

[3] Czestochowa University of Technology, Dabrowskiego 69,
42201 Czestochowa, Poland
olas@icis.pcz.pl

Abstract. In this paper, we study cache-efficient optimization and vectorization for the dynamic programming McCaskill algorithm, which computes the RNA partition function and base-pairing probabilities under a thermodynamic model. The McCaskill algorithm operates on the full ensemble of possible RNA secondary structures without pseudoknots, weighting them by their free energies to derive both the partition function and base-pairing probabilities. This task belongs to classical bioinformatics applications commonly benchmarked on multicore HPC systems. Well-known manual and automatic polyhedral code optimizations dedicated to dynamic programming tasks often avoid vectorization and focus solely on efficient loop tiling. As a result, such codes fail to exploit the vector computational capabilities of x86 processors and those available in newer architectures such as RISC-V. In this work, we demonstrate the generation of a readable, efficient OpenMP implementation of the McCaskill algorithm that leverages vector-level and cache-aware optimizations, outperforming related approaches. We analyze vectorization limitations on platforms lacking auto-vectorizing compilers, such as oneAPI, and propose an efficient implementation based on RISC-V vector intrinsics, demonstrating that hardware capabilities significantly exceed what current compilers can utilize.

Keywords: Vectorization · RNA folding · McCaskill's algorithm · Code optimization · RISC-V · Bioinformatics

1 Introduction

Compute-intensive applications must be rigorously optimized—through the exploitation of advanced SIMD/vector instruction sets, careful management of cache locality, and scalable multithreading—to realize the performance potential of modern multicore processors. A particularly noteworthy application domain of high-performance computing (HPC) is dynamic programming tasks in bioinformatics, which significantly hinder both manual optimization and automated compiler-based techniques [7,9]. Considerable attention has been devoted to optimizing dynamic programming for RNA folding [13], as it represents a fundamental case study in computational biology [6,9,17].

RNA folding is the process by which a single-stranded RNA molecule folds into a stable secondary structure through intramolecular base pairing, which determines its biological function. However, even basic algorithmic code, such as the Nussinov algorithm from 1978, already challenges existing automated optimization techniques on multi-core CPUs, particularly on emerging modern x86-64 and RISC-V platforms [7,12,16]. Modern CPU architectures require software to exploit not only parallelism but also memory locality and data-level parallelism via vectorization. This applies to both high-end x86 platforms with large caches and wide AVX-512 vectors, as well as emerging energy-efficient RISC-V architectures, where enhanced memory hierarchies and the RISC-V Vector Extension (RVV) play a similar role [14].

Recent studies, including our previous work [7] on optimizing the Nussinov algorithm across diverse multicore architectures, indicate that dynamic programming kernels are not fully memory-bound and exhibit sufficient computational intensity to benefit from SIMD execution. In this paper, we build on the insights gained from that study and extend them to a more complex computational scheme, namely the McCaskill algorithm [11]. We propose a computation scheme that enables cache-efficient and vectorization, building upon the authors' prior experience and insights from related work [9,12,16,18]. We demonstrate that none of the previously proposed solutions reported in the literature exploit vectorization for this algorithm and that this benchmark has not been evaluated on the increasingly popular RISC-V platform. Furthermore, we show the substantial optimization capabilities of modern x86-64 compilers, with particular emphasis on the oneAPI framework, and overcome the current limitations of available toolchains for RISC-V architectures [14]. In the experimental evaluation, we analyze computational speedups across varying problem sizes and assess scalability on modern 32-core Intel Xeon CPU Max 9462 and 96-core AMD EPYC 9654 architectures, as well as on two distinct RISC-V systems, 8-core Banana Pi BPI-F3 and 64-core Milk-V SG2042. We also point out the limitations of existing RISC-V compilation tools and propose an implementation of the McCaskill algorithm using RVV intrinsics in order to achieve the performance offered by the hardware.

2   Related Work

The McCaskill algorithm follows a Nussinov-like scoring scheme, which in turn enables the application of similar manual [9,10,17,18] and automatic (polyhedral) transformations [2,15] to those proposed for related dynamic programming kernels. These tasks share common structural properties: they typically construct a dynamic programming (DP) table over sequence indices (i, j), where entries correspond to subsequences and only the upper triangular region $(i \leq j)$ is evaluated, and their computations can be organized into block-level wavefronts.

Fekete et al. [5] were the first to parallelize the McCaskill algorithm on a computer cluster. Li et al. [9] showed that transposing the Nussinov dynamic programming matrix improves data locality on CPUs (referred to as *Transpose*) and revealed that GPU-oriented optimizations can be interpreted analogously to matrix multiplication. This approach was later extended by Zhao and Sahni [17] through the *ByBox* and *ByRow* schemes, with particular emphasis on cache optimization, and was then applied to the McCaskill problem [18]. *ByBox* is a cache-aware blocking strategy that groups and merges multiple dynamic-programming tiles into larger boxes, enabling wavefront execution with improved cache reuse and reduced memory traffic. To the authors' knowledge, this is currently the most efficient OpenMP implementation of the McCaskill algorithm.

In parallel, polyhedral compiler techniques were also advancing, aiming to optimize cache efficiency through loop tiling. This automatic loop transformation technique partitions iteration spaces into smaller blocks (tiles) to improve data locality. The McCaskill algorithm exhibits non-uniform dependencies, which classifies it as a non-serial polyadic dynamic programming (NPDP) problem. Researchers working on polyhedral approaches have highlighted the limitations of state-of-the-art optimizers based on the affine transformation framework (ATF) in inner-tiling, such as Pluto [3], when applied to NPDP kernels. To address these challenges, manual polyhedral transformations have been proposed, including Wonnacott's separation of the iteration space into problematic and non-problematic ("mostly tileable") regions [16], albeit limited to serial implementations, as well as the work of Mullapudi and Bondhugula [12], who identified opportunities to introduce reductions when parallelizing the NPDP recurrences. The limitations of ATF also motivated the development of source-to-source compilers based on the transitive reduction of dependence graphs and time-space tiling, as implemented in the *Dapt* compiler [2].

Unfortunately, these methods were not designed to utilize CPU vector instructions, and widely used implementations of the McCaskill algorithm, such as ViennaRNA Package [10], remain non-vectorized in their current form, relying on pointer-based data structures, complex control flow, and irregular memory access patterns that hinder effective SIMD vectorization. In our previous work, we proposed an optimization strategy for the Nussinov kernel that enables vector-level execution within a thread [7] on x86 and GPU platforms, and we subsequently investigated the resulting performance gains on the RISC-V architecture [14]. The experience from this work is applied to the McCaskill algorithm, which follows a more complex computational scheme.

3   Computation of RNA Partition Functions Using the McCaskill Algorithm

The McCaskill algorithm computes the partition function $Z = \sum_P \exp\left(-\frac{E(P)}{RT}\right)$, over all possible nested secondary structures P that can be formed by a given RNA sequence S. Here, $E(P)$ denotes the free energy of structure P, R is the universal gas constant, and T is the absolute temperature [11].

In this work, we consider a simplified formulation based on a Nussinov-like energy scoring scheme, in which each base pair contributes a fixed energy term E_{bp}, independent of its structural context. Under this assumption, two dynamic programming tables, Q and Q^{bp}, are constructed.

The entry $Q_{i,j}$ represents the partition function of the subsequence spanning nucleotide indices i through j, while $Q^{bp}_{i,j}$ denotes the contribution of structures in which nucleotides at positions i and j form a base pair, and is zero when such pairing is not allowed.

The McCaskill recurrences used to compute the tables Q and Q^{bp} are given below, where l denotes the minimal loop length:

$$Q_{i,j} = Q_{i,j-1} + \sum_{i \leq k < j-l} Q_{i,k-1} \cdot Q^{bp}_{k,j}, \tag{1}$$

$$Q^{bp}_{i,j} = \begin{cases} Q_{i+1,j-1} \cdot \exp\left(-\frac{E_{bp}}{RT}\right), & \text{if nucleotides } S_i \text{ and } S_j \text{ can form a base pair,} \\ 0, & \text{otherwise.} \end{cases} \tag{2}$$

Given these partition function terms, base-pair probabilities, as well as probabilities that a given subsequence is unpaired, can be computed according to the Boltzmann distribution [11].

As shown in Listing 1, the McCaskill kernel is implemented as a triple-nested loop with an inner accumulation over k.

```
for (i = N - 1; i >= 0; i--)
  for (j = i + 1; j < N; j++) {
    Q[i][j + 1] = Q[i][j];
    for (k = 0; k < j - i; k++) {
      Qbp1[k+i][j+1]=Q[k+i+1][j]*ERT*paired(rna[k+i], rna[j])
        ;
      Q[i][j + 1] += Q[i][k + i] * Qbp1[k + i][j + 1];
}}
```

listing 1: McCaskill algorithm

4 Optimization Strategy for the McCaskill Algorithm

The McCaskill algorithm is characterized by the fact that, when iterating over the k loop for a given (i, j) element, the computations can be grouped and executed in parallel within a single thread. This enables SIMD vectorization, either automatically via compiler directives or explicitly via vector instructions such as AVX on x86 architectures and RVV on energy-efficient RISC processors [14]. Hence, our objective is to achieve massive vector-level parallelization of the operations in the McCaskill algorithm.

Despite structural similarities in the code of the Nussinov and McCaskill algorithms, including the ability to be blocked and parallelized along diagonals, they differ substantially in their computational characteristics. McCaskill's code operates on floating-point matrices rather than integer-valued tables and requires the coordinated traversal of multiple dynamic programming matrices, notably the Q and Q_{bp} tables. All recurrences depend on nucleotide pairing functions over the alphabet $\{A, C, G, U\}$, and the resulting dynamic programming tables are typically sparse.

Zhao and Sahni [18] observed that the computation of the element $Q[i][j+1]$ depends on the values $Q[i][j]$, $Q[k+i+1][j]$, and $Q[i][k+i]$, which are independent and can therefore be computed in parallel, referring to it as the *OneArray* technique. At this point, one can observe a clear similarity to the Nussinov algorithm: the evaluation of the target element relies on the pair $Q[k+i+1][j]$ and $Q[i][k+i]$, while the element $Q[i][j]$ is precomputed before entering the innermost loop. This observation motivates the introduction of the notion of *problematic* pairing target blocks with the current tile, as well as *non-problematic* (or *almost-tileable*) instructions, as defined in the work of Wonnacott [16].

To effectively exploit cache locality, it is necessary to introduce block-based execution. We define this polyhedral approach as follows and generate a loop using Integer Set Library (ISL) tools [7].

$$
TILE_{MCC}(II, JJ) := \left\{
\begin{array}{l}
[ii, jj, i, j, k] -> [ii - jj, jj, i - j, j, k] : \\
0 \le jj \le \frac{N}{bb} \ \wedge \ \ 0 \le ii \le \frac{N}{bb} \ \wedge \\
0 \le i < N \ \wedge \ \ 0 \le j < N \ \wedge \ \ 0 \le k < j - i \ \wedge \\
ii \cdot bb \le i < (ii + 1) \cdot bb \ \wedge jj \cdot bb \le j < (jj + 1) \cdot bb \ \wedge \\
(ii = jj \wedge j > i) \ \vee \ (jj > ii)
\end{array}
\right\}
$$

$$(3)$$

The set $TILE_{MCC}(II, JJ)$ defines a two-dimensional tiling of the McCaskill dynamic programming domain, where (II, JJ) denote tile coordinates and bb is the tile (block) size. The problem size N does not need to be divisible by bb, as boundary tiles are handled separately.

The indices i and j range over the original $N \times N$ dynamic programming matrix, while k corresponds to the innermost summation dimension constrained by $0 \le k < j - i$. The tiling constraints $II \cdot bb \le i < (II + 1) \cdot bb$ and $JJ \cdot bb \le j < (JJ + 1) \cdot bb$ assign each (i, j) pair to a unique tile. The additional condition $((II = JJ \wedge j > i) \vee JJ > II)$ enforces execution only over the upper triangular region of the dynamic programming matrix, including the diagonal tiles with the restriction $j > i$. This formulation preserves the data dependencies of the McCaskill algorithm while enabling block-based execution and diagonal wavefront parallelism.

We use parallelization along diagonals, which corresponds to loop skewing, a typical strategy for NPDP-type problems [7]. The algorithm traversal is depicted in Fig. 1.

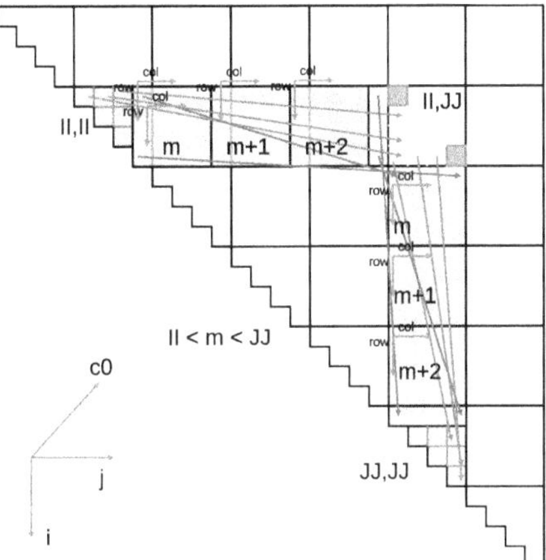

Fig. 1. Block-based (tiled) computation of the McCaskill dynamic programming tables with diagonal ordering. Indexing: (c0) denotes diagonals, (i, j) tile coordinates, while (row, col) represent indices within a tile.

Each computed block (II, JJ) depends on the diagonal blocks (II, II) and (JJ, JJ), as well as on pairs of blocks (II, m) and (m, JJ), where $II < m < JJ$ is called the left and bottom blocks [18]. The block pairs $(II, JJ) \rightarrow (JJ, JJ)$ and $(II, II) \rightarrow (JJ, JJ)$ are classified as *problematic*, as they are not profitable targets for parallelization. We therefore define problematic operations as those block pairs whose operands access values from the cells of the currently computed block (II, JJ). It is worth noting that such pairs are associated with triangular blocks located on the first diagonal. In Fig. 1, these are highlighted in red, the block under computation is shown in yellow, and the non-problematic block pairs are marked in green. Consequently, the largest portion of the computation - namely the pairs of blocks (II, m) and (m, JJ) - is identified as *non-problematic* and constitutes the primary candidate for parallel execution. To generate tiled code, we apply tiled wavefront scheduling using the transformation $[II, JJ] \rightarrow [II - JJ, JJ]$, where *II-JJ* indicates the number of diagonals.

At this point, it is useful to identify several aspects essential to characterizing the parallelization strategy. Blocks located on the first and second diagonals do not contain any non-problematic block pairs; such pairs appear only starting from the third and subsequent diagonals. The largest number of non-problematic block pairs is associated with the last block on the final diagonal. Conversely, the first diagonal contains the largest number of blocks, and the degree of parallelism (i.e., the number of active threads) decreases progressively toward the last diagonal, where it is reduced to a single block.

Blocks lying on the same diagonal have the same number of non-problematic block pairs. The order in which these pairs are evaluated can be rearranged by exploiting the fact that the update of $Q[i][j+1]$ is an addition operation and is therefore commutative and associative. Additional parallelism within non-problematic blocks can be exploited on GPUs or through vectorization on CPUs.

```
1  // The serial diagonal loop
2  for (int c0 = 0; c0 <= (N-1)/bb; c0++)
3     // parallel blocks on the diagonals
4   #pragma omp parallel for
5   for (int c1 = c0; c1 <= min((N -1)/bb, floord(N+c0-2, bb)); c1++) {
6    int jj = c1-c0;
7    int ii = c1;
8    double A[bb][bb], B[bb][bb], C[bb][bb], rna1[bb], rna2[bb];
9
10   for(int row=0; row<bb; row++)
11     for(int col=0; col<bb; col++)
12        C[row][col] = 0;
13
14   for (int m = jj+1; m < ii; m++) {
15      // data copying
16     for(int row=0; row<bb; row++){
17        for(int col=0; col<bb; col++){
18           A[row][col] = Q[bb * jj + row][bb*m  + col-1];
19           B[row][col] = Q[bb * m + row][bb * ii + col ];
20        }
21        rna1[row] = RNA[bb * m -1 + row];
22        rna2[row] = RNA[bb * ii + row];
23     }
24     //non-problematic statements
25     for (int row = 0; row < bb; row++) {
26        #pragma omp simd   // icpx   x86-64
27        for (int col = 0; col < bb; col++) {
28           double Cvalue = 0;
29          #pragma omp simd reduction(+:Cval)  // clang++ risc-v
30             for (int e = 0; e < bb; e++){
31             double v=B[e][col]*ERT*paired(rna1[e], rna2[col]);
32              if(v) {
33                 Qbp[bb * m - 1 + e ][bb * _si + col] = v;
34                 Cvalue += A[row][e] * v;
35              }
36           }
37           C[row][col] +=  Cvalue;
38        }
39     }
40   }
41
42 // For all cells Q(i,j+1)=Q(i,j)  in the target block (II,JJ)
43 // add the value ( C(i%b, j%b) and the rest of paired vals in
44 // problem. blocks {(II, II)->(II,JJ); (II,JJ)->(JJ, JJ)}.
```

listing 2: Parallel and vectorized McCaskill kernel (in OpenMP)

It is worth noting that when the nucleotides are unpaired, updating Q_{bp} is unnecessary, and updating Q can be omitted, as it does not contribute to the summation of the corresponding Q element. In practice, the value of Qbp is primarily determined by the outcome of RNA nucleotide pairing: it becomes nonzero only when both the Q term and the energy-related factor ERT are nonzero.

The computation of non-problematic blocks is illustrated in Listing 2. Each thread maintains a private array C, which must be initialized to zero before use. The operand values are loaded from the Q table into the auxiliary arrays A and B. Subsequently, each element of the block (II, JJ) accumulates a partial sum. At the same time, the corresponding value is written directly to the Qbp table. The number of paired non-problematic blocks can be determined from the diagonal index c_0 and is equal to $c_0 - 2$, which defines the number of iterations in the loop indexed by m.

In Listing 2, the loops in lines 25, 27, and 30 traverse the left and bottom blocks scanning indexes `{row, col, e}`, and the results are accumulated in the array C. These loops can be parallelized using a sum reduction on Q. The main difference between the proposed implementation and the *ByBox* approach of Zhao and Sahni [18] is that the target tile is not updated at every step. Instead, partial results are accumulated in local arrays; consequently, loops scanning non-problematic statements can be parallelized and preceded by appropriate pragmas, enabling SIMD vectorization of the multi-threaded code using AVX on x86 architectures and RVV on RISC-V processors.

5   Experimental Study: X86 Architecture

5.1   Methodology of Experiments

For the experimental study on x86 multicore processors, we compared our approach with the following OpenMP implementations:

- *ByBox* [18] combines pairs of left and bottom tiles to update the target tile at each step, while the base-pair table Q_{bp} is computed separately at the end.
- *Transpose* reuses the lower-left part of the array to support column-wise access, reducing memory usage and improving data locality [9].
- *OneArray* uses the rewritten recurrence relations from [18]; this scheme allows Q to be computed using a single array and enables diagonal parallelism.
- *Dapt* [2] is a polyhedral source-to-source compiler that applies 3D space–time tiling.

Other approaches, including Pluto-generated tiled code (serial-only) [3] and the *ByRow* scheme [18], were not considered further due to their extremely poor performance in practice.

On studied machines, we explicitly indicated the `#pragma omp simd` directive to the C++ compiler in order to enable vectorization of the loop iterating over the index variable *col*. For this purpose, we used the oneAPI compiler [8].

We analyze the possibilities for vectorizing the code. First, on x86 architectures, the oneAPI `icpx` compiler can vectorize the `col` loop. The variables `v` and `Cval` are private, the arrays `A` and `B`, as well as the function `paired`, are read-only, and the update of `C[row][col]` does not introduce any data dependencies. Particular attention must be paid to accesses to the `Qbp` array. Assuming that `bb`, `m`, and `_si` are constant, the write access has the form `Qbp[const + e][const + col]`, which is suitable for vectorization; therefore, these values do not overlap across threads. The value of `bb` is empirically set to 32.

5.2   Target Computing Platforms

We conducted the experiments with two multi-core x86-64 machines. The first one is equipped with an Intel Xeon CPU Max 9462 (the Sapphire Rapids HBM architecture), featuring 32 cores and 64 hardware threads, up to 3.5 GHz turbo, 150 MB L3 cache, 128 MB L2 cache, 3 MB L1d cache, and 2 MB L1i cache, as well as 128 GB of on-package HBM2e and 631 GB of DRAM. The second machine is equipped with an AMD Epyc 9654 CPU, featuring 96 cores and 192 hardware threads, operating at a base frequency of 2.4 GHz with a boost frequency of up to 3.7 GHz, and providing a cache hierarchy consisting of 64 KB L1 cache, 1 MB L2 cache per core, and 384 MB of shared L3 cache.

The code was compiled with the Intel oneAPI C++ Compiler 2025.0.4, `icpx` [8] using the flags `-O3`, `-qopt-report=max`, `-qopt-report-phase=vec`, `-march=native`, `-mavx512f` or `-mavx2`, and `-qopenmp`.

5.3   Experimental Results

Tables 1 and 2 present the measured execution times of the evaluated methods for Intel and AMD machines, respectively. Our approach, which uses vectorization only and no hyper-threading, outperforms the most efficient competing method, namely *ByBox*. Enabling AVX-512 provides a greater advantage over AVX2's 256-bit registers, demonstrating that our method benefits more from wider SIMD vectorization. For the Intel platform, the number of threads was chosen to match a configuration with hyper-threading enabled. For the AMD processor, the number of threads was set equal to the number of physical cores for related approaches. In all cases, the thread count was selected individually for each method to achieve the best possible execution time, ensuring a fair comparison that reflects the maximum performance potential of each approach. We observe that increasing the number of threads beyond the number of physical cores does not provide additional speedup for the SIMD version. The compiler report shows that the loops were successfully vectorized using SIMD, utilizing AVX-512 (8 double elements) and strip-mining for short loops. However, unaligned memory accesses and masked stores introduce overhead, reducing the achieved SIMD speedup due to memory inefficiencies and data dependencies. We also noted that the performance gap grows with problem size due to better parallelism, SIMD utilization, and cache blocking, while these effects are limited for small inputs.

The code generated by *Dapt*, as well as the *Transpose* and *OneArray* variants, is significantly slower than our approach. Compared to the CPU Max platform, the AMD platform offers a larger L3 cache and a higher thread count, resulting in better performance for both our approach and *ByBox*, indicating more effective processor utilization. For further investigations on the open and promising RISC-V architecture, we compared the proposed solution only with the best related method, *ByBox*.

Table 1. Execution time (seconds) for different implementations and input sizes on Intel Xeon CPU Max 9462.

Size	Ours AVX-512 32 threads	Ours AVX2 32 threads	Ours No vec. 64 threads	ByBox 64 threads	Transpose 64 threads	OneArray 64 threads	Dapt 32 threads
1000	0.03	0.04	0.09	0.04	0.03	0.03	0.12
2500	0.13	0.17	0.63	0.24	0.19	0.21	0.63
5000	0.86	1.02	2.19	1.21	1.71	2.22	5.48
7500	2.91	3.06	5.28	3.71	6.09	9.39	20.02
10000	6.27	7.57	10.94	8.41	15.89	24.25	56.41
12500	12.83	13.76	21.01	15.02	33.25	50.99	136.38
15000	17.52	22.81	33.61	26.56	59.87	94.49	268.86

Table 2. Execution time (seconds) for different implementations and input sizes on AMD Epyc 9654.

Size	Ours AVX-512 96 threads	Ours AVX2 96 threads	Ours No vec. 96 threads	ByBox 96 threads	Transpose 96 threads	OneArray 96 threads	Dapt 96 threads
1000	0.06	0.09	0.13	0.11	0.41	0.35	0.32
2500	0.26	0.33	0.41	0.38	1.18	0.47	1.17
5000	0.79	0.99	1.33	1.22	3.37	3.84	7.34
7500	1.97	2.44	3.43	2.75	9.71	15.27	29.11
10000	3.40	4.53	7.18	5.71	22.42	45.98	80.36
12500	6.01	8.36	12.71	10.65	43.75	98.21	198.04
15000	9.25	12.89	20.69	16.86	74.62	183.35	330.21

6   Experimental Study: RISC-V Architecture

RISC-V is an open-standard Instruction Set Architecture (ISA) that enables royalty-free CPU development and a common software stack. Although current RISC-V processors offer relatively modest performance, the architecture is rapidly evolving as a general-purpose platform, increasingly targeting HPC workloads. We conducted an experimental study on two different machines: the Banana Pi BPI-F3 and the Milk-V Pioneer.

```
1  for (int row = 0; row < bb; ++row) {
2    int col = 0;
3    while (col < bb) {
4      size_t vl = __riscv_vsetvl_e64m8((size_t)(bb - col));
5      vuint8m1_t vnt2 =
6        __riscv_vle8_v_u8m1((const uint8_t*)&rna2[id][col], vl);
7      vfloat64m8_t vacc  = __riscv_vfmv_v_f_f64m8(0.0, vl);
8      vfloat64m8_t vzero = __riscv_vfmv_v_f_f64m8(0.0, vl);
9
10     for (int e = 0; e < bb; ++e) {
11       vfloat64m8_t vB =
12         __riscv_vle64_v_f64m8(&B_elements[id][e][col], vl);
13       vfloat64m8_t vtmp =
14         __riscv_vfmul_vf_f64m8(vB, (double)ERT, vl);
15       uint8_t nt1 = rna1[id][e];
16       vbool8_t mp = paired_bits(vnt2, nt1, vl);
17
18       vtmp = __riscv_vmerge_vvm_f64m8(vzero, vtmp, mp, vl);
19       vbool8_t mBnz =  __riscv_vmfne_vf_f64m8_b8(vB, 0.0,vl);
20
21       vbool8_t mstore = __riscv_vmand_mm_b8(mp, mBnz, vl);
22       __riscv_vse64_v_f64m8_m(mstore,
23             &Qbp[bb * m - 1 + e][bb * _si + col], vtmp, vl);
24
25       double a = (double)A_elements[id][row][e];
26       vacc = __riscv_vfmacc_vf_f64m8(vacc, a, vtmp, vl);
27     }
28 vfloat64m8_t vC = __riscv_vle64_v_f64m8(&C[id][row][col],vl);
29     vC = __riscv_vfadd_vv_f64m8(vC, vacc, vl);
30     __riscv_vse64_v_f64m8(&C[id][row][col], vC, vl);
31     col += (int)vl;
32   }
33 }
```

listing 3: Execution of non-problematic statements using RVV intrinsics.

6.1   Target Computing Platforms

Banana Pi BPI-F3 is an industrial RISC-V development board based on the SpacemiT K1 processor [1], featuring eight 64-bit cores clocked at 1.05 GHz with an eight-stage, in-order, dual-issue pipeline. Introduced in late 2023, the CPU complies with the RISC-V 64GCVB architecture and the RVA22 standard and is the first commodity processor to support the RVV 1.0 vector extension, providing a 256-bit VLEN with a 128-bit×2 execution width. The platform employs a simplified memory hierarchy with private 32 KB L1 instruction and data caches per core and a shared 1 MB L2 cache (two 512 KB banks), backed by 4 GB of LPDDR4-2666 memory (up to 16 GB) connected via a single memory controller delivering up to 10.6 GB/s bandwidth. We upgraded the Bianbu OS to its third version (based on Ubuntu 25.04) and the `clang` compiler to version 20.

Milk-V Pioneer is a microATX developer motherboard based on the 64-core Sophon SG2042 RISC-V processor [4], which targets HPC workloads. The SG2042 operates at 2 GHz and is organized into 16 clusters of four XuanTie C920 cores connected via a 2D mesh network-on-chip (NoC). Each 64-bit C920 core implements a 12-stage out-of-order superscalar pipeline and supports the RV64GCV instruction set. Each core provides a private 64 KB L1 instruction and data cache, while a 1 MB L2 cache is shared within each cluster. All cores share 64 MB system-level L3 cache composed of 16 slices interconnected through the NoC. The processor integrates four memory controllers for 128GB of DDR4-3200, delivering up to 102.4 GB/s of bandwidth. The platform supports only the RVV 0.7.1 vector extension with a vector width of 128 bits.

6.2 Methods of Vectorization

With recent versions of the `clang` and `gcc` compilers supporting the RVV 1.0 vector extension, it becomes possible to rely on automatic compiler vectorization. However, on the Banana BPI-F3 platform, vectorization of the outer loop is inhibited by conservative safety checks and cost-model constraints, whereas it can be successfully vectorized on x86-64 systems. As a result, we enforce only vectorization at the innermost loop level using `#pragma omp simd reduction(+:Cval)`, explicitly declaring a reduction on the accumulation variable `Cval` (see Listing 2, line 29). In contrast, the `icpx` compiler adopts a more permissive heuristic, enabling more aggressive optimizations and relying on the programmer's assurance that the `#pragma omp simd` directive is safe for the outer loop.

The outer loop can nevertheless be vectorized using RVV intrinsics for Banana BPI-F3. The Listing 3 shows a modified loop from Listing 2 (Line 25) that loads data into vector registers corresponding to successive iterations of the `col` index variable. The computation is carried out in vector-length chunks determined dynamically by `vsetvl`. For each block of columns, nucleotide data in bit form are loaded into vector registers, and the accumulation vector `vacc` is initialized. The inner loop performs vectorized loads of the `Q` matrix, scales them by the constant `ERT`, applies a pairing mask based on the scalar nucleotide, and masks out invalid entries. Valid, nonzero results are selectively written to `Qbp` using masked stores, while fused multiply-accumulate operations update `vacc`. After the reduction over `e`, the accumulated vector is added to the corresponding entries of the `C` matrix and stored back to memory, and the loop proceeds to the next vector chunk with eight contiguous vector registers ($LMUL = 8$, $m8$). As a result, the kernel leverages both hardware register grouping and masked predication to coherently and efficiently combine operations on data of different widths within a single, integrated vector execution flow (Fig. 2).

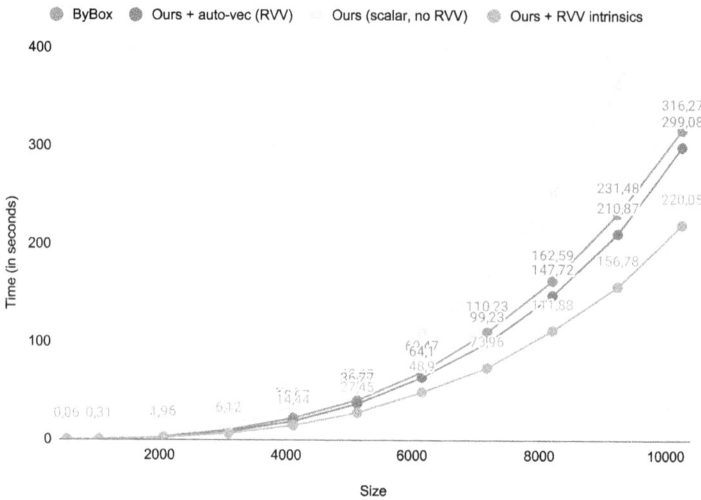

Fig. 2. Execution time (seconds) on Banana BPI-F3 using 8 threads.

On the Milk-V SG2042 processor (RVV 0.7.1), where intrinsics are not supported by stable compilers (available only from RVV 1.0), a manually optimized assembly version of the kernel was developed. In practice, the assembly variant follows the same principles as the intrinsics-based implementation: dynamic vector length, $LMUL{=}8$ to maximize throughput for float64 operations, and masked predication for selective stores and accumulation. The key difference is that, at the assembly level, precise manual control of `vsetvli` is required (with frequent switching between `e8,m1` and `e64,m8`), along with explicit maintenance of the mask in register `v0` at critical points of the computation. This ensures pipeline consistency and provides full control over the vector configuration and predication semantics in RVV 0.7.1.

6.3   Experimental Results

On the Banana BPI-F3 platform, we achieved automatic vectorization; however, `clang` only enabled vectorization after applying an additional reduction in the innermost loop. Figure reffig:banana illustrates the cost of this weaker form of reduction, which provides only marginal performance improvements over the related *ByBox* method. In contrast, by employing explicit RVV intrinsics, we were able to better exploit the potential of the eight-core system and significantly reduce the overall execution time by vectorizing the outer loop through chunk-based processing, achieving an improvement of nearly 80 s versus almost 300 s with the auto-vectorization for the largest problem size considered ($N = 10240$) (Fig. 2).

In turn, on the SG2042 platform, where only RVV 0.7.1 is available, and compiler auto-vectorization is not supported, we implemented hand-written vector code in assembly. This implementation outperforms the *ByBox* approach for all studied problem sizes, ranging from 512 to 10240, as shown in Fig. 3(a). None of the evaluated implementations scale efficiently to 64 threads, since the McCaskill algorithm is predominantly memory-bound and the SG2042 architecture relies on a mesh-based interconnect. Consequently, the best performance is achieved with 32–48 threads. Nevertheless, the proposed RVV-based implementation exhibits smaller performance degradations at higher thread counts compared to both the *ByBox* and scalar implementations, as illustrated in Fig. 3(b).

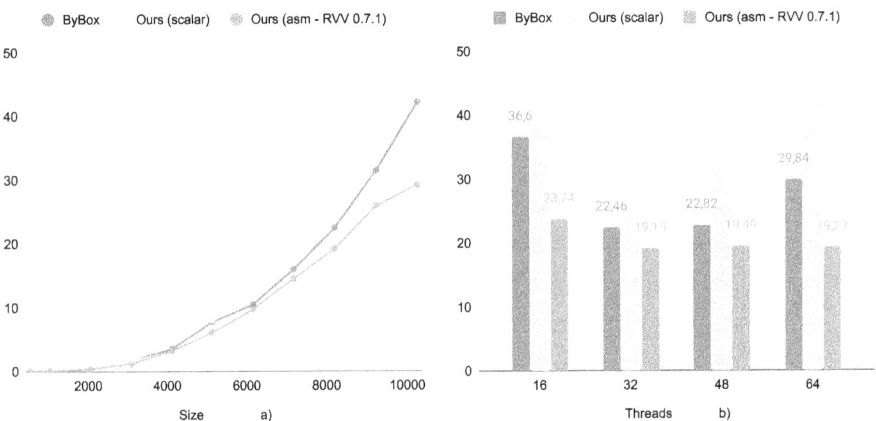

Fig. 3. Performance results on the SG2042 processor: (a) best execution time (in seconds) for different versions and problem sizes; (b) execution time (in seconds) for a problem size of 8192 using different numbers of threads.

7   Conclusions

In this paper, we present an efficient OpenMP implementation of the McCaskill algorithm for computing RNA folding probabilities. The proposed implementation supports both AVX and RVV instructions on two x86-64 and two RISC-V machines, respectively. Experimental results show that the achieved speedups significantly outperform the *ByBox* approach proposed by Zhao and Sahni. For RISC-V platforms, we demonstrate that improved vectorization is achievable despite limited auto-vectorization by employing manually vectorized implementations based on RVV intrinsics and, when necessary, hand-written assembly.

As future work, we plan to implement the maximum expected accuracy (MEA) for a given RNA sequence and exploit the potential of vector instructions more extensively. Furthermore, the proposed implementation can be ported to other multi-core platforms, such as GPUs and FPGAs, since loops containing non-problematic operations can be permuted and parallelized in two dimensions (loops over *row* and *col* variables). Additionally, we intend to investigate the energy efficiency of optimized NPDP codes on modern RISC-V and ARM platforms using the strategy proposed in this paper, as scientific computing workloads constitute a representative and demanding benchmark for evaluating the maturity and performance/energy efficiency of emerging processors.

References

1. Banana Pi BPI-F3. https://wiki.banana-pi.org/Banana_Pi_BPI-F3 (2024)
2. Bielecki, W., Poliwoda, M.: Automatic parallel tiled code generation based on dependence approximation. In: Malyshkin, V. (ed.) Parallel Computing Technologies, pp. 260–275. Springer International Publishing, Cham (2021)
3. Bondhugula, U., et al.: A practical automatic polyhedral parallelizer and locality optimizer. SIGPLAN Not. **43**(6), 101–113 (2008). https://doi.org/10.1145/1379022.1375595
4. Brown, N., Jamieson, M.: Performance characterisation of the 64-core SG2042 RISC-V CPU for HPC. In: ISC High Performance 2024 Int. Workshops. vol. 15058, pp. 354–377. LNCS (2024)
5. Fekete, M., Hofacker, I.L., Stadler, P.F.: Prediction of RNA base pairing probabilities on massively parallel computers. J. Comput. Biol. **7**(1–2), 171–182 (2000). https://doi.org/10.1089/10665270050081441
6. Frid, Y., Gusfield, D.: A simple, practical and complete o -time algorithm for RNA folding using the four-Russians speedup. Algorith. Mol. Biol. **5**(1), (2010). https://doi.org/10.1186/1748-7188-5-13
7. Gruzewski, M., Palkowski, M.: Cross-platform and polyhedral programming for Nussinov RNA folding. Futur. Gener. Comput. Syst. **169**, 107786 (2025)
8. Intel Corporation: Intel oneAPI DPC++/C++ Compiler. https://www.intel.com/content/www/us/en/developer/tools/oneapi/dpc-compiler.html (2024). Accessed 15 Jan 2026
9. Li, J., Ranka, S., Sahni, S.: Multicore and GPU algorithms for Nussinov RNA folding. BMC Bioinform. **15**(8), S1 (2014)
10. Lorenz, R., et al.: Viennarna package 2.0. Algorithms for Molecular Biology **6**(1) (Nov 2011)
11. McCaskill, J.S.: The equilibrium partition function and base pair binding probabilities for RNA secondary structure. Biopolymers **29**(6-7), 1105–1119 (May 1990)
12. Mullapudi, R.T., Bondhugula, U.: Tiling for dynamic scheduling. In: Rajopadhye, S., Verdoolaege, S. (eds.) Proceedings of the 4th International Workshop on Polyhedral Compilation Techniques, , Vienna, Austria (2014)
13. Nussinov, R., et al.: Algorithms for loop matchings. SIAM J. Appl. Math. **35**(1), 68–82 (1978)
14. Olas, T., Wyrzykowski, R., Olas, M., Pałkowski, M., Grużewski, M.: Towards the efficient use of RISC-V architecture in scientific computation (2026), manuscript submitted to Journal of Computational Science, No. JOCSCI-D-25-02945
15. Pałkowski, M., Bielecki, W.: Parallel cache-efficient code for computing the McCaskill partition functions. In: Proceedings of the Federated Conference on Computer Science and Information Systems (FedCSIS). vol. 18, pp. 207–210. IEEE / ACSIS (2019). https://doi.org/10.15439/2019F8, aCSIS, Vol. 18
16. Wonnacott, D., Jin, T., Lake, A.: Automatic tiling of "mostly-tileable" loop nests. In: IMPACT 2015: 5th International Workshop on Polyhedral Compilation Techniques, , At Amsterdam, The Netherlands (2015)

17. Zhao, C., Sahni, S.: Cache and energy efficient algorithms for Nussinov's RNA folding. BMC Bioinform. **18**(S15), (2017)
18. Zhao, C., Sahni, S.: Efficient computation of RNA partition functions using McCaskill's algorithm. In: Proceedings of the Federated Conference on Computer Science and Information Systems (FedCSIS), vol. 21, pp. 449–452. IEEE / ACSIS (2020)

QFredDet — Software Library for Computing Entropy of Continuous Variable Quantum Systems Using Fredholm Determinants

Marek Sawerwain[1]([✉]) [ID] and Joanna Wiśniewska[2] [ID]

[1] Institute of Control and Computation Engineering, University of Zielona Góra, Licealna 9, 65-417 Zielona Góra, Poland
M.Sawerwain@issi.uz.zgora.pl

[2] Institute of Information Systems, Faculty of Cybernetics, Military University of Technology, Gen. S. Kaliskiego 2, 00-908 Warszawa, Poland
JWisniewska@wat.edu.pl

Abstract. Fredholm determinants play a vital role in mathematics and physics, particularly in the theory of integral equations theory and random matrix theory. Recently, they have been proposed as an appropriate measure (especially for infinite dimensional continuous quantum systems) of quantum entanglement, which is one of the basic quantum information resources applied to the construction of the quantum computational machines. While the most studies rely on sequential numerical methods to compute Fredholm determinants, parallel programming techniques can be also effective. In this paper, we present an approach that leverages multi-core processors and GPUs, combined with an appropriate quadrature scheme, and is implemented in Python for broad accessibility. We also demonstrate how the proposed routines can be used to compute the von Neumann entropy for superposition of Fock states.

Keywords: Fredholm determinants · entropy computation for quantum systems · parallel computations · numerical quadrature

1 Introduction

In general, the Fredholm determinant is a mathematical concept used in functional analysis and integral equations. It is an extension of the determinant to infinite-dimensional spaces, especially for integral operators. It has long served as a practical tool in fields such as multivariate statistics, electrical engineering, and finance. More recently, it has found increasing applications in the field of quantum physics and computing. Fredholm determinants enable the numerical evaluation of certain probability distributions in random matrix theory, in particular the distribution functions of the Gaussian unitary ensemble [2]. They are also related to the Hamiltonian of coupled Painlevé V systems [19]. We can also utilize Fredholm determinants in analysis of one-dimensional fermionic chains [7]. Furthermore, they have been proposed as a potential measure of quantum entanglement [9].

In this article, we focus on the numerical calculation of Fredholm determinants. The function's implementation for computing the determinants has a cubic complexity but it requires values of quadrature (e.g. Gauss-Legendre or Clenshaw-Curtis) and the growing number of quadrature points causes significantly increasing time of computation, so we propose utilizing parallel approach in CUDA [13]. The solution presented in this work is based on Gauss-Legendre quadrature. It is implemented in Python using the Numba [11] and CuPy [3,14] libraries to enable efficient approximate computation of the Fredholm determinant. To the best of the authors' knowledge, the implementation of a parallel version of numerical procedure for the Fredholm determinant has not been reported in the literature so far.

The structure of this manuscript is as follows: Sect. 1.1 introduces the notations, symbols, abbreviations, and definitions used throughout the article. Section 2 provides a short overview of Fredholm determinants and revisits its fundamental applications. Section 3 presents serial numerical procedures implementing the calculation of Fredholm determinants. Then, the computational complexity of the mentioned method is analyzed what allows exposing how parallel techniques may be applied in this area. More precisely, we show in Sect. 4, how to carry out the parallel reduction to obtain an acceleration of the calculations. Section 4.2 presents an example of using developed implementations for Python. Conclusions are contained in Sect. 5. Acknowledgments and References are the last parts of the paper.

1.1 Notations, Symbols, and Abbreviations

Before starting the presentation of our solution concerning the application of parallel processing techniques to the calculation of the values of Fredholm determinants, a summary of the notation and the most important abbreviation symbols, and acronyms used in this work are collected in Table 1.

2 Fredholm Determinants

Fredholm's work [5] is undoubtedly the most important work that laid the foundations of modern analysis and operator theory. Erik Ivar Fredholm analyzed the solvability of the following equation of the second kind:

$$u(x) + z \int_a^b K(x,y)u(y)dy = f(x), \quad x \in (a,b), \tag{1}$$

where the function f and kernel K are assumed to be continuous functions. Fredholm also showed that recalled equation is uniquely solvable if the following determinant, today called Fredholm determinant,

Table 1. Some symbols, notations, sets and functions used in the paper

Notation	Description
Q	quantum state, $Q \in E(\mathcal{H})$
$d(z)$	Fredholm determinant
$d_Q(z)$	approximation of Fredholm determinant
$K(x, y)$	Kernel function for quadrature
$E_2(0, s)$	the probability that an interval of length s does not contain an eigenvalue of the Gaussian unitary ensemble
z	a complex or real number
δ_{ij}	Kronecker delta, $\delta_{ij} = 0$ if $i \neq j$ and $\delta_{ij} = 1$, if $i = j$,
$T_{d_q(z)}(K, z, a, b, m)$	computational complexity of Fredholm determinant routine
vEN(∞)	von Neumann entropy
vENH(Q)	von Neumann entropy calculated by the Fredholm determinant
vrENH(Q)	renormalized von Neumann entropy calculated by the Fredholm determinant
$\mathbb{R}$, $\mathbb{C}$, $\mathbb{N}$	sets of real, complex, and integer numbers,
i, j, k	integer numbers usually used as indices
m	the number of quadrature points
$1 \dots n$	means the sequence of $1, 2, 3, \dots, n$

$$d(z) = \sum_{k=0}^{\infty} \frac{z_n}{n!} \int_a^b \dots \int_a^b \det\left(K(t_p, t_q) \right)_{p,q=1}^n dt_1 \dots dt_n, \tag{2}$$

for $z \in \mathbb{C}$ is a function and $d(z) \neq 0$. Very often $d(z)$ is written in the following form:

$$d(z) = \det\left(I - zK \upharpoonright_{L^2(a,b)} \right). \tag{3}$$

Fredholm's work is utilized in many contemporary areas of modern science not only in the theory of compact operators but also in the physics atomic collision theory, inverse scattering, renormalization of quantum field theory, random matrix theory, combinatorial growth processes.

In [8,9], we demonstrated that the Fredholm determinant can be applied to extend the von Neumann entropy formula, derived using the theory of Fredholm determinants, in particular their standard regularization methods. The approach advocated in these works suggests employing techniques from the theory of Fredholm-type integral equations, including approximate methods, to develop controllable numerical procedures for computing Schmidt data associated with the Schmidt decomposition of solutions to the Schrödinger equations. It is also possible to show that von Neumann entropy can be expressed with the Fredholm determinant to cover the space of all, mixed states including as well, quantum states, which in the discussed two-particle system is the set of all non-negative trace class linear operators Q acting in the space $\mathcal{L}_2(\mathbb{R}^6)$ and obeying the condition $\mathrm{Tr}\,(Q) = 1$ (where $\mathrm{Tr}\,(\cdot)$ is standard trace operator). This formulation naturally enables a number of new applications, e.g. in the analysis of quantum key distribution [16].

2.1 Fredholm Determinants for Computing the Von Neumann Entropy of Quantum Continuous Variables States

Based on the results of [8], for a Hilbert space $\mathcal{H}$ of infinite dimension, $\dim(\mathcal{H}) = \infty$, and for $Q \in E(\mathcal{H})$, one can show that the von Neumann entropy of infinite-dimensional states takes infinite values:

$$\mathrm{vEN}(\infty) = \{Q \in E(\mathcal{H}) : \mathrm{Tr}\,(-Q \log Q) = \infty\}, \tag{4}$$

and moreover that this set is dense in $E(\mathcal{H})$ with respect to the L_1 topology.

However, for the complement set, i.e. for $Q \in \mathrm{vEN}(\infty)^c$ such that $\mathrm{tr}(-Q \log Q) < \infty$, one can provide a representation of the form:

$$(Q^{-Q} - \mathbb{I}) \in L_1(\mathcal{H}), \tag{5}$$

which allows one to prove that

$$\mathcal{D}(Q) = \det(\mathbb{I}_{\mathcal{H}} + \mathfrak{f}(Q)), \tag{6}$$

where $\mathfrak{f}(Q) = Q^{-Q} - \mathbb{I}$. It can be shown that $\mathfrak{f}(Q)$ is trace-class, and furthermore that

$$\mathrm{vENH}(Q) = -\mathrm{Tr}\,(Q \log Q) = \log \mathcal{D}(Q). \tag{7}$$

Referring again to [8], one can show that for any state $Q \in E(\mathcal{H})$ the condition $(Q^{-Q} - \mathbb{I}) \in L_2(\mathcal{H})$ holds, which leads to the definition of the normalized von Neumann entropy:

$$\mathrm{vrENH}(Q) = \mathrm{Tr}\left(-Q \log Q + (Q^{-Q} - \mathbb{I})\right), \tag{8}$$

which is continuous and finite with respect to the $L_2(\mathcal{H})$ topology.

Remark 1. Numerical counterparts of formulas (6) and (8) naturally require an appropriate choice of the kernel function K. This will be demonstrated by means of an example presented in Sect. 4.4.

3 Numerical Evaluation of Fredholm Determinants

In [2], a value of the determinant $d(z)$ (Eq. 2) is calculated using the determinant for the matrix sized $m \times m$ as Nyström equation $d_Q(z)$:

$$d_Q(z) = \det\left(\delta_{ij} + z w_j K(x_i, x_j)\right)_{i,j=1}^{m}. \tag{9}$$

wherein, if the coefficients w_j for a given quadrature are positive, the symmetrical variant of the determinant $d_Q(z)$ should be applied, i.e.:

$$d_Q(z) = \det\left(\delta_{ij} + z \sqrt{w_i} K(x_i, x_j) \sqrt{w_j}\right)_{i,j=1}^{m}. \tag{10}$$

Calculating $d_Q(z)$ needs the quadrature, however, according to [2] utilizing the GaussLegendre [18] or CurtisClenshaw [17] quadrature, we can generate a code for Matlab [12] or Octave [4] as a short function:

```
(1) function d = FredholmDet(K,z,a,b,m)
(2)      [w,x] = QuadratureRule(a,b,m);
(3)      w = sqrt(w);
(4)      [xi,xj] = ndgrid(x,x);
(5)      d = det(eye(m)+z*(w'*w).*K(xi,xj));
```

which allows solving Eq. 10 and is characterized by the complexity $O(m^3)$ (this results from the complexity of calculating the value of the determinant with the function `det`). A more detailed analysis of the computational complexity, that we want to conduct now, allows us to directly indicate the dependencies between the data and show that the parallel computational techniques may be fully utilized to obtain a significant acceleration of computations.

We utilize Python as the main programming language in this article, so the FredholmDet function's form is depicted in Fig. 1:

```
(1) def fredholm_det(K, z, a, b, m):
(2)      w,x=quadrature_rule(a,b,m)
(3)      w=numpy.sqrt(w)
(4)      xi,xj=numpy.meshgrid(x, x, indexing='ij')
(5)      d=numpy.linalg.det( numpy.eye(m)+z*numpy.outer(w,w)*K(xi,xj) )
(6)      return d
```

Fig. 1. Function fredholm_det implemented Python. It requires the quadrature_rule function to calculate a quadrature and kernel K function. At the beginning of each line, the ordinal number is placed to simplify referring to fragments of the source code.

This function is a counterpart of the original code given in [2] and also requires a function calculating quadrature: `quadrature_rule`. All vector and matrix operations are implemented by the use of the Numerical Python package – NumPy [10].

3.1   Computational Complexity

In general, the complexity of `fredholm_det` function, using symbols as in the implementation for Matlab/Octave, may be expressed as:

$$T_{d_q(z)}(K, z, a, b, m) = T_Q(a, b, m) + T_{\sqrt{w}}(w) + T_g(x)$$

$$+ T_{\det}(m, m) + \left(T_{eye}(m) + T_{zw}(z, w) + T_K(xi, xj) \right). \quad (11)$$

Particular markings T are assigned to the following code lines:

- $T_Q(a, b, m)$ – determines a complexity of line (2), i.e. the complexity of `quadrature_rule` function which calculates weights and quadrature's points in a range a, b with m points. If the Gauss-Legendre quadrature is applied, as in this work, then:

$$T_Q(a, b, m) = O(m^3). \tag{12}$$

- $T_{\sqrt{w}}(w)$ – line (3) corresponds to computing a root of quadrature's weights with a linear complexity depending on the number of points m: $O(m)$.
- $T_g(x)$ – line (4) refers to the `meshgrid` procedure which calculates a grid with the complexity $O(m^2)$.
- a complexity of line (5) has to be described as

$$T_{\det}(m, m) + (T_{eye}(m) + T_{zw}(z, w) + T_K(xi, xj)), \tag{13}$$

so in general we have $O((T_K(xi, xj) \cdot O(m^2)) + O(m^3))$, where calculating the kernel function is marked as T_K and this function may have a unit execution time but it is executed for each point in the grid sized $m \times m$. Additionally, it is dependent on the kernel function, therefore its complexity is not less than a quadratic function but a specific form of the kernel function can increase it.

Remark 2. The linear algebra operations related to the calculation of the argument T_{zw} can be expressed as a quadratic function. The entire calculation of the determinant is described as a polynomial of cubic degree. In general, we have here the complexity described by a third-degree polynomial, where the argument is T_K, i.e. the complexity of the kernel function. The kernel function in the case of more complicated kernel forms, what we emphasize here once again, can naturally only increase the degree of the polynomial, or even change the complexity class.

Assuming that the kernel function for a point on the grid has a unit complexity, the total complexity $T_{d_q(z)}(K, z, a, b, m) = O(m^3)$. This is a convenient complexity from a practical point of view what is also verified by the example of the procedure's NumPy version working time given in Sect. 4 (in Subsect. 4.1). $\square$.

4   Parallel Computations of Fredholm Determinant

In this part of our work, we introduce function `fredholm_det` realized in Python using the Numba and CuPy packages. Before the analysis of parallel implementation in Sect. 4.2, we present obtained results for the version based on NumPy package in Sect. 4.1.

After analyzing the computational complexity in Sect. 3.1, three areas in the `fredholm_det` function can be identified where parallel processing can be applied:

- calculation of quadrature weights and points,
- preparing matrix $m \times m$,

– computing of matrix determinant.

All three steps can be executed in parallel, with a significant reduction in computation time expected, especially for larger numbers of quadrature points. In the proposed solution, we use the Numba package to implement the second task, while the procedures from the first and third steps utilize the CuPy package to compute the quadrature points and, ultimately, calculate the determinant value for the prepared matrix.

4.1   The Basic Version Performance

It should be emphasized that `fredholm_det` function is characterized by sufficient efficiency $O(m^3)$ where m is the number of quadrature's points. We can easily show this, even without direct usage of parallel computing, by calculating the $E_2(0, s)$ value, i.e. the probability that an interval of length s does not contain an eigenvalue of the Gaussian unitary ensemble, what is given by the Fredholm determinant:

$$E_2(0, s) = \det \left(I - A_s \restriction_{L^2(0,s)} \right), \tag{14}$$

and

$$A_s u(x) = \int_0^s \frac{sin(\pi(x - y))}{\pi(x - y)} u(y) dy, \tag{15}$$

where the sine kernel $A_s u(x)$ was used. In the following part of the article, we apply this quantity as a synthetic benchmark to evaluate the performance of the proposed solution.

Results referring to the performance of procedure shown in Fig. 1 are presented in Table 2. The experiments were performed on two modern processors (AMD Ryzen 9 7950X (CPU 1), Intel Xeon W-2245 (CPU 2)) and in both cases, the dependence of the operating time on the number of quadrature points is visible. Therefore, the presented calculations also show a very good convergence of the function `fredholm_det`.

It should be emphasized that increasing the number of quadrature intervals, what is not justified in the case of probability described by $E_2(0, s)$, is characterized in this case by exponential complexity [1,2] because of the approximation of the Fredholm determinant value by the quadrature. Therefore, selecting e.g. 8192 quadrature points significantly increases the running time of the entire `fredholm_det` procedure, to an average of ≈ 250 s for the Intel Xeon W-2245 processor. The procedure of determining the quadrature points (in this case Gauss-Legendre approach) takes the most of the time: about ≈ 240 s. The remaining two computational tasks, i.e. preparing the matrix $m \times m$ and calculating its determinant, take only about 3.1–3.2 s.

In this case, it can be seen that if a given computational task related to the determinant $d_Q(z)$ requires a larger number of quadrature points, the computational time in practice, despite the use of modern processors and the NumPy package, requires several minutes of work. It is therefore reasonable to look for further possibilities of shortening the operation time, e.g. by using GPU systems.

Table 2. Performance characteristics of the basic Numpy version of the calculation for the basic example with probability $E_2(0, s)$, time in seconds (s). The column m describes the number of quadrature points, CPU 1 is AMD Ryzen 9 7950X processor (16 physical cores), and CPU 2 is Intel Xeon W-2245 (8 physical cores). In both cases, Python 3.11.9 and Windows 11 were used. The column Value provides probability values $E_2(0, s)$ for $s = 0.1$.

m	CPU 1	CPU 2	Value
5	0.00011020 s	0.00079250 s	0.9002570308592994
10	0.00011340 s	0.00102080 s	0.9002570308593463
20	0.00017330 s	0.00103600 s	0.9002570308593464
50	0.00056660 s	0.00360290 s	0.9002570308593462
100	0.00844520 s	0.02522680 s	0.9002570308593477
250	0.06502550 s	0.21752530 s	0.9002570308593448
500	0.28021040 s	0.73422160 s	0.9002570308593484
1000	0.84063120 s	2.20266480 s	0.9002570308593508
2000	4.87566096 s	12.7754558 s	0.9002570308593361
4000	40.5951504 s	76.6527348 s	0.9002570308593187
8000	243.3006925 s	252.954025 s	0.9002570308593004

4.2 Parallel Variant of Fredholm Determinant Implementation

An analysis the procedure `fredholm_det` (Fig. 1) reveals that line (2) and the procedure of calculating the determinant are characterized by complexity $O(m^3)$, whereas, the remaining code elements can be described by complexity $O(m^2)$. These mentioned three components may be implemented in parallel what will help to shorten the calculation time.

The first element that can be improved by using multiple computing cores of GPUs is the code from line (5), marked in bold (the NumPy package is represented by np):

$$(5) \quad \mathrm{d} = \mathrm{np.linalg.det}(\mathbf{np.eye(m)} + \mathbf{z} * \mathbf{np.outer(w, w)} * \mathbf{K(xi, xj)}),$$

which is responsible for preparing the matrix $n \times m$ from which we calculate the determinant. Since the number of quadrature points that can be used is limited in the practical case to several thousand, currently available GPU systems offering, for example, 16384 computing cores for the consumer NVIDIA RTX Geforce 4090 model (24 GB VRAM, 16384 CUDA Cores, clock approx. 2.5 GHZ), allow for full coverage of the computational task, what translates into a constant computational time for the number of quadrature points from 1000 to several thousand. In general, the implementation method uses the concept of a computational grid available in CUDA technology [13]. Figure 3 presents the applied construction of a computational grid (Fig. 2).

Importantly, even direct using of the computational grid, e.g. for $m = 4096$, means operating time of the order of 0.00040799 s (it should be noted that these

The 2D computational grid for computations of matrix
for the final determinant calculations

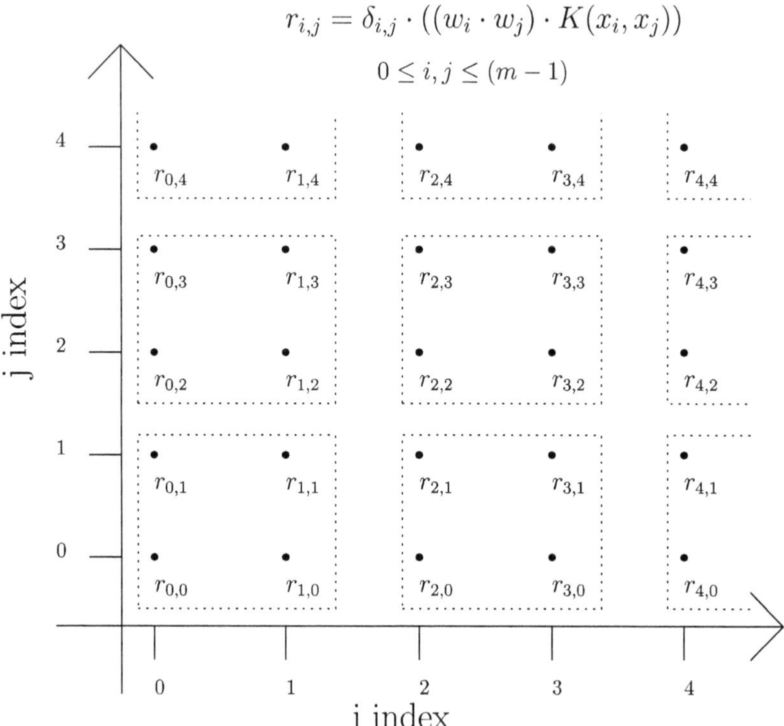

Fig. 2. An example configuration of the computational grid for executing the computation step from line (5) in the code from Fig. 1. Particular points represent elements of a matrix sized $m \times m$, and these coordinates are generated by the computational grid mechanism available in CUDA technology. All computations for individual points are performed in parallel within blocks, with each computational block outlined using dotted frames. Naturally, the execution requires weight vectors (variable w) and quadrature points (variable x) of length m. Although the direct approach to grid construction, as shown in the figure, it does not utilize shared memory (which could store temporary computations or data related to the vectors w and x), but still provides a significant practical reduction in computation time. For a large number of points – on the order of hundreds or even thousands – this approach can accelerate matrix preparation for determinant computation by a factor of two to three thousand times.

times refer to an already compiled computational kernel; the first execution of a CUDA computational procedure is always significantly longer), compared to about three seconds for the NumPy code, using double precision numbers. This means a speedup of over 5000 times for this single computational step.

The source code for $\mathbf{np.eye(m) + z * np.outer(w, w) * K(xi, xj)}$, implemented with the use of the Numba package, is relatively concise and selected parts are shown in Fig. 3. The function `fredholm_step_line5` fully realizes the mentioned fragment, where the role of the computational kernel K e.g. from Eq. 2 is played by the device function *d_ksinc*.

The implementation code fragments also provide the description of the kernel function: `d_ksinc`. The form of the kernel is:

$$K(x, y) = \mathrm{sinc}(\pi(x - y)). \tag{16}$$

It can be seen that its form in the implementation is not direct – although the Numpy package supports many special functions, the Numba package, which supports GPUs, unfortunately does not provide the definition of function `sinc`. This inconvenience does not affect the final performance.

Remark 3. The source code of the snippet in Fig. 3 may be found at [15].

4.3   Performance of Parallel Implementation

Figure 4 presents the results of calculations for different quadrature values. The GPU performance exceeds the CPU calculations for the number of points above 600 points. The reduction in calculation time for 4000 quadrature points is already significant, because it is twelvefold, and for 8000 it is already over fifty-fold. It should also be noted that the calculations are performed using double precision numbers and the graphics card used, i.e. the consumer model NVIDIA RTX 4090, offers significantly lower performance $\approx$ 1.2 TFLOPS for double precision calculations than for single precision ($\approx$ 82 TFLOPS). However, the number of available computing cores 16384, allows achieving high acceleration values for calculating the Fredholm determinant using many quadrature points. But, up to about 500 square points, it is easy to observe that the acceleration value is not better than a traditional processor, which is related to the fact that a traditional processor still has a much higher clock speed than GPU cores, which with less computation, GPU calculations will be significantly slower for small computing tasks.

The final acceleration values are influenced by the procedures for determining the eigenvalues during the calculation of the Gauss-Legendre quadrature points and the process of computing the matrix determinant value. Naturally, the time of executing these tasks determines the total time of the procedure calculating the value of the Fredholm determinant approximation, e.g. for $m = 8000$ the values (in fractions of seconds) that can be obtained are:

- time of calculating quadrature points: 2.6034144000 s.,
- matrix preparation: 0.00045769 s.,

```python
@cuda.jit(device=True, inline=True)
def d_ksinc(x,y):
    tmp=numpy.pi*(x-y)
    if tmp==0.0:
        return 1.0
    else:
        r=numpy.sin(numpy.pi*tmp)/(numpy.pi*tmp)
    return r


@cuda.jit
def fredholm_step_line5(w, x, m, R):
    i, j = cuda.grid(2)
    if i<m and j<m:
        wsi=math.sqrt(w[i])
        wsj=math.sqrt(w[j])
        tmp = (wsi*wsj) * d_ksinc(x[i], x[j])
        R[i,j] = d_kronecker_delta(i,j) - tmp

    ...


R = numpy.zeros(m*m).reshape(m,m)

w = numpy.ascontiguousarray(w); x = numpy.ascontiguousarray(x)
R = numpy.ascontiguousarray(R)

w_d = cuda.to_device(w) ; x_d = cuda.to_device(x)
R_d = cuda.to_device(R)

# preparation the computation grid
threadsperblock = (16, 16)
blockspergrid_x = math.ceil(m / threadsperblock[0])
blockspergrid_y = math.ceil(m / threadsperblock[1])
blockspergrid = (blockspergrid_x, blockspergrid_y)

    ...
fredholm_step1[blockspergrid, threadsperblock](w_d, x_d, m, R_d)
    ...
```

Fig. 3. Code snippets for computing the Fredholm determinant, specifically the fredholm_step_line5 function, which represents the matrix preparation in line (5) of the code from Fig. 1. The provided code was developed in Python using the Numba package.

– calculating of matrix determinant: $0.1987810\,\mathrm{s}$.

what, compared to $250\,\mathrm{s}$ for a traditional processor, is a significant benefit of using GPUs in the context of calculating the Fredholm determinant values.

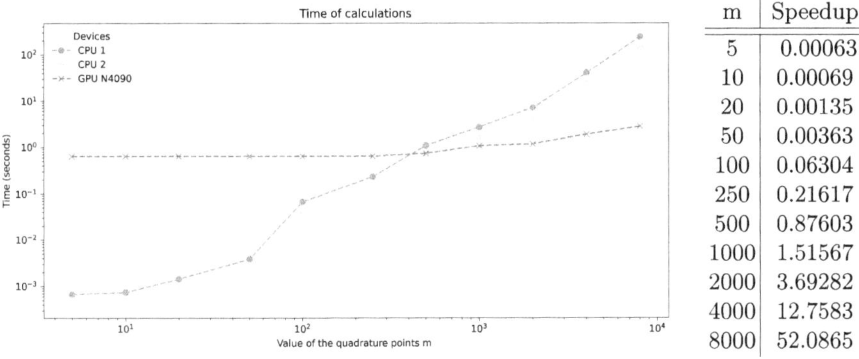

m	Speedup
5	0.00063
10	0.00069
20	0.00135
50	0.00363
100	0.06304
250	0.21617
500	0.87603
1000	1.51567
2000	3.69282
4000	12.7583
8000	52.0865

Fig. 4. Computation times (the graph has logarithmic axes) of the values for $E_2(0, s)$ for two processors CPU 1 and CPU 2 (identical to the "Basic Numpy" version and the NVIDIA RTX 4090 graphics card). The acceleration or deceleration values (between CPU 2 and GPU) for different numbers of quadrature points m are also given.

4.4 Entropy Calculation for Superposition of Fock States

In [6], authors propose calculating von Neumann entropy values for superposition of $|0\rangle$ and an arbitrary Fock state $|m\rangle$. Mentioned case is a binary superposition which may be expressed as:

$$|\psi\rangle = \frac{|0\rangle + z|m\rangle}{\sqrt{1 + z^2}} \tag{17}$$

where $z \in \mathbb{R}$. State $|\psi\rangle$ is subjected to unitary operation U which amplifies the Fock state $|m\rangle$:

$$U = e^{-v} e^{-\tau \hat{a}^\dagger \hat{b}^\dagger} e^{-v(\hat{a}^\dagger \hat{a} + \hat{b}^\dagger \hat{b})} e^{\tau^* \hat{a}\hat{b}}, \tag{18}$$

with $v = \ln \cosh |\xi|$ and $\tau = \frac{\xi}{|\xi|} \tanh |\xi|$. Finally, the entropy value may be defined as:

$$S(z) = \frac{1}{1 + z^2} S_0 + \frac{z^2}{1 + z^2} S_m. \tag{19}$$

Symbols S_0 and S_m stand for counterparts of states $|0\rangle$ and $|m\rangle$ in convex combination of mentioned superposition. That means the entropy here is a monotonically increasing function depending on the value of ξ.

Applying the numerical approach described in Sect. 3 to calculating the von Neumann entropy value requires specifying the kernel function that will be passed to the quadrature function. In the case of the Fock state, this can be a kernel of the form:

$$K(x, y) = \frac{\tanh(x - y)}{x + y}. \tag{20}$$

This allows us to obtain approximations, which are visualized in Fig. 5. Naturally, it must be noted that this is an approximation, so the value of the parameter ξ takes different values here, e.g., for $\xi = 0.75$. Calculating the value of the Fredholm determinant comes down to the following line of code:

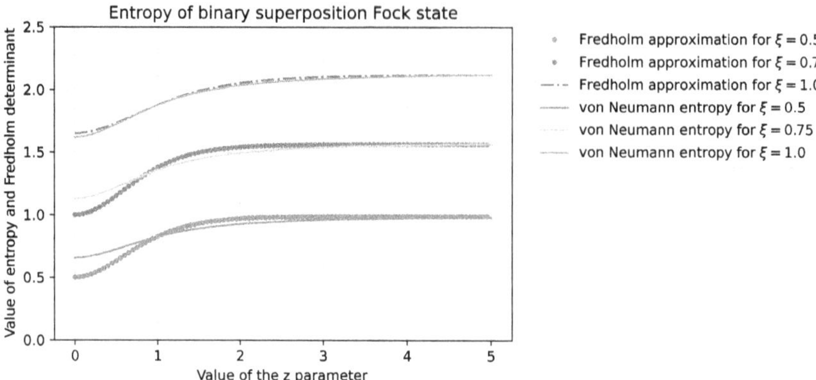

Fig. 5. Approximations of the von Neumann entropy values for the superposition of $|0\rangle$ and an arbitrary Fock state $|m\rangle$. The graph shows the values obtained using Eq. 19 and approximations calculated applying the Fredholm determinants. As one can see, as the parameter z increases, we obtain increasingly better approximations, and the overall behavior of the approximation correctly imitates the dynamics of changes in the von Neumann entropy value calculated by the formula Eq. 19.

```
max_r=5; val_of_z = entropy_with_fred_det( z , 1.5, 2, max_r)
```

where 1.5 acts as the ξ parameter and 2 is the number of quadrature intervals. The Python code for the entropy calculation function in this case is as follows:

```
def entropy_with_fred_det_xi075(r, z, m, max_r):
    a=0
    b=r*2
    w,x=gauss_legendre_quadrature(a,b,m)
    w = numpy.sqrt(w)
    xi,xj = numpy.meshgrid(x, x, indexing='ij')
    ker_mat = numpy.nan_to_num( kernel_fnc(r, xi, xj), 0.0)
    d = numpy.linalg.det( numpy.eye(m)
                          + z * numpy.outer(w,w) *  ker_mat )

    return d
```

5 Summary

The paper presents an implementation of a computational procedure based on Gauss-Legendre quadrature within the Python ecosystem, using the NumPy and CuPy libraries to enable GPU-accelerated computations. The proposed approach is applied to the calculation of the von Neumann entropy for continuous-variable quantum states. To the best of the authors' knowledge, this constitutes one of the first GPU-based implementations in this context. In contrast, the work of [2] provides general-purpose routines designed for CPU architectures. The achieved accelerations enable practical reduction of the computational time for those cases where many quadrature points must be used. It should also be emphasized that the use of the Numba and CuPy packages offers a relatively easy transfer of the problem of calculating the approximation of the Fredholm determinant to the Python language. In the case of a smaller number of square points, the NumPy package for a traditional processor (CPU) can also be successfully used in the calculation of the approximate value of the Fredholm determinant. Other numerical approaches can also be employed; however, they typically require the computation of eigenvalues. An advantage of the CuPy library is that this functionality is supported directly on the GPU.

Although only one quadrature was briefly presented in this article, the availability of the function calculating the inverse fast Fourier transform allows us to implement the approximation of the Fredholm determinant based on the Clenshaw-Curtis quadrature in a similar way. It is also worth emphasizing that the proposed solution is based on free and fully open Python environments and packages supporting calculations.

The application of techniques based on the Fredholm determinant also makes it possible, at the theoretical level, to formulate appropriate numerical procedures for computing the values of Schmidt coefficients in systems where one of the subsystems is described by a continuous, infinite-dimensional Hilbert space.

Acknowledgments. This work was co-financed by Military University of Technology under research project UGB 531-000091-W500-22 and by a subsidy for research projects in Technical Computer Science and Telecommunication discipline in University of Zielona Góra for year 2026.

Disclosure of Interests. All authors declare that they have no conflicts of interest.

References

1. Bornemann, F.: Numerical evaluation of Fredholm determinants and Painlevé transcendents with applications to random matrix theory. In: Workshop on Integrable Systems and Scientific Computing, 15–20 June 2009, ICTP (2009)
2. Bornemann, F.: On the numerical evaluation of Fredholm determinants. Math. Comp. **79**, 871–915 (2010)
3. CUPy: Cupy – Numpy & SciPy for GPU (2025). https://cupy.dev/
4. Eaton, J.W., Bateman, D., Hauberg, S., Wehbring, R.: GNU Octave version 5.2.0 manual: a high-level interactive language for numerical computations, (2020)
5. Fredholm, I.: Sur une classe d'équations fonctionnelles. Acta Mathematica **27**(none), 365 – 390 (1903). https://doi.org/10.1007/BF02421317
6. Gagatsos, C.N., Karanikas, A.I., Kordas, G., Cerf, N.J.: Entropy generation in gaussian quantum transformations: applying the replica method to continuous-variable quantum information theory. NPJ Quant. Inform. **2**(1), 15008 (2016). https://doi.org/10.1038/npjqi.2015.8
7. Gamayun, O., Lychkovskiy, O., Caux, J.S.: Fredholm determinants, full counting statistics and Loschmidt echo for domain wall profiles in one-dimensional free fermionic chains. SciPost Phys. **8**(3), 036 (2020).https://doi.org/10.21468/scipostphys.8.3.036

8. Gielerak, R.: Renormalized von neumann entropy with application to entanglement in genuine infinite dimensional systems. In: Quantum Information Processing, vol. 22, p. 311. (2023). https://doi.org/10.1007/s11128-023-04059-1

9. Gielerak, R., Wiśniewska, J., Sawerwain, M.: Infinite-dimensional quantum entropy: The unified entropy case. Entropy **26**(12) (2024).https://doi.org/10.3390/e26121070

10. Harris, C.R., Millman, K.J., et al.: Array programming with NumPy. Nature **585**(7825), 357–362 (2020). https://doi.org/10.1038/s41586-020-2649-2

11. Lam, S.K., Pitrou, A., Seibert, S.: Numba: A LLVM-based python JIT compiler. In: Proceedings of the Second Workshop on the LLVM Compiler Infrastructure in HPC, pp. 1–6. (2015)

12. MATLAB: 9.7.0.1190202 (R2019b). The MathWorks Inc., Natick, Massachusetts (2018)

13. NVIDIA: Cuda, release: 12.8 (2025). https://developer.nvidia.com/cuda-toolkit

14. Okuta, R., Unno, Y., Nishino, D., Hido, S., Loomis, C.: Cupy: a numpy-compatible library for nvidia gpu calculations. In: Proceedings of Workshop on Machine Learning Systems (LearningSys) in The Thirty-first Annual Conference on Neural Information Processing Systems (NIPS, (2017)

15. Sawerwain, M., Wiśniewska, J., Wróblewski, M., Gielerak, R.: Source code of examples of fredholm determinants calculations (2025). https://github.com/qMSUZ/EntDetector/tree/main/examples-fredholm

16. Szczepanik, W., Niemiec, M.: Optimizing routing in quantum key distribution networks using the artificial fish swarm algorithm. Int. J. Appl. Math. Comput. Sci. **35**(4), 667–675 (2025). https://doi.org/10.61822/amcs-2025-0047

17. Trefethen, L.N.: Is Gauss quadrature better than Clenshaw–Curtis? SIAM Rev. **50**(1), 67–87 (2008). https://doi.org/10.1137/060659831

18. Waldvogel, J.: Fast construction of the Fejér and Clenshaw-Curtis quadrature rules. BIT Numer. Math. **46**, 195–202 (2006). https://doi.org/10.1007/s10543-006-0045-4

19. Xu, S.X., Zhao, S.Q., Zhao, Y.Q.: On the fredholm determinant of the confluent hypergeometric kernel with discontinuities. Physica D **461**, 134101 (2024). https://doi.org/10.1016/j.physd.2024.134101

Mixed Precision Quantum Machine Learning on Photonic Quantum and Hybrid Quantum-HPC Systems

Mateusz Slysz[1(✉)], Krzysztof Kurowski[1], and Grzegorz Waligóra[2]

[1] Poznań Supercomputing and Networking Center, IBCH PAS, Poznań, Poland
{mslysz, krzysztof.kurowski}@man.poznan.pl
[2] Poznań University of Technology, Poznań, Poland
grzegorz.waligora@cs.put.poznan.pl

Abstract. We study mixed precision training in hybrid neural networks combining a photonic quantum processor with classical HPC computation. In hybrid quantumclassical models, gradients are noisy due to finite quantum measurements and classical rounding errors. We analyze gradient variance to examine how these noise sources affect training stability in a simple binary classification task, comparing full precision and mixed precision training. Results show that in low-shot regimes typical of Noisy Intermediate-Scale Quantum (NISQ) devices, quantum noise dominates and mixed precision does not harm training, while at higher shot counts classical numerical errors become increasingly relevant. These findings provide practical guidance for selecting numerical precision in hybrid quantumHPC workflows.

Keywords: Photonic Quantum Computer · Hybrid Quantum-Classical System · Quantum Machine Learning · Floating-Point Arithmetic · Mixed Precision · Gradient Variance

1 Introduction

Quantum Machine Learning (QML) [10] is an emerging interdisciplinary field that aims to harness the computational capabilities of quantum computers to enhance classical machine learning tasks, including classification, regression, and generative modeling [5,15]. In recent years, work on hybrid quantum-classical models has grown rapidly, as purely quantum models remain limited by current hardware constraints. Photonic quantum platforms, which encode quantum information in optical modes, have attracted particular interest owing to their potential for high-speed, room-temperature operation and intrinsic robustness to certain noise sources [4]. Photonic QML implementations have demonstrated competitive performance on classification and sampling tasks, indicating practical utility even on small-scale devices [11].

In variational QML, gradients are typically estimated via repeated circuit evaluations, which introduces stochastic noise that can overwhelm small numerical errors from classical computation [3]. In practice, a large number of measurement shots are required to average out this sampling noise, which increases the computational cost significantly on real quantum processors.

While substantial effort has focused on mitigating quantum noise and reducing shot complexity, comparatively little attention has been given to the role of numerical precision in the classical component of hybrid QML workflows. In classical deep learning, mixed precision arithmetic has emerged as a standard performance optimization technique, enabling substantial reductions in memory footprint and computational time while maintaining convergence behavior [7,12]. However, its interaction with stochastic gradient estimates arising from quantum sampling remains largely unexplored. Although mixed-precision quantum-classical algorithms have recently been proposed in contexts such as solving linear systems [8], to the best of our knowledge, there is currently no comprehensive investigation of mixed-precision training in hybrid QML workflows, where quantum measurement noise interacts with classical numerical precision.

In this work, we investigate mixed precision quantum machine learning on photonic quantum processors within hybrid High-Performance Computing (HPC) systems. We hypothesize that, in many regimes relevant to NISQ devices [14], quantum sampling noise dominates numerical precision error, enabling aggressive mixed-precision strategies that reduce classical computation time and memory requirements without detriment to training outcomes. We present an empirical study of mixed-precision training in a hybrid photonic quantum-classical machine learning environment deployed on an NVIDIA H100 GPU cluster integrated with an ORCA photonic quantum processor at Poznań Supercomputing and Networking Center.

2   Background and Problem Formulation

2.1   Variational Quantum Machine Learning

Hybrid variational quantum algorithms employ a parameterized quantum circuit $U(\boldsymbol{\theta})$ acting in an initial state $|0>$, where $\boldsymbol{\theta} \in \mathbb{R}^d$ denotes a vector of trainable parameters. For supervised learning tasks, the model output is typically expressed as the expectation value of an observable $\hat{O}$. In real quantum devices, expectation values cannot be evaluated analytically and must be estimated from a finite number of measurement shots N_s. The empirical estimator is given by

$$\hat{f}(\boldsymbol{\theta}, x) = \frac{1}{N_s} \sum_{i=1}^{N_s} o_i, \tag{1}$$

where the values of o_i are stochastic measurement outcomes sampled from the quantum device.

The model parameters are optimized by minimizing a loss function $L(\boldsymbol{\theta})$ using classical optimization methods. Gradients are commonly computed using the parameter-shift rule [15], which requires multiple circuit evaluations per parameter. As a consequence, gradient estimates are also reconstructed from finite-shot expectation values and take the stochastic form:

$$\widehat{\nabla}L(\boldsymbol{\theta}) = \nabla L(\boldsymbol{\theta}) + \epsilon_{\text{shot}}, \tag{2}$$

where ϵ_{shot} denotes sampling noise induced by finite measurement statistics.

2.2 Numerical Precision in Classical Training

Floating-point arithmetic represents real numbers using finite precision formats defined in the IEEE 754 standard [6]. In this work we compare standard FP32 arithmetic with the reduced precision BF16 format.

Reduced precision computation introduces rounding errors, which can be modeled as

$$\widehat{\nabla}L(\boldsymbol{\theta}) = \nabla L(\boldsymbol{\theta}) + \epsilon_{\text{fp}}, \tag{3}$$

where ϵ_{fp} denotes numerical rounding error introduced by limited precision.

2.3 Interaction Between Sampling Noise and Precision Error

In hybrid variational quantum machine learning, gradient estimates computed in mixed precision take the combined form:

$$\widehat{\nabla}L(\boldsymbol{\theta}) = \nabla L(\boldsymbol{\theta}) + \epsilon_{\text{shot}} + \epsilon_{\text{fp}}, \tag{4}$$

where ϵ_{shot} denotes the stochastic sampling noise of finite quantum measurements, and ϵ_{fp} is the numerical rounding error of a low precision classical computation. The relative magnitude of these two error sources determines their impact on optimization. When $\|\epsilon_{\text{shot}}\| \gg \|\epsilon_{\text{fp}}\|$, the effect of reduced numerical precision is expected to be negligible compared to the quantum sampling noise. In contrast, if the shot count is large and ϵ_{shot} is small, numerical precision may become a significant factor in convergence.

2.4 Shot Noise Scaling and Gradient Variance

To understand how quantum measurement noise and classical numerical errors affect training, we analyze gradient variance, defined as the variance of parameter gradients across mini-batches.

Consider a quantum observable $\hat{O}$ whose expectation value is estimated using N_s independent measurement shots. Each measurement produces a random outcome o_i with finite variance $\sigma^2 = \text{Var}[o]$. The empirical estimator $\hat{f}$ of the expectation value is given in equation (1). Since the measurement outcomes are independent and identically distributed, the variance of the estimator is

$$\text{Var}[\hat{f}] = \text{Var}\left[\frac{1}{N_s}\sum_{i=1}^{N_s}o_i\right] = \frac{1}{N_s^2}\sum_{i=1}^{N_s}\text{Var}[o_i] = \frac{\sigma^2}{N_s}. \tag{5}$$

Thus, quantum measurement noise decreases inversely with the number of shots. When gradients are computed via the parameter-shift rule, each gradient component is formed from differences of such expectation value estimates. As a result, the variance of gradient estimates inherits the same scaling behavior,

$$\text{Var}[\nabla L\left(\theta\right)] \propto \frac{1}{N_s}. \tag{6}$$

This $1/N_s$ dependence provides a theoretical baseline for interpreting experimental gradient variance measurements. Deviations from this scaling indicate the presence of additional noise sources, such as classical numerical precision errors introduced by mixed precision arithmetic.

By comparing FP32 training to mixed precision (BF16/AMP) training across different shot counts, we can determine which source of noise dominates. If variance is similar between FP32 and AMP, quantum shot noise is the main contributor ($\|\epsilon_{\text{shot}}\| \gg \|\epsilon_{\text{fp}}\|$), while larger fluctuations in AMP indicate that classical rounding errors are becoming significant. Systematically varying N_s and recording gradient variance for both precision modes allows us to identify the regimes where shot noise or numerical precision governs the optimization dynamics.

3   Experimental Setup

We evaluate mixed precision training in a hybrid quantum-classical scenario using a simplified binary classification version of the MNIST dataset [9], where the task is to distinguish between digits 0 and 1. Input images are normalized and flattened into 28×28 vectors before being fed into the network. This task provides a controlled environment to study the interaction between quantum measurement noise and classical numerical precision, while remaining computationally tractable on current hardware. All experiments were performed using the ORCA PT-1 [1,2] photonic quantum processors installed at the Poznań Supercomputing and Networking Center (PCSS). The ORCA PT-1 systems provide 8 optical modes (qumodes) and implement the boson sampling paradigm using a time-bin encoding of the optical modes. The devices operate in a single-loop architecture with 7 programmable beam-splitter parameters, as each adjacent pair of qumodes is connected by a single beam splitter. The system also supports computations in a double-loop configuration, which provides 14 programmable beam-splitter parameters. All experiments were performed on a high-performance computing node equipped with an NVIDIA H100 GPU and connected to the ORCA photonic quantum processor.

The hybrid model combines classical neural network layers with a photonic quantum processing layer implemented via the ORCA photonic platform. The classical pre-quantum block consists of fully connected layers designed to extract features from the high-dimensional input: we use two layers mapping $784 \to 64$ neurons, each followed by a Rectified Linear Unit (ReLU) activation. This block outputs the parameters required by the quantum layer. The quantum layer itself is implemented as a programmable interferometer (PTLayer) with $m = 6$ optical modes, using a time-multiplexed boson sampling architecture and photon-number detection to encode and process the classical features. Following the quantum layer, a classical post-quantum block maps the quantum outputs to a single logit for binary classification; the post-quantum block consists of one hidden layer with 64 neurons and a ReLU activation. Automatic Mixed Precision (AMP) [12] is applied on the classical blocks, while the PTLayer computations remain in full FP32 to preserve quantum numerical accuracy.

For each experiment, we vary both the number of shots $N_s \in \{10, 20, 50, 100\}$ and the numerical precision mode (FP32 or AMP BF16 for classical layers), while keeping all other hyperparameters fixed, including a learning rate of 1×10^{-3}, batch size of 128, and 10 training epochs. To evaluate the effect of numerical precision on training stability, we measure the final loss and the gradient variance across mini-batches for each combination of shot number and precision mode. This allows us to quantify the relative contributions of stochastic quantum noise and classical rounding errors in the hybrid training loop. The entire experimental pipeline is implemented in PyTorch [13], using a PTLayer wrapper to isolate FP32 quantum computations from AMP classical operations. The results for these runs are gathered in Table 1 and visualised on a plot in Fig. 1. Each configuration was evaluated over three independent training runs, and the reported gradient variances represent averages across these runs. The observed trends were qualitatively consistent, suggesting that the reported behavior reflects systematic effects rather than random fluctuations.

Table 1. Final loss, training time, and gradient variance for different shot counts and precision modes collected in experiments.

Shots (N_s)	Precision	Final Loss	Total Time [s]	Gradient Variance
10	FP32	0.00332	25.29	0.211
10	AMP BF16	0.00101	25.15	0.056
20	FP32	0.00039	31.25	0.0071
20	AMP BF16	0.00231	31.89	0.321
50	FP32	0.00034	50.55	$1.32 \cdot 10^{-5}$
50	AMP BF16	0.00065	51.02	0.0117
100	FP32	0.00029	80.70	$1.14 \cdot 10^{-4}$
100	AMP BF16	0.00177	81.78	0.0952

The hybrid model successfully learns the binary MNIST classification task across all tested shot counts and precision modes, with final losses below 0.01. Training under both FP32 and mixed precision (AMP/BF16) remains stable, although gradient fluctuations vary across shot regimes.

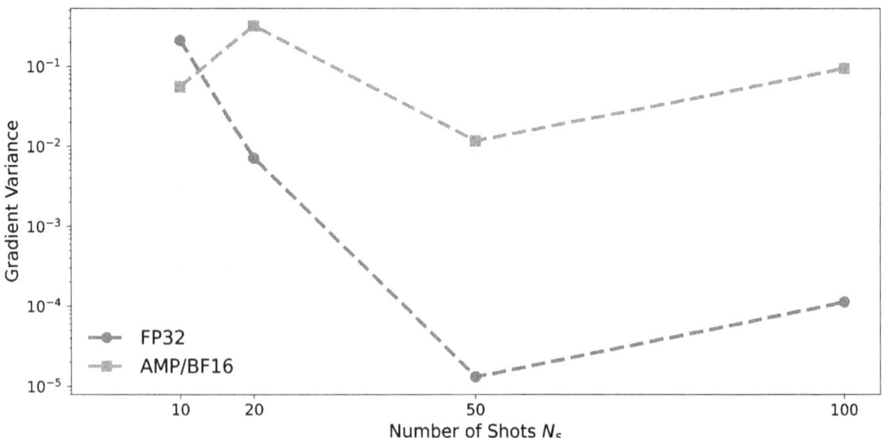

Fig. 1. Gradient variance of the hybrid photonic quantumclassical neural network as a function of the number of measurement shots N_s. Shaded regions highlight operational regimes: low-shot (blue) where quantum sampling noise dominates, and high-shot (red) where classical numerical precision becomes significant. (Color figure online)

We additionally measure total runtime as a function of the number of measurement shots N_s and numerical precision. These measurements allow us to analyze how quantum sampling noise and classical numerical precision interact during training.

4   Discussion

The experimental results confirm the expected inverse scaling of gradient variance with respect to the number of measurement shots N_s under full FP32 precision. As predicted by the theoretical analysis, increasing N_s systematically reduces stochastic fluctuations in the gradient estimates, closely following the ideal $1/N_s$ trend. This validates that quantum measurement noise behaves as statistically independent sampling noise in the studied regime.

In contrast, mixed precision (BF16/AMP) training exhibits deviations from ideal scaling. While gradient variance also decreases with increasing N_s, its magnitude remains consistently higher than in FP32 for moderate and large shot counts. This behavior indicates that when quantum shot noise becomes sufficiently small, classical numerical precision errors begin to contribute noticeably to gradient fluctuations. Interestingly, at very low shot counts, the variance under mixed precision does not significantly differ from FP32 values. In this regime, quantum sampling noise dominates the optimization dynamics, effectively masking rounding effects introduced by reduced precision arithmetic. As N_s increases and shot noise diminishes, the relative contribution of numerical precision errors becomes more visible, leading to a divergence between FP32 and AMP variance curves.

All these observations suggest the existence of distinct operational regimes. In the low-shot regime, optimization is governed primarily by quantum measurement noise, and mixed precision does not significantly degrade training stability. In higher-shot regimes, however, where quantum noise is suppressed, classical rounding errors can become comparable in magnitude, influencing gradient stability and potentially affecting convergence dynamics.

Finally, the observed total runtime increases approximately linearly with N_s, reflecting the direct proportionality between the number of quantum circuit evaluations and the number of measurement samples required for expectation estimation. These results suggest that, in hybrid photonicGPU workflows, optimizing shot allocation has a significantly larger impact on performance than reducing classical numerical precision. Mixed precision may still provide memory or throughput benefits in larger-scale models, however, in the present setting, quantum sampling remains the primary bottleneck.

5   Conclusions and Future Work

In this work, we investigated mixed precision training in a hybrid neural network combining a photonic quantum processor with classical computation on an HPC cluster. Our experiments on a binary MNIST classification task demonstrate that the interplay between quantum measurement noise and classical numerical precision governs training stability. In low-shot regimes typical of NISQ devices, quantum sampling noise dominates, enabling aggressive mixed-precision strategies (BF16/AMP) without degrading model performance. As the number of shots increases, classical rounding errors become more significant, highlighting the need for precision-aware algorithm design in hybrid quantumHPC workflows. From a practical perspective, this interplay provides guidance for precision selection in hybrid quantumHPC workflows.

For future work, we plan to scale to larger datasets and more complex architectures, including multi-class classification and deeper hybrid networks. In addition, utilising multi-GPU and multi-QPU setups could significantly accelerate hybrid computations, enabling the simultaneous parallelization of classical and photonic operations as initially demonstrated in [16]. Finally, extending these methods to other quantum machine learning tasks, such as generative modeling or quantum kernel methods, will help generalize our findings. Furthermore, investigating adaptive precision strategies that dynamically balance quantum noise and classical numerical accuracy during training represents a promising direction for improving efficiency and robustness.

Acknowledgment. We acknowledge the Poznań Supercomputing and Networking Center for providing access to the ORCA PT-1 photonic quantum systems and GPU cluster. This research has been funded by the Program of the Polish Ministry of Science and Higher Education "Applied Doctorate" realized in years 2022–2026 (agreement no. DWD/6/0142/2022) and by the Poznań University of Technology, Poland (project no. 0311/SBAD/0764).

References

1. AbuGhanem, M.: Toward scalable fault-tolerant photonic quantum computers. J. Supercomput. **82**(2), 51 (2026). https://doi.org/10.1007/s11227-025-08132-7
2. Bradler, K., Wallner, H.: Certain properties and applications of shallow bosonic circuits. arXiv preprint arXiv:2112.09766 (2021)
3. Facelli, G., Roberts, D.D., Wallner, H., Makarovskiy, A., Holmes, Z., Clements, W.R.: Exact gradients for linear optics with single photons. arXiv preprint arXiv:2409.16369 (2024)
4. Flamini, F., Spagnolo, N., Sciarrino, F.: Photonic quantum information processing: a review. Rep. Prog. Phys. **82**(1), 016001 (2019)
5. Havlíček, V., et al.: Supervised learning with quantum-enhanced feature spaces. Nature **567**(7747), 209–212 (2019)
6. IEEE: IEEE Standard for Binary Floating-Point Arithmetic. ANSI/IEEE Std 754-1985, pp. 1–20 (1985). https://doi.org/10.1109/IEEESTD.1985.82928
7. Kalamkar, D., et al.: A Study of BFLOAT16 for Deep Learning Training (2019). https://arxiv.org/abs/1905.12322
8. Koska, O., Baboulin, M., Gazda, A.: A mixed-precision quantum-classical algorithm for solving linear systems (2025). https://arxiv.org/abs/2502.02212
9. LeCun, Y., Bottou, L., Bengio, Y., Haffner, P.: Gradient-based learning applied to document recognition. Proc. IEEE **86**(11), 2278–2324 (1998). https://doi.org/10.1109/5.726791
10. Lloyd, S., Mohseni, M., Rebentrost, P.: Quantum algorithms for supervised and unsupervised machine learning (2013). https://arxiv.org/abs/1307.0411
11. Madsen, L.S., et al.: Quantum computational advantage with a programmable photonic processor. Nature **606**(7912), 75–81 (2022)
12. Micikevicius, P., et al.: Mixed precision training. In: International Conference on Learning Representations (ICLR) (2018). https://openreview.net/forum?id=r1gs9JgRZ
13. Paszke, A., et al.: PyTorch: an imperative style, high-performance deep learning library. In: Advances in Neural Information Processing Systems 32, pp. 8024–8035. Curran Associates, Inc. (2019). http://papers.neurips.cc/paper/9015-pytorch-an-imperative-style-high-performance-deep-learning-library.pdf
14. Preskill, J.: Quantum computing in the NISQ era and beyond. Quantum **2**, 79 (2018). https://doi.org/10.22331/q-2018-08-06-79, https://doi.org/10.22331/q-2018-08-06-79
15. Schuld, M., Bergholm, V., Gogolin, C., Izaac, J., Killoran, N.: Evaluating analytic gradients on quantum hardware. Phys. Rev. A **99**(3), 032331 (2019). https://doi.org/10.1103/PhysRevA.99.032331
16. Slysz, M., et al.: Solving combinatorial optimization and machine learning problems on hybrid near-term quantum photonic computers. Future Gener. Comput. Syst. **174**, 107934 (2026). https://doi.org/10.1016/j.future.2025.107934, https://www.sciencedirect.com/science/article/pii/S0167739X25002298

Author Index

GPSR Compliance
The European Union's (EU) General Product Safety Regulation (GPSR) is a set
of rules that requires consumer products to be safe and our obligations to
ensure this.

If you have any concerns about our products, you can contact us on

ProductSafety@springernature.com

In case Publisher is established outside the EU, the EU authorized
representative is:

Springer Nature Customer Service Center GmbH
Europaplatz 3
69115 Heidelberg, Germany

473182UK00002B/73